First Ladies

First Ladies

THE SAGA OF THE PRESIDENTS' WIVES AND THEIR POWER

1789–1961

CARL SFERRAZZA
ANTHONY

QUILL
WILLIAM MORROW
NEW YORK

It is the policy of William Morrow and Company, Inc., and its imprints and affiliates, recognizing the importance of preserving what has been written, to print the books we publish on acid-free paper, and we exert our best efforts to that end.

Library of Congress Cataloging-in-Publication Data

Anthony , Carl Sferrazza.
    First ladies : the saga of the presidents' wives and their power, 1789–1961 / Carl Sferrazza Anthony.
        p.   cm.
    Includes index.
    ISBN 0-688-11272-2
    1. Presidents—United States—Wives—History. 2. Presidents—United States—Wives—Biography. I. Title.
[E176.2.A58   1992]
973'.099—dc20   91-41976   CIP
[B]

Printed in the United States of America

5 6 7 8 9 10

To my parents, grandmother, grandfather, brothers,
sister, aunt, and the memory of Pauline

Preface

. . . the power behind the throne is *the*
power.

> —Maria Weston Chapman
> "How Can I Help to
> Abolish Slavery?" (1855)

IN ITS LARGEST scheme, this first volume, along with a succeeding one, attempts to be the first full chronicle history of the first ladyship. Book One opens with the period of May 16 through May 29, 1789, when Martha Washington was in a sense transmuted from private person to public persona, as she traveled from Mount Vernon to New York, assuming the role of the first First Lady. In Book Two, the saga concludes two hundred years later to the week, tracing the duties and role of Barbara Bush. In that month of May 1989, there was no notice of any kind recalling the first ladyship, yet a month previous a large public extravaganza celebrated the bicentennial of the presidency at the site of its inception, New York, culminating a reenactment that followed the coach ride north of the beloved general—along the same path Martha took two weeks later. As someone, now lost to time, once wrote, "Women are the forgotten men of history."

There seems to be some misconception that First Ladies prior to 1933 held little fascination for the public and press. Radio, and then television, may have proliferated information, but they also diminished national memory. The press of the "National Period" were so eager to visually present Dolley Madison to the public that one publisher placed her engraving on its magazine cover. The fashion industry attempted to solicit Louisa Adams's patronage by sending her a free bonnet—to wear in public, of course. They too have known they were not just the wives of public officials, but something quite different: Julia called herself "Mrs. President Tyler"; Abigail Adams wrote letters in which she examined her role. In obvious and helpful ways, the past has relevance to the present. This institution, albeit unofficial, has its own history and roots. The fifteenth generation of First Ladies may not realize it, but they have inherited certain customs indigenous only to their role, stem-

ming back to Martha. To deny them having had a "heritage" consequently voids a nation's full understanding of its own unique culture.
This is why I began with 1789, not 1901 or 1933 or even 1961.

What intrigued me most was their varying degrees of power.

How could a person of a gender once deemed "inferior," in a role
that tended to repress, in a position that was not official, in a situation
always scrutinized, usually criticized, and perpetually debated, exert influence on everyone from the presidents of the United States, Cabinet
members, senators, congressmen, Supreme Court justices, and governors to the czar of Russia, Pope John Paul II, and Mae West?

Here, the "first ladyship" is not viewed as a listless decoration orbit-
ing the presidency, but as an integral part of it. Only the First Lady and
the president determine the extent of her power, though frequently she
has operated without his knowledge or permission. There is an error,
though unavoidable, in viewing candidates' wives as mere hand wavers
and shakers. Think of Edith Wilson in 1916, Eleanor Roosevelt in
1932, Nancy Reagan in 1980. In light of the power they wielded, it
seems incongruous that the press paid relatively scant attention to them
during those campaigns. Quite often, *he* has got as far as a presidential
campaign partially because of *her,* whether through her financial security, political advice, or single-minded ambition.

Obviously, it would be impossible to give equal weight to each, so I
considered these questions: How much power did she exercise? How
much influence did she seek to wield, and how successful was she? Did
she exert so-called "apolitical" power over the general atmosphere of
the administration, her husband's personality and, consequently, the
lasting press and public impression of that presidency? Whether she
believed her power was merely "a woman's intuition," or she followed
the thought of Elizabeth Cady Stanton, who quipped, "Thank you,
gentlemen, there was no instinct about it. I did some hard thinking," I
only judged the power.

Because the final manuscript proved too vast to publish as one single book, this work is the first of two volumes, the second one to tell
the story from Jacqueline Kennedy to Barbara Bush. Martha Washington, Dolley Madison, Julia Tyler, Mary Lincoln, Julia Grant, Frances
Cleveland, Nellie Taft, Grace Coolidge, Eleanor Roosevelt, and Mamie
Eisenhower—all representing varying degrees of influence over the public and press, their presidents, and other officials—were those whose
lives I followed from beginning to end. In other cases—Abigail Adams,
Sarah Polk, Lucretia Garfield, Edith Roosevelt, Ellen Wilson, Florence
Harding, Lou Hoover, and Bess Truman—I concentrated mainly on
their tenure. The desire to put events in perspective also applied not
only to First Ladies in our memory but the early ones. We know Abigail
Adams's views, but what did Martha Washington make of slavery,
women's education, and the prickly international affairs of the era? So I

focused on certain women and aspects of their work or personalities that I felt have failed to emerge previously.

I also enjoyed writing about those women who relished life and enjoyed themselves despite the personal sacrifice. Essentially tough individuals, they grew as human beings, often opening their perspective and sometimes even changing their attitudes on public issues. By facing challenges with their own unique approaches, they consequently changed the public role. Clearly, they also enjoyed having influence, whether through timid clandestineness or outrageous boldness, consciously or unconsciously.

Another consideration was how well they embodied their eras. How did they respond to technology, to popular music, to current trends and issues? Though through an obviously privileged lens, some have uncannily, marvelously mirrored the epochal texture of the American heritage. So I've put great emphasis on the times, and one woman is used to represent each of the periods. Particular themes, like civil rights, women's issues, the press and public, technology—and how the women responded to or were affected by them—are woven through the two-hundred-year story.

In addition, this is a saga of intertwining lives, of friends and enemies, of rivals and allies. Amid the differences, there is that "sorority." It was commented upon as recently as Michael Deaver's 1987 memoir, which noted that Mrs. Nixon and Mrs. Onassis gave support to Mrs. Reagan, but it began with a visit that Abigail Adams made to former First Lady Martha Washington. It is curious, it is wonderful, and it's been what has managed to link all these very different women in the same role as a continuum. The scepter passing can be traced from the first George's wife to the new George's wife. It's a strong element in this work.

One element seemed to emerge as common to nearly every First Lady, regardless of era or crisis, no matter how bitter, disgusted or infirm, however tragically she may have departed or happily viewed retirement.

Almost every one of them missed the power.

Acknowledgments

THE MOST SPECIAL thanks to friends and colleagues Byron Kennard, Meredith Burch, Jim Elder, Donnie Radcliffe, Edward and Rita Purcell, and Hilla Del Re for their longtime interest, support, inspiration, and suggestions. Jay Dutton provided an example of how to get the job done to one's best capability. Agent Michael Hamilburg took enthusiastic interest in the project, and editor Lisa Drew had monumental patience and thorough commitment. She, along with David Means and Bob Shuman, put up with incessant requests.

For understanding through the difficult years of researching and writing the book, and scouting material, I am grateful to Glenn Pinder, Carrie and Sue Scott, Eric Michael, Duke Zeller, Bill Hitchcock, Amy La Guardia, Michael Del Villar, Alan Cohen, Louise Cayne, Barbara Zacharek, Donna Smith, Arlene Alligood, Josephine Cerone, Richard and Connie Brousell, Deanie Howett, Don Fraher, Jerry Haft, Virginia Blodgett, Peter Easley, Dean Hara, Peter Klein, Jacqueline Dubois, John Fitzgerald, Lyndon Booser, Scott Parker, Michael DiMauro, Louise Lang, Sally Blue, Camlyn Craig, Chris Edwards, Sarah Smith, V. V. Harrison, Lester Hyman, Kevin DiLallo, John Harper, Harry Stock, Sy Loewen, Brian Latker, Robin Roosevelt, Bob Till, Wesley O'Brien, and Michael Privitera.

Professional colleagues provided support, most especially Margaret Brown Klapthor, curator emeritus of the Division of Political History at the Smithsonian. Roger Kennedy, director of the National Museum of American History, curators Edie Mayo, Faith Ruffins, Herb Collins, Karen Mittleman, Kate Henderson, and staff member Marilyn Higgins gave helpful suggestions. Rex Scouten, former White House chief usher, now curator, Betty Monkman, and Bill Allman of the Curator's Office put up with frequent questions, always giving an answer. Charles Kelly and Mary Wolfskill of the Manuscript Division of the Library of Congress both went beyond and above in pulling items that would be helpful, and lent dimes for the copy machine. Bernard Myer and Gloria Hunter of the White House Historical Association kept an open door to "talk shop." Ellen Edwards of *The Washington Post* Style section was the first person there to appreciate my attempts to make history into relevant news. Bemused perhaps about presidents' swimming habits, she always gave a fair hearing. With academic perspective, Betty Caroli, author of a study on aspects of the role, shared insights, and Lewis Gould, author of the eminent study on beautification, took time to discuss our mutual interest at a conference.

Anne Rauscher of Mount Vernon led me to Mrs. Washington's letters, and John Riley provided vital information on that First Lady's arrival in her role. Robert Seager gave insights beyond his monumental joint biography of the Tylers. Julia Tyler's grandaughter-in-law, Paynie Tyler, brought to life a woman who lived over a century ago. Michael Berry, collateral descendant of Letitia Tyler, provided background on her. Frances Rainey, president of the Polk Auxiliary, sent an unpublished draft on Mrs. Polk prepared by Claudia Jack. Mary Benjamin and Chris Jaeckel distilled information for me from their firm's collection of Jane Pierce letters. Sally Cahalan of Wheatlands, and Salinda Matt, librarian of the Lancaster County Historical Society, provided information on Harriet Lane; Carl Angle of the Lake County Historical Society on Crete Garfield; Leslie Fishel of the Hayes Presidential Center and biographer Emily Apt Geer on Lucy Hayes; biographer Thomas Reeves on Ellen Arthur.

Jack Cadman, nephew of Frances Cleveland, generously shared his collection on her, and his cousin, Francis Cleveland, son of the president, provided marvelous recollections of his mother. His late sister, Marion Amen, also answered questions about their mother when I was just beginning my interest in the subject. Sylvia Jukes Morris, biographer of Edith Roosevelt, amid her own projects took time out to answer my questions. Michael Teague shared thoughts about his friend Alice Longworth, her stepmother, and her cousin Eleanor. The late Ethel Derby answered questions about her mother Edith Roosevelt, over the telephone. Largely in the spring of 1976, but upon occasion through the winter of 1978, I ran up phone bills for chats with the late Mrs. Longworth, and though I feared her barbs, she delightfully answered questions on Mrs. Harding, and we also touched on First Ladies Ida McKinley through Betty Ford.

The late Charles P. Taft answered questions about his mother, and William Seale shared some of his conversations with the late Helen Taft Manning. William Howard Taft answered questions about his grandmother's last years. Frances Wright Saunders, the biographer of Ellen Wilson, became a friend who commiserated about the perils of biography, and generously offered insights. Dr. Arthur S. Link, the Wilson expert, shared his recollections of Edith Wilson in her later years. Mary Clark, schoolgirl friend of the Tumulty daughters, provided reminiscences of the era. Dr. Joyce Williams provided information on Edith Wilson and Colonel House. Thanks also to Richard Di Danato. The late Louisa Kling answered questions over the phone on her aunt, Florence Harding, augmented by the great assistance of Herbert Garry and Richard West of the Harding Home. John Coolidge answered my questions in writing and over the telephone about his mother. George and Violet Pratt shared recollections of Mrs. Coolidge's work with the deaf at the Clarke School, of which Dr. Pratt is former president. Joan Haley shared some fond memories of Mrs. Coolidge. Thanks also to Dr. Lawrence Wikander of the Coolidge Memorial Foundation in Northampton, and Kathleen Donald. Mildred Hall answered questions by mail, and Robert Wood of the Herbert Hoover Presidential Library shared interesting and unknown aspects of Mrs. Hoover's remarkable life.

Splendid "J. B." West, former White House chief usher, granted a delightful interview in the spring of 1980, on Eleanor Roosevelt, and we subsequently talked of the other First Ladies with whom he worked, illuminating stories he touched on in his book. Thanks also to his hospitable wife, Zella. Kindly Eleanor Roosevelt Seagraves, namesake of her grandmother, also partook of the project for which I interviewed Mr. West, and answered many further questions. Gladys (Mrs. Todd) Duncan's astute observations provided new insight into Mrs. Roosevelt's civil-rights work. Elliott, James, and the late Franklin Roosevelt, Jr., provided answers to minute questions. Joseph Alsop gave insight into the relationship between Eleanor and Alice. The late Mae West responded to an inquiry about her admiration for the Roosevelts and Frances Cleveland. Edna Gurewitsch graciously offered recollections of Mrs. Roosevelt at the Kennedy Inaugural and of her last days. Reathel Odum, Mrs. Truman's social secretary, answered questions by phone and in writing, responding to a questionnaire I sent out to East Wing staff members. Thanks to the Honorable John W. Synder, Truman's secretary of the treasury, Mary Jo Collie, Mrs. Truman's secretary in her last years, and Jane Lingo, friend to Mrs. Truman. Clark Clifford graciously took time from his active schedule to speak with me about Mrs. Truman's political role.

Barbara Eisenhower Foltz is the personification of kindness. Her honest observations, wit, and gentle way of correcting misconceptions was impressive. Her son, David, spent a Sunday afternoon answering questions over the telephone about Mamie's political perspective in her last years. The late Milton Eisenhower gave me an entire afternoon in March 1984 full of humorous and warm but also pertinent stories about his sister-in-law, and clarified rumor by providing fact. Mary Jane McCaffree Monroe, Mrs. Eisenhower's staff director, provided tender and funny vignettes of her boss. Robert Grey, former secretary to the Eisenhower Cabinet, shared his perceptions on Mamie's political instincts.

I also want to especially thank the dedicated staffs of the presidential libraries. The FDR Library was patient with my many requests via telephone, as were the Ford and Truman Libraries. The Kennedy Library was able to guide me directly to the multitude of its sources. At the Johnson Library, Linda Hanson, Claudia Anderson, and Nancy Smith assisted during my short trip to Austin. At the Eisenhower Library, Thomas Braniger provided expert assistance on resources. Paul Schmidt and the audiovisual staff of the Nixon Archival Project provided filmed material. At the Martin Luther King Library, Mary Ternes guided me through its vast picture archives. I'd like to thank some journalists who've covered the East Wing: Helen Thomas, Nancy Dickerson, Liz Carpenter, Betty Beale, Sarah McClendon, Anne Cottrell Free.

And finally, I'd like very much to thank Jacqueline Kennedy Onassis, Lady Bird Johnson, Pat Nixon, Betty Ford, Rosalynn Carter, Nancy Reagan, and Barbara Bush for information on their early years. The late Mamie Eisenhower answered several questions by handwritten letters in 1976 and 1977.

In the flood of two centuries' worth of facts and legend, I've tried to wade through, investigate, discover the truth, then present it with balance. I did all the research, writing, and typing. If there should be oversights or errors, they're mine.

Author's Note

USE OF THE TERM "BLACK"

WHEN I READ a letter of Martha Washington's in which she referred to "blacks," I realized she was *not* being progressive. This presented a dilemma. If the book was to keep close to history as it progressed, what terminology would most accurately keep it within context?

I consulted with African-American, women's, and American culture historians about what terms to use. All agreed that it was proper to recognize the changing terms, but warned against using them in the text because the general reader—who might not first read an Author's Note—would be jarred to see archaic terminology, even within a historic context. Though it might be more historically accurate to use such terms as "African," "colored," and "Negro," in the end, I chose not to. To the modern eye, they would only offend, and perhaps detract from the larger story. When, in the 1960's, Lady Bird Johnson referred to the "Negro" in a speech, and, in the 1860's, Mary Lincoln wrote of the "oppressed colored race," the terms were proper in the context of the times, and without prejudice. Only in such cases—when I am quoting a source—is such terminology used. I also acknowledge the growing contemporary movement to shift terminology from "black" to "African-American," recognizing that such reference is not just a connotation of skin color, but heritage. As columnist William Raspberry noted, however, "It's not a universal sentiment" among "black" leaders themselves. So, I use the term "African-American" only in the last chapter, around the time of the Bush Inaugural, when the debate first began to reach the mainstream media.

USE OF THE TERMS "FEMALE," "WOMAN," "FIRST LADYSHIP," "LADYSHIP," "SORORITY"

Because this is a chronicle of women, I decided to use the terminology of gender appropriate to the era, specifically, the expression "female." In the early 1800's, schools, for example, were often known as "Young Female Seminaries." However, since some time before 1789, "woman"—often considered radical—was being used by some, its most famous articulation being Mary Wollstonecraft's *Vindication of the Rights of Woman.* That is why, on occasion, I've written "woman" prior to the 1840's. With Margaret Fuller's famous *Woman in the Nineteenth Century,* first published as a pamphlet in 1845, and the Seneca Falls Convention on women's rights in 1848, "woman" came into more mainstream usage. From that juncture onward, it is used in the text. Which brings me to the terms applied to the women of this book. "Lady" is used only rarely, usually in reference to women who would be, were, or had been First Ladies.

The title of "First Lady" seems to have evolved—from "Lady Washington" to "presidentress," among other cognomens—and as with other terminology, the term current with the period is used, changing in the text as it evolves. Reference to the "ladyship," and later, "first ladyship," is not sexist or royalist, but merely the distaff equivalent of the "presidency." The term "sorority" is used in reference to the groups of living former First Ladies and incumbent First Lady at any one given time.

USE OF THE TERMS PRESIDENTIAL "ADVISER," "ASSISTANT" CHIEF OF STAFF, "WEST WING," "EAST WING"

In the early days of the presidency, the many men who served as office help sometimes doubled as advisers, given the all-encompassing title of "secretary." Because the presidents and their staffs are secondary characters in this work, liberty was taken with the rule of keeping terms within context of the era. I clarify the role of the right-hand man by using presidential "assistant" or "adviser" as opposed to "secretary." If the "adviser" or "assistant" ruled all others as the closest in power to the president, I used the term "chief of staff," though it is a relatively new title. After Theodore Roosevelt's term, use of the term "West Wing" refers to the president's staff, and after Eleanor Roosevelt's "term," use of the term "East Wing" refers to the First Lady's staff.

USE OF THE PHRASE "THE PRESS AND PUBLIC"

There will often be references to "the press and public." Both are treated as entities with personae of their own. Unlike the presidency, the first ladyship was shaped, endured, and continues to evolve often because of "their" reactions, needs, and gentle guidance of the president's wife. How the citizenry and the journalists perceived the changing role and how the First Lady exerted power over them are just two dimensions to the sometimes uneasy relationship between the women in the White House and "the press and public."

SPELLING

When the grammar and spelling of some documents were incorrect [sic] was inserted. Effort was made to preserve the original texts verbatim because they retained an epochal flavor of the person and the era.

INTERTWINING AND TIME COMPRESSION

The story of the first ladyship, through the individual lives of the women, is presented as it unfolds, and I strove not to jump ahead. So, for those principal characters, rather than presenting their entire pre-ladyship lives in the time period when they were incumbents, their early years are written of in the context of when they lived them, woven and intertwined as individual strands traced throughout the larger tapestry. The same technique is used for their post-ladyship lives. However, there is a compression of time, used to summarize a particular period of their lives. For example, what Julia Grant did during the Civil War is compressed in paragraphs scattered through the chapters cover-ing Mary Lincoln's first ladyship. The same applies for her life as a widow in Washington during Frances Cleveland's tenure.

In presenting the pre- and post- threads, I always attempted to hook them to a future or former First Lady's interaction with or reaction to the incumbent First Lady, reinforcing the notion of the "sorority." Rather than just summarizing themes in one passage, I have woven them into a straight chronology. For example, Julia Tyler's battle for a presidential widow's pension over a several-year period is presented in several progressive segments. Depending on whom I'm focusing, the camera of time becomes either a microscope or a wide-angle lens. For example, the amount of space devoted to 1941 to 1943 is greater than 1841 to 1843, simply because Eleanor Roosevelt is a main character, while Letitia Tyler is not.

Contents

PREFACE   7
ACKNOWLEDGMENTS   11
AUTHOR'S NOTE   15
LIST OF ILLUSTRATIONS   23

PART I
THE FEDERAL ERA
1789–1801

PROLOGUE: MAY 1789   31
1. THE LADY IN THE COACH   35
2. "A VERY GREAT SOME BODY"   38
3. "THIS ELEVATED STATION . . ."   52
4. MRS. PRESIDENT   60
5. WARMONGER   64

PART II
THE NATIONAL PERIOD
1801–1817

6. "THE TENDER BREASTS OF LADIES"   75
7. THE QUEEN OF HEARTS   81
8. LEGEND   88
9. "AN INFLUENCE"   92

PART III
THE ANTEBELLUM PERIOD
1817–1849

10. QUEEN ELIZABETH   101

11. ". . . SUCH EXPECTATIONS . . ."   108
12. THE FEVER   115
13. "THE LOVELY LADY PRESIDENTRESS"   126
14. PRIM MADONNA   133
15. PHANTOM OF THE WHITE HOUSE   145

PART IV
THE MID-VICTORIAN AGE
1849–1865

16. IRON BELLES   151
17. VOLCANO DANCER   160
18. SECESSION!   168
19. MRS. PRESIDENT LINCOLN   172
20. A CIVIL WAR   182
21. 1865   194

PART V
THE GILDED AGE
1865–1886

22. RECONSTRUCTIVE COUNSEL   203
23. MRS. G.   209
24. THE BUSTLE OF POWER   214
25. SANTA LUCIA   225
26. DISCREET CRETE   235
27. WIDOWS AND WIDOWER, SISTERS AND BACHELOR   242

PART VI
THE GAY NINETIES
1886–1901

28. "YUM-YUM!"   253
29. FRANKIE   256
30. THE PRESIDENT-GENERAL   267
31. HOME AGAIN   275
32. USURPING CUCKOO   282

PART VII
THE PROGRESSIVE ERA
1901–1913

33. INSTITUTIONALIZING 295
34. THE CABINET WIFE 308
35. NERVOUS NELLIE 314
36. BEHIND THE SCREEN 324
37. 1912 331

PART VIII
THE GREAT WAR
1913–1921

38. THE ARTIST 343
39. THE MERRY WIDOW 350
40. MRS. WOODROW WILSON 356
41. "THE SHEPHERDESS" 360
42. QUEEN EDITH 366
43. "OUR REGENT" 371

PART IX
THE JAZZ AGE
1921–1929

44. THE DUCHESS 387
45. A SUNNY DISPOSISH 397
46. THE LADY IN RED 406
47. MAMMY 424

PART X
THE GREAT DEPRESSION AND WORLD WAR II
1929–1945

48. SCOUTING 435
49. CHARITY 439
50. ". . . OVERWHELMED AT THE MERE POSSIBILITY . . ." 449
51. ". . . IN WITH THE RADICAL!" 454
52. POWER AND INFLUENCE 462

53. 1940   485
54. "OUR ELEANOR"   493
55. UNPRECEDENTED   506

PART XI
THE ATOMIC AGE AND FABULOUS FIFTIES
1945–1961

56. "I HAVE NOTHING TO SAY TO THE PUBLIC"   517
57. THE BOSS   530
58. LOOK AHEAD, NEIGHBOR   545
59. IN THE PINK   551
60. SWEETHEART OF THE GOP   571
61. RACE FOR THE LADYSHIP   588
62. LADIES' DAY   599

    NOTES   605
    INDEX   669

List of Illustrations

29 Martha Washington COURTESY LIBRARY OF CONGRESS
39 Martha Washington walking in public with the president COURTESY LIBRARY OF CONGRESS
45 Martha Washington and Abigail Adams (dark hair, seated left) receiving guests COURTESY DAR MUSEUM, WASHINGTON, D.C.
47 A royal "Lady Washington" in commercial engraving COURTESY LIBRARY OF CONGRESS
53 Quaker widow Dolley Payne Todd COURTESY NATIONAL PARK SERVICE, INDEPENDENCE NATIONAL HISTORICAL PARK, PHILADELPHIA
62 Abigail Smith Adams PORTRAIT OF ABIGAIL ADAMS BY LYDIA SMITH COURTESY OF THE SOCIETY FOR THE PRESERVATION OF NEW ENGLAND ANTIQUITIES
73 Dolley Madison AUTHOR'S COLLECTION
78 Martha Jefferson COURTESY LIBRARY OF CONGRESS
84 Dolley Madison appearing as the first president's wife to grace a magazine cover, on the *Portfolio* COURTESY LIBRARY OF CONGRESS
91 Dolley Madison saving portrait of George Washington during War of 1812 COURTESY LIBRARY OF CONGRESS
99 Julia Tyler AUTHOR'S COLLECTION
101 Elizabeth Monroe AUTHOR'S COLLECTION
109 Louisa Catherine Adams AUTHOR'S COLLECTION
113 Mass-produced engraving of Rachel Jackson COURTESY LIBRARY OF CONGRESS
117 Mass-produced engraving of Angelica Van Buren COURTESY LIBRARY OF CONGRESS
119 Julia Gardiner, "the Rose of Long Island," appearing in the first personal advertising endorsement COURTESY OF THE MUSEUM OF THE CITY OF NEW YORK
120 Anna Harrison COURTESY LIBRARY OF CONGRESS
122 Letitia Tyler COURTESY MCCLURE PUBLISHERS
125 Julia Gardiner behind column as the cannon "Peacemaker" explodes on the naval vessel *Princeton,* fancifully portrayed by Currier & Ives COURTESY LIBRARY OF CONGRESS
127 Julia Gardiner Tyler in the first photograph of an incumbent First Lady COURTESY LIBRARY OF CONGRESS
132 Julia Gardiner Tyler portrayed in the first political cartoon involving a president's wife COURTESY TENNESSEE ARCHIVES
144 Sarah Polk, Dolley Madison, Harriet Lane, James Buchanan, and James Polk pose for a group photograph. COURTESY GEORGE EASTMAN HOUSE
149 Mary Lincoln COURTESY LIBRARY OF CONGRESS
152 Margaret Taylor, her unknown face conveniently covered by a handkerchief, at the deathbed of her husband COURTESY LIBRARY OF CONGRESS
153 Abigail Fillmore COURTESY LIBRARY OF CONGRESS
158 Jane Pierce COURTESY LIBRARY OF CONGRESS

160 Harriet Lane and James Buchanan at the 1857 Inaugural Ball COURTESY LIBRARY OF
     CONGRESS
165 Harriet Lane, drawn for the pictorial newspapers, appearing with the title "first lady"
     FROM LESLIE'S ILLUSTRATED NEWSPAPER
186 Mary Lincoln reviewing troops with the president and their son Tad COURTESY
     LIBRARY OF CONGRESS
192 Julia Grant meets Mary Lincoln in the East Room. COURTESY LIBRARY OF CONGRESS
201 Julia Grant COURTESY LIBRARY OF CONGRESS
204 Eliza Johnson AUTHOR'S COLLECTION
219 Julia Grant receiving guests AUTHOR'S COLLECTION
224 Outgoing First Lady Julia Grant's luncheon for her successor, Lucy Hayes COURTESY
     LIBRARY OF CONGRESS
226 Lucy Hayes COURTESY LIBRARY OF CONGRESS
232 Mary Lincoln as wandering widow COURTESY LIBRARY OF CONGRESS
236 Lucretia Garfield COURTESY LIBRARY OF CONGRESS
243 Lucretia Garfield preparing food for her wounded husband in the White House
     kitchens FROM LESLIE'S ILLUSTRATED NEWSPAPER
245 "Mrs. Ex-President Tyler" COURTESY VALENTINE MUSEUM, RICHMOND, VIRGINIA
247 Ellen Arthur COURTESY LIBRARY OF CONGRESS
251 Frances Cleveland AUTHOR'S COLLECTION
256 First Lady bride Frances Cleveland hugging her mother, Emma Folsom, with
     President Grover Cleveland in background FROM LESLIE'S ILLUSTRATED NEWSPAPER,
     COURTESY OF NATIONAL GEOGRAPHIC
257 Under a parasol, "Frankie" Cleveland is rushed by curious fans in St. Louis.
     COURTESY LIBRARY OF CONGRESS
264 "Frankie" Cleveland, victim of unauthorized commercial exploitation COURTESY
     NATIONAL MUSEUM OF AMERICAN HISTORY, SMITHSONIAN INSTITUTION
269 Caroline Harrison at the president's desk FROM LESLIE'S ILLUSTRATED NEWSPAPER
271 Caroline Harrison, first president-general of the DAR, with other founding members
     COURTESY NATIONAL SOCIETY OF THE DAUGHTERS OF THE AMERICAN REVOLUTION
     ARCHIVES, PHOTO COLLECTION
274 Live sketch of the deathbed scene of First Lady Harrison, drawn for the public by a
     newspaper correspondent COURTESY LIBRARY OF CONGRESS
279 Julia Grant as "Queen Mother" of Washington AUTHOR'S COLLECTION
283 Ida McKinley used on her husband's campaign paraphernalia COURTESY NATIONAL
     MUSEUM OF AMERICAN HISTORY, SMITHSONIAN INSTITUTION
287 Ida McKinley being wrapped in a shawl by the president before they review a parade
     COURTESY LIBRARY OF CONGRESS
289 Nelli Taft in native Filipino costume FROM RECOLLECTIONS OF FULL YEARS
293 Helen Taft COURTESY LIBRARY OF CONGRESS
299 Edith Roosevelt at her "office" desk COURTESY LIBRARY OF CONGRESS
304 Edith Roosevelt, Theodore Roosevelt, and "Princess" Alice Roosevelt, with the
     biggest bouquet COURTESY LIBRARY OF CONGRESS
317 Nellie Taft riding back with her husband after his Inaugural, setting a precedent
     COURTESY LIBRARY OF CONGRESS
325 The widow Galt, first woman in Washington to own a car COURTESY WOODROW
     WILSON HOUSE, A PROPERTY OF THE NATIONAL TRUST FOR HISTORIC PRESERVATION
333 Nellie Taft, circa 1912 campaign COURTESY LIBRARY OF CONGRESS
341 Edith Wilson PHOTOGRAPH BY HARRIS AND EWING; COURTESY LIBRARY OF CONGRESS

344 Artist Ellen Wilson behind several of her landscapes COURTESY LIBRARY OF CONGRESS

357 Edith Wilson, separating the president from his longtime adviser, Colonel House COURTESY NATIONAL ARCHIVES

363 Edith Wilson, second from right, working at the Union Station canteen, giving coffee to doughboys on their way to war AUTHOR'S COLLECTION

365 Young Eleanor Roosevelt and her husband, the assistant secretary of the navy, with two admirals COURTESY FRANKLIN D. ROOSEVELT LIBRARY

367 Edith Wilson receiving Christmas gift from World War I soldiers in France COURTESY LIBRARY OF CONGRESS

374 Edith Wilson, guiding the president COURTESY LIBRARY OF CONGRESS

384 Edith Wilson and Florence Harding ride together to Inaugural ceremonies, setting a precedent AUTHOR'S COLLECTION

385 Grace Coolidge COURTESY LIBRARY OF CONGRESS

388 Florence Harding giving short speech at the White House COURTESY LIBRARY OF CONGRESS

392 Florence Harding greeting wounded veterans at Walter Reed Hospital COURTESY LIBRARY OF CONGRESS

403 Grace and Calvin Coolidge with Nellie and William Howard Taft, microphone behind them COURTESY LIBRARY OF CONGRESS

411 Grace Coolidge at Easter Egg Roll, with Jim Haley, her Service agent, behind her at right COURTESY LIBRARY OF CONGRESS

421 Grace Coolidge, former teacher of the deaf, and Helen Keller COURTESY LIBRARY OF CONGRESS

433 Eleanor Roosevelt COURTESY FRANKLIN D. ROOSEVELT LIBRARY

436 Lou Hoover tilling the soil in Girl Scout uniform COURTESY LIBRARY OF CONGRESS

440 Lou Hoover working a sewing machine during the Depression COURTESY LIBRARY OF CONGRESS

459 Eleanor Roosevelt, in gold lamé gown, joins in an evening radio broadcast before attending reception. COURTESY LIBRARY OF CONGRESS

481 Eleanor Roosevelt and two black guard escorts at Howard University, in photo used against her in a racist pamphlet COURTESY LIBRARY OF CONGRESS

489 Eleanor Roosevelt addressing and acknowledging the 1940 Democratic Convention—the first First Lady to do so COURTESY FRANKLIN D. ROOSEVELT LIBRARY

492 Eleanor Roosevelt at her Office of Civilian Defense office COURTESY LIBRARY OF CONGRESS

498 The First Lady, in Red Cross uniform, behind the "Our Eleanor" during World War II in the South Pacific COURTESY FRANKLIN D. ROOSEVELT LIBRARY

501 Lady Bird Johnson, congressional wife, circa mid-forties COURTESY LYNDON B. JOHNSON LIBRARY

513 Mamie Eisenhower COURTESY NATIONAL MUSEUM OF AMERICAN HISTORY, SMITHSONIAN INSTITUTE

525 Jimmy and Rosalynn Carter on their wedding day, 1946 COURTESY JIMMY CARTER LIBRARY

526 Bess Truman, Frances Cleveland (Preston), Harry Truman, Herbert Hoover, and Edith Wilson at Princeton University Bicentennial COURTESY PRINCETON UNIVERSITY LIBRARY

531 Bess Truman christening a plane at one of her rare speeches ABBIE ROWE, NATIONAL
     PARK SERVICE; COURTESY OF HARRY S TRUMAN LIBRARY

533 Bess Truman and her Independence Tuesday Bridge Club visiting her in Washington
     COPYRIGHT THE WASHINGTON POST; REPRINTED BY PERMISSION OF THE WASHINGTON,
     D.C., PUBLIC LIBRARY

542 Mamie Eisenhower in her cornfields in the garden of the French château where she and
     the general lived while he was head of NATO COPYRIGHT THE WASHINGTON POST;
     REPRINTED BY PERMISSION OF THE WASHINGTON, D.C., PUBLIC LIBRARY
     Newlyweds Ronald and Nancy Reagan pose for Hollywood fan magazine photo.
     COURTESY LIBRARY OF CONGRESS

546 Betty and Gerald Ford campaigning in 1952 with Mamie and Ike COURTESY GERALD R.
     FORD LIBRARY

550 Outgoing Bess Truman shaking hands with incoming Mamie after the former's tour of
     the White House for the latter COPYRIGHT THE WASHINGTON POST; REPRINTED BY
     PERMISSION OF THE WASHINGTON, D.C., PUBLIC LIBRARY

555 Mamie Eisenhower meets the press at her first and only press conference. COPYRIGHT
     THE WASHINGTON POST; REPRINTED BY PERMISSION OF THE WASHINGTON, D.C., PUBLIC
     LIBRARY

558 Newlyweds George and Barbara Bush, circa 1948 COURTESY THE WHITE HOUSE

560 First Lady Eisenhower takes the podium from President Eisenhower, to cheering crowd
     COURTESY WIDE WORLD PHOTOS

570 Former First Ladies Edith Wilson, Eleanor Roosevelt, and Bess Truman at Washington
     dinner COURTESY LIBRARY OF CONGRESS

577 The young Senator John F. Kennedy chatting with former First Lady Grace Coolidge
     COURTESY CLARKE SCHOOL FOR THE DEAF, CENTER FOR ORAL EDUCATION

579 Senate wife Jacqueline Kennedy campaigning for Stevenson at the 1956 Democratic
     Convention COURTESY WIDE WORLD PHOTOS

584 Mamie Eisenhower and her "Rock of Gibraltar," Second Lady Pat Nixon COURTESY
     DWIGHT D. EISENHOWER LIBRARY

586 Mamie Eisenhower promoting her "project," the American Heart Association
     COPYRIGHT THE WASHINGTON POST; REPRINTED BY PERMISSION OF THE WASHINGTON,
     D.C., PUBLIC LIBRARY

595 Jacqueline Kennedy at press-conference discussion of women's, health, and educational
     issues during 1960 campaign COPYRIGHT THE WASHINGTON POST; REPRINTED BY
     PERMISSION OF THE WASHINGTON, D.C., PUBLIC LIBRARY

602 The Kennedy Inaugural was also the largest gathering of First Ladies in history—
     eight—including (left to right) Pat Nixon, Mamie Eisenhower, Lady Bird Johnson,
     Edith Wilson (behind Mrs. Johnson), and Jacqueline Kennedy. Not pictured, but
     present, Bess Truman, Eleanor Roosevelt, and Betty Ford. COPYRIGHT THE
     WASHINGTON POST

. . . the . . . historian . . . will put be-
fore us the men and women as they actually
lived, so that we shall recognize them for
what they were—living beings.
        —Theodore Roosevelt
        President, 1901–1909

PART I
The Federal Era
1789–1801

If you have any learning, keep it a profound secret, especially from the men,
who generally look with a jealous and
malignant eye on a woman of great parts
and cultivated understanding.
—*A Father's Legacy to His*
Daughter (1775)

Prologue: May 1789

Once made equal to man, woman becomes his superior.
—SOCRATES

ON THE LAST day of April in the capital city of New York, George Washington, heroic general of the Revolution for the American colonies' independence from Great Britain, places his hand on a Bible, repeats a simple oath, and becomes enpowered as the head of state of this new "democratic" government, the first such leader of these United States. Along the route from his Virginia estate, Mount Vernon, up to New York, he was feted in a grand procession of testimonial dinners, toasts, pyrotechnical displays, and musical tributes. Appropriately enough, he travels alone, as if familial connection would somehow ennoble him less, and permit them escape of public notice. How he is to be addressed is a current issue of debate. Something more than a title, however, seems lacking. As the days flow into May, about three weeks after his arrival a curious anticipation stirs in the public, in the press, and in the general.

May 1789. On the royal courts, three women sat.

In faraway Russia is Catherine the Great. She'd come to power by marrying the right man, and, widowed, she now reigns with unbridled autonomy. Catherine has herself declared empress, leads victorious battles against the Turks, and widens Russia's borders. The French thrash to and fro as they wrestle Providence's will to dethrone King Louis and Queen Marie Antoinette. Marie wasn't responsible for *"le déficit"* that the rousers, in their call for liberty, named as one ripe reason for revolution. Yet, in royal robes and lofty coiffure, she's become a hated symbol, almost universally so after her involvement in the "Affair of the Diamond Necklace." She has manipulative power as well as style, influencing Louis to resist the National Assembly's attempt to abolish the feudal system and not to relent to calls for restriction of royal prerogative. In the "democracy," based on the ancient Greek notion of justice, Marie will be tried—and will meet the grisly slicer, in view of "the press and the public." Then there is Charlotte, wife of England's George III. A coarse German with a flat mouth, her role seems confined to protecting George in his precarious mental state, not for power but as a devoted wife. To this mother of fourteen, barely able to speak English, a nursing smock seems more appropos than regalia.

Three wives of leaders, females of power, each playing different roles, are Catherine, Marie Antoinette, and Charlotte.

The American immigrants have such legends in their heritages. The Spanish knew of Isabella who funded Columbus, and Maria Luisa Teresa, whose power over her feeble king ruined the treasury. The French had Margaret, who left court to travel alongside Louis IX on the Seventh Crusade, attempting to involve herself in politics. The Swedes in Delaware named Christiana after their queen, a linguist and athlete. The Scottish Margaret had so helped the poor that she was literally canonized. In Africa, some tribes were matriarchal. Even natives knew the power. In the Iroquois nation, families lived in the squaws' longhouses. Renowned through the ages, England's Elizabeth was more powerful than most kings, and immigrants to North America were mostly English.

The colonies had already experienced such women. There was the outspoken Bay Stater Mercy Warren, and Hannah Winthrop, the governor's wife, appointed by the colony's General Court in 1775, along with a "farmeress" to question Tory women. The husband of the farmeress, a member of the Continental Congress, wrote her, ". . . you are now a politician and now elected into an important office, that of judgess of the Tory ladies, which will give you, naturally, an influence with your sex . . ." This wife hoped that democracy would give all women rights, and admonished him, "I desire you would remember the ladies and be more generous and favorable to them than your ancestors! Do not put such unlimited power into the hands of the husbands . . . If particular care and attention is not paid to the ladies, we are determined to foment a rebellion, and will not hold ourselves bound by any laws in which we have no voice or representation."

"I cannot say that I think you are very generous to the ladies," she badgered in another missive, "you insist upon retaining an absolute power over your wives. But . . . we have it in our power not only to free ourselves but to subdue our masters, and without violence throw both your natural and legal authority at our feet." As the American Revolution continued, so had she: "If our men are all drawn off and we should be attacked, you will find a race of Amazons in America . . . if General Washington and his whole army should be cut off I hoped that an army of females would oppose him." And she broached the subject of women being elected to political office: "Patriotism in the female sex is the most disinterested of all virtues—excluded from the honors and from offices we cannot attach ourselves to the state or government from having held a place of eminence—even in the freest countrys our property is subject to the control and disposal of our partners, to whom the laws have given sovereign authorities—deprived of a voice in legislation, obliged to submit to those laws which are imposed upon us, is it not sufficient to make us indifferent to the public welfare?"

The same woman, in the position of the wife of the American ambassador to England, had recently reported how Charlotte, swathed in silver and purple, had seemed embarrassed at receiving her. So thought "farmeress" Abigail Adams, of late the wife of the vice president. Democratic government promised no monarchy. While not all questions had been resolved, it was decided that there would be no George the king. Just George the president. Perhaps some Americans hoped that the presidency would inhibit the unchecked power that queens had held through the centuries.

And now, a month later, seemingly out of the blue, the East Coast buzzed with frenetic anticipation. In Baltimore, a doctor's brother arranged for pyramids of fireworks. In a Philadelphia ballroom, tricolored bunting was being hung. In New York, the expectant air was thickest. A festooned barge docked near noisy Wall Street. Oarsman in white uniforms would have the privilege of rowing the same vessel that had carried Washington.

For progeny, a king must always have a queen. But what of a president? Americans knew they didn't want George and Charlotte. Just George and Martha.

The Lady in the Coach

IT WAS THREE o'clock on the afternoon of May 16, 1789, and on the oval drive of pebbles, in front of the buff-stoned, red-roofed manor house of Mount Vernon, "everything seemed to be in confusion—packing—and making all the necessary preparations for the intended peregrinations to N.Y." So wrote young Robert Lewis in his diary as hefty trunks were heaved onto the coach.

Bob was a dutiful nephew. His uncle George, now president, had entrusted the young man with the responsibility of escorting a particular female up the East Coast. For a full two months, plans had been under way for this special journey. The first detail was securing the proper coach. Bob wrote his uncle that his "grandmother was very well disposed to lend the carriage, but on condition that it should be returned when of no further use to my aunt." The offer was turned down. On May 3, one William Heth, agent of traveling coaches, was so proud of his "particular and pointed arrangements" that he wrote President Washington, "I flatter myself, that she will experience no other inconvenience from not having her own Coachman & Horses, than will naturally arise from *female apprehensions*, on being drove by *Strange* coachman, with *Strange* Horses." Heth had contracted with the reliable Gabriel Van Horne, who ran a successful post line from northern Virginia to Philadelphia, arranged for the rental of horses, coaches, and drivers for private trips, and owned many taverns along the way. Van Horne was honored by this particular contract, and so worried about the precarious route between the Potomac and Susquehannah rivers, that to "Aid the Safe Conveyance" he would "do the Honour of Attending her . . ."

Now, the coach was about to depart, and Bob Lewis noticed how "servants" and "field negroes" appeared "to take leave of their mistress—numbers of these poor wretches seemed much greatly agitated . . . aunt equally so." The short, snow-white-haired woman, just a few weeks short of turning sixty years old, spent the next day in nearby Alexandria, arranging final details of her private life. She was taking two grandchildren, George, eight, and Patsy, ten, with her. In the dark of five two mornings later, Bob watched the "pathetic and affecting scene," children "a bawling" as they left their mother. Everyone involved seemed to sense that this was to be no ordinary journey.

Four hours later, they arrived at the Potomac River ferry and crossed to Georgetown in such a strong current that his aunt became extremely alarmed. Once there, she "preferred walking up to the tavern," instead of being driven. The trip was delayed for two hours when the frightened horses "so baulked" that they broke from the reins, and ran away. Van Horne sent for replacements and fixed the coach. By 1:00 P.M., they arrived in Bladensburg, Maryland, stopping briefly for "a cold cut with some wine." Three hours later, the party arrived at a Major Snowden's home, where they stayed the night. Because of the exacting "arrangements" of her schedule, the stout woman in mobcap and "fine Hartford brown" homespun turned down a kind offer to rest through the next day.

She was evidently anxious this particular day of May 19, as the coach headed out in the morning with Snowden escorting on horseback for about ten miles. As they prepared to near the city limits, Bob noticed that his aunt "shifted herself here, expecting to be met by numbers of Gentlemen out of Baltimore . . ." She seemed to be bracing for some unspoken metamorphosis, from the private person of a grandmother and aunt to something *public*. Rain clouds literally gathered above. Having looked forward to a pastoral retirement with her husband the general, the woman peering out the coach window wasn't particularly joyous about her journey's purpose. Perhaps the only certainty of what she faced was what they'd call her. The Continental Army soldiers and then the colonists had been formally addressing her as "Lady" for over a decade. She herself neither encouraged nor used it, but admirers had nothing but British nobility from which to find a reverential title, perhaps out of some notion that as the most revered female in the colonies, this wife of America's greatest hero was their representative in Charlotte's court.

After descending a valley affording a breaktaking glimpse of the Elk Ridge hamlet, orchards and meadows tucked about the meandering Patuxent River, President Washington's wife, in what would seem like her last moment of calm, boarded a boat to cross.

As they traveled the river, it suddenly turned treacherous; "the wind by this time had risen almost to a storm—the waves running very high, the boat took in a great deal of water which frightened my Aunt a good deal," Bob recorded. He, Van Horne, and the ferrymen, managed the vessel, safely, to the other side.

As the "Lady" with wooden and metal dentures debarked, there awaited an official party of five "Gentleman from Baltimore who had come out for the purpose of escorting Mrs. Washington into town," including a doctor, a captain, and a colonel. A messenger arrived to inform her that a welcome was being prepared by Margaret Carroll, sister of the president's wartime aide-de-camp, at her countryside home. The growing group "formed ourselves in line of march" and proceeded with regal simplicity to Mrs. Carroll's, where they consumed "a large bowl of salubrious ice punch" in fifteen minutes. While the men repaired to the city, the "Lady" stayed behind to rest briefly. In private.

Later this day of May 19, as soon as her coach entered Baltimore, Martha Dandridge Custis Washington realized how thoroughly she had lost her cherished private life and been thrust into public as she had never been before. The stragglers who'd cheered the coach became a crowd by the time it pulled up before the town home of friends Dr. and Mrs. James McHenry.

A special "tea reception" had been prearranged in her honor, and regardless of whether she wished to endure it, Martha proceeded "as she had promised," retired to a room to change from her summer clothes into grander dress. Then, descending the staircase, this private person was feted as "this truly respectable personage," as one newspaper reporter termed her. Martha made her first officially public appearance as "Lady Washington," the president's wife. At the reception "a number of Ladies," the assiduous Bob Lewis wrote, "assembled to pay their respects to Mrs. Washington, the names of which are too numerous to insert . . ." The public gathered outside for an "elegant entertainment" and a fireworks display in Lady Washington's honor, "judiciously managed" by Dr. McHenry's brother. The *Maryland Journal* and *Baltimore Advertiser* noted that besides fireworks "before and after Supper . . . she was serenaded by an excellent band of music, conducted by Gentleman of the Town." The news was dispatched and carried across America by the *Gazette of the United States.* Bob was blunter: "[T]o sleep was impossible . . . we were serenaded until two o'clock in the morning . . ."

Lady Washington and party arose at five, "to avoid any parade that might be intended." They headed out for Philadelphia, Van Horne having turned over the coach to a Mr. Kerlin as the roads improved. This time, as they neared Philadelphia in the afternoon, the *governor,* with *two* military troops, and a group of women in smaller coaches escorted Martha into the city. Near Gray's Ferry, about a hundred prominent Philadelphians honored her at a "collation" at a local inn. Crowds flanked the coach as it rolled down the streets. Bells pealed. Then, giving equal importance to the "Lady" as they did her husband, a thirteen-gun salute boomed rapid fire. Cheers went up: "God Bless Lady Washington!" It was all reported in the *Pennsylvania Packet.*

The May 26 *Pennsylvania and Daily Advertiser* noted that the public adulation "recalled the remembrance of those interesting scenes, in which, by her presence, she contributed to relieve the cares of our beloved Chief, and to soothe the anxious moments of his military concern—gratitude marked the recollection, and every countenance bespoke the feelings of affectionate respect." Here, Martha began to realize she was now more than herself, fulfilling some sort of government "role." Although few females in *any* position would have done so, the realization that she was now somehow different prompted the quiet woman to formally acknowledge the public. Martha delivered her only speech, extemporaneously. "She arose," one account stated, "and standing in the carriage, thanked the troops who had escorted her, and the citizens also." It was the first public act in the role. She was less certain how to react to citizens and reporters who trailed her as she privately shopped for "new fashioned" shoes at "Mr. Whiteside's fancy dry goods store." She was recognized.

From Philadelphia, a Mr. Mercereau drove the coach, now including Martha's friend Marcia Morris and her two daughters, with the "Troops of the Light Horse" escorting. *Daily Advertiser and Gazette* dispatch reporters trailed the coach. In two days, they arrived at the Elizabethtown, New Jersey, wharf, and Lady Washington was escorted by the governor to the dockside, where the festooned forty-seven-foot presidential barge with thirteen liveried oarsman and two snapping flags awaited. There, too, she was rejoined with George. As the oarsman rowed the Lady with precision timing, rounding the southern tip of Manhattan's Battery, another thirteen-gun cannon shook the sky in her honor. Slicing through the clearing smoke, the barge pulled up carefully to Peck's Slip, where ruddy Governor Clinton gregariously extended his hands in welcome along with a formal committee.

The shouts of "God Bless Lady Washington" began. Reporters focused on her fashion, the *Gazette* noting "she was clothed in the manufacture of our Country, in which her native goodness and patriotism appeared to the greatest advantage." The private Martha seemed adjusted to reading her name in public print, writing, nonplussed, to a niece, "the paper will tell you how I was complimented on my landing . . ." As she headed into town, Lady Washington was impressed by "the great parade" around her.

It was May 27, 1789. The queen had arrived.[1]

− 2 −

"A Very Great Some Body"

IF PROVIDENCE ITSELF had divinely intervened, a woman who better looked and played the part could not have been found.

She seemed always surrounded in white—white muslins, white satins, white dusters, white mobcaps, white hair. The simplicity made her classic, in the words of one European, like a "Roman matron." If she

did not adapt well to the latest style of the Continental beau monde, she had an inbred, timeless grace. Somehow, here in this kindly yet staid grandmother, there was an absolutely brilliant balance between Queen and commoner. A woman who was equally herself through the already legendary winter at Valley Forge and the regal English courts of Williamsburg gentry. She was filled with as much humility as grandness. She was somehow both democratic and not so much elitist, but august. In her role as wife of George Washington the combination seemed to be precisely what the Americans envisioned. Martha was as noble as George, but her naturalness seemed apparent, whereas he stayed noble.

She even made her own coffee in the morning.

She had been born on June 13, 1731, daughter of wealthy tobacco farmer and English immigrant John Dandridge, maturing on the outskirts of Williamsburg, a belle in the court of the royal governor. Martha's education lacked lessons in grammar and writing, a fact that embarrassed her. Sensitive to public knowledge of this deficiency, she dictated her public correspondence, then hand-copied it with perfect spelling. Amid Williamsburg's statesmen, she was comfortable and familiar with politics. Legend claimed that she was bold, riding her horse onto the steps of a home, slapping an officer who made an impertinent remark, and pursuing a wealthy bachelor, tobacco heir Daniel Custis, *twenty* years her senior. Against his father's wishes, he married the seventeen-year-old, and they had four children. Only a son survived adolescence. When Custis died eight years later, Martha became perhaps the wealthiest female in the colony, inheriting an estate and a property of seventeen thousand tobacco acres, along with several hundred slaves. Martha controlled her business, firing off pointed letters to London tobacco merchants, demanding tersely that they get her "an uncommon Price" for her shipments.[1]

The relationship that developed between Martha and George Washington, then a British officer, as commander in chief of Virginia's forces—was complex. At twenty-seven, Martha married him less than two years after being widowed. It was a respectful, not passionate romance. Martha wanted a father for her children; for George, Martha's business ventures held undeniable appeal. Her family, George wrote, had "disgust at the news" of their union, but she married for herself, not the Dandridges. Affection grew, and just after their engagement, George wrote Martha, "Since that happy hour when we made our pledges to each other, my thoughts have been continually going to you as to another self."[2]

An underlying tension developed when the marriage proved barren. George claimed Martha was incapable of further childbearing, and said that if she died first and he remarried "a girl," he could produce heirs. There was no evidence that Martha was jealous over his earlier affection for their neighbor Sally Fairfax, though it was *after* his marriage that George wrote Sally that nothing could "eradicate from my mind those happy moments, the happiest of my life, which I have enjoyed in your company."[3]

When George became general in the American Revolution, rumors circulated that Martha was a Tory, one newspaper stating that "being a warm loyalist" she'd separated from him, and "lives very much respected" in New York. Martha, however, defended herself and the colonies' right to war, saying, "I foresee the consequences . . . domestic happiness suspended . . . property of every kind put in jeopardy by war . . . But what are all these evils when compared with the fate of which the Port Bill may only be a threat? My mind is made up; my heart is in the cause . . ."[4]

Asserting her loyalty was likely a partial motivation for her annual winter treks to George's side, in Cambridge, Morristown, Valley Forge, and Middlebrook, New York. She was a conspicuous presence. At headquarters, she was entrusted with military secrets by George as he pressed her into clerical service, copying his correspondence. She discussed the war with statesmen and military leaders, writing nonchalantly, "I have been to dinner with two of the Generals, Lee and Putnam." Pierre Etienne du Ponceau recalled a meeting he and Baron Von Steuben had with her: "Our conversation was on general subjects . . . she reminded me of the Roman matrons of whom I had read so much about . . ."[5]

Martha knew confidential military movements, revealing to her sister, "Lord Dunmore, with part of his fleet, was to come to General Howe at Staten Island; that another division of Hessians is expected before they think the regulars will begin to attack on us. Some here begin to think there will be no battle after all. Last week our boats made another attempt on the ships up the North River, and had grappled a fire-ship to the *Phoenix* ten minutes, but she got clear of her antagonist and is come down the river. On Saturday last our people burnt one of the tenders. I thank God we shan't want men. The army at New York is very large, and numbers of men are still going. There is at this time in this city 4000, on their march to camp, and the Virginians are daily expected." She nevertheless ended with the "wish there was an end to the War." Her inspection of shelled Boston in 1775 made her shudder at war's devastation.[6]

Martha had no fears of the 1775 threat of Virginia's royal governor to capture her at Mount Vernon as a war hostage, but George was incensed. "I can hardly think that Lord Dunmore can act so low, and unmanly a part, as to think of seizing Mrs. Washington by way of revenge upon me." Unlike Martha, who acquiesced to leaving their home and visiting family, the general was frightened. His nephew Lund reassured him that "she does not believe she is in any danger . . . ten minutes notice would be sufficient for her to get out of the way." Lund's suggestion that "she has often declared she would go to the camp if you would permit her" may have been another reason that the general granted her permission to travel with him. Living at the front was no less a threat than capture, but at least Martha could oversee camp life—and that she did.[7]

She became nationally known as a result of the Revolution. The *Virginia Gazette* of August 2, 1777, reported that, upon her arrival on a brief visit to Williamsburg, "she was saluted with the firing of cannon and small arms . . ." At Valley Forge, a regiment was named "Lady Washington's Dragoon." Already that title had become affixed. The more she traveled, the more attention she attracted. "I don't doubt," she wrote her sister, "but you have seen the figure our arrival made in the Philadelphia paper—and I left it in as great pomp as if I had been a very great some body." Not only was she becoming as widely known as George, she was being regularly mentioned in newspapers, a rarity for any female. She was the recipient of gifts as honors to her personally. The Pennsylvania Assembly had given her a coach that once belonged to Governor William Penn. The city of Williamsburg remembered their native daughter by presenting her with a gold medal. Perhaps the most brilliant of intended gifts, and one that might later have raised controversy, was "an elegant present" from Marie Antoinette. The French ship carrying it, however, was captured by the British, and the item later appeared at auction.[8]

Since Martha had enjoyed this popularity, by 1789 it was not public adulation that presented uncertainty for her, but rather a public role. Once settled in New York, she was frustrated by the limitations her position placed upon her, particularly the protocol established in her absence, forbidding the president and his wife to dine at private homes. Even her return social calls to prominent women who left their cards must be limited. This, to a woman accustomed to managing the vast business of a plantation and traveling the coast independent of her husband for nearly two decades, was a shock. Resentfully, she wrote, "I live a very dull life here and know nothing that passes in the town. I never go to any public place . . . indeed, I am more like a state prisoner than anything else. There is certain boundaries set for me which I must not depart from . . . and as I cannot do as I like, I am obstinate, and stay at home a great deal."[9]

Several months later, she thanked a friend for a letter that gave her "more satisfaction than all the formal compliments and empty ceremonies of mere etiquette." She revealingly added, "I am only fond of what comes from the heart." Reflecting on her role, Martha continued, "The difficulties which presented themselves . . . entering upon the Presidency seem thus to be in some measure surmounted . . . my new and unwished-for situation is not indeed a burden to me . . . I sometimes think the arrangement is not quite as it ought to have been; that I, who had much rather be at home, should occupy a place which a great many younger and gayer women would be prodigiously pleased."

She concluded with a complacent philosophy on the role. "I do not . . . feel dissatisfied with my present situation. No. God forbid! For everybody and everything conspire to make me as contented as possible in it. Yet I know too much of the vanity of human affairs to expect felicity from the splendid scenes of public life. I am still determined to be cheerful and to be happy, in whatever situation I may be; for I have also learned from experience that the greater part of our happiness or misery depends upon our dispositions, and not upon our circumstances . . ."[10]

Since the capital was being moved to Philadelphia late in 1790, the Washingtons lived in New York for just a year, in two different residences. Lady Washington soon settled into a daily schedule. Her grandson recalled that she was "an uncommon early riser, leaving her pillow at day-dawn at all seasons of the year, and becoming at once actively engaged in her household duties." After breakfast with the president, she returned to her room for an hour, reading all newspapers delivered to him. Then it was "paying calls." During her first years in the role, Martha held afternoon receptions on Tuesday and Friday afternoons, for special callers. Later it was reduced to just Tuesday. Supper was at three, and formal dinners while Congress was in session were held on various days, save Friday, Martha's reception night. Other evenings, the Washingtons indulged in theater, their entrance into the presidential box heralded by the playing of a grand air, "The President's March," at which the entire audience would rise. Some nights they attended the assemblies, George engaging in the minuet, Martha never dancing. She, who admitted to always having a complaint, said "I have not had one half hour to myself since the day of my arrival."[11]

Martha spent her rare private moments with an escort, friend, or two grandchildren, prowling the museum or waxworks, taking in a ventriloquist show, pestering a painter who promised portraits she commissioned, and playing the lottery. Later in the term, hairdresser Lawrence Marcey would set her coiffure in the morning at the presidential mansion. On one occasion, when the president was ill, Martha went as his representative to a public memorial service for the late General Nathaniel Greene, "of a patriotic nature," standing alongside members of Congress, government officials, and the Society of the Cincinnati.[12]

Martha's role as protective wife met its first challenge just two months after her ladyship commenced. When the president developed a large tumor requiring surgical removal in July, the presidency faced its first dilemma of a suspended executiveship. Martha helped alleviate the fear by taking quiet control behind the scenes. Rumor claimed that it was she who immediately ordered the rope drawn across the street to keep carriages and pedestrians away from the house, straw laid on the streets to muffle noise, and guards placed near the house to keep hawkers from loudly selling their wares. As George recuperated, she guarded him as they rode in their carriage, from which she had the seats removed so he could lie comfortably on his side. She cared for his health as her husband, not the president, but the situation established that a sick president was still chief, regardless of what others claimed as impairment.[13]

"Though I may not have a great deal of business of consequence," she admitted, "I have a great many avocations of one kind or another which imperceptibly consume my time." She began calling these years her "transitory life" and "lost days," and though she felt the greatest pressure by being on display at public events, Martha never canceled. "I have been so long accustomed to conform to events which are governed by public voice that I hardly dare indulge any personal wishes which cannot yield to that." Fortunately for her, the only event at which Martha had to meet personally with the vast, often motley public hordes was at the New Year's Day open-house reception, begun that first year. As time passed, she not only grew confident in her role, she evolved into a democratic "queen."[14]

Martha dressed elegantly but plainly, without the ruffled European high style popular in the Federal Era. Lady Washington never attempted to lead fashion, though she acquiesced to support a campaign to wear clothing made only in America. She was frugal when it came to personal items, hand-copying musical pieces rather than buying extra sheet music, but she insisted on "bigger and thicker" false teeth. Her standards were met, the vice president's wife, Abigail Adams, noting her "Teeth beautiful."[15]

Of necessity, she had a staff. Polly Lear, the wife of the president's chief aide, served as Lady Washington's unofficial social secretary for part of the administration, writing and sending invitations. "She did everything in her power," wrote one chronicler, "to relieve Mrs. Washington . . . she assumed the burden of the details connected with the drawing-rooms and other social functions, matters which Mrs. Washington, with her strong dislike for the formality necessary to her position, was only too glad to be rid of." Tavern owner Samuel Fraunces oversaw all dinners, entertainments, and teas—public and private. Bob Lewis continued to serve unofficially as her escort and assistant.[16]

Martha ruled supreme at her Friday receptions, deciding they should be auspiciously formal, which would hopefully establish respect for democracy's presidency, particularly in Europe. It seemed more permissible in the class-rigid New York. When the capital was moved from there, the *Gazette* reported that upon leaving the city, "Mrs. Washington appeared greatly affected . . ." Philadelphia, however, was a city she truly loved and in which she had many intimates. Martha was more

self-assured and relaxed here, frequently visiting the private homes of
her Revolutionary Era friends, like Marcia Morris, whose home the
Washingtons rented. The High Street mansion from which Lady Washington now reigned was perfectly Federal. Mr. Morris suggested that "it
is of great Importance to fix the Taste of our Country properly . . . your
Example will go very far . . . everything about you should be substantially good and majestically plain . . ." The house had "an external
aspect marking it as the abode of opulence."[17]

The staid atmosphere at Martha's Friday "levees" remained. An an-
nal recalled them as being "arranged in as formal a manner as that of
St. James or St. Cloud. Always an aristocrat, Mrs. Washington's administration . . . was but a reproduction of the customs and ceremonies
of foreign heads of government, and her receptions were arranged on
the plan of the English and French drawing-rooms . . . Reared as she
had been, a descendant of . . . the English nobility—aristocratic,
proud and pleased with her lofty position . . . her influence extended to
foreign lands."[18]

Guests entering the receiving hall were formally announced at the
entrance. Women were escorted to Lady Washington, where they made
"a most respectful curtsy." The president's wife made acknowledgment
only by stiff nodding. Guests were then led to chairs arranged in a
semicircle, she at the meridian. They were instructed to sit silently,
ignoring all others. The president passed by the ladies' chairs, speaking
a few polite words. The women were then led into another room,
where buffet tables of cakes, candied fruits, spiced meats, and tea were
spread out before them.

Men were welcome, and many "foreigners and strangers of distinction" came "all anxious to witness the grand experiment that was to determine how much rational liberty mankind is capable of enjoying, without that liberty degenerating into licentiousness." There were none of the bawdy flirtations and card games by candlelight here as there were in other society homes. The liveliest moment of Martha's Friday occurred when one woman's headdress feathers enflamed while brushing against a chandelier. Martha retired at nine, and the levee was over.[19]

Lady Washington was said to have protested some of the protocol that would dictate future presidencies—seating guests by rank, shaking no hands, accepting no invitations—but Colonel David Humphreys, Washington's assistant, who'd been secretary of legation in Paris, exerted his influence. Lady Washington, however, began to take on a few airs of her own.[20]

She drove about publicly in Philadelphia in a London-made yellow coach with affixed richly gilded medallions, pulled by cream-colored horses, and attended by liveried grooms in white and scarlet, the Washington colors. On each of its four panels was painted a lavish illustration of the four seasons, the artwork of Italian painter Cipriani. In the windows hung Venetian blinds, and the interior was lined with black leather curtains for privacy on rainy days.[21]

Annually, Lady Washington and the president attended birthday balls in his honor, akin to European ceremonies held for kings. A French nobleman, the duke de la Rochefoucauld-Liancourt, said, "I have seen balls on the President's birthday, where the splendor of the rooms, and the variety and richness of the dresses did not suffer in comparison with Europe." Martha was anxious to send out engravings of her picture being mass-produced by a printer, who asked her not to rush him. She wore, and was portrayed in, a peculiarly high-crowned headdress known, according to the Annals of Philadelphia as the "Queen's Nightcap." While the engraving pictured an undeniably queenly figure who little resembled the real person, it was a momentous occasion. For the first time, a president's lady was pictured by the press for the public. Around the oval engraving was printed what had become her unofficial but formal title. Martha never demurred when Vice President John Adams called her "the presidentess" or when another addressed her as "Lady President." The Gazette even went so far as to suggest "Marquise," but it was now engraved, "Lady Washington," and used by all loyal Federalists, the party of Washington and Adams.[22]

Regardless of what some anti-Federalists despised as royal symbols, Martha's queenliness was received with understanding and admiration across the sea by Europeans, part of the purpose for a royal touch. Ruthey Jones, a Belfast admirer of Martha's, had a gift hand-delivered to her, having "long wished for a safe opportunity" to send it. The countess of Buchan sent a medallion paste portrait of the president. German nobleman Andreas Everardus van Braam Houckgeest presented

Martha with an unusual set of Chinese export porcelain, on the borders
of which were the encircled names of the fifteen states, forming a round
chain. In the center, in large letters, were Lady Washington's initials.[23]

John Fenno, the rabid Federalist publisher of the *Gazette*, unwittingly sparked press criticism of Martha when he began naming society
females as "Lady" rather than "Mrs." in his paper. Anti-Federalist papers immediately attacked, the *Albany Register* editorializing of Martha's
Fridays: "We also find that Levees, Drawing-Rooms, &c. are not such
strange, incomprehensible distant things as we have imagined; and I
suppose, that in a few years, we shall have all the paraphernalia yet
wanting to give the superb finish to the grandeur of our AMERICAN
COURT! the purity of republican principle seems to be daily losing
ground." Others called them "court-like levees" and "queenly drawing-
rooms."[24]

The Lady was accused of "aping royalty." David Stuart wrote Martha that many Virginians criticized her Fridays as "awkward imitations
of royalty" with "more pomp than at St. James, and that your bows are
more distant and stiff." Anti-Federalist Albert Gallatin sarcastically
called Martha "our most gracious queen." Congressman Thomas
Rodney criticized that she was not royal *enough:* "In old countries, a
Lady of her rank would not be seen without a retinue of twenty persons." Another engraving showed the Martha of "Fine Hartford brown"
homespun now swathed in ermine and ruffled silks. Senator William
Maclay viewed Martha's role as a direct threat to democracy's stability:
"Levees may be extremely useful in old countries, where men of great
fortune are collected . . . But here I think they are hurtful . . . From
these small beginnings I fear we shall follow on nor cease till we have
reached the summit of court etiquette, and all the frivolities, fopperies
and expense practiced in European governments."[25]

Once the first attack was fired, press and public criticism of Lady
Washington seemed permissible.

In the face of such critics, Martha sustained the persona, considering it vital to the dignity of the presidency, but though she didn't take
the berating personally, she did give careful heed to conduct that could
be misinterpreted. She decided against using her father's coat-of-arms
seal on her letters, after going to some trouble in getting the impression. She bragged that many of her dresses were "manufactured . . .
from the ravellings of brown silk stockings and crimson damask chair
covers," and when the gowns became worn, they were unravelled into
thread spools.[26]

While Martha relaxed in friendly Philadelphia, she, like others of
her class, was largely unaware that beneath the colorful society existed
an entire gray world. For here, with religious tolerance, the Quakers
flocked and flourished. Dressed in plain clothes, advocating peace, and
eschewing show of any form, the Quakers were of liberal philosophy,

scorning severely the ownership of any slaves, and educating females equally with males.

One Friend, Virginia native John Payne, had freed rather than sell his slaves before emigrating to the city in 1783. His wife, Mary, shared equal responsibility in supporting the family, and in their previous home in North Carolina, where their daughter Dolley had been born in 1768, she assumed a position of authority as a chief clerk in their meetinghouse. Their daughters were given educations in language, math, and philosophy. Like many impressionable youths recently arrived in the mecca, Dolley had been tempted with the colorful fashions of the elegant females she saw pass before her, and was stupefied at the vast citizenry of America's most populated city. "I saw more people in my first half hour in Philadelphia," she later wrote, "than I had in my whole life." She, too, was noticed, and her ample figure was said to "wreak havoc with the hearts of Quaker lads." Curiously, she made a vow never to marry, but instead to remain independent of men. Not so her sister Lucy, who "fell" in the eyes of the Quakers by suddenly marrying George Steptoe Washington, a favorite nephew, and employee, of the president's.

George and Martha found themselves the unwilling financial and emotional foster parents to many of their nephews and nieces. Their material needs strained the Washingtons' resources, and employing relatives was often their only alternative. Financial constraint was a reason Martha longed for retirement at the end of George's term. When forced to contend with the prospect of a second term in 1792, he was said to have consulted Martha. She preferred he not run, but came to terms with it, later writing, "I cannot blame him for acting according to his ideas of duty in obeying the voice of his country."

Martha was present on March 4, 1793, in Philadelphia's Federal Hall, to witness the understated second Inauguration. The mood was tense, owing in part to the recent murders of Marie Antoinette and Louis XVI. Secretary of State Thomas Jefferson and fellow anti-Federalists favored friendly alliance with the new French government, while Vice President Adams recommended restraint.[27]

At receptions, Martha always reserved the seat to her right for Adams's wife, Abigail, and if anyone else took it, the president told that person to get up. With Martha, the fine-featured, brown-haired, brown-eyed Abigail found herself "much more deeply impressed than I ever did before their Majesties of Britain." The two women enjoyed vacationing and traveling together, but rarely discussed politics. Abigail attended public House of Representatives debates on the assumption of state debts and offered advice to John when he discussed procedures in the Senate. While home in Massachusetts, she took an informal poll of reaction to Jay's Treaty for John, adding that she suspected sympathizers with the new French government were trying to manipulate the public.

Her dislike of the French, and suspicion that the anti-Federalist press and Jefferson followers were undermining the American government, grew into open hatred. She even felt that when "Mrs. Washington was abused for her drawing-rooms" by the *National Gazette*, there was a far more devious political plot behind it. Abigail used her son, John Quincy Adams, who was serving as minister to Holland, to obtain confidential international information, and she channeled it, along with her fears, to other Federalists.

Next to Abigail, Martha seemed apolitical. Shrewdly, she was merely masking her nimble observations. In one letter, while she said that "we have not a simple article of news but politics, which I do not concern myself about," Martha added, "I wish you could see the papers that come here every week." Politics infused its way into her life.[28]

The president had "impressed her with his views so thoroughly that she could not distinguish her own," and though she held her tongue in public, Martha was said to discuss politics with him. Her grandson said she partook the president's "thoughts, councils and views" and "inspired confidence" in his policies. During the few times they were separated, George's letters to Martha mentioned public affairs, and she kept abreast. While he was coping with the Whiskey Rebellion, Martha reported confidentially to a niece, "The insurgents in the back country have carried matters so high that the President has been obliged to send a large body of men to settle the matter, and is to go himself tomorrow to meet the troops."[29]

While she called herself "no politician" who "likes to read the newspapers," Jefferson termed her keenness "estimable." She seemed most concerned about international relations. When asked about British-American relations, Lady Washington wrote, "The difficulties and distresses to which we have been exposed during the war must now be forgotten. We must endeavor to let our ways be the way of pleasantness and all our paths Peace."[30]

She was not so pacified toward the French, and there was a claim that when Jefferson and his supporters wanted to assist France in its war with England, invoking the Treaty of 1778, Lady Washington said that since France had overthrown the government that had negotiated the treaty, it was now void. Treasury Secretary Alexander Hamilton had forwarded the same theory. She also offered the point that Jefferson had never seen active duty, whereas Hamilton had, and that American neutrality must be maintained. In March 1794, she paid close attention to the new French government's representative. "There is a new French Minister arrived about ten days ago," she wrote. "He . . . can't speak a word of English. He will soon learn if he stays here. As far as *we* can judge . . . he is very agreeable a man."[31]

Martha was blatantly pro-American, and pointedly offered her opinion to a returning friend: ". . . that you arrived from Europe with all your prejudices in favor of America I have no doubt, for I think our country affords everything that can give pleasure or satisfaction to a rational mind . . ." Daily, she read a multitude of regional newspapers. While reading a Richmond paper, she noticed the mention of a new congressman, and thought it important to mention in an otherwise social letter. She kept an almanac at all times, and regularly purchased a variety of informational pamphlets. Among her collection of books was a copy of *General View of the Agriculture of Argyl . . . Drawn Up for the Consideration of the Board of Agriculture and Internal Improvement.* In New York, she attended some lectures. And political rhetoric fascinated her. In New York, she wrote the governor's wife that "finding that Congress will contrary to their usual practice on Saturdays assemble tomorrow, proposes to Mrs. Clinton to visit the federal building . . ." Mrs. Clinton accepted, and the females went to hear the political debates at six—not in the afternoon, but morning—on a Saturday.[32]

Martha respected differing opinions. When Dutchman Gijsbert Hogendorp criticized the president to her face, he said she received him "in dismal silence . . . but has not a bad opinion of me for not adoring her husband; she has eyes more perceptive than her husband; she has made many piquant remarks to me that reveal to me that she is not irritated by what I say, as she would be if I were wrong." When told she was smarter than George, Martha couldn't help but smile.[33]

While she listened to all viewpoints, Martha was a rabid Federalist who mistrusted "Democrats" like Jefferson. Legend claimed that upon seeing a wall scuff, Lady Washington angrily cracked, "It was no Federalist! None but a filthy democrat would mark a place with his good-for-nothing head in that manner." Her closest friendships were with Federalists Marcia Morris and Eliza Powel.[34]

Martha called George "Pappa," in private and "General" in public. He referred to her as his "amiable consort," who shared her opinions with him alone. In public, she was mute on politics. When she did speak—on anything—it came out nearly inaudibly. An aide to General Steuben said she had "a certain goodness of heart, but . . . squeaks so damnably that there is no hearing her."[35]

Martha's mental skills lay elsewhere than political Abigail's. She was a genius as a business manager, a matter that was regionally inherent. Plantations like Mount Vernon had to be orchestrated not merely as homes but businesses. It was an agricultural society foreign to Abigail's New England. One observer recorded, after visiting Martha at Mount Vernon, "She is a very sensible Lady . . . The people here all intent on commerce and trade—seem to have no taste for the Sciences, or Literature . . . profoundly ignorant with respect to learning, but sagacious and cunning in every other respect . . ."[36]

While perhaps mentally unchallenged by her, Martha's well-being remained vital to George, and he relied upon her presence. That is why he wanted her with him in those oppressive, unhealthy dog days in the summer of '93, when suddenly, without warning, the still air of Philadelphia racked with terror into a state of emergency. All because of mosquitoes.

— 3 —

"This Elevated Station . . ."

PANIC BROKE OUT in the streets. Yellow fever was spreading, person-to-person, without regard to rank, race, religion. The dead bodies of rich, vain females of society and poor, humble charladies ended up together on the same cart, carried through the filthy alleys, avoided by all. Some who carried "the fever" died immediately. Others lingered. The insidious disease had gripped the city, and stopped the government.

The president did not want Martha to leave his side. Her "presence," as her son had written George, during a smallpox outbreak in the midst of the war, would "alleviate the Care and Anxiety which public Transactions may occasion." Those who could afford to fled the harbor city for the countryside. The government was relocated to Germantown, and that is where George brought Martha. Others were not so lucky. One Isaac Heston, assistant to Quaker lawyer John Todd, described the plague:

> You can not imagine the situation of this city. How deplorable. It continues to be more and more depopulated, both by the removal of its inhabitants into the country, and by the destructive fever which now prevails. They are dying on our right hand and on our left . . . in fact, all around us. Great are the numbers that are called to the grave, and numbered with the silent dead . . . there is hardly a smile to be seen in the countenance of any person walking in the streets. Those who have not removed are afraid to see anybody, even the nearest friends, and keep themselves closely confined in their houses, and this city never wore so gloomy an aspect before . . . the Doctors are now differing about the disorder and the methods of curing. Some of the presses are stopped . . . the Governors of New York and Maryland have published their proclamation, enjoining the strictest search to be made of every person that arrives from Philadelphia. Politics, that run so high lately, are now all laid aside, and almost everyone who have property are making their

wills . . . To see a hearse go by is now so common that we hardly take notice of it . . . We live in the midst of death.

Within days Heston himself was dead. His employer, John Todd, had removed his wife, Dolley, their son Payne, and newborn William to the country to keep them from the fever while he stayed and nursed his parents, who had the fever.

Under the pressures of "parental dictation" from her late father, whose business had utterly failed, Dolley had married Todd in 1790, but told friends that "no sublimary bliss whatever should have a tendency to make me forgetful of friends I so highly value." Now, suddenly, in September 1793, the fever killed her infant son, husband, father-in-law, and mother-in-law, all within three and a half weeks. At twenty-five years old, Dolley Payne Todd found herself a widow with a child. Her widowed mother, who had opened her house to boarding congressmen, independently supporting herself, left town to live with the George Steptoe Washingtons at their Virginia estate. Dolley, Payne, and her sister Anna, who lived with her, were alone and near poverty.

The widow Todd, however, was determined to survive it all. She fought her husband's brother who was withholding the estates of his parents and her husband. After her volley of polite but ignored letters, she penned a final one: "As I have already suffered the most serious inconvenience from the unnecessary detention of my part of my mother-in-law's property and of the receipt books and papers of my late husband, I am constrained once more to request—and if a request is not sufficient—to *demand* that they may be delivered this day." John Todd had once written that Dolley was fully capable of understanding law, working as his legal assistant. With New York congressman Aaron Burr, who befriended her while he boarded at Mrs. Payne's, as her attorney, Dolley received her share, and eked out an existence in the devastated city. By early winter, the mosquitoes that spread the fever had died. The city was never to revive its lively spirit, its population of thirty-seven thousand reduced by death and fear by more than half. Seventeen thousand had left. More sobering was the news that five thousand had died in five months.[1]

Though Lady Washington was qualified by war's experience to nurse the sick, being in Germantown quite possibly saved her life. Her benevolence nonetheless manifested itself with her "adoption" of the Revolution veterans. In fact, her only interference in the administration were "her many intercessions with the chief for the pardon of offenders" who were veterans. By directing her interests toward the veterans, she planted the notion of a president's Lady having a public responsibility. A visitor remembered how emotional Lady Washington became about the issue: "It is astonishing with what raptures Mrs. Washington spoke about the discipline of the army [and] . . . [W]hat a pleasure she took in the sound of the fife and drums, preferring it to any music that was ever heard."

During the war, in her plain muslin, Martha had become most famous for organizing sick wards and provoking Morristown ladies in silk into rolling bandages from tableclothes and napkins, and making and repairing uniforms. As the president's wife, she regularly doled out cash to veterans, and her grandson remembered that on national days veterans "were seen to file off toward the parlor, where Lady Washington was in waiting to receive them, and . . . were cordially welcomed as old friends, and where many an interesting reminiscence was called up of the headquarters, and 'the times of the Revolution.'" If they appealed, Martha interceded. On one occasion, veterans "repaired . . . to headquarters" to call on the president, all the while knowing he'd be unable to see them. It was "the good lady" with whom they actually wanted to speak. "Each one had some touching appeal," and they were shown into a servant's room, where refreshments were brought. When Lady Washington finally came in, she presented each with "some little token" of money. Whenever she appeared before a public crowd, veterans in the throng cheered her, and she enjoyed repeating that "it had been her fortune to hear the first cannon at the opening, and the last at the closing, of all the campaigns of the Revolutionary war." Soldiers had always escorted her carriage, and she always mentioned the "poor soldiers" who lacked "sufficient clothing and food," ending one letter, "Oh how my heart pains for them."[2]

During the war, Martha had headed a unique mobilization of the colonies' females, calling for them all to donate and collect money for the relief of the soldiers. Her plea had immediate appeal in Philadelphia, where thirty-six women held a meeting to decide how best to implement it. The *Pennsylvania Gazette* announced the plan that donations would be collected by an appointed "Treasuress" in the counties, all of whom answered to the governor's wives, who in turn reported and sent the donations to Lady Washington.

The president's wife was an influence over American females, as evidenced by the May 1793 request of the editors of the Philadelphia *Ladies Magazine*. As a new publication, the magazine was attempting to build a circulation, and the editors wrote Martha to "beg your acceptance of the 1st volume . . . and request that we may have the pleasure of considering you in the future as an encourager and patron of the Work." Mercy Warren wrote to Martha that she, in her role as "President's Lady," "by general consent, would be more likely to obtain the suffrages of the sex, even were they to canvass at election, for this elevated station . . ."[3]

Mrs. Washington enjoyed the company of young political wives like Mrs. James Monroe, wife of the Virginia senator, said to be at the center of those "years of the magnificently gay Philadelphia" and called a "smiling little Venus." But if Martha traded food "receipts" with Elizabeth as a fellow sister of the old Dominion, she did so under a false impression. Mrs. Monroe was a born and bred New Yorker whose several generations of Dutch parentage secured her a position in society. She was no democrat. Her father had been a Loyalist officer; her brother served in the redcoat army. Her grandmother, Hester Carmen Le Grand, had run her own business, and cousin Lord Ashburton headed Baring Brothers in London. Her grandfather owned most of Harlem. One sister was married into the wealthy Gouvernour family, another into the famous Knox family; a third was the wife of the grand chamberlain to the king of Denmark. When her native Virginian husband, James, was attempting to run for office, Elizabeth spent little time in the South, staying instead with her family in New York. Rumors that Monroe actually planned to move to New York contributed to his defeat in a race for the House of Delegates in 1786, and while his 1790 Senate election brought them to Philadelphia, Elizabeth spent the entire 1790–91 social season in New York.

Martha would bear more direct influence over the life of one particular Philadelphian daughter of Virginia, Widow Todd, kin by marriage. In the early summer of '94, Lady Washington summoned the widow to her court. "Dolley, is it true that you are engaged to James Madison?"

Mrs. Todd, indeed being courted by the Virginia congressman, was taken aback. She denied it.

"If it is so," Martha pressed, "do not be ashamed to confess it;

rather be proud; he will make thee a good husband and all the better for being so much older. We both approve of it; the esteem and friendship existing between Mr. Madison and my husband is very great, and we would wish thee to be happy."

After a full investigation through her agents into Madison's investments and wealth, Dolley did indeed marry "Jemmy," a short, gray, quiet man seventeen years her senior. While she admitted that he was the man she most "admired," shrewd Dolley nevertheless retained the Todd home as her property. The rent financed her expensive clothing tastes—and tobacco snuff—both of which she now indulged freely. For wedding a non-Quaker, she was "read" out of her faith. In reflection on how Quakerism attempted to "control me entirely, and debar me from so many advantages and pleasures," she felt "my ancient terror revive in great degree." She shed her grays, and began dressing in white satin, silk, and cotton dresses.

Politics was a positive factor in her marriage. As a congressional wife, Dolley was immediately thrust into the role of hostess to great statesmen, duly impressing everyone from Vice President Adams to the French legation. Her amazing adaption manifested itself as she glided comfortably into serious discussion with ambassadors, senators, and judges, and became a "social politician," using seemingly social dinners as a means of persuading opponents and gathering information for her husband. When Federalist Samuel Dexter was heatedly arguing with Madison over his changed opinion on an issue, Dolley invited Dexter to dinner. He neutralized his stridency.

Dolley exerted her own influences, too. It was perhaps no accident that just before their marriage, Congressman Madison made a persuasive speech against an excise tax on snuff. It was likely Dolley's first political handiwork.

Though the union was barren, it gave Dolley the freedom to always travel with her Jemmy, a rarity for political wives. She began to take an interest in the issues he faced, and Jemmy delightedly shared everything, providing books to study, asking her opinions, and recalling the days' events in Congress. This was indeed a rarity for a man at that time. Dolley retained her basic Quaker principles of religious tolerance, pacifism, abolition, faith in humanity, self-reliance, and equal education for females, and Jemmy began learning from Dolley as well. They grew as partners, and a passionate love blossomed.[4]

Publicly and privately, a familial bond also developed between Mrs. Madison and Lady Washington. Not only did they trade food receipts, as did Elizabeth Monroe with both of them, but Martha gave Dolley a prized porcelain milk jug given to her as part of a set from a French count.

Lady Washington concurred when it came to equal education, endeavoring to provide her nieces and granddaughters the most thorough schooling available, particularly pleased with Miss Graham's in New York, where her granddaughter Nellie studied with daughters of prominent families like Anna Symmes of Long Island.

Still, Martha preferred boys. When it came to her rambunctious grandson "Little Wash," who was nearly expelled from Princeton for misconduct, Martha ignored it. But when niece Maria flashed her temper after being placed in a disciplining school by Martha, the latter was angered about "how ill she had behaved . . . had I known it before I should have reprimanded her very seriously—she has always been a spoiled child . . ." Sometimes Martha could be cruel. When she discovered some giggling girls under her bed, Lady Washington "haughtily arose, [and] in imperious tones demanded if . . . curiosity were full satisfied and ordered them out of the room." They retreated backward in terror, one girl falling and breaking her arm. On another occasion, Martha asked a friend to get her some metal collars that clamped the necks of girls straight which "expands the chest & prevents those ridiculous distortions" that teenage girls bashfully took to hide their growing bosoms.

Lady Washington could strike submission even in George. He told Charles Thompson, secretary of the Congress, that "Mrs. Washington, if she knew I was writing to you in the style of an invitation, would, I am certain, adduce arguments to prove that I ought to include Mrs. Thompson, but before she should have spun the threads of her discourse, it is more probable I should have nonplussed her by yielding readily to the force of her reasoning."

On the question of female equality, Martha believed strongly that females must exercise independence. In a 1794 letter she admonished a young niece to depend only on herself, not men:

> . . . there are few people that can manage more than their own business. I very sincearly [sic] wish you would exert yourself so as to keep all your matters in order yourself without depending upon others as that is the only way to be happy—to have all your business in your own hands without trusting to others . . . look upon this advice in the friendly way it is meant, as I wish you to be as independent as your circumstances will admit and to be so, is to exert yourself in the management of your estate. If you do not no one else will. A dependance is, I think, a wretched state and you have enough if you will manage it right.[5]

Martha's toughness led to a subtle battle of child custody for some of her grandchildren. Her son Jacky's wife had born four girls and "Little Wash." After Jacky's death, Martha insisted to her daughter-in-law that she be allowed to adopt grandchildren Nellie and "Little Wash" as her own. The widow, pressed for cash, relinquished the children. Sadly, she later wrote another relative, "shake hands with my dear boy . . .

don't let him forget he has a mother." As it happened, Martha's influence may have proved better. One granddaughter raised by her natural
mother not only made a rather rash and unfortunate marriage (Martha
refused to attend the wedding, and tried to prevent Nellie from attending), but maintained an adulterous affair with an army officer, disguis-
ing herself in a uniform to get into the barracks.

Rather than leading a formal cause on behalf of needy women, however, Lady Washington chose to help by making personal contributions
to everyone from a wife raising her husband's bail to an unemployed
actress, a beggar, and an insane female. Her attitude toward blacks,
slave or "freedman," was not so beneficent; she maintained the view
that they were all innately servile even after her exposure to a variant
perspective in the North.[6]

When someone remarked that the Washingtons treated their slaves
well, the president's secretary, Tobias Lear, added with a murmur, "But
they are still slaves." Martha's sole concern for blacks in bondage was
their efficiency as servants, and she felt a mistrust of all blacks as a race.
Writing of one freedman servant, she advised a friend to ascertain that
he was "trustworthy, careful of what is committed to him, sober and
attentive," because these traits were "essential requisites in any large
family, but more so among blacks—many of whom will impose when
they can do it."

"Black children," wrote Lady Washington, "are liable to so many
accidents and complaints that one is heartily sore of keeping them. I
hope you will not find in him much sass. The Blacks are so bad in their
nature that they have not the least gratitude for the kindness that may
be showed them . . . . [T]he women that wash, they always idle half
their time away about their own business and wash so bad that the
clothes are not fit to use."

When Martha's slave Oney Judge ran away from Philadelphia, the
president's wife was angered. Bewildered by the concept of slave liberation, she insisted that the president try to recover Oney. When Oney
was finally located in a New Hampshire freedman community, it was
reported back to a shocked Martha that she was not living with the
Frenchmen who was said to have taken her, but had expressed "a thirst
for freedom." She was never recovered as property.[7]

On the issue of alcoholism, Martha was enlightened, having personally witnessed its effects on George's brother. About another alcoholic,
she sympathetically wrote, "It is improbable that things can go on tolerable if Mr. Henley is always drinking brandy. Everything he has must
suffer," and she thought, "he has but little affection for them [his fam-
ily] or he would devote his time to take care of them rather than to be
always drinking." She hoped his children "will . . . not follow their
unhappy Father's bad example." Such personal utterances remained private. As she neared the end of eight years as First Lady, Martha had

clearly managed to differentiate between public persona and private person. That was illustrated by her later destruction of all her private letters. [8]

The First Lady's admirers included no less a public wife than her companion and "elected" successor, Abigail Adams, who fondly wrote that "we live upon terms of much friendship." (The two women even took a three-day vacation together at "the Jersies.") When John Adams was elected president, he was taken aback by Martha's uncharacteristic expression of politics, as she congratulated him "affectionately" and "went further and said more than I expected." In Adams's race against "Democrat" Jefferson, Martha had nothing but contempt for the latter, but remained publicly neutral on the campaign. In the wings of the electioneering, Abigail trembled at the thought of having to be so politically mute.

Abigail thought Martha had a better figure than herself, with "modest and unassuming, dignified and feminine" manners. Mrs. Adams imagined that she lacked such attributes, but it was no fallacy that she lacked Martha's apolitical placidness. Abigail's entire married life had been a political partnership. Now, even that secure role would be changed. As the new "Lady," she was to be essentially absent, suffering illnesses, once near death from yellow fever. She would be spending more time home in Quincy, Massachusetts, than at the presidential mansion. Consequently, her crucial role as adviser to the president would be conducted largely by mail. The liberal optimist of the Revolutionary Era was a far different female from the fifty-two-year-old who shook with pessimistic fears and paranoia when she considered the responsibilities coming her way. "I feared a thousand things which I pray I never may be called to experience. Most assuredly I do not wish the highest post. I never before realized what I might be called to," she'd written just after President Washington's near-fatal illness in 1790. [9]

Just one day before leaving the ladyship, Martha wrote to a friend that the "winter has been very severe here, and upon the whole dull; but it is now moderating and drawing to a close, with which the curtain will fall on our public life, and place us on a more tranquil theater." Aware of her place in history, conducting herself as queen to the end, Lady Washington climbed into her coach, with George, and headed south, past Baltimore, to her beloved Mount Vernon and private life.

Abigail was still in Quincy on John's Inauguration Day, writing him, "My feelings are not those of pride or ostentation, upon the occasion. They are . . . a sense of the obligations, the important trusts, and numerous duties connected with it." Regarding herself, Abigail felt "Lady Adams" should emulate "Lady Washington," but said she'd rather be bound and gagged and shot like a turkey. "As to a crown . . . I shall esteem myself peculiarly fortunate, if, at the close of my public life, I can retire esteemed, beloved and equally respected with my predecessor." Yet Abigail thought herself less "Lady" and more co-president. John actually encouraged that thinking, calling her "my dearest Partner . . . my best, dearest, worthiest, wisest friend in this World . . . I think you shine as a Stateswoman . . ."

But John Adams was also acutely aware of his wife's vitriolic opinions, and willingness to express them. The president gently reminded her, "Let us hold our tongues."[10]

– 4 –

Mrs. President

SHE WAS ". . . sick, sick, sick of public life," and said, "[I]f my future peace and tranquility were all that I considered, a release from public life would be the most desirable event of it." She believed it "requires courage and firmness, wisdom and temperance, patience and forebearance to stand in such a conspicuous, such an elevated position." And yet, she had realized the inevitable: "I expect to be vilified and abused with my whole family when I come into this situation. . . ." When a friend called the ladyship "splendid misery," Abigail admitted, "She was not far from the truth."[1]

Abigail Smith was the child of politics. On November 23, 1744, she was born into a prominent Massachusetts family, famous for its history of public service. Her grandfather had served twenty-one years in the state's House of Representatives and Supreme Court. Abigail's education included philosophy, mathematics, the classics, and economics—all of which she was taught by her father and his father in their vast libraries. She was unsatisfied with her education, later lamenting, "My early education did not partake of the abundant opportunity which the present day offers . . . which our common schools afford." By seventeen she was discussing the impact of England's new King George.

At twenty she had married lawyer John Adams, eventually bearing four children, John Quincy, Thomas, Charles, and "Nabby." From the beginning, it was decided that Abigail would stay home, raise the family, and manage their farm, investments, and finances. But when John was elected to serve in the first Continental Congress in 1774, she was welcomed as adviser in absentia. She wrote to John on the intricate details of government structure and world economics with more savvy than most congressmen. Between Quincy and Philadelphia, their partnership was conducted by mail. During the Revolution, she had

watched the nearby Battle of Bunker Hill, melted pewter to make bullets, and was even consulted by her husband's colleagues in Congress.
John told her she was "a heroine, and you have every reason to be."
Left alone with four sickly children, she resented being far from the seat
of power, and a deep-rooted struggle had begun in her, private versus
public life, family versus politics. But it was John who never let her
political input stray too long. When she wrote him that family illnesses
kept her from reporting local political news, he admonished her.[2]

When Adams left America in 1778 for Paris, to serve as minister,
Abigail had hated being left behind. To stay as involved as possible,
John reported classified information to her, and sent his private journals. "I dare say," he wrote, "there is not a lady in America treated
with a more curious dish of politics than is contained in the enclosed
papers . . . by no means let them go out of your hands." For her part,
Abigail kept him informed on elections and legislation. She had finally
sailed for London in 1783. That's when she met Charlotte. When she
visited Paris with John when he was conferring with Thomas Jefferson,
she commenced her own friendship with Jefferson, offering her advice
that they seek larger loans from the Dutch government when bank-
ruptcy threatened America. Europe rounded out Abigail's perspective.
She hated Shakespeare, loved Handel, and had her "delicacy wounded"
at the ballet as females danced, "showing their garters as if no petticoats
had been worn."[3]

Perhaps as a result of exposure to Charlotte's court, Abigail rather
liked formal titles, and whimsically noted that when a Federalist suggested she be called "Autocratix of the United States," he should know
"I was always for equality as my husband can witness." But even the
pompous president-elect thought she went too far when she had her
family coat of arms prominently painted on the presidential coach. She
demurred and had it taken off, joking, "I never placed my happiness in
equipage."

But her uncertainty about her role was no joke. She explained that
"the situation in which I am placed [is] enviable no doubt in the eyes of
some, but never envied or coveted by me." Her first reaction was to
write for advice from her "most amiable predecessor" whose ladyship
had been "exemplary and irreproachable." Speaking her mind in public
was Abigail's first fear: "I have been so used to freedom of sentiment
that I know not how to place so many guards about me, as will be
indispensable, to look at every word before I utter it, and to impose a
silence upon my self, when I long to talk."[4]

When she was in Philadelphia, her day began at 5:00 A.M., as she
contended with correspondence and the household. Afternoons, she
returned social calls and greeted the public. She dined with John every
night except Tuesdays and Thursdays, when her drawing-room salons
were held. Mrs. Adams never hid her resentment at having to privately

finance public entertaining, and tried at every opportunity to save her money. Indeed, it was a guarded secret that when the Quincy tax collector came to call, the president's wife had no cash with which to pay him. Still, Lady Adams—as she was immediately titled—felt that as president's wife she had a responsibility to help the needy. Following Martha's example and making it part of the role, she explained, "A man cannot be an honest and zealous promoter of the principles of a true government, without possessing that good will towards man . . . ."

In Philadelphia, Abigail was acknowledged as a public figure. When a group of Federalists paid a formal call on her, she proudly presented them with a cockade ribbon, the party symbol. When Indian chiefs came to greet the president, they wanted also to meet Abigail because, as one chief told her, "duty [was] but in part fulfilled until he had also visited his mother." A volunteer light-infantry company petitioned to be organized under the name of the "Lady Adams Rangers." On one occasion, as she rode over the cobblestones of Philadelphia, people of all ranks bowed or removed their hats. Even the Quakers respectfully acknowledged her "in their way." The most startling recognition of the President's Lady was on her initiative when she served as the president's representative at an official government event. Heading north, Abigail stopped at a New Jersey federal army site, toured the camp thoroughly, and even reviewed the troops, like the president. "I acted," she boldly wrote him, "as your proxy."[5]

Try as she might, Abigail was unable to conceal her power over the president. Her grandson explained that she, "even upon public affairs, had at all times great weight with her husband is unquestionably true, for he frequently marked upon her letters his testimony to their solidity . . . Whenever she differed in sentiment from him, which was sometimes the case, she perfectly well understood her own position, and that the best way of recommending her views was by entire concession . . ." In instances of the president's imprudence, "She was certain that a word said, not at the moment of irritation, but immediately after it had passed, would receive great consideration from him. She therefore waited the favorable time, and thus, by the calmness of her judgement, exercised a species of negative influence, which often prevented evil consequences from momentary indiscretion." But it was her letters that offered the strongest opinions. "My pen," she wrote John, "is always freer than my tongue. I have wrote many things to you that I suppose I never could have talked."

Her views became so notorious that a merchant quoted her in making his argument before a town-meeting debate. She was mortified. "I could not believe that any gentleman would have so little delicacy or so small a sense of propriety as to have written a vague opinion and that of a lady, to be read in a publick assembly as an authority. The man must have lost his senses. I cannot say that I did not utter the expression . . . but little did I think of having my name quoted . . . It will . . . serve as a lesson to me to be upon my guard." It was the first time that a president's wife's opinion was subject to public discussion.[6]

As word of Abigail's power spread, she was faced with a deluge of patronage requests. She alone decided whether to recommend the names to the president, and was angered when he opened some of her mail. "The President has agreed that he will not open any more letters to me," she wrote her sister, "and will be satisfied with such parts as I am willing to communicate." Some of her husband's foes were alarmed. Albert Gallatin said a friend of his "heard her majesty as she was asking the names of different members of Congress and then pointed out which were 'our people.'" Gallatin dubbed her "Mrs. President, not of the United States but of a faction." One senator noted that "the President would not dare to make a nomination without her approbation."[7]

News of her power likely leaked through her unusual method of refuting criticism. Regularly, she sent letters and articles to friendly newspaper editors with requests to publish them, directing which passages to quote and which words to change to hide her identity. Abigail didn't seem to mind having her name in the press. While home, she asked John, "Tell me who inquires after me as if they cared," and was flattered to learn that there were regrets in *two* newspapers about her absence.

When, however, the rabid Democrat editor Benjamin Bache's *Aurora* parodied the president and his wife as "the Happy Old Couple" of the English Ballad "Darby and Joan," and as being too aged and incapable for politics, and then, in 1798, sarcastically referred in his newspapers to Abigail's crying at a theater performance, Abigail's famous temper was riled. She loathed Bache, claiming he was the leading agitator of the influx of revolutionary French immigrants working secretly to overthrow the American government. She wanted him imprisoned. "The vile incendiaries . . . and . . . base, violent and calumniating abuse," she felt, could be handled by special legislation. "But nothing will have an effect until Congress passes a Sedition Bill . . . I wish the laws of our country were competent to punish the stirrer up of sedition, the writer or printer of loose and unfounded calumny . . ."[8]

Bache indeed represented a movement undermining John Adams's attempts to steer America from allying with France. But far more threatening were Federalists who wanted the president to declare war on France because of that country's belligerence on the high seas. Those Federalists were reactionary radicals.

Among them was Mrs. President.

– 5 –

Warmonger

WHEN ON MARCH 4, 1798, the important dispatches sent from American commissioners in France arrived at the President's House, Abigail read them. The very next day she wrote, "I see not but war is inevitable. This morning for the first time dispatches have arrived from our Envoys . . . The French papers are full of abuse . . . Every deception is made use of to exasperate the publick mind against America and to prepare them for hostilities."

While the Lady knew all in March, the dispatches were not released to Congress until April, and to the public until July. They revealed that the French were willing to negotiate if a bribe was made to three unofficial agents of French foreign minister Tallyrand. The agents were identified only as "X, Y, and Z," and the scandal became known as the "XYZ Affair." Abigail was incensed at the offer, "[b]ut what a fine answer was made to X. Y. Z. by Mr. Charles Pinckney! 'Millions for defence, but not one cent for tribute!'—this is the toast from Georgia to Maine!"

Divisive feelings ran high, and when threatening letters were sent to the president, Abigail was disturbed. "With the temper in a city like this, materials for a mob might be brought together in ten minutes." Soon after a fight broke out between Federalists and Democrats at the State House, a guard was posted at the President's House and the streets around it were patrolled, no doubt prompted by Abigail's fear of assassination.

Through the early summer, Abigail pressed John, as many did, to sign the Alien and Sedition Acts. Often anti-Catholic, and mistrustful of French immigrants, she felt that ". . . in times like the present a more careful and attentive watch ought to be kept over foreigners. This will be done in the future if the Alien Bill passes without being curtailed and clipt until it is made useless." Whether the president truly approved of the bills, he signed them. There was no doubt in Abigail's stand, and her hatred of Bache came to sweet revenge. He published a forged letter of John Adams, was arrested on June 26, 1798, on a charge of libeling the president, and finally jailed.

Abigail still beat war drums, though John held out. "Indeed we are all but at war," she persisted. "Intercourse with France forbidden, the Treaties declared void and no longer obligatory—navy building, and three frigates already at sea—a capture made! . . . All we need is a declaration of war." She boldly admitted, "And—though the President must not hear me say this!—one undoubtedly would have been made— ought to have been made." Had the Lady been president that tense summer of '98, or managed to persuade her husband as she often did, war would have been declared, and the new United States' very existence would have seriously been threatened.[1]

At every chance, however, President Adams carefully averted aggressions. When, that next winter, he appointed Democrat William Vans Murray to help negotiate with the French, some Federalists protested. The most telling factor, however, was that Abigail was absent when he made the appointment. At this crucial moment, that wasn't lost on angry Federalists. John wrote her that her power was being publicly recognized—and missed. "Oh how they lament Mrs. Adams's absence! She is a good counsellor! If she had been here, Murray would never have been named nor his mission instituted! This ought to gratify your vanity enough to cure you!"[2]

The possible French invasion of the South was a real fear, though negotiations with France were promising. When Charles Pinckney was appointed to command American troops in Georgia, another Federalist Lady belligerently laced into the French.

Martha Washington was enjoying retirement, telling a friend that "New York and Philadelphia was not home, only a sojourning," and how she felt like a child "just released from a taskmaster." As "an old-fashioned Virginia house-keeper" she said she was "steady as a clock, busy as a bee and as cheerful as a cricket." Nonetheless, Lady Washington found herself still celebrated, quite apart from George. Georgetown College's president invited her to the school's "first essay of our juvenile stage." George was invited, too, but it was really hoped Martha would come—with or without him. President DuBourg added that she was revered "for her personal virtues" and "possess[ed] the next claim after him to the highest reverence."

Martha kept a keen eye on the real estate development of the District of Columbia, across the Potomac River from their home, where the permanent national capital was being planned. She reported to a friend, "For the purposes of a purchase in the Federal City that period will now, I dare venture to say, be too late (although we were told by one of the Commissioners the other day, that the Public buildings were going on with great activity). It is possible however, that some of the best situated lots may be disposed of in the interim but even of this nothing can be said with certainty."

In the most remarkable of her post-ladyship letters, however, Martha stridently expressed political opinion. Now removed from public scrutiny, her frankness proved her astuteness on foreign affairs, and her hatred of the French. While her faulty grammar somewhat obscured the meaning of some sentences, her reference to an American negotiation and the resistance of the French is clear.

She wished that "the newly proposed Negotiation may divert more serious movements; but from a faithless Nation, whose injustice and ambition know no bounds short of its power to accomplish them, little is expected from this Negotiation. If the proposition should be acceded to by those who wish for a permanent Treaty. Arrogance or deception, as is the best calculated to promote the views of the Directory seem to be the only Rule of the French government at present. Of course nothing is to be expected from their domineering spirit when uncontrolled by events—as too many unhappy Nations of Europe, and recently the poor Italians have experience to the entire annihilation of their Government."

In the end, President John Adams resisted all pressure, and kept the nation out of war.

For Martha, the end of 1799 was marked by an unexpected tragedy. "The General" died, and the entire nation mourned. The time it would take to travel from Philadelphia to Virginia prevented John and Abigail from attending the funeral, but one adopted daughter of the Old Dominion came, and offered condolences to Martha. It was the first time anyone could recall seeing Dolley Madison cry.

Congress made sudden plans to bury the late president in their Capitol Building, in the new Federal City on the Potomac between Virginia and Maryland in the Columbia District, now named "Washington, D.C." Nobody had bothered first to inquire whether that was acceptable to Martha. On the last day of the eighteenth century, she somewhat bitterly wrote to the president, "Taught by the great example which I have so long had before never to oppose my private wishes to the public will, I must consent to the request made by Congress, which you have had the goodness to transmit to me [but] in doing this, I need not, I can not, say what a sacrifice of individual feelings I make to a sense of public duty."

Adams sent "the sentiments of that virtuous lady" in full to Congress, adding, "It would be an attempt of too much delicacy to make any comments upon it; but there can be no doubt, that the nation at large, as well as . . . the . . . government, will be highly gratified by any arrangement which may diminish the sacrifice she makes of her individual feelings." Whether it was a trade-off for her sacrifice or an honor for her contributions, Congress got the message. On April 3, "an act to extend the privilege of franking letters and packages" to Martha was passed.

Martha took widowhood in her philosophical way, helped by the wave of national sympathy. To Governor Trumbull, she wrote, "When the mind is deeply affected by those irreparable losses which are incident to humanity the good christian will submit without repining . . . but in the severest trials we find some alleviation to our grief in the sympathy of sincere friends . . ."[3]

Lady Washington was still held as a virtuous example by her countrywomen, but Abigail wasn't as successful, even in her attempts to influence fashion. "So far as example goes, I shall bring in the use of silks," she confidently wrote her sister. "At my Age I think I am priviledged [sic] to set a fashion." She was particularly disgusted at the new French vogue of high waists, exposed bosoms, and flimsy white fabrics, a style adopted and beloved by none other than Democrat Dolley Madison, now living in political retirement with Jemmy at his Virginia estate, Montpelier. When one so-dressed female entered Abigail's drawing room, she condescendingly noted that "every eye in the Room had been fixed upon her, and you might literally see through her . . . they most of them wear their Cloaths too scant upon the body and too full upon the Bosom for my fancy. Not content with the show which nature bestows, they borrow from art, and litterally [sic] look like Nursing Mothers."[4]

Abigail was modest about sexuality. She was mortified when her widowed sister remarried a younger man and a cousin wed "an able bodied sea captain." By middle age, she thought "the hey day in the blood" should be "tame." In France, she had been horrified to learn of rampant premarital sex and dozens of abandoned bastards. Though John had a heartier attitude, she kept him at bay, saying age should subdue "the ardor of passion" and be replaced by "friendship and affection." But even in their courting days, when he told her not to cross her legs, Abigail prudishly retorted that "a gentleman has no business to concern himself about the Leggs of a Lady." Yet, while he was in Europe, and she joked about his finding warmth with a "frozen Laplander," Abigail, unknown to John, conducted a flirtatious correspondence with another congressman, Lovell of Massachusetts. At times, she shocked herself. When lonely, she enjoyed it.[5]

She retained her interest in female progress by reading the latest theory books on equality, like the radical Mary Wollstonecraft's *Vindication of the Rights of Woman* (John called her "a disciple of Wollstonecraft") and *Bennett's Strictures*, which advocated better education for females. Abigail angrily noticed in a book on morality that it made females subordinate: "I will never consent to have our sex considered . . . inferior . . . Let each planet shine in their own orbit. God and nature designed it so—if man is Lord, woman is Lordess—that is what I contend for."

"No man," the Lady reflected on the success of John Adams, "ever prospered in the world without the consent and cooperation of his wife." While the president didn't argue that point with her, in private he told his son Thomas, "There can never be any regular government . . . nation, without a marked, subordination of mothers . . . to the father." But he added carefully that his opinion was "between you and me." If Abigail heard about it, John said it would "raise a rebellion."

In practice, Abigail conceded, "However brilliant a woman's talents may be, she ought never to shine at the expence of her Husband." Nor be elected to federal office. "Government of States and Kingdoms, tho God knows badly enough managed, I am willing should be solely administered by the Lords." As she aged, her feminism abated, save for the issue of equal education.

Abigail developed a curious propriety of conduct as Lady. When John in December 1799, delivered the first State of the Union speech given by a president before a joint meeting of Congress, daughter Nabby went to hear him from the conspicuous public galleries, but the president's wife didn't think it proper to attend herself.[6]

Other political wives asserted themselves. In France, Elizabeth Monroe, now a diplomat's wife, had been accorded tremendous public responsibility by her husband in a successful plot to have Madame de Lafayette freed from jail. Officially, Monroe could not intercede, but his wife could make a gesture indicating American displeasure at the Frenchwoman's imprisonment. He arranged for Elizabeth to visit Madame de Lafayette, conveyed by his carriage, boldly marked with the American seal, in full public view. Word reached French officials immediately, and Madame de Lafayette was freed. Soon Elizabeth was publicly recognized as a power, and solicited with innumerable requests, like that of a Madame Doré, who needed bail for her husband's release from prison.

Elizabeth reveled in the exclusive snob appeal of European court life. In Paris, while it was true that she patriotically nursed "like a sister" the cantankerous dying expatriate Tom Paine, she also managed to witness the regal splendor of Napoleon's self-crowning ceremony at which he declared himself emperor. Her daughter Eliza was placed in a French school, where she began a lifelong friendship with Empress Josephine's daughter. The Monroes lived in a classic château, the Folie de la Bouexière, with formal gardens designed by Chevaulet. Elizabeth's two closest female friends were Madame de Corny, wife of one of

Lafayette's associates, and Madame de Vallette, a friend of Voltaire's. She was beloved by the French for adapting to their habits instead of remaining a stubborn American. Politically, she had developed a tactful diplomacy. Parisians dubbed her *"la belle Américaine."* In London theaters, when she entered the Monroe box, Elizabeth was greeted by "a storm of cheers" and the playing of "Yankee Doodle." Mrs. Monroe became more celebrated on the Continent than she ever would be in America, where females like Abigail looked very disdainfully upon haughty European manners.[7]

Abigail thoroughly disapproved of her new daughter-in-law, English-born, Catholic-educated Louisa Catherine, wife of John Quincy. Though several years passed before they met, Abigail, with a nativist prejudice against the foreigner, judged Louisa "Anti-American." "I would hope," she wrote to John Quincy, "for the love I bear my country that the Siren is at least *half-blooded.*" Indeed, Louisa's father was American merchant Joshua Johnson, but that fact didn't matter to anti-Adams newspapers like Boston's *Independent Chronicle*, which wrote that young John's "negotiations have terminated in a marriage treaty with an English lady . . ." A humiliated Abigail sent the clipping to her son with a rebuttal from the *Centinel.* Louisa, in Europe, was equally angered that the "scorpion tongue of political slander assailed me."

The Louisa situation worsened in Abigail's view when word got back to her that the new Mrs. Adams was the popular dance partner of royalty and was being called "Princess Royal" at the Prussian courts in Berlin. Other stories linking the family with royalty began blooming. Besides the Democratic press calling John Quincy "the American Prince of Wales," a rumor spread that only after George Washington had intervened did President Adams stop one of his sons from marrying one of English Queen Charlotte's daughters, plotting a new Anglo-American empire.

When Louisa's father returned to America financially ruined, his in-laws sought to halt potential criticism, and he was appointed as "Superintendant of Stamps" in Washington, D.C. Abigail was an unabashed nepotist, even in the face of rebuke, getting her brother-in-law appointed as Quincy postmaster, and supporting her son-in-law's several and varied nominations for federal jobs.[8]

With her own children, Abigail held impossible standards, once instructing her husband to "not teach them what to think, but how to think, and they will learn how to act." As Abigail headed south to Washington, D.C., and the new President's House, she stopped in New York to see her son Charles, who was dying of alcoholism. "He was beloved," she wrote, "in spight [sic] of his Errors, and all spoke with . . . sorrow for his habits." Abigail's brother, as well as her other son, Thomas, also suffered from alcoholism. While she sympathized with them, she herself eschewed the use of drugs or alcohol to combat pain.

When she had insomnia, she began to use laudanum, a sedative, but stopped after recalling how Patrick Henry had become addicted in a similar situation.[9]

When she joined John in Washington, becoming the first Lady to live in the President's House, Abigail was shocked not only at its inadequacies, but at the use of slaves. It was an issue upon which she and Martha Washington never agreed.

Before she had left Quincy to assume her duties, Abigail had placed her freedman servant, James, in a local school, knowing what the repercussions might be. Sure enough, "Neighbor Faxon" told the Lady that if she persisted in having James educated, the other boys would be denied an education, for they certainly wouldn't attend school with a black. Abigail rebuked, "This, Mr. Faxon, is attacking the principle of liberty and equality upon the only grounds upon which it ought to be supported, an equality of rights . . . I have not thought it any disgrace to myself to take him into my parlor and teach him both to read and write." Before the Revolution, Abigail suggested abolition. As vice president's wife, she had refused to hire slaves from their southern masters as servants. But here, on her first trip to the South, she personally witnessed the effect. From her window in the President's House, she observed "slaves half fed and destitute of clothing" forced "to labor, whilst the owner walked about idle."[10]

She deemed the new mansion unfit for occupancy, claiming that in New England it would have been completed with more efficiency, but she made use of the great unfinished audience room to hang her drying laundry. The mansion, however, was suitable enough for congressional leaders to be properly entertained, and a private letter describing the interiors proves that the Adamses did so in style. An amazed Mr. Cushing wrote:

> We dined at the President's on the 7th with the Judges & a large circle of ladies and gentlemen . . . We also had the pleasure of dining there without company on the 8th . . . I have had a good opportunity of traversing the house which may truly be said to be magnificent. It is built of white stone. The length is 160 feet. The height of the rooms are 21 & the length of some . . . are 38 feet . . . The window curtains of two of the rooms are white, with a narrow cornice of gold. The fringe has colours intermixed with the white. The walls being also white displays an elegance that exceeds anything that I have seen before. The drawing room is an oval on the second floor. The window curtains 3 sofas & 3 doz chairs are of crimson damask. The situation is one of the best in the City . . . which space is to be laid out with trees etc& for pleasure walks . . .[11]

The Adamses' occupation was to be short, John losing his reelection bid. Abigail was more concerned about the Federalist infighting, blaming Alexander Hamilton and his radical right wing, whose hatred of the French and love of the English she viewed just as dangerously as pro-French Democrats. Disgustedly, she called them "Brittania & Gallia." She was also "disgusted with the world and the chief of its inhabitants," who "do not appear worth the trouble and pains they cost to save them from destruction." Disgust didn't mean ignoring the chance to make money. She played the market against Adams's defeat and Jefferson's election. Although stocks fell sharply after election day, the president's Lady advised her son not to sell, but rather to buy: "I think they will rise again."

Perhaps it was her way of acknowledging that old friend but political rival Jefferson would be a better president than Aaron Burr, another rival, and the vice president—elect. So friendly were the Adamses and widower Jefferson that he paid a courtesy call on Abigail, and she later invited him to dinner in the mansion that was soon to be his home. At the dinner, in which he took her arm as escort, she warned him of plotters within his party, and recalled that, "at this he laughed out, and here ended the conversation."[12]

Before leaving town, Abigail made a sentimental trip across the Potomac to visit her comrade Martha, who had sent venison and other vittles to use at dinners in the President's House. Since George's death, Martha had become lonely, inviting political cronies now in the capital, to sojourn with her. ". . . the sight of an Old Friend," wrote Abigail, "soothed my heart."

At Mount Vernon, the Lady chronicled Martha's relationship with her three hundred slaves. "In the state in which they were left by the General, to be free at her death, she did not feel as tho' her Life was safe in their Hands, many of whom would be told that it was in their interest to get rid of her. She therefore was advised to set them all free at the close of the year. If any person wishes to see the baneful affects of Slavery as it creates a torper [sic] and an indolence and a Spirit of domination—let them come and take a view of the cultivation of this part of the United States."

As she looked at Martha and then herself, Abigail realized that under present conditions, they were lucky not only to be white, but to have been females in a very unique role. "I shall have reason to say, that my Lot hath fallen to me in a pleasant place, and that verily I have a goodly Heritage . . ." As different as their backgrounds and views of the Lady's role were, Martha and Abigail had shared a very privileged experience. They would always have that bond. During Abigail's visit to Martha, something else had occurred.

A "sorority" was formed.

In afterthought, Mrs. Adams realized that her power to help others, like slaves, would be limited once she left her ladyship. "I can truly and from my heart say that the most mortifying circumstance attendant upon my retirement from public Life is, that my power of doing good to my fellow creatures is curtailed and diminished, but tho' the means is wanting, the will and the wish remain." The "power of doing good" was now part of the role.

Visitors to Mount Vernon now found a bolder Lady Washington. One 1801 caller noted that she "converses without reserve & seeming pleasure on every subject." Another said she "loves to talk and talks very well about times past." Freed from public scrutiny, and George's commanding presence, Martha emerged without inhibitions. While she knitted, the former Lady discussed her favorite subject, international politics, one guest recording that "the extensive knowledge she has gained in this general intercourse with persons from all parts of the world has made her a most interesting companion, and having a vastly retentive memory, she presents an entire history of half a century."[13]

President-elect Jefferson also paid respects to the Lady across the river. Though Jefferson pronounced political females unnatural, he considered Martha and Abigail in a different class, as he did the savvy wife of his secretary of state nominee and protégé, James Madison, retired from Congress since 1797. In the interim, Dolley Madison had been emerging. She now wore silks in her favorite color, bright yellow, rouged her cheeks, and bedecked her head with plumes and wig pieces. And she still used snuff. Dolley and Jemmy joined Jefferson in visiting Martha. If she hadn't known her personally, Martha would never have recognized the former Quaker of gray bib and bonnet.

All that was very different by May 27, 1801, when President Jefferson scribbled an urgent third-person note to Dolley, asking if she would "be so good as to dine with him to-day, and to take care of female friends expected." It was a seemingly minor call to duty that would change history.

As she was departing, Abigail may have been thinking about Dolley, whom she knew as a congressional wife from Martha's Fridays. In February, just before heading home to New England, Abigail was certain her record, and Martha's, would stand well in history, compared to this new young woman. "I feel not any resentment against those who are coming to power and only wish the future administration . . . may be as productive . . . as the two former ones have been," she wrote. "I leave to time the unfolding of a dream. I leave to posterity to reflect upon the times past; and I leave them characters to contemplate."[14]

Indeed, posterity would remember Abigail Adams.

But not as lovingly as it would Dolley Madison.

PART II

The National Period
1801–1817

. . . there are appropriate duties peculiar to each sex, yet the wise Author of nature has endowed the female mind with equal powers and faculties, and given them the same right of judging and acting for themselves . . . Women have an equal right, with the other sex, to form societies for promoting religious, charitable and benevolent purposes . . . But of all studies most necessary and most natural to women is the study of men.
—HANNAH MATHER CROCKER
Observations on the Real Rights of Women (1818)

"The Tender Breasts of Ladies"

"THERE IS ONE secret," Dolley Madison revealed, "and that is the power we all have in forming our own destinies."

If ever a woman would exert power to change her destiny, it was Dolley, buoyant, gregarious, witty, ebullient, progressive-minded Democrat. With mirth in her heart and joy on her face, she nonetheless had a serious agenda behind those merry, fluttering violet eyes. And she loved a party.

Jefferson sensed this when he invited her to serve as his official hostess, but he didn't foresee the power she could exert even over politics. *Had* he known this, it is doubtful he would have raised her star. "The tender breasts of ladies," he wrote in 1780, "were not formed for political convulsions and . . . ladies miscalculate much of their own happiness when they wander from the field of their influence into that of politics."

After seeing the women of France so openly involved in politics, Jefferson had written, "Our good ladies, I trust, have been too wise to wrinkle their foreheads with politics. They are contented to soothe and calm the minds of their husbands returning ruffled from political debate. They have the good sense to value domestic happiness above all other . . . There is no part of the earth where so much of this is enjoyed as in America." It was a sentiment harbored by repressed emotions. He in fact wrote of Marie Antoinette's power, "had there been no Queen, there would have been no revolution."

By 1801, Jefferson had been widowed for twenty years. The irony is that had Martha Wayles Jefferson lived, she would likely have prevented Thomas from becoming president. She exerted a posthumous power so strong that he could never publicly come to terms with her. Outside of his family, he neither discussed nor wrote of his dead wife. Martha, daughter of wealthy English immigrant John Wayles, had been born just outside Williamsburg. By Betty Hemings, his half-white slave, Wayles fathered another daughter, Sally. Martha was described as a tall, auburn-haired "model of graceful and queenlike carriage." She was a gifted harpsichordist, and it was her musical talent that attracted Thomas Jefferson. They married on New Year's Day 1772. Upon Wayles's death, Martha inherited 135 slaves, which was how her half-sister, the three-quarters white Sally Hemings, came to Jefferson's Monticello.

Jefferson, enraptured with Martha, "the cherished companion of my life," showered her with the finest horses, furniture, pianoforte, and exotic fruit trees money could buy. With other women and men, she gambled freely on whist card games. Aristocractic Martha enjoyed the privileges of landed gentry, but she immediately compromised Thomas's philosophies as America entered the Revolution. A granddaughter revealed that Martha "had a vivacity of temper which might sometimes border on tartness . . . She commanded . . . respect by . . . considerable powers of concentration."

The marital strain reached an apex during his 1775–76 tenure in the Second Continental Congress. Because Jefferson destroyed all of her letters, Martha's reaction to his authoring the Declaration of Independence is unknown, but she never acquiesced in his pleas to join him in Philadelphia. Pregnant six times in ten years—with only two children living to maturity—she pleaded poor health as her excuse. The fact remained that she was quite well enough to journey to the tidewater of Charles City from Monticello, in mountainous Charlottesville over precarious roads by lone carriage, unescorted by Thomas, to be with her sister. In '76, Philadelphia, that hotbed of patriots, was safer from British attack than Charles City. Martha obviously had no interest in being among anti-Loyalists. Using her health as an excuse, Jefferson resigned from Congress just two months after authoring the Declaration. This agitated many of his colleagues, who knew that his participation in the war effort was crucial.

In '79, Jefferson relented to accept Virginia's governorship. Martha reveled in her popularity in social Williamsburg, reigning from the royal governor's mansion, playing the harpsicord "very skillfully," and "in all respects a very agreeable, sensible and accomplished lady." But when Lady Washington asked the governor's wife to lead her state's drive for the soldier-relief program, Mrs. Jefferson, in her only extant letter, while publicly supporting the Revolutionary cause, seemed evasive:

> Mrs. Washington has done me the honor of communicating the enclosed proposition of our sisters of Pennsylvania and of informing me that the same grateful sentiments are displaying themselves in Maryland. I undertake with cheerfulness the duty of furnishing to my country women an opportunity of proving that they also participate of those virtuous feelings which gave birth to it. I cannot do more for its promotion than by enclosing to you some of the papers to be disposed of as you think proper.

In mentioning the "duty" and begging off that she "cannot do more for its promotion" than pass on information, Martha distanced herself. She did not mention her health.

In 1780, Thomas was offered the chance to work with Benjamin Franklin as the commissioner to Paris. It was an honor, but indirectly Martha prevented his accepting. He later excused himself by saying, "Such was the state of my family that I could not leave it, nor could I expose it to the dangers of the sea, and of capture by the British ships then covering the ocean." It was completely contrary to his immediate decision less than four years later, after Martha had died, when he took his daughter Patsy to France. His other child, Maria, was sent across the very same dangerous ocean Jefferson had said he feared sailing with his family. Maria was only eight years old, and sent alone, except for her half-aunt, the slave Sally Hemings. Patsy was placed in a convent, and Maria put in Abigail Adams's care.

Later, the daughters married congressmen, who both stayed with Jefferson in the President's House. On long visits, the daughters sometimes served as hostesses there, but neither lived permanently in that residence with him, or ever expressed interest in politics. He would have considered it very unseemly. Did Jefferson transfer to them an earlier resentment of Martha's interference in his career? Was there a reason for his refusal to free his sister-in-law, and reputed mistress, Sally Hemings? Nobody knew. Jefferson destroyed all material remembrances of Martha, save for a silhouette, a few lines of poetry, and a lock of her hair. Even in death, he blurred her memory, having her gravestone inscribed not in English, but in Latin.[1]

Mrs. Madison, of course, knew none of this. Had she known the president's attitude toward political women, she tactfully might have adhered to his notions and not emerged as publicly. As surrogate Lady, she had already gone public, and political. John Quincy Adams, now a senator, recorded that she gave him a ride to the Capitol in her carriage as *she* was on *her* way to take in Senate debates. The French military attaché, Colonel André de Bronne, wrote that "Mrs. Madison has become one of America's most valuable assets . . . The Secretary of State and his lady are so inseparable as his duty permits." It was Dolley who caused a minor diplomatic stir when she returned criticism to the sharp British minister's wife, whereas the president never spoke up to defend himself. As a symbolic gesture, Dolley halted entertaining during the Barbary Wars. She headed a drive to provide supplies for the Lewis and Clark expedition of the West. The public reception on July 4 found her "amusing myself with the *mob.* " During one of their rare separations, Dolley broached to Jemmy the subject of her being kept informed of international politics:

I wish you would indulge me with some information respecting the war with Spain, and the disagreement with England, which is so generally expected. You know I am not much of a politician, but I am extremely anxious to know (as far as you think proper) what is going forward in the

Cabinet. On this subject, I believe you would not desire your wife to be
the active partisan . . . nor will there be the slightest danger, while she
is conscious of her want of talents, and the diffidence in expressing those
opinions, always imperfectly understood by her sex.

Madison replied with the straight facts: "The power of deciding
questions of war and providing measures that will make it is with Congress and that is always an answer to Newspapers."[2]

Jefferson, with all his reservations about women in public life, was
so comfortable with Dolley that he permitted her to include his bedroom on her tours of the mansion for her friends. And in his own way,
he first established an official recognition of the role of Lady. In his
revision of presidential protocol, *The Canons of Etiquette To Be Observed
by the Executive,* he listed Rule 12, which read, "The President *and his
family* [author emphasis] take predecence everywhere in public or private."[3]

The president would have been taken aback had he visited Mount
Vernon in the first year of his tenure. There, an increasingly lorn Martha Washington welcomed aging Federalists, and became increasingly
outspoken on politics. One visitor, William Curtis, recorded, "We were
all federalists, which evidently gave her particular pleasure. Her remarks were frequently pointed and sometimes very sarcastic on the new

order of things and the present administration. She spoke of the election of Mr. Jefferson, whom she considered as one of the most detestable of mankind, as the greatest misfortune our country has ever experienced. Her unfriendly feelings towards him were naturally to be expected . . ."

Martha had evolved from Lady to a grand, uniquely American version of a Queen Mother, and a pilgrimage to her became a must for aspiring politicians and their wives. Upon return from Europe, John Quincy and Louisa Adams spent a night with Martha *before* dining with Jefferson and the Madisons. Though they were Democrats, Martha warmly welcomed the Madisons again, and encouraged her granddaughters' friends, like Margaret Smith of Calvert County, Maryland, to cross the river and visit as well.

The visits, however, were oftentimes sad. Martha "in gloomy solitude" took "melancholy" daily walks to George's nearby grave, placed in what was thought to be a temporary tomb. She hated to see people leave. "Mrs. Washington urged us," wrote one visitor, "to tarry to dine, but we were obliged to return to Washington. She was likewise pressing in her invitation to make her another visit before the close of the session . . ." Mrs. William Thornton wrote that "Mrs. Washington asked me to stay longer . . . and hoped it would not make it so long again before I came to see her," and Sally Foster Otis bluntly said, ". . . it was very difficult to get away. She urged us in the most flattering manner to remain a few days with her."

Visitors noticed how deteriorated Mount Vernon had become. Although George Washington's will stated that his slaves would be freed only after Martha died, he overlooked the emotions of human chattel. Thus, Martha, a paranoid old woman, had found herself surrounded by several hundred slaves eagerly awaiting her death.

When the end finally came to the great Lady Washington on May 22, 1802, it was widely reported in the national press. One eulogy included a rather accurate wood engraving of her and remarked that "her claims to celebrity rest *not solely* to her connection with that distinguished patriot . . . In all his public cares and duties . . . she took a deep interest . . . she was always a helpmate."

Hearing the news, Abigail Adams was saddened, but had her own bad news. Meeting Louisa for the first time, the matriarch thought her a weak European, ill-prepared for the world of politics upon which Abigail was advising her son. There was also the heartbreaking situation of her beloved elderly black maid, who was slowly dying in severe pain. Unable to find others willing to nurse her, Abigail took it upon herself to see that her last days were comfortable. Amid her trials, Mrs. Adams had a change of political heart. She supported Democrat James Madison for president in 1808.[4]

The coming election stirred both joy and anger in Dolley. Her desire to become the bona fide Lady of the White House, as the presidential mansion was now frequently called, was made clear when Jemmy's candidacy was threatened by none other than James Monroe, husband of her colleague Elizabeth, who had welcomed Dolley as an overnight guest at her home, and in turn received pickled gooseberries from Mrs. Madison. Dolley had previously depended upon Elizabeth, among others, to buy her magnificent Parisian costumes. But by July 1807, when Monroe permitted his name to be circulated as a rival for the nomination, Dolley thought Elizabeth was responsible, and privately told her sister Anna that she had never really trusted nor liked *"la belle Américaine."* Dolley had no hesitation in speaking, according to John Quincy Adams's diary, "upon the electioneering now so warmly carried on, in which she spoke very slightingly of Mr. Monroe."

Though Elizabeth had nothing to do with it, lewd rumors of a scandalously graphic nature were being circulated by the anti-Madison press. Dolley's full figure and intimacy with Jefferson fueled the fires of the campaign "sex scandal" hovering around her. Earlier gossip claimed that Dolley was Jefferson's mistress, since she and Jemmy had lived briefly in the White House with the president before buying their own home. Even Abigail spoke to defend Dolley. The scandals spread largely through gossip, but some innuendo was printed by a Baltimore newspaper.

It was said that the reason the Madisons were childless was that he was impotent and she oversexed; that Dolley was happy only when surrounded by men, and she and her sister Anna were pimped by Jemmy into service for Jefferson and foreign diplomats to win support from the president and European nations; that Dolley had relations with Democrats who could deliver electoral votes; that with Dolley's approval, Anna was intimate with Madison, and her husband, Massachusetts Congressman Richard Cutts, accepted the condition with the promise of a Cabinet position. Cutts was so angered that he challenged the editor of the *Boston Federalist*, which reprinted the claims, to a duel.

Meanwhile, Congressman John Randolph of Virginia spread the scandals in Congress by alluding to them in his speeches, and wrote of Madison's "unfortunate matrimonial connection." Dolley was deeply wounded by it all, and wrote her husband that she would forever "resolve not to admit a gentleman into her room unless entitled by age and long acquaintance." Dolley's sister Lucy wrote that Federalists "abuse us all in the lump" but that outright lies could "seldom injure much." Jefferson's reaction on being "unfeelingly traduced in the Virginia papers" with Dolley was amused shock. He "thought at my age and ordinary demeanor would have prevented any suggestions in that form . . ."

Madison won his party's nomination and the election against

Charles Pinckney, who claimed he "was beaten by Mr. and Mrs. Madison."

In afterthought, the loser mused, "I might have had a better chance had I faced Mr. Madison alone."[5]

− 7 −
The Queen of Hearts

AMONG THE SEVERAL thousand citizens attending the 1809 Inaugural, one shed a spiritual brilliance so strong that it was she, not the president, upon whom all others craned their necks to cast their curious eyes. Dolley Madison was the first Lady to witness her husband's initial swearing in, but it was her new title that was rippling through the throng on this sunny day that marked the primary difference. The Lady had become "Lady Presidentress."

Her warm presence was also symbolic of the new type of power relationship that was now to reign. As in the Washingtons' marriage, Jemmy and Dolley shared an interest in entertaining, but, like the Adamses, they also shared opinions, state secrets, and politics. On her first night, Lady Presidentress was already exerting social power. Her friend Thomas Tingey, Navy Yard chief, was tentatively planning the first "Inaugural Ball," and timidly asked whether she and Jemmy would attend such an event. The answer was a swift, twinkling yes. The ball was advertised in The National Intelligencer, and tickets were sold to the public.

The Lady Presidentress also exerted political power.

The nations of France and England were then at war. Both nations' ministers to America showed up at the Inaugural dinner. There was frenzy among the State Department protocol officers. Should France or England get the seat of honor next to the Lady Presidentress? Complimenting both and offending no one, Dolley took her seat right between the two ministers. The next day, the Intelligencer reported the playing of a new song, "Mrs. Madison's Minuet." It was was the first time a president's wife was the subject of popular music.[1]

The immediate White House family consisted of the Madisons, her son Payne, who was boarded for a while at a Baltimore Catholic school, sister Anna and her husband, Congressman Cutts, and widowed sister Lucy Washington, who later remarried in the first White House wedding. The three sisters were dubbed the "Merry Wives of Windsor," all raising eyebrows for their rather bold habit of rouging heavily and using tobacco snuff in public. The Payne sisters were a quartet when another, Mary, married to a Virginia congressman, was around.

In polite circles, snuff was confined largely to gentlemen's use, but Dolley had been enjoying it for years and saw no reason to discontinue it now, just because she was a public figure. That honesty, and her forthright, easy manner, proved to be the very reason for her popularity. In short, Dolley was comfortable with herself, loved to laugh and to make others laugh. She treated all humans, regardless of race or social standing, with dignity. From deep within came a tranquillity that managed to radiate out to all who came near her. Through personal crisis, Dolley had already come to implicitly accept that, in life, change was inevitable and often uncontrollable. She made adaptation an art.

The Madison relationship continued to operate in the White House. An early riser, Dolley supervised all domestic details before breakfast with the president. Until noon, she received callers and kept pace with her wide correspondence. Sometimes Jemmy dropped in to see her to "get a right story and a good laugh." Afternoons were spent making calls throughout the wide-spread and still-unpaved city. When not entertaining, the Madisons dined and then read together. Before the Library of Congress received their new books, the president routed them to Dolley first, for her pleasure and comments. One evening a week, however, Lady Presidentress shone at her roaring, wonderfully mad public reception. It was known as "Mrs. Madison's crush," or simply "Wednesday Night."[2]

The first "Wednesday Night," held on March 30, 1809, set the tone for all others. Dolley successfully managed to appear as a grand queen in magnificent costumes, but being completely informal, she also appeared truly democratic. "Wednesday Night" kept her in touch with the public, but it also served an unspoken political motive. Statesmen knew that they had a good chance of quietly discussing issues with the president by gathering about him in his discreet corner, away from the din.

Meanwhile, through the reception rooms, Dolley, unlike her predecessors, meandered about, joking with and greeting each of her guests, who were fed from groaning buffet tables upon which sat domes and pyramids of her favorite dessert, ice cream in warm pastry shells. Jefferson had introduced the French sweet to her, but it was essentially Dolley who popularized it, as congressional wives began asking for her "receipt," and used it when they went back to the provinces. From there it spread to local households.[3]

The Lady Presidentress also hosted special political dinners for about thirty guests. These were particularly important to Jemmy, who placed his wife—not himself—at the head of the table, next to the key statesman. In this way, she managed to get an opinion or persuade the politician to consider the president's views. And there were her "dove parties"—informal but exclusive gatherings of Cabinet, Senate, and Congressional wives; current political events were among the topics discussed. The individual women were carefully selected by Dolley for a specific though unnamed tactic—gathering opinions from the statesmen's wives that might reflect their husbands'.

Women played an integral part in Dolley's politics. Within a short time of her Washington residency, she had cultivated friendships with two women who would prove crucial to the press coverage of the administration: Margaret Bayard Smith, wife of Samuel Smith, original owner of the country's first national newspaper, the *Intelligencer,* and Sarah Gales Seaton, wife of its co-editor, William Seaton. When Margaret later asked Dolley for permission to write her biography, Mrs. Madison tactfully said, "[I]f a Biographical Sketch must be taken . . . your pen would be more agreeable to me than any other . . . ," and Mrs. Smith also veiled her as the heroine of her novel *What Is Gentility?* They served each other's purpose, but they were also friends. Consequently, Dolley became national news. *Intelligencer* stories about her wit, fashions, and parties were read across the young nation, by men and women alike, and regional publications followed suit. Even the anti-Madison *New England Palladium* carried a flattering account of one of her receptions. One magazine, *Port Folio,* was so eager to portray Mrs. Madison that its editors had a woodcut engraving copied from her portrait, and used it to illustrate their cover, making Dolley the first president's wife to grace a publication.[4]

Unlike her predecessors, Dolley genuinely enjoyed her public. She conversed easily "on books, men and manners, literature in general and many special branches of knowledge," and recalled all names and faces. At the White House, she welcomed everyone from steamboat inventor Robert Fulton and actor George Cooke to Indian chiefs and her friend the scandalously lascivious Elizabeth Bonaparte—who went without underpants and dampened her gown to show off her buttocks. For children, Dolley started the Easter Egg Roll on the Capitol grounds. When two old western ladies came just to meet her and interrupted the presidential breakfast, Dolley obliged them with kisses. At her friend Mary King's wedding, Mrs. Madison became the first president's wife to take part in a tree-planting ceremony, pitching soil on a sickle-pear sapling.

This love of being among the people extended to her appearances at card games and the racetrack, indulging her publicly known predilection to gambling. She appeared in the audience at her husband's speeches, at a ship launching, dancing assemblies, and fund-raisers. When told that "everybody loves Mrs. Madison," she retorted with what was so plainly evident: "*Mrs. Madison* loves *everybody.* "

The immediate effect of her fame was effusiveness. Dolley received an outpouring of gifts—from tiger skins to counterpanes—which spurred the commercial exploitation of the president's wife, as an un-

authorized writer used Dolley's name to sell his book, and a banker, Jacob Barker, named one of his merchant ships *Lady Madison*. It also made her a human figure to whom the public could address its grievances or affection when hesitant to do so with the president, as if she shared the presidency. One writer told Dolley she had "a precious talent committed to thy trust by the King of Kings." The postmaster of New Orleans sent her, as if she were president, an official military report.

This all made the role of president's wife thoroughly celebrated at a time when women remained demurely private. Though Martha and Abigail had been recognized as public figures, they were largely unresponsive. Dolley, a citizen's diary noted, was the best female "to dignify the station which she occupies." Dolley Madison built upon a role to create a *position*.[5]

Though the Lady Presidentress didn't personally foster any parallel to the queen, it was thrust upon her by a loving public—"every inch a Queen," as one admirer put it. It was her friend New York Congressman Samuel Mitchell who put monarchial notions in perspective: "She has a fine person and a most engaging countenance, which pleases, not so much from symmetry or complexion as from expression. Her smile, her countenance and her manners are so engaging, that it is no wonder that . . . with her fine blue eyes and large share of animation she should be, indeed, a QUEEN OF HEARTS."[6]

Always, however, her outward trappings were balanced by the greater value she placed on the human soul. As a child, she'd run through the woods and lost an emerald secretly given her by a non-Quaker grandmother. She realized the folly of materialism. One of her favorite passages was key to her personality: ". . . our vanity may enamour us with rank . . . but who can love genius and not feel that the sentiments it excites partake . . . of its own immortality."

Dolley's only regal symbol was her grand state carriage, but her Yardwood Washing Machine, which she was not above using herself, settled any whisper of pretension. Clothes, nonetheless, remained one of the most important factors in Mrs. Madison's life, her Achilles' heel being French fashions. Dolley ordered them through William Lee, the American consul at Bordeaux, who complained he did nothing but "waddle round Paris and cutt from the magazines of fashion," and her consultant was the French minister's wife. Her gift to pregnant friend Mary McKean was a huge trunk of Parisian baby clothes. Though Jemmy was angered at a particular shipment that carried a two-thousand-dollar duty, she paid for most clothes from her property rents. But it was the turban with which she wrapped her head that became her trademark.

Dolley's outrageous turbans with foot-long birds-of-paradise feathers were said to cost one thousand dollars annually. So addicted to these turbans was she that she even napped in them—without feather. The turban became Washington's latest fashion rage.

Mrs. Madison's fashion influence wasn't lost on merchant John Jacob Astor. He sent her clothing gratis from his American Fur Company, "from motives of patriotism." The Rubenesque figure of this woman who admitted to "eat heartily . . . and never feel . . . worse for it," snugly tucked into the flimsy high-waisted, low-busted Empire gowns, raised eyebrows. As one observer delicately put it, "her sylphic form 'thinly veiled' displays all the graces of a Venus . . ." Another said that "her soul is as big as ever and her body has not decreased." Dolley found the comments flattering. When she encountered another former Quaker and commented on his "absent broadbrim," he retorted, looking at her bosom, "And here's to thy absent kerchief." Others, scrutinizing her, rhapsodized, "The woman adorns the dress," and "Tis not her form, tis not her face, it is the woman altogether."[7]

Abigail Adams thought otherwise, writing, "With respect to Mrs. Madison's influence, it ought to be such as Solomon describes his virtuous woman's to be—one who should do him good and not evil all the days of her life,—so that the heart of her husband may safely trust in her . . . Since Dolley Madison adopted the new fashions and seemed in every way delighted with the French influenced manner . . . we may assume . . . Madison enjoyed . . . 'luxuriant feminine displays' . . ." Quite disapprovingly, she concluded, "I believe I may say with safety that her predecessors left her no evil example."[8]

As effusive as she was, Dolley remained taciturn on politics. Part of the reason Jemmy confided to her the conversations of Cabinet meetings, congressional reports, military maneuvers, and diplomatic dispatches was her utter discretion, underscored during the sensitive period of Aaron Burr's banishment to Europe. The very man who had introduced the Madisons became persona non grata when it was discovered that he was plotting to undermine the government. Apprehended, tried for treason, but acquitted, Burr was banished to Europe in 1808. Dolley wrote only that "I have nothing . . . to tell you . . . about Burr," and after his arrest tersely commented he would probably be convicted. When his daughter Theodosia tearfully attempted to get Dolley to influence the president in permitting Burr to return, she got no support. Or so it seemed. One story said Dolley was the "most potent factor in facilitating" his return, and had earlier rendezvoused secretly with him in a nearby garden to silently hear out his defense.[9]

Dolley, who regularly led a file of women to House debates, held a power over politicians besides Jemmy. Once, watching anti-Madison Congressman John Randolph rave, she thought it "as good as a play," but interceded between him and Congressman John Eppes, who planned to duel each other over a political argument and even "converted to compromise" their debate. She particularly cultivated friendships with Congressmen Henry Clay and John Calhoun, young leaders of the "War Hawks," who were calling for war with England, since that nation was capturing and impressing sailors from American ships into their own service. Mrs. Madison knew that the "War Hawk" voting block would be crucial to Jemmy's reelection in 1812. Again she socialized for political end, pointedly sharing her snuff with Clay, a fellow dipper.

Jemmy shared information with her, once sending her "intelligence just brought us." They together feared the outcome of a situation unfolding into a crisis, the British hijacking of American ships. Jemmy shared the news of secret negotiations between England and America with her, and Dolley reported it to the Cutts, along with the depressing prospects of war and optimistic nationalism. She said her "spirits have been low in these troublesome times. No Constitution heard of yet; the Hornet went to take dispatches and to let them know our determination to fight for our rights . . ."[10]

While war clouds gathered, Dolley was busy with patronage, evidently exercising power over the Cabinet. She was informed—no doubt by Jemmy—of Senate confirmations and post-office designations before they were made official and kept abreast of nominations and appointments. She made particular strides in attempting to help secure Treasury secretary Albert Gallatin an appointment to a peace commission. She also had advance knowledge that the appointment would not be approved. Only once did she belie her access, when she wrote that a situation was "a little calmer . . . or rather I hear less about it." As word got out that "through Mrs. Madison one could obtain . . . access to . . . her distinguished husband," letters requesting jobs fell upon her in a flurry. She successfully influenced the promotion of a War Department bookkeeper to chief accountant, and the appointment of Anthony Morris, a friend, to Spain on a diplomatic mission. Another friend, Joel Barlow, was made the American minister to France. She managed to get the conscientious objector son of an old Quaker friend Debbie Pleasants freed from prison. Yet even the presidentress's power got stuck in red tape. "I have waited," she wrote impatiently, "[for] a speedy appointment from the secretary in favor of W. Williams, but . . . none . . . have been made . . . *when* is the question that cannot be answered. I will continue to remind him [Cabinet member] of the . . . merit of the applicant and however tedious the suspense may seem, I think success must crown him at last."

She didn't always grant favors. Dolley couldn't help Barbara Peters, who begged protection from a crafty lawyer, and a Harriet Hawley who ventured "to ask a favor . . ." Even author Washington Irving, who expected his kindness toward the presidentress—whom he called "a fine, portly buxom dame"—would get him a diplomatic post was flat disappointed when Dolley felt used and did nothing for his career. If there were administration critics, she wanted to hear them. After securing an advance copy of Robert Smith's anti-Madison pamphlet, *Address to the People of the United States*, she read it, and sniffed it was "too impertinent to excite any other feeling than anger" in her. Yet her letters remained so discreet as to render their meaning obscure to outsiders, as when she admitted she was "acting in his [Congressman Mitchell's] department" during the representative's absence.[11]

Mrs. Madison kept abreast of the opposition tactics through her network, begging one friend to be open "in laying their [the opposition's] claims before me" though "no one shall see statements but myself." Besides seeking experts' opinions, the presidentress used her public for informal polling, emphasizing in her report of some campaign news to Anna that "[a]ll this is from the people, not from the Cabinet," but added with the savvy of a populist, "yet you know everything vibrates there." Dolley saw the election not as a race between men, but marital couples, confiding in Anna confidently, "The intrigues for President . . . go on, but I think may terminate as they last did. The Clintons, Smiths, Armstrongs, etc. are all in the fields . . ." Though she noted, "All are busy electioneering," Dolley later confessed, "I do not admire the contentions of parties, political or civil, tho' on my own quiet retreat I am anxious to know all the maneuverings of both, the one and the other, so be not timid." Federalist senator Pope remarked that Mrs. Madison made "a very good President, and must not be turned out."

Her instincts proved correct when the War Hawks threw their thirty-eight votes to Madison. Dolley was later credited for holding Jemmy "back from the extreme of Jeffersonianism and enabled him to escape the terrible dilemma of the war. But for her Dewitt Clinton would have been chosen President in 1812."[12]

On April 1, after England's continued belligerency, Congress had passed a ninety-day embargo on all British vessels within U.S. jurisdiction. Mrs. Madison followed each minute development as closely as anyone in the Department of the Navy. She reported to Anna, "I wrote you that the Embargo would take place three or four days before it did . . . and General Dearborn will leave in a few days . . . Congress will not adjourn, I believe, though it has been much spoken of . . ." But, as she detailed in a subsequent letter, something more ominous was emerging from the seas: "Before this, you know of our Embargo—to be followed by War! Yes, that terrible event is at hand . . . our appointments for the purpose are mostly made and the recruiting business goes on . . ." To another she tersely replied, "I have nothing . . . more agreeable to tell you from the seat of government."

War had been declared on June 19. Personally, Dolley was prepared and was hoping Congress would hasten its declaration, revealing "I have always been an advocate for fighting when assailed . . ."

And Presidentress Dolley frankly admitted that "tho' a Quaker, so I keep the old Tunisian sabre within reach."[13]

– 8 –

AMID WAR'S ANXIETIES, Dolley found herself the government figure having to placate nervous merchant John Jacob Astor. Astor promised to continue supplying Dolley with free tea and wine because of, as he wrote her in the third person, "Mrs. Madison's assurances that all Mr. Astor's ships should arrive . . . from Canton . . . with valuable Cargoes." The shipping businesses of merchants like Astor were now jeopardized with the sea war.

Dolley also counted military leaders as her confidants, her particular favorite being General William Henry Harrison, who failed to bring his wife, Anna, former schoolmate of Nellie Custis, with him when he journeyed from his Indiana Territory home to meet with the president. When Harrison's character was under scrutiny and a military dossier on him was being prepared, the presidentress offered her unsolicited support, sending classified War Department information to Kentucky's Governor Shelby, explaining that "such a testimony in favor of . . . Harrison and such facts and explanations will dispose of charges against his military character . . ." When Harrison was immediately ordered back West by the president after a short visit, Dolley told her husband that she "laid my command on him [to stay] and [he] is too gallant a man to disobey me." Jemmy thought she was joking. That night Harrison danced at Dolley's reception.

From the White House, Mrs. Madison cheered soldiers on to fight, and kept her social schedule in full swing to keep morale boosted. It was during these stressful months that Dolley evidently delivered several "public patriotic addresses." She could often be called upon to say a few things, and on one recorded occasion during the war she "made a little speech for the men, presenting an 'elegant standard.'"[1]

If publicly she lifted morale, privately Dolley was alarmed. In the spring of 1813, the Parliament buildings of Toronto were burned by Americans. The destruction of Washington was the announced revenge. Destruction by fire.

Dolley was barely able to "describe . . . the fears and alarms that circulate around me . . . all the city (except the Cabinet) have expected a visit from the enemy . . . we are making considerable efforts for defense . . . five hundred militia . . . are to be stationed on the green . . . the twenty tents already look well in my eyes . . . One of our generals has discovered a plan of the British . . . to burn the President's House . . . I do not tremble at this, but feel hurt that the admiral . . . should send me word that he would make his bow at my drawing-room very soon."[2]

Suddenly, without warning, in the midst of this terror, the president's assistant, Ned Coles, fell ill. Dolley Madison, presidentress in wartime, assumed his responsibilities. Then, just after Coles left his job to seek recuperation, the president himself fell deathly ill and was disabled. Though details were sketchy, in May 1813 Dolley Madison may have assumed some responsibility in the administration of the executive branch.

Even in the midst of war, Dolley's primary concern was for Jemmy's recuperation. She was cautious about what was said and done concerning the situation, later guardedly granting, "I could tell . . . many curious things . . . but as people say I have my opinions etc&&. I must not trust my pen." The only scrap of evidence that she was in control was a terse message that she wrote and sent to a hostile Senate committee clamoring to see the president after postponements: "James Madison is sorry that a continuance of his disposition will not permit him to see the committee of the Senate today." She did so only to protect the president.[3]

Through all these new trials, Dolley helped others in their pleas. Francis Scott Key needed Madison's permission to board an enemy ship in his attempts to secure the release of a captured friend, Dr. William Beanes. It was on this mission that Key witnessed the firing on Fort McHenry. Legend persisted that it was Dolley who persuaded Jemmy to grant Key his permission, resulting in the poem "The Star-Spangled Banner," afterward set to the music of an existing ballad.

By August 1814, the terror of war became real. A stronger Jemmy left Dolley in the White House on the morning of the twenty-fourth to be with the troops at nearby Bladensburg. Late morning found her planning a dinner for the president and military leaders on their return from what she was certain would be success at Bladensburg. In between her preparations, Dolley vaulted up the attic stairs to the roof with her binoculars, looking for some sign of the army.

Instead, she saw panic-stricken Washingtonians fleeing with their possessions packed in carriages, and heard the distant sound of firing cannons.

She tried to stay calm. Just weeks before, a woman had driven up to the White House, let down her hair, and screamed she would hang Madison with it. A story circulated that British general Ross had recently appeared dressed as an old woman at a White House reception, looking over the house he planned to burn.

But one rumor was terrifyingly personal. Admiral Cockburn had announced his plan to take Dolley hostage and parade her through the streets of London.

If Dolley was directly threatened, Elizabeth Monroe, wife of Madison's most recent secretary of state, was quite safe at her Virginia home, away from the tension. While she and Dolley often gambled at "loo" together, and even strolled down Pennsylvania Avenue on warm evenings with mutual friends, they were associated by politics only. It was sister Anna and "French John" Sioussat, her general manager, who remained devotedly at Dolley's side.

As the muggy afternoon wore on, the mayor of Washington three times bade her to evacuate. Three times she refused. To flee would signal defeat. Then she received alarming pencil dispatches from Jemmy informing her of the British proximity to the capital.

She later recalled how she "lived a lifetime in those last moments waiting for Madison's return, and in an agony of fear lest he might have been taken prisoner . . . I confess that I was so unfeminine as to be free from fear, and willing to remain in the Castle. If [only] I could have a cannon through every window . . . my whole heart mourned for my country."

Running with French John through the rooms just recently redecorated so lavishly—her ladies' parlor in her trademark color of sunshine yellow, the Oval Room, the dining room where her "Wednesday

SAVING THE PORTRAIT OF WASHINGTON.

Night" buffet tables had groaned—Dolley realized everything had to be sacrificed. *Almost* everything.

In what would become her most single famous act, Dolley ordered that George Washington's Gilbert Stuart portrait be removed from the wall and given to friends for safekeeping. Then she gathered copies of important state documents, ordered her carriage made ready, collected what silver she could, took her boxed scarlet velvet curtains, and, disguised as a farm wife, jumped into her chariot, "flying full speed through Georgetown, accompanied by an officer carrying a drawn sword."

As the frenzied seconds had ticked away, there was one other item she had considered important enough to rescue for posterity. Before she fled the White House, Dolley Madison ran into her ladies' parlor and grabbed a winsome portrait of herself.[4]

- 9 -

"An Influence"

WHEN THE BRITISH arrived at the house, they discovered that their intended hostage, Mrs. Madison, had eluded them, and they had to satisfy themselves with one of her seat cushions, shouting "pleasantries too vulgar to repeat," according to an observer, about the absent presidentress. Lewdly referring to her shapely derriere, Admiral Cockburn carried the chair cushion off with him, so he could "warmly recall Mrs. Madison's seat."

Then they set the fire, burning out all the interiors, leaving a gutted bare shell. A rainstorm saved the four walls.

Meanwhile, over the next several hours Dolley would attempt unsuccessfully to link up with Jemmy at various local homes, trudge through a rainstorm, be expelled from shelter by a spiteful tavernkeeper's wife, suffer verbal abuses, sleep in a tent, and convince an officer to permit her to cross the Potomac river by raft after revealing her true identity. When her eyes finally saw the sight of the still-smoldering White House timbers with "unroofed, naked walls, cracked, defaced and blackened by smoke," Dolley "violently" railed that she "wished we had 10,000 such men . . . *to sink our enemy to the bottomless pit . . .*" For months she would burst into sobs when she thought of the fire.

The Madisons moved temporarily into nearby Octagon House, where the peace treaty of Ghent was approved by the president on February 15, 1815. It was a night of revelry, music, and shouts of "Peace! Peace!" As usual, the immobile crush was clinging to Dolley, said that night to be "the observed of all observers . . . in the meridian of life and queenly beauty . . ." She was also now a national heroine. At an earlier reception, the flag of the captured British ship *Macedonian* was placed before her, not the president.

When she joined Jemmy at a public ceremony in Annapolis, where he dedicated the navy's seventy-four-gun *Washington*, the presidentress attracted more attention than he or the ship did. Abigail Adams, shed of her conservative Federalism, wrote proudly of the Madisons' actions, and Dolley was again in the newspapers, praised in a poem, "The Bladensburg Races":

> Now Mistress Dolly [sic] (careful soul!)
> Two wrapper-bags had found
> To hold the sword and chapeau-bras
> And Keep Them Safe and Sound.

It concluded:

> Now long live Madison, the brave,
> And Armstrong, long live he!
> And Rush! And Cutts! Monroe and Jones!
> And Dolly [sic], long live *She*![1]

At a reception for General Andrew Jackson, celebrating his victory in the Battle of New Orleans, Dolley was equally heralded. Few noticed the fat, quiet female who arrived with the general. She was a religious zealot who felt anxious in places where the sinful might be reveling, and stayed in the background. She had no interest in public life or recognition and just wanted to have her husband at her domestic side at their Nashville, Tennessee, home, "the Hermitage." She was his wife, Rachel. No newspapers seemed, at the moment, to show any interest in her or her background, but Sarah Seaton wrote that a "dilemma" and "debate" arose among official Washington as to a "question of propriety" involving Rachel. Mrs. Seaton thought Mrs. Jackson to be "totally uninformed in mind and matters." The war was over now, and Mrs. Jackson did not want to see Andrew again depart. Andrew felt a deep, protective love for his wife, who traveled with her Bible. But he was torn about retirement. He obviously enjoyed the limelight, and felt strongly about politics. He would return Rachel safely to Nashville. Then he would go off again.[2]

Behind the felicitations of the postwar era lurked a dark side to Dolley's ebullience. It was her son, Payne, an alcoholic and gambler. Instead of attending Princeton, as previously planned, he had been sent with the Peace Commission to Europe, where it was hoped he would take life more seriously. Rather, Payne gallivanted on the Continent with a forty-eight-year-old German authoress, fell in love with a Russian princess (who was said to be abducted and "never seen again"), was titled "the American Prince," and absolutely refused to write to his parents. It was a disturbing situation, which would have devastating repercussions.

Meanwhile, in America, Dolley was said to be influencing one of the government's most important decisions. A discouraged president had considered relocating the capital back to Philadelphia, but Mrs. Madison evidently insisted that the Founding Fathers had chosen Washington for its central location. One legend quoted her as proclaiming, "We shall rebuild . . . The enemy cannot frighten a free people." She personally surveyed the burned federal buildings and initiated a move for volunteers to help rebuild the city. Dolley added her own postscript to the spirit of regeneration. She evidently had a dress made from the red White House curtains she had taken before fleeing.[3]

It was after the war effort that the presidentress assumed leadership in a welfare issue that afflicted many communities, the first formally organized project of a president's wife. Dolley had been known to set certain mornings aside for visits to "the poor of the district," and was said also to be "desirous to promote the cause of general literature [i.e., to eradicate illiteracy]," but it was the plight of the Washington City Orphans Asylum that caught her special attention. On October 10, 1815, the *Intelligencer* announced a meeting for its formation:

> The Ladies of the county of Washington and neighborhood are requested to meet in the Hall of Representatives, this day, at 11 o'clock, A.M. for the purpose of joining an association to provide asylum for the destitute orphans . . . it is hoped that the Ladies will show the interest . . . to supply to them . . . the place of the deceased parent . . . It is . . . hoped that there will be a full and punctual attendance . . .

At the meeting, Mrs. Madison was elected the "first directress" and donated twenty dollars and a cow. She herself commenced an arduous year of cutting and sewing orphans' clothes, setting an example for the gathered females, proclaiming it "delicious work." Dolley helped attract "[e]very female in this City . . . from the highest to the lowest" to work for the asylum, and when they raised enough funds they built it, just a block from the White House; the cornerstone was laid by Dolley's friend Maria Van Ness. The presidentress's interest was likely prompted by lifelong confidant Eliza Lee, whose husband was judge of the local orphans' court.[4]

Such efforts created a bond between Dolley and the city's women of all classes. It was Mrs. Madison who not only first led women into attendance of congressional debates and Supreme Court deliberations, but also the horse races. Her "dove parties" were for government *wives* only. When one day she decided that she wanted to eat at an infamous oyster house that was closed to women with the exception of prostitutes, her request was granted. Jemmy sent word by courier to the restaurant, it was cleaned up, and Dolley appeared the next day, her purpose not to break barriers but to eat oysters. It resulted in the opening of the restaurant to all women.

Dolley extended social invitations to include statesmen's wives and daughters, traditionally barred at Jefferson's stag affairs. At her receptions, both sexes freely conversed with each other as they never had before. With her example, women began attending luncheons, orations, and other public events. Dolley had a particular fascination in listening to sermons given by women in the halls of Congress.

During the Jefferson years, French minister Turreau, in drunken stupors, physically abused his wife. Dolley wrote to Anna that she had "heard sad things of Turreau, that he whips his wife, and abuses her dreadfully. I pity her sincerely . . ." Therefore, at receptions, an indignant Mrs. Madison showered attention and pity on Mme. Turreau. For diplomatic reasons, she grudgingly permitted the minister to attend her receptions, but Turreau was one of the few individuals for whom Dolley had utter contempt and treated rudely. She later expressed anger at the treatment of females by society. "Our sex," she confided to a niece, "are ever losers when they stem the torrent of public opinion." It's doubtful Jemmy told her that he approved State Department funds for a prostitute when the Tunisian ambassador requested one. Dolley did not respect loose females. When asked about a particular one with a tarnished reputation, Mrs. Madison minced no words: "She is a hussy!"

While commenting that "a lady seldom can speak freely to or on the subject of her fancy," Dolley was an equal in her marriage. "The capacity of the female mind for studies of the highest order," James Madison willingly admitted, "cannot be doubted . . . and the saddest slavery of all was that of the conscientious woman." The Madisons shared a fascination for the rare professional woman, later receiving warmly British educator and writer Harriet Martineau, whose "enlightened conversation Dolley relished." Jemmy told Martineau that "no distinction . . . should be made between men and women in equality of the mind," and she observed how Dolley fully shared in all business transactions.

When the controversial journalist Anne Royall arrived unannounced to see Dolley, in what would be the first press interview ever of a president's wife, she was rudely dismissed by a relative. Mrs. Madison overheard the trouble at the front door, and invited Royall in, spending the day with her, granting the interview, and even cleaning Royall's boots. When yet another woman writer, Elizabeth Lummis Ellett, was writing a book on Revolutionary Era women, she asked for Dolley's cooperation. Lying about her age, Mrs. Madison claimed she was but a mere child at the time, but would "look forward with much interest" to a book on "that distinguished class whose exploits and sacrifices well deserve to be commemorated."[5]

Dolley Madison became the single greatest influence on women in her time. Women frequently wrote and visited her, asking her advice, opinions, permission to use her name, and approval of projects. A young female wrote the presidentress that she was the "representative of our sex in every female virtue," and was personally "an influence" on the writer's life. One gentleman explained that he wanted her to help promote his book because he knew no woman who held "so distinguished a place . . . You are one of the Favored Few who to do good, need but will it. The elevation of your Rank, together with . . . your spirit . . . gives you an Influence which no other Lady can pretend to especially among the Fair Sex of our Country . . . I had rather have a few lines from Mrs. Madison than from a whole Bunch of Bishops.[6]

Not everyone loved Dolley. Her ego and clothing were criticized ("still fond of admiration—loads herself with finery and dresses without any taste") as was her figure ("fat, forty, but not fair"), and her informality ("without distinction either in manners or appearance"). Though she accepted criticism of her public life as part of the role, Mrs. Madison defended herself against personal untruths. When a seamstress told decorator Henry Latrobe that Dolley disliked his work for her, she wrote an astringent response:

> The varnished tale . . . of . . . my conduct . . . has been insufficient to assure your judgement . . . and as it is one of my sources of happiness never to desire a knowledge of other people's business . . . I shall be strict in my examination of the servants . . . I wish to know those who have taken the liberty to misrepresent me . . .[7]

Dolley had no response to criticism of her use of slaves as human candles, holding torches at a reception, and decried as "a barbarous Egyptian display." Nor was there an answer to the charge of Madison Hemings, son of Jefferson's slave Sally, who claimed that when he was born, Dolley had begged Sally to name him for her husband, and she would give her a "fine present." "Like many promises of the white folks to the slaves," Madison Hemings later wrote bitterly, "she never gave my mother anything."

Dolley was a member of the American Colonization Society, which opposed further slavery and supported freedman resettling in Africa's Liberia instead of their remaining in America as second-class citizens. Abolitionists resented the notion that any American should be sent to another country rather than change the attitudes of the society in which blacks had lived for generations. Dolley's attitude toward slavery was conflicted. Her family had sacrificed all their life's comforts for the freedom of slaves, and that sense of justice was ingrained in her. And yet the Madisons owned slaves.

At Montpelier, Dolley went to all ends in permitting slaves to live freely, viewing "human chattels as human creatures," and expressed the opinion that "the black-hued had emotions like unto those of the more fortunately hued." When Mrs. Madison bought a slave, David, she did so reluctantly, and "it was understood that at the expiration of five years he is to become free . . ."[8]

Mrs. Madison had personally experienced intolerance in fashionable Philadelphia, where Quakers were often ridiculed for their oddly plain ways, and it gave her a sensitivity to other religious minorities. Dolley, who wore such a large cross around her neck that she was quite often mistaken for a Roman Catholic, later frequently invited the nuns of the Visitation to her home, befriending a Sister Gertrude in particular. Dolley formed many close friendships with the prominent Roman Catholic families of Maryland, and sent her son to a strict Catholic academy run by the bishop of Baltimore. Her husband appointed the first Jewish diplomatic representative, Mordecai Noah, and, with Dolley, frequently attended the interdenominational "sabbaths in the speaker's chair," religious services held in Congress.[9]

In so many respects was Dolley a woman of the people that, as the end of her administration neared in March 1817, there was a pervasive melancholia throughout the city when James Monroe was elected to succeed Jemmy. No woman could ever replace Dolley. As hostess for Jefferson's eight years and Jemmy's eight years, she served longer than any in the White House. Part of her success was an implicit understanding of the dual life the role fully entailed. "Be always on your guard," Dolley once quoted Jemmy, "that you become not the slave of the public nor the martyr to your friends."

"Talents such as yours," Eliza prophesied in the very last letter Dolley received as presidentress, "were never intended to remain inactive." Soon after returning to Virginia, Dolley would admit, "Washington would no doubt be my preference."

The end of this golden era of Jefferson and the Madisons also marked the beginning of a new one.

As Elizabeth Monroe prepared for her ladyship, a Washington friend confided to Dolley that she had "so filled" her role as presidentress "as to render yourself more enviable this day than your successor." Another Washingtonian asked Mrs. Madison, "Do you know? or do you not know, my beloved Dolley, that your absence is more and more lamented; that your urbanity, benevolence and cheerfulness . . . will long be sought for in vain."[10]

These gloating sentiments, with their implied snipes at Mrs. Monroe, by females who now fancied themselves indispensable Washington society, were not at all lost on Elizabeth.

Dolley remained tactfully silent. Though the Madisons owned a town house facing the park across from the White House, there would be no sign of the Queen of Hearts for years. Her absence from the capital during the Monroe years was in itself telling. The queen was being usurped by "a smiling little Venus" from New York who would do everything in her power to diminish, and eventually eradicate, all signs of the queen's touch. Virginia charm was about to be replaced with Continental aristocracy.

As the Madison entourage rolled away in the dust, headed for the blue mountains of Virginia's piedmont, James and Elizabeth Monroe were preparing their private home on Pennsylvania Avenue, now the temporary White House, for the unfit masses about to crowd its elegant rooms crammed with the fine furniture of deposed French nobles. But there was one chair, not the least prominent, which sent a clear indication of things to come to those who knew its origins. It had once belonged to another powerful lady, Marie Antoinette.[11]

Among the many illnesses from which Elizabeth Monroe claimed she suffered was one the public prognosticated as "queen fever."

It would prove contagious.

PART III

The Antebellum Period 1817–1849

All men are privately influenced by women . . .
What Woman needs is not as a woman to act or
rule, but . . . to unfold such powers as were given
her . . . Women have taken possession of so
many provinces for which men has pronounced
them unfit, that . . . it is difficult to say just
where they must stop . . . Woman has always
power enough, if she choose to exert it, and is
usually disposed to do so . . .

—MARGARET FULLER
Woman in the Nineteenth Century (1845)

Queen Elizabeth

THE INAUGURAL RECEPTION at the Monroe house once again had eager Washingtonians craning to see their new presidentress. Unlike Dolley, she hadn't been at the swearing-in ceremony. And whereas Mrs. Madison had reigned at her Inaugural Ball, Mrs. Monroe, said to be "a little too New York," failed to appear and greet the crowds in her own home.

Washington society and congressional wives, eager to call and be called upon by Elizabeth, perhaps justified her absence because the restored White House wouldn't be opened to the public until the 1818 New Year's Day reception. They were duly aghast at their first glimpse into some of the rooms of the renovated White House. It was more palace than home, with no attempt to re-create Dolley's sunny Anglo-

American country-house comfort. Everything was gilded and regal—in a word, French. There were *two* special Bellange chairs, resembling thrones, with enclosed side panels—while other chairs of the set were open. As guests looked to the chilly Lady, surrounded that first New Year's Day by her sisters and daughter, they noticed her highly rouged cheeks and her unmistakably French embroidered costume in the high Empire style, part of a recent trousseau rumored to cost fifteen-hundred dollars. Elizabeth acknowledged guests "in the etiquette of the Old World . . . with a little nod of the head." In private, the Monroes spoke French. Publicly, they suggested "a uniform for the heads of departments and officers of the government." Unarmed guards were placed at the White House doors to dissuade improperly dressed citizens from seeing the First Family.[1]

The immediate outrage, to both official and unofficial Washington wives, came from the Monroes' eldest daughter, Mrs. Eliza Hay. Mrs. Hay announced that neither she nor her mother would conform to the Madison tradition of paying or returning calls. The excuse was that Mrs. Monroe was "in poor health," although the exact nature of Mrs. Monroe's illness remained an enigma. When she made her rare appearances in public, her youthful beauty always drew comment. This was obviously not a female ravaged by the most common disease, tuberculosis. Her "illnesses"—save arthritis—were never explained, and many doubted there was anything really wrong with her except snobbery. The secret, however, had less to do with the fact that she was ill and more to do with the illness itself.

Evidence indicated that Elizabeth Monroe may have had epilepsy, a condition then so mysterious that the Monroes perhaps kept it hidden in fear of misunderstanding. The fact is that she was alternately in good, then bad, condition, in public and private, and sometimes unavailable for weeks at a time. It was not a matter of age either. There were references to the "indisposition of Mrs. M" while she was in her twenties and thirties.

James Madison, too, had suffered, early in life, from a mysterious illness that included frequent fainting spells, lack of coordination, and "fits." Elizabeth Monroe's symptoms were similar to the former president's. Why was her public contact limited, and then further screened? Why did Eliza Hay assume some of the hostess responsibilities? Throughout her life, Elizabeth, one careful chronicler recorded, "suffered from convulsions which left her unconscious," and the illness was "of a chronic character." James Monroe wrote that "her health is impaired by many causes," and he spent several years in vain trying to have it cured. Elizabeth's only confidantes were her three sisters and two daughters, forming a protective closed circle. She made trips to the same mineral spring as Madison had; this was also the spring to which Martha Washington had brought her epileptic daughter. There were few instances of Elizabeth's appearing outside of the White House. When she did meet the public at home, she barely spoke.

In one letter, the president wrote frankly of Elizabeth's sudden blackout "convulsions," which rendered her temporarily unconscious. On one occasion, she fell into an open fireplace in a room where she had been left alone, and was badly burned. Epilepsy was in fact called "the falling sickness."[2]

Of course, no explanations were given. Meanwhile, the openly condescending Eliza dealt with the public. She told a charity-ball committee that she would accept their invitation only on the condition that they didn't acknowledge her presence in print. When someone kindly inquired of her husband, she impatiently told them, "He is dead. And I'll hear nothing more of it said." When she managed the plans for her younger sister's White House wedding, she announced it would be exclusively "in the New York style," that no diplomats and congressmen were to be invited, and even their gifts not be acknowledged.

But criticism fell upon Elizabeth, who was accused of consciously attempting to turn her role into that of a queen. Secretary of State John Quincy Adams's wife, Louisa, wrote old John Adams that Elizabeth was always dressed "in the highest style of fashion and moved not like a Queen—for that is an unpardonable word in this country, but like a goddess." Congressman Harrison Otis recorded that he "dined at the palace, and at the right hand of the Queen who was most exceedingly . . . conversible." Another observed that the president's wife was "serene and aristocratic . . . too well-bred to be moved by anything—at least in public."

Neither Dolley's "Presidentress" title nor Martha's "Lady" title were ever applied to this woman. She was simply Mrs. Monroe. But though the words were unspoken, it was understood that America now had its own first Queen Elizabeth.

Louisa Adams admitted that "tastes differ and dear Dolley was much more popular." Though Queen Elizabeth followed Dolley's example by inviting Mrs. Van Ness and the Orphans' Asylum ladies committee to meet with her in the White House, nothing ever came of it. Mrs. Monroe never served dinner in the "harvest home style" of Dolley, but rather "in the English style," with one butler per guest. She could not have been pleased to learn that some confused foreigners thought that Dolley Madison was still the official White House hostess, or that many sought an invitation to the Madison estate over the White House.[3]

For her part, Dolley remained silent about Elizabeth. She was now thoroughly involved in helping Jemmy prepare his papers on the Constitutional Convention. Harriet Martineau observed the Madisons at work and discussing politics, noting of Dolley, "She is a strong minded woman, fully capable of entering into her husband's occupations and cares; and there is little doubt that he owed much to her intellectual companionship, as well as to her ability in sustaining the outward dignity of his office."

Abigail Adams was also being remembered, but in a manner that shocked her. She learned that some of her Revolutionary Era letters were going to be published by a Judge Vanderker. "A pretty figure I should make. No. No. I have not any ambition to appear in print. Heedless and inaccurate as I am, I have too much vanity to risk my reputation before the public." She firmly put a stop to Vanderker's enterprise.[4]

Meanwhile, in Washington, a social attitude became a political issue. Complaints about the calling rules of "Queen Elizabeth" reached President Monroe, specifically from indignant European diplomats, and on December 29, 1817, the president held a special Cabinet meeting to consider questions of diplomatic receiving. Taking her cue, Elizabeth held her own Cabinet meeting, by summoning Mrs. Secretary of State Louisa Adams to the White House on January 22, 1818. Commanded by a quick note to call at once, Louisa heard out Mrs. Monroe's complaints about the complaints. Elizabeth stood firm about her social policy: She would neither pay nor return calls from anyone, regardless of rank. Callers could present themselves at the White House on Tuesdays at 10:00 A.M. to be greeted by Mrs. Hay, who *might* return calls. She advised Louisa to set her own individual policy.

Even the secretary of state was commanded to appear before the "queen," recording that on December 12, 1818, he was summoned before Mrs. Monroe "sitting in counsel," as she "seized the opportunity" to snappily complain that the Senate wives were not only making no "first visits" to her, but none whatsoever. When the Monroes left town for the annual public open house on July 4, 1819, it was the last straw. Elizabeth was boycotted.[5]

"The drawing room of the President," it was recorded of the first event of the 1819 autumn season, "was opened last night to a beggarly row of empty chairs; only five women attended, three of whom were foreigners . . . Mrs. Adams, the previous week, invited a large party . . . at which there were not more than three ladies." The rudeness now directed at his wife prompted the president to hold another Cabinet meeting on December 20, 1819. It was agreed that the president, vice president, and Cabinet were "free to pursue the course of conduct dictated by their sense of propriety respectively."[6]

Louisa Adams, a woman who never intended to insult anybody, was in a quandary. She didn't want to offend Elizabeth, whose slippers she hoped to fill, but neither did she want to be placed in disfavor by senators' and congressmen's wives, whose husbands' support was necessary for her political ambitions. She wrote to her mother-in-law, sagacious Abigail of Quincy, who advised her to follow the lead of the Cabinet. As for Elizabeth, Abigail predicted that she wouldn't get away with a lean social calendar, and was surprised that her "queen fever" showed little sign of abating. "In my day," she wrote, "if so much stile [sic], pomp and Etiquette had been assumed the cry of Monarchy, Monarchy would have been resounded from Georgia to Maine."

Abigail seemed forlorn. The woman who had made news now had to resign herself to reading news in the papers. She was bored without power, writing, "It is better to have too much than too little. Life stagnates without action. I could never bear merely to vegetate," but admitted that an old female's mind could be like "a sieve." She followed politics through letters from John Quincy, but broke down to admit that "Much . . . might we moralize upon these great events, but we know but in part and we see but in part. The longer I live, the more wrapt in clouds and darkness does the future appear to me."

She liked Monroe's international policy of intervention, but was particularly pleased with her son's rising star. In the end, Abigail had managed to overcome old bitterness. "I am determined to be very well pleased with the world, and wish well to all its inhabitants. Altho in my journey through it, I meet with some who are too selfish, others too ambitious, some uncharitable, others malicious and envious, yet these vices are counterbalanced . . . I always thought the laughing phylosopher [sic] a much wiser man, than the sniveling one." Abigail Adams died peacefully, in 1818.[7]

Abigail had been correct in her predictions. Eventually, the indignant diplomats returned to Elizabeth's court. And the queen had changed, too, attending the public ball at Brown's Hotel on James's second Inaugural. At a public dinner, she was pronounced magnetically beautiful, amiable, and witty by Auguste Levasseur, assistant to the marquis de Lafayette, who was making his grand American tour in 1824.

Mrs. Monroe made her own rules when it came to personal friends. The leathery-skinned religious fanatic "Mrs. General Jackson," uncouth by Washington society's standards, was a world apart from regal Elizabeth, and yet, on her second trip to Washington in 1824, Rachel was warmly welcomed by Mrs. Monroe. Elizabeth frequently asked James to include her best wishes to Mrs. Jackson when he wrote the general, and Rachel did the same when the general wrote to the president. To her credit, Mrs. Monroe considered character more important than social status.[8]

Elizabeth's political power remained a mystery. Certainly through her social dicta she helped strain diplomatic relations, however temporarily. John Quincy Adams said Mrs. Monroe was a "partner" and "companion" of "accomplishments" for Monroe. The president himself admitted that she was "the partner of all the toils and cares . . . exposed in public trusts abroad and at home . . . devoted to the honor and interest of . . . country . . . her burdens and cares must have been great . . . It was improbable for any female to have fulfilled all the duties . . . in such cares . . . with more attention . . . than she has done." As the wife of the creator of the Monroe Doctrine, which warned Europe against further colonization in the Americas, Elizabeth had always been right on the scene. That she understood the importance of silence as a foreign officer's wife, and exactly who was, and was not, a political ally, is unquestioned. There were claims that during her husband's negotiations with Spain for the purchase of Florida, Elizabeth "played her part on the diplomatic side," and that she "followed with close attention the charting" of the Monroe Doctrine. One private 1815 letter, however, written to her by son-in-law George Hay, suggests that she may indeed have played some political role.

Hay wrote Elizabeth with political urgency, enclosing a letter from the governor of New York's wife, pleading, "[we] beg you to give us your opinion on the proper course to be pursued after consulting Mr. Monroe. In your deliberations on the subject, you will take into view one fact which is that John R[andolph, a Virginia congressman] and myself have no communication together and that there is a point of difference between us." Hay, a prominent attorney who successfully tried Aaron Burr, added a frantic postscript: "We wish for an immediate answer if of six lines only." What her "opinion" was, and what was the issue, however, remained a mystery.

Elizabeth did act with a decisive independence from James. After the president had turned down an invitation from the French minister, Elizabeth was then invited to attend as his proxy. John Quincy Adams noted that "the question with regard to Mrs. Monroe" was first raised by officials, and since "we could have no deliberation," it "was therefore left to her own decision." Adams continued, "The President went and consulted her, and she said she did not think it proper for her to go any place where it was not proper for her husband to go." Elizabeth, then, was shown the deference of being permitted to make her own decisions, even if the response was predictable.[9]

But Elizabeth's legacy was her insistence on defining her own ladyship, regardless of what predecessors did or what criticism might ensue. After an election, of course, one could do as one wished, but when "electioneering," one became a chameleon to public will—even though one might despise the very idea of public life. Enter Louisa Adams.

In January 1824, Mrs. Adams held her famous ball in honor of General, now Senator, Jackson, parading about the room on his arm. It was the commencement of her long months of "campaigning" for her husband's presidential bid, and a brilliant diplomatic move, too, for Jackson was also running.

Running for the presidency had been an unsystematic procedure since 1800. It was Congress that nominated candidates, with members meeting as a nominating convention. The year 1824 marked the last time this unpopular selection process occurred (national conventions would soon evolve), so it was to congressmen and their wives that Louisa Adams turned for support.

Louisa had been "campaigning" all along, using the Dolley technique as a social politician. She was quite literally her husband's "campaign manager." She curried the right congressional wives, always "Smilin' for the Presidency," calling cards in purse, prepared by her husband with, as she whimsically remarked, "as much formality as if he was drawing up some very important article to negotiate in a Commercial Treaty." In the election year, she hosted dinners for sixty-eight congressmen. Every single Tuesday night between December and May, she held open house with fine wine, lavish food, and musical entertainment.

Louisa's campaigning was not limited to the capital. In Philadelphia, she was visited by prominent congressmen and journalists, whom she joined in dissecting the Monroe Cabinet. She advised her husband to campaign actively there and "show yourself if only for a week . . . Do for once gratify me," she wrote rather resentfully, "I implore you and if harm comes of it I promise never to advise you again." A new, though temporary, power was given Louisa, whose personal political opinions were now actively sought by others. At weekly congressional debates, she wrote, "Even my countenance was watched at the Senate [as I was] hearing Mr. Pinckney's speech . . . If my husband's sentiments are to be tried and judged by such variations the gentlemen will have hard work." Calling it "my campaign," in Maryland she wrote that she was "most solicitous" to family and friends supporting John Quincy "in his interest. Maryland it is said will be his."

While Louisa was successful at debating both Henry Clay and Andrew Jackson, the latter's wife had no such skill. It was only after the election that Rachel had made her second Washington sojourn, staying at the fashionable Gadsby's Tavern, where she met fellow boarder and celebrity Lafayette, paying calls, going to the theater, and testing the waters by attending carefully chosen social affairs like Elizabeth Monroe's drawing room. She had done so well that the last event she attended before returning home was Adams's Inauguration.

But already there was something unsettling about her presence. The day after Rachel appeared at a ball, Andrew angrily wrote of the "wickedness" of "investigation" into the character of "an innocent female in her declining years . . ." There were questions about Rachel's background, and he thought them aimed at his political ambitions. It wasn't that she was "a little inclined to corpulency," or that she suffered from bronchial and heart trouble. Or even that, in the privacy of her luxurious hotel room, the country woman Rachel, in modest clothes and white veil, pulled out her long clay pipe and smoked. No Washingtonians seemed bothered that she, as Jackson wrote, "spends her time on sundays at church, on thursdays at prayer meetings . . ."

Now more than ever, Rachel frantically insisted that Andrew get out of politics, and stay with her at the Hermitage. There was a dark, scandalous secret that she feared revealed.

For intellectual and talented Louisa, the ladyship would signal the most tragic period in her life. John Quincy had a brilliant mind, but he was a cold, demanding, and inconsiderate husband. His use for Louisa ended with his election. He had once sniped, "There is something in the very nature of mental abilities which seems to be unbecoming in a female." Though he loved her in his own private way, he married the wrong woman.

Just as Rachel's husband's ambitions took precedence over hers, so, too, did Louisa's. Mrs. Adams had no desire to be the Lady.

"For myself," she poignantly noted, "I have no ambition . . . the exchange to a more elevated station must put me in a prison."[10]

- 11 -

"*. . . Such Expectations . . .*"

"THE MORE I bear, the more is expected to me, and I sink in the efforts I make to answer such expectations," wrote the new president's wife, known without title simply as Mrs. Adams. Except for receptions, Louisa was ignored. She took to her room, and along with her deep depression she developed breathing problems because the room was heated with burning anthracite coal, which caused choking and coughing. Her depression, she continued, "passes for ill temper and suffering for unwillingness and I am decried an incumberance [sic] unless I am required for any special purpose for a show or some political maneuver and if I wish for a trifle of any kind, any favor is required at my hands, a deaf ear is turned to my request. Arrangements are made and if I object I am informed it is too late and it is all a misunderstanding."

The mansion represented loneliness. "There is something in this great unsocial house," she told her beloved son George, "which depresses my spirits beyond expression and makes it impossible for me to feel at home or to fancy that I have a home any where." The only time she had with her husband, at breakfast and dinner, was spent reading newspapers to themselves. A marital breach developed only four months after they entered the White House, and they summered apart

for several-month stretches, their rare letters to each other signed formally with their full names. He cared only for his work. "Family is and must ever be," she wrote bitterly, "secondary consideration to a zealous Patriot."

When Louisa did entertain, she did so brilliantly, with the European air that was, of course, her very self. A gifted musician, she sometimes played her harp and piano for guests, but with self-imposed isolation, and struggling with menopause, Louisa's severe mental depression kept her hidden for weeks at a time. She called herself "a prisoner in my own house" and said the "dreadful tedium of an almost entire solitude" was unbearable. "The habit of living almost entirely alone," she wrote, "has a tendency to render us savages . . . isolation is an evil . . . and one likely to be productive of insanity in a weak woman." She ate chocolates obsessively and found an outlet in satirical play-writing, parodying her husband as an uptight egotist who repressed his wife. She wrote poems about the folly of society and the illnesses of females. She began her autobiography, which she called *Adventures of a Nobody.*

Slowly, within her writing, a latent feminism was aroused in her bitterness over a world in which man controlled female, no matter how capable the female might be. "That sense of inferiority which by nature and by law we are compelled to feel and to which we must submit," she angrily wrote her husband just a few years earlier, "is worn by us with as much satisfaction as the badge of slavery generally, and we love to be flattered out of our sense of degradation." Anger rose in her when she read of an Irish immigrant girl who had been sexually abused by her master, and the president's wife wrote two fictional poems about the poor girl, who commits suicide when her hopes that the master will marry her are dashed.

This same defensive spirit burst out when the press took shots. Once, she had laughingly told John Quincy to "[p]ut a little wool in your ears and don't read the papers," but when Duff Green of the pro-Jackson *United Telegram* detailed the fact that the Adamses had bought a billiard table with public funds, and pro-Adams papers worsened the situation by declaring it was for Louisa's use and was "a common appendage in the houses of the rich and great in Europe," she struck out against the fable that she lived in "regal magnificence." Then, Jacksonian Russell Jarvis, in the *Daily Telegraph,* declared that Adams had "pimped" the family nursemaid for Czar Alexander of Russia. Louisa took aim and wrote a detailed account of her life, defending herself, her father, and her marriage in the June 2, 1827, issue of *Mrs. A. S. Colvin's Weekly Messenger.* The dirtiest campaign yet was about to begin, and drag the candidates' wives into public debate.

What Louisa perhaps feared more than the slanders were the *truths.* Her niece Mary, an unabashed tease, had dated two of the Adams sons and ended up marrying a third, alcoholic John. Louisa once warned him, "I am sorry to say there are many of my sex who address themselves alone to those passions which are the most easily excited . . ." Son Charles was sexually active with a mistress of the lower classes, and like his father, who had sought out prostitutes in his youth, he had trouble controlling his physical desires. Another son, George, used opium to fall asleep. When Louisa stumbled across one of their books of pornography, she felt that "debased by loathsome and disgusting pictures of nature or of vices, our actions and our thoughts will become gross and indelicate, destroy all relish for moderate and virtuous enjoyment, and render us unfit for any society but the lowest and most degraded." None of the family sordidness became public knowledge.

Once again, however, Louisa campaigned. On her annual vacation away from the president, she passed through Baltimore, Philadelphia, and New York, gathering political support, serenaded at her hotel room, and rushed by Philadelphia politicians with requests for personal meetings. She was told confidentially that Adams would "have Pennsylvania" if only he campaigned. Again, Louisa pressed her case to John Quincy to get out of the White House and campaign, even mapping out her own campaign route for him from Washington to Boston. His refusal to do so, she wrote him, "embarrasses me very much." This time, however, he paid dearly for ignoring Louisa. He lost to Jackson.

In the end, the loss spared Louisa further humiliation. In her liberation, she fought for others', later becoming openly involved in the fight for freedom not only of slaves, but also females. Her reaction to Jackson's election was both politically astute and contemptuous. "Popular governments, are peculiarly liable to factions, to cabals, to intrigue. The people may often be deceived for a time by some fair-speaking demagogue, but they will never be deceived long."

But if 1828 brought joy to Louisa, it brought terror to Rachel Jackson, who had suffered mercilessly at the hands of Adams supporters.[1] Rachel cared nothing about repressions, politics, or society. The '24 campaign had given her more than a life's worth of trauma. But '28 would devastate her. The words that had been whispered were now verbalized in speeches and printed in handbills—"bigamist," "adultery."

The documentation of events preceding her first husband's filing for divorce on the grounds that she had committed adultery with Jackson disappeared mysteriously after the election, so the truth remained obscured. Rachel had believed herself to be divorced, but technically she was a bigamist. She and Jackson were sexually involved after their first marriage, but before their second and valid one. The first "marriage" consisted of unofficial vows in a love ceremony performed in territory under Spanish rule, where Protestants couldn't legally wed.

Rachel's adultery could not be disproven by any written records, only the oral arguments of friendly "eyewitnesses." Rather than address the bigamy, Jackson forces made their case by arguing that such charges were unchivalrous against so religious a woman as "Aunt Rachel." When the first anti-Rachel pamphlet, *Truth's Advocate*, appeared, from Cincinnati, Jacksonians had already prepared *The Friends of Reform and Corruption's Adversary* and the Nashville Jackson Committee pamphlet for distribution. When an editorial rehashing the Robards divorce appeared in the *St. Louis Post Dispatch* and *National Banner* and *Nashville Whig*, the well-organized Jacksonian network of orators had already been making national speeches, the most famous being delivered by Thomas Kennedy: "[T]he wife of his [Jackson's] bosom has been wantonly attacked . . . to think that the affectionate partner . . . should be represented as faithless and worthless . . . is not such conduct abominable?"

Unlike the apolitical woman whom enemies portrayed, Rachel had been raised amid politics. As a child, she had met Washington and Jefferson in their homes, while traveling with her father, a Virginia aristocrat and member of the House of Burgesses, and she relished his stories of Revolutionary politics. She was exposed to all races and classes. She was taught to read and write, and took an interest in current events.

When she was twelve, her family relocated to the dangerous region that would become Tennessee. During her early adulthood and marriage to the insanely jealous Lewis Robards, her world became limited. Travel back East was arduous, and few females, once settled on the plantation, surrounded by slaves, family, and homespun comfort, had any desire to leave.

Over time, Rachel became complacent. Personally, she didn't even consider herself equipped for the role of presidential wife. She wasn't high society. She was in poor health. A committed Fundamentalist, she often infused religion into politics, an unpopular perspective in world-lier Washington. Jackson's victory celebration in New Orleans fore-shadowed how Washington might react to Rachel. A cartoon appeared of her standing on a table being lassoed like livestock into a corset, and she was called a bobbing "fat dumpling" when she danced. She had appeared so rustic that Mrs. Edward Livingston was called in as her sartorial and social aide.

Rachel's religious-political influence had manifested itself during Andrew's short stint as governor of Florida, persuading him to declare edicts banishing the demon spirits on Sundays. He resigned the gover-norship, "as Mrs. Jackson is anxious to return home . . ." Nevertheless, as Senator Thomas Hart Benton recalled, Rachel Jackson possessed the ultimate gift of political wives, "a faculty—a rare one of retaining names and titles in a throng of visitors, addressing each one appropri-ately . . ."

Rachel also exerted a strongly negative influence over Andrew's pursuit of fame, with letters meant to induce guilt. "Do not," she ad-monished him, "let the love of country, fame and honor make you forget you have one [a devoted wife] . . . You will say this is not the language of a patriot, but it is the language of a faithful wife . . ." And ". . . never make me so unhappy for any country. You have served your country long enough. You have gained many laurels . . . Oh Lord of Heaven, how can I bear it!" Sometimes Jackson resented her pos-sessiveness and gently scorned her. "The Patriotism of the family," he wrote of fellow soldiers' wives, "does them great honor."

At first, Rachel planned on staying home. "I had rather be a door-keeper in the house of God than live in that palace in Washington," she wrote. "For Mr. Jackson's sake, I'm glad; for my own part, I never wished it" . . . In a short time, her attitude shifted. She added, "I wish never to go there and disgrace him." Rachel knew what was being said about her. Though isolated in Nashville, she voraciously read every newspaper, book, or magazine that dealt with current politics, and transmitted political information to her husband in letters, even news taken from opposition press. During the campaign, she wrote with un-characteristic defensiveness, "My mind by trials hav [sic] been severe. The enemys [sic] of the Genls [sic] have dipt [sic] their arrows in worm-wood and gall and sped them at me . . . prayers I ofered [sic] up for

their repentance [sic]—but wo [sic] unto them of offences [sic] . . .
theay [sic] had Disquieted one that they had no rite [sic] to . . . Now I
leave them to themselves. I feare [sic] them not." Now, she wanted her
husband to win; she had no fears of defending herself—or speaking her
mind, even to her imposing general. During the election, according to
one Judge Bryant, a friend of Rachel's, when Andrew was reading an
opposition paper's pronouncement of his mother as a prostitute who
followed the army during the American Revolution, General Jackson
came in cursing. Rachel looked him in the eye, pulled herself up and
disciplined him with a simple "Mr. Jackson!" As a chronicler recalled,
"He was subdued in an instant, and did not utter another oath."

Her vindication would represent the triumph of Jacksonian democracy for the new powers of the westerner. Men like Frederick Dent,
staunch Jacksonian, migrant from Maryland to Missouri, who became
so wealthy that he retired in mid-life, with thirty slaves to support his
thousand-acre farm, "White Haven." His daughter Julia, born there in
1826, matured amid southern comforts, having the privilege of a pri-
vate-school education that entailed even "history, mythology and the
things," she said, "I happened to like." Julia was an unusually powerful
girl, physically and psychologically. ". . . believe you can and you
can," she told her timid sister.

But even in the West, political and social schisms were becoming sharp. In contrast to Dent, there was Robert Todd of Lexington, Kentucky, who used his wealth to support candidates like intimate Henry Clay, and to call for eventual abolition. Todd was as rabid a Whig as Dent was a Democrat. His daughter Mary grew up in far worldlier surroundings than Julia Dent, eight years her junior. Mary Todd, who abhorred the slavery that afforded her an exceptional education in French and world affairs at Dr. Ward's prestigious coeducational boarding school, would consider herself polished compared to parvenus like the Dents. In Washington, however, she'd have been called western.

Western females infiltrating Washington were being organized into a defense circle for their president's wife by Jackson supporter John Eaton, who wrote to Rachel that even more "[l]adies from distant— from remote parts of the Union will be here—brought essentially and altogether on your account and to manifest to you their feelings and high regard: they will be present to welcome and congratulate you . . . By all means then come on; and as you have had to bear with him the reproaches of foes, participate with him in the greetings of his friends." Rachel chose a white Inaugural gown, but fate forestalled her vindication.

She suffered a heart attack, died, and was buried in the gown on Christmas Eve, weeks before the Inaugural.

Jackson was devastated. "I try to summon up my usual fortitude, but it is vain. The time, the sudden and afflicted shock, was as severe as unexpected." But he was also enraged at those he believed secretly led the smear campaign on Rachel, "whom they tried to put to shame for my sake." Rachel's niece, Emily Donelson, came to the White House with her uncle to fill the role of hostess. Within a short time, however, Emily was sent back home to Tennessee because of another woman, Peggy Eaton.[2]

Peggy Eaton had a past with men in the navy. The daughter of a Washington tavernkeeper, she had known the Jacksons, and they liked her country manners and musical ability. Most others scorned her. Her marriage to John Eaton, Jackson's secretary of war, made her a Cabinet lady to whom at least civility was due. The Cabinet wives, and nearly all Washington society, refused to give Peggy her due, regardless of her closeness to the president. Jackson furiously railed against his Cabinet to convince their wives to welcome Peggy. To him, the scorn Mrs. Eaton received had been intended for his wife. Peggy's honor was Rachel's honor. When even Emily refused to treat Peggy kindly, she was replaced with his adopted son's wife, Sarah. When the Cabinet refused to bend, however, Jackson saw implications of disloyalty. Rachel Jackson's influence extended posthumously as the Jackson Cabinet were all—save the postmaster general—asked to resign. Others in government who were even suspected of in any way speaking unchivalrously of the late Mrs. Jackson were on risky ground. As one reporter later recorded, "Probably into no other administration of the government . . . has personal feeling had so much to do with official appointments as in the offices emptied and filled by Andrew Jackson. It had only to enter his suspicion that a man had failed to espouse the cause of the beloved Rachel, and his unlucky official head immediately came off. It was told that Mr. Watterson, the Librarian of Congress, had told, or listened to something to the detriment of Mrs. Jackson, and Mr. Watterson was immediately disposed."

The uproar over Rachel's suitability as Lady and the Eaton affair clearly indicated that Americans, or more precisely, Washingtonians, had expectations of a queen.

What they would get was a Queen Mother.

Dolley was coming back.

- 12 -

The Fever

SHE SAID SHE felt as if "awakened after a dream of twenty years." Dolley Madison had left in an era of horse and carriage. Now, there was a canal pulling travelers down to Maryland, and a railroad steaming them up to New York. After Jemmy's death in 1836, Dolley had pined longingly to return.

Hours after word was out that Dolley had moved into the Madison home on Lafayette Square, across from the White House, streams of callers—prominent and common—came to pay homage. "Ah! Madam," one told her, "your successors have been sickly, tame, spiritless and indifferent . . ." Dressed in her now-unstylish Empire gowns, with dyed false curls hanging from her faded turbans, Dolley was a living memory of the past, a link to the days of the early republic. She regaled the young with stories of Washington and Jefferson, and became a regular at the White House. No incumbent Lady ever expressed jealousy over her presence at their receptions. Rather, Mrs. Madison enhanced them.

Dolley being Dolley, however, her social comeback had a political purpose. She would now lobby Congress to purchase for the government her husband's papers on the writing of the Constitution. She needed money desperately, her son having run her into near-poverty with his reckless drinking, gambling, womanizing, and strange money-raising schemes. While Congress debated whether to buy part or all of the papers, and for how much, friends of the Queen Mother were slipping her money, and food into her cupboard. In time, the secretary of state's wife would "extract a few pens" from the department for Dolley, and Congress would vote her the franking privilege. Pens and postage, however, did little to alleviate her problem. So, on a seemingly social call, Dolley dolled herself up and went to see the president.[1]

Martin Van Buren's wife, Hannah, described as "a woman of sweet nature but few intellectual gifts," with "no love of show . . . no ambitious desires, no pride of ostentation," had died nineteen years before her husband became president. The widower, father to four single sons, often escorted Dolley to social events, but planned to remain single. Nevertheless, Mrs. Madison had a goal. When her young South Carolina cousins Angelica and Marian Singleton were in the capital for the '37 social season, Dolley arranged a private dinner for them at the White House. Marian found the Van Buren boys to be "pleasant, unpretentious, unpretending, civil amiable young men." With chiseled features, large dark eyes, swanlike neck, and antebellum corkscrew curls, twenty-one-year-old Angelica, a student of Philadelphia's prestigious Madame Greland's Seminary, soon had young Abraham Van Buren completely under her spell. They married within months. The White House got its hostess, but Dolley could sell only part of the Madison papers, and received $30,000, a comparative trifle of the worth.

Angelica's wealthy father, Richard, had raised her amid all the trappings of aristocracy on a storybook plantation, Home Place, with impressive steeds, a racetrack, lush, manicured lawns, and a mammoth manor house. Established as Lady of the White House, she consulted Cousin Dolley with a breathless plea for guidance—"I am very anxious to see you for a few minutes to consult you on a very important matter." She wrote Marian of how "this bustling place" filled her time with "high bred, civil belles and proper and agreeable beaux—native, foreign and migrant." She freely used the president's franking privilege. Angelica's premiere was the '39 New Year's Day reception, at which the *Boston Post* reported she was "a lady of rare accomplishments . . . free and vivacious in her conversation . . . universally admired." Symptoms of queen fever became full-blown when Angelica took her postponed honeymoon that spring. It was no simple trip north. It was a grand tour of the Continent.[2]

No incumbent presidential Lady had ever gone to Europe, and it presented a prickly situation for its kings and queens. Should she be received as American royalty? Another of Angelica's kin happened to be Andrew Stevenson, minister to the Court of St. James. He arranged for formal presentation of the Van Burens to the new queen, Victoria. Angelica was received in an exquisite white satin gown she ordered designed, and Victoria liked her immensely. Also in England at the

time was Angelica's pretentious brother-in-law, dubbed "Prince John" by the anti–Van Buren Whig press. The Van Buren trio sauntered their way to France, trailed by the press, and were received as royalty at St. Cloud by King Louis Philippe. Privately, Mrs. Stevenson pitied "the unfortunate being whose duty or necessity it may be to give the rousing shake . . . to awaken" Angelica "from such dreams . . ." At both Victoria's and Louis Philippe's court, Angelica witnessed the royal "tableau" form of receiving. The female monarch would set herself and a bevy of virgins apart, posing with bouquets, dressed in long-trained white gowns. Like waxworks, they remained still, high on a platform, as guests were announced at the door. The female monarch and her circle never shook hands.[3]

Rich American girls on the grand tour were becoming a familiar sight on the Continent. Blessed with money, social status, and conversational arts learned at the young ladies' academies, such girls sought, with the chaperoning of an older female, the finer pleasures of the Old World, and perhaps a husband. No American beauty better personified this than Miss Julia Gardiner of New York, who toured for a full year starting in September 1840—but only after she was treated to a visit at Angelica's White House. The hasty retreat to Europe, however, had been prompted by a scandalous publicity stunt of Julia's that disgraced her society parents.

Descendant of English merchant Lion Gardiner, who purchased his own island off the tip of Long Island, Julia was born into wealth and society on the property in 1820. Her father, David, was a Whig state senator; her mother, Juliana, a domineering Scottish heiress. Julia was educated in French, ancient history, and music at Madame N. D. Chagaray's Institute in New York City, and made her debut in 1835. With large, expressive brown eyes, svelte figure, and luxuriant brown hair pulled tightly back from her face, she was ravishing, flirtatious, and clever. In New York, East Hampton, and Saratoga, Julia was known as "the Rose of Long Island."

Julia had a naturally winning personality, peppered with a bewitching wit and sense of ridiculous fun. And yet, one sensed almost a giddy frustration. She was extremely bright and incisive, but as a young society woman, she was cast in a coy demeanor. Her power was consciously exerted through personality.

Bored with baronial life on Gardiner's Island, "the Rose" somehow, in 1839, made secret arrangements with a mediocre clothing store to model for an advertisement. The lithograph handbill had a fashionably dressed Julia carrying a handbag with the loud news, "I'll purchase at Bogert and Mecamby's No. 86 Ninth Avenue. Their Goods are Beautiful and Astonishingly Cheap." At the bottom of this very first example of celebrity personal promotion was her cipher, the rose. The ad stirred a society storm, quickly followed by a "Romeo Ringdove" poem, smack on the front page of the Brooklyn Daily News.

Julia and her equally cunning sister, Margaret, were whisked off to Europe by their humiliated parents. It proved no respite for "the Rose." Crossing the Channel, Julia was romanced by Sir John Buchan. In England, there were a German baron and a War Ministry officer; in Brussels, a Belgian count. In Spain, Julia was thrilled to be staying in the same hotel as Christina, former Spanish queen. In Italy, she was duly impressed with old Pope Gregory and a smoldering volcano crater at Vesuvius. It was, however, the pageantry of Louis Philippe's court that left the greatest impression. Margaret wrote of the queen's "headdress . . . fancifully arranged with diamonds of great brilliancy, and a bird of paradise." Julia would never forget St. Cloud.

Neither had Angelica Van Buren.

At the very moment the Gardiners were sailing the Atlantic, Angelica was assembling her European court, dressed in white, seated on a raised platform, with three ostrich feathers—the insignia of the Prince of Wales—in her headdress. She copied the "tableau," with a circle of similarly dressed "ladies-in-waiting" set back apart from the masses, in the end of the Oval Room, to be viewed with awe. In Europe, Julia read of Angelica's Buckingham on the Potomac in the American newspapers devoured with interest by homesick Yankees.

President Van Buren did nothing to stop Angelica, himself serving

European menus and wines—as had most presidents. Combined with the depression of 1837, it was all the Whig party needed to destroy his reelection bid. Portrayed as a callous king, he was publicly rebuked in the famous "Gold Spoon" speech by Whig congressman Charles Ogle. In the speech, Angelica, veiled as a member of Van Buren's "court," was accused of suggesting congressional appropriations for formal White House gardens, after having toured Versailles and "rich and sumptuous parks and gardens belonging to the Crown of England." Ironically, Mrs. Van Buren's visibility helped firmly establish the role of Lady of the White House in the public's mind. The first engraving showing all the president's wives or hostesses as a group, from Martha Washington to Angelica Van Buren, in individual oval portraits, all linked together by garlanding, was struck and mass-produced in 1842.[4]

Meanwhile, the Whig candidate, General William Henry Harrison, whose victory over Indians at the Battle of Tippecanoe had made him a national hero, was being billed as a simple man. Among Harrison's most ardent supporters was young Mary Todd of Kentucky, whose political capabilities were remarkable for a female. "I suppose like the rest of us *Whigs,*" she wrote a friend after the campaign, "though you seem rather to doubt my faith you have been rejoicing in the recent election of Gen. Harrison, a cause of . . . vital importance to our prosperity— This fall I became quite a *politician,* rather an unladylike profession, yet

at such a crisis, whose heart could remain untouched while the energies of all were called into question?"

Harrison's own wife, Anna Symmes, was interested in politics. Former schoolmate of Martha Washington's granddaughter, Anna was extremely well read, and was particularly noted as an avid consumer of all the political newspapers and journals that she could get hold of while living at her frontier home in Indiana Territory. There, she also was afforded the opportunity of conversing with the many politicians and military leaders who visited her husband. But Mrs. Harrison had doggedly opposed William's candidacy, saying, "I wish that my husband's friends had left him where he is, happy and contented in retirement." Her command was no gentle whisper. Harrison strictly followed her edict of not permitting business to be conducted on Sundays, explaining, "I have too much respect for the religion of my wife to encourage violation." One observer noted, "She rules the General apparently." She decided against coming to Washington for the Inaugural, planning instead to journey in May, when road conditions improved for traveling from the West. Meanwhile, her daughter-in-law Jane served as temporary hostess.

The world was shocked when exactly one month to the day after his Inaugural, President Harrison died. Anna decided against attending his Washington funeral. In Europe, Julia and Margaret Gardiner fashionably wrapped their left wrists in black mourning crepe. Their brothers, Alex and David, maneuvering behind the scenes in New York politics, had both voted for Harrison. Alex wrote his family about Vice President Tyler being summoned to Washington, "drawn from the bosom of his family" in Virginia, and assuming the presidency. Tyler was a mild Whig, and many in the party, including Mrs. Harrison, were distressed with his taking over as their party leader. Anna was quite pleased, however, with the congressional award to her of the franking privilege—and twenty-five thousand dollars—as a presidential widow. At first she had little use for Tyler. In time, she used his sympathy and her power as presidential widow to persuade him to make political appointments for family members. Privately, she would write that "his Administration has been a bad one."[5]

John Tyler's wife, Letitia, entered the White House as a paralytic stroke victim. She had for years entirely run the complex business of their plantation, and made all the financial investments. Her role as businesswoman was rightfully credited as the reason Tyler was able to remain solvent and pursue politics. Although never questioning slavery, Letitia was sensitive to women, and wanted her female workers toiling only in "milder employments," leaving all fieldwork to men. In the White House, though largely confined to her bedroom with reading at her side, she seemed still to play the role of adviser, as well as exert influence over the hostess role, which was literally performed by her spirited daughter-in-law, a former actress, Priscilla Cooper Tyler. Priscilla recalled that from her room, the president's wife directed both the entertaining and household management.

Demure to the point of mysterious, Letitia Tyler was an Anglican lady of the manor, who nevertheless advised her husband behind-the-scenes. One daughter recalled that "I have frequently heard our father say that he rarely failed to consult her judgement in the midst of difficulties and troubles, and that she invariably led him to the best conclusion." The president himself later admitted that "brought before the tribunal of her judgement . . . all her actions are founded on prudence."

Although Mrs. Tyler's stroke evidently took her power of speech in its first stage, she regained it, and overall, as President's Lady, Letitia was apparently not quite as meek as romanticists fancied. Described as having "an acute nervous organization and sensitive temperament," she was remembered as being able to "converse with visitors on current topics, intelligently." At one point, she may even have attended the theater in Washington with several members of her family, as Priscilla wrote specifically of noting Letitia's velvet dress while they sat together watching the show. Letitia Tyler also let it be known that "because I am ill is no reason why the young people should not enjoy themselves."

While the President's Lady "modestly shrank from all notoriety and

evaded the public eye as much as possible," she obviously read more than her Bible, having definite opinions about how frequently and specifically the women of her family should be mentioned in the press. Regarding a vague social notice in the *Madisonian* newspaper journal of March 17, 1842, one daughter said, "Anything more particular would have shocked her delicate sense of propriety . . ."[6]

As hostess, Priscilla Tyler depended greatly upon the wisdom of Mrs. Madison, a frequent guest at Tyler social affairs, both private and public. On many occasions, the president's hostess sent her carriage across the street for Dolley to use. Her alcoholic son having quickly squandered the $30,000 Congress had paid her for part of her husband's papers, the indigent Queen Mother had no carriage of her own, barely able to survive on the small dribbles of money that she borrowed while waiting for Congress to buy the remaining papers. Dolley had left Washington temporarily for Montpelier in hopes of overseeing profits from the small farm there. She knew nothing about loans or interest or mortgage, floating by as best she could in the complicated world of finance. She returned permanently to Washington in October 1841. The next year, she made her first trip to New York, marveling at the wonder of railroad trains, but not for pleasure alone. She paid an embarrassing visit to an old friend, financier John Jacob Astor, asking for a loan. She was forced to sell part of Montpelier. Still Congress did nothing.

While Dolley went up to New York, the recently returned Gardiner girls went down to Washington. On the train, a "handsome portly" gentleman threw "several furtive glances" their way, but unfortunately Congressman Millard Fillmore was already married. They also met John Tyler, Jr., who invited them to visit in the White House, and so, on the magic night of January 20, 1842, a thrilled Julia met the president, who, as she later recalled, paid her a "thousand compliments" while other guests "looked and listened in perfect amazement." Avidly drawn to intrigue, Julia was excited this night because "[t]he President's break with the Whigs had been the occasion of unprecedented political excitement." February, however, found a bored Julia back on Long Island, consulting her copy of the new book *Wealth and Pedigree of the Wealthy Citizens of New York City*, which only listed families whose incomes exceeded $100,000. Money, and the fear of lack of it, were as important to Julia Gardiner as love.

That same year, her brother Alex registered as a Democrat and planned to enter politics through New York's Tammany Hall. The Gardiners agreed with Tammany's fear that abolition would clog the white job market with freedmen, and Julia therefore had no ethical conflict with slavery. Tyler, a president without party support, would use any connections he could get to Democratic Tammany. For Alex, his family's friendship with the Tylers, though minor, might prove useful. The Tylers and Gardiners could work together, politically and socially.

Amid this, the Tylers privately agonized over Letitia Tyler's deteriorating health. After only one public appearance, she died in the White House in September 1842. "Nothing," Priscilla wrote, "can exceed the loneliness of this large and gloomy mansion, hung with black, its walls echoing with sighs."

She was the first incumbent President's Lady to die, so Letitia Tyler's funeral was of considerable public acknowledgment. The mansion was hung with official mourning, newspapers carried notices of her death and burial plans, her coffin lay in state in the East Room, an official "committee of the citizens of Washington" accompanied her casket from the capital to its resting spot in Tidewater country, Virginia, the city's bells were tolled, and "a crowd of her beneficiaries" gathered at the low gate, "sobbing, wringing their hands, and every now and then crying out, 'Oh the poor have lost a friend.'"

By December, Julia had returned to Washington, intrigued with "a young bachelor of 50," Congressman James Buchanan, as well as Congressman Francis Pickens, Supreme Court Justices John McLean, Smith Thompson, and Henry Baldwin, and naval officer Richard Waldron. Daily, she visited the House to hear debates, commencing her political education. It was hard for her to concentrate, however, when Congressmen like Richard Davis came from the floor to woo her. One day when his vote was called and there was no response, congressional eyes focused on the large plumage in the visitors' gallery. "Mr. Speaker," joked Roosevelt of New York, "Mr. Davis has gone to the gallery to study horticulture."

These men paled when compared with the president, and Julia relished the widower's growing attentions toward her. On February 7, he asked her to play cards alone with him. By evening's end, the president, thirty years her senior, was chasing Julia down the stairs and around tables. Days later, he planted three kisses on Julia's cheek, as noted by Margaret, who only received two. At the Washington's Birthday Ball, President Tyler cornered the betassled damsel and asked her to marry him. "I said, 'No, no, no' and shook my head with each word which flung the tassel of my Greek cap into his face with every move."

Gossip sparked, some "salacious," said one chronicler.

It was said that Tyler would think of "resigning the Presidential chair *or at least sharing it with J.*" In New York a story circulated that Julia would marry Tyler only if he was elected in 1844, and on good faith she would campaign for him in the fashionable northern watering holes. Alex immediately wrote pro-Tyler newspaper articles at Julia's insistence. This had obvious advantages for the president, but Mother Gardiner had reservations about Tyler's lack of great wealth.

Meanwhile, Mrs. Madison was still gently battling Congress. Perhaps out of guilt, but certainly because of veneration, she was awarded an honor considered to be the greatest bestowed on any American woman. The *Washington Daily Globe* of January 8, 1844, reported that Congress had unanimously decided that "whenever it shall be her pleasure to visit the House, she be requested to take a seat within the Hall." Dolley was thankful, but she would have preferred "compliments even higher." Her patience was being tried as she continued to sink into debt. She wanted money.[7]

Nevertheless, the Queen Mother attended every event to which she was invited as an honored guest, keeping anxiety to herself, smiling and making merry remarks. At seventy-seven, she was in excellent health, and sallied forth from gala to gala. She joined President Tyler, the Gardiners, and four hundred others, on February 28 for a fifteen-mile cruise down the Potomac on the naval ship *Princeton*. The momentous event of the day was to be the firing of the famous massive cannon "Peacemaker," the world's largest and an object of the navy pride. Peacemaker was fired twice during the morning and afternoon, delighting those gathered about it.

At about three in the afternoon, a sumptuous lunch, below deck in a reception area, was announced. Julia stayed on deck until told, "The President wishes to take you into the collation which is just served. I suppose you will have to obey orders." She headed to the reception, asking her father to join her. She was met with a glass of champagne. Toasts followed. The Queen Mother chatted with Margaret. The president toasted the navy. Mirth and laughter rang out. Meanwhile, the

ship had just passed Mount Vernon, and Peacemaker was to be fired one more time. Senator Gardiner came down briefly to bid Dolley a hello, then returned upstairs while the president attempted to break away and witness the firing. When his son-in-law William Waller broke into a sea chantey, however, he tarried.

Within seconds, there was an deafening blast. A sailor let out a bloodcurdling scream for a surgeon. Billowing black smoke drifted below deck. Pandemonium broke out.

Peacemaker had backfired and exploded, spewing chunks of hot metal into nearby spectators, and instantly killing the secretarys of state and the navy, and Senator Gardiner.

Julia fainted, and was carried across the gangway to another vessel by Tyler. She awoke, became hysterical, and nearly threw herself and the president into the icy river. Queen Mother Dolley calmly remained on the ship, helping to dress wounds. By the time she returned home, her little house was filled with anxious friends. "She came in quietly, with her usual grace," remembered a niece, "spoke scarcely a word—smiled benignly."[8]

While Julia, in mourning, grew closer in the comfort of the president, 1844 proved to hold even more struggles for Mrs. Madison. In May, Congress stalled again, giving her the honor of sending the very first message on Morse code after the inventor himself, but her financial situation worsened to the point of desperation. She had to sell the rest of Montpelier. When one of the slaves there wrote to her of their fear that families would be broken up, Dolley had a special stipulation provided in the sale, allowing the families to continue living together on the property. Several individual slaves came to live with her in Washington, where she eventually arranged for their freedom, one by one. When she struck the deal allowing the families to remain together, Mrs. Madison did not refer to them as "slaves" in her contract, but "black people." Her history of kindness toward blacks—now increasingly called "coloreds" with the influx of Haitian immigrants—was repaid at the end of the year when one of her former slaves, now a freedman, Paul Jennings, gave *her* money. Meanwhile, she tried to get the president to appoint her son to a diplomatic vacancy. Tyler gently told her Payne was "not fitted for the office."[9]

If the Peacemaker incident was the shock of the winter, the quick, short vows exchanged in a dark Fifth Avenue cathedral on a steamy June afternoon proved the thunderclap of the year. The tiny female stood by the side of a man who could have been her father. He was a mystery man, having slipped into a local hotel under the darkness of the eve previous. All hotel servants had been detained that night, not allowed to leave. If they recognized him, they couldn't tell anyone.

Wearing her crown of white roses, the veiled woman had just undergone an ancient ceremony. But it was more than a wedding.

Julia Gardiner had just eloped with the president.[10]

It was a coronation.

- 13 -

"The Lovely Lady Presidentress"

EVEN JULIA TYLER admitted that John "seemed to fill the place" of her father.

Reactions ranged from shock to laughter. Tyler's daughters—several of whom were older than their new stepmother—were disapprovingly stunned. Former President, now Congressman, John Quincy Adams parodied the "May-December" match as the laughingstock of the capital. One New York newspaper joked that the president's "arduous duties" were just beginning.

"I have commenced my auspicious reign," the new Mrs. Tyler wrote with mock hauteur," and am in quiet possession of the Presidential Mansion . . . this winter I intend to do something in the way of entertaining that shall be the admiration and talk of all the Washington world."

First she made the mansion presentable, using money from the pri-

vate sector—her mother. For her regal strolls, the lovesick president ordered an elegant Italian greyhound from the consul at Naples. She drove about, pulled in a royal coach and six white matching Arabian steeds. While in town, Margaret assisted as social secretary. Among Mrs. Tyler's orders was that the Marine Band should play "Hail to the Chief" whenever she and the president appeared. Wanting to preserve her image for posterity, Julia became the first incumbent president's wife to pose for a daguerroetype, the earliest form of photography, though she wasn't the only Lady to do so. Dolley Madison posed for several, dressed in old turbans, with white tulle filling necklines where bosom had once bulged.

Even ambitious Julia felt no competition with the Queen Mother. They got along famously. Julia invited Dolley to visit her at the president's home, Sherwood Forest, near Williamsburg and took counsel from her predecessor, applauding that "Mrs. Madison added a new dimension to Washington society." Dolley was among those present at the convivial White House wedding reception Julia held for herself. The sorority endured.[1]

Though she would serve for only eight months, Mrs. Tyler had an impact on the role, unabashedly viewing it as that of a queen, copying the impressive scenes of Louis Philippe's court. And for the first time since Mrs. Madison, a president's wife was given a title: Lovely Lady

Presidentress. It was a more flourishing version of Dolley's, dubbed by the press, apropos for the antebellum romanticism of the Fabulous Forties.

One reporter recorded, "The lovely lady Presidentress is attended on reception-days by twelve maids of honor, six on either side, dressed all alike . . . Her serene loveliness receives upon a raised platform wearing a headdress formed of bugles and resembling a crown . . ." The dozen misses were dubbed "the vestal virgins." Seated in a large armchair, Julia nodded to guests who were formally announced, as they passed before her. Jessie Fremont, a senator's daughter, noted with wry understatement, "Other Presidents' wives have taken their state more easily."[2]

Julia's prowess pervaded from her oval Blue Room court into the East Ballroom. There, for the first time, something scandalous to a few, daring to most, occurred and its impact was felt throughout the nation. Julia Tyler danced publicly.

Having learned the dashing polka in Europe, which was now the rage in New York, Mrs. Tyler decided to introduce it in provincial Washington. She "opened" her receptions with a four-step dash across the East Room with courtly ambassadors and brave Cabinet members. A few years previous, the president had warned his daughters that it was bad form to dance. The indecorum of it to some was based on puritanical forbiddance of the opposite sexes touching each other's bodies in public. But Mrs. Tyler merrily polkaed, even at private balls outside the White House, recording that "almost everything in the Polka depends upon the fascinating expression of countenance . . ."

As word spread, the polka became popular in dance rooms across the country. A New York composer, Lovel Purdy, wrote a series of dance tunes to the presidentress entitled "The Julia Waltzes." When the first fourteen hundred copies of the sheet music sold out because, as Julia wrote, they were "so popular," she instructed Margaret to ask friends, "Have you seen the Julia Waltzes which are just out? dedicated to Mrs. Tyler. They are quite beautiful." Margaret was less than enthusiastic when she learned that Purdy wanted the Lovely Lady Presidentress to get him a foreign consulship.

Dance was literally sweeping the country. In Springfield, Illinois, the temperamental belle of Lexington, Mary Todd, had been living with her sister, Elizabeth, and her husband, Ninian Edwards, attending cotillions and balls. Her beloved father's remarriage had alienated her from him when she was eight years old, and she felt that her childhood was "desolate," and that boarding school had been her only real home. But she still shared a rabid Whigism with her father, and she wanted Henry Clay to be president. Though she dated the ambitious lawyer Stephen Douglas, Mary announced that "I would rather marry a good man—a man of mind—with a hope and bright prospects ahead for position—fame and power than to marry all the houses [of] gold . . . in the world."

While Mary danced, a gangling lawyer, Abraham Lincoln, watched from the sidelines. "Miss Todd," he nervously told her, "I want to dance with you in the worst way." Later, with trampled slippers below her voluminous gown, witty Miss Todd jested, "And he certainly did." This tall man—whom Elizabeth Edwards called the plainest in Illinois—and the belle married in 1842, political ambition being one of their common denominators.[3]

The Lady Presidentress was extremely conscious of her public impression. She, and her entire "court" of twelve energetically attended events in private homes and public places. At the dedication of the new St. Mary at the Navy Yard in October 1844, she arrived an hour and a half late, trailed by dutiful Cabinet members, ambassadors, naval and war officials and their wives. By ceremony's end, she had instigated a row between the navy and war secretaries over whose department was superior.

Mrs. Tyler made even more scandalous history by "hiring" a press agent, heeding her mother's warnings, "You must not mind any objections made of you in the newspapers. You will not escape censure. Do your best." Julia did more than her best by befriending the already smitten F. W. Thomas, dandy bachelor and New York Herald correspondent, who was instructed, as Margaret wrote, "to sound Julia's praises far and near . . ." It was Thomas who concocted the "Lovely Lady Presidentress," title, and the nation read of her reign through Herald dispatches reprinted in other papers. His reporting was sycophantic adulation. On November 21, he said she was "the most accomplished woman of her age" and her court rivaled "that of Charles II or Louis Grand." Another of his showers of adulation had Julia "far more beautiful and younger, and more intelligent [than], and more Republican [than], and quite as popular with the people" as Queen Victoria, deeming Mrs. Tyler "a spirit of youth and poetry, and love, and tenderness, and riches, and celebrity, and modesty . . ."

Unlike her predecessors, Julia sought publicity, and grew testy when it wasn't forthcoming. "Can't it get into the New York papers that Mrs. President Tyler is coming to town accompanied by Mrs. ex-President Madison?" she impatiently wrote Thomas. Neither was she amused when he guessed the reason for her being "rosy and fat" in print. She was indeed not pregnant.[4]

Julia was the most publicly receptive Lady since Dolley. The entire nation seemed to be swept away by her audacity. She accepted all of their gifts, including an Arabian steed from a naval commodore. Pleas poured in: "One good word from your mouth would make us happy and comfortable," begged someone from Julia's hometown. Others, from females like Ohioan Lucy Murphy, New Yorker Esther Gibbons, Virginian Mary Smith, asked her for executive clemency for their menfolk, for pardons, military leaves, patronage, money. She examined each request, and passed on with approval to the president and Cabinet those she wanted considered. When the presidentress received letters from hardened criminals begging for suspension of death sentences, she was tickled. Her most famous success actually made it into the paper. It was Mrs. Tyler who managed to persuade Mr. Tyler to commute the death sentence of "Babe," the notorious New York pirate.[5]

To some, it appeared that the presidentress was mere decoration for the waning administration. That was perhaps the impression she wanted to leave, but though just twenty-four years old, Mrs. Tyler possessed tremendous instinct. With a president willing to meet all her demands, she held a power over him. As a ravishing coquette, she held estimable sway over members of the Cabinet, Congress, and Supreme Court. *Sans* president, she dined at the home of the navy secretary, strategically sitting between the secretary of state and attorney general, finding both "exceedingly agreeable," and having "together a pleasant flirtation." Tyler joked that he "must look for another Secretary of State if Calhoun is to stop writing dispatches and go to repeating verse." Whether consciously or not, she used her sensuality to influence issues, which unfortunately misled one chronicler to later falsely accuse that Julia's lobbying was a "feat she accomplished partly in the bedrooms of men other than her husband." There was no evidence to support that slander, though another's estimate that she had "the decisive influence that stems from the boudoir" of her husband was accurate. The Tylers' love for each other was all-encompassing enrapture, despite their thirty-year age difference. There was, however, one piece of Mother Gardiner's advice that Julia took to heart: "Be a politician and look deep into the affairs of state." The presidentress proved a genius as a social politician, instinctively realizing that she could exert more power in the East Room than in the halls of Congress. Her entertainments all had political motives. Counseled by brother Alex and the president, she curried with élan the favor of specific legislators for administration objectives.

Shortly after Julia's honeymoon, a nervous Margaret, with as much interest as Alex in seeing Tyler run successfully for the presidency in 1848, chided her sister that the clan had "not heard of any gifts of offices from you and I fear the time will slip by unheeded . . . you will not be able to look back with the satisfaction of having made a single person happy or grateful. You do not seem anxious to exhibit your power." Alex's objective was to create a support machine for Tyler among New York Democratic leaders. Through Julia, he was shortly given control of New York's Suffolk County appointments. As her most eminent chronicler wrote, "Throughout Alexander's correspondence and conversations with the President on patronage matters, Julia acted as intermediary. She relayed names, jobs, and patronage decisions back and forth between New York and the White House. Often she made clear her personal preferences."

Alex realized that Senate confirmation of Tyler appointees was crucial, and Julia declared to him, "I will make as many friends as I can among the Senators." Though he told her that "some of the applications made for these places, and they are numberless, exhibit strange hallucinations," both siblings found themselves embroiled in a publicly embarrassing gaffe. The trouble began with Alex's Suffolk County patronage. Cousin John D. Gardiner wrote to Julia, suggesting his son Samuel for appointment to the collectorship of the port of Sag Harbor. Julia approved and took it to Secretary of State John Calhoun for action. Gardiner was appointed, replacing incumbent Henry T. Dering, whom Mrs. Tyler dislike anyway, because "he has never immortalized me in Rhyme." When cousin John N. Dayton, an anti-Tyler Democrat, got wind of the planned appointment, he frantically persuaded the Sag Harbor postmaster into a coerced deception to warn Julia that Cousin Sam was actually *anti-Tyler*, while he, Dayton, was pro.

Now, Julia was frantic. Alex was humiliated and Calhoun angry, having already approved the appointment. To keep the locals quiet, Cousin Dayton was suddenly nominated for, and elected to, the New York State Assembly. Then, quickly, Alex recommended Ezra, Sam's brother, for the collectorship. In his haste, Alex had failed to realize that it was the wrong Gardiner cousin. Sheepishly, he wrote to the president that "if Ezra has already been appointed the matter is not worth a second thought." In the end, Dering was restored. Angered at being duped, Julia moved on to a new issue.[6]

Mrs. Tyler made the annexation of Texas—her husband's driving ambition—her tally, using her powers over the decisive legislators. "At least fifty members of Congress paid their respects to me, and all at one time . . ." she wrote Mother. Julia was warming the cold foes of annexation. Texas became a state when Tyler circumvented constitutional complexities by proposing a "joint-resolution," which required a majority in both houses. Julia's work was to help convince House and Senate members to support annexation. When the Tyler proposal was first printed, she distributed copies in town and by mail to New York, noting it had a "prodigious sensation," and gasping, "Oh! if it will only have the effect of admitting Texas!"

From Julia, Alex received updates of the progress of congressional legislation and advice on how to proceed at Tammany. When the Texas issue was brought up for debate on the House floor, the Lady Presidentress prominently bustled into the visitors' gallery, arousing ripples of delight among weary legislators. At a dinner, she cajoled Supreme Court Justice John McLean toward public support, as "a matter of honor." Calhoun grunted "There is no honor in politics," but McLean had been a beau of Miss Gardiner's just two social seasons past. "We will see," she cooed to Calhoun, as she slipped McLean a scrap upon which she had scribbled "Texas and John Tyler," her suggestion for an after-dinner toast. "For your sake," the curmudgeon sniveled. The glass was raised, the toast was made.

Word of Julia's Texas lobbying diffused, and she became forever
linked with it in public. A popular ditty with the opening "Texas was the
Captain's bride, Till a lovlier one he took . . ." made the rounds. Further acknowledgment came in the way of the first political cartoon linking a presidentress and an issue. It fancied a fork in a road, with Tyler in
the middle. One road led to reelection and the White House, but the
president was shown more interested in following the other, which had
Julia strolling down a primrose path marked "Texas." Newspaper jokes
referring to Tyler's "annexation" meant both Julia and Texas.[7]

In the end, Texas's statehood was considered her work as much as
the president's, and Tyler gave his presidentress the "immortal gold
pen" he used to sign the Texas proclamation. She attached it to her
necklace and displayed it publicly and proudly. At a dinner honoring
the Texas success, President-elect Polk and his wife, Sarah, were present. Julia had dutifully called upon her successor several times after the
latter's arrival in town, though the notion of her being replaced
wounded her soaring ego. She could not have forgotten that "Sahara
Sarah" (as Julia's chronicler so aptly dubbed Mrs. Polk) had been conspicuously absent from one of the most stunning evenings in White
House history, her Grand Finale Ball of February 18, 1845. As F. W.
Thomas told Julia, "Your ball to be is all the talk, and . . . many beautiful things said of the Lady Presidentress."

Somehow, three thousand social beings crammed themselves into
the mansion that shimmering night. As Margaret waxed, "We were as

thick as sheep in a pen." The Lady Presidentress was regally decked in "white satin underdress embroidered with silver with bodice en saile and over that a white [cape] looped up all around with white roses and buds—white satin headdress hat embroidered with silver with three ostrich feathers and full set of diamonds." And she still managed to not only "open" the dancing with the secretary of war, but also gallivant across the ballroom with the ambassadors of Spain, France, Russia, Austria, and Prussia. At ten, the dining room doors were opened and "such a rush, crush and smash to obtain entrance was never seen," Margaret sighed, but "only two glasses were broken."

Though Alex was not present, he published—with Julia's notes— an "eyewitness" account of the ball for the *New York Plebian,* comparing her to the queen of France. "As to his beautiful bride," he editorialized, "whom I a stranger saw from time to time in foreign parts, I can scarcely trust my pen . . . Tonight she looked like Juno . . . which no Court of Europe could equal . . ." Sibling Margaret, the exhausted social secretary, boasted, "All acknowledge that nothing half so grand had been seen at the White House during any Administration, and fear nothing so tasteful would be again."

Not everyone loved Julia. The growing religious-revivalism element chastised her drinking and dancing. The conspicuous absence of Sahara Sarah at the ball, where one thousand candles were burned and ninety-six bottles of champagne were drunk, was not lost on the president. Mrs. Polk offered "indisposition" as her excuse. "Imagine," John sniffed to Julia, "the idea of her being able to follow after you."[8] Others weren't so hasty in dismissing the new Lady. The card-playing, snuff-taking Queen Mother, one of Julia's guests at the Grand Finale Ball, may have welcomed the newcomer. With political change, there was new promise that Congress would finally heed the desperation of impoverished Dolley Madison, still battling to sell her husband's papers. She managed to amuse herself with the current rages of phrenology— the "reading" of one's skull bones—bowling, and autograph collecting. She was a whiz at whist, the card game favored by her equally venerable sorority sister and card partner Louisa Adams. Poverty, however, was not in the least bit amusing. At worst, Mrs. Polk offered hope.

Dancing, music, and alcohol were anathema to Sahara Sarah, a rigid Calvinist. Although she attended Julia's March 2 Cabinet dinner, when the smoke cleared after Mrs. Tyler's ball, Mrs. Polk could say with a clear conscience that she had never been a party to irreligious antics. Sarah was just as fond of expensive gowns as Julia, but with sweeping edicts she would cure the curse of queen fever. To Sarah, her husband's Inaugural was a religious occasion, deemed by the will of God, and she was determined that *her* reign would commence solemnly.

Julia Tyler was droll to the end. As if mourning the arrival of Sarah, she exited the house in "black with light black bonnet and veil"—she was still in fact mourning her father. But it was the Lady Presidentress's departure from the city that rivaled her sensational entrance. As a mammoth fire roared through the sky, destroying the National Theater and other buildings in its wake, Mrs. Tyler's carriage headed out, not to fashionable New York, but south, to her husband's Virginia plantation, worked by slaves. The scourge of Sarah's morality watered the flames. Julia Tyler's spark died down.[9]

But it was still smoldering.

— 14 —

Prim Madonna

IT RAINED ALL day.

The new president murmured his address like a eulogy to a "large assemblage of umbrellas." The somber Inaugural of James Knox Polk on March 4, 1845, ushered in an funereal era. It seemed that the only smiling face among the very important persons attending the swearing in was Queen Mother Dolley Madison, riding in a closed carriage up Pennsylvania Avenue to the Capitol, past sparse crowds, as part of an official Philadelphia delegation. She had witnessed the ceremony of John Adams, back in 1797, a half-century ago. Mrs. Madison could be counted on to radiate her extroverted warmth, even to a damp ceremony.[1]

Sarah Polk was acknowledged as a serious politician, more partisan and outspoken than her husband. At the ball that night, dancing and music stopped when she entered the ballroom. Word had already been spread that the religious zealot disapproved of all "ungodly" pleasures. At forty-one, the Tennessean was a bright matron with corkscrew curls and dark features, often called "a Spanish Madonna." Her expensive taste managed to reflect itself, despite her Puritanism, and she dressed in rich velvets with trains and plumed headdresses. She was wealthy and meant to stay so, replacing White House servants with newly bought slaves and rearranging the basement into their sleeping quarters as a cost-efficiency measure; Sarah was always able to justify moral conflicts of religion and commerce.

But she was reflective of the times. A national religious revivalism was sweeping America. The times were fraught with tensions between North and South, centered on the slavery question. Some Northern women formed abolition societies, while in the South slavery was defended as not only an economic need, but a humanitarian one—the explanation being that "blacks" led happier lives supported by masters than they would have if freed and left to fend for themselves in a segregated society. The Polks owned vast slave-run cotton plantations.

Acridly judgmental, yet showing flashes of enlightenment, Sarah possessed an ambition that had few bounds. Daughter of a wealthy Tennessee merchant, she received an excellent education at perhaps the most superior girls' school in America, Moravian Female Academy in North Carolina. Her husband later remarked that "had he remained the clerk of the legislature she would never have consented to marry him." The marriage remained barren. Whether the Polks, religious views notwithstanding, eschewed procreation by birth control or were physically incapable of procreating was unknown, but the situation afforded Sarah the chance to be a total political partner to James. "Their character," said a friend, "gradually expanded, unfolded, and rose under the mutually stimulating, helpful, and elevating power of thoroughly congenial daily intercourse, in which one was exactly complemented by the other."

Sarah was with James in Washington for most of his term as speaker of the House. "Indeed," she surmised, "the Speaker, if the proper person, and with a correct idea of his position, has even more power and influence over legislation, and in directing the policy of parties, than the President or any other public officer." To her credit, Sarah rarely permitted convention to prohibit her discussion of national politics with her husband's colleagues. She developed a network of Democratic congressmen and Washington civic leaders who would all prove to be helpful in the path to the White House, but Sarah carefully prefaced her opinions with "Mr. Polk believes . . ." Hiding her stridency became necessary. "I never will forgive him" was her initial response to those who disagreed with her. "Mrs. Polk," it was said, "early learned to be silent where anything was at stake."

Sarah assumed the most powerful position a Lady had yet, serving as the president's private assistant. She said, "[H]e set me to work." She read all the national and local newspapers, gazettes, and magazines, marking articles that *she* considered most important for the president, and leaving them on a chair outside his office. Thoroughly political, in one instance, just prior to his nomination, she even managed to sublimate her moral code when it conflicted with currying helpful Democrats.[2]

When James was unable to accept invitations, Sarah frequently went in his stead, unescorted. When, however, her friend Josephine Seaton held an important reception that James couldn't attend, Sarah steadfastly refused to go. There was something telling in Mrs. Seaton's scold that she had invited "Mr. Buchanan, a bachelor senator . . . and Colonel King, another bachelor . . . those two old Democrats to be company for you, and behold, you did not come!"[3]

Superficially, it seemed that the race for the '44 Democratic nomination was the source of tension between the bachelors and Sarah.

James Buchanan of Pennsylvania was promoting the candidacy of William Rufus Devane King of Alabama, against Polk. Below the surface, however, something far more personal provoked Sarah's reluctance to face the two men. Legend claimed that Buchanan had remained single because the fiancée of his youth, Ann Coleman, daughter of a millionaire, had allegedly committed suicide after a "misunderstanding . . . [of] a peculiarly sensitive nature," and he vowed never to marry. Even friends questioned that. Hannah Cochran, of Buchanan's hometown, wrote in December 1819 that the whole town knew Buchanan loved the Coleman money more than Ann. The story most circulated was that "the lady committed suicide in a fit of jealousy, believing he had ceased to love her." He destroyed all of their letters, and his most thorough chronicler said he carried a guilt about women, while another wrote of Buchanan's "inability to return affection adequately," and use of Ann as a "romantic legend . . . to shield himself" from committing to women. "Ever after," Roy Nichols contended, "he had the ill-equipped bachelor's eagerness for feminine attention to hide his peculiar lack."[4]

A far more secret tale of Buchanan's love life persisted, however, with accounts substantiated by letters. Whatever manifestations it might have taken, Buchanan maintained a longtime relationship with King. Buchanan had met King in 1821, when he was elected congressman, while King, five years older, was serving as senator. In Washington, they took lodgings and lived together for sixteen years. King, also a lifelong bachelor, of "fastidious habits and conspicuous intimacy with the bachelor Buchanan," began raising eyebrows. King's campaign biography bragged that the "six feet high" senator's "fine colloquial powers, and the varied and extensive information which he possesses, render him a most interesting companion."[5]

Sometime after 1834, Buchanan evidently became involved with a female member of his longtime family friends the Kitteras in "some kind of romantic affair, which like most of his episodes with women remains more of a mystery than a story." Again, any letters between the two were destroyed. "One can discern," Buchanan's biographer continued, "that the affair in progress had little mark of the divine passion . . . Rather [it] suggests a marriage of convenience in the making." During the courtship, however, King wrote his roommate that "the anxieties of love" were interfering with his Senate life. Buchanan's marriage never took place. By 1836, Buchanan wrote that he and King were being referred to as "the Siamese twins," and that others called King his "wife."[6]

Tyler had appointed King as minister to France, against his personal wishes to stay in Washington. As soon as he arrived, King wrote to Buchanan, "I am selfish enough to hope you will not be able to procure an associate who will cause you to feel no regret at our separation. For myself, I shall feel lonely in the midst of Paris, for there I shall have no

Friend with whom I can commune as with my own thoughts." Two months later, he wrote that upon being presented to the king, he "was mortified and provoked with myself on finding that I possessed so craven a spirit . . . and caused me to regret still more that I ever consented to accept of a situation for which I am so illy qualified. All of this is for yourself alone, from whom I disguise nothing. But it has determined me absolutely to avail myself of the earliest occasion which offers to get back to my country and permit our high spirited and proud people to be represented here by some one who had more of the spirit of a man . . . Why do I not hear from you? Packet after packet arrived but brings me no letter, thus verifying the old adage, out of sight out of mind . . ." King concluded, "[B]elieve me to be as ever devotedly yours."[7]

President Jackson, whose word Sarah cherished, had once declared King to be a "Miss Nancy." But it was another Tennessee Democrat, and Jackson-Polk supporter, Congressman Aaron V. Brown, who snidely relayed political gossip to his frequent correspondent and ally Sarah Polk during the race for the 1844 Democratic nomination. Brown called his January 14 letter one "of innuendo," marked it "confidential," and focused on an argument between King and Buchanan:

Mr. Buchanan looks gloomy and dissatisfied & so does *his better half* until a little private flattery . . . excited hopes that by getting a divorce, she might set up again in the world to some tolerable advantage. Since which *casual* events, which she has taken for neat and permanent overtures, *Aunt Fancy* may now be seen every day, triggered out in her best clothes and smirking about in hopes of seeing better terms than with her former companion . . . a Calhoun man . . . in the presence of Mr. Buchanan and *his wife* and some others, advanced the opinion that neither Mr. Calhoun nor Mr. Van Buren had any chance to be elected. This of course was highly indecorous towards *Mrs.* B[uchanan] . . . it would be better of course not to irritate Colo. K[ing]—but considering his former course of life, his associations and future aspirations we conclude that silence might not conciliate . . ."[8]

Because of her faith, Sarah refused to attend the theater, cotillions, concerts, card parties, and horse races. Accepting Buchanan, regardless of his *reputed* life, however, could and would serve the Polks' purposes. Whatever reservations Sarah may have had about him personally during the campaign, Buchanan's appointment as her husband's secretary of state proved politically expedient. She evidently approved the choice.

Mrs. Polk believed that God had preordained her, as well as all humans, for their roles in life. Of her role, she explained: "The greater the prosperity the deeper the sense of gratitude to the Almighty . . . My heart never yielded to wordly honors or self-vanity;" "I recognize nothing in myself; I am only an atom in the hands of God."

Prior to the Inaugural, Sarah received a letter from a self-proclaimed religious "fanatic," Leonard Jones, who referred to "the favorite doctrine of female supremacy," the Bible, advising her to consider her role "with the Lord for a fair and just interpretation . . ." Hinting at Mrs. Tyler's conduct, he believed that "greater worth and wisdom will be expected . . . you will have to be more than human . . . the Presidency is no idle thing . . . commence it now, in the multitude of counsel . . . [I] hope the characteristic of your administration may be to feed hungry, cloth[e] the naked, visit sick in prison and take the stranger in." With such support, Sarah's crusade pervaded the presidency.

The edicts fell swiftly. No hard liquor would be served at the White House. Band concerts for the public were forbidden, the president demurring that "Sarah directs all domestic affairs, and she thinks that is domestic." She banned all dancing, sharply retorting to a female who questioned her move, "To dance in these rooms would be undignified, and it would be respectful neither to the house nor to the ofice. How indecorous it would seem for dancing to be going on in one apartment, while in another we were conversing with dignitaries of the republic or ministers of the gospel. This unseemly juxtaposition would be likely to occur at any time, were such an amusement permitted." Even an admirer found Mrs. Polk "a little too formal and cold."[9]

Sunday was the Lord's day. When the Austrian plenipotentiary called to present his credentials at the White House on a Sunday, he was turned away. Sarah did not even permit her husband to conduct business on the Sabbath. And Mrs. Polk had the president attend services at her church, the Presbyterian, even though he was a Methodist and steadfastly refused to convert to her Calvinism. Going to church was a stylishly divine experience for the president's wife. She always arrived fashionably late, making a conspicuously sweeping entrance, once "covered from the neck down in a floor-length coat of heavy black silk moire; her angled, wide-brim hat, also black, was crossed diagonally by a large white ostrich plume." On at least one recorded occasion, Sarah spent over six hundred dollars in the purchase of Paris gowns.[10]

From the religious press, there was rapture: "A profanist of religion, Mrs. Polk deeply realized the responsibility of her position. Exposed to the temptations of life in their most alluring forms, it required . . . her to adjure the maxims and customs of an ungodly world . . . thanks to Providence and her own pious heart . . . expectations have not been dissappointed [sic]." The *Nashville Union* sang Sarah's virtues with a veiled attack on Julia Tyler. "The example of Mrs. Polk can hardly fail of exerting a salutary influence. Especially does it rebuke the conduct of those ladies who professing godliness, nevertheless dishonor its profession by their eager participation in the follies and amusements of the world."[11]

At Sherwood, "Mrs. Ex-President Tyler"—as Julia now fancied herself—planned a triumphant return to Washington, realizing that Sahara

Sarah was no threat. When Margaret learned that Mrs. Polk planned not to redecorate, she wrote Julia, "What monstrously small people they must be!" Rumors had begun in Washington that the Tylers were divorcing, and Mrs. Tyler felt like "choking the perpetrator of the scandal." But she neither returned to Washington nor attacked journalists. She bore her first of seven children, and fretted over the havoc maternity wreaked with her figure. Nevertheless, Julia enjoyed motherhood. Even the children were reminded just who she was, as she sang a nursery rhyme that ran a line, "Rock-a-by baby, your cradle is green; Father's a nobleman, Mother's a queen." Though she still made madcap dashes to New York, Mrs. Tyler was evolving a pronounced southern lifestyle, provided by the comforts of slavery.[12]

Not everyone found Sarah exemplary. "Public comment," wrote one later chronicler, "became more pronounced until her attitude was discussed from every angle, and the consensus of general opinion was to the effect that her private religious views were wholly personal and should not be intruded into national affairs nor should established national functions be either curtailed or modified to conform to them."

For all her moralizing, Mrs. Polk tended to a slight hypocrisy. She said it was undignified for a Lady to travel with the president and meet the common man. Yet, in May 1847, she went ahead and traveled quite publicly with him on a trip to the University of North Carolina, grandly feted in Richmond and Petersburg. She demurred about joining Polk in his tour of the Northeast, only to travel to Tennessee at the same time. Equally untrue was her claim that she accepted no gifts— even refusing bouquets from the federal conservatories, moaning, "Oh, I have lost so many pretty things . . ." The diary of a niece who lived in the White House with her revealed that Aunt Sally indeed took the gift of an unusual glass bonnet presented by a manufacturer.[13]

One particular presidential wife told the truth with particular emphasis. Old Mrs. Madison enjoyed regaling listeners with stories of yore, but remained conscious of her own place in history. In 1848, Dolley was quick to take deserved credit for saving the Washington portrait during the War of 1812: "I acted because of my respect for . . . Washington—not that I felt a desire to gain laurels; but, should there be a merit in remaining an hour in danger of life and liberty to save the likeness of anything, the merit in this case belongs to me."

Dolley was invited by Sarah to White House dinners and receptions, always escorted by the president. The sorority duo took carriage rides together, and spent hours talking about the White House. The clout of having Mrs. Madison as an ally wasn't lost on Mrs. Polk, but Dolley used Sarah equally well. The support of the Polks might help her cause with Congress, which *still* refrained from the full purchase of the Madison papers. One day at her house, with a bevy of congressional wives circling her, Mrs. Madison asked Mrs. Polk, whose carriage had pulled up outside, to come in. The wives were angry that Sarah wasn't paying calls. "Now, Mrs. Madison, we leave it to you; don't you think so young a lady as Mrs. Polk ought to return visits . . . Did you not return and make visits when you were in the White House?" Dolley was no fool. She wouldn't place Sarah in an embarrassing situation, and thereby threaten her own presidential favors. "Yes, my children, I did," she rhapsodized, "but one parlor would then contain all who came to my receptions . . . Now there are so many people in the city that it is an impossibility to return the calls that are made on the President's household."[14]

Not only congressional wives, but the president himself sometimes became annoyed with Sarah. Whenever she was judgmental, gentle James smiled softly at her, which she "well understood to mean disapproval of her inconsiderateness." Sometimes, he rebuked her. "Sarah, I wish you would not say that. I understand you, but others might not, and a wrong impression might be made." Their arguments weren't confined to questions of religion. On at least one issue—national banking—Sarah was progressive, and she bickered with him over his opposition to the national bank. When Mrs. Polk had to search a trunk for coins, she snapped at him. "Don't you see how troublesome it is to carry around gold and silver? This is enough to show you how useful banks are." James wearily retorted to her, "[Y]ou've turned your politics . . . but all I want now is that money."[15]

Others noticed her power over the president. James Buchanan, while touring with him, wrote her, "[W]e have gotten along as well as could be expected in your absence." Vice President George Dallas felt misplaced, as if the president's wife, not he, was the second most important political leader of the nation. "She is certainly mistress of herself," he sarcastically noted, "and I suspect of somebody else also." One friend, Judge Catron, encouraged Sarah's "lectures" to the president about his "inordinate" and "irregular" work schedule, and reported, "All sides seem to vye in vaunting you . . ." A New York newspaper editorial remarked on "the legitimate influence of a pious wife . . . his guardian angel." Even opponent Henry Clay told Sarah, "All agree in commending . . . your excellent administration." She replied, "I am glad to hear that my administration is popular."[16] Sarah's consciousness of her role further strengthened its public notions. A relative, Mrs. Knox Walker, served as social secretary. The President's Lady headlined a February 12, 1846, "Ball for the Benefit of the Poor" at Carusi's Hall.

A congressional page noted how frequently Mrs. Polk attended House debates, and Congressman Franklin Pierce said he relished ruminating politics with her more than with other men. She so chatted on about issues throughout dinner that her ignored meal often had to be reheated for her. "Knowing much of political affairs," an account read, "she found pleasure in the society of gentlemen; and someone remarked that 'she was always in the parlor with Mr. Polk.'" She was able to escape the societal limitations because, as Judge Catron told her, "You are not the one, Madam, to have the charge of a little child; you who have always been absorbed in political and social affairs."

There was no question of her handiwork in the executive branch, and she admitted to using her influence on patronage during her tenure, and often "writing and rewriting speeches and letters" for her husband. Of her role, she admitted, "I will neither keep house, nor make butter . . . I always take a deep interest in State and national affairs."[17]

In her role as the president's assistant, she often gathered information for him and espoused his views. Just days after he signed the act establishing the Territory of Oregon, negotiated from the British, she wrote him, "I do hope when you receive this note you will not say to yourself that your wife is as annoying as the office-seekers . . . I saw Mr. Buchanan last evening; he was full of foreign news, but I learned nothing very specific." One observer, Henry Gilpin, felt that "she has both the sagacity and decision that will make her a good counsellor in some emergencies." The emergency had come days after the Inaugural, when Mexico, protesting Texas annexation, broke off diplomatic relations. Polk ordered General Zachary Taylor to the U.S. Mexican border on the Rio Grande. A year later, he declared war.

Sarah was perhaps an influence in the president's declaration to gain more territory in the Southwest, as well as to obtain the western territory as far as the Pacific Ocean. The "Manifest Destiny" publicly espoused by the Polks was part of the belief that God had decreed America to be a chosen land, and to gain what they could to further develop the blessed nation. The war rallied the president's wife. She hosted a full schedule of political dinners with retaliation at the Rio Grande as the topic of discussion, and the purpose of persuading dissenters. One guest recalled her "patriotic sentiments" when "a gallant lieutenant, just [back] from the bloody but glorious conflict at Monterey," came to her. Mrs. Polk asked him to recall the noble fight, highlighting the virtues of godly war. The guest was stunned at her observation "that whatever sustained the honor and advanced the interests of the country, whether regarded as democratic or not, she admired and applauded." She became popular with the war's General Pillow, who gave her an expensive pearl fan, and General Worth, who presented her with a portrait of Hernán Cortés, first conqueror of Mexico. "I regard," Mrs. Polk later declared, "the results following the Mexican war, that is, the adding of California and New Mexico to the territory of the United States, as among the most important events in the history of this country . . . Of course, there were some opposed to it; there is always somebody opposed to everything."[18]

Even in conquered Mexico, she became legendary, and appeared on a strange lithograph in the Catholic region. Elizabeth Fremont recalled a Mexican home where hung on the wall were lithographs of "the

'Three Marys' of the Bible and a fourth individual, one of "still another Mary . . . in a flaming red dress and ermine tippets, a pink rose in her hand, and underneath the inscription: "Mary, Wife of James K. Polk, President of the United States!"[19]

During the war, Sarah Polk's role as assistant to the president was not merely as a supporter. One intimate said she comprehended the president's most "abstruse and complicated political questions," and took "pains to inform herself on these subjects" and "quickly comprehend their plans . . ." The president never assembled a kitchen Cabinet of advisers or formed political friendships. He all but ignored his Cabinet, writing in his diary, "I have conducted the government without their aid. It is only occasionally that a great measure or new question arises upon which I need the . . . advice of my Cabinet." Polk did, however, trust his wife's judgment on the political aspects of the war, admitting, "None but Sarah knew so intimately my private affairs." Polk's chronicler claimed Sarah was his "political counselor, nurse and emotional resource."[20]

Freshman Whig congressman Abraham Lincoln opposed Polk's war, and his "spot resolution" called upon the president to precisely define just where American property had been desecrated by Mexico. Lincoln and his wife, Mary, had traveled to Washington together in the late fall of 1848, stopping first in her hometown of Lexington, where they discussed the war with Henry Clay, who, like Mary, feared the spread of slavery. There, Lincoln for the first time saw the horrors of slave trade. His former law partner recalled that it was Mary, however, who was "endowed with a more restless ambition than he. She was gifted with a rare insight into the motives that actuate mankind . . . much of Lincoln's success was . . . attributable to her acuteness . . . and influence."

Lincoln's 1847 campaign had been Mary's as well. Friend Ward Lamon said he was "convinced that Mrs. Lincoln was running Abraham beyond his proper distance in that race . . ." The Lincolns entered Washington on December 2, the height of the social season, and Mary stayed through April. Certainly, like other congressional wives, she attended the White House New Year's Day reception, as well as the weekly functions at which her distant relative Dolley Madison remained the center of attention.

In the capital, Mrs. Lincoln showed the first trace of a particular flaw. After she left, Abraham wrote her about several bills that had been sent to him. "I hesitated to pay them, because my recollection is that you told me when you went away, there was nothing left unpaid."[21]

War changed other careers. Lieutenant Ulysses S. Grant, fighting under General Zachary Taylor, missed desperately his fiancée, Julia Dent. Julia, who suffered from insecurity over her crossed eyes, found comfort in dreams, even envisioning her absent lover represented by her tall bedpost. On her own, Julia began meeting politicians like Webster, Clay, and Van Buren in St. Louis, where they came to orate. Julia confessed to being "superstitious," but she was also quite determined. She married "Ulys" in 1848, and they set up a humble life together, riddled with poverty and depression over it. Time and again, Julia would serve as Ulysses' armor against their desolate prospects.[22]

Other tough women were fighting poverty as well.

Though still privately desperate for cash, Dolley Madison raised money for public causes—chairing a committee to raise funds for a proposed Washington Monument, serving as "patroness" for a fund-raiser ball for the Washington Orphans Asylum, her project of White House days, subscribing to raffles, and offering her personal letters of famous statesmen for the rebuilding of the burned Pennsylvania Academy of Fine Arts. For struggling artists, she posed her famous but—as she called it—"wayward face," so they could make and sell copies of the Queen Mother, and introduced them to other potential clients. She, along with Martha Washington, became one of the few women whose likeness graced the first register of nationally prominent Americans. Personally, she found solace from her vagrant son and pecuniary anxieties in converting to Episcopalianism at St. John's Church on Lafayette Square—"the Church of the Presidents."

Louisa Adams, now a rabid abolitionist who served as her husband's assistant in gathering abolition information, served as Dolley's religious witness. "There are few Ladies," the sixth president's wife said of the fourth, "who retained their power over the heart of mankind so long as she has through the winning attraction of her manner and conversation." Although Sarah Polk also praised Dolley as "first among our . . . Ladies," she had exerted no influence with legislators on Dolley's behalf. Mrs. Madison was at the point of pawning her silverware and paintings when once again fate intervened.

One quiet night in the second week of May 1848, Dolley Madison was roused by the screams of a frantic neighbor. The Madison house was on fire. Calmly, the Queen Mother, just a week shy of eighty, yelled, "The papers, the papers first!" Dolley permitted herself to be carried out only when assured that the papers would be rescued. Her niece said that Dolley laughingly recalled being taken "from a war bed to the cold grass with her bare feet and her best velvet dress thrown for her to put on at three o'clock in the morning!" Congress finally took action on the remaining Madison papers.

On her eightieth birthday, her wish was granted. Congress bought the papers for twenty-five thousand dollars. Lest Dolley spend it on her unbalanced son, Payne, most of it was placed in an account, with James Buchanan as one of her trust officers. Dolley took to Buchanan and his niece Harriet Lane who, when on leave from the Georgetown Convent School, regularly visited the Queen Mother. Sarah Polk liked Harriet as

well, and the three generations of women posed for a daguerreotype, together with the president and Buchanan, who, Sarah thought, "had many of the cranks of a bachelor."[23]

While the gained territory of the Mexican War had brought slavery more into focus, Sarah continued to maintain that the sale of human beings was the will of God. One day, while working with the president in his office, she looked out the window. "Mr. Polk," she declared, "the writers of the Declaration of Independence were mistaken when they affirmed that all men are created equal." Pointing to the blacks working on the lawn, she continued, "There are those men toiling in the heat of the sun, while you are writing, and I am sitting here fanning myself, in this house . . . surrounded by every comfort. Those men did not choose such a lot in life, neither did we ask for ours; we were created for these places." She saw herself as a businesswoman, not a racist. Agriculture was the South's economy, and slaves kept it from collapsing. Sarah Childress Polk was untroubled that her slaves indirectly paid for her beautiful Worth gowns.

However, she was troubled by the "Massacre at Haun's Mill" of twenty Mormons, stating to her husband, "I object to the practice of polygamy too, still I can't help but pity them. They have suffered so much at the hands of 'civilized' people." As far as the growing movement for recognition of her sex, Sarah Polk was less interested. Mrs. Polk declined to send her support to the Seneca Falls convention on "woman's" rights. A generation of females became "women" with the publication of the radical

Woman in the Nineteenth Century, written in 1845 by Margaret Fuller, "feminist" reformer, and widely published five years later.[24]

On July 4, 1848, the U.S. treaty with Mexico was delivered to the president. Along with the Oregon Treaty, it added eight hundred thousand square miles to America. Afterward he was joined by America's most cherished woman, the great Queen Mother, at a ceremony laying the cornerstone of the Washington Monument, with Mrs. Madison in a prominent seat on the dais and the curious clustering near.

The undisputed hero that summer was General Taylor, who was being run as the Whigs' presidential candidate, against the wishes of his wife, Margaret. Even the strident Taylor supporter Mary Lincoln broke polite tradition by publicly traveling with her husband in his speaking-tour campaign for Taylor. Julia Tyler met "Old Zach" at a Richmond reception, but was more amused by the fact that people paid more attention to her. Mrs. Polk said his "opinions as expressed, I hope, have not been well considered . . . a well-meaning old man . . . he is uneducated, exceedingly ignorant of public affairs, and, I should judge, of very ordinary capacity." Nevertheless, the election made Margaret Taylor successor to Sarah Polk.

At the last Polk White House reception, it was Dolley Madison who eclipsed everything. Some may have thought the Queen Mother a bit dotty by now, but she proved them wrong. There, in her old home, again on a raised platform as if she were a museum piece, the eighty-year-old woman was wearing a very low-cut décolleté gown, baring shockingly young arms, neck, and bosom. She hadn't been seen like that since the sounds of the cannons of the War of 1812 had boomed from those windows. It was her one new fashion purchase with the congressional money, an ensemble in white satin with her old trademark, the plumed turban, fringed in the same material and twined about her head. Few might have realized that night as they gazed upon the seemingly indestructible legend that the end of an era was so close—for Dolley, and for the nation.

– 15 –

Phantom of the White House

MARGARET TAYLOR'S SLAVES were kept upstairs, out of public view. But if nobody saw her slaves, neither would they see her.[1]

Some said she was forced to stay on the attic floor, hidden away by a family embarrassed by her frontier idiosyncrasies. They said that she puffed tobacco from a long-stemmed western corncob pipe. They claimed she hated politics and politicians, and had never been to the East. She was said to be an uncouth "poor-white of the wilds." Why else would a president's wife be a phantom?[2]

Mrs. Taylor was to play an unusual role as president's wife. In private, she was matriarch of the mansion, but to the press and public she would remain utterly unrecognized. Her role may have led her to make the even more curious decision not ever to sit for her portrait or even a "photograph." Determined to somehow picture the woman, some zealous engraver drew a spurious portrait of her that abounded in several versions, even superimposing the imaginary face on another woman's body. Regardless of gossip, Mrs. Taylor would not deny or confirm anything. The press and the public knew nothing about her.[3]

Earlier in her life, "Peggy" had decided on a public over a private role. She trudged with her husband in pursuit of his army career, and sent her children for long stays with relatives until their maturity, when she enrolled them in superb eastern schools. Those years took her through some of the beautiful but dangerous wild territories of North America, living in swamp tents and forest forts. Because of Indian raids, she had learned how to use a gun for self-protection. She was accustomed to the "[P]rofanity, ribaldry, and blustering braggadocio" of soldiers."

By the time "Old Zach" was being considered for the Whig nomination for the presidency, Peggy was ready for retirement, and so strongly opposed his nomination that she prayed Henry Clay would get it. In a "dreadful frame of mind," she made a morbid prediction that it might be the Democrats' "plot to deprive me of his society, and shorten his life by unnecessary care and responsibility." But she went to Washington, on a separate and less grand route than her husband, for the Inauguration, contrary to rumor that she wasn't there. She made it clear, however, that her daughter Betty would serve as hostess.[4]

The public's fancy of a phantom pipe-smoking poor white was in reality a daughter of Maryland aristocrats and girlhood friend of Martha Washington's granddaughters, who became "actively ill" at the smell of smoke. She was not an ignorant woman. She had made extended visits to the polished cities of Washington, Philadelphia, and New York, journeyed as far south as Florida, as far north as Niagara Falls, and as far west as Minnesota.

A rare visitor described Mrs. Taylor as a "most kind and thoroughbred Southern lady." Upstairs in the private rooms, not the attic, she received special guests, and "took every opportunity to drop a good word in company that might help her husband." She entertained political visitors with the president at eight in the evenings. She was the only woman at a stag dinner hosted by Vice President Millard Fillmore, where politics was undoubtedly the sole subject. She knitted near the president while he held political discussions, absorbing all she heard, and at dinners was remembered as "capably sharing in her part of the conversation." It is likely that the president's wife influenced her husband's decision in appointing Reverdy Johnson, whose wife was her kin, as attorney general. A Senate wife wrote that Margaret was "full of interest in the passing show."

Mrs. Taylor actually did partake in several public ceremonies, like greeting a Baptist Sunday school group on the Fourth of July and accepting life membership in the American Sunday School Union in November. In the first year of the administration, she went out daily, to attend services at St. John's Episcopal Church and sometimes visit family friends in Virginia and Maryland. Zachary never pushed her to assume any public role, recalling her sacrifices throughout their army years. "You know," he told Senator Jefferson Davis, "my wife was as much of a soldier as I was."[5]

While some Washingtonians lamented Mrs. Taylor's lack of social interest, they mourned the passing of America's most beloved woman. On July 12, 1849, Dolley Madison died peacefully in her sleep. Her last words were a reassurance to a worried niece. "My dear, do not trouble yourself about it; there is nothing in *this* world worth caring for."

On July 16, the remains of one of America's last links to the Federal Era lay in state at St. John's. Hundreds lined up to pass by the open coffin and view the wizened Queen Mother under the eerie glow of candles. For a woman who was technically a public figure, as president's wife, for only eight of her eighty-one years, the reaction was phenomenal. District of Columbia police marshals organized the "state" funeral; the city council passed a "Resolution of Respect." All federal government departments sent a representative to the ceremony, and a procession of officials, said to have been "the largest yet seen in this city" and headed by the president, marched from church to cemetery. It was at the funeral, according to legend, that the very first public utterance of a title that would be reserved for the president's wife was spoken. President Taylor eulogized the great Dolley Madison by saying, "She will never be forgotten, because she was truly our First Lady for a half-century."[6]

The "Lady," the "president's lady," "presidentress," "Mrs. President" fell by the way as this new title captured the public's fancy and affixed itself to whomever the current president's wife might be. Almost embarrassed by it, the woman in question would rarely use the title to refer to herself, but the "unofficial" title would quickly circulate. The mere mention of it would come to represent the power of a particular woman in America.

The First Lady.

PART IV

The Mid-Victorian Age 1849–1865

Mrs. A. Lincoln.

There has been a long standing dispute respecting the intellectual powers of the two sexes . . . share with men the sceptre of influence . . . without presuming to wrest from him a visible authority . . .

—SARAH HALE, editor, *Godey's Lady's Book* (1850)

Iron Belles

IF MARGARET TAYLOR attended Dolley Madison's rites, she would not have been identifiable by sight. Ironically, had she attended the state funeral held that next July, it would have been both her first and last publicly acknowledged appearance. Her strange prediction that the president would die in office came true. It was a "heart-piercing" scene. "The tearing of Mrs. Taylor away from the body nearly killed me—she would listen to his heart, and feel his pulse, and insist he did not die without speaking to her." She became hysterical, having the ice preserving his body removed three times so she could gaze upon him. She refused to permit embalming, and she could not be moved to attend his memorial service. Senator Davis's wife watched over the widow, who, upstairs in her room, endured "all the torture," and, "worn to a shadow," lay on her bed without talking, "but trembled silently from head to foot as one band after another blared the funeral music" and "the heavy guns boomed . . . to announce the final parting."[1]

Taylor's death posed a curious dilemma for romantic engravers. The First Lady was there when the president died, but nobody knew what she looked like. Conveniently, it was a death scene. Mrs. Taylor was shown in a widely distributed engraving, in full dress and cap, sitting prominently at her husband's bedside, crying, and covering her face with a large handkerchief.

By autumn, the new president, Millard Fillmore, was joined by his erudite partner, the tall, red-haired Abigail Powers, the first president's wife to come out of poverty and the first to have earned her own living, as a professional teacher. She even started the first public library in her town in the Finger Lakes region of New York State by selling two-dollar subscriptions. One of her students had been the young carpenter Fillmore, and it was she who taught him how to write and speak correctly, and study geography with a map. In middle age, she taught herself French and took piano lessons. Her mind was active and curious.[2]

When the Whigs nominated Taylor and her husband, Abigail followed the campaign closely, writing her daughter Mary that "General Taylor's course gives the Whigs a great deal of trouble, and they had an indignation meeting last night. Your father, being cooler, thinks they are going too far, but they are in great excitement." As First Lady, she

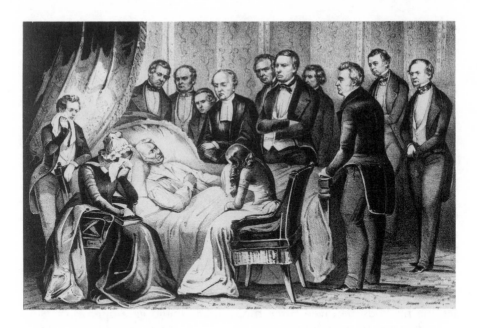

exercised her power over the president to make him seek, and get, a congressional appropriation for the very first permanent White House library. It was Abigail who spent several months carefully choosing the books' subjects, including science and government. Intellectual benefit was the factor she used in deciding what rare public events she would be seen at. With a bad ankle that disabled her from standing on receiving lines, and suffering from bronchial ills, Mrs. Fillmore presided at formal political dinners but had Mary play hostess at the mass public receptions. Yet Abigail made it her business to appear at concerts and lectures, greet Hungary's liberationist Louis Kossuth, and attend the Washington premiere appearance of "Swedish Nightingale" Jenny Lind. The First Lady paid a call on Lind, then had her to the White House, where Mrs. Fillmore asked the diva intellectual questions about Sweden. The First Lady was now invited to attend public events of all kinds with the president and was even sent a free ticket to "Señor Spinetto's 100 Learned Canaries." She did not attend. The public was also increasingly more aware of what the First Lady looked like. Copies of Abigail Fillmore daguerreotypes were "a popular early seller," particularly among women.[3]

Some of Abigail's earlier letters reveal the intensity of her relationship with Millard. "I have spent the day at home," she reported. "Have felt more than usual lonely tho' not unhappy or discontented. Your society is all I have thought of." And she added, almost routinely, "Have finished studying the maps of ancient geography." In another, she was "happy and proud in the thought that your heart is firm, and

that no fascinating female can induce you to forget whose whole heart is devoted."[4]

Mrs. Fillmore's greatest role was as political adviser to the president. When they were apart, he wrote her about political developments every single day, and she, in turn, offered her opinions. He had come to rely upon her. One friend wrote that "Mrs. Fillmore was a woman who had read much and was well-informed on all the topics of the day, and Mr. Fillmore had the highest respect for her attainments, and has been heard to say he never took any important step without her counsel and advice."[5]

Some believed that her deep humanitarianism had influenced the president to end the violent flogging permitted in the navy, and she was more adamantly opposed to slavery than he was. In fact, the most important advice she gave him concerned his most vital decision, whether to sign the Fugitive Slave Bill.

The bill would enable slave owners to reclaim their runaway slaves even in free territory. Abigail Fillmore urged her husband not to sign the bill. Not only was she morally opposed, but she realized it would be the end of his career. One chronicler bluntly wrote that Abigail told him "that . . . it would be the death blow to his popularity in the North, and that the great portion of his political friends would be alienated . . . Indeed his wife . . . made it clear to him." But hoping the bill might postpone civil insurrection and further regional deterioration, Fillmore signed it.[6]

Other women disagreed with Abigail. "Mrs. Ex-President Tyler" became an international newsmaker once again, this time on the sensitive slavery question. In February 1853, she wrote a pointed letter to British women, led by the duchess of Sutherland, who called on southern women to end slavery. Julia had it published in American newspapers, and later reprinted in Europe. In this letter, Julia Tyler showed her biased savvy with an unsparing, acid pen:

Spare from the well-fed negroes . . . one drop of your superabounding sympathy to pour into that bitter cup [Ireland] which is overrunning with sorrow . . . relieve many a poor female of England, who is now cold, and shivering . . . I reason not with you on the subject of our domestic institutions. Such as they are . . . We prefer to work out our Destiny . . . The African under [English] policy and by her laws became property. That property . . . [now] constitute[s] a large part of Southern wealth . . . We meddle not with your laws of primogeniture . . . although they are obnoxious to all our notions of justice . . . We are content to leave England in the enjoyment of her peculiar institutions; and we must insist upon the right to regulate ours without her aid. I pray you to bear in mind that the golden rule of life is for each to attend to his own business, and let his neighbor's alone!

Again, Julia was a celebrity to some, receiving congratulations from even "Sahara Sarah," and immortalized in "Oh Susanna!" lyrics: "Oh, Lady Sutherland, To comfort you I'll try. Mrs. Tyler gave you what was right, But Duchess don't you cry."[7]

Julia Grant was equally comfortable with slavery, though she lived in a border state where tensions ran high. Others, like Mary Lincoln, became more fervent in their sentiments about stopping slave states from entering the Union. But Mary was also careful to refrain from being too outspoken and jeopardizing her husband's rising political star. It was she who "put her foot down . . . with a firm and emphatic No" to Abraham's offer from the Whigs to assume the governorship of Oregon. She had higher ambitions. So Mary shrewdly pointed out that Lincoln "desires . . . that slavery shall not be extended, let it remain where it is." Only privately did she speak of her belief in eventual emancipation.[8]

In her own way, Mrs. Fillmore exercised independent power. Through the First Lady, her brother David was awarded a presidential commission in his hometown of Sanderly City, even though both siblings knew that the president scorned nepotism. There was also the case of a blind New Orleans woman, Helen De Kroyft. Mrs. Fillmore recommended the prominent Dr. Turnbull to her, and arranged for the woman to be treated by him. The *Daily Delta* printed the cured woman's thanks to Abigail.[9]

In her new library, Mrs. Fillmore created a salon, where invited statesmen and authors could join her family and friends and discuss current issues. Among her circle were Charles Dickens, William Makepeace Thackeray, and Washington Irving, and the latter two were her escorts to the Inaugural of Fillmore's successor, Franklin Pierce, in 1853. Pierce had been elected with Senator King of Alabama— Buchanan's roommate—as his vice president. When suddenly King was taken seriously ill, the president-elect privately wrote to Buchanan about him, saying that "an interchange of thoughts with Colonel King (whose returning health is a source of great joy to me) would also be peculiarly pleasant and profitable . . ." King, however, died shortly after.[10]

Adding to the funereal atmosphere in the capital was the sudden death of Abigail Fillmore, still in Washington.

Mrs. Fillmore's unpredictable but steadily worsening health had not been an excuse to get out of a public role. On her birthday in 1849 she had written, "Perhaps ere another anniversary, I shall be numbered with the dead—I feel a presentment that I shall not see many more."

For the first recorded time in history, an outgoing First Lady attended the Inaugural of her husband's sucessor, and it was on the public stand, in the open, raw air that Mrs. Fillmore caught a chill resulting in bronchial trouble. It was not serious, because she was quite active and all over town in the time that followed. Her days were filled with well-wishers who invited themselves to her Willard Hotel suite (where she had lived with her husband during the 1850 social season when he was vice president), but inconvenienced her, as she was in the midst of packing and sorting. Besides attending dinners and receptions with her husband, she was preoccupied with her Fillmore sister-in-law Olive, and brothers-in-law Cyrus and Calvin, who were staying at Rensselaer's Hotel in Georgetown. It was during a shopping trip with her daughter that Abigail became seriously ill and had to return to her suite. She would never leave again.

Her lungs rapidly filled with fluid, and she had breathing troubles. Doctors were called in from Baltimore. "After the first week," Millard wrote to his sister Julia Hall, "she talked very little. She, however, listened to conversation and especially to reading with her usual interest. I read to her a great deal by way of amusing her and diverting her mind from the nausea with which she was annoyed." Not long after, however, Mrs. Fillmore started going deaf, due to a high fever. She had to sleep with her head on a table, keep her chest upright for two weeks because of the collecting fluids, and was walked about when she was conscious. She had no sleep for long hours, and fatigue set in.

President Pierce sent a message over to the Willard with the news that Jane Pierce knew one particular White House servant, "Abby," who had "been so long with your wife" that she might be of some comfort to the former First Lady. Mrs. Pierce "begs you to command" if they could be of any such assistance. In reply, Fillmore described his wife's ghastly condition: "She is indeed very sick . . . her thoughts hold out beyond all expectations and I hope and pray that it may continue until her lungs shall be so far restored as to enable her to take rest in a reclining posture. Over this her fate seems to hang . . . Mrs. Fillmore feels very grateful for the generous offer of Mrs. Pierce to permit Abby to come and assist her, but . . . We have two excellent nurses . . . I cannot be too thankful that this terrible calamity did not fall upon me during the last few days of my administration—when either she or the public business must have been neglected."

Abigail Fillmore died on March 30, and immediately upon getting the news by messenger, the Senate officially adjourned in mourning. One stranger from North Carolina, a W. A. Graham, would write Fillmore that Abigail had performed her role "in a manner acceptable and admired throughout the country." Beyond the bare facts of her birth, marriage, children, and death an obituary added that she was "a lady of great strength of mind, dignified manners, genteel deportment, and of much energy of character." She was laid in state at the Willard, and the President and Cabinet came to pay their official respects.

Though it was most likely by virtue of the fact that she had just left the First Lady role, public response to Mrs. Fillmore's death was another great recognition of the first ladyship. Letitia Tyler had been an incumbent. Martha Washington had been an icon, apart from being the president's wife. Dolley Madison had been a living legend, the most popular and famous former First Lady. Abigail Fillmore was less known, yet still a former First Lady, and that was a status which was now undeniably of public importance and acknowledgment. Less than a year before, Louisa Adams's death had been reported in the first edition of *The New York Times,* and six months before, even the reclusive Margaret Taylor's death was noted in the public press. Death preoccupied the era in every way, and unfortunately for the new administration, it was unable to shake the specter of the grim reaper.

Though melancholic, Jane Appleton Pierce, when she so chose, was as much an iron belle as Abigail Fillmore. The daughter of two famous and wealthy New England families who made fortunes in textiles, Jane was imbued with the warped religious fanaticism of her father, a Bowdoin College president who killed himself by sacrificial fasting. A beautiful woman, with finely chiseled features, pale ivory skin, and raven hair, Jane became maudlin about politics' ruination of her life—particularly after a short stint as a congressional wife. Her influence over husband, Franklin, was not insignificant. She managed to force him to refuse Polk's offer to become attorney general. Pierce had somewhat embarrassingly explained to the president that "the responsibilities which the proposed change would necessarily impose on her, ought probably in themselves to constitute an unsurmountable objection to leaving our quiet home for a public station in Washington."

While he promised her that he would not do so, Franklin secretly kept his name prominent in politics, and drank. "Oh, how I wish he was out of political life!" Jane moaned. "How much better it would be for him on every account!" When he was nominated for the presidency, Jane stopped to contemplate her role as First Lady. "If what seems so probably is to come I pray that grace may be given where it is and will be much so needed." She nevertheless paid close attention to Franklin's remarks on issues, once revealing to a friend that the candidate didn't always tell the press what he really thought: "I just tell it to you because I liked his true answer best . . ."[11]

When he was elected president, Jane discovered the disturbing truth that he'd *actively sought* the nomination while telling her he hadn't. A breach in the marriage ensued, but Jane agreed to serve as First Lady, rationalizing that the presidency would be beneficial to her beloved son, eleven-year-old Benjamin, over whom she hovered obsessively. Two months before the Inaugural, Bennie was killed in a train wreck, crushed before her eyes. She first hysterically refused to go to Washington, blaming her husband for the death. Then, more calmly, she rationalized that God had killed the boy so Franklin could have no distractions. When her family, which included a senator, pleaded that she had to go, Mrs. Pierce headed south, but at Baltimore left the train, would go no further, and missed the Inaugural.

When she finally arrived in town, Jane was escorted by her friend and aunt-by-marriage Abby Means. Mrs. Means assumed the public hostess role. Jane kept upstairs, refusing to appear at large public events for two years. . . . She ordered mourning bunting placed indefinitely in the state rooms, and halted the Saturday night Marine Band concerts because they interfered with her prayer hours, as she prepared for the Sabbath. In her darkened room, the First Lady wrote letters to dead Bennie, asking his forgiveness. So consumed was she with mourning that any real role was suspended for half the term. Mrs. Pierce was so determined to reach him that she called in the famous mediums the Fox Sisters for a White House séance. (Other women, like Julia Tyler, enjoyed making contact with the spiritual world—a fad running high in the fifties—on their own. One night Julia hosted a party to contact "the other side," but only managed to levitate a table. More seriously, Julia relied upon her self-described ability to foresee the future through her dreams.)[12]

Gradually, however, the reality of her role cracked light into Jane's darkened life. As she wrote her sister, "The last two nights my dear boy has been in my dreams with peculiar vividness. May God forgive this

aching yearning that I feel so much . . . Mr. Pierce is burdened with
cares and perplexities . . . He has but three large dinners yet, at all of
which I have appeared, but not at the evening [public] receptions . . .
Little interruptions are very abundant here, and I do not accomplish
half I wish to, either in reading or writing . . . I came accidently upon
some of my precious child's things . . . but I was obliged to turn and
seem interested in *other things* . . ."

Strange as it seemed for this woman, one of the "other things"
proved to be the political world of her husband. Close friend Nathaniel
Hawthorne visited and took her on boat cruises. She sensed competition when the war secretary's wife, Varina Davis, made her home the
center of the social scene. At private White House dinners, Mrs. Pierce
was escorted by other politicians, and was familiar enough with Senator
Stephen Douglas to introduce him to others, prompting him into political conversation. She took carriage rides with Mrs. Davis, made semi-
official trips to the Virginia springs with the president, and even
showed wit about a friend's overcrowded room; "Well it *is* very social."
The First Lady's sudden appearances regularly in the visitor's gallery to
listen to Senate debates and deliberations must have been a great surprise to those who knew who she was.

Elihu Burritt, a famous peace proponent of the day, was delighted
by the First Lady's lively conversation on the Crimean War, as she

asked many specific international-affairs questions when he brought up the notion of American intervention.[13]

The First Lady evidently opposed her husband's signing of the Kansas-Nebraska Act, which permitted the new territories the option by vote to permit slavery and provoked a bloody battle in Kansas. Though she was summering at the shore when he signed the act, when she returned, Mrs. Pierce directly involved herself. Upon receiving a letter from the wife of an imprisoned abolitionist accused of treason, Dr. Charles Robinson, Jane persuaded the president to free the man. In response to one of her letters, Franklin opposed Jane's favoring war with the South if it seceded, rather than permitting slavery to continue.

Publicly, however, Jane continued to minimize her role by maintaining mourning. It kept people at a distance, and furthered sympathy for her. "Her woe-begone face," one woman observed, "banished all animation in others . . . she broke down in her efforts to lift herself . . ." Mrs. Pierce had skillfully manipulated her role, thereby forfeiting traditional duties without a trace of criticism. She cast a permanent pall on the administration and rendered Pierce's political career—which she so detested—and Washington—which she viewed with condescension—obsolete in her sphere.[14]

Romantics claimed that Mrs. Pierce was so helpless she had to be carried from the White House at the administration's end. In truth, she walked out, rather happily, and stayed in town for two months after, enjoying its spring. She would spend several years traveling through Europe and the Caribbean, under the guise of seeking health, carrying with her a box containing locks of hair of her "precious dead." The malaise of the ladyship, however, dissipated with the election of James Buchanan, whose niece Harriet, fresh from Victoria's court where "Nunc" served as ambassador, was lively and witty.[15]

Buchanan's election wasn't won without jibes about his marital status, one ditty running, "Who ever heard in all his life, Of a candidate without a wife?" There would be many women, however. "Buck" gathered around him loyal Cabinet members and their wives as his "family." There was promise of brilliant social life, though political differences were uncomfortably glaring as well. The Inaugural Ball featured dancing belles and gentleman, and a sumptuous buffet dinner. The walls twinkled with gold stars and were festooned with tricolors. Harriet, in white gown and pearls, was dubbed "Our Democratic Queen." Amid the laughing faces, however, the Russian minister, Baron de Stoeckl, swirling the French minister's wife to a waltz, wore a somber expression. He recalled Tallyrand's ominous murmurings to King Louis Philippe just prior to the 1830 revolution.

"Sire," de Stoeckel whispered between the melodic strains of the music, "we are dancing on a volcano."[16]

– 17 –

Volcano Dancer

CURVACEOUS, BLOND, VIOLET-EYED Harriet Lane came with a dossier of impeccable credentials. A few years previous, she'd presented herself to Victoria in one hundred yards of white lace, diamond tiara, and snow-white ostrich plumes. Becoming a court favorite, Harriet was even pressed by Victoria to marry an Englishman and stay. The queen decreed that Harriet be given the rank of ambassadorial consort, rather than the lower position awarded to women relatives.[1]

In the White House, Harriet recreated Julia Tyler's royal tableaux, dressed in white, carrying a mammoth bouquet of roses, nodding to guests, murmuring with her "gracious chill" to friends. The household staff consisted almost entirely of English servants. Invited guests were expected to follow a rigid dress code. Harriet spent every cent of a congressional appropriation to redecorate in her rich tastes, with primary colors brilliantly reflecting artificial gaslight at the elegant evening soirees, rooms aglow in the height of Victoriana. She loved to dance the Austrian quadrilles, the "Germans," the fast polka, and the grand waltz. She corresponded with nobility and took holidays *only* at the fashionable spas. Julia Tyler seemed reincarnated. She was equally—in the words of one observer—"naughty." When a "young gentleman once warmly expressed the thoughts that her hands were fitted to play the harp or guide the path of the Empire," she flirtatiously shot back, "or awake to ecstasies the living lyre."[2]

Only twenty-seven years old, Miss Lane was a cunning political partner to her uncle, a northerner with southern sympathies. Her father and mother—Buchanan's sister—died when Harriet was young, and she eventually became his ward. Her uncle shaped her into a spiritual daughter, supervising her rigorous education at the Georgetown Academy, where she studied with Tennessee congressman Andrew Johnson's daughter, Martha. When Buchanan was secretary of state, fifteen-year-old Harriet was "allowed to listen" to the conversation of politicians he gathered. He "began training her to observe these people and to learn from observing. Then he would discuss government questions with her . . ." Once she was subtle to artful politics, Buchanan shared his secret ambition to become president with her, warning her *"but this is for yourself alone."* Harriet admitted that "Uncle . . . places such confidence in me that he gives himself no uneasiness."[3]

Buchanan was so confident of Harriet that during the 1852 election he had asked her to meet with the leader of western Pennsylvania Democrats, David Lynch, the mayor of Pittsburgh. Harriet had begged James to allow her to campaign actively, and the Lynch conference proved that Miss Lane was a "figure in the political world" and that "Buchanan listened to her opinions." It was not until the '56 campaign that presidential candidates' wives were used in a public role. That year, Republican John Fremont's campaign had buttons carrying the slogan "Oh Jessie!," a colloquialism for "Oh hell!" and the first name of Fremont's wife.[4]

Harriet's White House power with the president was obvious. They spent their mornings "together, usually reading the newspapers, she incidentally absorbing his statesmanlike view of the political questions," and he "permitted her to attend his [Cabinet] conferences." As one contemporary carefully chronicled, Harriet was keenly "aware of the political currents of the day and because of her training, [intelligence], official position, and her personal relationship with the President, she could not escape having some influence on his public policies. People believed that Buchanan listened to her opinions and that she had his full confidence . . ." But before they even left the presidency, that would become a dubious distinction.

One woman observer said that in Harriet's "affection he found the only solace of his lonely life. For her sake he condescended to unbend in public . . . She was his confidante in all matters political and personal."[5] But Miss Lane could never provide what a partner might have for "Old Buck." Bachelorhood had turned Buchanan into a fussy and irritable fellow of highly affected manners. He had to squint and tilt his head to see from one eye. He dressed in impeccably stiff clothes. He insisted upon the finest food, wines, and flowers. Inevitably, innuendo about his past stirred. There were descriptions of a weak and feminine man; one visitor made much out of nothing by saying Buchanan was often "arrayed in a long dressing-gown and slippers." A less veiled description told of his "shrill, female voice, and wholly beardless cheeks." It was further stated that "he is not by any means, in any aspect the sort of man likely to cut, or attempt to cut his throat for a Chloe or Phillis [sic] . . ."

When Buchanan himself wrote about his idea of being married, he admitted, "I feel that is not good for a man to be alone, and should not be astonished to find myself married to some old maid who can nurse me when I am sick, provide good dinners for me when I am well, and not expect from me any very ardent or romantic affection." However, the president never married. The oddest tale was that he was engaged to the now-widowed Sarah Polk, which she heatedly made a point of denying. His guilt about women was so known that "it was a common joke" that one could gain "political favor" by sending a woman with a fabricated woe to "Buck."[6]

Buchanan preferred gentlewomen to abolition women, whom he bitterly blamed for stirring up the slavery issue. Besides Harriet and her friends, there was the presence of two stellar Cabinet wives, Mary Ann Cobb of the Treasury and Kate Thompson of the Interior, both coy and keen southern hostesses. Unknown to the public was also the quiet but regular presence of southern belle Katherine Ellis, whom most knew as Harriet's friend. Buchanan dearly cherished the company of Mrs. Ellis, who had served as a sort of daughter to her uncle precisely as Harriet did. Her uncle happened to be the late Senator King, Buchanan's old roommate.[7]

Though Pennsylvanians, Buck's and Harriet's friends and lifestyle were southern, save for the fact that they never owned slaves. As tensions rose during the first year of the administration between northern abolitionists and his southern slave-owning friends, Buchanan found himself compromised. He walked a tightrope as threats of southern secession grew. On the social front, Harriet also delicately avoided the subject of slavery and the widening chasm, as if it were not a polite subject to raise in her presence. One contemporary said she was "[S]ilent whenever it was possible to be silent, watchful and careful, she made no enemies, was betrayed in no entangling alliances, and was involved in no contretemps of any kind."

Privately, Harriet opposed secession, and yet "she became convinced that immediate emancipation would end in more widespread slavery. To hurl the Negro into the whirlpool of society totally unprepared for freedom would increase the rate of poverty and disease, which not only would cripple the Negro but could devastate the nation as a whole." She supported the president's belief that moderates could agree on "a course of action to eclipse the emotionalism of the extremists."[8]

If she avoided the welfare of blacks as an issue, Harriet spoke out quite publicly about the native American Indian. Her most publicized concern was the arts (she became the first White House hostess to invite artists as dinner guests, and under her influence a lobbying effort was launched for a national art gallery, to which she later donated her vast collection of masterpieces as well as offering advice on what should be sought and collected) but it was Indian welfare on which she focused.

Harriet had first been taught about the often-avoided issue of Indian welfare by the nuns in her school. In that environment, she also became aware of religious intolerance, and even considered converting to Roman Catholicism. Her sense of tolerance about minorities fully blossomed in England when she began to study, collect, and promote Indian arts at a time when African and Oriental art were just being recognized. She also formed permanent friendships with public-service and government leaders including the dowager marchioness of Wellesley, who worked with her husband on his Catholic Emancipation campaign and Reform Bill of 1832, and the dowager duchess of Somerset, who worked with her husband on rural housing projects and repeal of the Corn Laws.

Harriet consciously emulated the reformers and sought to influence lawmakers on behalf of the Indians. She became a colleague of American reform movement leaders—Job Tyson, advocate of prison reform, Augustus Schell, founder of the New York Institute for the Blind, Nahum Capen, founder of the Massachusetts State Board of Public Education. Through them, Harriet kept abreast of welfare work and in turn informed them of the conditions of Indians.

As word spread of her advocacy, Harriet received pleas for influence from Indian tribes. A Chippewa leader begged her to stop the illegal liquor trade and the expulsion of missionaries from the reservation by dishonest federal agents. She not only looked into the case, but started efforts of her own to meet the tribe's educational and medical needs. Shortly thereafter, "Nunc" informed her that she was being hailed as their "great mother" and that "Harriet" was becoming a namesake for Indians' babies.[9]

Harriet was widely known through the nation, a fact not lost on exploiters. Her shapely bosom, which so daringly brimmed over in the "low-neck lace bertha," helped make that style the most popular in America. The song "Listen to the Mockingbird" was dedicated to her. She became the first Lady of the White House since Julia Tyler to appear as a public person officiating at a formal event when, as the "observed of all observers," she christened the battleship *Lancaster*. Her full name was bestowed upon "flowers, perfumes, garments, poems, songs, pet animals, horses, neckties, ships, clubs and societies." When, however, she twice used the navy's revenue cutter *Harriet Lane*, the first of several press attacks were set off. "Nunc" wrote her angrily of the "newspaper criticism of yourself. This is most ungallant and un-gentlemanly. The practice, however, of employing national vessels on pleasure excursions . . . is a fair subject of public criticism. You know how much I condemned your former trip . . ."[10]

Harriet Lane was of interest not only to the public but to the press. Journalists in particular helped to make her a full-fledged celebrity, per-haps because it had been a dozen years since a young, attractive woman of social polish had been in the role. The May 8, 1858, edition of *Harper's Weekly* carried an illustration of "Miss Lane, Our Lady of the White House," which ran ten by six and a half inches across the nearly four-column page.

The oddity of a bachelor president seemed in no way to have af-fected the status of President's Lady in Miss Lane's case. Harriet would recall that her uncle had no hesitation in bestowing upon her all the conditions usually devolving upon a president's wife, yet at the same time he "often waived the social conventionalities which hedged in the presiding lady of the mansion." One journalist observed that Harriet Lane "occupies a position in the palatial residence of her eminent rela-tive *similar to that which Queen Victoria and the Empress Eugenie oc-cupy* . . ."

With the increase in newspaper correspondents now in the capital, Harriet Lane was news, for example, in the *Deseret News* of Salt Lake City, in its October 31, 1860, edition and the St. Louis *News* three months later. She appeared too in *The New York Times* "Washington Society" column. But it was the reference to her in the March 31, 1860, edition of *Frank Leslie's Illustrated Newspaper* that would make historic precedent as the first time the term "first lady" was used in public print.

In that issue, *Leslie's* carried a full-page illustration of Harriet in the greenhouse, with the following lead: "The subject of our illustration, from the semi-official position which she has so long sustained with so much honor to herself and credit to her country, may be justly termed the first lady in the land."

For just over a decade, according to legend, since Mrs. Madison's 1849 funeral, the term "first lady" had been a verbal expression. Now, it was taking on semi-official usage. Once again, several months later, *Leslie's* used the expression in reference to Harriet, as Buchanan's "ami-able niece, the lady of the White House, and by courtesy the first lady in the land." The regular use of the term thereby gave continuity to the title, at least, for the moment, in Miss Lane's case.[11]

Whether her high public profile was part of the issue or not, increased petty snipings underlined the growing animosity toward Buchanan and Lane. The *New York Tribune* disparaged the president's sending of Harriet's portrait engraving to the *Almanac de Gotha*, for inclusion in the social register of European nobility. At a White House reception, Alabamian Mrs. Clement Clay sarcastically told Miss Lane that she was "a poet's ideal of an English dairymaid . . . fed upon blush roses and the milk of her charges."[12]

Harriet's relationship with her uncle became strained. She liked enticing men, but turned down the marriage proposals that followed, finding them "dreadfully troublesome." She resented her uncle's habit of opening her mail—after doing which he once scribbled, "Opened by mistake. I know not whether it contains aught of love or treason." Harriet told a friend that she was uncomfortable having young men court her under her uncle's nose. In 1859, she left him for three summer months. "I do not care how long she stays," he told friends, "I can do very well without her." That bothered Kate Thompson. "Who can expect anything better from such a hardened Bachelor!" she wrote to Mary Ann Cobb.[13]

Mrs. Cobb called the president "Old Gurley" behind his back, and sarcastically wrote of "Miss Lane, the model of an American girl!!" One reader of Kate's letters believed that she had an "unease bordering on revulsion" for Buchanan. When Mary Ann was away from Washington, Buchanan insisted her husband, Howell, stay with him for several weeks, and Cobb was in the uncomfortable position of trying to leave and fetch her in Georgia, "whether the President will permit me or not." In the end, Cobb had to send his assistant to escort his wife back, because Buchanan didn't want to be left alone and wouldn't let him go.

In another letter, Kate, according to one chronicler, "implies something unhealthy, too, in Buchanan's close attentions to Howell Cobb, during his wife's absence." She wrote to Mary Ann, "The President has taken complete possession of him since you left and drives there nearly every day & when he is missing, the President calls upon him . . . he has gained no additional freedom by your going home." When Mrs. Cobb left Washington the next summer, Mrs. Thompson wrote her of Buchanan's "*overpowering*" reaction to her departure, adding "I have a great [deal] to say on this subject which I must keep until I see you." The ladies' relationship with "Buck" would end all too soon. And bitterly.[14]

Besides the 1860 election, in which Democrat Stephen Douglas was running against Republican Abraham Lincoln, the autumn promised an event of supreme social importance. Queen Victoria had given permission to her eldest son and heir, Edward, Prince of Wales, to visit the United States. Both Harriet and the president were giddy with plans for the prince's White House reception and Washington itinerary. By the time the October visit arrived, the president's many enemies were complaining that he was more concerned with soirees than secession.

Harriet served as the prince's Washington escort, taking him to dilapidated Mount Vernon to view the graves of George and Martha Washington, and to Mrs. Smith's Young Ladies Institute, insisting he be shown the gymnasium where the young women physically exercised, a controversial notion. In a game of tenpins, Harriet beat the prince. She was unsuccessful, however, in convincing the president to host a White House dance, which he thought might provoke criticism. But to accommodate the retinue of the nineteen-year-old "peachy-cheeked beardless boy," President Buchanan permitted his own bedroom to be used. As thanks, Victoria sent engraved prints of the royal family.[15]

But while Harriet Lane twirled to a calm waltz at a private dance with the prince, the volcano began erupting beneath her.

When Lincoln learned that he had won the election, his joyous shout to his wife was revealing: "We are elected!" With his success, however, South Carolina made good on a threat and, five days before Christmas, seceded from the nation. Weeks earlier, Buchanan had told Congress that the government had no power to prevent it. Meanwhile, his official "family" began abandoning him. The secretary of state resigned because Buchanan had refused to reinforce Fort Moultrie, South Carolina. War Secretary Floyd resigned under suspicions that he had been transferring excessive amounts of federal arms to southern arsenals—within weeks he would become a Confederate general. Buchanan sent word that Carolina's Fort Sumter would be defended. A day after Moultrie was abandoned by the Union, rebel troops occupied it. Three days later, the arsenal at Charleston was also taken.

The hurt that cut Buck deepest was the departure of the Cobbs and Thompsons. Cobb's December 8 resignation was "a personal heartache." Harriet was sent to change Cobb's decision, begging him to stay in the "family." He would not reconsider. Mary Ann went back to Georgia. Kate Thompson was in turmoil. On December 15, she wrote Mary Ann that Harriet and the president felt that "their old friends are many of them deserting them . . ." She did, too, when her husband resigned on January 8. Kate wrote Mrs. Cobb that ". . . *all their* old friends are thrown off . . . I feel as light and happy as a *bird I am out, yes out of the Union* too."[16]

Now, even the personal fact that Buchanan was single was turned publicly against him with maliciousness. In an anonymous January 4 letter to Congressman Edward McPherson, a Philadelphian referred to the president in feminine terms, which he equated with political weakness: "I do not share in the confidence which some entertain in poor Betsy Buchanan," the letter read, "She is very weak, and I fear, very bad . . . the share of leaving it to *her* [the pronoun "his" is crossed over] Cabinet whether he should or not recall her troops! Let her publicly deny (if she dare) her compact with the S.C. rebels, not to increase her force!" The writer then asked if the congressman received "a posted letter" titled "Unhappy Man!" that was "sent to every member of Congress." Buchanan's portrait had to be removed from the Capitol to stop its defacement. Congress abolished the franking privilege for former presidents to spite him.

Buchanan's humiliation drew Harriet closer as "a fit adviser in difficulty, a sympathetic companion in sorrow . . . and the comfort, at last, of his lonely hearth." But she was attacked, too. New York papers accused her of stealing White House portraits and state gifts presented by the Japanese envoys, when in reality she merely took her own royal family engravings and some stuffed birds. There was innuendo that she had overspent the 1857 congressional appropriation for redecoration. It was soon rumored that England would remain neutral on secession because of Harriet's friendship with the queen and sympathies with the South. Her closest friend resentfully wrote Harriet for failure to secure her husband a last-minute government appointment. As she prepared to leave, Harriet said it all made her "feel very sad." Ironically, her term was dubbed "that gayest administration."[17]

By February 1, seven southern states had seceded. The last hope of keeping the Union together rested in an emergency "Peace Convention" that was called. Toward the end of the month, President-elect Lincoln would be there from Illinois.

And Mary Todd Lincoln was coming to Washington.

It was therefore no surprise when word circulated that *another* political wife was coming with *her* husband, who would help lead the peace talks. On February 2, she excitedly bustled into the lobby of the Brown's Hotel with husband, nursemaid, and two youngest children in tow. Her bags were stuffed with silk gowns. She did not favor secession, but rather a brief separation permitting the South time to devise Constitutional amendments.

Revelry filled the ballrooms of Washington. Southern aristocrats, the social lions of Washington, hosted bittersweet farewells, in between packing possessions and crying good-bye.

"Perhaps," the woman mischievously scribbled from her hotel room, "I am here during the last days of the Republic."[18]

The "Lovely Lady Presidentress," formerly of the White House, "Mrs. Ex-President Tyler" lately of Virginia, had returned.

— 18 —

Secession!

RECEPTION AFTER DINNER after ball, Julia Gardiner Tyler was the center of all attention. "You ought to hear the compliments that are *heaped* upon me," she bragged. "I haven't changed a *bit* except to improve." She was still ravishing at forty. And enjoying an active intimacy. At seventy years old, John Tyler fathered his last of fifteen children, Julia's seventh.

After calling at the White House, Julia raved about her coup of having the president return the call. Harriet Lane soon followed, for an afternoon tea with her predecessor. One political opinion they shared was doubt of President-elect Lincoln's ability to hold the Union together. On February 23, Lincoln met with John Tyler in the Willard, Julia as always accompanying him to his destination, then departed. Sometime later, across the same lobby passed the woman Julia would dismiss as inferior. The object of her derision rested in her room with her three sons. Mary Todd Lincoln had arrived, but her reputation had preceded her.[1]

No candidate's wife had participated so fully in a presidential campaign. Mrs. Lincoln attended rallies where her husband was speaking, and harshly criticized rival Democratic candidate and former beau Stephen Douglas as "a very little, little giant by the side of my tall Kentuckian . . ." She believed that giving a "brave, whole-hearted fight" made "one feel better." She was at Abraham's side on Ohio campaign trips, and the candidate deferred to her judgment in choosing his official campaign portraits. She warmly received journalists who came to the Springfield, Illinois, Lincoln homestead, one observing that she was "quite confident of her husband's election." As Mary herself wrote a friend, "I scarcely know how I would bear up, under defeat. I trust that I will not have that trial."

Her campaign appearances weren't as shocking as her post-election, pre-Inaugural boldness. On a trip to New York, she demurred on none of her strong opinions, one incredulous politician recalling that "Mrs. Lincoln's journey is considered very much out of place, the idea of the Presidents wife kiting about the country and holding levees at which she indulges in a multitude of silly speeches is looked upon as very shocking . . ." The observer wrote, "Among other interesting speeches of Mrs. L" was her boast that she would help choose the Cabinet. [2]

It was no exaggeration. From New York, in a confidential letter she affirmed that Lincoln mustn't appoint one Norman Judd to the Cabinet. "Perhaps you will think it no affair of mine, yet as I see it . . . Judd would cause trouble . . ." Rumor claimed that she threw a tantrum when her husband hesitated to make a political appointment she desired. Another charged that she took gifts "for the use of her influence . . ." Lincoln read his Inaugural speech to her first—though there was no evidence that he changed the copy because of her suggestions. Journalists seized upon the subject of her power, and one *New York Times* editorial praised her: ". . . the country may congratulate itself upon the fact that its President elect is a man who does not reject, even in important matters, the advice and counsel of his wife."

Despite threats against their lives, Mary insisted on accompanying Lincoln in his appearances from the Midwest to Washington. She was thrilled to meet former President Fillmore in Buffalo, and his son Powers, an attorney who roomed with fellow lawyers Grover Cleveland and Oscar Folsom. Ohio crowds beseeched Lincoln to coax Mary out on the train's platform, Pennsylvanians applauded her at the station. In Poughkeepsie, Mrs. Lincoln gamely raised her windowshade in return for the crowds' shouted greetings. But among the smiling faces were suspicious stares. [3]

Never before had the press so thoroughly covered a President-elect's wife. And no woman had assumed the role under more trying circumstances. Unfortunately, Mary Lincoln was a woman sensitive to criticism now in a role very vulnerable to it. Rumors had already begun that the ambitious native Kentuckian secretly sympathized with the

South, and would use her influence against the Union and abolition. Southerners considered her a traitor, northerners mistrusted her. Harriet Lane bitterly reflected Washington's preconceived notion of Mrs. Lincoln: "They say Mrs. L. is awfully western, loud & unrefined."[4]

At the Inaugural Ball the First Lady, grandly dressed in blue hooped gown and with a feather in her hair, danced the quadrille with the defeated Douglas. Newspapers reported that her gown was just one of her compulsive purchases made in an orgy of spending. Mary refused to be dismissed with snide remarks about her background, her allegiance, her taste. Unfortunately for Mrs. Lincoln, it was the wrong time to play the great lady.

By the 1860's, the capital was becoming a mecca for women "journalists." Often catty, these regional correspondents kept themselves working by describing—or imagining—the activities and behavior of the First Lady. Every minor gaffe of Mary Lincoln's was to be magnified, every purchase exaggerated, every act of charity misinterpreted. It was they who would destroy her, these women whom she denounced—not unjustifiably—as the "vampyre press."

Mary Lincoln was nervous yet cool, tedious yet lively, a bundle of conflicting complexities. She was intelligent and talented, gifted with witty, vivid language. Her mind had a tremendous capacity for detail. She was highly literate, reciting Shakespeare and poetry from memory, translating German and French works by Victor Hugo, studying astronomy. She spoke perfect French, was a student of opera, adored the theater, and had worked hard to establish a library in Springfield. She had impeccable fashion and decorating tastes.

Unfortunately, coupled with these attributes was her abyss of insecurities. She suffered from myriad feelings of inferiority regarding her physical appeal, capacity to be loved, western background. And money. Rather than shrink from notice, however, Mary asserted herself, manifesting all her faults in a baffling pattern of effusions and outbursts. She had a raging temper, suffered from excruciating migraine headaches and hallucinations, and could be hysterically oversensitive. Thunderstorms left her terrified for hours. Mrs. Lincoln suffered from an undiagnosed ailment that often flared to extremes after eating sweets, later termed "diabetes." She believed in spiritualism, confident that "the other side" sent messages through dreams and signs. She was depressed by her prophesy "that poverty was my portion."[5]

There was also the compassionate Mrs. Lincoln whom few were to ever know. When her carriage injured a little boy, the First Lady took time from her schedule to frequently visit the child in the hospital with gifts and soft, gentle words of encouragement. Her son Robert observed of her being in often-torturous pain, "It is really astonishing what a brave front she manages to keep when we know she is suffering . . . She just straightens herself up a little more and says, 'It is better to laugh than to be sighing.'"[6]

Her greatest political ability was a skillful judgment of individuals jockeying to get close to the president. She could sense those ambitious men who postured as friends to her husband but were merely using him. And yet, when it came to her own supposed friends, Mary often trusted the shadiest of characters.

The White House executive and house staffs had never dealt with such a perplexing woman, presidential assistant William O. Stoddart explaining, "It was not easy at first to understand why a lady who could be one day so kindly, so considerate, so generous, so thoughtful and so hopeful, could, upon another day, appear so unreasonable, so irritable, so despondent, so even niggardly, and so prone to see the dark, the wrong side of men and women and events." From her first day in the White House, however, in the face of an already mounting pack of critics, Mary Todd Lincoln "assumed and held her rightful position as lady of the mansion."[7]

Unfortunately, Mary's first mistake as chatelaine immediately highlighted her worst liability, her compulsive spending binges.

After inspecting every White House room, she calmly explained that "no one has the interest of the place more at heart than myself," but tearfully confided to buildings commissioner B. B. French that she overspent by sixty-seven hundred dollars the twenty-thousand-dollar congressional redecorating appropriation. The public was never to learn of it, for French skillfully hid the excess cost in other accounts. The decorating occurred at the most inappropriate moment possible. On April 12, 1861, Fort Summer, held by the Union troops, was fired upon by rebels. Lincoln ordered seventy-five thousand militia for active duty. Mary Lincoln was in the indefensible situation of being a southerner married to the Union president. Virtually every male relative of hers joined the Confederacy to fight against her husband's armies in the Civil War.[8]

The initial fear was invasion of Washington, but when Union commander General Winfield Scott urged that Mrs. Lincoln and her two youngest sons, Tad and Willie, leave town immediately, the First Lady refused. After she was ordered not to leave the White House grounds without a guard, there was a spate of criticism about the spending of war funds to guard a president's wife. When a young family friend was killed in one of the war's battles, his funeral march was dedicated to the First Lady. But when she appeared at a subsequent funeral dressed not in black, but half-mourning purple, she was excoriated, prompting her snapping defense of her fashion tastes: "I want the women to mind their own business. I intend to wear what I please."

As she looked about her, Mary realized she had enemies. In the Cabinet, her two foes were Secretary of State William Seward, and Treasury Secretary Salmon Chase. She made no attempt to hide her belief that their sole ambitions were to use Lincoln for their plans to succeed him. They, in turn, both resented her openly expressed declaration that the Cabinet formed before the war should be dissolved in favor

of a new one. She considered Seward weak on abolition. He attempted
to control the planning of her state dinners, considering Mary un-
polished in social graces. Chase's daughter-hostess, Kate, fomented the
hostility by audaciously receiving her friends in one White House room
while the First Lady was receiving her guests in another. Even from the
capital prison, Mrs. Lincoln was maligned. Augusta Heath Morris, a
leading hostess imprisoned when it was learned that she was a rebel spy,
through her letters and grapevine fueled the rumor that Mary was also
one.[9]

The two men most devoted to the president, assistants John Hay
and John Nicolay, were the most antagonistic to Mrs. Lincoln. The
duo and the First Lady bristled at the sight of each other, she placing
demands on their already overburdened schedules, and they attempting
to usurp what she considered her rights as First Lady. The assistants
dubbed her "La Reine," and "the Hellcat." All the staff soon learned
that Mrs. Lincoln was inclined to fire people quickly. When the steward departed, Mary—considering herself responsible for the house—
tried to have his salary turned over to her, in payment for her job. It
was the only instance of a First Lady seeking government compensation
for her role. Her attempt failed, but provoked a rumor that she was
firing staff in order to divert money to pay for her wardrobe.

Enemies intriguing to discredit and overthrow, malicious arrows of
rumor—all left her undaunted. Mary Lincoln was *the* First Lady, and
nobody but Mary Lincoln directed her role. And while the critics of a
strong female were many, her toughness was admired by others, and
seemed rather to endear her. B. B. French found her "a smart, intelligent
woman & [who] likes to have her own way . . . I was delighted with her
independence . . . There is no denying the fact that she is a curiosity . . . Mrs. Lincoln is—Mrs. Lincoln, & no body else, & like no
other human being I ever saw. She is not easy to get along with . . ."[10]

– 19 –

Mrs. President Lincoln

THE FIRST LADY'S day began with the president's at an eight-thirty
breakfast. After she toured the house and gave directions to servants,
she returned to her room, and behind her business desk began her correspondence—all public mail first screened of threats and crank letters
by the protective Stoddart. Her wide correspondence ranged from coun-

try cousins to national political allies, whom she informed of Cabinet deliberations and war progress, while also soliciting their opinions and assistance. She often ended with *"entre nous,"* or even "burn this letter."

In the early afternoon, she stole a brief moment of solitude in the greenhouses. During the day, if she wanted to discuss an issue with the president, "she did not hesitate to go to his office . . . [as] his helpmate and comrade and . . . she would [go] often," remembered Colonel Crook of the staff. After a carriage ride, she greeted visitors. They were often legislators finishing up business with the president. Her busy schedule precluded even relatives from visiting without an appointment.

Dinner was at eight. She then spent time with Tad and Willie, and afterward she finally descended to the Red Room to pore over political journals and regional press. Crook said she "read the newspapers carefully and kept informed not merely of the great war . . . but of changing political conditions, and of important events throughout the world . . . and had very clear and strong ideas concerning them." Thursday was her reception night, after which, at about eleven, the president would come "tell her the news from the front. They would discuss the battles, the retreats, the victories, the defeats—all the main developments of the day and evening—with calm thoughtfulness . . ." On such nights, the Lincolns didn't go to bed until after midnight.[1]

Initially, Mary relished her role: "how every moment is occupied . . . This is certainly a very charming spot . . . every evening our blue room is filled with the elite of the land . . . I am beginning to feel so perfectly at home, and enjoy every thing so much." With some of the public, she was popular, several even naming babies after her, but the day after the Inauguration one woman entered Mary's life and became a trusted friend. She was black, a former slave and a gifted seamstress, Elizabeth Keckley. A friend recommended "Lizzie," and Mary, needing a confidante as much as a dressmaker, immediately hired her. The two women formed an immediate bond.

Both had suffered much already; both had lost children. Lizzie possessed tremendous sensitivity, patience, and the rare ability to listen. For the agitated Mary, she was a tranquil godsend, often acting as a second mother to the rambunctious Lincoln boys. Lizzie became Mary's solace. Mary meanwhile perceived something wondrous in Lizzie. Here, in her "mantuamaker," was the precise sort of human being that determined Miss Todd had once—with her abolitionist grandmother—helped to escape on the Underground Railroad to freedom in the North. Mary's gentleness to those she always called "the oppressed colored race" was heartfelt, but with Lizzie at her side, her hatred of slavery would bravely blossom. To Mary, Lizzie embodied the benefit of abolition. Mary may have been hypersensitive to personal criticism, but she would always publicly defend justice. To the woman who rarely complimented others, Elizabeth Keckley was "a remarkable woman."

The fact that the best friend of the white First Lady was a black woman stirred polite disapproval even among abolitionists, and cruel parody among the coarser lot. A racially offensive cartoon appeared with the representation of Mary and Lizzie's friendship as commencing an era of miscegenation, but even when persistent rumors that Mary had black blood became particularly strong, she stood by Lizzie. For a First Lady who agonized over personal criticism, it was rather a brave and sterling trait.[2]

As dressmaker, Keckley was kept busy. Mrs. Lincoln was fanatical about her appearance. Her saucy blue eyes always darted to the finest cuts, boldest colors, priciest bonnets, fans, gloves, handbags. When she browsed amid the glass-cased merchandise at Washington's famous Galt's store, she compulsively made dozens of purchases, not just from Galt's famous silver pieces, but from its diamonds, onyx, and pearl jewelry, too. In her auburn hair, she usually wore a crown of red and white roses. Plump, but with marvelously rounded white shoulders and bosom, she was handsome in massive hoopskirts, long trains, and low-cut necklines, prompting the president to remark, "Mother, it is my opinion, if some of that tail were nearer the head, it would be in better style." Others were more caustic. An Oregon senator viciously re-counted, "The weak minded Mrs. Lincoln had her bosom on exhibi-tion, and a flower pot on her head, while there was a train of silk dragging on the floor behind her . . ."[3]

Mrs. Lincoln believed that dressing well was vital to her role— regardless of debt or wartime. When some Union women asked her to join their boycott movement of foreign textiles, like cloth, she first sought the advice of the president and Treasury secretary, and was told that the government needed the money that came from duties on im-ports. That was her justification for her expenditures. "I must dress in costly material," she told Lizzie. "The people scrutinize every article that I wear with critical curiosity." It became an obsession.[4]

Accepting the proffered free use of a private car from the president of the B&O Railroad, the First Lady made a splash when she forayed to New York on gleeful shopping binges. Her veil failing to foil reporters, who cornered her in the aisles of A. T. Stewart's and Lord & Taylor, she ignored their questions about her purchases, some of which she carried in hand. Without answers to their questions, rebuffed reporters merely fabricated their copy, claiming that she bought clothes she hadn't bought, and inflating the prices of the items she had purchased. When she bought luxurious purple state china, and decided to purchase a separate set for herself, she was accused of using federal funds for personal use. Her interest in fashion wasn't lost on some merchants who commercially exploited her. One created a Mary Lincoln bonnet with pictures of the president on the drawstrings, then sold copies in his street window. When she accepted gifts from retailers (who later charged her premium prices for other items), she was accused of taking gifts for political patronage.[5]

It was on a trip in August 1861 to New Jersey's shore that Mary Lincoln's notorious role was dramatized. It was the first public trip of a First Lady without a president. The *New York Herald* recognized its importance, and sent a special correspondent to cover the First Lady's appearances, which included her inspection of beachfront lifeguard stations, a musical concert in her honor given by a choir of little girls all dressed in white, a reception, and a "Grand Ball." Afterward, the man who conceived the stations, former Governor Newell, was appointed their superintendant because of Mary. The *Chicago Daily Tribune* and *Philadelphia Bulletin* defended her being so visible, while the *Herald* focused on public fascination with her: "Others occupying the same high position . . . have failed to excite a similar interest." She won the ultimate compliment when reporter Ben Perley Poore compared her to legendary Dolley Madison.[6]

While her sarcastic Confederate sister Anne called her a "Queen," and some of the public addressed her as "Mrs. President," Mary called herself "Mrs. President Lincoln," especially when giving orders to officials. But it was after her New Jersey trip that "first lady" was again used in public.

In reference to Mrs. Lincoln, the term "first lady" first appeared in the press on August 8, 1861, after Mary's state dinner for France's Prince Bonaparte. The *New York Herald* waxed on about "this Kentucky girl, this Western matron, this republican queen" who "puts to the blush and entirely eclipses the first ladies of Europe." Soon the reference to the American president's wife was more direct. The *Sacramento Union*'s Washington correspondent Noah Brooks was defending Mrs. Lincoln with the expression in his commentary: "It is not a gracious thing to refute these things, but the tales that are told of Mrs. Lincoln's vanity, pride, vulgarity and meanness ought to put any decent man or woman to the blush . . . which they so glibly repeat concerning the first lady in the land." The general public also began using the term. In a letter, philanthropist Carl Schurz described Mary in German—"The first lady was overwhelmingly charming . . ." Now in use for two presiding ladies of the White House, the term became permanent.[7]

At the Bonaparte dinner, the prince was so taken with Mrs. Lincoln and her perfect French that some credited her power over him as being a factor in keeping France neutral, rather than supporting the Confederacy, as initially feared. One of those who took notice was Henry Wikoff, a pretentious dandy and informer for the *Herald*. He managed to meet, flatter, and befriend her quickly. Though ignorant of his secret role for the Herald, the First Lady flattered his ego, as she did with other journalists, in the hope that their politeness toward her might be reflected in print.

By ingratiating himself, Wikoff became privy to some personal secrets. As her first full social season began in the fall of 1861, Mary steeled herself against inevitable critics, Wikoff posing as her supporter. But when just months later the Herald published portions of the president's as-yet-undelivered congressional address, all hell broke loose. Someone had stolen a copy of the speech for the Herald. Congressional investigation ensued, and Wickoff, already a suspect, was subpoenaed. He wimperingly admitted telegraphing parts of the address. After a few days in prison, he admitted to receiving the material from Watt, the White House gardener.

Word circulated in the prison why Wickoff was there. In her cell, Mrs. Morris stepped up her slander campaign against the First Lady. Writing now to newspaper editors, Morris said that as a "Confesh" spy, Mary had actually slipped the papers to Watt the gardener, thereby betraying her husband. While there was no truth to the rumor that Mary was a spy, it is not so certain that she didn't pass the papers to Watt. Shortly thereafter, the fired Watt attempted to blackmail the president for twenty thousand dollars in exchange for three incriminating letters written by Mary. A wealthy Lincoln friend bought the letters for fifteen hundred dollars. Obviously, the letters contained some scandal, but once bought, they disappeared. Mary's entanglement in the affair, however, would haunt her.

Mrs. Lincoln's flirtatiousness and men's flattery were troublesome. Just a few months earlier, when William Wood, the acting commissioner of public buildings, who owed his appointment to Mary, traveled with her to New York, gossip linking them in romantic intimacy was nearly printed. The president received an anonymous warning that if Wood was confirmed for the permanent position, enemies would begin "circulating scandal about your most estimable Lady and Mr. Wood. They say the papers of this country and Europe will teem with it . . . was ever anything so diabolical heard of before?" Wood was not confirmed.

And Mary Lincoln didn't let the scandals stop her from playing a very active political role.[8]

Mrs. Lincoln's refusal to submissively sacrifice independent thought and action was one reason Abraham Lincoln was attracted to her. He respected her right to her own opinions, and their relationship was based on equality. It didn't mean they always agreed, particularly on politics. In the '56 campaign, for example, she opposed his support of Republican Fremont by boosting for Fillmore, the candidate of the conservative anti-Catholic American party. She thought Abraham was "monomaniacal" about honest politics, and too trusting of politicians.

Some said she "often gave Lincoln hell" and that "ferocity" characterized her political badgering of him, but more astute appraisers said there was a "moving undertow of their mutual ambitions," and Lincoln "was enormously proud of her." One family friend observed that "Lincoln thoroughly loved his wife. I had many reasons to know this in my intimacy with him, and she therefore wrought a great influence over him."[9]

In the early days of his administration, the president made no attempt to keep his wife from offering her opinions, because he knew that she was motivated only by instinct to protect their personal and political well-being. Against his wishes, she persisted in having a guard provided for him during their summer excursions to the nearby rural Anderson Cottage at the Soldiers' Home, the first official presidential retreat. Lincoln patiently endured her hysterical outbursts with a deep understanding, and a relative believed they made him love her "perhaps all the more, for this human frailty which needed his love and patience to pet and coax the sunny smile to replace the sarcasm and tears . . ." He called her "Molly" or "Mother," and she called him "Father." The couple still shared physical intimacy, although some enemies circulated a story that Mary refused to let the president share their bed for three consecutive nights until a certain gentleman was appointed lieutenant, and Lincoln pressed his war secretary to approve it. Mary confessed that while they were of "opposite natures . . . scenes are novelties with us." She didn't deny they occurred.[10]

Lizzie Keckley recalled one night when Mary's jealousy of other women even being near the president provoked a row, and the First Lady took control by ordering a protocol change so that the president would escort her rather than the ranking woman guest on state occasions. Ironically, one issue the couple disagreed on was Mary's notion of holding public receptions but halting state dinners as a cost-reduction war measure. The president argued against it. "Public receptions," she declared, "are more democratic than stupid state dinners—are more in keeping with the spirit of the institutions of our country, as you would say if called upon to make a stump speech." Point made, she won.[11]

The Lincoln partnership lent itself to her political advisory role, and once she found Cabinet members whom she trusted and would listen to her, Mrs. Lincoln formed alliances. As with Dolley and Julia, Mary's greatest power was patronage. In less than three weeks as First Lady, she fired off a letter to Secretary of State Seward. Though mistrusting him, she disliked Secretary Chase even more, and she used a patronage opportunity to also subtly stir rivalry between the two, perhaps to tumble Chase:

Col. Mygatt . . . comes to us highly recommended, as a gentleman, and an earnest Republican. He was an applicant for the collectorship of the

port of C[leveland] that place was given by Gov. Chase to another although he had been one of his earnest supporters. He desires the consulship of Honolulu & brings the highest testimonials from prominent
men in Ohio. It would be gratifying, if his request would be granted.
Trusting you will pardon, the liberty I have taken . . .[12]

Though she didn't specify whom "we" meant, Mary often implied
that the president had given her permission to make requests. Preoccupied with the war, he likely did not. Mary asserted vast independent
power in choosing officer-seekers *she* considered pro-Lincoln, and did so
without necessarily consulting the president. Sometimes, as in the case
of a man she recommended for Springfield quartermaster, the president
did review her choices. "I submitted it to President Lincoln," she told
the applicant's mother-in-law. "I presume, the appointment will be
made." In other cases, she pulled rank by using official War Department
stationery, adding the postscript "By order of President through War
Department," but signing her own name. In another case, regarding the
military position of one Thomas Stackpole of the White House staff,
she wrote Major General John E. Wool that Stackpole's appointment
was "duly appreciated by the President & myself." Then, she solicited
the signature of her husband, who did as she asked, and signed beneath
her name.

Like Abigail Adams and Julia Tyler, Mary Lincoln had no guilt
about nepotism. One of her sisters' husbands, William Wallace, was
appointed a paymaster of volunteers; another, Ninian Edwards, received a government job in Springfield. Cousin Lyman Todd was made
Lexington postmaster. She even got her minister appointed to a State
Department position in Scotland.

The fact was, Mrs. Lincoln had remarkable success with her power.
Whether it was her answered command to have another "agent" position created in the already filled Treasury Department, requesting that
the War Department make a policy of first employing honorably discharged soldiers, arm-twisting the New York collector of customs to
hire one of her favorites for the Custom House, or asking an Internal
Revenue confidant of hers at the Philadelphia office to see one of her
subjects, this First Lady held sway in administration of government departments. Lincoln evidently didn't stop her. For minor appointments,
he approved her actions; for more important positions, he listened to
her opinions and made his own decisions.[13]

Most Cabinet members carefully avoided crossing her, and an almost frightened navy secretary Gideon Welles nervously chuckled as he
approved every one of her known recommendations to him. Even the
brutal war secretary Edwin Stanton was no match for Mrs. President
Lincoln. He cantankerously bellowed at the first few memos she sent
him as petty female meddling. She retaliated by sending him published

accounts of his disagreeableness. Just after the Inauguration, Stanton recalled how "one of those indescribable half loafers," came to his office with a card from Mrs. Lincoln requesting that he be appointed to the commissary corps. Stanton blew up. "There is no place for you, and if there were, the fact that you bring me such a card would prevent my giving it to you." Then he tore up the First Lady's card. The next day, the man appeared again, this time with a letter from her with the same request. Stanton shredded the letter, and marched over to see the First Lady.

"Yes, Mr. Secretary," she tersely told him, restraining her famous temper, "I thought that as wife of the President I was entitled to ask for so small a favor." Stanton replied, "Madam, we are in the midst of a great war . . . If I should make such an appointment, I should strike at the very root of all confidence of the people . . ." Mary played wounded coquette. "Mr. Stanton, you are right, and I never will ask you for anything again." Stanton claimed that she didn't. He lied. Within two years, he would be approving the First Lady's demands for relief of a wounded soldier, a job in the War Department for a friend, and the reinstatement of a West Point cadet. All she did was couch her requests in Victorian furbelows: ". . . may I not rely on your great kindness of heart, in, giving him another trial?"[14]

The president relied upon her observations. Though he once told her, "I give you credit for sagacity, but you are disposed to magnify trifles," he gave her power. "My husband," she admitted, "placed great confidence in my knowledge of human nature." Lincoln was interested in her shrewd assessments, and he learned from her what he could. He, in turn, confided in her, to an extraordinary degree, his political strategies, positions, and estimations of fellow statesmen. Every night they discussed events in the privacy of their bedroom. In public, she almost slyly became his most crucial, often subtle, operative.

Seward was her first target. She had disliked him long before the Inaugural, and just weeks after it, she lashed out at him. "It is said that you are the power behind the throne—I'll show you that Mr. L is President yet." Mary demanded that he be fired.

"Seward is worse than Chase," she told the president. He tried to calm her. "Mother, you are mistaken; your prejudices are so violent that you do not stop to reason."

She retorted, "Father, you are too honest for this world! . . . You will generally find it a safe rule to distrust a disappointed, ambitious politician. It makes me mad to see you sit still and let that hypocrite, Seward, twine you around his finger . . ."

In her view, Salmon Chase was equally guilty of political treachery. Mary believed the news of one secret informer who told her that it was less likely that Seward was the one spreading gossip and "more likely [it] emanated from the Treasury Department . . . for I have traced many of them to the special friends of . . . Chase . . ." Mary wanted him fired because Chase "was anything for Chase." The president wearily retorted that "if I listened to you, I should soon be without a Cabinet." The heated banter subsided.[15]

General George McClellan, leader of the Union Army, recalled how the president came to him on September 8, 1861, "to ask me to pardon a man that I had ordered to be shot, suggesting I could give as a reason in the order that it was by request of the 'Lady President.'" On occasion, she admitted that he "enjoined upon me to be quiet." Mary even once revealed her power as she coyly apologized for it, to *Herald* editor James Gordon Bennett:

> From *all parties*, the cry, for a "change of Cabinet comes. I hold a letter, just received from Gov. Sprague, in my hand, who is quite as earnest, as you have been on the subject . . . if my . . . Husband were here, instead of being with the Army of the Potomac, both of these missives, would be placed before him, accompanied by my womanly suggestions . . . I have a great terror of *strong* minded Ladies, yet if a word fitly spoken and in due season, can be urged, in a time like this, we should not withhold it.[16]

"Mrs. President," as one escort called her, often swept into the Capitol Building and seated herself in the visitors' gallery for hearings and debate. On one particular day, she took in a joint meeting of both houses of Congress. It was here, on Capitol Hill, that she made one of her most loyal friends, Senator Charles Sumner of Massachusetts. When he perceived her emotions as she spoke of slavery, Sumner felt a kindred spirit, and became her tutor in the legal aspects of abolition, while Lizzie illustrated the personal aspects of it. The bachelor senator and the First Lady shared many interests, and a relationship began.

They both wanted equal opportunity for freedman and harsh treatment of the South if reconciliation came. They were opera devotees and shared a box together for performances. They enchanted each other with discussion of American literature. Sumner shared observations and recollections of his diplomatic career, and read her his private correspondence with foreign statesmen. They were clearly smitten, and there was a flirtatious quality to this affair of the heart, of which the president had no jealousy. "I was pleased," Mary recalled of Sumner, "knowing he visited no other lady . . . and that cold & haughty looking man would insist upon my telling him all the news & we would have such frequent and delightful conversations."[17]

In the press, Mary's political role was roundly criticized. The *Springfield, Massachusetts, Republican,* for example, said, "Her friends compare Mrs. Lincoln to Queen Elizabeth in her statesmanlike tastes and capabilities . . . She has ere this made and unmade the political fortunes of men . . . Nothing escapes her eye . . ." When the *Herald,* in a mood of charity, rebuked those critical journalists, Mrs. Lincoln gratefully wrote its editor, "My own nature is very sensitive; have always tried to secure the best wishes of all . . . need I repeat to you, my thanks . . . when I meet, in the columns of your paper, a kind reply, to some uncalled for attack, upon one so *little desirous* of newspaper notoriety, as my own inoffensive self."[18]

In February 1862, on the night of a rare White House ball, the Lincoln's eleven-year-old son Willie, who had been ill, relapsed into a high fever. Tad, the eight-year-old, was precocious and loud. Robert, eighteen, was an almost dour Harvard student. But Willie was remembered as "lovable . . . bright, sensible, sweet-tempered and gentle-mannered." Throughout the evening of her ball, the First Lady, resplendent in white satin and black lace, managed a smile at guests as the Marine Band played. Alternately, she and the president hurried upstairs to check on Willie. From that night on for several days, Mary kept a bedside vigil, to no avail.

Little Willie died.

"We loved him so," the president said simply, with the knowledge that thousands of sons were dying on battlefields. Mary, however, was devastasted beyond consolation. Her prostrate hysterics were quieted by lapses as she lay on her bed, stunned. She suffered convulsions. She refused ever again to enter the Green Room, where Willie was embalmed. Her husband hired a nurse to watch Mary. He pleaded with Mary's sister Elizabeth to come and comfort her, and then begged her to stay indefinitely.

Just four days before Willie died, Mary suffered a particularly vicious attack in the form of a published poem, "The Lady-President's Ball," by Eleanor Donnelly, a bitter account of a fictitious soldier who was dying on the street, looking into the mirthful White House. It juxtaposed the low compensation to families of killed soldiers with Mary's lavish style. On the heels of this appeared a sarcastic editorial by journalist Mary Clemmer Ames, who claimed that while American women "sewed, scraped lint, made bandages," Mrs. Lincoln "spent her time rolling to and fro between Washington and New York, intent on extravagant purchases for herself . . ." For entertaining during wartime, Mrs. Lincoln was vilified, but when she halted weekly band concerts, she was also criticized. The vilest rumor to be printed was that she beat her children. She received few sympathy letters about Willie. As a result of all this, Mary's fragile temperament cracked. She suffered from what was later termed a "mild nervous breakdown," and "severe depression."

So distraught was she that one day her husband gently placed his arm around her, and spoke carefully, pointing.

"Mother, do you see that large white building on the hill yonder?

Try and control your grief, or it will drive you mad, and we will have to send you there."

It was a lunatic asylum. [19]

— 20 —

A Civil War

THE FIRST LADY found relief in spiritualism. She began gathering information about "the other side," and believed that "a very slight veil separates us, from the 'loved & lost' . . ." She began consulting mediums, and actually held a White House seance. One medium, Madame Laurie of Georgetown, warned her that "the Cabinet were all enemies of the President, working for themselves," and they'd have to be dismissed. Did Mrs. Lincoln need any further proof of the power of mediums? At the same moment Mary was placing faith in crystal balls, Julia Tyler was receiving messages from "the other side" through her dreams. [1]

Weeks before Willie Lincoln died, not far away in the Confederate capital of Richmond, former President Tyler was taking his seat as a member of the rebel Congress. Though seventy-one, Tyler was in good health, and managed to travel from his tidewater manse, Sherwood Forest, without Julia. On the night of January 9, however, "Mrs. Ex-President Tyler" had a frightening premonitory dream that her husband was ill. She rushed to Richmond. He was fine. Six days later, he died, precisely as her extrasensory perception predicted he would.

This aging coquette found herself mistress of an estate in danger of Yankee troop invasion, bills mounting around her, slaves starting to run for freedom, and her status as First Lady diminished in official Washington, where she was now viewed as the powerless widow of a secessionist, particularly inconvenient at that very moment. War had become fairly *un*chivalrous.

Her immediate, frantic concern was to get herself and her younger children to the safe haven of Mother Gardiner's on Staten Island, in New York, but letters were blocked at the Mason-Dixon line, and General McLellan's troops were sweeping near Sherwood.

Working her connections as the Battle of Richmond raged, however, Julia miraculously arranged for the general to order a *guard* placed around Sherwood. And she broke the stalled mail to Mother by having her letters hand-delivered to Leesburg, and sent to Baltimore for regular delivery in New York. Others of the sorority were suffering with the war.

Ensconced at the former president's Hudson River mansion, Angelica Van Buren remained a southerner at heart, sending blankets to imprisoned Confederates at an Elmira, New York, prison. Embittered Harriet Lane, now married and living in Baltimore, remained a Unionist, but like "Nunc," was upset at the devastation of the Alabama home of the late Senator King, which his niece Katherine Ellis had to evacuate. Louisa Adams had died in Washington, fighting for abolition, while Margaret Taylor died a comfortable southern widow, with slaves freed only upon her death. Taking an abolition stand, Jane Pierce saw the beginning of the conflict, and disagreed with her southern-sympathizing husband. Anna Harrison, nearly ninety, lived only to encourage her grandson Benjamin to fight for the Union.

Sarah Polk, crumbling along with her aging mansion, in which she would live for nearly a half-century of widowhood, publicly declared her property, marked by a rickety iron fence, as neutral territory because she was a president's widow. Privately, she'd say that "my sympathies" were with "the lives of the people with whom I always lived, and whose ways were my ways . . ." Sensing the demise of slavery, she sold her cotton plantation and slaves in 1860. Mrs. Polk made a great profit before the chance was missed. Those blacks not sold, she hired out to work, keeping them as property. The high infant-mortality rate of her slaves never moved her to secure medical care for them, and though women like Julia Tyler—who was herself indifferent to religion—offered religious training for her slaves if the slaves desired, pious Sarah did not. She would have no financial woes during the War Between the States.[2]

Another Julia, this one born to the South but wed to the North, struggled with slavery and secession. The wife of Union brigadier general Ulysses S. Grant—who was making a sudden and estimable reputation for himself in the war—she owned four slaves. As a child, she had grown emotionally close to those owned by her father, and sneaked them money for tobacco. "I think our people were very happy," she wrote, adding "the young ones became somewhat demoralized about the beginning of the Rebellion, when all the *comforts* of slavery passed away forever." There was obvious tension between Julia and her abolitionist mother-in-law. "Ulys" respected Julia's independence, and never asked her to surrender her slaves, although since they traveled with her— except for when she leased them while in free territory—they remained conspicuous. Julia loved her slaves as people and treated them as family, but as time went on, Mrs. Grant would find her slaveholding increasingly compromised her husband, and her own as-yet-unstated ambition. "When reading patriotic speeches," she admitted, "my blood seemed to course more rapidly . . ." Like Mrs. Lincoln, Julia Grant craved prominence.

In the 1860 election, Julia professed loyalty to the Democrats—which she just as quickly admitted was because her father was one. "My dear husband Ulys," she recalled, "read aloud to me every speech for and against secession. I was very much disturbed in my political sentiments, feeling that the states had a right to go out of the Union . . . and yet thought it the duty of the national government to prevent a dismemberment of the Union, even if coercion should be necessary . . ." While "reading aloud the papers" and discussing the war, Ulys was also forcing Julia to no longer avoid, but confront, her loyalties.

Mrs. Grant became angered with southern friends, and she remonstrated them for sneaking mail through enemy lines. Their condescending smiles and "we know you will not" in response to her threats to report them left her frustrated. Julia Dent Grant was emerging as a shrewd woman. Someday she would herself prove, to friend and foe, that she had power. Admittedly, at times she could be "dreadfully puzzled by the horrid old Constitution," but boasted, "I was all right on the duties of national government."

While Ulysses had struggled from tannery to real estate, Julia had been the sole booster of his morale. She had been forced by their reduced lot to clean her own floors and feed her chickens. In her view, the Grants deserved not just better, but best. When he became the Galena, Illinois, recruiting chairman, she herself made his uniform. When he left for the front, he took heart in the fact that "Julia takes a very sensible view of the present difficulties . . . and will not throw a single obstacle in the way . . ." She took to calling him "Victor" for Italian military hero Victor Emmanuel, but did object to his tobacco addiction, and often threw out his cigars.

When her mother said Ulys was "made for great things," Julia went further. "Wait until . . . [he] . . . becomes President."

Julia had power over Ulys. He found her physically appealing, despite her badly crossed eyes and stumpy figure. When separated, he had once admitted, "You can have but little idea of the influance [sic] you have over me Julia, even while so far away. If I feel tempted to do any thing that I think is not right I am shure [sic] to think, 'Well now if Julia saw me would I do so' and thus it is absent or present I am more or less governed by what I think is your will."

Julia's extrasensory perception and dreams held momentous significance for her, and she claimed even to have complete visualization of Grant's upcoming military battles. Uncannily, her predictions often came true. Always she sensed power in her path. Once, during a period of stressful poverty, she asked herself, "Is this my destiny?" and claimed a "silvery light" came over her and responded, "No, no this is not your destiny!" Julia Grant had gone from great comfort as a daughter to the depths of poverty as a wife. Behind her ambition was a longing for such wealth that material insecurity would never again threaten her.

For now, her "destiny" was as an army wife, who frequently lived in camp, calming her Grant. As a camp nurse, she was shaken by the sight of gangrene, injured, shell-shocked, and amputated soldiers, the smell of antiseptics, the specter of young death. Sentiment was always her hubris, and Mrs. Grant returned to her husband's headquarters each day "laden with petitions for discharges." Finally, he "positively prohibited" her continued work there. "I hear of these all day long and I sent for you to come that I might have a rest from all this sad part," he admonished her. "I became so absorbed in these poor fellows, the wounded, the sick and the dying," Julia later revealed, "I could think of nothing else."[3]

Nursing the injured catalyzed Mrs. Lincoln back to a public role. Something genuinely tender was struck in the relationship between soldier and First Lady. She spent nearly every day walking through the hospital aisles of long rows of cots, herself distributing fresh fruits, and placing bouquets at each pillow. She took dictation from men missing arms. A newspaper noted, "It may not be known that Mrs. Lincoln has contributed more than any other lady . . . from her private purse, to alleviate the sufferings of our wounded soldiers," without "fear of contagion and the outcries of pestilence . . ."

It was extremely rare that such an account reached print. Mary wanted her charity to remain private. As Stoddart noted, "She rarely takes outside company with her upon these errands, and she thereby loses opportunities. If she were worldly wise she would carry newspaper correspondents, from two to five, of both sexes, every time she went, and she would have them take shorthand notes of what she says to the sick soldiers and of what the sick soldiers say to her . . ." The First Lady also privately raised one thousand dollars for the wards, through the president obtained citruses to prevent scurvy, and had fresh bread sent from the White House kitchens to malnourished men. When a hamper of wine was sent to her, Mrs. Lincoln sent it to the hospital.

Soldiers responded by naming a "Camp Mary Lincoln." One passing regiment offered a military salute to her as she reviewed them with the president and Tad, and the scene was illustrated for *Harper's Weekly*. Yet there were those who sarcastically dubbed her "the Yankee nurse." When her visits were "treated by surgeons as impertinent meddling," she hurtfully retreated, saying she would do nothing that might incur "the displeasure of the Surgeons and others in authority . . ."[4]

"Will we ever awake," she asked as the war dragged on "from this hideous nightmare?" Displaced from the wards, she plunged into military affairs, encouraged by the president's sharing of military news and

secrets with her. Her first victim was General McClellan. She wanted him out, and from New York wrote the president that "Many . . . would almost worship you, if you would put a fighting General, in the place of McClellan . . . McClellan & his slowness are vehemently discussed." It encouraged Lincoln's already low opinion of the general, and in fact McClellan was removed from command within a week of her letter.

During the Battle of Bull Run in July 1861, she had gone to the White House roof to hear the distant sounds of battle. Now, she determined to go to the battlefront, suggesting to the president that they visit General Hooker's nearby encampment. The *Sacramento Union* reported, "The thoughtful wife of the President . . . ought to have the credit of originating the plan of a tour through the Army by the President, as she saw what an excellent effect would be given to the troops . . ." To General Daniel Sickles, Mary wrote that she regretted a missed chance to talk "Virginia affairs" with him.

On a visit of Fort Stevens, she unleashed furious hell on Secretary Stanton when bullets flew around her as she stood on the parapet. "I can assure you of one thing, Mr. Secretary, if I had had a few ladies with me the Rebels would not have been permitted to get away as they did!"

She even showed interest in military supplies, once sending a Kentucky colonel a pair of revolvers and a saber, remarking, "On every field the prowess of the Kentuckians has been manifested." On another occasion, she asked Assistant War Secretary Thomas Scott to "favor me with the authority," to direct the Baltimore quartermaster to buy several hundred Kentucky horses being offered for sale, "at government prices, subject to Government inspection," because "it would gratify me, to see the horses used from my native state . . ."[5]

Mary Lincoln's enduring legacy, however, went largely uncredited. By the summer of 1862, she had become an unabashed abolitionist. It became her issue, and not since Abigail Adams had a First Lady advocated human rights so convincingly, and with such commitment. Martha Washington had helped veterans, Dolley Madison, orphans, and Harriet Lane, American Indians. Now, Mary Lincoln involved herself with black welfare. In fact, "Mrs. President Lincoln" became so devoted to her cause that she risked a scandal of national and political proportions.

She diverted funds.

The First Lady quietly had one thousand dollars that was allocated for soldier care given instead to her work on behalf of "all the oppressed colored race." She had found a public outlet in the Contraband Relief Association. Mrs. Keckley, who said she "knew what freedom is, because I know what slavery was," had suggested the formation of a branch group in her own church, and had introduced the First Lady to its goals. Members were both black and white, and their mission was to provide temporary welfare for freedman, many of whom managed to drift North but needed assistance in housing, education, and employment. On trips North, the First Lady spoke as a fund-raiser for the association to wealthy private citizens. The "project" seemed even to be the purpose of one excursion to New York. She herself gave an initial two-hundred-dollar donation, and made "frequent contributions . . ."

Her devotion to helping blacks reached in all directions. A great number of her patronage successes were on behalf of former slaves. She wrote letters of introduction—once, for the Reverend Mr. Hamilton, another time for Mrs. Johnson, who, in Mary's words, was "an estimable colored woman . . . an active nurse . . . who had once been a slave," adding that both were "genteel and intelligent . . ." She openly grieved over the premature death of abolitionist and Illinois congressman Owen Lovejoy. The First Lady lobbied by mail Senator Sumner and others to publicly speak against a rumored Cabinet appointment of one General N. P. Banks, because he was not an abolitionist. And she became the first First Lady to welcome blacks as White House *guests*, permitting a Sunday School festival group to use the South Lawn for a picnic, ordering the staff to "have everything done in the grand style" for them.

But she did not restrict black people to the lawn. The Lincolns opened the doors of the White House rooms to blacks. Mrs. Lincoln publicly received a black nurse "who brought a gift as a testimonial of the appreciation of her race." The most prominent black orator and leader of the day, Frederick Douglass, was invited to take tea with the president.

Mary recalled how Sumner told her "he wishes my husband was as ardent an abolitionist as I am." Another abolitionist, Mrs. H. C. Ingersoll, went further, and said Mary's exposure to slavery was more horrifying than anything Lincoln could have experienced. "Of slavery," Ingersoll wrote, "her expressions were strong enough to satisfy any abolitionist." Sumner's friend and fellow abolitionist Jane Grey Swisshelm, the highly respected publisher of *Saturday Visitor,* was initially uninterested in meeting Mary because of what she believed of the gossip. But Swisshelm changed her mind after several lengthy conversations on abolition legislation. "I recognized," Swisshelm later recalled, "Mrs. Lincoln as a loyal, liberty-loving woman, more staunch than even her husband in opposition to the rebellion . . . she was more radically opposed to slavery" than the president and she "urged him to Emancipation as a matter of right, long before he saw it as a matter of necessity." Abraham Lincoln's cornerstone achievement was Mary Todd's as well. On New Year's Day 1863, the president signed the Emancipation Proclamation.

When a friend congratulated her, the First Lady responded ecstatically of "emancipaton, from the great evil, that has been so long allowed, to curse the land. The decree, has gone forth, that 'all men are free,' and all the perfidious acts . . . cannot eradicate the seal, that has been placed on the 'Emancipation Proclamation.' It is a rich & precious legacy . . ."[6]

And yet, publicly, she demurred when people credited her own achievement on emancipation. Swisshelm observed that "I never knew a woman who more completely merged herself in her husband. Whatever aid or counsel she gave him, in her eyes his acts were his own, and she never sought any of the credit due to them." The Emancipation Proclamation was a high point for Mary in Washington. That was quite definitely not the emotion for the woman who slipped into the dark capital six nights later. Through yet another gentleman admirer of yore—now luckily the *Union*'s General Dix—a precious pass South was secured by Julia Tyler.

On January 7, Julia left Washington for Sherwood. Much as she would have enjoyed seeing her old beloved White House, even the former Lovely Lady Presidentress wouldn't have the gall to pay a visit to Mrs. Lincoln. Instead, in the Confederate capital of Richmond, she visited Varina Davis, the other First Lady. Julia was now determined to sell Sherwood, and give up her fervent adoption of Dixie as bill collectors became impatient. She planned on safely settling in with Mother Gardiner and financial security in New York. Before doing so, she hoped to sell her Sherwood cotton for inflated prices, but when her coach stopped at a northern border and she wouldn't take an oath of allegiance, the former First Lady was refused passage.[7] The Confederates began suffering war losses. That July, the little Pennsylvania farmtown through which so many Rebels passed north became the sight of the decisive blow to the Confederacy. It was called Gettysburg.

As the battle there raged on, the First Lady lay semiconscious, not in the White House but in a military hospital.

While at the Soldiers' Home, Mary had learned of the battle, and headed back into town to be with her husband. During the ride, her carriage became detached and she was thrown from it, smashing the back of her skull on a stone. She was rushed to a nearby medical unit. Someone had sabotaged the carriage.

Days of physical agony followed. The wound was open for some time, and the skull exposed. It became infected, and suppurated, and had to be reopened. Robert would later admit that "mother has never quite recovered from the effects of her fall."[8]

But by autumn, Mary was back in New York, buying with a vengeance, bustling through the garlanded columns of Lord & Taylor, spending well beyond her means. Another woman was walking the same marble aisles. Lord & Taylor was a shop preferred by the recently returned "undergrounder," who now sometimes used an alias.

Mrs. Ex-President Tyler decided that her options to either concentrate on selling cotton or escape to New York were of equal importance. She broke two laws in one wink. Unable to get North legally, she did so illegally, by boarding a blockade runner out of North Carolina for Bermuda, where she reveled in the high life of the elite self-exiled Confederate community there. Meanwhile, her cotton bales were shipped to Naussau and sold for high prices. After two weeks on the island, Mrs. Tyler secured passage on a flag-of-truce ship to New York. In New York, Julia sent flirtatious letters to an imprisoned friend, and became active in the underground "Copperheads," a sympathy movement for Confederates. Shopping, however, proved a better tonic for Julia than passing out "Copperhead" leaflets. At her mother's Staten Island home, she found turmoil. Julia's Unionist brother David bickered with her bitterly. When he struck Julia, Mother Gardiner, banished him. David would not forget.[9]

Shortly after Mrs. Lincoln finished up *her* shopping and returned to Washington, a familiar face brightened her life. Her dear sister Emilie Helm, now widow of a Confederate soldier, had come to visit Mary with her three small children. When the president was informed that like Mrs. Tyler, Emilie had refused to take an oath of allegiance at the border, he issued the command, "Send her to me." Mary and Emilie were extremely close. Thankful just to be together, they avoided war talk because, as Emilie scrawled in her diary, it was "like tearing open a fresh and bleeding wound and the pain is too great for self-control . . . This frightful war comes between us like a barrier of granite closing our lips but not our hearts, for though our tongues are tied, we weep over our dead together and express through clasped hands the sympathy we feel for each other . . ." The sight of her deteriorated sister that spring of 1864 overcame Emilie.

When she entered Mary's room quickly, Emilie was shocked at "the frightened look in her eyes" One night, "Little Sister" was awakened when the First Lady, smiling broadly but with tears streaming from her shining eyes, whispered that dead Willie "comes to me every night, and stands at the foot of my bed with the same sweet, adorable smile he has always had . . . You cannot dream of the comfort this gives me." She told Emilie that Willie once brought her other dead son, Eddie, and her brother Alec, a Confederate killed in the war. The president one night gently told Emilie, "I hope you can . . . spend the summer with us . . . you and Mary love each other—it is good for her to have you with her—I feel worried about Mary, her nerves have gone to pieces; she cannot hide from me that the strain she has been under has been too much for her mental as well as her physical health."

Emilie was worried. "It is unnatural and abnormal, it frightens me. It does not seem like Sister Mary to be so nervous and wrought up. She is on a terrible strain and her smiles seem forced. She is frightened about Robert going into the Army."

Robert was of the age to fight, but Mary tearfully begged the president not to send him, crying, "I am so frightened he may never come back to us!" The issue renewed Mary's vulnerability to criticism. One day while she and Emilie entertained General Sickles and New York's Senator Harris, the latter sharply asked why Robert wasn't fighting. "If fault there be," she admitted, "it is mine . . ." Harris then turned on Emilie, provoking her to retort, "[I]f I had twenty sons, they should all be fighting yours."[10]

Of Mary's immediate Todd family, four brothers and three brothers-in-law were Confederate soldiers. She had only contempt for them, and said she hoped they would all be killed, because "[t]hey would kill my husband if they could, and destroy our Government—the dearest of all things to us." When sister Martha came to Washington, demanding to see Mary, she was refused, but the president issued her a return pass South. One newspaper, however, said that the real reason Martha White had obtained a White House pass was to transport large medical supply trunks South. The most absurd allusion questioning the First Lady's true loyalty was a smear that rebel spies came by ladder to her bedroom window, from which she passed them military secrets. As Mary bitterly explained, "I seem to be the scapegoat for both the North and the South![11]

Mrs. Lincoln's wish to see the war end came closer to fruition on March 12, 1864, when Ulysses S. Grant was appointed General in Chief of the Armies. It was a role his wife knew *they* would fill, and

Julia Grant prepared for her White House presentation and first meeting with Mary Todd Lincoln.

Julia remained self-conscious about her crossed eyes, which made her stride in a sideways crablike gait, but she was a witty conversationalist, excellent dancer, and graceful horsewoman. She was warmhearted, spontaneous, and genuine. Like Mrs. Lincoln, Mrs. Grant loved the theater, and she loved money. She had an equal weakness for New York fashions and décolletage; her husband was as unsuccessful as the president in his protests over such bosom exposure. From the Grant suite at the Willard, Julia proceeded to the White House in a gown that would rival Mrs. Lincoln's, accompanied by Grant's military assistant, Adam Badeau.

Though often tardy, on this occasion Mrs. Grant arrived on time. When she was passed up in the receiving line rather unceremoniously, Badeau repeated her name to President Lincoln: "Mrs. General Grant." Lincoln looked at her with "infinite kindness." Mary sized up Julia then effusively engaged her in conversation, telling Badeau to please Mrs. Grant by taking her through the conservatories for a private tour. The meeting of the two women stirred enough public interest that an artist memorialized the moment by mass-producing a large engraving of the event, placing their husbands in the scene for undeniably further market appeal. When Julia's son, after seeing the uniforms of Washington and Jackson in a museum, asked if his father's clothes were there too, she replied, "Not yet, Jess dear."[12]

Shortly, however, the First Lady bickered about Grant with the president: "He is a butcher . . . not fit to be at the head of an army," Mary complained. "[H]e . . . manages to claim victory, but . . . loses two men to the enemy's one . . . should he . . . remain in power, he would depopulate the North. Grant, I repeat, is an obstinate fool . . ." The president upbraided her, "Well, Mother, supposing that we give you command of the army. No doubt you would do much better than any general that has been tried."[13]

In Grant's spring campaign, his hundred-thousand-man Army of the Potomac swept through Charles City, Virginia. On May 7, Sherwood was taken and occupied by a black brigade commanded by General Wild. Julia Tyler's manager was imprisoned, and from New York a desperate Mrs. Tyler fired off a plea to President Lincoln that he be freed, tugging on his heartstrings by using Mrs. Lincoln as a ploy. "By the memory of my Husband, and what you must be assured would have been his course in your place, had your Wife appealed to him, remove from me these causes for anxious suspense."

Lincoln merely passed on her request, but while it got bogged down in the slowness of government administration, Sherwood was overrun by blacks: A schoolroom was set up in the hall where Julia had danced; the smokehouses and barns became home to drifters; mirrors, busts, and

GRAND RECEPTION ✦ NOTABILITIES ✦ NATION.
AT THE WHITE HOUSE 1865
Dedicated to Mrs. Abraham Lincoln,
by the Publishers of Frank Leslie's Chimney Corner?

china were smashed or stolen; silks were torn from the sofas; her ornamental gardens were dug up for vegetable planting. Julie was less concerned with sentiment than resale values. Again she fired off a missive
to Lincoln, this time pointedly. "Will President Lincoln have the kindness to inform Mrs. (Ex-President) Tyler whether her home on the
James River can be withdrawn from the hands of the negro . . . and
restored to the charges of her manager . . . though her estate has been
subjected to wreck and devastation within doors and without . . ."
While she was at it, Mrs. Ex demanded that the Union pay rent on her
country home, Villa Margaret, which its soldiers had now occupied.

Like Mrs. Madison, the widow Julia was gravely concerned about
money. As Mother Gardiner's health began sinking rapidly, Julia was
reminded of the vast fortune that might also slip away if her estranged
brother David was kept in the will. In Julia's presence, lawyers came to
Mrs. Gardiner's deathbed with a new will, *sans* David, as she went in
and out of lucidity. Then Julia lifted her dying mother from her bed,
holding her steadily as she signed the new will. Mother fell back, dying
four hours later.[14]

Mrs. Lincoln's trouble was the election campaign. There was a new
rumor, printed in the *Crisis,* which claimed that she'd become drunk
with Russian sailors on a yacht in New York. Lies could enrage her, but

the truth terrorized her. The charge of accepting bribery for her political patronage was technically true. The First Lady had taken gifts from many seeking political favors, and she naively accepted them as tokens of esteem rather than obligation. As First Lady, she had been offered limitless credit at stores. In one 1864 New York trip alone, it was said, "From the early hours until late in the evening, Mrs. Lincoln ransacked the treasures of the Broadway dry goods stores."

Now, she was twenty-seven thousand dollars in debt.

She knew that if her husband lost the election, more than his career was at stake. Hysterically, she told Lizzie, "If he is reelected, I can keep him in ignorance of my affairs; but if he is defeated, then the bills will be sent in, and he will know all." She begged A. T. Stewart, "soliciting as an especial favor" of a "delay of . . . my account." Fear that political rivals of Lincoln would learn of her debts, she devised a panicked scheme: "The Republican politicians must pay my debts. Hundreds of them are getting immensely rich off the patronage of my husband, and it is but fair that they should help me out of my embarrassment." She approached friends like the commissioner of agriculture, whom she had helped get the position. "Oh, that lady has set here on this here sofa and shed tears by the pint a begging me to pay her debts," he said, "which was unbeknownst to the President." She spun a web of intrigue by sharing political secrets with a host of politicos, whom she then barraged for either personal loans or declared support for Lincoln. Politician George Ashum's letter to General Banks illustrated: "There can be no doubt but that Mr. C[hase] is desperately bent on supplanting the President . . . I have had but little conversation with him directly on the subject, but Mrs. L——— keeps me thoroughy informed of every-thing . . ."

Some of these men perhaps feared that she knew too much about their own political chicanery, and feared blackmail. So, some of them "donated" money to her, made loans, or put off creditors. Still it was impossible for Mary to surmount her enormous debts. At one point, she even considered selling the manure on the White House lawn as fertilizer to pay the bills.[15]

But if Mary's finances didn't then become public, other attempts were being made to create an issue out of her. The New York World revived the "crockery businesss" of the cost of her china. One Democratic worker admitted, "I have been writing out all the bad things I have heard of Lincoln and his wife, hoping to get them into the papers . . ." Plans for an organized anti–First Lady publicity campaign were confirmed by B. B. French: "Rumors are about, that the Democrats are getting up something in which they intend to show up Madam Lincoln." The attorney general's diary referred to "a secret pamphlet . . . levelled agst. Mrs. L." Even anti-Lincoln Republicans circulated leaflets to congressmen and soldiers condemning the president through his wife. The threat of a widespread smear, however, never materialized.[16]

Mrs. Lincoln explained, "All that I ever did was acutated by the purest motives, but where there are designing wicked men & I truly may say women—such acts are so often misinterpreted . . ." Her interest in power waned: "My position, requires my presence, where my heart is so far from being." When a reporter offered to praise her in an editorial, the First Lady poignantly broke down. "Oh, it is no use to make any defense; all such efforts would only make me a target for new attacks. I do not belong to the public; my character is wholly domestic, and the public have nothing to do with it. I know it seems hard that I should be maligned, and I used to shed many bitter tears about it, but since . . . Willie died—all these shafts have no power to wound me . . . that I had wronged no one, that is all I have wished . . ."

Election day was bleak. Between jaunts over to the War Department Telegraph Office for vote returns, Lincoln noticed his depressed wife: "She is more anxious than I am." When she learned that he had won, Mary told Lizzie, "I almost wish it were otherwise. Poor Mr. Lincoln is looking so broken-hearted, so completely worn out, I fear he will not get through the next four years."

At the Inaugural, she watched the new vice president, Andrew Johnson, take his oath under the influence of medicinal alcohol. In her eyes, it was a strike against him. But something more was bothering her in March 1865. The First Lady seemed to sense some omen, even though a Union victory was now almost certain.

On some strange impulse, Mary Todd Lincoln ordered one thousand dollars' worth of new black mourning clothes.[17]

– 21 –

1865

TWO WEEKS AFTER the Inaugural, Mary Lincoln joined her husband on a visit to Grant's headquarters in City Point, Virginia, to inspect and review troops. For Julia Grant, it was a social coup, but she was in for a surprise if she expected a personal triumph among the wives of other military leaders also there. By Mrs. Lincoln's definition, a First Lady ranked higher than a General in Chief's wife.[1]

Since 1862, Julia had been living in camp with Ulys whenever his army was stationary. The Confederates monitored her movements, and she once came perilously close to capture by General Van Dorn. When separated from him, Julia kept Ulys's morale high with letters "full of ambition of what you expect of me," he once wrote her. In turn, he shared with her not just military information but his goals, adding that they were confidential.[2]

Julia had an influencce over the general. Besides persuading him to pardon some deserters, she could modify his drinking habits. One observer praised her "quiet firm control," while General Porter said she was a "woman of much great intelligence, and exceedingly well informed upon all public matters." Primitive army quarters didn't prevent her physical affection either, Porter chronicling that the Grants "would seek a quiet corner of his quarters of an evening, and sit with her hand in his, manifesting the most ardent devotion; and if a staff-officer came accidentally upon them, they would look as bashful as two young lovers . . ." Though he unfolded his detailed military map to reveal the secret movements that would finally crush Dixie, Julia made no attempt, according to Badeau, "of influencing his military decisions . . . except in regard to individuals . . ."[3]

Even outside of camp, Mrs. Grant was now being treated as an important person. War Secretary Stanton sent her telegrams with army movement information. At a Georgetown party, her opinion on Grant's "Paducah" program to bring the South back into the Union was sought. At one point, she was seriously considered as a possible mediator for Grant with Confederate General Longstreet's wife, a role she begged Ulys to allow her to play because "of the desire I always had shown for having a voice in great affairs." When he told her, "The men have fought this war and the men will finish it," she became "silent, indignant and disappointed."[4]

Word of her power spread through the army. One contingent of officers, whose military plans differed from Grant's assignment of Sherman to Vicksburg, asked Julia to be "mediator" between them and her husband. Generals Hurlbut, Marsh, and McPherson, who wanted Grant to reassign colleague Rosecrans to another duty, approached her because, as the latter said, "We want to reach the General's ear through you . . ." She did so. In camp, she also favorably impressed the national war-news correspondents. That, combined with the fact that there had been considerable talk of Grant for president against Lincoln in '64, undoubtedly nettled Mary Lincoln. When asked if the general would run, Mrs. Grant had "said most emphatically that her husband would not think for one moment of accepting a nomination." That meant for the moment. Mary Lincoln knew political vagueness when she heard it.[5]

Mary Lincoln had little use for women as a group, or for a national movement for their equality in voting, property laws, professions, and wages. Her involvement with female public citizens came through either war effort or helping single individuals. Through Mrs. Swisshelm, Mary joined women's committees for charitable events like the "Sanity Fair" fund-raisers for nursing supplies. When Swisshelm asked the First Lady to approach Secretary Stanton with a proposal to supplement the army with a female nurse corps, the First Lady "was willing to cooperate." She helped women get Treasury Department jobs and War Department permission to visit male kin in military schools. Independently, Mrs. Lincoln wrote directly to the governor of New York pleading the case of Mary Real, a woman sentenced to hard labor after being found guilty of murdering her husband when she discovered he had a mistress. When a woman was a victim, Mary seemed stirred. But those that she sensed were in any way as ambitious as herself were a different story.[6]

As soon as Mrs. Lincoln was settled at City Point and receiving callers, Julia came to see her. The First Lady was seated on a sofa, engaged in conversation. When she rose, Julia took her seat. When Julia looked up, she heard the voice of an angry Mrs. Lincoln. "How dare you be seated, until I invite you?" Julia fumbled, and rose. Mrs. Lincoln cooled down, invited Mrs. Grant back to share the sofa, and they were wedged in tightly together. After a very uncomfortable moment, Julia rose and "quietly" took a nearby chair. By this time, the president had no doubt told Mary that on a previous visit to the Grants, he and Julia had seriously discussed the possible peace terms.[7]

The day after the sofa incident, the two women were being driven in a rickety ambulance carriage over knee-deep mud, hitting bumps and smashing their bonnets, on their way to join their husbands at a military review. Impatiently, Mrs. Lincoln attempted to leave the carriage and walk. Julia persuaded her not to. When Badeau, their escort, made small talk about their excursion and mentioned that General Griffin's wife had received permission to be with the men, Mary flared: "What do you mean by that, sir? Do you mean to say that she saw the President alone? . . . I never allow the President to see any woman alone . . ." An uncomfortable Julia found herself placating Mrs. Lincoln. The next day, again in an ambulance, headed to a review of General Ord's troops, Mary noticed his wife on a horse, near the president. "What does that woman mean?" Mary shouted to Mrs. Grant. "Does she suppose that he wants her by the side of him?" The smiling Mrs. Ord came up to the First Lady, who instantly "insulted her . . . [with] . . . vile names" in front of everyone there.

Suddenly, Julia snapped back to defend Mrs. Ord.

Without missing a beat, Mary Lincoln spewed her accurate suspicion on Julia Grant: "I suppose you think you'll get to the White House yourself, don't you?" A mortified Mrs. Grant pulled herself up, saying she was quite satisfied with the position she had. Mary gave her one more dig. "Oh! you had better take it if you can get it. 'Tis very nice."[8]

Mary Lincoln made a second trip on April 5 to Julia Grant's camp, after visiting the captured Richmond with a group including Senator Sumner. Once again, the president's wife and the general's wife found each other's unwanted presence. Just as the First Lady was discussing the fall of the Confederacy, Mrs. Grant entered. Mrs. Lincoln turned to her guests and drolly asked, "Suppose we ask Mrs. Grant. Let *her* answer this important question . . . What should be done with the Confederate President . . . in the event of his capture." Rather than confuse Julia, as she probably intended, Mary's question gave Mrs. Grant a chance to display her emerging savvy. "I would trust him," she said, "to the mercy of our always just and most gracious President." Julia would proudly recall how the "gentleman" told her "it was a most diplomatic answer." She did not mention Mrs. Lincoln.

Both women toured Richmond. Mary, who received her requested tour of Varina Davis's evacuated Confederate White House, suspiciously remarked it was still full of "enemies," and spoke of harsh retribution against the conquered. Julia responded with emotion. "I fell to thinking of all the sad tragedies of the past four years . . . homes made desolate . . . hearts broken! How many youth sacrificed! . . . And tears, great tears, fell from my eyes."

On the presidential transport *River Queen*, Mrs. Grant attempted again to be friendly. From the forward cabin Julia instructed an aide to offer Mary, on the outside deck, a comfortable upholstered chair. The First Lady glared at him, and refused his offer. As far as Julia was concerned, it was the last straw. Mrs. Grant moved to the *Martin*, and the ladies occupied separate vessels, known as "Mrs. Lincoln's Boat" and "Mrs. Grant's Boat," Mary insisting that her own always lie nearest the dock. Julia was wounded when she was pointedly left off the invitation list of Mary's planned party on the *River Queen*. Just before the party began, however, Julia ordered the *Martin* to take her on a twenty-mile pleasure trip, along with the one military band—which angered Mary, since her party would have to go without music. As the *Martin* passed the *River Queen*, the bandleader asked Mrs. Grant if there was anything special she wanted to hear. She "coolly" responded, "Yes, play 'Now, You'll Remember Me.'"[9]

Upon return to Washington, celebrating the end of the war, Mary confided to Lizzie about the president, "I have a presentiment that he will meet with a sudden and violent death." She was shaken by his recurring dream of his own funeral and death at the hand of an assassin. She even softened her attitude toward Grant. He was the Union's national hero, having signed the peace treaty with the Confederates. She invited him—without Julia Grant or President Lincoln—to promenade by carriage with her through the illuminated capital on April 13. Since she had been pointedly left out, an insulted Julia Grant insisted that under no circumstances would they accept the First Lady's invitation, personally extended by the president, to join the Lincolns the very next evening for a performance of *Our American Cousin* at Ford's Theater. Julia's no was ironclad. They would leave the night of the fourteenth to see their children in New Jersey.

On the day of the fourteenth, after the premature announcement that the Grants would attend the theater with the Lincolns, a seedy-looking fellow knocked on Julia's door at the Willard, and presented a bouquet and message "from Mrs. Lincoln" that "she will call for you at exactly eight o'clock." To Julia, it sounded like "a command." She told him no, and to "deliver my message to Mrs. Lincoln . . ." Julia instantly felt something askew. She knew Mary wouldn't be sending her flowers. She sent a frantic note by messenger to Ulys, pleading with him to be ready to leave town. She had three of his staff officers, who called on her that day, urge him to be prompt. "I do not know," she wrote, "what possessed me to take such a freak . . ."

While lunching in the Willard restaurant, Mrs. Grant noticed four men. One of them was the "messenger." Another strained to eavesdrop on her. "I thought he was crazy," she recalled. By dusk, Julia felt ominously "glad" as she and the general headed for the station. When a man on horseback rode up beside their carriage, then turned around and rode toward them, staring at the Grants, she recognized him as one of the men from the restaurant. The Grants caught their train and left Washington.[10]

Meanwhile, back at the White House, Mary Lincoln was dressing for the theater. Just two weeks before, she had again exercised her powers by hastily approving an order assigning local policeman John F. Parker to White House duty. He was to guard the Lincolns' theater box during the performance that evening.

Accompanied by their last-minute companions, Clara Harris, daughter of the New York senator, and her fiancé, Major Henry R. Rathbone, the president and First Lady arrived for the performance, settling into their chairs in the flag-draped box. At his post, Parker grew restless. He walked away, leaving the narrow passage to the presidential box unguarded, not noticing the tiny drilled hole in the entry door. At the beginning of the third act, Mrs. Lincoln slipped her hand into her husband's. She held it tightly. Seconds later, there was a shot. And suddenly, Mary Lincoln's hysterical screams ripped through the hushed theater.

Mary reached for her husband before he fell to the floor. Some witnesses said she fainted; others claim she ran about the box like a trapped animal. She went into shock. A doctor came. Both Lincolns were brought across the street to a private home. There, Mary alternated between uncontrollable sobbing spasms and calling her husband by nicknames. He was unconscious. Her beloved intimates—Sumner, Lizzie, son Tad—gathered there for her, but she acknowledged none. Through the night, the president's life ebbed. As dawn broke, it began to rain. At seven-thirty in the morning, Lincoln died. He was brought back to the White House. Mrs. Lincoln could recall no details. She rested in a bedroom, requesting any bedroom but hers or the President's.[11]

The Grants had been waiting in a Philadelphia restaurant for the ferryboat to take them to New Jersey. Anticipating his plate of oysters, Ulys was instead handed a telegram. "Is there anything the matter?" Julia asked. "Yes, something very serious has happened. Do not exclaim. Be quiet and I will tell you. The President has been assassinated . . ." Mrs. Grant recalled that "the whole land . . . now filled with . . . woe." She firmly believed that the men she saw at the Willard that day were part of a ring of conspirators to kill Lincoln, his Cabinet, and her husband. Her description of one man fit that exactly of John Wilkes Booth, the president's assassin.

Not far from Mrs. Grant in New Jersey, about to return to Washington for the funeral, another woman was confronting a new fate. It was also raining on Staten Island.

Fifteen hours after Lincoln was shot, an armed trio, carrying "swords and clubs" burst into the Gardiner home, finding "Mrs. Ex-President Tyler" in her mother's parlor. They demanded her "Rebel flag," and eyeing an innocent handkerchief hanging on the wall, the muddy-booted mob mounted chairs, ripped it off the wall, and made off into the night. Two days later, the *Herald* reported, "You are aware that we are blest with . . . Mrs. Tyler . . . She seems to be successful in passing the lines of our army, and of returning at her pleasure . . ." Julia instinctively knew that her brother David was behind the raid. He had begun a vicious court battle with her over their mother's property. Living in New York might not be the best thing for her.

Mrs. Lincoln did not attend her husband's East Room service, but upstairs, through the nights, she had endured the hammering construction of the catafalque. From her window, she saw her husband's coffin depart. Among the noises, inevitable murmurs floated about her. Some thought her prostrated refusal to attend the funeral was undignified. Meanwhile, the coffin, proceeding to Springfield, stopped in New York City. There, it passed a house where the window view of three-year-old Edith Carow was blocked by her friends Elliott and Theodore Roosevelt.

Few people paid sympathy calls on Mary. One who did was turned away. "With my heart full of sorrow, I went many times to call on dear heart-broken Mrs. Lincoln, but she could not see me." So wrote Julia Grant.[12] Upstairs, Mary Lincoln was trying to reassemble her life. Queen Victoria had written her, but the new president, Andrew Johnson, had not. She would not forget that. She wept to Lizzie, "God . . . what a change!" Did ever woman have to suffer so much and experience so great a change? I had an ambition to be Mrs. President;

that ambition has been satisfied, and now I must step down from the pedestal." Nearly sixty boxes were brought upstairs as Lizzie helped her friend pack. Mary dispensed with very little. Every item now represented equity.

But Mrs. Lincoln did not forget the people of her "cause." She gave two of the president's canes to black abolitionists Frederick Douglass and H. H. Garnet. Another went to Sumner. She presented a fourth to black servant William Slade. To his wife, and to Lizzie, Mary gave her bloodstained clothes from April 14.[13]

Meanwhile, the unguarded downstairs rooms she had decorated were looted. Curtains were cut, tassels yanked off. If Mary thought that her departure would at least end the press criticism against her, she was mistaken. As her packed boxes were being carried from the house, yet another smear campaign was just beginning. She was accused of stealing government property. Many in Congress assumed she had enough material comforts, and wouldn't deserve any more than the twenty-five thousand dollars it would award her at year's end.

As Mrs. Lincoln penned last-minute requests to President Johnson on behalf of staff members, she could see the building of a grandstand directly in front of the house. A grand military review was planned, with Grant as hero. While the widow's immediate plan was to live in a Chicago boarding house, "roving generals," she sarcastically wrote, had "elegant mansions, showered upon them." The Grants had been given homes in Galena, Illinois, and Philadelphia.[14]

Mrs. Lincoln would later indirectly reflect poignantly on her role: "You should go out every day and enjoy yourself . . . Trouble comes soon enough . . . you must enjoy life, whenever you can . . . knowing full well by experience that power & high position do not ensure a *bed of roses . . .*" On May 23, heavily veiled, completely in black, Mary Todd Lincoln descended the White House steps. There was no ceremony, no committee, no military escort, only Lizzie, who would accompany her to Chicago. Lizzie recalled sadly how "there was scarcely a friend to tell her good-by . . . The silence was almost painful." As they rounded out of the drive, the once-powerful First Lady left the White House forever.[15]

Forty-eight hours later, Julia Grant took to the review grandstand. Behind her loomed the empty mansion she had come to know. She hoped to know it better.

PART V

The Gilded Age 1865–1886

The queens in history compare favorably with the kings.

—ELIZABETH CADY STANTON, SUSAN B.
ANTHONY, and MATHILDA GAGE
History of Woman Suffrage (1881)

Reconstructive Counsel

FOR OVER TWO months, there was no First Lady in residence. President Andrew Johnson had only the company of his daughter Martha Patterson, wife of the family's native Tennessee senator. A friend of both Harriet Lane and Sarah Polk, she knew the distaff role. As her father's confidante, she'd wired him when word had reached the family of Lincoln's murder: "Poor Mother, she is almost deranged fearing you will be assassinated."[1]

On August 6, 1865, a small carriage finally pulled up to the North Portico, and feebly, an emaciated, tiny gray-haired woman with a white lace shawl stepped out. If the curious citizens watching thought that she too was ill to take an interest in her new life, they were mistaken. Her warm brown eyes glistened with fascination as she shuffled up the white front steps. The war had deteriorated Eliza McCardle Johnson, only fifty-five. Suffering from tuberculosis, she had to pause on the state floor to catch her breath before ascending the stairs. When the family—which included Martha, her husband, and two small children, daughter Mary Stover and her three children, sons Robert and Andrew, Jr.—went upstairs, all deferred to the First Lady's choice of room. She chose the one directly across from the president's office.

From the beginning, she would relinquish the public hostess role to her daughters. "My dears," Eliza Johnson pointedly told reporters who gathered at one of her rare public appearances, "I am an invalid."[2]

Daughter of poor Scottish immigrant shoemakers, Eliza was said to have received a fine education at the Rhea Academy in Greenville, Tennessee, her hometown. At sixteen, she noticed a young man walking into town, and told friends, "I might marry him some day." She did, and became the wife of tailor Andrew Johnson. She changed his life, teaching him to read and write properly, doing simple math, sharpening his speaking ability, encouraging his interest in local politics, and helping him prepare his speeches. She also managed their estimable investments and real estate.[3]

Mrs. Johnson had been to Washington only once before, during the 1860–61 social season. When war broke out, she returned home in the perilous role of loyal Unionist. Tennessee was, at various times, claimed by both North and South during the war. When the Confederates held

Greenville, Eliza's home was confiscated, and she moved to daughter Mary's nearby farm. Because her husband was a senator, her life was threatened. In May 1862, Major General B. Kirby Smith ordered the family expelled from the area. Eliza Johnson briskly responded, "I am informed that you require that I and my family pass beyond the Confederate state line in thirty-six hours! . . . I cannot comply with the requirement." Her boldness won her a stay of five months.[4]

Eliza finally evacuated, and after a harrowing three weeks of wandering, which included verbal abuse, military antagonism, and occupation of an abandoned cottage near railroad tracks, she and the family reached Nashville, welcomed by the senator. Mrs. Johnson hadn't seen him for nearly a year, and had feared that the stories that he had been killed were true. The trip had broken the infirm woman, whose breathing difficulties required hours of inhaling turpentine fumes from a pine-knot fire. But when her alcoholic son Robert went berserk in his Ohio military unit, Mrs. Johnson made the journey to Cincinnati alone to assist officials dealing with him.[5]

Though housebound as First Lady, she kept a regular schedule. After breakfasting alone, Eliza was joined by the president for a half-hour meeting where they discussed his schedule and appointments. Late mornings, she made a slow tour of the house. In the president's room, she inspected his wardrobe, making sure everything was in place. In the kitchens, the unpretentious woman chatted amiably with the staff, "as though she wished to have a hand in making the doughnuts and pies!" Her public mail, including many patronage requests, was handled by Martha. Afternoons, she devoured national newspapers, administration papers, and political journals in her room. She was never available to the press.

Eliza was rarely seen in anything but the finest clothes, designed in the city, but she hadn't lost her humility, gently treating the staff "just as members of the household," regardless of race. When the black servant Slade was dying, she prayed for him, and sent his family food from the White House. At what was the most stressful time in his life, she asked her husband to visit Slade at home, and he went. She maintained a silent power over the president.[6]

One observer said the Johnsons "seemed as two souls and minds merged as one." When his famous temper raged, she placed her hands on his shoulders, and cooled it with a simple "Now, Andy . . ." She walked into the president's office whenever she wanted to discuss an issue or offer advice. And as she sat in her room sewing, she kept her door open. Eliza always knew with whom he was meeting. Colonel Crook described the First Lady as "a woman of far more than usual power . . . but absolutely inflexible when it came to a matter of principle and through her husband's life exercised a very great influence upon him . . . she appreciated to the full the exalted position her husband occupied . . . perhaps because her intellectual powers were so wide she . . . understood this better than he . . . Her influence was a strong one . . ."

As First Lady, Eliza played a crucial role as political adviser. One chronicler asserted, "I should not wonder if Andrew Johnson did not consult his wife . . . more than he did any fellow statesman." A Greenville resident called her the president's "counterpart," while a Reconstruction expert said Mrs. Johnson throughout the congressional trials "remained his [Johnson's] most trusted counselor." Her influence likely manifested itself in his conciliatory Reconstruction policy, and his 1865 Proclamation of Amnesty, a pardon to nonleaders of the Confederacy who would take an oath of Union loyalty.

Another woman also offered the president Reconstruction policy advice, unsolicited though it might be.[7] Hands full, purses empty, Julia Tyler was having a difficult time, and considered moving to Europe, where the cost of living was lower. Julia felt obligated to assist the destitute Varina Davis and other impoverished Confederates with monetary gifts, but she had her own problems: Several of her children were scattered in schools around the world; the court battle begun by her brother was draining her in legal fees; Mother Gardiner's home was still threatened; the desecrated Sherwood was costing money, not bringing in revenue. Still unsuccessful in her attempts to convince the War Department to purchase Villa Margaret, she tried to influence the president to take pity on the beaten southerners—namely herself. "Now, President Johnson," she lectured, "you can redeem yourself in the hearts of your real fellow countrymen, your brave and noble citizens of the South, whose blood runs in your veins . . . the right way . . . of . . . peace and mercy—with a memory of the terrible trials and suffering . . ."[8]

It was precisely Johnson's conciliatory policy that made him the enemy of radical Republicans, whose legislation he vetoed. But it was his replacement of radical War Secretary Stanton with General Grant that they deemed an unconstitutional usurpation of their power. The radicals brought Articles of Impeachment against him, the hearings beginning in February 1868.

Into this arena, Julia Grant played social politics, sometimes with skill, sometimes not. The general had decided against their keeping the Philadelphia home, partially because Julia said that "one could not expect me to be happy confined within the walls of my new home." They settled in Washington, where a thrilled Julia held court while Ulys was in the delicate position of respecting yet remaining distant from the president, guarding his own aspirations. At a dinner after the January Senate session considering whether the legislature should move to reinstate Stanton, Mrs. Grant was particularly attentive to one Congressman Schenck, whom she carefully kept engaged in banter. Schenck slipped and told her that reinstatement efforts were likely.

Other times, Julia's stubborn craving for the spotlight placed Grant in embarrassing situations. When he tried to maintain distance from the president without public statement, Julia overcame his protest and attended a White House reception. The Grant presence that night was taken as a sign of loyalty to Johnson. She sympathized with the Johnsons, saying that the "trials savored of persecution," and argued politically that it was "a dangerous precedent" in weakening the presidency.[9]

The First Lady carefully followed the technicalities of the trial through her newspapers. During their morning meetings, the president and his wife discussed the legal proceedings, and she "counseled cheerfully, [and] never doubted the outcome," said one observer. She insisted to the president that he follow his conscience, regardless of consequence. All the while, Eliza was also amassing a mammoth archival record of her husband's presidency. Though disgusted at cartoon and editorial lampooning of her husband, she read even hostile stories, clipping all printed sources that came her way. One writer affirmed that the "assiduity with which she collected current facts," on the impeachment trials would be "one of the best sources for the public" on the controversy.[10]

As the nation followed the trials through their newspapers, one lady—who read the dailies voraciously to see if there should be mention of herself—particularly despised Johnson. Mary Lincoln was now residing in her own Chicago home, purchased with the money Congress had given her. When Lincoln's estate was finally settled, Mary was living with an annual income of seventeen hundred dollars. She was fighting with a committee over her husband's eventual burial memorial, and considered smoking cigarettes to calm her nerves. When she walked alone near the lake, she contemplated suicide. To the charge that she stole from the White House, she stated that it was Harriet Lane who'd done so. Galt's bought back some of her jewelry, but she had no buyers for her Inaugural gown.

Mary considered herself "homeless," and with her two sons "Living Monuments of a Nation's Ingratitude." Her objective was to secure a permanent annual pension, and her letters pleading for it were literally stained with tears. As a recluse, she spent her time penning strategies to congressmen, political bosses, newspaper editors—anyone who she felt would help her cause. She pointed to the "Harrison precedent," which had provided Anna Harrison and Margaret Taylor with substantial pensions, and asked one friend to tell men in Congress that "Chicago residents had told him about her condition." A handbill even circulated asking for donations, but rumors persisted that she was rich, one claiming that she was writing her memoirs for money.

She called President Johnson "that miserable inebriate," and thought his first congressional address "dwelt very lightly" on Lincoln's death. She believed that a circular sent to her that said Johnson had been part of the murder conspiracy was true. "Did not Booth say," she wrote a friend, "'There is one thing, he would not tell.'" She even wrote to "that family" in the White House, requesting that some small china pieces that were left behind be sent to her. She thought it a travesty that people believed "Johnson—is carrying out President Lincoln's policy." What particularly hurt her was "his feelings towards the oppressed race," recalling an incident in which she said "he is endeavoring to ignore all the good . . . and returning the slave, into his bondage." When Johnson toured Chicago, she left town. Ulysses and Julia Grant's postured modesty didn't fool Mary. "Gen. Grant," she wrote sarcastically, "to judge from his extensive wanderings over the country, his mind, is evidently, gradually realizing, what he may become in the future—I think, he had better let 'Well' enough alone. He makes a good general, but I should think, a very poor President."[11]

Mary soon found herself enmeshed in public scandal. Lincoln's former law partner William Herndon, on a lecture tour, humiliated her by claiming that Abraham's only true love had been Ann Rutledge. Mrs. Lincoln became the first president's widow faced with the rumors of "another woman." She defended herself privately, saying it was "music in my ears, when . . . my husband . . . said I was the only one he cared for . . ." She was correct in asserting that "Anne Rutledge is a myth . . ."[12]

In her desperation for money, Mrs. Lincoln went ahead with a scheme to sell her clothes. Consigning gowns, undergarments, furs, and other items to a seedy New York resale store, she permitted it all to be displayed to lure buyers, justifying, "I might as well turn them into money, and thus add to my income . . . It is humiliating to be placed in such a position, but, as I am in the position, I must extricate myself as best I can."[13]

The former First Lady traveled to New York with Lizzie Keckley, who as a black was refused rooms in hotels to which Mary had become accustomed. Mary Lincoln was indignant about segregation. So, with "my best friend" she shared rooms in a hotel attic. When reporters learned the purpose of Mary's presence, they created the "Old Clothes Scandal," vilifying Mrs. Lincoln for so degrading herself. She said that had she "committed murder in every city," the criticism couldn't be worse, as they made "political business of my clothes." Most of the support that she'd had in Congress was lost. No clothes were sold. She again considered suicide. The *Tribune* went so far as to predict that Mrs. Lincoln would end up in an asylum.

Meanwhile, in hopes of helping Mary's reputation, Lizzie wrote her memoirs, *Behind the Scenes.* This only worsened the situation, by revealing intimate details of the Lincolns, and the book was lampooned by racists as *Behind the Seams.* Mary Todd Lincoln had had enough. She bitterly resented the American government and citizenry and cursed "vampyre press." In 1868, she left America, and sailed for a new life, in Europe.[14]

As Mary left her troubles behind, Eliza Johnson's were resolved on May 26, when the final vote on the Articles of Impeachment found the president innocent. Colonel Crook, at the Capitol, was estatic. He ran the full length of Pennsylvania Avenue to the White House. He knocked on Mrs. Johnson's door. A small voice told him to enter. Crook blurted the news to Eliza:

"He's acquitted!" I cried, "the President is acquitted!" Then the frail lady—who looked frailer than ever—rose from her chair and in both her emaciated hands took my right hand. Tears were in her eyes, but her voice was firm and she did not tremble once as she said: "Crook, I knew he'd be acquitted. I knew it . . . Thank you for coming to tell me" . . .[15]

After the trials, White House social life assumed a flourish, and the First Lady managed to attend more public receptions. It was Julia Grant who attested to Eliza's visible presence, contrary to rumor that she never appeared. Julia said the First Lady was "retiring, kind, gentle," and "came into the drawing room after the long state dinner to take coffee and receive greetings of her husband's guests. She was always dressed elegantly and appropriately." At a children's party, she was described as a "lady of benign countenance and sweet and winning manner," but with a "sad, pale face and sunken eyes," seated in a "republican court-chair of satin and ebony." The First Lady also attended the first White House State Dinner for a woman monarch, Queen Emma of Hawaii. In the receiving line, when Eliza tired of standing, she merely asked for a chair, and continued to receive, seated.[16]

Mrs. Johnson had no regrets about her limited public role. "It's all very well for those who like it," she said, "but I do not like this public life at all. I often wish the time would come when we could return to where I feel we best belong."

Talk of Grant for president predominated politics, and though Julia coyly claimed that after seeing Johnson endure impeachment, her ambition cooled, "And yet, I had the reputation of having urged the General to accept!" But by the time Grant won the 1868 election, she admitted, "I became an enthusiastic politician." Now, ambitious Mrs. Grant would sail into the coveted position, relishing the house, the press, the gifts, and the power. "First Lady-elect" Julia's first decision was getting New York Senator Roscoe Conkling to help write the Inaugural speech.

On the Inaugural stand, after taking the oath as president, Ulys turned to the new First Lady, shook her hand, and remarked, "And now, my dear, I hope you're satisfied."[17]

– 23 –

Mrs. G.

JULIA GRANT'S PRIMARY role was partner to her husband. She never hesitated to interrupt him, to send a little note, or to call him over at a reception to discuss a trifle. He loved to tease her, and she would respond with mock horror. When he challenged her to scale a high fence around their summer house at Long Branch, New Jersey, she accepted the dare. The stout woman bounded over the fence like a gazelle, and smugly planted herself on the terra firma, to the amazement of the president. Theirs was an intimate, nurturing relationship. Neither hesitated to display affection. She had decided that as, in her words, "a plain little wife" she would get her crossed eyes fixed. Gently, Grant tugged her close to him. "Did I not see you and fall in love with you with these same eyes? . . . They are mine, and let me tell you . . . you had better not make any experiments, as I might not like you half so well with any other eyes." Because she traveled with him on as many of public excursions as possible, they were rarely separated. He affectionately called her "Mrs. G."[1]

Julia impressed Crook as "energetic, and lively of spirit, and very active indeed . . ." Her schedule was crammed with family breakfast and lunch, staff meetings, personally answering most of her heavy correspondence, private visits, shopping, and carriage rides. At night, she broke precedent by often dining outside the house. She retired by ten. She had charities, but no "project."[2]

Because of Grant's fame, his family received more press attention than their predecessors. Sometimes Julia's press was unflattering, as when she was described as "fair, fat and forty," but Mrs. Grant implicitly understood—and thoroughly enjoyed—the increased interest in the ladyship. She became the first First Lady to always acknowledge reporters and to issue a press release—declaring her disinterest in being "fashion dictator."[3]

Often the First Lady would appear in a receiving line, having forgotten an earring, fan, glove, or handkerchief. A friend, Mrs. Logan, said, "She often failed to remember that Mr. and Mrs. So-and-So had been twice married, were or were not temperance leaders, Protestants, or Catholics . . ." Because of her bad eyesight, she bumped into guests and furniture.[4]

Yet few women basked so comfortably in the limelight. Never had she received so much attention, but never did it intimidate her. "My life at the White House," she said in a later interview, "was like a bright and beautiful dream, and we were immeasurably happy. It was quite the happiest period of my life . . . I am a woman and the life at the White House was a garden spot of orchids, and I wish it might have continued forever, except that it would have deterred others from enjoying the same privilege."[5]

The power vilified in Mary Lincoln was welcomed in Julia Grant. The times had changed. The war was fading. Julia Grant was popular because she embodied the indulgent, naively hedonistic Gilded Age, a First Lady who so perfectly reflected the garish era for American women as an ideal. In that characterization, Julia Grant became the first First Lady satirized in literature, in Henry Adams's novel *Democracy*.

Industrialization in the postwar period had been a boon to massproduced women's fashion, and styles changed faster. Julia's little Watteau hats were tilted on a mass of fake puffs, "rats," and curls. She weighed her gaudy self down in diamonds from Galt's, where she often went herself to choose her jewelry. In violet, blue, and black satin gowns, Julia encased herself in the new look of thick-laced, fringe-trimmed, heavily beaded protruding metal wires known as the bustle. It hid well the effect of her gargantuan twenty-nine-course dinners.

Mrs. Grant enjoyed socializing with the leading robber barons of the day—and many of them lavished welcome gifts on her. Though she escaped press censure, even when implicated in political scandal only six months after she became First Lady, the unscrupulous activities of two of her ruthless friends, Jay Gould and Jim Fisk, attracted enormous publicity. Earlier in the year, they displayed Julia in their Fifth Avenue theater box, and entertained her and the president at the seashore. The First Lady soon questioned her "friends." The scandal involved her directly. She only vaguely recalled it as "dark clouds in the bright sky . . . that dreadful Black Friday."

The two men, along with Grant's sister's husband, Abel Corbin, attempted to illegally profit by cornering the gold market with the latter as their insider. When the gold panic struck Wall Street in September 1869, the president received an urgent letter from Corbin asking him not to interfere in the crisis. Soon after, Grant came upon the First Lady writing a letter to Mrs. Corbin. He bluntly told his wife that while she was at it, Julia should tell her to warn Abel that he would be ruined if involved in the scam. Julia signed it "Sis," instead of using the presidential surname, shrewdly keeping her distance. Grant then released a flood of gold via the Treasury, thereby breaking the cornered market. Corbin immediately warned Gould to pull out of the deal, though Julia's letter was not brought up. Traders moved to sell their "phantom" gold," and thousands were ruined.

The First Lady obscured her involvement by writing, "The papers seemed to say I knew something of it, but I did not . . ." During the ensuing congressional investigation, Fisk claimed that "Mr. Gould . . . sold $500,000 of gold belonging to Mrs. Grant, which cost 33 [$133], for 37 [$137], or something in the neighborhood, leaving a balance in her favor of about $27,000 and . . . a check had been sent." The possibility existed that Corbin and Gould had just told this to Fisk in order to drag the First Lady's credibility into the miasma, but Fisk's testimony convinced the prosecutors that he honestly believed Julia's speculation was true and that she accepted the money "with equanimity." Committee Democrats wanted to have the First Lady testify about whether the Corbin account was also, in fact, hers. Republicans blocked it.

Nevertheless, the question of one particular delivery of twenty-five thousand dollars in cash made to Mrs. Grant at the White House remained unanswered. A clerk later claimed that the decimal point of the transacted money might have been misplaced and that the amount had been twenty-five dollars. But even Grant's most scrupulous chronicler, William S. McFeely, questioned why the First Lady needed to have received "cash in the mail unless someone could not write a check?" It was never fully determined to what extent, if any, the First Lady had been involved in Black Friday.[6]

One intimate defended Mrs. Grant by saying she was "incapable of hypocrisy or deceit," but added that the First Lady was "quick to see the best side of a proposition." Others, namely her nemesis Mrs. Lincoln, suspected that Julia was involved, and relished revenge: "Fisk . . . testifies before the banking committee that *Mrs. Grant's* portion was to be $500,000!!! . . . As, in the midst of all my wickedness & transgressions, I never indulged in gold speculations, perhaps a more dreadful than *Mrs. L*—may yet occupy the *W.H.* . . . ."

In self-imposed exile, the nomadic former First Lady made an aimless trail from one German, Italian, French, and British address to another, grand hotel to tavern, seeking refuge, anonymity, and peace. Removed from America, she nevertheless read the *"hostile American"* paper, keeping an eye peeled out for news of being awarded her sacred presidential widow's pension, which she felt was "my due" but unlikely. "Doubtless they are *tomahaw[k]ing* me *now*, to slay afterwards," she wrote of the press. Europeans were not as vulgar to her as *"our nouveaux riches!,"* which she recognized immediately in Europe because they wore *"Full dress"* while sightseeing. People like the Grants.

When her few friends in Congress found unspoken resistance to Mary's pension request, she acknowledged the power Julia Grant could exercise on her behalf. Through Sally Orne, friend to the two First Ladies, Mary got word of her deplorable condition to Julia. "Mrs. L." first approved the plea to "Mrs. G." that Sally wrote on Mary's behalf, concluding that "the letter to Mrs. G is admirable beyond expression . . . could not be surpassed for womanly persuasion—*if it is* read and *made use of* in *the same* spirit *as* in which it was written, my lot, pecuniarily will be miraculously changed." When no word came, she lost her patience. In a letter marked "Private and burn" to Sally, she said she hoped "Mrs. Grant has had the GRACE, to reply . . ." She ranted on about the Grants' *"utter* indifference and heartlessness . . . They are intensely SMALL selfish people & it will be more than fully realised, ere *their* administration is over . . ." When Congress appropriated money for Julia's White House refurbishment, Mary bitterly wrote of "living in an uncarpeted apartment—ill in bed without a menial to hand her a cup of cold water." A week later, again desperate, she wrote to Sally, "Even the Grants *will be excused—if they will work* . . ." When, on May 2, 1870, a bill was introduced to award Mary an annual pension, she was ecstatic. But it only caused the vicious rumor mill to churn again, tearing unmercifully at her. American newspapers had fresh gossip that she was to marry a rich German count, who was after her prospective pension.

When she read a newspaper in Frankfort's English Reading Room that said the pension had been stalled because she was living "royally" in Europe, she collapsed on the spot. But in December, when the Pensions Committee approved her three thousand dollars a year, Mrs. Lincoln regained her sense of power. She was unsatisfied, and she was coming back to fight for more.[7]

As Mary disembarked in New York in May 1871, an archrival was at the moment planning to leave town for good. Mrs. Ex-President Tyler's attack on Washington was unsubtle. Julia Tyler took a house in Georgetown in 1871. Like Dolley Madison, she established herself as Queen Mother in capital society, her rebel taint fading but adding an appropriate dash of spice. Mrs. Tyler had no use for a mediator to exercise power. She barraged the Grants directly, offering Villa Margaret for sale to the government, without pulling punches. Even though the villa was "shorn of its beauty," Mrs. Ex suggested, "It seems to me a desirable piece of property." Grant wasn't interested, and Mrs. Tyler had to sell at a disappointing loss. Though she eventually won her court battle against her brother, legal fees consumed most of her award.

If they despised Mary, the press loved Julia, who left a trail of reporters in her wake. Her first visit back to the White House since before the war was a heralded event, lacking only trumpets. Julia Grant rolled out the red carpet for Julia Tyler. At White House women's receptions, the two Julias received, side by side. The sorority flourished. A year previous, with her panache for publicity, Mrs. Tyler personally carried in, and donated, a portrait of herself as presidentress to Mrs. Grant. The First Lady, perhaps uncertain whether displaying it in public would antagonize old Unionists, hung it in the upstairs hall. It was the beginning of a First Ladies portrait collection.

With the press "frequent in their allusions to me," and citizens telling her "your witchery—your beauty . . . have enlightened the President and softened him to the South," Mrs. Tyler claimed that she was secure with radical Republicans. When her son rebuked her Yankee socializing, Julia rebuked *him* in a remarkably philosophical letter that captured her ability to adapt and enjoy life, regardless of momentary circumstance:

> I went, and the consequence was the handsomest attentions . . . as the ladies crowded in at the reception and were introduced to me as "Mrs. Ex-President Tyler." I was enthusiastically received by those who had formerly met me . . . I was taken by surprise . . . at the warmth of my old acquaintances—with the gulf of so many years between. The fact is . . . the only way now to get along is to take the world as you find it and make the best of it. It will be the means of satisfying your feelings much better than by *showing* them your dislike . . . That is the way to *triumph* and to make your enemies even speak well of you.

Mrs. Tyler found solace in Catholicism, and when she converted to the Roman Church, she incited an avalanche of press and mail. She had not, however, returned to Washington for hosannas and a holiday. Her return had been consciously timed *only* after congressional beneficence had altered Mrs. Lincoln's fortunes. Her comeback having achieved good press, Julia launched her last battle. Mrs. Ex wanted a pension, too.[8]

Tactfully, Mrs. Tyler undoubtedly managed some compliment for Julia Grant's monstrous redecoration, described as "Greek Revival Mississippi Steamboat." Mrs. Grant's cohort in the heinious desecration was her husband's former private secretary, the loyal Orville Babcock, now commissioner of public buildings. The First Lady was understandably flabbergasted then when a "Whiskey Ring" rumor became the second great scandal to rock the administration, all the more damaging because Babcock had been an old confidant. On a trip to St. Louis, the Grants, publicly squired about by Babcock, were even entertained by one of the conspirators.

Initially, on impulse, the First Lady urged the president to detail one of his aides to Babcock's trial, signifying administration faith in his innocence. Then, evidently, Julia had private information confirming Babcock's guilt. Part of her motivation in influencing the president to offer support was to test the validity of Babcock's self-proclaimed innocence. When Babcock turned down the offer, the First Lady said she was "glad." When Babcock managed to elude conviction, the president considered offering him back his former position as secretary. But it was the First Lady who later admitted, "It was I who protested against this . . ." Babcock did not return.

Adam Badeau, in considering Mrs. G.'s advice to Ulys to rid the Administration of questionable characters, wrote that the "president would not overthrow a man whom he trusted though there were occasions when it would have been better for him had she succeeded."[9] In two terms, Ulysses S. Grant was to be the president who made the most Cabinet appointments.

But Julia Grant was to be the First Lady who influenced the most Cabinet dismissals.

- 24 -

The Bustle of Power

JULIA GRANT'S FIRST major coup had resulted directly from her social alliance with the grand and famous Hamilton Fishes of New York, aristocrats who needed neither the money nor the position of a Cabinet post. Grant knew nothing substantial of Fish, but ever since the war Julia had been sizing up the couple, and she saw to it that Fish became secretary of state. It was an appointment of great significance, for Fish would serve every day of the two terms. Her second Cabinet "appointment" proved less enduring.[1]

Rumor was afloat at the beginning of the administration when A. T. Stewart, owner of the famous store preferred by Mesdames Lincoln, Tyler, and Grant, was appointed Treasury secretary. Gideon Welles wrote that "Stewart's silks and laces, scandal says, were potent in the appointment." Though the president claimed that he had not consulted anyone on the appointment—"not even Mrs. Grant," her friendship with Stewart held a sense of security for her when the Cabinet was formed. When an obscure law that forbade a Treasury secretary from being "engaged . . . in any trade or commerce," was raised, Stewart had to relinguish the position. The First Lady was quite displeased.[2]

But more Cabinet members incurred her wrath than soothed her ego. When Postmaster General Marshall Jewell openly opposed the president's public stance on Babcock, the First Lady wanted Jewell fired for disloyalty, also suspecting that he would run against Grant if there were a third-term election. "Ulys, how can you let a man like that stay in your Cabinet?" A year later, Jewell was gone. From the beginning, she had disliked Interior Secretary Jacob Cox, who'd created discord by advocating civil-service reforms in opposition to the president. To the First Lady, that was nothing short of betrayal. When Mrs. Cox anonymously mailed a newspaper editorial criticizing Grant's civil-service views, she inadvertently mailed it in a monogrammed envelope. Julia angrily sent it back with a note: "Returned to Mrs. Cox, with the compliments of Mrs. Grant." When Cox suddenly resigned a year and a half after entering his position, the New York Herald wryly added that it was partly due to "little disagreements and unpleasantness in the female department . . ."[3]

Attorney General and Mrs. George H. Williams met with a similar fate. Mrs. Williams, an overtly ambitious woman, gadded about town in a Gilded Age carriage with liveried coachman, paid for by Justice Department funds. Shortly after, when her husband was then nominated by the president for the chief justiceship, it became apparent that confirmation was unlikely. Mrs. Williams, desperate to become "Mrs. Chief Justice," lied to Mrs. Fish that she knew about federal funds the president had misused for the reelection of Senator Roscoe Conkling. When letters referring to shady dealings of the First Lady's sister's husband—James Casey of the New Orleans Custom House—arrived for Mrs. Grant, she correctly suspected the attempted blackmailer to be Mrs. Williams. Within five months, the attorney general was gone.[4]

Another treacherous Cabinet wife prompted a further Grant scandal, once again involving the First Lady. This concerned War Secretary William Belknap and his attractive third wife, Puss, sister of his *second* wife and friend of Mrs. G.'s. Mrs. Belknap's gowns, emeralds, and coral-headed parasols became infamous in Washington, attracting speculation. Inquiries into rumors of the secretary's graft were in fact provoked by his wife's sumptuous lifestyle. Belknap's department included management of all Indian post traderships, and he'd awarded his second wife with one. With that appointment, she made clandestine arrangements with a third party to permit the incumbent trader to keep the job to the annual tune of twelve thousand dollars. Mrs. Belknap's cut was half the amount, and after her death, the new Mrs. Belknap kept receiving the kickbacks. Furthermore, Belknap created several other such contracts with friends. One such friend turned out to be none other than John Dent, Julia's brother.

When the scandal broke, Mrs. G. was stunned as "red-mouthed rumor held high carnival in the capital." Puss pleaded with Julia to visit, as a sign of her faith in the Belknaps. After Black Friday and the Whiskey Ring, Mrs. Grant moved with more caution, claiming she'd "been counseled not to go . . ." Instead, she welcomed Puss at the White House with "tears falling thick and fast." But, Mrs. G. directly questioned Puss's reasoning for keeping secret her transactions. She felt "much sympathy" for Puss, but gave no public support. Belknap was out.[5]

Julia Grant was never timid about exercising power, in one case bragging that "I always flattered myself that I rendered my husband and the country a very great service in advising the President to veto the all-important Finance Bill that was almost convulsing the country . . ." In the process of "influencing" the president, however, she wreaked havoc with both supporters and foes of the Finance Bill. While Julia was shopping in New York, A. T. Stewart rushed her into his office and asked if the president was going to veto the "infamous" bill. Julia casually assured Stewart that Ulys would veto anything that might "reflect dishonor." She offered the same assurance to some men who badgered her at her hotel about "another bill which they said would bring great prosperity to the country . . ." When she returned to the White House and found a flood of letters addressed to her about "the bill," she angrily "reproached" the president "for not informing me sometimes of state affairs, telling him how very embarrassing it was for me to be obliged to give such equivocal answers." After he explained the complicated details involved in unpaid war loans of the government, she exclaimed, "Why, Ulys, it is your bounden duty to veto this bill. You will be burned in effigy if you sign it or veto it, and I would rather be burned for doing right than wrong." He vetoed it.[6]

The First Lady voiced her opinion on Supreme Court appointments as well. Close friend to Edwin Stanton, she had grave concern for his failing health and, pulling rank, made special inquiry to the Surgeon General about the best environment for Stanton to regain health. Switzerland was suggested, and Mrs. G. presented her plan to make Stanton ambassador there. When Grant felt overseas duty would prove too stressful, Julia urged the chief justiceship. Ulys concurred, but Stanton died several days after being told of his nomination. Shortly, at a public event, Mrs. G. scouted for "my choice" for another nominee, and spotted Roscoe Conkling. As the ceremony broke up, she ordered him to her carriage and told him, "Senator, if it were with me, I should know exactly where to place the robes of justice." She did so before even consulting the president. When she finally told him, Ulys responded, "You have anticipated me, for I am going to offer the appointment to Conkling." In the end, Conkling refused it.[7]

Mrs. G. made it her business to stay informed on all phases of national politics, whether it was attending Senate hearings, reading through the president's mail, meeting with Cabinet members, senators, justices, or diplomats, even interrupting presidential conferences. After floating seemingly innocent questions to individuals about men the president should have in mind for an appointment, she reported back the information to Ulys, along with her opinions. If he withheld information from her that she felt necessary, she went directly to the Cabinet or the executive staff. Recipient of many patronage requests, she would whip off a short note of "Ulys—please do make this appointment," and often produced jobs.

Nepotism carried no evil overtones for her. Her son Fred was appointed assistant to General Sherman, accompanying him on a Grand Tour of Europe. A sister's husband was made marshal of the District of Columbia, another got the collectorship of the Port of New Orleans. The First Lady's brother George was given the appraisership of customs at San Francisco; her brother John, the New Mexico Indian tradership. Yet another brother, Fred, was put on the federal payroll as one of the president's secretaries.

The president's daughter, simple, lovely Nellie, only thirteen when she entered the White House, proved to be the family member, however, who had international attention focused on her. Mrs. Grant was taken to task for pushing Nellie into public society long before she'd fully matured emotionally. Heralded as a princess royal, the forlorn teenager enjoyed the ensuing publicity less than her parents. At sixteen, she was sent on a Grand Tour of England, met the queen, and became engaged to an Englishman. Mrs. G. became more concerned with the pomp, gifts, and gowns of a White House wedding than the emotional judgment of the bride. After the hoopla, Nellie found herself doomed to be a proper wife to a less than proper Algernon Sartoris. After spending time with the newlyweds, writer Henry James felt that he could not "sufficiently deplore the barbarous conduct of her mother leaving such excellent soil so perfectly untilled." He based his character Daisy Miller on Nellie.[8]

Paradoxically, though she spent more effort on developing Nellie's style rather than her substance, Julia Grant had "feminist" attitudes toward both her First Lady role and women in general. She was incensed whenever someone questioned the ability and equality of women. Since childhood, when she "often heard my mother say she always felt her unworthiness and incompetency," Mrs. Grant was sensitive to women's roles. In St. Louis, she had attended a lecture by famed Swedish author Fredrika Bremer, whose life's cause was equal rights for women. During the war, Julia had discussed politics with women who'd also "not submit" to the notion that it was only a man's subject. Adam Badeau considered the First Lady "a woman who understood other women."[9]

When her husband had arranged to sell their Washington home before moving into the White House, Julia was enraged. "I had enjoyed my independence too long to submit quietly," she boldly declared. Turning on Ulys, she retorted, "I have nothing to say in this matter? . . . if I decline to sign the deed, what will the consequences be?" Grant laughed, saying casually, "Oh, nothing . . . except it would be a little embarrassing to me; that is all." Infuriated, she sarcastically retorted, "Oh, is that so! Well, I will not sign it." At this, Grant responded stiffly, "[V]ery well, I will send word . . . that my *wife* will not *let me* sell the house." Julia wasn't joking. "Very well, you may do so." The house was not sold.[10]

Neither would Mrs. G. permit cracks at women's expense in her presence even when made by men other than Ulys. When Admiral Porter continually repeated that a mutual friend was "a regular old lady," Julia burst out angrily at the "great disrespect" "We women" were being shown. Her indignation emerged during her public trip with the president to Utah, heart of the Mormon Church, which practiced polygamy. When she met its founder, Brigham Young, the First Lady called polygamy her "one objection to your people [and] to you," and further pointed out it was "prohibited by the laws of the country and would have been wiped out long ago . . . except through charity for the young and innocent that would necessarily suffer . . ." While she found polygamy the lesser of evils compared to a spate of bastard children, Mrs. Grant warned Young that the closing transportation gaps would force its demise.[11]

In her relished hostess role, Mrs. G. placed the political wife in the public arena, bringing a strong consciousness of their importance as individuals, not merely connubial fixtures. She ordered that when the wives of the Diplomatic Corps arrived, they were met by the secretary of state's wife, when officers' wives came through, the wives of the

secretaries of war and the navy greeted them. In time, Julia expanded her concept to include Senate, Congressional, and Supreme Court wives. At her afternoon receptions, women of all socioeconomic backgrounds were encouraged to attend, and "chambermaids elbowed countesses," to shake the hand of the First Lady. The only, odd rule was that everyone wear a hat.[12]

During Grant's 1872 reelection campaign, Victoria Woodhull became the first woman to run for the presidency, on the Equal Rights ticket, but Susan B. Anthony, a leader of the suffrage movement calling for women's right to vote, decided against supporting both Woodhull and Horace Greeley in favor of the president. That wasn't lost on the First Lady, and the two women eventually became friends. Thereafter, Mrs. Grant privately supported women's right to vote. Though she issued no public statement of support, Mrs. G. gave it in subtler ways. When a group of nationally prominent women, including most of the First Lady's friends, signed a public petition *against* suffrage, the name of Julia Dent Grant was glaringly missing. She nevertheless remained less convinced of the benefits of women working.[13]

As far as civil rights went, Julia retained her family's southern attitude. When her brother Fred was appointed Inaugural Committee chairman, he billed the ball as a "private party," which managed to keep blacks excluded. When one James Smith, the first black West

Point cadet, was unmercifully harassed with the intention of getting him to leave, Julia's son Fred, in the same class, joined the ring of students who mistreated him, telling a man trying to mediate that "no damned nigger will ever graduate from West Point." When Smith was denied entry to the traditional ball, it raised the ire of abolitionists. Julia Grant was prominently in attendance, without a troubled conscience. As the controversy raged over attempts to expel Smith on contrived grounds, the First Lady was blissfully present at graduation.

Mrs. Grant seemed to take the attitude that the black was not worthy of full equality, but paradoxically, she refused to offer support, publicly or privately, to her white supremacist brother Louis's race for the governorship of Mississippi. With her exposure to minorities, there lurked a sense of justice in Mrs. G. She called the famous order that Grant wrote expelling Jewish traders from Tennessee "obnoxious," and when he was reprimanded by Congress for it, she said it was "deservedly so, as he had no right to make an order against any special sect." She felt very strongly about helping blacks on the White House domestic staff invest in their personal financial security, demanding that they buy property in the District while it was still cheap. When Harris, a dining-room waiter, lagged in her orders, she threatened "so decidedly" and "meant every word that she uttered." She told him, "If you do not go out and select a home and commence paying for it, I will buy one for you myself; and I will take out of your wages each month enough to pay the installments." Harris bought a house.

In her own naive way, Julia supported racial equality. When she was preparing for her first ladies' reception, an usher ran in to urgently ask "if any colored people call, are they to be admitted?" Julia, "after a moment's thought," said, "This is my reception day. Admit all who call." For a First Lady, it was a bold move, yet when she wrote that "no colored people called, however, nor did they at any time," Julia added that it showed them to be "modest and not aggressive." She remained unaware that police obstructed her order by preventing blacks from even walking through the White House gates.[14]

One woman who might have taken advantage of the Grants' attitudes toward blacks was now a comparatively subdued shadow of her former self. Upon Mary Lincoln's return to America, her son Taddie had died suddenly. It was the setback that broke her. Her behavior became peculiar. She wandered erratically, first to Canada, then to Florida. She kept lights burning in her room all night, fearing something ominous. Unknown to all, her consumption of sugar also set off her severe diabetes. She hallucinated, and her migraine headaches became more painfully intense. She believed Indians were pulling wires through her eyes, and needles of fire were floating in her brain. Paranoid, she carried thousands of dollars in cash in her petticoats. She panicked that she had no money, then began a round of spending for useless items. One night, she ran partially naked into a hotel elevator.

When son Robert held her, she accused him of trying to kill her, and threw him off. Heartbroken at her condition, Robert called for hearings to declare Mary Todd Lincoln insane. In court, with tears streaming down his face, he whispered, "She has no home . . . She has been of unsound mind since the death of her husband." Throughout, Mrs. Lincoln sat calmly, almost remote.

There was no defensive cry when the court determined that the former First Lady of the United States was "to be committed to a State hospital for the Insane." The name "Mary Lincoln" was entered into the Cook County Court's "Lunatic Record." Later that night, she finally went ahead with a long-considered threat. Mrs. Lincoln attempted suicide. When the poison she obtained failed, she returned for more. Were it not for a suspicious pharmacist who gave her a harmless liquid, she would have killed herself.

On the morning of May 20, 1875, Mrs. Lincoln was taken to a private woman's sanitarium. There, she began almost immediately planning for her release. She quietly mailed several letters to people who might help her. Her sister Elizabeth, and Illinois's first woman lawyer, Myra Bradwell, petitioned for a second trial, and the former First Lady was declared sane and competent. Embittered toward Robert, she resumed full control of her estate, and moved in with Elizabeth. Throughout the ordeal, Mary Lincoln had refused to admit to any insanity, but she was humiliated. "I cannot endure to meet my former friends," she calmly reflected. "They will never cease to regard me as a lunatic. I feel it in their soothing manner. If I should say the moon is made of green cheese, they would heartily and smilingly agree with me . . . I cannot stay." Gently but firmly, she concluded, "I would be much less unhappy in the midst of strangers." In September 1876, she returned to Europe.[15]

While Mary Lincoln began packing to leave America, the nation was itself turning inward to celebrate its centennial at a Philadelphia Exposition, and Julia Grant was planning her most conspicuously public appearance yet. She steadfastly upheld her belief that the role of First Lady was public and must be acknowledged as such, equal to the wife of any foreign nation's leader. She was visibly angered at exposition officials when they failed to do so.

On opening day, the president and Mrs. Grant were joined by the emperor and empress of Brazil. Then, an official asked the empress to join the two men in placing her hand on the starting valve of a mammoth Corliss engine. The First Lady was livid. "I, too, was there . . . I, the wife of the President of the United States . . . was there and not invited to assist in this little ceremony, which opened the centennial celebration of America's independence. I wonder what could have prompted this discourtesy to the wife of the President of the United States . . ." She was further angered when the empress was chosen as the president's escort through the exhibits, but was mollified by the chance to defend American industry to the emperor. As they came to a large pyramid of native tobacco, he questioned its worth. The First Lady, though despising Ulys's smoking, explained that tobacco, ". . . quiets the nerves . . . soothes one and promotes sleep . . . [and is] a great assistant to digestion." When he argued that exercise was best for digestion, she retorted, "Oh, Your Majesty, you are quite away behind the times. The whole energies of the United States are now bent upon inventing laborsaving devices."[16]

This was one First Lady who loved her role and everything it entailed. By 1876, Julia had already had a full seven years. She made no secret of her support of a Grant third term, and vigorously lobbied her husband to seek one. He seemed uncertain. No president had sought a third term.

It was not uncommon for Mrs. Grant to be present as the Cabinet gathered for a meeting. The fact that they were meeting on a Sunday, however, brought out her honed suspicion.

Standing just on the other side of the door, Mrs. G. paced, waiting, anxious to know the subject under consideration, instinctively realizing it was something important.

As soon as the president opened the door, he handed a messenger a letter. Julia begged to know what had been discussed. He stalled her by fetching and lighting a cigar. Impatiently, she demanded, "What is it? Tell me."

"You know what a to-do all the papers have been making about a third term. Well, I have never until now had an opportunity to answer," the president explained. He had called the Cabinet to read to them his letter to the press stating that he would not be a candidate for a third term.

Julia was stunned. "And why did you not read it to me?"

He shrugged. "Oh, I know you too well. It never would have gone if I had read it."

Julia shrieked, "Bring it to me now." The president explained it was too late. She was heartbroken. "Oh, Ulys! was that kind to me? Was it just to me?"[17]

As Julia mourned the inevitable, she read news of the wife of the Republic candidate for the 1876 presidency, Mrs. Rutherford B. Hayes. That teetotaling, modest pillar of piety, Lucy Hayes. One story in the *New York Herald* commented that Mrs. Hayes was "most attractive and lovable . . ." Like Julia, she was a midwesterner. There, the similarities ended.

Lucy Hayes was as interested in politics as Mrs. G., but embodied the more conservative, religious element of the party. She had sharply opposed the gentle Lincoln-Johnson Reconstruction policy. She despised Grant when he offered her war-hero husband an insultingly minor position. As a congressional wife, Lucy had been a familiar sight at House debates. As the Ohio governor's wife, she made war orphans, mental institutions, and reform schools her projects. If "elected," Mrs. Hayes would be the very first First Lady with a higher-education degree, being a graduate of Cincinnati Wesleyan Female College. As a student, she'd shown interest in women's rights. She had the education, experience, and potential to be a visible national leader of a cause.

The election, however, was disputed. Neither Hayes nor Democrat Tilden had won the requisite electoral votes, and it was decided that a bipartisan Congressional Electoral Commission would count the disputed votes of three states. Held at the Capitol, the commission hearings became a popular spectator's sport during the winter of 1877, and a familiar pair of brown eyes were ensconced to drink it all in. The outcome could affect her.

Julia Tyler, beset by financial disaster after the '73 panic, had had to relinquish her Georgetown apartment and return to Sherwood, but that didn't prevent her from taking lengthy working trips to Washington as she kept lobbying in the Capitol halls for her sugarplum pension. Mrs. Ex-President Tyler, now dressed in perpetual mourning, became so familiar that she was winsomely preserved in a massive canvas group portrait entitled "Electoral Commission of 1876." She would hang smiling in the Capitol forever now, surrounded by the famous, including Lucretia Garfield, wife of an Ohio congressman.

The *other* Julia "attended their sittings" as well, "much interested" in the commission proceedings. Mrs. G. even had a plan to keep herself indefinitely in the White House. "My policy," she declared, "would have been to hold the fort until another election could be held." Ulys teased her, "It is lucky you are not the President. I am afraid you would . . ." One day, however, she made it clear whom she did not want filling her high-button boots. When she read that "Louisiana had elected a Democratic governor, and yet her [the state's] vote for President was to be counted on the Republican side," Julia declared it "wrong and incompatible." This perhaps could make her case for another election. She burst in on Ulys's meeting with several senators to ask, "What does this mean? . . . Oh, Ulys, do you permit this?" "I?" he told her. "I have nothing to do with it. The whole subject is in control of a committee of Congress . . ." She turned for sympathy to the senators, one of whom obediently harrumphed, "As you say, Madam, the two seem incompatible."[18]

Upon suggestion, Mrs. G. and the president decided to take a Grand Tour of Europe, the Middle East, and Asia, a continuance of the adulating public life she was unwilling to sacrifice. While she packed upstairs, citizens streamed through the state rooms below her. Her redecoration, along with the centennial, had swelled the numbers of tourists, one of whom, Edith Carow, wrote to her friend, the sister of her secret love, Teddy Roosevelt, "Today, for the first time I went to

the White House . . . how unlikely it is that . . . I shall ever [again]
come in contact with [it] . . ."[19]

When Hayes was declared victor, Grant invited him and Lucy to
stay overnight at the White House. They instead decided to just come
to dinner on Saturday, March 3. Because the Inaugural fell on Sunday,
and there were rumors that the Tilden people might storm the ceremony with their candidate, Hayes was secretly sworn in after dinner.
The next day, when Lucy Hayes invited Mrs. G. to be *her* guest at the
public ceremony, the latter "politely declined," declaring, "No, I have
already witnessed two inaugurations." When asked if she was "going to
vacate the house" during the ceremony, she said, "No . . . I am not."

Mrs. Grant was determined to delay leaving her role quite literally
to the very end. Quickly, she devised a new scheme. *She* would be First
Lady, one last time, for the new First Lady. Minutes ticked by, but Julia
Grant instantaneously ordered an impromptu "Inaugural Luncheon." It
would be the first of its kind. It was all devised swiftly. She would greet
the Hayeses, then they would retire properly to the Blue Room. Only
then would Mrs. G. bid adieu.

That inevitable moment finally came. Julia had planned to say, "My
house is yours," but opted for the more prosaic, "Mrs. Hayes, I hope
you will be as happy here as I have been for the past eight years." She
was fighting back tears. As she walked through the door, she thought,
"How pretty the house was! Flowers on the table . . . sunlight falling
through the lace curtains . . ." Onto the steps of the North Portico she
descended. There, the staff crowded to catch a last glimpse of this lady

they'd truly loved. Julia Grant had technically lived in the mansion longer than any of her predecessors. Four chestnut horses champed their bits, waiting. Finally, she entered the carriage.

At the train depot, there was a little speech in her honor. A Michigan senator proclaimed in front of the crowds, "Mrs. Grant, I wish to thank you, Madam, in the name of the Republican Party, for the propriety and dignity with which you have conducted and presided over the Executive Mansion during these eight years past." Julia remained silent, and bowed her head, thinking. "[T]his straw was the lever which opened the floodgates of my heart." As the train pulled out, she stood on the rear platform with beloved Ulys, waving her scarf. As the sight of her public dimmed, Julia sought her parlor car. She burst into tears. Flinging herself onto a sofa, she "wept, wept, oh, so bitterly." Ulys came to her.

"Oh, Ulys, I feel like a waif, like a waif on the world's wide common." Indeed, a new, unpredictable journey in Mrs. G.'s life lay on the tracks ahead. She would travel the entire globe, the first former First Lady ever to do so.

Julia had intently protected her castle against the onslaught of Lucy. Insult added to injury of being replaced when Mrs. Grant learned that Mrs. Hayes, as governor's wife, had banned liquor from her public entertainments, and that temperance advocates hailed the political hope of a dry White House. For Julia Grant, who served her wickedly intoxicating "Roman Punch," of champagne and Cointreau, it was all rather like the shuddering demise of Babylon. For the next four years, Julia Grant would not set foot in the White House save for one dinner. But that didn't mean she didn't plan to return.[20]

— 25 —

Santa Lucia

HAD MRS. GRANT accepted Mrs. Hayes's invitation to stand by her side at the Inaugural ceremony, she'd have noticed, in a stanchioned area, the increased core of notepad-scribbling women correspondents who now covered the president's wife as a regular beat. They stared sweetly at this new modestly smiling First Lady who wore no jewelry, and whose pure black hair was parted in the center and pulled back tightly in a plain bun. One woman wrote with much expectation that

Lucy represented "the new woman." Bright and natural, Mrs. Hayes could prove to be just that.

Mary Clemmer Ames, a reporter who had helped destroy Mary Lincoln by incorporating fabrications in her stories, decided that she liked the prim Lucy, and rhapsodized about Mrs. Hayes "with that tender light in the eyes which we have come to associate with the Madonna." She wondered what *Vanity Fair* magazine would do in their illustrations of Lucy: "friz that hair? powder that face? . . . bare those shoulders? shorten those sleeves? hide John Wesley's discipline out of sight. . . ?"

A *Cleveland Plain Dealer* editorial retorted, "Every one praises the way Mrs. Hayes plasters down her hair, and enthuses over her Columbus cut dresses. It is all very well now, until the novelty wears off . . . in 90 days she will be picked to minute shreds." One dressmaker asked a Cabinet wife to please ask the First Lady to wear clothes less solemn than her frequent plain dark outfits, covering her completely from wrists to neck, and white tulle suffocating the one open spot at her throat.[1]

But no fashion magazine could fiddle with the distinct Lucy Hayes, the most pious woman in the role since Mrs. Polk, although never as sanctimonious. Lucy would, nevertheless, earn a more critical ephithet than "Sahara Sarah" by damning the demons from the White House. Whereas Sarah had still permitted wine to be served at state dinners,

Lucy banned all spirits. Mrs. Hayes had long led her life by religion, but privately so, without proselytizing. Personally, she was warm and kind, exceedingly thoughtful to White House staff of all races. It was in her public persona that her rigid edicts of morality, regardless of consequence, emerged. She could be unforgiving, and even admitted of herself that "love your enemies is not prominent in my character." Morally outraged at the love affair between married Kate Chase Sprague and Roscoe Conkling, she disapproved of others being friendly toward them. She carried on a petty feud with vain Harriet Blaine. Such ambitious women were the antithesis of Lucy Hayes's charmed but narrow circle. Clearly, the First Lady saw her role as a chance to be the exemplar of morality.[2]

On Sundays, Lucy attended services at Foundry Methodist, specifically refusing to join Julia Grant's more fashionable Metropolitan Methodist. The First Lady involved herself in local church activities, attending class meetings and prompting the children to sing at Sunday School. In the evening, she walked back to church with one of her sons or a close friend. Most nights there was hymn-singing around the piano. Colonel Crook claimed that the First Lady also disapproved of smoking, dancing, and card parties. The hypocrisy of what some claimed was the "stolen" election of her husband troubled none of the pious admirers who hallelujahed the end of Mrs. G.'s halycon days.[3]

Mrs. Hayes enjoyed her role as hostess, but like Mrs. Grant found that the social schedule had grown so that she needed assistance. The bevy of young matrons who often stayed with the family, mostly nieces, were used as social aides, one Emily Platt even serving as an unofficial social secretary. Lucy invited Ohio friend and congressional wife Ida McKinley to lunch several times, and the woman even served as mistress of the White House for two weeks in Lucy's absence. But it was the invitation to the daughter of Hayes's former law partner that would change the course of the young woman's life. "Nothing in my life," she recalled, "reaches the climax of human bliss I felt when, as a girl of sixteen, I was entertained at the White House." Miss Helen Herron, progressive, talented, insightful, emotional, and brazenly ambitious, vowed to someday return to the house, not as a guest, but as First Lady.[4]

As far as public correspondence, the new First Lady's mail was screened of the heavy numbers of requests for financial and other aid, but with the help of a clerk from the president's staff, her two sons who worked for their father, or one of the many women relatives staying with her, Lucy did get a sampling and, in some cases, she scribbled her responses for the clerks. There was also now a machine that enabled the president and First Lady to respond to more public letters than ever before. And if she had the new "typewriter" as a means of streamlining her First Lady role, Lucy was also the first to have the great marvel of the age—the telephone—at her disposal. It was demonstrated by Alexander Graham Bell for President and Mrs. Hayes, and one was installed on the premises. It was Thomas Edison's "phonograph," which first managed to preserve sound on record cylinders, that seemed to capture Lucy's imagination, and its demonstration by the inventor kept her up until 3:30 in the morning. Unfortunately, neither the First Lady nor her husband had their voices recorded on disk. It was also a blessing, in light of their ban on liquor, that the Hayes years saw the final installation of a permanent running-water system in the White House.

With a two-month perspective, Mrs. Hayes considered her new life "strange," unable to believe that "really and truly I am the same person that led a humble happy life in Ohio," and though she said it came "natural and easy . . . sometimes my *native modesty* gives me severe twinges. . ." She seemed uneasy in the role, saying that "without intending to be *public* I find myself for a quiet mind her own business woman rather notorious." In the private letter to her son, she admitted that among "my views my hopes" she prayed that "'Righteousness and Temperance' will cover the land . . ." On politics, Lucy believed, "The colored people have a better and fairer prospect of happiness and prosperity now than ever" under the controversial Hayes order to remove federal troops from the South, part of a deal struck between Republicans and southern Democrats on the Election Commission who voted for Hayes with the understanding that he remove the troops. It put the South back under the control of white men. Some believed blacks were again "enslaved" in everything but name.[5]

Many southern Democrats, like the Wytheville, Virginia, lawyer, John Bolling, were pleased. His daughter Edith, born in 1872, recalled talk of "before the war." After emancipation, her father had gone to the federal troops, demanding food for "the wards of the nation." When food was brought home, neither Edith's mother nor grandmother would touch it. It was from the Yankees, and they were too proud. Their learned mistrust became naturally embued in the little girl, whose formal education went wanting for lack of funds. Grandmother Bolling, recalled Edith, was "strong in her likes and dislikes . . . She simply did, or did not, like you . . ." Miss Bolling felt her own life was influenced by the old woman more than by any other human being. Edith's early impressions of the freedman echoed her background: "Dressed in calico dresses and big white aprons the chicken vendors smiled as only darkies can smile, revealing the generous white teeth and something of the happy-go-lucky nature of the negro of the South."[6]

Mrs. Hayes felt the needy were best helped through private charities. She demurred from adopting any one cause, though she visited Hampton College for black women, paid for one Indian girl's education, and collected $125 from Cabinet members for a poverty-stricken veteran, among other individual acts of kindness. It was not long after the Hayes ban on alcohol that she decided to detach herself from any notion that temperance was her "cause." Very quickly, she had learned that it was an issue that stirred controversy, and unwittingly swept her into the eye of the storm.

There was a political motivation to the edict. As a child, the First Lady had signed and kept a pledge of temperance. The president, conscious of her feelings, found it a good public reason to ban liquor. Though Lucy was said to be "the power behind the throne" on the decision, Rutherford claimed that he had not been pushed, and admitted that it was expedient to keep temperance advocates as Republicans, rather than having them defect to the Prohibition party. Perhaps that was a reason Lucy withstood the ensuing ridicule, for though the president claimed it was his decision, Lucy took the rap.[7]

Never before had a First Lady been subjected to such parody. As one approached the White House, a nearby bar called the Last Chance opened up. As one left the White House and passed the bar, the reverse sign advertised its name as the First Chance. Verse at the First Lady's expense proliferated, like the one in Chick Magazine: "Ever the Marine Band plays/At the feasts of Mrs. Hayes./What but a Marine Band oughter/Usher in the guests to water?" Cartoons pictured a tight-faced marm, smiling in a water bottle, grimacing in a wine decanter. A poem, "Lemonade," appeared, and a story was published claiming that Lucy was upset at the sight of a glass of red liquid until the president told her it was only lemonade with a mashed berry, not wine. She would forever become the notorious "Lemonade Lucy."[8]

The religious press praised her virtues. A schoolbook text used Lucy as a moral example to children. A support testimonial to Lemonade Lucy's reign began its circulation among American celebrities for their signature. Sarah Polk, who joyously met the first temperance First Lady since herself when the Hayeses made a southern tour, gladly affixed her autograph. Mrs. G. would not.[9]

Though Secretary of State William Evarts, a fellow Ohio Republican, joked that "water flowed like champagne," the ban had serious repercussions. President Hayes fired Simon Wolf, a German Jew, from his position as recorder of the District of Columbia because he belonged to a German-American club whose members drank, and had dared to venture close enough to Lucy to present her with a bouquet. The liquor traffic between the United States and Siam was strictly limited. The President signed an unpopular law prohibiting liquor sale at army bases. Finally, there was the case of the Women's Christian Temperance Union banging their drums and sharpening their hatchets. When it was disclosed that Mrs. Hayes was a member of the group, Lemonade Lucy became their Santa Lucia, and they used her as a heroine to promote their cause.[10]

Mrs. Hayes distanced herself from the WCTU. She agreed to meet or entertain them, but she absolutely refused to be swayed by their rallying call to defeat the demon rum. She was extremely angry when they used her to promote their cause under the guise of a national subscription of ten-cent contributions for a larger-than-life portrait of her. In the portrait, painted by Daniel Huntington, a water jug was drawn into the background. Publicly, Mrs. Hayes claimed she had never wanted to make temperance a "cause." As she explained to a friend, "I trust I am not a fanatic, but I do want my influence to be always in favor of temperance . . . It is true I shall violate a precedent; but I shall not violate the Constitution, which is all that, through my husband, I have taken an oath to obey."[11]

Many of the women in the temperance movement also happened to be suffragists, and this element began pestering the First Lady to help promote the cause of women's rights. Without raising any controversy, Mrs. Hayes could easily have advocated the education of women. She was a living example of its benefit. Increasingly, women were attending college, and pursuing careers as nurses, teachers, musicians, and clerical assistants.

One girl, Frances Folsom of Buffalo, took her education very seriously. Though her father, Oscar, had died, his bachelor law partner, Grover Cleveland, raised the child—his ward—with intelligence and care, even buying her baby carriage. As she grew, he took her everywhere he could. Members of the male Beaver Island Club recalled him leading the "chubby little 'Frank' Folsom" by the hand across the club's lawn. Besides being utterly devoted to Oscar's widow, Emma, Cleveland was also concerned about the college education of Frances, who was blossoming into a tall, graceful dark-haired beauty. As she prepared to enter Wells College, where she would study French and German, the example of Lucy Hayes could have been inspirational to "Frankie."[12]

As a student herself, Mrs. Hayes had once believed in pay equity between the sexes, but now resisted offering even the most minor encouragement to women using their talents. The First Lady's own college chum Rachel Bodley, eminent dean of the Women's Medical College, tried to coax Lucy, as the "genuine educated, Christian American Woman," into showing her support for women's education by inviting her to commencement at the medical school. Mrs. Hayes merely made a later, momentary stop there. She was equally uninterested in commending women who had fought the system to become successful in business. Journalist Emily Briggs told the First Lady that women should be told whether she favored "the progress of women in the high road of civilization or whether you are content because destiny lifted you to an exalted position, so high and far away that you cannot hear the groans of the countless of our sex . . ." By her smiling silence, Mrs. Hayes was evidently quite secure in being "far away."[13]

Many believed that Mrs. Hayes secretly wielded a heavy magic wand over her husband's policies. One politician called her "shrewd," while another claimed she was the president's confidante "in important questions of State," and had "most decided opinions about public affairs, and could express them in vigorous fashion." President Hayes was claimed to have been "ever eager to gain her sanction before adopting a new plan or policy." When the First Lady was briefly out of town, one newspaper sarcastically ran notice that "Mr. Hayes will, during the absence of Mrs. Hayes, be acting President . . ." Another publication called her "the most popular member of the Cabinet . . ." Rutherford Hayes himself admitted, "I don't know how much influence Mrs. Hayes has with Congress, but she has great influence with me." The truth was that while Lucy had a postmistress reinstated who was fired for her temperance advocacy, she refused to use nepotism and get a job for her own brother. Lucy rarely intervened in government, though it was easy to see how her public believed their woman would move heaven and earth if motivated.[14]

With this in mind, Mrs. Ex-President Tyler made regular appearances back at the White House, seeking her sorority sister's powerful backing to get her pension. At a February 1878 reception, Lucy invited Julia to receive guests with her. "That's right," one of her sons wrote Julia, "go it while you can!" Earlier, Mrs. Ex had believed Hayes's election was a fraud, but changed her tune quickly when William Evarts, her former attorney, was appointed secretary of state. Julia stepped up her pension efforts in 1879, while Evarts was still in office. "Do you not think," she wrote him, "now would be a favorite time to suggest that the only two other Presidents' widows now living shall be generously allowed the same pension that Mrs. Lincoln receives?"[15]

When Mary Lincoln read that she was being used as a precedent by Julia Tyler, she was livid. "I observed," she wrote her nephew, "a little paragraph in the papers that Mrs. John Tyler, was applying very vigorously for a Pension, from OUR government. A woman, who was so bitter against our cause during the War, with much northern property & money—as well as the South—but so fearful a Secessionist—Our Republican leaders will, I am sure, remember ALL THIS—& the Country will not have fallen upon such 'evil times,' as to grant her impudent request."[16]

Mary's angry reaction to Julia Tyler's plea may have been the result of a realization that it could hurt the chances of her own new fight, this time for an *increased* pension. Mary was now an invalid recluse, living in a shabby, tiny room in Pau, France, where she took a bad fall and damaged her spinal cord. Through an ironic twist of fate, the Grants swept into Pau with pomp, staying at an elegant mansion just blocks away from Mrs. Lincoln.

Along with Ulys, Julia was in the midst of the long festival of a

world tour. In England, she dined with Queen Victoria, telling the monarch that she understood what it was like to be a leader. In Spain, she audaciously accepted the offer to wave Queen Isabella's royal scepter and try on her crown. In Pau, the Grants were being feted by Americans there for several days. Julia claimed that she learned "the night before we left that Mrs. Abraham Lincoln was there and I was very, very sorry we had not learned this sooner." But, she added tersely, "it was now too late to make her a visit."

The Grant party rolled through the Middle East, where Julia struck a minor score for equality. In Cairo, she was disappointed to learn that women of the royal family couldn't appear publicly. "I at once," Julia wrote, "declared it to be a very hard and unjust custom." Other events on the tour were not so memorable. In India, Grant got raving drunk and, in front of British naval officers, became sexually aroused by the women there, but attacked Julia! Lord Lyton said that "this remarkable man satiated there and then his baffled lust of the unresisting body of his legitimate spouse, and copiously vomited during the operation. If you have seen Mrs. Grant you will not think this incredible." Through all the world, however, Julia seemed anxious about her return to America before 1880. It was another election year, and Mrs. G. was staging her comeback.[17]

The election of a new president—and First Lady—held promise for

Julia Tyler as well. Her hopes that Lucy Hayes might help in her pension fight proved futile. Mrs. Hayes never acted in any way that might compromise her husband. To her, the ladyship was a role to be gingerly manicured to the traditional values of the submissive wife, though the opportunity was given her to do much with it. She seemed to emulate predecessors from the distant past, and when she learned that there was a move to have presidential portraits commissioned for the White House, Mrs. Hayes saw to it that government funds were used to also paint Martha Washington and Dolley Madison. Still, her distinct personality, strong sense of history, reams of press on her family life and temperance policy, all brought a tremendous public consciousness of the official role of First Lady and what the entity should embody. One aspect of the role that she *did* expand was that a First Lady should publicly travel.

In Philadelphia, Lucy Hayes visited six educational institutions on a scheduled tour, and out West she joined the president in going down into a coal mine, all of which helped extend the role to include regular press coverage, and even more illustrations of her First Lady activities in newspapers, a practice begun with Mrs. Lincoln.[18]

Startlingly, when she later assumed presidency of the Woman's Home Missionary Society, Mrs. Hayes became the first woman who had been First Lady to deliver formal, prepared public speeches. In that role, she consistently fought any association of the group to the suffrage movement, and in one memo ordered that they not introduce any resolutions approving suffrage. Most of her speeches, unfortunately, encompassed the most offensively patronizing racist notions then prevalent. In one she would declare that "First in importance" were the "unfortunate of our own race," before blacks, Indians, Spanish-Americans, and even Mormons. Two years later, Lucy said, "If our eyes are to be gladdened by the sight of heathen lands rapidly becoming Christian, we must direct our efforts . . . to protect from heathenism our own land . . . we see the paganism of other lands—of Asia, of Africa, and of Europe—which has poured in upon our shores . . ."

The speeches would become more vigilant: "Not less than five millions of people are now added to the population of our country in each ten years by emigration from foreign lands. Among them are no doubt persons of education, or morality, and of religion, who . . . with our language and institutions, will in good time become valuable citizens . . . As to a multitude of others, it may truly be said that the missionary to pagan lands will find nothing more hostile to Christian civilization than the evil influences which immigration brings into the very bosom of our American society. Home Missions seek to protect our own land from imported heathenism." Then she spoke out on the American black: "It is represented by well-informed and conscientious observers that the colored people increase more rapidly than the white in proportion to their number, and that the proportion of the ignorant and unchristian does not diminish." But she concluded that instruction "can only be imparted by female teachers . . ."

Her last speech contained a minor point for the women's movement, when she spoke of "the crime against women that now holds Utah [polygamy] . . . There surely never existed such an offense against women . . ." She then appealed to fanatical fears by warning that blacks, "At their rate of increase . . . before the end of the century . . . will exceed in number the total population of the United States." Finally, she directly assailed the immigrants from southern and western Europe, most of whom were Catholic and Jewish. "For the most part, in the first century after the Declaration of Independence immigrants were from the most civilized nations of Europe, and were seeking liberty and land for homes. Now, however, an increasing number come or are brought from the less enlightened European nations and from heathen countries, seeking simply better wages, and caring little or nothing for land or homes. They are sadly lacking in education and religion, and are by no means well fitted for the citizenship of a republic." Unlike the curious Julia Grant and Mary Lincoln, Lucy Hayes showed no interest in seeing lands and cultures past her narrow shores. She never left America. As the Hayes term came to an end, she ironically wrote about herself ". . . four years is long enough for a woman like this one."[19]

As the electioneering for the 1880 Republican nomination heated up, Mrs. G. returned to America, thrilled by the serious talk among party leaders that Ulys had a chance of being nominated. Several weeks before the Chicago convention, they moved to their Illinois home, Julia full of "suspense," in the tallying of delegates, "sounding like the campaign manager . . ."[20]

Mrs. G. said she felt certain Grant could win because "all told me so, but I knew of the disaffection of more than one of his trusted friends." If he wasn't nominated, she said, "then let it be so, but he must not withdraw his name—no, never." She "entreated" him to put in an appearance at the convention. He refused to. "Oh, Ulys," she argued, "how unwise, what mistaken chivalry." He was incredulous at her ambition. "Julia, I am amazed at you." Without Mrs. G.'s knowledge, Grant withdrew his name from circulation. When she was invited by nominee James Garfield's wife, Lucretia, to visit at her Mentor, Ohio, home, Julia tersely declined, adding "the hope that all your most sanguine anticipations many be realized." Mrs. Garfield was realizing nothing sanguine just then. She learned of the nomination when a swarm of people suddenly rushed her lawn.[21]

The Grants settled in an expensive New York hotel, but according to Julia they were "poor." When wealthy friends bought them a sumptuous town house, they formally presented it to *her*, knowing the former president wouldn't accept charity. Julia, of course, took it. Again it was

Julia who accepted on Ulys's behalf an offer of partnership in an invest-ment business with one Ferdinand Ward. It was a hasty decision. And fateful. [22]

Another woman in New York that winter, not off Fifth Avenue near Julia but downtown in a seedy hotel, was trying to find relief with Turkish, electric, and Roman baths. Mary Lincoln now had to be bodily lifted from bed to bath. From her room, the emaciated woman, now partially blind, calmly continued her fight for a pension increase, instructing newfound friends just which congressman could be trusted. Congress was in fact considering increasing her pension to five thou-sand dollars, with an extra bonus of fifteen thousand dollars. As Mrs. L. barraged from the North, Mrs. Ex attacked from the South. "I am forced," Julia Tyler begged Congress, "to seek the aid that was not denied Mrs. Lincoln . . . I can no longer contend without as-sistance . . . Surely the Widow of a President . . . deserves your con-sideration." When, early in 1881, she was awarded only twelve hundred dollars annually—less than half of Mary Lincoln's pension—Mrs. Tyler only then began her Waterloo. [23]

Meanwhile, Republican candidate's wife Lucretia Garfield was fight-ing her own battle against the press invasion of her family's privacy, and permitted only one formal photograph of herself for use by the Garfield campaign. Nevertheless, she became the first candidate's wife to appear on a campaign poster.

When the candidate one day returned home with several reporters seeking her out, they found the "home-loving little woman" scrubbing a room, in old bonnet and rolled sleeves. Cleaning her hands of the suds, she told the reporter under condition that it not be published that "if the General is elected it will mean four years of almost killing work . . ." [24]

Brilliant Mrs. Garfield would shortly find herself an unfortunate prophet.

– 26 –

Discreet Crete

When Garfield won, Lucretia responded that "it is a terrible respon-sibility to come to him and to me." Emotionally and politically, the Garfields were spiritually bonded partners. Earlier that summer, she had written him, "I don't want you to have the nomination merely because

no one else can get it, I want you to have it when the whole country calls for you . . . My ambition does not fall short of that."[1]

One of the reasons Lucretia may have been uncomfortable with public inquiry into her life during the campaign was a not entirely groundless rumor of impending divorce. During their marriage, James had declared to her that it had been a mistake to wed, he was not the husband type. Crete had been frigid toward her union, but within her, as her diary illustrated, she was a warm, sensual woman, unable to verbally express herself. Later on, when James had an affair with a Lucia Calhoun of New York, Crete discovered his "fire of . . . lawless passion," and wrote him, "I shall not be forever telling you I love you when there is evidently no more desire for it on your part than present manifestations indicate." Eventually, their depth of character transcended the mistakes, and a euphoric love blossomed between them. Crete was youthful and spoke in a whispery voice. She had a high forehead and cheekbones, deep-set, luminous eyes, and was an attractively thin forty-eight-year-old brunette. They were still lovers in the White House.[2]

Crete, as James always called her, was earthy but wise. Hearing the story that Maine senator James G. Blaine had got his wife pregnant before their marriage, she gently responded, "My opinion of Mr. Blaine would be rather heightened than otherwise by the truth of such a story;

for it would show him not entirely selfish or heartless." But that controlled scholarly air was deceiving. She was a wise politician. It was
Crete who insisted that Blaine be made secretary of state, and he wrote
Garfield that "I wish you would say to Mrs. Garfield that the knowledge
that she desires me in your Cabinet is more valuable to me than even
the desire of the President-elect himself." Her advocacy had the successful effect of placing Blaine under obligation. When Thaddeus
Pound was being considered for a Cabinet position, however, Lucretia
stopped it because of some earlier scandals involving his wife. She liked
Blaine not only because he'd been kind to his wife; Crete recognized
the political value of allying with him.[3]

Descendant of German Disciples of Christ, daughter of a farmer,
and founder of the Eclectic Institute, from which she graduated, Crete
was raised strictly and religiously. Though expert at Greek and Latin,
she wondered whether her erudite studies were useful in the real world,
and thought time spent learning linguistics might possibly be better
used in studying more practical things. One newspaper emphasized that
"she was trained for an industrious career. She worked to get an education; then she taught school, that she might release her parents from
the burden of her support . . . She was, early in life, a bread winner."[4]

Living in Washington for nearly two decades as a congressional
wife, Crete knew capital life well, but she and James belonged to the
literary Burns Club, preferring intellectual salons to society. Though
she taught their children how to read the classics, and nurtured their
spiritual and intellectual growth, Crete nevertheless maintained a sense
of detachment. "Life begins in isolation and intense individualism," she
later wrote. "Influences and surroundings may mold and modify that life
but they in turn may be transfigured by qualities and characteristics
which belong to it by inheritance."[5]

Mary Clemmer Ames believed the new First Lady had "a strength of
unswerving absolute rectitude her husband has not and never will
have." Another reporter said Crete was "in all senses the 'helpmeet' of
her husband, his companion in all sorts of studies and reading, his confidante and advisor in all things . . ." Crete once told James, "Very
many men may be loved devotedly by wives who know them to be
worthless. But I think when a man has a wife who holds him in large
esteem . . . he has reason to believe in his own worth." He equally
valued Crete, particularly as First Lady: "I have been wonderfully
blessed in the discretion of my wife. She is one of the coolest and best-
balanced women I ever saw. She is unstampedable. There has not been
one solitary instance of my public career when I suffered in the smallest
degree for any remark she ever made . . . many times such discretion
has been a real blessing."[6]

Just before the Inauguration, in New York under the secret name of
"Mrs. Greenfield" as the guest of politician Whitlaw Reid, Crete

learned from him and Blaine of the dubious support from the New York "Stalwart" faction of the party, Vice President-elect Chester Alan Arthur among them. Crete quickly reported to James, "You will never have anything from these men but their assured contempt, until you fight them *dead*. You can put every one of them in his political grave if you are a mind to & that is the only place where they can be kept peaceable."[7]

The hostess role of First Lady interested her only to the extent it could focus attention on literary and fine arts. Before the election had even been won, Crete began keeping a very detailed file of notes on authors, artists, poets, and sculptors, listing their achievements with abbreviated critiques, planning to have them brighten White House events. One friend recalled how the First Lady was "interested in modern movements" with "a larger vision of life." Another described her "thorough culture" and called her "reserved, yet affable, and with the distinguished trait of genuineness. There is not a trace of affectation about her." Crete was upset, however, when a newspaper announced that she spoke "French and German fluently, [and] is said to be the first President's wife able to talk with foreign diplomats in the court language of Europe," considering this offensive to her predecessors who had fluently spoken foreign languages.[8]

Blaine urged the Garfields to end Lucy Hayes's "village society," but the First Lady didn't feel up to being a social lioness, tearfully telling the president, "I hope I shall not disappoint you." One newspaper account backhandedly praised her by saying, "Her qualities of heart and mind are those that pass for less than their value in what is termed society life . . . not given to saying of sharp things that sound clever . . ." But Crete's White House diary accounts proved that when it came to political power, she was certain and tough.[9]

When a snobbish social arbiter tried to breeze in and see the new First Lady, the doorkeeper stopped her, saying Mrs. Garfield had changed Mrs. Hayes's calling hours and the woman couldn't see Mrs. Garfield without an appointment. After the woman haughtily wrote to the First Lady, she tartly responded, ". . . unless he were disrespectful in manner he was only acting under orders," but admitted, "I may have blundered in my method of getting this to be understood." When the woman warned that Democrats "who are so afraid of 'Republican Imperialism'" would raise a furor over the changed time, Crete said the "attempt at intimidation" was "petty criticism which might worry me, if I would let it."[10]

She took equal offense at a "genuine fanatic" temperance woman who told the First Lady that "'all reforms must come from the better classes,'" and hoped that she'd continue the Hayes edict. Crete said *that* was "new to my mind . . ." and firmly explained that "drinking wine at a respectable dinner was so small a factor in bringing about the intemperance of the country that I felt there was great inconsistency in giving it so much prominence." The president delighted in her force. "Crete grows up to every new emergency with fine tact and faultless taste."[11]

Extremely astute politically, she was particularly sensitive to cloaked maneuverings of both national leaders and their wives, as well as the stealthiness of "Stalwarts," headed by Conkling.

On March 22, the president confided in her that Blaine was angry over Garfield's appointments of Stalwarts, and surrendering to Conkling. He then told her he'd immediately appoint some of the New Yorkers Blaine wanted in the administration. The next day, the First Lady noted, "The new list was sent in and the two New York factions stood looking into each other's eyes astonished and enraged, but feeling themselves thoroughly fettered and outwitted. The Conkling faction may make a struggle yet, but before the country they are powerless." "The New York muddle thickens," she penned later in the week, fearing it might cause trouble for the president, and "sorry that it will probably alienate Vice President Arthur altogether." Toward Conkling, she was "indifferent—perhaps the truth is, I am glad of it . . . his power . . . is only used to gratify his own vanity and selfishness, and to bolster up his hates . . . no true loyalty . . . nor patriotism in him, and history will write him down for . . . a peacock."[12]

The president consulted his wife on political matters, revealing even "the profound State secret" that no extra congressional session would be called, as well as the confidential news that two Cabinet officers were resigning. Crete, perhaps more than her husband, was a true partisan. In reference to a Senator Thurman, she wrote," We have always been good friends notwithstanding political differences," saying that when a rare Democrat was appointed to a position, it was "'over the party walls in Politics.'" Though she realized support from all factions was vital, she considered loyalty a priority, and her reference to the Cabinet as "our political family" emphasized that. To her, Blaine was the most loyal.[13]

Blaine was the subject of the First Lady's one and only press interview. Like Mrs. Grant, she was willing to meet with the press without Victorian inhibition and discuss politics. She described her interviewer, political journalist Miss Withington, as "sentimental and visionary," when Miss Withington informed the First Lady that "she was afraid the President was too much influenced by his advisors . . . that she did not quite trust Mr. Blaine." She proudly recorded that "I made her understand that the President knew . . . the men around him . . . and I took the opportunity to make her know that I regard Mr. Blaine as—not only . . . brilliant . . . but . . . full of good impulses . . . great magnanimity, and sterling worth . . ."[14]

She was quite amused when Harriet Blaine, with her deserved reputation for bitchiness, troubled to restrain herself in the First Lady's presence, writing of the night when a "Mrs. Senator" told Mrs. Blaine that she was "a good Republican in the Senate but now that her husband is in the Cabinet she would be glad to compel the Senate to do anything to please the Democrats . . ." Crete was drawn to political women like herself. She delighted in detailing the feistiness of Mrs. Senator Mahone, whom the First Lady said was "a politician from the brisk determined way in which she called Senator Don Cameron of Pennsylvania to an account for failure to deliver some paper she had intrusted to him . . ."[15]

Mrs. Garfield quickly became the victim of patronage requests. A Miss Bryan "in her artless girlhood" was seeking for her father a position at the Berlin mission, and had the wisdom, wrote Crete, "to make the request of me." Inevitably, the suffrage question arose. The First Lady "took interest in women's rights," but was "repelled" by the idea of active lobbying for the cause, and "even rejected proposals for dress reform," like those proposed by women like Victoria Woodhull, "seeing in them the opening wedge to free love and the weakening of family ties."[16]

Lucretia Garfield's conviction that women could achieve equality rested in the belief that they must first think of themselves as equal, and she personally reminded her husband that equality was her right: "You have been king of your work so long that maybe you will laugh at me for having lived so long without my crown, but I am too glad to have found it at all to be entirely disconcerted even by your merriment. Now, I wonder if right here does not lie that 'terrible wrong,' or least some of it, of which the woman suffragists complain. The wrongly educated woman thinks her duties a disgrace, and frets under them or shirks them if she can. She sees man triumphantly pursuing his vocations, and thinks it is the kind of work he does which makes him grand and regnant; whereas it is not the kind of work at all, but the way in which and the spirit with which he does it."[17]

For her, the imposed role of mother had its frustrations. "It is horrible to be a man," she admitted, "but the grinding misery of being a woman between the upper and nether millstone of household cares and training children is almost as bad. To be half civilized with some aspirations for enlightenment and obliged to spend the largest part of the time the victim of young barbarians keeps one in perpetual ferment." Now, finally, as First Lady, she found some of those cares were removed, and she planned a project. She would historically restore the White House.[18]

One journalist recalled that the First Lady "was most often found in the Congressional Library where she studied," and the president recorded one visit there with her to research the White House rooms. More than any of her predecessors, Mrs. Garfield was conscious of living in a house "among the shadows of the last eighty years." When a visitor described to her recollections of Mary Lincoln receiving foreign ministers upon the news of Richmond's fall, Crete said, "These little scraps of reminiscence that I gather up now and then lend this old place a weird charm that I fancy might grow into a solemn silence with me."[19]

On Good Friday, she recorded, "I think I have enlisted both Mr. Nordhoff and Mr. Harper to support me"—a slip she quickly corrected—"or rather *the President* in making a plea to Congress to rebuild during the summer following this. With much less money than a new house would cost this might make a magnificent house." She began her project with a New York visit to see decorators' wares, also making an unusual inspection of "the electric baths" with the "possibility of introducing one in the White House."[20]

In New York, Crete immediately realized just how renowned the First Lady role had become, as well as public expectations of it. Under her heading of "Blundered," she wrote that she regretted that she had "allowed Miss Ranson to take us to the City Hall to see Alexander Hamilton's portrait, and she, poor woman! committed the mistake of presenting me to some of the officials, and the penalty is that this P.M. I am announced as having called on the Mayor at City Hall. I wonder if I shall ever learn that I have a position to guard! Spent the rest of the day shopping."[21]

On April 26, Crete was receiving afternoon callers at the White House when one, Charles Guiteau, a pesty office-seeker, engaged her in conversation. He found her "chatty and companionable." Others were noticing Mrs. Garfield simply because she was quite frequently in the public eye. Previous to the New York trip, the First Lady had made a public appearance with the president and navy secretary at the Navy Yard, for an inspection tour of "the workshops," where she "examined the new method of obtaining steam power by the evaporation of ammonia." This was not the stuff of children's hospitals and ladies' teas. It was immediately apparent that Mrs. Garfield was going to be quite public, always at the president's side.[22]

Suddenly, in early May, it was all cut short. When newspapers remarked that "she kept herself secluded from public gaze," it was finally disclosed that the First Lady had malaria.[23]

Crete lay in bed, barely conscious. The president, beside her nearly every hour, admitted, "My anxiety for her dominates all my thoughts, and makes me feel I am fit for nothing." Amid his work and the infighting of the party, James Garfield's sole concern was for his wife. He could not administer without her.

The presidency seemed suspended, the president of the United States confessing, "[A]ll my thoughts center in her, in comparison with whom all else fades into insignificance."[24]

– 27 –

Widows and Widower, Sisters and Bachelor

WITHIN WEEKS, as spring bloomed in the capital, Mrs. Garfield emerged from her brush with death, and decided to recuperate at the Jersey seashore. On June 18, as the president escorted her to the train, one of those in the ogling crowd had gone there with a mission, but later admitted, "Mrs. Garfield looked so thin, and she clung so tenderly to the President's arm, that I did not have the heart to fire upon him." So wrote Charles Guiteau, a familiar face at the White House, who had routinely been denied patronage for a government job. Guiteau felt sympathy for Crete, but ominously added, "It will be no worse for Mrs. Garfield, dear soul, to part with her husband this way than by natural death."[1]

When the president entered the train depot on July 2, to leave to join Crete, Guiteau stepped right up to him and fired his pistol. Crete's earlier political instincts proved chilling as the assassin yelled, "I am a Stalwart! Arthur is now president!" Wounded but conscious, James was rushed to the White House, where he told Mrs. Blaine, "Whatever happens, I want you to look out for Crete."[2]

The First Lady rushed on a special train straight through to Washington. As she entered the White House, she was so overcome with grief that two men had to support her. But once inside the president's bedroom, now set up hastily as a hospital ward, she took control. When James spoke of dying, she stopped him. "Well, my dear, you are not going to die as I am here to nurse you back to life; so please do not speak again of death."[3]

In moments of emergency, the sorority endured, once again cutting across political differences to bolster a sister. Among the thousands of letters of support Crete received was one from the feeble but spry Sarah Polk, offering "hope for recovery of President." Summering on Long Island, Julia Tyler, who had already sent a telegram, now comforted Mrs. Garfield in a long, kind personal letter. "I am not content in dispatching a telegram to express my deep sympathy for you in this dreadful occurence [sic] which has befallen your family & the nation, but must do the justice myself to further add . . . how heartfelt is the instinct I feel in your heavy affliction. May it be the Will of the Heavenly Father to avert the worst! . . . may your strength & fortitude be

equal to the demand . . . In this hamlet by the sea whence I so sadly pen these lines, but one feeling pervades the community on this 4th of July—that of anxious sorrow . . . In . . . trust that tomorrow will bring us a happy relief . . ."4

Lucretia endured a wearisome routine through the muggy summer. When she wasn't at James's bed—where doctors were attempting to locate the bullet—she was in the kitchen preparing some of his food. She sent word through the press that "anything printed about her husband be sent to her." She penned a poignant little poem, "To the Poplar Tree Outside the President's Window." Stalwart Vice President Arthur kept his distance, solicitous of her intention of giving the impression that the president still ran the government. Arthur didn't assume presidential duties.5

As the miserably muggy Washington summer dragged, the First Lady's role became legendary across the world, one newspaper chronicling:

". . . she has gone on [as] the most hopeful person . . . [so] that it was feared she did not realize the danger . . . 'What can save him?' she asked the doctors. 'Only a miracle,' she was solemnly told. 'Then that miracle will be given, for he must live,' she said, and quietly returned to her post at the bed . . . she . . . was only unnerved when delirium set in and her husband failed to recognize her. Soon his mind cleared and she asked to be left alone with him, and what passed between them is not known, but she was happier afterward and he was better . . . On every side her praises are heard . . . As a representative American woman her country people are proud of her. She fitly represents the best qualities of her sex, and is an honor to a nation, which, more highly than any other in the world, esteems women . . . Her control over herself is supreme . . . she has proved herself greater than the demands of the situation. It is well, for her own sex . . . to stop and consider this fact, and to secure personal benefit from the knowledge."[6]

With the promised therapy of salt air, the president was moved to the shore in September, but the First Lady's unspoken fear became reality. On the day he died, she broke down for the first time, wailing, "Why am I made to suffer this cruel wrong!" Julia Tyler tried to console her "sister," hoping Crete would be comforted that the late president "has now a *martyr's crown.*"[7]

Though Mrs. Ex mourned, there was a silver lining for the sorority. A subscription drive for Mrs. Garfield and her children would reap $300,000, and word came from Congress of a $5,000 annual presidential widow's pension. And not just for Crete. On March 31, 1882, with uncharacteristic benevolence Congress voted Mary Lincoln, Julia Tyler, and Sarah Polk the same award.

When the news that they were being considered for the pension reached Mary and Julia, they reacted characteristically. Mary Lincoln, still in New York, was suspicious that her congressional enemies "would try to prevent [President] Arthur from *signing* it." Julia wrote one of her covert letters to the editor. In the *Washington Post,* an anonymous "Lady Subscriber" suggested Congress award the Widows $10,000 annually, so "they may . . . meet the requirements their actual position in the society of the country imposes upon them—and let there be no invidious distinctions . . ." When she got her first five-thousand-dollar check, Mrs. Ex was quite satisfied, and went on her perennial shopping binge, returning to the capital in time for the 1882 social season's close. At the White House, the former Lovely Lady Presidentress was asked by the new hostess, Mary McElroy, the widowed president's sister, to do the honors of receiving guests nearly forty years after her own reign, joined by Harriet Lane, now the widow of a Baltimore lawyer, living at nearby 1738 M Street.[8]

Chester Arthur's White House suited not just Julia Tyler but Julia Grant, honored with the general at the first formal dinner of the new president. On Arthur's arm, in diamonds and white lace, Mrs. G. was conscious of the lavish, expensive changes Arthur had made to her decorating project. In 1884, there would be some vague talk of Grant running, but conveniently about this time Julia—told that "I was a better politician than the General"—dreamed that a carriage pulled her in front of the White House, paused, and moved on. "After that,"

wrote Julia, "I gave no more thought to the subject." In New York, she satisfied herself as a leading society matron, befriending millionaires, dining at Delmonico's, summering at Long Branch, coaching through Central Park, and attending the theater. She settled into a lifestyle she had long sought, and was about to lose.[9]

Unknown to the Grants, their investment firm with Ferdinand Ward was collapsing, he having taken out loans beyond his capacity for repayment. The firm failed. Ward fled the country. In their luxurious house, Mrs. G. and Ulys faced the worst depths of poverty since their early married life. Julia bore up, accepting a thousand-dollar "loan" when a friend slipped it to her, commended by President Arthur for donating relics to the Smithsonian, and carefully observing Ulys as he began his memoirs for money. She began to think of her own version of their lives.

Money was now useless to Mary Lincoln. She just wanted peace. Returning to the Springfield home of her sister Elizabeth, she kept to her room, her eyes unable to endure light. Children outside chatted about the "crazy woman" in the upstairs room where the shades were always drawn. Suffering from paralysis, the bedridden Mary lay on one side of the bed, and other being "the president's place." Covered with boils, blinded, unable to move with comfort, she died on July 15, 1882—as she had lived—in pain. Her casket lay downstairs a few feet from where she had married.

Curiously, Mary's last battle was against suffrage. The woman who had once written that "men have the advantage of us women, in being able to go out, in the world and earning a living," opposed a woman's right to vote. Just a month before leaving New York, Mary Lincoln had noted that "Susan B. Anthony & other suffrage women" were staying in her hotel, but to a friend who had sent her a "spirituelle brochure" opposing suffrage, Mary wrote that she concurred. She felt American women had equal rights, even in "insolence," and suggested that "our strong minded sisters" go to Europe and see women at hard labor. She said suffrage should be treated with "wholesome neglect," because if given the vote, women would "behave in so inconsequent a manner as to reduce the whole matter to an absurdity." Nevertheless, she refused to sign an antisuffrage petition.[10]

The organized antisuffrage movement had among its flock the sitting lady of the White House, Mary Arthur McElroy, member of the Albany Association Opposed to Women's Suffrage. A woman "of a decisive manner when giving orders . . . she knew exactly what she wanted, and how she wanted it done; and she never hesitated to express her wishes clearly." President Arthur, however, refused to give Mary the protocol rank reserved for the president's wife. It was left empty, out of respect for his late wife, Ellen Herndon, who had died just a year and a half before.[11]

Gracious Ellen Arthur would have been perfect in the hostess role. Daughter of the Virginia aristocracy, raised in Washington, and even playing on the steps of widowed Dolley Madison's house, she was described as "one of the best specimens of the Southern woman," who assisted her husband's career as she "visited and kept up his list of friends." At their fashionable Lexington Avenue brownstone in New York, Mrs. Arthur had worked for prestigious charities, and befriended both old money and nouveaux riches, from Roosevelts to Vanderbilts. She had been a guest at Lincoln's second Inaugural and Nellie Grant's White House wedding. One friend had recalled that "Mrs. Arthur was a very ambitious woman. There was no happier woman in the country than she when her husband was made collector of the port of New York."

In her own right, she had been a celebrity as soprano of the New York Mendelssohn Glee Club, singing throughout the metropolis at performance halls. It was while waiting for her carriage after a concert that she caught a chill that developed into the pneumonia that killed her. But all had not been as beauteously engraved as the seemingly perfect vignette looked. During the war, when Arthur had been salaried as New York quartermaster, Ellen never hid her loyalties to the South. When a rebel cousin was in a northern prison, Chester had obtained permission for Ellen to visit her kin discreetly. Arthur joked that she was his "little rebel wife." But it wasn't an easy laugh. He eventually felt the need to resign. With his time spent increasingly in nurturing Republican connections, she began to resent her loneliness. Ellen Arthur was on the verge of filing for separation when she died.[12]

"Honors to me now," the widower confessed about the presidency without Ellen, "are not what they once were." In the White House, he kept a cherished hand-tinted photograph of the bonny Ellen in his room; a new rose was placed before it each day. At his New York home, her room was kept as she had left it, needle in place for her sewing, bookmark on the last page she read. To St. John's, he donated a stained-glass mirror in her memory. The light behind it was kept on all night, so he could see it glowing from the private rooms on the top floor of the White House, across the street. When he was approached by temperance leaders to not serve liquor at the executive mansion, his response spoke equally of his hesitancy not to discuss the memory of his wife. "Madame, I may be President of the United States, but my private life is nobody's damned business." He left the White House on March 4, 1885, remaining a widower.[13]

His successor, the corpulent, walrus-mustached Democratic governor of New York, Grover Cleveland, was also single, becoming the first unmarried president since Buchanan. When the news of his election came to him at the governor's mansion, he was encircled by women, including his married sister Mary Hoyt, single sister Rose Elizabeth, and Emma Folsom, comely widow of his former law partner, recipient of his loyal devotion, and to whose daughter, Frances, he was surrogate father and legal guardian.[14]

Albany wasn't the only town celebrating the return of the Democrat. Patronage jobs long held by GOP loyalists were quickly turned over to the steadfast members of the Democratic party who supported Cleveland, from California to New England. In Vermont, for example, mechanical engineer Andrew Goodhue was appointed steamboat inspector for the Lake Champlain Transportation Company by the president. For the Burlington Democrat, his wife Lemira, and six-year-old daughter, Grace, it meant a higher salary and prestige in the small college town of the University of Vermont. Goodhue regaled his little girl with legends and stories of tranquil Lake Champlain. Its peaceful calm metaphorically reflected in the gentle spirit of both father and daughter. Early on, it was noticed that Grace had a perceptive ability to understand people, with curiosity and love of life.[15]

The winds of change brought a stern presidential sister-cum-hostess to the helm, Rose Cleveland. With "masculine manner," she was considered a "bluestocking," being a graduate of Houghton Seminary, a professional college teacher, lecturer, and author. With the prominence of her role, Rose's book, *George Eliot's Poetry and Other Studies*, eventually earned her more than twenty-five thousand dollars in twelve printings. She was hostessing only as a favor to her brother. Personally, she was "a little grim," and some people found her "purposeful movements rather terrifying." On receiving lines, she passed the boredom by mentally conjugating Greek verbs. She nevertheless had strong views on her public role as example, resuming the Hayes edict, in part, by banning wine, and publicly supporting the suffrage movement. Rose even had a taint of the era's bigotry against many of the immigrants now coming from certain countries, "warning against his [Cleveland's] too frequently appointing Catholics to public office."[16]

Besides her circle of professional and reform-movement women friends, Rose welcomed the perennial Julia Tyler, who swooped into town for her annual sojourn. Following her tradition as seasonal Queen Mother, Mrs. Ex helped Rose receive at a White House reception. That very same spring of 1885, Miss Cleveland entertained Emma Folsom, who brought her twenty-year-old daughter, then on school break and preoccupied with her upcoming college graduation from Wells in June, and planning a Grand Tour of Europe with her mother some months later.[17]

Inevitably, Emma Folsom's visit volleyed a titter of gossip that she was to be the president's bride. To even the most practical observers, it seemed logical. He was a gentle and careful protector. He had managed her investments. They'd been friends for twenty-five years. Mrs. Folsom would not answer questions about the president's ardor. Still, by the time she sailed for Europe in late 1885, many were certain it was to purchase her wedding trousseau, "and study court life."[18]

Other secretly engaged women were sailing to Europe. Edith Carow had quietly accepted the marriage proposal of her childhood sweetheart, Theodore Roosevelt. Edith would claim that she had turned him down several times earlier, and he then went ahead and married Alice Lee of Boston, who had died three years later, the day after giving birth to a daughter named Alice. Burdened with the guilt of remarriage after widowhood, Theodore kept their plans secret. Edith's mother had moved to Europe after her alcoholic husband's death, and expected her daughter to assist her in the transition. Teddy and Edith would wed in England at the end of the year.

Another recent widow was also considering a move. At the moment, Julia Grant was in deep mourning at Mount McGregor, near Saratoga, New York. The general's book had provided well for her, but it was posthumous honor. Ulys had died a protractedly painful death from throat cancer. He'd finished his opus, *Personal Memoirs of U.S. Grant,* just days before dying in 1885. At his services in New York, President Cleveland led a host of dignitaries, among them presidents Hayes and Arthur. Mrs. G. was too bereaved to attend the impressive state funeral. But Julia had much to be soothed by. Within two years of its publication, royalties of Ulys's book had totaled $450,000. In February 1886, her friend Mark Twain handed her the largest royalty check in history—$200,000. Just two months before, without having to stage lobbying efforts like Mrs. Lincoln and Mrs. Tyler, Julia Grant was awarded the established five-thousand-dollar presidential widow's pension. She was an extremely wealthy woman. Her only concern was where to settle. She was not the sort to stay on a mountaintop.[19]

Meanwhile, as spring 1886 burst in Washington, the rumored betrothed of President Cleveland was finishing up her European tour, making purchases of new gowns. Spring fever brought fresh capital gossip. One rumor actually broke into print. To published reports, the president only vaguely responded, "I don't see why the papers keep marrying me to old ladies all the while . . ." It was a subtle clue. Many now were certain that Emma Folsom would be the new First Lady. Even Eugene Field abetted national gossip with his ballad "Sister Rose's Suspicions," posing Rose as questioning Grover, "And is it true, as eke 't is said, That you have made your mind to wed?" The *New York Herald*'s headline cover blazed: WASHINGTON GOSSIP—SOCIETY INCREDULOUS ABOUT THE PRESIDENT'S MARRIAGE—WHAT IF IT PROVE TRUE? Still no official word came from the White House on the president's intentions toward the Folsom woman. By now, the once-silly gossip had become a serious, full-blown national question.

The press managed to learn that Emma Folsom's boat was arriving back in the United States on May 27. As the startled Emma and her daughter debarked, they were rushed by the press. With the presence of the president's assistant Colonel Lamont *and* Rose Cleveland there to whisk and cloister them away at the Gilsey House hotel, there was no denying the gossip to be truth.

Finally, the next night, an official White House statement was released. The president was not marrying Emma Folsom.[20]

He was marrying her twenty-one-year-old daughter.

PART VI

The Gay Nineties
1886–1901

There was much interest among the ladies in reading of the lives of early Presidents' wives. Those who knew realized that the power itself lay in their province.

—Henry Adams
Democracy (1886)

"Yum-Yum!"

BEFORE ISSUING HIS public statement, President Cleveland privately aired his hopes on what role his new wife would play: "I have my heart set upon making Frank a sensible, domestic American wife and would be pleased not to hear her spoken of as 'The First Lady of the Land.' . . . I should feel very much afflicted if she gets many notions in her head." He feared most a "huntdown" by the press "animals" of the "defenceless girl, as if she were a criminal."[1]

The nervous bridegroom needn't have worried about "Frank's" notions. It was the press, whom he derisively called, "the gang," and the public who were to shape her into more than just a First Lady. Out of the wisps of half-truths and intrigue about an innocent, unaffected college girl called Frances, a full-fledged Celebrity was being created.

The wedding would take place at the White House, in the Blue Room, on June 2. As Rose icily told reporters, it was to be "a very private affair." The press was barred, which made them work even harder at producing new daily copy for the columns, even if they had to make it up.

Each satin footstep of the young lass was recorded. She was called everything from "The Bride-Elect," to "Yum-Yum"—the latter cognomen taken from a musical number in the Gilbert and Sullivan hit *The Mikado*—but "Frankie" seemed the most popular nickname. Her hairstyle of a low-slung knot, covering her shaved nape, was the rage, dubbed the "à la Cleveland." Little was printed of "who" Frankie was, as opposed to "what" she now represented. In fact, Miss Folsom never did speak with the press.

Alongside advertisements for Buffalo Bill's Wild West Show and corset sales, as well as stories of violence in Northern Ireland, cocaine addiction of the wealthy, and pressures on professional women (under the headline DEGENERATED WOMEN), there were stories on the wedding cake's "plain" frosting, the bride's seasickness, the amount of her luggage, and the fact that an old piece of veiling found in her ship stateroom was torn to pieces by souvenir hunters, soon after Miss Folsom vacated. There was a serious account of the "thirteen barrels of cut mums . . . five wagonloads of . . . roses, azaleas, geraniums, heliotropes" with which the White House was festooned. Another story went into reams of detail on the white satin wedding boxes that were ordered from Tiffany, which subcontracted with the Spooner Manufacturing Company, which had to pay its shopgirls double to work feverishly and secretly on the boxes. An Illinois congressmen now fretted about his campaign promise to get one of his women constituents married to the president.

Though a *New York Times* story quoted an Englishman who was "shocked and disgusted at the freedom, levity and fulsomeness attending to the affair," a *Washington Post* editorial defended the intrusions. "Everybody is gossiping about the White House wedding. Men and women are interested in an affair which has never before been witnessed and the curiosity manifested is neither vulgar nor impertinent: it is merely the penalty which those occupying high stations always have to pay." The president still refused to invite even one reporter to witness the event.

While the *Times* believed that "the orderly" Washingtonians would consider the wedding private, the *Post* advised that at the moment of the wedding, every single home and church bell "should sound forth a wedding peal, that every battery, either afloat or ashore . . . should welcome her with thunders of fort and of fleet (cannons, horns and sirens) . . . every national flag should be unfurled . . . every home . . . should bear additional light . . ."

Meanwhile, when President Cleveland appeared in New York to review the Decoration Day parade, thousands were amused as every passing band played "He's Going to Marry Yum-Yum." People were crazed to see Frankie, and several churches were "dangerously crowded when it was reported" that she might appear. Miss Folsom stayed in her "number 8" room (which was widely printed in newspapers), amused by press drawings of her because they "do not bear the slightest resemblance," and received a flood of letters, one of which, from a common worker, asked her to teach the president of "the amelioration of the laboring classes." When she arrived in Washington the morning of the wedding, some members of the press actually glimpsed her, giggling at them from a landeau window.

In the White House, Frances readied her fifteen-foot-trained white gown with orange-blossom trim in Julia Grant's favorite "South Room," looking before Dolley Madison's mirror, surrounded by a sense of her predecessors. At the last minute, a concession had been made to the press, allowing them to take a peek at the flower arrangements, done up as a Victorian jungle. The buzzing crowds swelled, covering the lawn, peering into the open windows, ogling the arriving guests. By six, the "thoroughly democratic" crowd, which ranged from "ragged street arab" to "well-to-do merchant and his wife" to "rough bricklayer" to "clerk" all shuffled into place, clustering around the house. One account claimed, "The gates were left wide open. Everybody could come in and everybody who was disposed entered the wide portals and passed up the wide asphalt drives."

"Suddenly," a reporter recorded, "the strains of the wedding march floated through the open windows . . . 'the service has begun' was whispered from mouth to mouth. At the same time came the booming of cannon . . . the merry peal of bells . . . Then . . . a tantalizing hush within the walls . . . the strains of the 'Bridal Chorus' . . . the ceremony was over." Bandleader John Philip Sousa played Gilbert and Sullivan, but the president asked him to change the printed title of a program piece, "Student of Love." He also removed the word "obey" from the vows. No need to provoke snide remarks about robbing the cradle.

The president, wanting to "avoid the number of newspaper men" at all costs, managed to foil them as he and Frances slipped to Deer Park, Maryland, a quiet country spot, but there found that "leading papers of the country had their representatives here almost as soon as he arrived." The "Peeping Tom" reporters aimed their spyglasses toward the love cottage's bedroom. All efforts were made to dissuade the press. Detectives wouldn't let them stand stationary. No local hotels made rooms available to them. Still they persisted, churning stories like "Mrs. Cleveland Fishes," which carried the warning that "she is disposed not to give up." Other exploitation began. A reputed Folsom cousin, "Agnes," who sang at the Casino Theater as "the pretty waitress," enjoyed a brief moment of fame. A Washington merchant sold his surplus of luggage by lettering FRANCES FOLSOM CLEVELAND on the pieces and placing them out on the street. E. B. Barnum & Company advertised their clothes by running an ad with a cartoon of the president and Miss Folsom taking the vows. A drawing of Emma Folsom's kiss for her bride-daughter made a magazine cover.

Meanwhile, congratulatory cables were thrown as scraps to a press starving for copy. European factory workers, woman presidential candidate Belva Lockwood, Queen Victoria, Odd Fellows disappointed over the relinquished bachelorhood, and Mrs. Joseph Pulitzer, who assured, "Of the many congratulations you will receive today, none will be more sincere than mine," all sent messages. Grover, perhaps at Frankie's thoughtful prodding, did not forget her new sorority. First Ladies Tyler, Polk, Grant, and Garfield were all sent engraved White House announcements.

When the president did acknowledge reporters, he chastised them for repeating "ridiculous" stories "manufactured out of whole cloth," and soon after wrote to the New York Evening Post that the press had "used the enormous power of the modern newspaper to perpetuate . . . a colossal impertinence . . . not as professional . . . tattlers, but as the guides and instructors of the public in conduct and morals . . ." He may have been rude, but he was right. The Washington Post, however,

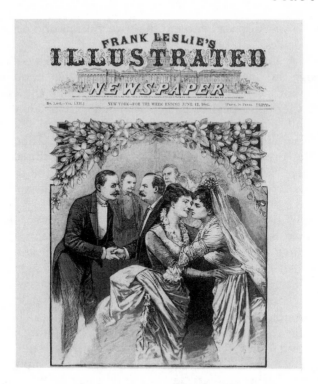

offered a warning to the president who dared consider his public First Lady a mere private citizen, stating that "privacy about a private matter does not suit the American people who, since the advent of modern journalism, have no private matters." If the Clevelands thought that the besieging of their private lives would peak upon their return to the White House, they were quite mistaken.

The honeymoon was over.[2]

– 29 –

Frankie

THE NATIONAL OBSESSION with Frances Cleveland assumed proportions never before seen in America. Her marriage was the closest event in presidential history to a marriage in the British royal family. With the sophistication of communications, American journalism had come of age, and its primary subject was young, pure, innocent, and ravish-

ing. Christened as "Frank," she had legally changed her name to Frances, but the press and public persisted in calling her Frankie. She
absolutely hated it.

Almost immediately, there was warranted concern about Frankie
being stampeded as gawking crowds shoved each other to stare at her.
At her first reception, several women fell back dangerously into the
Marine Band. People stood outside the house or on the lawn to try and
glimpse her. The most astounding phenomenon was the moment she
appeared on a stand at a St. Louis ceremony. At the mere sight of her
parasol, literally hundreds of people stormed the stairs, scaled a wall,
clung to carvings, and smashed a barricade, just to see Frankie. No First
Lady had *ever* caused such a reaction. The entire world saw her in
church and at any number of other places through the illustrations in
weeklies like *Leslie's* and *Harper's*. To the public, she was an entity, a
symbol. Initially, Frances viewed it all as a manifestation of benevolent
interest. Suspicion was foreign to her nature.

She was tall and thin, with pale skin and rosy cheeks, and sapphire-
blue eyes fringed by long, thick black lashes. Her lips were full and red,
her chestnut hair wavy and abundant. Others noticed that she had
"some mysterious inner force" of peaceful spirituality. "It is . . . comparatively easy . . . for a beautiful woman to captivate men," said one
woman author, "but to please women is quite another thing . . . [They]
admire her grace and beauty, but . . . naturalness and cordiality . . .
has won their hearts."[1]

She played the piano, spoke French and German and read Latin, and was adept at photography with her own camera. She had a Buffalo accent, pronouncing roof as "ruff" and root as "rutt." Having taken a childhood pledge, Frances did not drink, but didn't inflict her abstinence on others. She merely had her glass always filled with Apollinaris mineral water. Eventually, a time came when she would sip a liqueur, but added, "I feel horrible taking a brandy after signing that pledge." She was a quick wit, making "things lively." Englishman Cecil Spring-Rice recalled her dry humor when she recounted an event at which the public were to hear her husband speak and stare at her good looks. When they arrived, the president had a sore throat, and she had a bandage over her eye. She taught her French poodle to understand French.[2]

Some questioned the intelligence of the "girl." The editor of Harper's wrote confidentially about her bewilderment over Frances's "bond" with the erudite Mrs. Henry Watson Gilder. "It did not occur to me that there was anything in Mrs. Cleveland." Rose Cleveland clarified, "My new sister is a woman capable of great development; a much stronger character than appears on the surface. She is a superior person."[3]

She had a coy charm. When the editor of the Philadelphia Public Ledger told her at his farm that she could choose one of his dairy cows as a gift, she picked "Grace," and he retorted, "I never thought you'd pick the best one!" Coming upon some house staff in her room dancing while an engineer banged away on her piano, Frances reprimanded only with a look, then joined them.[4]

Her thoughtfulness to people of all races and classes earned Frances a deserved comparison to Dolley Madison, but one creative manufacturer linked the First Lady to the saintly figure of Martha Washington looming kindly behind her on a mass-marketed postcard. It was Grover, however, who instructed her, "You will find that you get along better in this job if you don't try anything new." Mrs. Cleveland agreed to essentially play hostess, and when the president spied her successfully handling throngs at her first reception, he chortled, "She'll do! She'll do!" She shook tens of thousands of hands by "tilting her forearm upwards in a playful and almost girlish gesture." Privately, the First Lady was assisted by a social secretary, Minnie R. Alexander—the first nonfamily member called in to help a First Lady—and the first form letters were drafted to deal with the deluge of thousands of fan letters sent to this president's wife. The role was a tremendous responsibility for the mere twenty-one-year-old. A friend later recalled, "To be who she was meant to deny herself many harmless and pleasant things permitted others" her age, but she learned "self-denial" easily.[5]

The president's overprotectiveness sometimes appeared like a twinge of jealousy. He was insulted when the New York Fire Department invited the First Lady, and not *him*, to a ceremony to present some fire flags. Defensively, he wrote, "I have not the slightest doubt that I would have been very welcome . . . my wife, because she is my wife, was expected to appear before the city of New York, in its streets, in the most public way possible, and assume a prominent role without reference to the presence or absence of her husband and without the least participation on my part . . ." Grover claimed it was Frances's decision "whether she was willing to assume such a public role, entirely independent of her husband, and . . . her judgment and feeling were against it . . . Her social duties . . . [are] very exacting . . ." As First Lady, Mrs. Cleveland was never to make a separate public trip.[6]

Though she led no specific cause, Mrs. Cleveland sent money and supported the WCTU's "Hope and Help" project, and took especial concern in supporting aspiring musicians, an interest sufficiently well known to the public that she became the recipient of many original scores of music, composed in her honor. In one case, she sponsored a young violinist to study in Berlin, and the girl became the first American to win the prized Mendelssohn Stipendium. She also "showed a genuine concern for women who worked, and . . . helped a struggling friend, who taught music to support herself, by obtaining several pupils for her." Mrs. Cleveland's interest in music was real, and when opera singer Adelina Patti paid a call on the First Lady, she told Frances her voice had the proper "timbre" for professional singing.[7]

It was another multilingual pianist besides Frances who admitted, "Music was the absorbing interest . . . the inspiration of all my dreams and ambitions." Although Miss Helen Herron graduated from the Cincinnati College of Music, she had gone to work as a teacher before marriage, and organized a salon where "intellectual and economic" issues were debated. That's where she had met the jolly lawyer William Howard Taft. He'd become mesmerized by this remarkable young woman who sometimes insisted on paying for her own share of a rented rig, and had sought employment to be financially independent of her father. Taft wrote, "She has done this without encouragement by her family, who thought the work too hard for her . . . she chafed under the conventionalities of society which would keep a young lady for evening entertainments. She wanted to do something in life and not be a burden. Her eagerness for knowledge of all kinds puts me to shame. Her capacity for work is just wonderful."

"Nellie," as she was called, made no secret of her ambition. On a trip to Washington during the Cleveland administration, she received a letter from her Taft: "I wonder, Nellie dear, if you and I will ever be there in any official capacity? Oh, yes, I forgot; of course we shall when you become secretary of the treasury." Will needed Nellie, admitting to her that "it is an awful question for you to solve whether you will put yourself in the keeping of a man." He begged, "[D]o say that you will try to love me. Oh, how I will work and strive to be better and do better, how I will labor for our joint advancement if you will only let me." They married just seventeen days after the Clevelands.

Nellie was remarkably free of any bigotry. When a black porter came to visit her father-in-law, Will asked her if she'd be offended. Nellie broke into laughter at the very thought of it. "I didn't mind," she wrote, "but the black butler of the house was rather shocked." Equally, she showed no intolerance toward the many Jewish families who offered help in her "organisation and management" of the Cincinnati Orchestra Association, which afforded her "a practical method for expressing and making use of my love and knowledge of music."[8]

Frances was akin to Nellie. When approached by a black woman who founded the Washington Home for Friendless Colored Girls after discovering two starving girls eating out of a garbage can, to help the home get started, Frankie immediately accepted and tried to interest other white women. The First Lady was also the most visible member of the Colored Christmas Club, a charity providing food to poor local children, by personally distributing gifts and sitting with them through a Punch and Judy show.[9]

Though she avoided suffrage, Frances became the first real example for women since Dolley Madison. No First Lady within anyone's memory had enjoyed such popularity with women of all ages. "The women's party, in the field won't count," wrote one woman, "unless they take Mrs. Cleveland for their candidate—then!" Perhaps the single act that won her the universal respect of lower- and middle-class women was her initiation of a special Saturday afternoon reception, conceived for working women.[10]

Not long after she began them, an official urged her to stop her special receptions, explaining that "about half of all the women . . . are clerks from the department stores and others—a great rabble of shopgirls. And of course a White House afternoon is not intended for them." Mrs. Cleveland became extremely angry, but held her temper. "Indeed!" she snapped. "And if I should hold the little receptions . . . other than Saturday, they couldn't attend, because they have to work all other afternoons. Is that it?" The smug official smiled. "That's it exactly." The First Lady gave strict orders that nothing should ever be scheduled to interfere with the Saturday receptions "so long as there were any store clerks, or other self-supporting women and girls who wished to come to the White House."[11]

Frances kept abreast of the professional and personal lives of her fellow Wells alumnae, and accepted the offer to serve as a Wells trustee, a position she'd hold for nearly a half-century. She believed that education was a means of achieving equality, and eventually became publicly active in that cause, assisting women in gaining education and professional employment and maintaining a network by helping to found the

University Women's Club. She was later instrumental in urging New Jersey to "open up educational opportunities for girls, like young men." Partly due to her efforts, the New Jersey College for Women was founded.[12]

Women with special requests made Frances their patroness. From a group identified only as "Your Mothers" came a plea to help an "industrious" single mother with two children who had "successfully taken the civil service examination," and was looking for "a position under the government." "Will you not bring your innate sympathy in her behalf through your husband [and] have her placed in office. . . ?"[13]

The interest American women took in Frankie's doings prompted Laura Holloway, author of the first history of the First Ladies, *Ladies of the White House*, in 1881, to update the book so Mrs. Cleveland could be included, and spurred the writing of Mary Gordon's 1886 *From Lady Washington to Mrs. Cleveland.* The books brought renewed focus on the more elderly members of the sorority, all of whom took interest in their new young member.

When the Clevelands visited Tennessee, the infirm Sarah Polk insisted on rising, "for there was a distinguished precedence for this in Dolley Madison rising in John Quincy Adams' presence . . ." The two women compared notes on how the role had changed. Julia Grant also liked Frances. Mrs. G.'s years immediately following the general's death were spent fighting a movement to have Ulys's remains transferred to Arlington Cemetery, and making lengthy holiday from Europe to San Diego, still restless about where to settle.

Among "Frankie's" most eminent admirers was the other White House bride, Julia Tyler. Now that she had finally won her pension, the waltz had slowed down for Julia. Gray-haired, heavier, she remained the center of attention amid a large and happy brood of descendants, her wicker basket full of fried quail legendary among them. Strongly disagreeing with her son Gardie's continued pro-southern sentiments, Mrs. Ex had mellowed back to being woman of all the people. Though now living in Richmond, she said she was still "the subject of great attention from the society people" during her seasonal visits to Washington. She had left town a month before the Cleveland wedding, but Julia Tyler met Frances Cleveland at an afternoon ladies' reception during the spring 1887 season, in what would prove her last visit to the White House. When a misaddressed letter from Crete Garfield inviting Julia to the unveiling of a President Garfield statue in Washington on May 11 finally reached Mrs. Tyler in Richmond, she responded that she had already left town by that date, but regretted not sharing Crete's "sad participation." She would never again return to Washington.[14]

Like the Tylers, the Clevelands were openly affectionate. When reunited after several days' separation, they "kissed each other tenderly," in front of Harvard president Eliot, and Grover had "tears running down his cheeks." Frances knew and forgave that her husband had, admittedly, likely fathered an illegitimate son, having been informed while in college of "the Buffalo scandal" by her mother. It had no effect on her marriage. Frances would later write Grover that "my heart is full of gratitude for what the years of your life have meant to me. You know how dearly I love you. You do not not mind me saying it over, any day . . . so I repeat it and repeat it . . ."

Still, she was quite independent. According to Crook, though Frances "deferred" in many matters to her husband, she "possessed a keen mind and could see straight through things which would baffle many women." When she was legally required to be questioned to determine that she was not being pressured by her husband into co-signing a deed, her husband respected her right. When a companion asked her if the president would go fishing with him, Frances asserted, "No one goes out of this house on Sunday." After waiting for her to join him in a scheduled drive together, Grover angrily threw down his coat and gloves, resolving not to go. As Frances shouted, "I am ready now," he quietly picked up his hat and gloves and went driving.[15]

Her influence on him began to have political effects. One Cabinet wife said, "You may depend that the President will not work himself to death now. He has begun a new life . . . you may look for a decided change in favor . . ." One account asserted that she "did bring him in contact with people and ideas he had never considered before . . . eased his lonely concentration on the minutiae of his work . . . could and did make his relations easier with congressmen who had been offended when, as they felt, he was unreasonable about political concessions."[16]

President Cleveland was adamant that "a woman should not bother her head about political parties and public questions, and that she should be content to rule in the domain of the house." Though it was said that Frances "laughingly turns from politics," by the mere nature of her position, it crept into even domestic questions. The only way she managed to get the president out of an ugly tawny suit was to remind him that Irish Catholics, who were mostly Democrats, considered orange the symbol of their hated British Protestant enemies. When Frances warned that he'd "certainly lose the Irish vote," her "argument prevailed!"[17]

Cleveland clearly saw the political advantages of his wife. On July 21, 1888, as members of the House were making speeches just previous to voting on the important Tariff Bill, the First Lady was prominently present, listening intently from the visitors' gallery, as her absent husband's representative, and would personally report back to him. One account said Frances was "the soul of the administration . . . an integral part . . . which subdue[s] even the bitterest political opponents; she has but to show her . . . winsome manners to . . . bridge every pitfall . . ." Frances's personal power was apparent to Cleveland's political enemies as well. And it was no light matter to them.[18]

Republican Chauncey M. Depew conceded "that it will be harder for us to win against both Mr. and Mrs. Cleveland." The wife of a prominent Republican leader said she felt "dreadfully guilty, as if she were conspiring to increase" the popularity of the Cleveland administration, because she openly admired Frances. One Republican said, "I detest him so much that I don't even think his wife is beautiful." For fear of it backfiring, the opposition press avoided making hay of her, and even Eugene Field, who had delighted in razzing Rose in verse, made no "reference to Mrs. Cleveland." But more threatening political elements who hated Cleveland were already setting in motion secret plans to counteract Frances's political advantage. They were not alone.[19]

Interest in Frances hadn't slackened, and exploiters began offering gifts. When it was learned that she played the piano, she was flooded with piano-manufacturing company requests to let them give her a piano and advertise her use of their product. Gifts like fifty shares of stock in a milling and mining company were returned. S. Oppenheimer & Bros. "were led to believe" that the First Lady "would be pleased to examine" their improved sewing machines at "a private view . . ." Even members of the public seized upon every bit of trivia revealed about Frances. When news was made out of the fact that she enjoyed the conservatories, she received a letter from a Republican Senate wife, Caroline Harrison, on behalf of the Agriculture Department's Division of Botany, asking, "Will you be kind enough to give me . . . when you can spare them, specimens of your orchids? . . . I will prepare and mount them myself . . ." for the "National Herbarium."[20]

Up to ninety dollars a month was being spent on women's daily hairdressing, "à la Cleveland" remaining the popular vogue, and Frankie was lauded for setting "the example of simple and becoming hairdressing." "Tens of thousands" of "Frankie" photographs were sold and found "in nearly every home." Women imitated her pose when they sat for photographs. As initially timid advertisers now began to brazenly use "Frankie's" name and picture without permission to sell their soaps, perfumes, candies, liver pills, ashtrays, and even ladies' underwear, things got out of hand. One offensive magazine ad, which blatantly lied that her complexion was due to the use of a certain brand of arsenic pills, set off a series of indignant letters to Frances, chastising her for commercializing her role. She'd never even heard of the company.[21]

A congressional bill was introduced in 1888 to enact that any individual or corporation "who shall publicly exhibit, use or employ the likeness or representation of any female living or dead, who is or was the wife, mother, daughter or sister of any citizen of the U.S. without the consent in writing of the person whose likeness is to be used shall

be guilty of high misdemeanor and shall upon indictment be fined not less than $500, nor more than $5,000, and stand imprisoned until fine and costs are paid."

Perhaps the lawyers in Congress realized that, although technically Frances was a private citizen and not an elected public official, she was indeed a public figure. The bill never passed, and manufacturers took its failure as a cue to step up their exploitation of "Frankie" ads. With Congress's decision, the field was open, without legal recourse against advertisers. With the worst charge being impropriety, all the White House could do was dissuade. It could not sue. The president personally berated one Leo Oppenheim, who used Frances's name "in the most indecent way," in an *Albany Evening Journal* ad. "I suppose we must always have . . . dirty and disreputable fellows," Cleveland rebuked the exploiter, "but I shall be surprised if you find such advertising profitable . . ." There was little else the Clevelands could do. The problem became affixed to the role.[22]

Mrs. Cleveland's fashions became the subject of public debate. After one admiring newspaper described the First Lady in a dress with "waist cut low in the neck, and the arms were bare from the shoulder to the elbow," the WCTU demanded that, as a moral example for young women, she stop wearing such gowns. Mrs. Cleveland didn't respond, and continued to wear her dresses. The WCTU went ahead anyway and distributed a flyer at its convention claiming that the First Lady *had* stopped wearing low-cut gowns. Other arbiters fiddled with Frances's clothes. When two reporters found themselves in the empty capital one summer without a story, they devised the fable that Frances hated the bustle, stopped wearing it, and that the contraption would soon meet its final demise. It did. And even Frances stopped wearing it.[23]

The fear for the First Lady's personal security, even in the house, hadn't abated, but when she left the mansion, it was worse. "More than once," wrote a chronicler, she would arrive at an out-of-house destination "trembling . . . after running a press gauntlet." Even a vacation was ruined, as she was, according to Grover, "continually watched and lied about," and he planned to cut short the respite because he wouldn't "subject my wife to that treatment."[24] There was but one answer. The president and First Lady moved out of the White House, living there only during the social season, December 1 to March 31. Just previous to his marriage, President Cleveland bought a pastoral farmhouse two miles from the White House to "escape this cursed grind." Though the First Lady called it Oak View, the press called it Red Top, because of the newly painted roof. Red Top, as well as their Cape Cod summer home, Grey Gables, was barred to the press. "Mr. Cleveland," wrote the Massachusetts governor, "was very particular that no photographs should be taken of his family or of the interiors of his home."[25]

Occasionally, the president's frustrations burst out in public. Once, chastising reporters who focused only on Frances while he was delivering a speech, Cleveland yelled out about "those ghouls of the press." For herself, Frances accepted the invasion of her privacy with more equanimity, even levity. When the small daughter of one of Frances's Wells colleagues wondered if the First Lady was as popular in Washington as she was in her native western New York, Frances mocked child talk: "Yes, dese peoples down here loves Mrs. Cleveland as good as us folks up dere do."[26]

But the press's simmering resentment began to boil. For both Democratic and Republican enemies of the president, the campaign of 1888 proved to be the best chance to strike at him politically through Frances. One woman believed that her "popularity makes her the most potent factor in the administration which the Republicans have to face and fight against."[27]

That is exactly what they did.

The very day after Henry Watterson publicly escorted Mrs. Cleveland to the theater, "there began to buzz reports . . . [a]t first covert," romantically linking him with Frances, which soon "gained in volume and currency until a distinguished Republican party leader put his imprint upon them in an after-dinner speech, going the length of saying 'the newly-wedded Chief Magistrate had actually struck his wife' and forbidden me the Executive Mansion." When she heard the tale, the First Lady was privately "shocked and outraged."[28]

Every "little trip" of the First Lady's "was construed into a permanent break" from her husband. When the president slipped out of the White House for a private carriage ride, often to Red Top to join Frances, callers were told he was out and might not be back "until night— perhaps not until the next morning." Enemies twisted this "with such cunning" to "hint that President Cleveland indulged in periodical dissipation." The actress Mae West would long after recall hearing as a child the dirty lyrics to a Bowery vaudeville routine about "hankin' for Frankie" with a lewdly retouched photograph of the First Lady hanging above the piano. Quick to follow was the publication of the novel *The Honorable Peter Sirling*, which thinly veiled the president as a character who assumes the paternity of his law partner's bastard son to spare the feelings of his partner's legitimate daughter. Of course, Frances's father was long dead by the time she married. It didn't matter to a gullible public and scheming enemies. Rumors spread. Just prior to the Democratic Convention, the vilest story burst.[29]

A Massachusetts Baptist minister, one C. H. Pendleton, proclaimed from the pulpit that the president physically abused the First Lady.

While the convention was meeting, a printed pamphlet with the charges was distributed to delegates with an anonymous senator as a reputed witness. The pamphlet was believed to be the work of anti-Cleveland Democrats. When a Maggie Nicodemus wrote Frances about the pamphlet, it was the last straw. The First Lady took the opportunity to defend her marriage, publicly, in newspapers.

"I can only say in answer to your letter that every statement in the interview which you send me is basely false, and I pity the man who has been made the tool to give circulation to such wicked and heartless lies. I can wish the women of our country no better blessing than that their homes and their lives may be as happy, and that their husbands may be as kind and attentive, as considerate and affectionate, as mine." It was only the second time a First Lady had issued a "press release." Cleveland was nominated, but his nomination failed to stop the rumor mill. When another rumor circulated that the president also "pummeled his mother-in-law" and "exiled her to Europe," the vacationing Emma Folsom was more brittle than her daughter. "All this is beneath notice, and is a matter best treated with contemptuous silence . . . I suppose they counted on the fact that the President and his wife would not deign to utter a word in reply . . . It is all a foolish campaign ploy without a shadow of foundation."[30]

Some now openly diminished Mrs. Cleveland's influence in the campaign. She appeared in a cartoon on the cover of *Judge* magazine in October 1887 as the Queen of Hearts, holding a rose and a scepter, portrayed as Cleveland's greatest "drawing card." "What a pity it is for

Grover," the copy ran, "that Hearts are not Trumps in politics." There were, however, Cleveland supporters who saw the use of "Frankie's" celebrity as beneficial. Frances Cleveland became the first First Lady to be a subject of comment at a convention, a speaker invoking her name from the podium and "elicit[ing] such rounds of applause that men lost their heads." Without their candidate's permission, some Cleveland managers ordered posters, flags, emblems, handbills, plates, and cards manufactured with her image, placed above and between the president and vice president, as if she were running for the office of First Lady. Frances Cleveland Influence Clubs were organized by women working for the party.

The Republicans countered by placing the picture of Mrs. Benjamin Harrison, their candidate's wife, on campaign paraphernalia, like tablet covers and a fanlike card that flipped over to reveal her quote of admiration for "Little Ben."[31]

Caroline Harrison "won," but being a good loser, Frances hosted a welcoming dinner for her and her family.

On Inauguration Day, just moments before she left "forever," soon to take up residence in New York, a composed Frances Cleveland dropped an extremely rare hint of her hidden ambition. To servant Jerry Smith, she revealed her plan, almost calculating so. "Now, Jerry, I want you to take good care of all the furniture and ornaments in the house for I want to find everything just as it is now when we come back again."

Jerry gasped at this prediction, but Frances, one observer thought, "departed defiantly" from her role.

Frances Folsom Cleveland was certain. "We are coming back just four years from today."[32]

— 30 —

The President-General

ADEQUATE LIVING QUARTERS were important to Caroline Harrison.

To that end, she became the first First Lady to skillfully and publicly manage her "project." She personally called a meeting with the secretary of state, worked in tandem with an engineer-architect drawing designs for a new White House, and gained the support of Harriet Lane and the general public by holding a press briefing and politically allying herself with Senator Leland Stanford and Congressman Seth Milliken to lobby for a congressional bill to completely overhaul and expand the White House into a gargantuan monstrosity with tipped greenhouses, lumbering wings, and grand fountains. When the final vote came, it was frustrating. Though it passed the Senate, the speaker of the House, Thomas B. Reed of Maine, had refused to let the bill come to the House floor for a vote because President Harrison had ignored Reed's choice for collectorship of Maine. Caroline had to make due with minor funds to clean the house.[1]

The living quarters remained crammed full of her family, which included a son, his wife, and daughter; a daughter, her husband, and two children (including the most famous of the brood, "Baby McKee"); her aged father; and her widowed niece and social secretary, Mary Lord Dimmick. Crook called them "home bodies." Others were less kind.[2]

Senate wife Julia Foraker said, "The opening nineties saw the old regime, Anglo-Saxon, conservative, making its last stand at the White House. The Harrisons gathered . . . women who could give all their time to social perfections undistracted by suffrage, divorce, interior decoration or other extraneities . . . We still exchanged recipes . . . changed our dresses exhaustingly—often during the day, and were, altogether, as conventional as a sideboard." Of the First Lady, Harriet Blaine sniped, "Her American Majesty . . . is too much given . . . to making everybody comfortable." Cecil "Springy" Spring-Rice wrote his friends the Theodore Roosevelts that Caroline and Ben Harrison were "small and fat . . . They said they were glad to see us, but neither looked it." Caroline *was* motherly, but she also had a droll sense of humor. When a butler appeared with one of his trouser legs up, showing his underwear, the First Lady asked if he were adopting the British custom of knee breeches, and if so, why with just one leg?[3]

Caroline's activities reflected her domestic role—though when electric lights were installed, she was too frightened to touch the switches. She inspected the house from dank basement to cobwebbed attic, screaming every time her assistant shot a rat. She uncovered, identified, and tagged past First Ladies' china, grouping pieces of them for eventual public display. A gifted watercolorist and deft with her own pottery kiln, she designed the Harrison state china and taught the process in special classes. She also hosted French classes, and bred her beloved orchid, popularizing it for matrons. Critics laughed at all this, parodying her as a mindless homebody, saying she cooked her own family's meals in the kitchens. The jibes deeply wounded this woman of substance.

Mrs. Harrison, a graduate of what would become Ohio's Miami University, had worked for the welfare of all people, a product of the growing belief that women should take an active role outside their homes. If her primary public role was exemplary goodwife, she was privately a political power. Conscious of all political subtlies, she joined

Ben in publicly reviewing a parade of organized-labor workers, mostly Irish immigrants, as well as a "Blaine Day" parade composed of "dusky faces as well as fair." She knew her husband's stand on issues, and even promoted them by sending out copies of one of his speeches to Republican leaders.[4]

Benjamin Harrison was said by intimates to have "often talked State matters over with her. He did not always do so, but, as a rule, when time and opportunity permitted, would discuss with her the principal plans of his administration . . . [and] like all men of keen perceptions and good executive tact, [he] saw that a woman's intuition was often more valuable in matters of statecraft than a man's logic. He did not hesitate to talk over with Mrs. Harrison a great many affairs of state and her advice was frequently found of value." When the Sherman Silver Act was passed in Congress and the president signed it, it was to Caroline that he wrote immediately about its importance.[5]

Caroline had her share of press criticism. In 1890, the millionaire postmaster general John Wanamaker and several of his Philadelphia friends gave a rambling Cape May cottage to the First Lady. It immediately incited public criticism that a president's wife should not accept such valuable property from a politician and private interests, though, after the fact, the president claimed that the original plan was for him to *buy* it from them. In Gilbert and Sullivan verse, a poem was published, implying that Harrison, using his wife as an excuse, had accepted the house as a bribe. When the First Lady assumed occupancy of the twenty-room beach house, the ridicule continued, the *New York Sun* suspiciously asking, "Who are those generous individuals that have bestowed upon MRS. BENJAMIN HARRISON a cottage at Cape May?"[6]

Caroline was also parodied in an unflattering commercial exploitation, in a QD girdle fastener advertisement. An accurate sketch of her was used with the proclamation that she was "A Boon to Woman [of the] Anglo Saxon Race." Some time after, coming to consult her, Colonel Crook found her in a depressed mood after reading a newspaper. "Oh . . . what have we done! What have we ever done that we should be held up to ridicule by newspapers . . . cruelly attacked . . . made fun of, for the country to laugh at! If this is the penalty . . . I hope the Good Lord will deliver my husband from any further experience."[7]

Caroline Harrison, however, would endure as the first First Lady to publicly associate herself with struggling women's organizations, the Women's Medical Fund of John Hopkins School of Medicine and the Daughters of the American Revolution, both founded on feminist principles of full equal rights—one for education and the other in public affairs. Both groups needed the publicity a First Lady brought them. On suffrage, Caroline was open-minded, and supported the hiring of family friend Alice Sanger as the first woman stenographer to work for a president.

The Medical Fund was a drive by prominent American women to raise the necessary $500,000 for Hopkins Medical School, only on the condition that women be given full and equal opportunities in pursuing medical educations and careers. Mrs. Harrison headed the national committee from Washington, as a network of fifteen urban areas were targeted for fund-raising. Curious about the feminist movement, and openly supportive of women's "political activities," a "shrewd" First Lady saw "great political potential" when the DAR formed, with founders from the ranks of government workers, and hoped to make it a "powerful political force for women." To begin to build a unified lobby of women's influence in government, Caroline accepted the offer to become their first president-general. By inviting the group to meet in the Blue Room, guiding the election of officers to women with political connections, listening to their objectives, and supporting "every move that had political implications," the First Lady helped the DAR immediately establish credibility.[8]

The group was founded because men—the Sons of the American Revolution—had promised to include, then excluded, women from membership. What made Caroline's role even more important was her delivery of her own prepared speech before the DAR, the first instance of an incumbent First Lady speaking publicly from her own text. She focused on woman's power:

We have within ourselves the only element of destruction; our foes are from within, not without. It has been said "that the men to make a

country are made by self-denial," and is it not true, that the society to
live and grow and become what we desire it to be, must be composed of
self-denying women? Since this society has been organized and so much
thought and reading directed to the early struggles of this country, it has
been made plain that much of its success was due to . . . women of that
era. The unselfish part they acted constantly commands itself to our
admiration and example. If there is no abatement in this element of
success in our ranks, I feel sure that their daughters can perpetuate a
society worthy the cause and worthy themselves.[9]

The founding of the DAR represented a recent surge in patriotism and
interest in American heritage. On April 30, 1889, Mrs. Harrison
joined her husband on Wall Street in New York for the reenactment of
George Washington's Inaugural, on the centennial of the presidency.
At the grand ball, Caroline Harrison was joined by Julia Grant, Frances
Cleveland, and Mary Arthur McElroy, all of whom were given special
V.I.P. viewing boxes overlooking the waltzing. And Martha Washing-
ton was not completely ignored during the Centennial of the Presi-
dency. She became the only First Lady to appear on U.S. currency.
On a special series of one-dollar bills, Martha was substituted for
George.

On Memorial Day, 1890, Richmond's elite attended the unveiling of the equestrian statue of General Lee. Also there, in the thick of the throng, was Miss Edith Bolling, who found the trip to the city from her rural home to be "exciting and unexpected . . . my first visit to a city," she later recalled, "and it seemed to me a seething mass of humanity and distractions." Miss Bolling's irregular education prompted her stay in Richmond as an 1889 student at Miss Powell's School. Formal education, however, never played an important part of Edith's life. Her thoughts turned to conventional subjects, like finding a husband.[10]

The society debs and Virginia bluebloods whom she met in her brief term in Richmond made it glaringly and materially obvious that Edith Bolling was, by comparison, desperately poor. The fact was that she came from a family of eleven children, and they all lived in a humble house, along with her grandmother and other momentarily indigent relations. She had tremendous potential—brightness, wit, the power of observation and persuasion—but the destitute Bollings had to make a choice between paying for an education for their sons or their daughters. Edith Bolling was never to have the privilege of any long-term formal schooling. To a girl from the hills with dreams of greater things in the metropolis, Wytheville, Virginia, seemed to be the end of the earth. A man could prove the quickest escape route.

By her mid-teens Edith had grown to her willowy height of five foot nine inches and admitted to making an impression in her "tight-fitting" Henrietta dress. She had a large bosom, and was "on the threshold of my first serious love affair."

Lobbyist or carpetbagger, some unnamed Yankee "representing some Northern capitalists," she recalled, came to call on her older sister and, "he told me afterwards, fell in love with me as soon as he entered the room." She was sixteen. And he was thirty-eight. As Edith stated, "He was a New Yorker and he had money." She began to see him every single day, and made note of his "fine horses," and how he "entertained in a much more elaborate style than our modest townspeople." Edith politely termed their spending evenings together in the hills as "moonlit picnics on top of the mountain," and their private moments as "imitation love," but her parents were "worried over it." The relationship persisted for about a year, at which time, Edith said, "I began to realize that a new element had come into my life. Romances," she coyly wrote, "were not all in books." Whatever transpired, the romance was abruptly stopped by her parents.

But there was no stopping Miss Edith Bolling. She had learned that she could make men respond.

As a southern girl's ambitions flourished in Richmond, a Yankee queen's was dimming there. In July 1889, sixty-nine-year-old Mrs. Ex-President Tyler suffered a stroke at the same hotel where, years before, her husband had died. Offered brandy for relief by unfamiliar doctors gathered about her bed, she managed one last tastefully autonomous opinion, shook her head, and demurred. "Tea." It was her last word. Her illness was reported over technology's *bon ton* of long distance—the telephone.[11]

As Mrs. Tyler's lively spirit was missed in Washington, Edith Bolling was making hers felt. In 1890, on her first visit there, she fell in love with capital life as fervently as Julia had. "A new world was opened up to me," she later wrote. Edith boarded with a sister who was married to Alexander Galt, of the old Washington family. Edith met his cousin Norman, who fell instantly in love with her. After his father's sudden death, Norman inherited a percentage of the family's famous Galt's jewelry and silver shop, and bought out everyone else.[12]

Caroline Harrison had made sure her Ben was bundled up for the driving rain that had plagued his Inaugural. "No inauguration pneumonia for him!" she'd cracked, referring to his grandfather President William Harrison's death. But neither the president nor doctors could help Caroline as she became noticeably weaker by early 1892, just previous to the president's campaign for reelection. She had cancer. While the First Lady spent the campaign summer resting at the Adirondacks, her "opponent," Frances Cleveland, was so excited that her husband was running again that she stayed up until 3:20 A.M., when the news came that Cleveland was nominated. She pronounced the dawn sunrise "a good omen."[13]

The Clevelands had been enjoying New York, now as parents of a daughter, "Baby" Ruth, born on October 3, 1891. The birth of the infant had inspired international attention, an avalanche of poems, proclamations, parodies, and the naming of a candy bar. Among the well-wishers was sorority member Julia Grant, who came over to Frances's house from her own, to drop off a "little top" for the baby, with her calling card and congratulations. (Birth in other political homes, however, prompted political rivalry that same year. When Edith Roosevelt and Nellie Taft were due at the same time, Nellie had her child first, and smugly wrote, "I see that I got ahead of Mrs. Roosevelt and feel quite proud.")[14]

The public had retained their fascination with "Frankie." When she won a *Morning Journal* poll as the most popular woman in New York, she asked that the prize of a silver wreath be sold and the proceeds given to charity. Grover griped she'd have been "better pleased if she had not involuntarily appeared as a contestant," but her fame extended beyond the metropolis. Augusta Female Seminary instructor Dr. W. W. Moore, lecturing students on "Internal Beauty," used "Frankie" as his example of spiritual beauty "because she carries sunshine wherever she goes."[15]

The '92 campaign, however, lacked the impression of wives. Out of respect for Mrs. Harrison, who died just before the election, Cleveland declined to campaign actively. He refused to permit new Frances

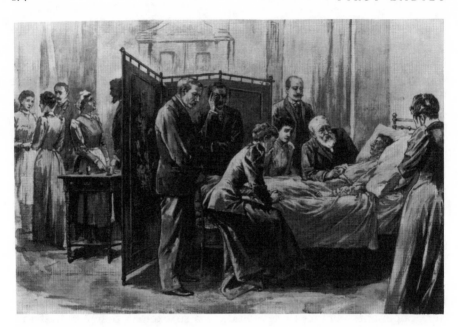

Cleveland Influence Clubs from forming, so she wouldn't be used "to exert political influence." He even resisted *Once a Week* magazine's request of her photo, "exceedingly anxious to shield her . . . from any . . . political campaign." When, at four in the morning, the Clevelands learned that they would be returning to the White House, the only former First Lady to be reinstated tossed a rare quote to the press: "Mr. Cleveland's pleasure was not demonstrative. He seemed to be simply in the enjoyment of a perfect satisfaction."[16]

As a "Frankie" fan, Julia Grant thoughtfully dropped her Republicanism for the moment to congratulate the returning First Lady, "admissible," she wrote, now that "the struggle . . . is over." Julia was also leaving New York and staging a long-anticipated comeback. "Dear Washington," she rhapsodized, "how I love you, with your beautiful, broad, generous streets and blue skies! The sun shines always there for me." Mrs. Grant would purchase a gleaming white marble mansion on grand Massachusetts Avenue, and ensconce herself as the capital's Queen Mother, just as Mrs. Madison and Mrs. Tyler had done.[17]

Everyone anticipated "Frankie's" new lease. Just before she returned, a commercial postcard was printed and sold, showing Mrs. Cleveland and her husband in front of the White House with the inscription "Home Again."[18]

The public, the press, and the exploiters were gleeful. As far as "Frankie" was concerned, they would pick up where they left off, only this time it would be worse.

– 31 –

Home Again

FRANCES CLEVELAND WOULD recall that in 1886, she was "not fright-ened at all," but in her second term "was a little uneasy," because "I knew more by that time." One staff member, however, observed that her natural maturity had given her "security and confidence," and that she discharged the role with "vim and dash." Even her fashions mir-rored her metamorphosis from student to young matron. She now dressed in the height of the Gay Nineties, in tight-fitting hourglass-figure gowns, fluffy feather boas, and large picture hats jauntily tilted over one eye, all replacing the image of virginal white décolleté of her girlish years.[1]

The Clevelands' return to the mansion was in name only. Since they'd sold Red Top, they rented another rural property, Woodley, again living in the White House only during the social season. Though Frances resumed the hostess role, she never sacrificed her voracious and varied reading. In the midst of planning a state dinner, for example, she wrote a friend, "Whatever do you suppose I'm finding time for with the other things I'm doing? Reading McCauley's History of En-gland . . ." She received thousands of letters, and in time she had a typewriter taken up to her "office" desk, typing her public correspon-dence herself. Eventually, a federal clerk, George Cortelyou, was as-signed to assist her in social planning.[2]

Women again looked to "Frankie" as a role model, and she imme-diately revived her women's receptions on the first Saturday of her new term. She was prominent during the visits of two women heads of state, extending "various courtesies, formal and informal," to eighteen-year-old Princess Kaiulani of Hawaii. She expressed "considerable sympathy" to Kaiulani's political "effort to accede to the Hawaiian throne from which the Hawaiian people had deposed her aunt, Lilioukulani," and the princess later approved a press release in which she publicly thanked "your fair First Lady . . ." When the queen regent of Spain, Princess Infanta Eulalie, swept grandly into Washington, occupying three hotel floors with her entourage of nineteen, Mrs. Cleveland paid a call on her, the first such recorded act of a First Lady for a visiting head of state. At the White House State dinner honoring the queen regent, Frances directed all floral decorations, and even some desserts, in the red and yellow colors of the Spanish flag. Harriet Lane, now working to help establish a national art gallery, was among the guests Frances invited for that evening.[3]

In some respects, the president relaxed his overprotectiveness toward his wife. When once greeting a male visitor who asked why she wasn't there, too, Grover smilingly responded in mock horror, "Why, somebody might carry her off." With the economic crisis facing him in his first few months back in office, it was now the First Lady who protected her spouse. As electrician, and later usher, Ike Hoover recalled she fretted over the president as if he were a child: "Never would she permit herself to be placed first; always it was he." The economic situation worsened during the summer. The nation's gold reserve had been rapidly declining in April, and stocks on the New York Exchange began plummeting into the worst dive the nation had yet experienced. On June 27, the market crashed, and the Panic of 1893 began. Mrs. Cleveland was concerned for those who would be affected, but felt unable to grasp the complicated financial issues, later telling her nephew, "I didn't understand it then, and I don't understand it now!"[4]

But in secret, Frances Folsom Cleveland would play a crucial role that actually helped prevent a further panic on Wall Street, which could have undermined America's stability. The president was suffering from unusual mouth pains in his upper left jaw, which required surgery. He had cancer.

The Clevelands decided to keep it secret, even from aides, and especially the press, for fear of the alarm it might spark on America's shaken economy and the world market.

Boarding a friend's private yacht on July 1, Cleveland was operated on at sea, dosed with nitrous oxide and opium. By the time the yacht arrived at his Buzzard's Bay summer home five days later, his improved appearance was able to fool the already suspicious press. There, the First Lady, who was seven months pregnant, monitored his health, and was angered when she found him eating a peach, which could bring infection to the fresh wound. "Wouldn't you think," she reprimanded, "a *child* would have had more sense. . . ?"[5]

Mrs. Cleveland was kept fully involved in all the medical details, and was part of the covert plan to keep the press and public deceived. She deftly handled questions about the president's absence, wrote some of his letters for him, and carefully concealed his illness. When Governor Russell of Massachusetts sent the president a salmon, the First Lady took it upon herself surreptitiously to respond. As "housekeeper," she told Russell, it was "my privilege to thank you." She continued, "The President has not been writing at all . . . He came here completely worn out." She dismissed rumor by camouflaging her husband's illness as "rheumatism," and drolly added, "If the country hadn't been so inconsiderate as to get up this financial trouble, which necessitated the early session of Congress, and he could get another month here away from worry, I think he would be thoroughly rested . . . we insist upon his returning [to Buzzard's Bay] when he gets things running in Washington." In private Frances was not so lighthearted. She admitted that the cancer operation had been "a narrow escape."[6]

With a rubber jaw fitted to perfection, the president returned in time for the special congressional session, sending a blunt request that Congress repeal the Sherman Silver Act. He believed this would end the Panic. It did not. Increasingly, the president depended upon the refuge of his family, which was growing. On September 9, Frances gave birth in the White House to Esther, the first presidential child to be born there. Two summers later, another daughter, Marion, was born. In the first Cleveland term, many American baby girls were named "Frances." Now, "Ruth," "Esther," and "Marion" became the most popular choices.[7]

Frances doted on her daughters, even playing on the floor with them in front of servants accustomed to staid matrons. She herself often took Ruth to a kindergarten run by her friend Frieda Bateman at the German embassy. Whenever she was away, she left a note, read to them by their nurse. "Mother missed kissing her babies good night tonight," she wrote them in one letter, "but she hopes they are all sound asleep by now." Mrs. Cleveland did all she possibly could to protect them from the curious, but discovered that the public could be just as intrusive with innocent children as they had been with an innocent bride. Once, glancing out a window, Frances saw "Baby Ruth" being handed from one to another group of about twenty sightseer tourists on the lawn while the nurse stood by, helpless. On another occasion, a determined tourist had to be prevented by force from snipping a lock of Ruth's hair as she passed through the corridor in her nurse's arms. Finally, the gates of the grounds were closed to the public for the remainder of the term.

The order was received with "great indignation" and "considerable protest," and the First Lady "suffered much perturbation and annoyance in consequence, especially when it was boldly asserted that her little girl was a deaf mute, was deficient in faculties, or otherwise afflicted from public attention." While once receiving at her Saturday reception, Mrs. Cleveland saw Ruth pass the door and called her over to "let the ladies see that she was not minus arms, legs or fingers."[8]

Frances became justifiably wary of the public. When, at Grey Gables, some telephone workers appeared, prepared to install a new line, she refused to permit them to begin before first checking with the president. LONG DISTANCE PEOPLE HERE GOING TO PUT TELEPHONE IN HOUSE, she wired Grover in Washington, DID YOU ORDER IT?[9]

A month afterward, while he was still in Washington, Frances Cleveland took an alarming situation into her own hands, directing an official order, specifically requesting that the president not be told. On July 11, 1894, she wrote to a Secret Service official, H. T. Thurber, "I don't by any chance, want to have a word of this to get to the President because he is worried and anxious enough . . . ."

She had been with Ruth and Esther when told of "three different very tough looking men on different parts of the place," which "had no kind of a watchman." The suspicious characters slipped away by noon, but reappeared later. Municipal authorities had "quite a time" getting the men off the Cleveland property, and placed a local night guard there, fearing "the men are after the children." The First Lady admitted that, "it troubles me," and thought it best "to have a Secret Service man or detective sent . . . ." It was the first recorded threat against a president's child.

She did "not want to be silly but the times are so queer and everything seems so uncertain that it looks to me only right to take every precaution even to the extent of going too far . . . There are never toughs or strangers in this vicinity—it is entirely a new thing. For myself, I shouldn't worry, but the children—that is another matter . . . ."[10]

With high unemployment and lingering economic malaise, the times were indeed fraught with turmoil. The president discussed the economy's effect on the unemployed poor with friend Richard Watson Gilder and the First Lady. Gilder responded that the poor were probably better off than they had been, but Frances shrewdly observed that "the poor did not care anything about comparisons as to present and former conditions."[11]

Though an ardent Democrat, Frances was apolitical when it came to the sorority. Crete Garfield had begun spending social seasons in town, living just down the avenue from Julia Grant. A confirmed widow, when it was rumored that she was to remarry, Crete said she was humiliated "that anyone could believe me capable of ever forgetting . . ." her martyred husband. She was extremely frugal, dunning her daughter for a loaned penny stamp, converting her Washington property into a boardinghouse, and fretting over whether butter made on her Ohio farm would fetch high prices. When the railroad planned to expand near her farm, she determined to retain the right of way. ". . . am I not greedy?" she joked. Frances Cleveland invited Crete to a White House luncheon, and the two First Ladies spent the afternoon of March 29, 1894, together. Julia Grant did likewise, welcoming Crete in February 1896.[12]

Frances invited Queen Mother Grant, with Harriet Lane, to an 1894 dinner. Mrs. G. had no hesitation in pulling her patronage requests on presidents. She had asked Grover Cleveland "as a lasting favor to myself" to appoint her son Ulysses as a member of the Interstate Commerce Commission. Though the appointment wasn't made, Mrs. Grant remained a visible and respected figure at the White House.

Julia was a very wealthy woman now. Besides her annual $5,000 pension and the continued royalties from Ulys's memoirs, she had sold her New York home for $130,000, while the Washington mansion had cost her only $50,000. On trips to New York, she visited with newly found friend Mrs. Jefferson Davis, and dined at her son Fred's house with important Republicans like the Elihu Roots, Mark Hannas, and Theodore Roosevelts. One of Theodore's cousins even married Julia's granddaughter. But since widowhood, Julia Grant had become more introspective.

Concerned that social life was becoming too excessive, Mrs. G. told the press that she thought women should devote more evenings to family. She became closer to Susan B. Anthony, lunching with her and, after some misgivings, supporting suffrage. Mrs. Grant was now consciously planning to leave a strong mark on history by becoming the first First Lady to have her memoirs published. After she granted an interview with reporter Frank "Carp" Carpenter, he described her "pleasant voice," as she spoke of the "wonderful events of her life." However, Julia's memoirs proved to be too frank for some publishers, who felt her sharp estimations of many living public figures were out of place for a woman's market. In the nineties, she shrank "from the final task of publication" when she considered the "criticism, controversy and misunderstanding which it might provoke." Instead of abandoning the project, however, she took to rewriting it. In old age, Mrs. Grant had discovered that she wrote well, and enjoyed it. She began to write articles for popular magazines of the day, urging readers, in one, to vote Republican.[13]

Frances rose above partisanship not only for her sorority, but also included Theodore and Edith Roosevelt as dinner guests. Roosevelt had been appointed to the Civil Service Commission. He returned to New York as president of the board of police commissioners, but soon came back to the capital as assistant secretary of the navy. Mrs. Roosevelt was becoming highly political and, escorted into dinner by the president, she wrote "As the only Republicans present we felt rather out of it and had to be most guarded in our conversation." Dinner chat was likely confined to children—the Clevelands' and her own brood.[14]

Besides her own children, however, Edith had the burden of long visits from Theodore's brother's daughter, Anna Eleanor, to their recently built Long Island home, Sagamore Hill. In many ways, this niece was like another daughter to "Uncle Ted," arousing jealousy in his own daughter, Alice. Like Alice, just eight months her senior, Eleanor, as she was called, was not to have the closeness of her real mother, who died when the girl was eight. With all her heart, Eleanor clung to her beloved father, but Elliott was a severe alcoholic. On one excursion she made with him to his club, he got drunk, and a doorman had to take her home. Rarely did she admit that she had seen her father in such condition. But nothing diminished him to his "Own Darling Little Nell."

The Roosevelts realized Elliott was too irresponsible to care for Eleanor, and she was shifted about the families even before his death in 1893. But, she recalled, he always "lived in my dreams," and "was the center of my world . . . He dominated my life as long as he lived, and was the love of my life for many years after he died." Edith made no overture to raise Eleanor, having little interest in other people's children. She suggested that the girl be sent to boarding school in England, because "I do not feel she has much chance[,] poor little soul." Edith wrote of Eleanor, "[S]he is very plain. Her mouth and teeth seem to have no future. But the ugly duckling may turn out to be a swan."[15]

Nobody questioned the beauty of the outgoing First Lady, who now even publicly danced with abandon, tiring out old senators. Increasingly, Frances's dark beauty was maturely offset by sparkling sets of diamonds from Galt's, where she also bought many service items for the White House. Julia Grant also indulged at Galt's, a patron since her ladyship. The presence of women like Julia Grant and Frances Cleveland in the store was now a common sight for the owner's wife, Mrs. Norman Galt. Edith Bolling had become a respectable Washington tradesman's wife. "We were the best of friends," she later admitted of Norman, "and I liked him immensely, but I did not want to marry anyone." She had nevertheless remained available during the years of the second Cleveland term, living just two blocks from the White House. Norman's "patience and persistence overcame" Edith, and, in 1896, "after four years of close and delightful friendship," she married him.

Mrs. Galt clearly was impressed with the aura of a First Lady. One day, Frances Cleveland dispatched a quick note to Galt's, asking, "If you have anything in flat gold round lockets to hold two pictures, about an inch in diameter, will you kindly send me by bearer some to look at with prices attached?" It was a routine request, typical of many others, but because it was from the First Lady, Edith Galt saved it forever.

Edith's first "society" outing had occurred before her marriage, when she attended a special one-night performance of Adeline Patti's at Albaugh's Opera House. It is likely that Patti admirer Frances Cleveland was also in the theater that night. Behind the counter at Galt's, where she often worked with her husband, or in a theater was, however, as close as Edith could get to powerful women like that. "Trade" people almost never became part of the world of embassy balls and select dinner parties. Except, perhaps, for the most ambitious.[16]

Even though Frances was on her way out, pleas were still forthcoming, even from Republicans concerned with the imperial fight for Cuba. "If you could do anything to influence the President to act and carry out the will of the American people," wrote a New York woman to the First Lady, "you will merit the gratitude of all true American women. Belligerents' rights granted those brave fellows in Cuba who are fighting against desperate odds for their liberty as our fathers did! . . . aid the wounded Cubans . . . through the . . . Red Cross society. You being the first lady in the land surely are in sympathy with the sentiments and enthusiasm of American women in a noble work and duty . . . use your influence . . ." It was signed, "Mrs. Theodore Roosevelt."[17]

As Frances's last Saturday reception for working women neared—a custom no First Lady would revive—her still-obsessed public realized it was the last chance to see her. Helen Nicolay said that "for two hours people of high and low degree" passed through the rooms at a rate of twenty-five per minute. Three thousand people showed up for her "hearty handshake" and "quick wit." But the real evidence that Frances both was beloved by all and that she cared for all peoples without distinction to race, was the welcome appearance of "coloured people [who] came through, both men and women . . . [and] two Indians . . ." Frances's gloved hand was blackened from the thousands of handshakes, but "she regarded it with an amused smile [and] . . . asserted that she was not at all tired."[18]

Of all the First Ladies he would serve, Ike Hoover said Frances was the most "brilliant and affable . . . it was a pleasure to even know her . . . Here we had a lady who took real pleasure in seeing people."

The staff was heartbroken that she was leaving. Frances had invited the Republican president-elect William McKinley and his wife, Ida, to a special dinner in their honor, but at the last minute Mrs. McKinley was indisposed. There were already murmurings that there was something strange about the new First Lady.[19]

The next day, Mrs. McKinley was well enough to attend her husband's Inaugural. She did not join her husband at the White House to meet with the Clevelands, but went directly to the Capitol. While the two presidents left through the front door, Frances would leave through the back, by the south entrance, to go directly to the train station, headed for Princeton, where the Clevelands were retiring. At eleven o'clock that day, she had sent word through the entire house that she wanted all the staff gathered so she could say good-bye to these friends. While the little ceremony, the first of its kind, was taking place, she spoke of how she had first come there "practically a girl, and was now leaving a mature woman."

And then Frances Folsom Cleveland lost her official composure. She "wept as if her heart would break."[20]

— 32 —

Usurping Cuckoo

IN THE MIDST of frock-coated cronies and Inaugural committeemen, the new president's ears pricked up. A determined little bird of a woman in black fluttered into the dark, garish marble White House hall. "Major!" she called her husband. "Major, where are you? . . . Oh! there you are! We'd better start now, the luncheon is announced, and all are ready." It was the new First Lady, Ida McKinley, calling for her husband. He listened to her immediately.

That night, at the Inaugural Ball, all eyes were on the diminutive Mrs. McKinley, who took the president's arm as she proudly promenaded through the parting throng for the grand procession in diamonds and white satin. Without warning, she fainted and fell unconscious. Calmly, without explanation, devoted husband William swept her up and back to their new home. Reporters and socialites alike were left to wonder about the odd departure.[1]

Ida's low visibility during McKinley's 1896 campaign, conducted largely from their own front porch, actually worked in his favor. "Ladies often came with their own husbands" to meet him, and his utter devo-

tion to Ida was used by Republicans as a virtue that qualified as presidential compassion. But her only rare appearances on the porch stirred rumors. Some campaign officials felt it was vital to deny the varied stories well circulated in Missouri and Kansas that Mrs. McKinley was an English spy, a Catholic fanatic, a mulatto, a hopeless cripple overcome by insanity, and a victim of wife-beatings. Campaign manager Mark Hanna's brother, however, said, "We are of the opinion that it would do harm to answer the slanders on Mrs. McKinley . . . it would make the matter worse . . ." But there was a public-relations effort to contain the rumors about her from spreading, via a campaign biography of Mrs. McKinley, the first of its kind for a candidate's wife.[2]

The staff had been told that their new mistress was "an invalid," but the tenacious woman was not an arthritic in a wheelchair, nor hidden behind closed windows like a tubercular. She was sprightly, with no dread or depression of her new, demanding role. Crook recalled that Ida was usually "up and about the White House, doing her part, in every way desirous of aiding her husband so far as her physical disability would permit."[3]

That "physical disability" was never named to anyone, even to family. It was stated only that she suffered from womanly "nervous" ills. Only a few dared to whisper the well-guarded secret that Mrs. McKinley was a victim of "the falling sickness." Of her excruciating headaches, memory absences, mouth-foaming, blackouts, facial convulsions, only one thing was known about this mystic illness. It was incurable. First Lady Ida Saxton McKinley was an epileptic.

Physicians didn't understand epilepsy, or how to treat it. Mrs. McKinley's condition was particularly baffling, and her husband had sought every possible method of relieving her symptoms. In Ida's case, however, the line between real illness and personality was a fine one. She often acted infantile, and was a demanding and determined individual. Unpredictable, irrational, and jealous of any woman who neared the president, she made her embarrassed friends cringe. Her epilepsy may have been used as an excuse to restrain her, for when she was either in physical pain or throwing a tantrum, the First Lady was dosed by the doctors with barbituates, bromide sedatives, lithium, and other powerful narcotics. Though the medical records proved that she was put on sedatives, it was done so quietly that no staff ever recorded it.

When she was drugged, her personality became milder, her mind duller, and her appearance like that of a smiling mannequin. It was ghoulish, but there was little else that could be done because she insisted on fully playing the public role of First Lady. She would not relinquish the glamorous position to any of her young and able nieces. Her ego needed constant affirmation. The president denied her nothing. If she had a seizure in public, he calmly placed a napkin over her head until it was over. At this, Ida resumed the conversation, ignoring the lapse and expecting her conversants to do the same. But once, after William had taken a card from her hand during a game of euchre because she blacked out, she snapped, "Who played that card for me?"

The First Lady was not frightened by the press, to whom she was unceasingly gracious and occasionally made herself available for interviews. Her magnificent and rich gowns were always mentioned in the press—as was their cost. With an independent inheritance of $70,000 as First Lady, Ida was perhaps the wealthiest of presidents' wives, and spent $10,000 for her White House trousseau. Her fashion tastes were in fact the only target of public censure. Ida McKinley's trademark aigrette, made of short, cut feathers of the endangered egret bird, brought a protest from the Audubon Society.

No newspaper during her tenure ever printed the word "epilepsy" in reference to her. But again, the tense air about her illness meant she was treated with extreme caution. Few were so indelicate as to mention the fact that while Mrs. McKinley refused to go to church because crowds might upset her "illness," she enjoyed vaudeville shows at the far more crowded theater.

The staff did notice, however, how the First Lady's illness "was a constant source of anxiety" to the president, "and because of her nervous disorder she was physically unable to endure, much less inspire in others, an atmosphere of singing joyousness." Ignoring her condition, she wanted to meet all the important statesmen who came to see the president, and be present at every public event. It made him quite nervous. One staff member called him a "martyr."[4]

Ida Saxton had always been perspicacious. She had received an excellent education at women's private high schools and Brooke Hall Seminary, made a sweeping tour of Europe, exploring places her chaperon had deemed improper for ladies, and received a unique education in finance through her father, a prominent Ohio banker with political and journalism connections. He thought women should know as much about finance as men, and hired her first as a clerk, then promoted her to cashier. After marrying McKinley, she bore two daughters who died as little girls. This, and the unexpected death of her mother, caused what was evidently a nervous breakdown. Just when she began showing manifestations of epilepsy wasn't certain, but after her breakdown, she became an "invalid."

Though Mrs. McKinley never did express support for or disapproval of suffrage, her greatest public association with women was her White House reunion of Brooke Hall classmates, which received much press notice. Her education had given Ida "candor and womanly independence." An example was being established for young American women. Since Lucy Hayes, all First Ladies had sought, and achieved, a higher education comparable to college. The striving for equality through education was now a socially acceptable goal. Grace Goodhue, the Vermont Democrat's daughter, entered the University of Vermont during the first fall of the McKinley term. There, she organized and founded the Pi Beta Phi women's sorority for the entire state, and was known on campus as a "lively extrovert, with an unquenchable taste for good times, an infectious laugh and a knack for endearing herself to others." Her tranquillity marked her unpretentiousness. "I was born," she admitted, "with a peace of mind."

She was also about to leave her secure parents' home and the community of Burlington for an ambitious professional career as a teacher of the deaf. In order to prepare herself, she was going to Northampton, Massachusetts, to study at the Clarke Institute.

At the institute's training school, Grace Goodhue's career began to flourish. She taught lip-reading, first to primary-school children, and later to junior-high students. Her three years there developed in her a deep empathy for the handicapped and hearing-disabled. Years later, George Pratt, a former president of the institute, and his wife, Violet, recalled her growth there. "She was a professionally trained teacher who knew their language, though she took time to understand all people. Her love of deaf children was lifelong and she believed they could be taught to talk, and must be given full command of all communications." Unlike the more popular belief that the deaf should communicate through sign language, Grace's "philosophy was to teach them to learn the spoken language. Her activities at Clarke, and later on, for the deaf always underlined her feelings for their eventual merging into mainstream of life."

While at Clarke, she made the acquaintance of another Vermonter, who was and would forever remain to observers the very antithesis of the chatty, vibrant, chestnut-haired, hazed-eyed Grace. Though he was not deaf, the pale, thin red-haired lawyer appeared to some to lack the ability to communicate his emotions. He was painfully shy, and appeared stone cold. But Calvin Coolidge had poetic passions deep within his soul. Grace was intrigued as he pursued her. One friend joked that having taught the deaf to hear, she might cause the mute to speak.

Not all American girls received American educations. Miss Eleanor Roosevelt was sent to England, as Aunt Edith suggested. There she studied under the kindly, wise Marie Souvestre, headmistress of the Allenswood School. At the elite institution, Eleanor found a loving and warm circle of friends, and was influenced by Souvestre's interest in politics. The girl's narrow view of the world was beginning to widen, though on the surface, in every way, she still reflected the conventional society girl.[5]

The idealized American wife, the First Lady also managed to conceal her true self while maintaining a veneer. She spent most of her time furiously active, whether knitting, scrubbing jewelry, or playing cards. The president and she ate all meals together. Afternoons she received callers, but to say that meeting her was a bizarre experience would be a gross understatement. Following a group of schoolgirls, congressional wife Ellen Slayden and a friend, Mrs. Maxey, began "an experience more pathetic than pleasant," by walking down "a dreary grey corridor" where Ida sat "enthroned." Slayden hauntingly recalled:

The first glimpse . . . made me ashamed of coming. She sat propped with pillows in a high armchair with her back to the light. Her color was ghastly, and it was wicked to have dressed her in bright blue velvet with . . . hard white satin spangled with gold. Her poor relaxed hands, holding some pitiful knitting, rested on her lap as if too weak to lift their weight of diamond rings, and her pretty grey hair is cut short as if she had typhoid fever. She shook hands with us lightly, but didn't speak until the words "Mrs. Maxey of Texas" seemed to strike her and she then said in a faraway tone, as if talking to herself, "That's a long way off." Mrs. Maxey murmured some commonplace . . . and she went on, saying, "I've had a great deal of experience." I expressed the hope she felt no ill effects from the cold at the Grant memorial parade in New York last week and again she said, "No, I've had a great deal of experience, my husband was in Congress a long time, and then he was governor of the state." She was rambling on in the same strange tone when we saw other visitors coming and slipped away as gracefully as we could . . .

[she] ought to have been hidden from the . . . curious . . . Her voice was . . . refined, and her face . . . childishly sweet.[6]

At dinners, Mrs. McKinley was controlled by being seated next to the president, a breach of protocol. On formal receiving lines, the First Lady was cradled in a massive blue velvet chair. Seated and sedated, she nodded to guests as he passed callers nervously into self-described "Second Lady" Jennie Hobart's handclasp "until the affair was over."[7]

Since the McKinleys spent almost every hour together, except when he was in the office or meetings, it was natural that Ida came in frequent contact with his political world and allies. She had influenced his earlier public stance on temperance. During one of their daily carriage rides together, the president matter-of-factly discussed a major tariff bill with her, saying he thought it would pass by either six or seven votes. It wasn't so much that she was interested in politics as that she wanted his attention always focused on her. Ida McKinley said, "It seemed that without a speech, he knew a wish when I formed it," but just in case he was momentarily diverted from her, she reminded him. On one reception line, when he was engaged in animated conversation, Ida stared at him and tugged his arm so he would pay attention only to her. When they played cards, he always permitted her to win—because he knew she did not like to lose. When he was absent for a brief while, longer than he had promised, he returned to find her "sobbing like a child."[8]

One intimate reported that the First Lady "deeply appreciates the thoughtfulness that prompts him to leave Cabinet meetings or other important councils . . . to seek her . . . No matter of State could ever engross the President so as to make him forget his delicate wife for an hour." For her part, Mrs. McKinley was a staunch defender of her husband, and severe critic of his political opponents. A friend, Opha Moore, affirmed that Ida was a better judge of politicians than the president. When she learned that some visitors were Democrats, Ida railed against the Clevelands, who, in her view, had exploited the presidency by making money on the sale of their first home. It was announced that a Captain Heistand would be appointed the president's military aide, but Ida couldn't stand his bossy wife. He was not appointed. She pulled no punches about politicians who she felt were using the president to further their own ambitions, once lashing out at the war secretary's wife, "I know one of you wants to be in my place, and that's Mrs. Alger." A witness said, "The poor woman is not so imbecile . . . she sees some things intensely . . ."9

As America asserted itself as a global power, declaring war on Spain after the sinking of the Maine in 1898, the First Lady "was greatly distressed because her husband was worried; and of course this added to his anxiety." He could not be with Ida as often as she wanted him to be, and her demands added unnecessary stress to the already desperate president. Looking after her, "as if she were a child," he became her willing lackey. Crook said, "When she wanted a pen, or a needle, or a book to read, all she did was say so, and the President would start at once, hurrying after it all as quickly as possible . . . it was . . . pathetic . . . [since] the affairs he was carrying . . . could hardly fail to change the . . . relations of United States with all the rest of the world." Her only role in the ordeal was a solo trip to Baltimore for a memorial to those who died on the Maine. She also attended most of the dinners her husband hosted for congressional leaders whose support he needed, listening to the discussions of war. The success of Admiral Dewey— whom she insisted on meeting—at Manila Bay, however, meant a victorious early end to war, and "the load of sadness" lifted off Ida.

The First Lady took a serious interest in the taking over of the Philippine Islands, and influenced the president on some accounts. One reason McKinley appointed General Leonard Wood in 1899 as commander of the army division in Cuba was because Wood had, as White House doctor, gained Mrs. McKinley's confidence. Ida was directly responsible for a DAR officer's appointment to a Philippines welfare commission. While State Department officials conferred on how to govern the Philippines—an issue many people noticed that the First Lady was informed about—she intervened. Ida arbitrarily selected the wild tribe of the northern Luzons as ideal for experimental Christian missionary teachings. "Mrs. McKinley talked ten to the minute about converting the Igorrotes," remembered William Beer, a McKinley adviser. It was not idle chatter. Ida "implored" an important social worker to see what the Presbyterian board of foreign missionaries could do. For whatever

reason, the First Lady was "lured" in "what could be done" for "women and children of the Orient." She went to the top, to the president.

By the time a member of the president's five-man Philippine Commission wired him that the island people should be allowed to follow their own religious beliefs, it was too late. McKinley told a group of Methodists that "we could not leave them—the Filipinos—to themselves—they were unfit for self-government . . . there was nothing left for us to do but to take them all, and to educate . . . and uplift and civilize and Christianize them." White House aide Benjamin Montgomery "boldly declared" that Mrs. McKinley's "incessant talk on the conversion of the islanders influenced the President's decision to retain the Philippines."[10]

The woman who took an active role in bringing dignity to the Philippines without condescension was Nellie Taft. Her freedom from racism became a political advantage when Will was appointed chairman of the commission establishing a civil government there. The voyage to the islands was itself thrilling, and she was inspired to "risk my life" surfing at Hawaii's Waikiki Beach. Nellie frankly admitted that "when you see a beautiful, slim, brown native, naked save for short swimming trunks, come gliding down a high white breaker, poised like Mercury, erect on a single narrow plank—it looks delightfully exhilarating."

In the Philippines, Nellie learned government principles from the ground up, and became adept at debating and defending federal policy from constitutional specifics when critics argued that the United States should not be stamping itself so imperially upon the Philippines. She said she "met the Constitution face to face" when her husband said she could not accept gifts, but as an unsalaried nonofficial she made her case to the White House, and the decision was reversed. What she wanted, she usually got.

When Taft was appointed governor-general, Nellie held sway in the fabulous Malacanang Palace, with no apologies about being grand. "I had not been brought up with any such destiny in view," she admitted, "and I confess that it appealed to my imagination." She was one of the few white women who "insisted," she wrote, "upon complete racial equality for the Filipinos."

At the time, American military leaders, under instructions from General Arthur MacArthur, refused to treat the natives with even a semblance of civility, viewing them as an inferior race. Nellie strove to change that even before she landed when Will wrote, "I need your assistance in taking a different course . . . Its political effect will be very considerable . . ." Every day, natives came to see this progressive yet decorous woman, and "though their customs are not always like ours," Mrs. Taft stood her ground in support of "inter-racial social experience," even learning a native dance, "the rigadoon." She tackled the high infant mortality rate by making it "her own problem." First convincing native mothers to accept medicine and food provided by the American government, she then organized Drop of Milk, to distribute sterilized milk. Nellie Taft literally saved lives. Later, the young children who benefited from her project admiringly flocked about her at receptions. Riding precariously on a horse, she adventurously fought torrential rainstorms to become the first white woman to explore the isolated Luzon mountain region, and pridefully noted that while the men had "long, murderous-looking spears" the women were "the burden-bearers." They fascinated her, because "they take to education eagerly." She recalled the "beautiful" men's "physical development," and even noted the colors of their "G-string," as she called it. On another mountain climb, she joined in a song about Mint Juleps. This was a frank, hearty, and rare woman.

Nellie was also exposed for the first time to the "elaborate and beautiful forms of the Roman Catholic Church." She later sent her daughter to Catholic school, and when her husband was sent to the Vatican as an envoy, she believed it possible to maintain a church-state alliance and "soothe the feelings of American Catholics . . . yet not shock the conscience of any Protestant."

But Nellie was frustrated by the limitations placed upon her sex. She was herself capable of holding political office. Perhaps this slight resentment at society developed her cynical humor. Unlike her jovial husband, sons Charlie and Bob, and daughter Helen, she didn't laugh easily. "I and my matter-of-factness have afforded them life-long amusement . . ."[11]

One thing Nellie shared with Ida was a love of music. Mrs. McKinley even approved a White House performance of the new sound of ragtime, but she didn't make music or anything else her "project," in the erratic role of leading a specific cause. However, she had her own

unique way of being visibly productive for the public's good. An ob-
sessive crocheter, the First Lady made thirty-five-hundred pairs of bedroom slippers to send as fund-raising items for the hundreds of charities
that pressed her for a donation. The slippers became high-priced auction items, raising large sums of money for groups, particularly the
Ladies' Aid Society. A friend said it was Ida's "surest defense against
ennui and depression . . ."[12]

McKinley won reelection in 1900, with his new vice president,
New York governor Theodore Roosevelt, most famous as leader of the
"Rough Riders" who stormed San Juan Hill during the war. He was
present at the White House for its centennial celebration on December
12, 1900, when "a dazzling white model, an adaptation of one of Mrs.
Harrison's discarded plans," was displayed on "a red-draped platform,
palm-banked, before the President, Mrs. McKinley, Admiral Dewey,
the cabinet, the Supreme Court and 22 governors . . ." There were
revived hopes that the White House would be enlarged, but Ida had no
enthusiasm for the expansion plan, and "served notice" to Iowa's Senator Allison that "no hammering" would take place while she was
there.[13]

At the Inaugural, Ida McKinley was joined by the new Second Lady
Edith Roosevelt, who detested "camera fiends," of which there were
many that day. When those ladies returned to the White House for
luncheon, they were met by none other than Queen Mother Julia
Grant, in the odd role of greeting the incumbents on the front portico.
As was Crete Garfield, Julia Grant was a favored matron of the
McKinleys. She had been at the president's side in 1897 when Grant's
Tomb was dedicated, as well as at the Philadelphia unveiling of a Grant
statue in 1899. After the latter event, leaning on a cane, Mrs. G. was
honored with Ida McKinley at a private luncheon. She still hoped to
have her memoirs published, and when Andrew Carnegie expressed interest in buying them for publication, she asked $125,000 for the "very
valuable little book" that cost her "months of labor . . ." He wasn't
buying at that price.[14]

Also at the Inaugural was Edith Galt, attending with Norman. It
was her first such ceremony. Mrs. Galt was familiar with the First Lady
because some of Ida's diamonds, a picture frame, and a vase all came
from Galt's. At the Inaugural Ball, seated in a large armchair, overlooking the crowd, the First Lady was so sedated that she could hardly have
noticed the young woman "perched on the arm of the chair" who was
then told that she "ought not to." It was the new vice president's
daughter, Miss Alice Roosevelt. Though she was a defiant problem to
her stepmother, Edith, she aptly dubbed her father's new boss and wife
as "usurping cuckoos." She pondered, "in the terminology of the insur-
ance companies, what sort of a 'risk'" they were.[15]

Ida's precarious health had earlier taken a turn for the worse. Her seizures had become more severe, and she was confined to a wheelchair, unable to receive. Rather than permit a substitute to serve as First Lady, however, she canceled the social season. By June 1901, she was well enough to make a cross-country tour with her husband, but in San Francisco, an unhealed infection in her finger spread through her body, and at one point it seemed certain that she would die. Through her tenacity and expert medical attention, Ida survived, but a scheduled trip to Buffalo's Pan-American Exposition was postponed until September. Ida was now keeping a diary. One day that summer, just before departing from a short vacation in Canton, Ohio, she wrote what would seem like a premonition: "I wish we were not going away from home."

The postponement to Buffalo played fatefully against her. There, on September 6, the president was shot by an anarchist. He wailed, "My wife, be careful how you tell her! Oh, be careful!" As one Cabinet wife recalled, though he fought to live, McKinley had "lived in close, stuffy rooms" because Ida hated the cold. He didn't exercise because Ida occupied every second of his leisure. And, wounded, "he had not sufficient vitality to recover." As he lay dying, the real shock was Ida's sudden transformation. By his side, she comforted like a nurse. When he died eight days later, she calmly took the train to Washington, seated beside the coffin. In the East Room, she prayed alone at his coffin unassisted. She firmly descended the Capitol steps after the funeral, looking ahead stoically and without hysterics.[16]

As a staffer recalled, "To the amazement of her physician and other attendants, Mrs. McKinley bore up surprisingly . . . and her physical condition occasioned little anxiety . . ." Ida left Washington for good, with the official party, for her husband's burial at Canton without having to be sedated.[17]

She lived for another six years without seizures.

As the White House windows were flung open, and the bracing autumn air rushed in, the cloying stagnation of McKinley's stogies and Ida's violet perfumes wafted out with the romanticized century they so personified. The new First Lady, waspish Edith Carow Roosevelt, rose at dawn, dressed in her starched whites, and even in subzero weather marched in jaunty unison with her bully president during their morning constitutional.

The forty-year-old Mrs. Roosevelt did not look forward to "this life of confinement," but added, "I suppose, in a short time I shall adjust myself to this." She hadn't wanted the role. She had tried to stop Theodore from running for mayor of New York and accepting the vice-presidential nomination. But if she didn't want the role, there were many other women who did.[18]

Helen Taft was soon to return from the Philippines. The "century of miracles" was just beginning.

PART VII
The Progressive Era 1901–1913

And who are responsible for the men?

Are not the women, the wives and mothers of the nation, the bearers of this great burden of responsibility?

No nation has ever risen, or can rise above the level of its women, and in no other country is this truth more obviously demonstrated than in our own beloved and favored land.

—MARGARET E. SANGSTER
Introduction, *Presiding Ladies of the White House* (1903)

Institutionalizing

MISS ALICE ROOSEVELT, who had an uncanny habit of "losing" her maid and escort, was finally lured to the White House by stepmother Edith with the promise of her debutante ball there. "In one way you will find this a hard position but in others it will be delightful, and can do much for you that has been financially impossible otherwise . . ."[1]

The "problem" of Alice was Edith's most challenging as "private person," a clear distinction she made from "public persona." In both public and private, however, Mrs. Roosevelt was assisted by one Isabella Hagner, "social secretary," the first salaried government employee answering to the First Lady as her boss. It was all part of the Roosevelts' institutionalizing not just the White House and presidency, but the ladyship as well. Ironically, though Edith Roosevelt was to be one of the most private First Ladies, she helped begin to establish the notion of the First Lady role as a public, semiofficial government entity. Roosevelt's ascendance marked not only America's emergence as a global superpower, but the modern presidency and first ladyship.

Besides Alice, there were the five other children, ranging from the darling terror Quentin, four, to Ted, Jr., who turned fourteen the day before his father took office. Intense public interest in the family strengthened Edith's priority of being a protective mother and wife. And yet, within the traditional limitations of "devoted wife," she had to be rather untraditional, for her husband was Theodore Roosevelt. With new territories in the Philippines, Panama, and Puerto Rico, as well as leadership in industry and technology like the Edison voice grapher, "moving picture" nickelodeon shows, electric horseless carriages, and "flying machines," the United States took to the world stage. Roosevelt realized that the presidency must symbolize this modern America, proud of its heritage but conscious of its progressive future.

Ample congressional funding for the White House renovation was finally approved. Some thought the house, in the new scheme of things, should serve merely as the executive offices, and the residents should live in a new mansion, but T.R. publicly stated that he and Edith believed that a president's family "should live nowhere else than in the historic White House."[2]

The house remained woman's domain, and that national example to women, the First Lady, would have to guide its metamorphosis into a serene shrine. Edith Roosevelt fully controlled the impression of the modern presidency; she would manage an almost theatrical stage setting of imperial flags, seals, and eagles, against classical white-pillared lines, to serve the purpose the presidency now called for, in earning respect. Even before Congress had officially approved funding, the First Lady had held a meeting with Charles McKim of the architectural firm McKim, Mead and White. The so-called "private" third floor of the house was still the arena of grimy office-seekers and cigar-chomping politicos who came to meet with the president or his staff. The family found itself having to make do with the limited private rooms on the floor, and the vast open hallway that ran the length of the house, down into the office space, as their only living-room area. In her suggestions for the renovation, Edith's priority was to separate the public from the private, as she did with confidence in her First Lady roles.[3]

And yet, within this emotionally unexpressive woman there existed a myriad of complexities and pursuits that she brought to the role.

She was healthy and strong, standing ramrod straight, with an imperious chin, brown eyes, and thin auburnish hair. Her face was that of a sturdy matron, with a prominent large nose. The most athletic First Lady yet, Edith "did not believe in letting weather conditions interrupt plans for riding or walking." Dressing in vogue was unimportant to her. One society leader commented, "The wife of the President, it is said, dresses on four hundred dollars a year, and she looks it." Alice described the First Lady as having a "withdrawn, rather parched quality." A niece found her "imperturbable as a Buddha," a wife who could "dominate" the president "by withholding the outward and visible signs [of] affection." A nephew admitted to being "rather terrified" of her. One staff member called her influence "a sort of luminiferous ether, pervading everybody and everything." As one friend said, "You could live in the same room with Edith for fifty years, and never know what she was really thinking."[4]

Edith as much as admitted to one son that though "one should not live to oneself . . . It was a temptation to me . . ." Yet she remained the only person who had complete influence over the president. The stakeout of her "office" room connecting right into T.R.'s study was proof of her power. If the president was still working at 10:30 P.M., the First Lady would shrill, "Theodore!" The president would reply "Yes, Edie!" and stop his work. Even Alice admitted that Edith "had a very calming influence on him . . ."[5]

She could manage him like a child, even doling out his twenty-dollar-a-day allowance. When a friend asked if the president was going to accompany her and the children back to Oyster Bay for a short respite, the First Lady responded, "For Heaven's sake, don't put it into

Theodore's head to go too; I should have another child to take care of."
She called him "my fifth boy."[6]

Colonel Crook said Edith had a "great . . . capacity for carrying
through her share of her husband's life, in addition to her own particular duties . . ." Though not interested in government issues, Edith
could discuss them, if Theodore chose to during their evening meetings. One observer said she had "the art of always giving the impression
of being interested and pleased in the affairs of the moment whether
she really felt so or not."[7]

One chronicler felt that Edith's influence was "negative," adding
that she "never told him what to do, but merely what to avoid." Edith
was pragmatist to T.R.'s positive optimism. He had barely won his battle with her to control his own career and her influence worried Theodore's sisters, Corinne and Bye. Corinne particularly "did not regard
her childhood playmate as quite the angel that Theodore did." The
sisters resented that Theodore was made to feel guilty about politics
when contrasted with family life.[8]

Still, as niece Eleanor recalled, "Uncle Theodore made no major
decision in foreign or domestic policy without first discussing it with
Auntie Bye." Edith, naturally, resented this. She insisted that Bye and
Corinne be required to make appointments, like anybody else who
wanted to see the president. Even with this edict, Edith frequently insisted that Theodore saw too much of his sisters. He acquiesced silently.
Edith, said Alice, "usually called the shots . . ."[9]

Theodore and Edith spent hours alone together in conference most
nights, and during the day he often consulted her between his appointments. She expressed disapproval of certain individuals meeting with
the president by absenting herself from welcoming them. "I don't dislike him," she would say, "I just don't want to live in the same world as
him." If Theodore specifically requested her to greet such people, she
might refuse, saying she had a headache.[10]

Ike Hoover thought her "a great help to her husband in an indirect
manner," saying her forte was to "win" conferees "over to his point of
view by her tact and consideration." If Theodore was occupied when
officials arrived, they joined Edith first. As her knitting needles clicked,
her sharp eyes and ears caught every innuendo of their discussions. Like
Sarah Polk, Edith read through newspapers, magazines, and journals,
then shuttled them to the president, marked with "any item which she
thought he should know about." Most important, Mrs. Roosevelt had a
good relationship with the president's assistant, William Loeb. The
First Lady "had great confidence in him and often . . . [sought] . . . his
assistance in bringing the President round" on issues. Through Loeb,
Edith could subtly get her views across to the president.[11]

Roosevelt believed women's destiny was marriage, instead of any
"makeshift and starveling substitute." Nevertheless, he had once ex-

pressed the opinion that women might be allowed to retain their maiden names, and deserved equal education. Though Edith felt marriage was "far better in every way for a woman than independence," she also believed that a bad union could be "hell on earth." Far better, she thought, to remain single than be "lonely in a mismatched marriage." She cherished autonomy but simultaneously enjoyed being a traditional wife, recalling pleasurable evenings when the president and advisers settled "world affairs" while she would "meekly listen as becomes our sex and position." For her, the role of public lady was not at the price of being a private wife: "Being the centre of things is very interesting, yet the same proportions remain . . . I have not been forced into the 'first lady of the land' model of my predecessors."[12]

The president agreed, saying, "[S]he has combined to a degree I have never seen in any other woman the power of being the best of wives and mothers, the wisest manager of the household, and at the same time the ideal great lady and mistress of the White House." He further bragged, ". . . Mrs. Roosevelt comes a good deal nearer my ideal than I do myself." T.R. acknowledged her power, saying, "[E]very time I have gone against Edie's judgement, I have gone wrong," but he also questioned the coolness of the woman whom he once called "Her Ladyship."[13]

Public notice of her private life was Edith's greatest fear, but with seemingly untroubled grace, at every turn, she tried to deflect interest in her family by willingly performing as a full-fledged public figure, thereby increasing the citizenry's awareness of the entity of First Lady. That prominence had been unquestionably furthered by her hiring of Belle Hagner. Obviously, the federal government itself gave recognition to the ladyship by allocating fourteen hundred dollars for Hagner's annual salary. There had been no published civil-service bulletin listing the position, and in name, she was an employee of the presidential staff. Mrs. Roosevelt realized that requesting the government to salary an employee for the First Lady could provoke criticism.

The First Lady knew Hagner, who had worked part time for sister-in-law Bye, and had initially contacted the secretary to help with Alice's debutante ball. Perhaps as a trial balloon, Hagner worked only several hours a day for the First Lady. But once routinely established as Mrs. Roosevelt's employee, Hagner became full time, even working some Saturdays. No criticism ensued, and the concept of a First Lady's staff was established. Hagner became "the chief factor at the White House . . . her sphere has broadened until it is sort of head aide, general manager, and superintendent." Hagner endeared herself.[14]

Edith also formalized the position of chief usher by hiring Thomas E. Stone. All house help answered to this manager, who answered to the First Lady. Although the title "First Lady" had been in use for a half century now, and the press regularly referred to presidents' wives as

such, Edith did not assume the formal title. Even on calling cards, she remained officially "Mrs. Roosevelt," whereas Mrs. Cleveland had her initials engraved onto "Executive Mansion" stationery. Yet when a special invitation went out to guests, the cameo engraving of the First Lady appeared on it, alongside the president. That was a first. The stationery, her working office, the social-secretary and chief-usher roles, all furthered the institutionalization.

With her passion for privacy, the First Lady tightly controlled her correspondence, once instructing a correspondent, "I have answered this so destroy it." She said she "could not bear the idea" that her letters might ever be published. To patronage requests from the public, she sent a standard response: "While many of the cases brought to Mrs. Roosevelt's attentions appeal to her sympathies and excite her cordial interest, she has made it a rule not to take any part in Government affairs . . ." That was not entirely true, for privately, those few appeals that she favored were forwarded to departments or commissions.

In her hostess role, Edith transformed dinners from haphazard Victorianism to dignified restraint, and initiated a ceremonial processional of president and First Lady, descending the new grand staircase to trumpets. Edith remained untouched, without escort of her husband's arm, hands at her side. Not wanting to shake hands, she clutched a large bouquet. As her renovation got under way, the First Lady ordered that it be completed as quickly and cheaply as possible. When McKim brought detailed plans for Edith to study, she looked at them hastily, comprehended little, and reemphasized her time and economy priorities. Nobody dared cross Edith, not even the president. As the couple examined the floorplans, the president marked his approval of proposed changes, but when he came to the State Dining Room, she curtly reminded him that the "housekeeping end of the establishment" was her business. He stopped red-penciling.[15]

In the midst of renovation, the president received a letter from a former occupant. Frances Cleveland wrote to see if a lost book had shown up in the shuffle. "It seems a small matter with which to trouble the President—just a book—but after all as valuable an edition of Dante sent by the King of Italy to the President isn't such a little thing—and I feel perfectly sure you will be willing to get the hunt going." T.R. ordered an earnest search, and a book was located and sent to her. Frances timidly responded, "I could not trouble you again about the Dante, but I want to thank you and tell you that the one sent is not the right one . . . With greetings to Mrs. Roosevelt . . ." He ordered yet another search, and "if nothing comes of it [,I] will look after the matter personally . . ." Three months later, he wrote her that "no trace of it has come to light . . . Mrs. Roosevelt joins me in kindest regards to yourself . . ."

When someone asked Frances if she'd like to be First Lady again, she referred to the old surly stories. "What! There where my husband was accustomed to drag me about the house by the hair and where my children were blind, deaf and deformed? Never!" She was fulfilled in Princeton as mother, wife, and sponsor of musical concerts, where "nobody disputed her position . . . [in] the community." The only event to mar her tranquillity was the death of daughter Ruth in 1903. (Among those who sent their sympathy was Lucretia Garfield, now working full time on the collection, preservation, and publication of her late husband's papers.) Ruth's death prompted the Clevelands to sell their old Cape Cod home and begin summering in Tamworth, New Hampshire. The family had grown with the birth of two sons, Richard and Francis.

The Princeton community suited Frances's warmth. In 1902, she wrote to a neighbor that it was "so good a turn" to get a letter from him. The neighbor had just been installed as the president of Princeton University. His name was Woodrow Wilson. Part of his success, however, was due to his plump, soft-voiced wife, Ellen, whom Frances liked very much.[16]

A native Georgian, Ellen Axson had been a bohemian. She studied logic, and taught herself trigonometry. Unsatisfied with her education at Rome Female College, Ellen determined to study painting at the Art

Students League in New York. There, her world continued to widen, from museum visits to theater. She taught black children in a mission over a saloon, and eventually went to hear the "sinful" Henry Ward Beecher preach. In school, she sketched nude models. She subscribed to The Nation, keeping abreast of politics, which she admitted "quite exercised" her. Ellen even attended lectures unescorted, a horror to Woodrow, the native Virginian law student she had met and who was in love with her. At first, she remained wary of romance, believing that women "give much and receive little . . ." At one point, friends had called her a "man-hater," but Woodrow respected her ideas of equality, and after marrying, Ellen became a partner in his academic career, even translating complicated monographs for him. "It would be hard to say," Woodrow told her several years later, "in what part of my life & character you have not been a supreme and beneficent influence. You are all-powerful in my development." In most ways, she was the stronger of the two. Woodrow's passion was sometimes uncontrollable, and he admitted to her that his "anatomical" needs were as strong as his emotions.

The Wilsons and their three daughters moved to Princeton in 1890, when Woodrow took a professorship at the university. His "critic and mentor" continued to contribute to his work with "insight." Ellen's vast knowledge of literature, politics, and history provided his speeches and lectures with excellent passages. She ventured where other women didn't: keeping a pistol at her bedside; trying a cigarette; going to New Orleans's Mardi Gras without any male escort. Mrs. Wilson noticed changes affecting women. On a trip to Europe, she wrote her husband, "This is certainly the woman's century! They have taken possession of the earth! . . . women of all nationalities . . . all, all equally emancipated!"

As university president's wife, she raised money to provide women's rooms at the gym, facilities and staff at the infirmary. At Woodrow's installation ceremony, Ellen practiced equality by welcoming Booker T. Washington with as much open warmth as she did Mark Twain. She also promoted friendships with "bright" women who boosted Woodrow's ego. "Since you have married someone who is not gay," she told him, "I must provide for you friends who are." When he began a full love affair with one Mary Hulbert Peck, however, Ellen reputedly warned him of the consequences of continuing it, and would admit it was the only unhappiness he ever caused her. Wilson referred to the "affair" as an "error" and "madness of a few months." Ellen burned some letters from the period, and buried the Peck affair to circumvent any ammunition some future foes might make of it.[17]

Edith Roosevelt also considered her opponents. As the renovation neared completion, she became vigilant about costs. Overspending an already large budget on a project so visible to the press and public could evoke harsh criticism of her, and have severe political repercussions on her husband's plans for 1904 reelection. Regardless of what had to be cut, the First Lady wanted to avoid both personal press and political implications. Over McKim's protests, the house was decorated with cheaper goods and older, historical furnishings. From Galt's, Edith ordered some small china and silver pieces.

At the store, there were more Bollings than Galts. Mrs. Galt had persuaded husband Norman to hire her brothers in the shop. Norman and Edith had their first child, a boy, in October 1903. It was a difficult childbirth, and Edith was hospitalized. The baby died in a month, and she was unable to bear any more. At this time, however, she evidently met Cary Grayson, a gallant Virginian then studying obstetrics.

In time, Mrs. Galt was again living life to the fullest with the substantial income the store afforded. There were summer trips to Europe, with nights at the theater and opera. In Paris, she became a devotee of Monsieur Worth, outfitting herself in his annual fall and spring collections. Worth said her curves were so perfectly Rubenesque that she would make a wonderful model for him. Yet, with all the glory, there was a spiritlessness in Edith Galt. Her marriage lacked passion. Socially, she might as well have *lived* in Europe, for she remained outside any power circle in the capital, besides which she claimed that politics held no interest for her. She made no attempt to see the renovated White House, just a few blocks from her home. Perhaps she had heard that its newness was unpleasing to many Washingtonians who'd been going there for generations.[18]

Mrs. Roosevelt's initial impression was also disappointing. The old house lacked that sense of history the Roosevelts relished. When McKim planned to banish historical items because they clashed with his stark walls, Edith said no. She ordered McKim to place the portraits of "all the ladies of the White House, including myself, in the downstairs corridor," along which she had also placed past First Ladies' china pieces in display cabinets. Julia Tyler beamed from her frame, as did "Sahara Sarah" Polk, and "Lemonade Lucy" Hayes, among others. The portrait hall was a very public recognition of the First Ladies' roles. Martha Washington's painting remained in the East Room, and Dolley Madison's inferior posthumous representation by Andrews was banished as a gift to the Cosmos Club, headquartered in Mrs. Madison's old Lafayette Square house.[19]

The oversized family portrait of the Grant family, which they donated when they departed in 1877, was too mammoth a canvas to hang in the lower corridor. Perhaps a portrait of Julia Grant might have been donated. That was never to occur, for at the moment Edith Roosevelt was moving back into the house, Mrs. Grant was dying, a few blocks away. She had taken a great interest in the Roosevelts, and in the summer of 1902, from Saratoga Springs, Mrs. G. had written to T.R.

that she had "just had your Cambridge speech of June 26th read to me
. . . and I cannot resist sending you my own excited congratulations. It
is indeed fine." Roosevelt responded that her letter "pleases me and
touches me, and I thank you for it."

But Julia Grant's weight had finally caught up with her as she developed heart and kidney troubles. She died just before midnight on December 14. Her *New York Times* obituary, headlined A WEALTHY
WOMAN, made the front page. Julia's estate was nearly $250,000. Mrs.
Grant's funeral and burial at Grant's Tomb in New York featured the
president, naval and army officers, and political figures in attendance.
At her Washington memorial service, she was eulogized with a comparison to Martha Washington, but while remembered fondly across the
nation, Mrs. G. was not as widely appreciated as she had wished. Her
memoir of "ruthless candor" lay unpublished. [20]

Julia's death created a vacuum for a Queen Mother of Washington.
Lucretia Garfield was no longer in town. Crete had decided to try the
balmy weather of Pasadena, which was quickly becoming a utopia for
wealthy elderly women. Here, Crete became the leading citizen, even
attending the first Rose Bowl parade there, on New Year's Day, 1902.

Meanwhile, the building of a white marble structure, Union Station, also furthered the new status of First Lady, by its inclusion of a
series of high-ceilinged, gold-leafed, ceremonial rooms with presidential
seals to be used as a grand entry for both president and his wife. A
special suite was built for First Ladies to prepare themselves before making their way through massive wood doors that opened out into a semi-
circular marble alcove, ideally designed as a ceremonial white setting
for the gathered photographers. [21]

As far as photographs were concerned, Edith was conflicted. She
knew her role made her subject to the press, but she hated it. And
there was the gall of a private problem now going public:

Alice.

"Princess" Alice was crowned by the press on February 25, 1902,
when Miss Roosevelt christened *Meteor*, the yacht of the German
prince Henry, brother of Kaiser Wilhelm. Though Edith was also there
as part of the official proceedings, Alice was center of the international
press attention and public curiosity, and got the larger bouquet. The
frenzy snowballed. In the Progressive Era, there was no star like the
"princess." She became an idol to women around the world, completely
eclipsing Edith as the most written about, discussed, debated, praised,
and criticized American female. Shortly, an entire "Alice industry" was
set in motion. When it was discovered that a particular gray-blue was
her favorite color, "Alice blue" was born. The fashion industry rushed
to turn out materials in the same color. Sheet music for the hit song
"Alice Blue Gown" became impossible to get because it kept selling
out. Another composition, "Alice, Where Art Thou?," was played by

every band everywhere she appeared. Alice became the most popular
name for baby girls.

The First Lady realized that there was no way to stop photographers
from snapping Alice once she stepped outside the White House gates,
so, attempting to exercise some control over the dilemma, she chose
several select camera artists, like Frances Benjamin Johnston, to do
their work on her turf, under her conditions—posed photographs—
which were then released to the newspapers and magazines who requested them. Though the First Lady and her children all had their
pictures taken, Alice's remained the most requested. The First Lady
despised personal publicity. "Why do they want a photograph of
me? . . . They only need a picture of the President," Alice recalled her
"waxing very indignant . . ."[22]

"One hates to feel that all one's life is public property," the First
Lady wrote about the increasing number of news stories about her family, which had the direct affect of prompting public mail. National interest was piqued on the most personal of matters. "You can't think
how much anxiety pervades the country about the children's education," she wrote her husband. "I receive letters from schools and tutors
every day." The president protested press intrusions, writing to the editor of the New York Sun that ". . . I am living here with my wife and
children just exactly as you are at your home . . ." Edith's solution was
to have Belle act as a sort of First Lady press secretary, occasionally
releasing information, but only to reporters in "good standing." This
solution worked for press interest in the family, but not Alice, who,
often away, disobeyed her stepmother by speaking directly to reporters.

From the First Lady's perspective, it was just one of many differences she had with her stepdaughter.[23]

Mrs. Roosevelt's aesthetic taste brought a superior sense of the arts to the White House. Her weekly musicales for women included Pablo Casals, Ignacy Jan Paderewski, and the Vienna Male Voice Choir, and these musicales became a mode of entertaining copied by many Washington hostesses. Edith also took the arts to government, Belle Hagner writing "that largely through her influence Congress passed the bill which laid the foundation of a national gallery . . ." As one of the most literary of First Ladies, Edith often prompted her bright guests ". . . into informal frank discussions of the subjects uppermost in their interest . . . a luncheon at the White House . . . was an education and an adventure."[24]

Unlike at Frances Cleveland's Saturday receptions, however, Edith's guests were socially and racially restricted. Those women interested in attending would send a letter, or leave a calling card, from which Belle drew up a draft guest list. Then the First Lady combed through it carefully, pruning out those she considered undesirables. Since it had been a dare among capital prostitutes to attend First Ladies' receptions, Edith "was determined that no person of bad reputation receive the hospitality of the White House." As far as middle- and lower-class working women were concerned, if they managed to obtain an invitation, they could be denied entry at the door by being deemed "improperly" dressed. Black women were not at all welcome. Although T.R. had invited Booker T. Washington as his lunch guest, at Edith's receptions, "Negroes were excluded."[25]

Edith made it clear that the White House under her regime would make moral judgment a standard. Sexual permissiveness was anathema to her, and Washington's reputation as "a wicked city" tremendously "disturbed" her. With husbands boarding in town *sans* wives, and single "government girls available," adultery was rampant. A seedy section—once occupied by General Hooker's division during the Civil War—specialized in "hookers." To eradicate immorality, the First Lady initiated a rather unconventional custom, "Cabinet meetings" with Cabinet wives, ostensibly for social purposes.

Tuesdays, eleven to noon, they gathered about their knitting leader, who, "determined to purge the social scene of unacceptable names," used them as a "sort of genteel secret police," with their responsibility to gather intelligence on "immorals" in guest lists. "No Senator's son, whatever the number of his millions," it was recorded, "could marry a chorus girl and expect her to move in official society . . ." Dismissed just before noon, the wives were rarely invited by Edith to stay for lunch.

Mrs. Roosevelt wouldn't tolerate any sexual shenanigans, and "could and did" refuse admittance to those who "transgressed her code of upright conduct," regardless of position. At one "Cabinet meeting," the First Lady announced that a ranking wife was to be cut from her guest lists if she continued her illicit affair with an embassy official. The romance—as far as the First Lady was told—was broken off, and the woman continued to receive invitations. Edith even dictated her morality on visiting royalty when she refused to meet Grand Duke Boris of Russia, a scandalous womanizer. Private affairs, however, often remained private, and even Edith's spies didn't nab all sinners. Alice Roosevelt remembered that in the Washington of that time, "Homosexuality and lesbianism were quite fashionable . . . people put bells and flowers in strange places and had affairs with their poodles."[26]

Among those students gathered around their teacher was one rather willful pupil. Nellie Taft was now the war secretary's wife, and wrote that the gossip of the Cabinet meetings was of "supposed . . . interest to us all . . ." They were obviously not of interest to her, but she dutifully attended, as part of her "job." Nellie's resentment toward Edith Roosevelt may have been heightened by the fact that the First Lady thought the replacement of War Secretary Elihu Root with Taft was a great mistake, considering him too much of a yes-man.

To be a Cabinet wife answering to Edith Roosevelt was not what Nellie wanted for herself. She was indignant when someone told her that she may have been "a queen" in Manila, where her husband had been governor-general, but in Washington she was "just nobody!" She wrote, "I didn't expect to be and didn't expect anybody to consider me 'just nobody,'" and thought a Cabinet position, "a curious and peculiarly American sort of promotion . . . with . . . such diminished advantages." Nevertheless, she undertook with energy the traditional Cabinet wife duties of receiving calls, dropping off folded cards (indicating that one had personally called), sending out flat cards, taking tea, hosting lunches—in short, doing the circuit. For so bright a woman with political ambitions and feminist beliefs, it was tedious, tiring, and frustrating. "The life of a 'Cabinet lady,'" she wrote with the frank shortness that characterized her, "is one of rather monotonous stress." Nellie wanted to be First Lady.

Only a few Cabinet wives had ever been politically prominent, and only four had earned the crown. Now, a powerful and ambitious woman using her position to pave the way to the White House subtly wrote that "such a life gave us an opportunity for meeting many interesting men and women who contributed much to the sum total of what the world seemed to have in store for us."

The price of Mrs. Taft's greatness was perpetual anxiety. She fretted about everything, imagined or real, that was out of her control. She admitted to having been "very near to a nervous breakdown." Her greatest fear was that Will would accept Roosevelt's offers to serve on the Supreme Court—an overture she made him turn down. When he had accepted the Cabinet offer, she said, "This was much more pleasing to me . . . because it was in line with the kind of work I wanted my husband to do," and "the kind of career I wanted for him and expected him to have . . ."

One night President Roosevelt teasingly hinted where Taft's career might lead, envisioning something hanging above Will, either the presidency or the chief justiceship. "Make it the chief justiceship," Will responded. "Make it the presidency," Nellie commanded. Mrs. Roosevelt would have no part in Nellie's coy politicking.

To Mrs. Taft, Edith's moral concerns must have seemed prudish. But it was a false impression.[27] In fact, as First Lady, Edith twice became pregnant, though miscarriage intervened. She would later shock a young relative by referring to "that wonderful silky private part of a woman." Lucy Hayes had been offended by the Watts painting of nude women and sent it to the Corcoran Gallery. Mrs. Roosevelt retrieved it, and hung it before her hall desk, where visitors and children saw it.

Edith's public sternness was not intended for those who maintained discrete personal lives. She never questioned one particular employee who entered her inner circle and became a beloved friend. Major Archibald Butt, White House military aide, factotum to the First Lady, was about as intimate with her as any nonfamily member could ever be. At forty-two, the genial Archie, with perfectly groomed hair, lived in privacy with his friend, Francis Davis Millet, a gifted painter, sometime art instructor in Rome, and fellow bachelor. Butt was witness to many private scenes between the Roosevelts, but recorded them only in private letters to his mother and sister. He liked Edith, and she him.[28]

More common staffers were less fond of the First Lady. To Ira Smith of the mailroom, Edith "had a rather overbearing attitude towards the staff in general . . ." Ida McKinley had always permitted the young men on the staff to play baseball on the South Lawn at lunchtime, but when they first did so under the Roosevelts, Edith "looked out the window and was shocked to see young men with their coats off disporting themselves on 'her' lawn." The First Lady immediately called Rudolph Forster, executive clerk, who told her it would not happen again. Not satisfied, she telegraphed the president, who was at Yellowstone National Park. The president wired that "a reprimand was being dispatched." That was still not enough. She even felt, as Smith wrote, "that we ought to be deprived of our annual leave. The President eventually agreed with her and issued the order," which he quietly dropped soon after. To Smith, it was glaringly evident that Alice "didn't get along especially well with Mrs. Roosevelt," and his sympathies "were on Alice's side . . ."[29]

On occasion, Alice served a purpose. In 1903, Edith, suffering from neuralgia, relinquished the First Lady role to Alice when a French commission arriving in the United States on the warship *Gaulois* required formal welcome by the president and First Lady. Sometimes, she helped Edith foil reporters' requests for fashion information. The "princess" could describe the same dress in so many different ways that they seemed all like different gowns. But Alice's increased publicity posed a potential liability to T.R.'s 1904 election.

The antics were no longer innocent incidents; they became real embarrassments—like the time she appeared in public court, giving moral support to a driver who broke the speed limit on the assumption he could do so because *Alice* was his passenger. The most appalling crisis was both the story *and* photographs of Alice taking cash from a bookie, and waving to a jockey as she hung on to a railing with her escort, a coarse, cussing Irishman, at the racetrack. A single photographer had snapped shots of her picking up winnings, and both the *New York World* and *Journal* made efforts to buy prints. Frantically, the White House contacted the newspapers' offices, which gave in to the president's demand that they suppress the photographs.

Alice's troubles had suddenly worsened in the summer of 1902, with the landing of a vessel carrying a cousin. In unrelenting comparisons with Alice, most felt the cousin was leading the proper life. Miss Eleanor Roosevelt had returned from Europe.[30]

– 34 –

The Cabinet Wife

UPON ARRIVAL IN the port of New York, Eleanor headed for Grand Central Station to catch the train north. As she settled into her Pullman coach, she heard a young man call her name. It was one of the many Roosevelts who lived on the Hudson, and he escorted her over to say hello to his unmoved mother, in another car, covered in black mourning veil from head to toe. The kindly attention nevertheless flattered Eleanor, whose insecurity was partially based on her feeling that she lacked beauty. Forced to live through what she considered the ordeal of a debutante ball at the end of 1902, she was brought near to a "nervous collapse." After the debut, she finally traveled down to visit the White House. With Alice, she served tea, watched the New Year's Day callers, and attended the theater with the very same cousin whom Eleanor had met on the train. Later in that month of January, he invited Eleanor up to Hyde Park for his birthday party. His name was Franklin D. Roosevelt.

In Washington for both the 1903 and 1904 seasons, Eleanor often stayed with her aunt Bye, whose home the president, sometimes with the First Lady, often visited to consult his sister on political issues. They were often joined by Corinne. "They all talked on political questions," Eleanor recalled, and her three aunts, "in all their own ways, made their contributions to what was always stimulating talk."

Eleanor seemed more impressed by Auntie Bye's mind than Cousin Franklin's heart. The cousins had known each other since childhood, an oft-repeated family story being that on a visit to Hyde Park, Eleanor's mother had allowed her to play piggyback with Cousin Franklin. In 1898, at a Christmas party, he had chosen the shy girl to dance with him above the many beauties in the room, and asked permission of his dominating mother, Sara, to invite her back next year, adding, "Cousin Eleanor has a very good mind." Eleanor was interested only in a social life that involved social service. In New York, through the Junior League, a recently formed organization of debutantes working for the poor, she became a teacher at the Rivington Street Settlement to the poor immigrant children living in tenements on the Lower East Side.

Living with her cousin Susan Parish, on East Seventy-sixth Street, Eleanor braved the elevated public train downtown to the tenements. She had become a member of the Consumers League, which made inspection tours of the "sweatshops" where immigrants worked under life-threatening conditions. Her first assignment shook her with fear, for she believed, "I had no right to invade their private dwellings, to ask questions . . ." Nevertheless, she "walked up the steps of my first tenement . . . I saw little children of four or five sitting at tables until they dropped with fatigue . . ." Immediately felt was a deep empathy for the disadvantaged, as well as a determination to do something about them.[1]

In this respect, Eleanor was like Uncle Ted. From reformers, he learned of the misery in the tenements, and spoke out against such injustices. His vigorous attack on greedy corporations earned him the cognomen of "trust-buster." By the 1904 election year, there was no question that he would achieve a second term in the White House. T.R. received his nomination notification at Sagamore Hill, where behind a screened window Edith and Alice, the latter recalled, "had to be hidden out of sight, like houris in the harem, while the men performed their stately minuet outside . . . tribal rites in which we had no part . . . My stepmother accepted it as perfectly natural." The one moment Edith wished she had involved herself was election night, when her husband announced, upon victory, that he would not be a candidate in 1908. Had she known what he was to announce, she said she wouldn't have allowed it, for it handicapped him with Congress.[2]

Just after the election, Edith did play a crucial role as diplomat. The First Lady maintained independent friendships with those in international affairs, the president finding her one day casually lunching with both the war secretary and the Mexican ambassador. Though T.R. once said she was "intensely anti-anglomaniac," her alliance with English diplomat Cecil Spring-Rice proved historic. When Russo-Japanese tensions broke out openly in 1905, Roosevelt needed expert information on the situation. The president, who did not get along with the British ambassador, suggested Spring-Rice replace him, an appointment denied by England. Therefore, T.R. made a secret plan to have "Springy" report from Russia with firsthand accounts. There could be a serious international repercussion, however, if word leaked of T.R.'s arrangement. The First Lady became their mediator.

Springy's reports were sent as "letters" to Edith, which she read, conveying the information to the president. Filled with frank, often horrifying accounts of life in Russia, and news of diplomatic circles, it was all highly classified. The clandestine correspondence continued for a year, and Springy teased Edith, "But you are quite a politician now, aren't you . . ." Along the same lines, she maintained a voluminous correspondence with the ambassador to England, Whitelaw Reid, who lengthily reported to her on "political intrigues, and the course of events on the European continent." As Owen Wister succinctly put it, "She was the perfection of 'invisible government.'"[3]

On Inauguration Day, the First Lady arranged for relatives and Cabinet wives to have seats at the swearing-in ceremony and tickets to the ball. Besides Edith and Eleanor Roosevelt, and Nellie Taft, Edith Galt was also present at the ceremony, but watching behind the fences with the masses, though she still feigned interest in politics. Eleanor was impressed, since she "never expected to see another inauguration in the family!" Continuing a tradition since Martha Washington, Edith's ball gown was made in America of native fabric. Upon its completion, she ordered both the cloth from which it was made and the pattern destroyed, thereby avoiding the publicity that would ensue if copies were manufactured. When the designer released information to a reporter, Edith was livid, and shot back, "Greatly annoyed by your advertisement of my gown in New York Sun . . . Fear this makes it impossible for me to employ you again." Deep blue with gold medallions, the gown had a thick, three-foot gold-embroidered robe. Because of its heaviness, the Inaugural Committee cut the procession down to five minutes, and offered Edith the use of "two powdered youths to act as train bearers." She declined.

Just thirteen days after the Inaugural, on Saint Patrick's Day in New York, the First Lady was in the midst of another mob scene. That day, at Susan Parish's home, the president gave his late brother Elliott's daughter, Eleanor, away in marriage to Franklin, a fifth cousin. Uncle Ted wrote Eleanor, "Married life has many . . . trials," and advised Franklin, ". . . No other success in life—not the Presidency, or anything else—begins to compare . . ."4

A far less imposing wedding that year was Grace Goodhue's to laconic lawyer Calvin Coolidge. He cut the honeymoon short, claiming he wanted to show off his "prize" back in their adopted domicile of Northhampton, but Grace knew, "It was his first political campaign which drew him." In less than three years, there were two sons, John and Calvin, Jr. Mrs. Coolidge would assume many fatherly roles, since Calvin stayed mostly in Boston after his election as representative in the Massachusetts General Court in 1907. Among other activities, Grace taught her sons how to play baseball, her favorite sport. She followed the professional leagues, and was a loyal fan of the Boston Red Sox, going to Fenway Park during her rare visits to Calvin. When he was in Boston, Grace was always on his mind, and he bought lavish clothing and hats for her.5

Other women had no intentions of marrying. Alice, the unwed deb, had now been "out" in society three years. As a means of keeping her out of Washington, Theodore and Edith permitted her to travel as a quasi-representative to fairs in New Orleans and Chicago, and on a Puerto Rican vacation. But her greatest "tour" was as the first president's daughter sent as part of an official government junket, from the Pacific islands to the Orient. The trip only increased her fame worldwide, and cartoons, rhymes, and poems satirized the journey. Her "guardian" was Secretary Taft.

Nellie Taft had traveled with Will to see the work on the Panama Canal, but decided against going to the Orient, the unspoken reason being Alice. Nellie tartly wrote that the excursion "was destined to be slightly overshadowed as a Congressional party by the personality of Miss Alice . . ." When European newspapers' "somewhat lurid accounts . . . of Mr. Taft and Miss Alice" reached her, she became quite jealous, sniffing, "One German paper went so far as to announce that Miss Roosevelt was undoubtedly engaged to be married to her father's War Secretary." But there was a bit of Alice in Nellie, who also had enjoyed cigarettes and liquor in her youth, and still knew how to get what she wanted. After futile arguments that she was the war secretary's wife, Nellie was still unable to get porters to haul her luggage to a departing train until she invoked the name of the princess. "You must have heard of him. He's travelling now with Miss Alice Roosevelt." Suddenly, an entire crew of porters emerged. The train was even held. Afterward, her children unmercifully teased her as "*The* Mrs. Taft whose husband was travelling with Miss Alice Roosevelt."

Meanwhile, Alice had become intrigued with fellow traveler and close Taft ally Nicholas Longworth a Cincinnati congressman. Will wrote Nellie that Alice and Nick "indulge in conversations on subjects that are ordinarily tabooed between men and women much older than they are and indeed are usually confined to husband and wife." He timidly asked Alice if she and Nick were engaged. "More or less, Mr. Secretary." More was the case.

Alice and Nick's February 16, 1906, wedding was unrivaled in press attention, but the First Lady refused to admit a single reporter. Cousin Franklin attended the event, even fixing Alice's train for photographers, but Eleanor, six months pregnant with her first child, was prohibited by society etiquette from appearing at social events. As the bride was departing for her honeymoon, Edith ruefully told her, "I want you to know that I'm glad to see you leave. You have never been anything but trouble."[6]

Unlike Alice, Edith did not make conspicuous solo public tours. She did join T.R. on his 1905 southern tour, was honored in her own right at two receptions, and traveled with him to inspect the building of the Panama Canal. There, she described natives as "little groups of chocolate drops," and "poor little scraps of humanity," expressing approval of segregated housing built for the white workers of, as she put it, "the better class," while flimsy huts were the only quarters provided for blacks. With her sense of noblesse oblige, the lower classes were the recipients of Edith's generosity, and through Jacob Riis, she kept abreast of the welfare needs of immigrant families, and sent checks, but she made no tours of tenements.[7]

Not all friends praised her instincts. Henry Adams focused on her imperiousness, smirking that she "needed a crown," and even Theodore would remark that "people think I have a good-natured wife, but she has a humor which is more tyrannical than half the tempestuous women of Shakespeare." Nevertheless, in her role as president's wife, she was superb as she argued against his stridency, defensive speeches, and rash public statements. "We all knew," daughter Ethel said, "that the person who had the long head in politics was Mother." Perhaps the best but most secret example of her enigmatic power was how Edith managed, without the president's knowledge, to make certain that Secret Service agents were always placed unobtrusively close to him. T.R. was never to know. "I doubt if I was ever happy," she later said, "for there was always that anxiety about the President."[8]

Such anxiety, however, was coming to an end. With the primaries of 1908, Edith knew her first ladyship was limited. Amid the election season, however, another sorority member was also in transition. On June 24, Grover Cleveland died, and Frances was widowed at forty-three years old. Though Edith was unable to attend the Princeton funeral, the president was there, calling on Frances after the service. Daughter Esther recalled, "My mother was sitting in a large chair in her bedroom that day . . . He [Roosevelt] went down on his knee and kissed her hand." When Roosevelt named a portion of the San Jacinto National Forest after Cleveland, the former First Lady responded, "As you suggest, forest preservation was one of [Cleveland's] . . . strongest interests . . . it is very gratifying to me . . . I thank you . . ."9

T.R. dealt head-on with another political woman, a Cabinet wife. In a second meeting with Nellie Taft, the president invited Secretary of State Elihu Root to join in, and Nellie, mistrusting Root, took his presence as indicative of other influences bearing down on Roosevelt. Indeed, T.R. told her that if Will didn't actively seek the nomination, the more vigorous Charles Evan Hughes might receive the presidential blessing. Furious, she wrote her husband that Roosevelt "seems to think that I am consumed with an inordinate ambition to be President . . . I felt like saying, 'D——— you, support whom you want, for all I care.' But, suffice it to say, I did not . . ." When the genial Taft told Root that ideally the president should have a third term, Nellie was further enraged. Roosevelt told Will that Nellie misinterpreted the meeting, and that he had only wanted Taft to actively seek organized support.

Mrs. Taft, however, believed "that this is all a part of his scheme to get himself nominated," and asked Will to stop making "any more speeches on the Roosevelt policies . . ." For a year before the election, Mrs. Taft had been traveling with Will, watching his every move, listening to his every speech, but it was not openly called "campaigning." When they happily played bridge, fear suddenly overcame her when she realized it was Sunday, and she imagined the headlines: TAFT PLAYS CARDS ON THE SABBATH DAY. On a three-month official world tour, she gamely spent nearly two weeks in a train across Siberia, expecting the "open spaces" to be "endless monotony" that would "depress me." It did not. Rather, her natural curiosity about different cultures was further aroused, particularly in a nation from which so many immigrants were coming to America.

On the day before the Republican nomination in Chicago, the slight, brown-eyed, brown-haired Nellie with her regal posture sailed confidently through the marble-columned halls of the State, Navy and War Department Building, into her husband's office. There, throughout the day, she waited for reports via a telephone connection hooked up with the convention. The next day, when Taft was nominated, she was the first to congratulate him.

When they were separated during the campaign, Will wrote daily to Nellie, as he always did when they were apart. Mrs. Taft said that "he poured into them all the politics and the turmoil of the hour, together with lengthy comments . . ." In one news photograph, she was seen focusing attentively to his speech, sitting right in the front row, the only woman among men. Her stern brow scrutinized his delivery through a lorgnette, her presence reminding the ambivalent Will that she wanted to win. "The ups and downs of such a campaign, the prophecies, the hopes, the fears aroused by favorable and opposing newspapers were all new and trying to me," she admitted, "and in a way I think I was under as great a nervous strain as my husband was . . ."[10]

Nevertheless, Mrs. Taft's genius political maneuverings paid off. Will was elected. But if her having finally achieved her life's ambition made some think that she'd calm down, they were wrong.

She gave a whole new dimension to the expression "Nervous Nellie."

– 35 –

Nervous Nellie

UPON VICTORY, MRS. Taft immediately de-Roosevelted the White House. She announced that all the white ushers in their frock coats would be replaced with black servants in blue livery. Only after Mrs. Roosevelt spoke up on behalf of the longtime employees did Nellie reluctantly acquiesce, retaining some, transferring others. She ordered staffers to shave off mustaches or beards, prompting Alice Longworth to wonder what she'd do with "bearded ladies." She stopped Edith's use of catering companies, and hired a terrorizing housekeeper, Elizabeth Jaffray, whose eagle eye would direct all meals prepared in house. Certain White House rooms were closed to tourists. Ike Hoover said there was "a disposition to change things for the sake of changing . . ."[1]

But there was something about this bold midwesterner that Archie Butt liked, and defended. Of the Roosevelts, he said, "To hear them talk, one would think that . . . Mrs. Taft was not even civil . . ." To press criticism of her changes, Nellie was defensive. "Each new mistress of the house has absolute authority . . . and can do exactly as she pleases . . ."[2]

Mrs. Taft was appalled that the president was still using horse and carriage, and paying for it himself. She pressed for, and won, a twelve-thousand-dollar congressional appropriation for presidential transportation, and planned on having four elegant automobiles—a White steamer, Baker electric, and two gleaming royal Pierce-Arrows—at her disposal. When Butt informed her that she would have to settle for modest Ford Sixes at twenty-eight-hundred dollars each, she was undaunted. Pierce-Arrow was asked to provide the Tafts with a discount.

The company agreed only if they could publicly advertise that they supplied the White House. In a dramatic departure from anything her predecessors would have even considered, Nellie Taft struck the deal, willingly opening herself to commercial exploitation. A similar bargain was struck with the White Company. A half-page *Washington Post* advertisement selling White Steamers told drivers they should buy the car because "Those in whose judgement the Nation has the most confidence have selected the White Steamer for their personal use, thereby stamping it as 'the correct car.'"[3]

Patronage was her next chore. When Will was considering one particular individual, Helen vetoed him as a "perfectly awful man." When the president-elect tried laughingly to dissuade her, Nellie cut him off: "I won't even talk about it." There was the case of Henry White, Roosevelt intimate and American ambassador to Paris. The Tafts had honeymooned in England while White was a diplomat there, and had asked him for tickets to Parliament. Instead, they received tickets to the king's stables. Nellie believed it was a purposeful slight, and White lost his position because of it. Nick Longworth, under consideration for ambassadorship to China by Taft, was not appointed because Nellie disapproved of Alice.[4]

William Howard Taft was so blasé about his wife's power that he once sent her a note addressed "Memorandum for Mrs. Taft—the real President from the nominal President." It was a serious memo regarding her patronage decisions: "If you are going to give Gist Blair a place in this Administration you had better talk with the Attorney General about him. He has the power of appointment over in his Department. Don't come to me, who have very little influence in this Administration."[5]

Except for patronage, however, Nellie said she began "to neglect the political affairs which had for many years interested me so intensely. Perhaps with my husband safely elected I considered all important affairs satisfactorily settled. At any rate I found little time at the moment to worry about . . . what policies should be pursued during his administration." That decision, however, fatefully crossed purposes with her husband, who wrote at the same time, "with the troubles of selecting a Cabinet and the difficulties in respect to the revision of the tariff, I feel just a bit like a fish out of water. However, as my wife is the politician . . . she will be able to meet all these issues . . ."[6]

The end of the Roosevelt regime was sad even to Democratic cousin Franklin and his wife, Eleanor, who visited two months before the Taft Inaugural. Eleanor was going through her own torture with mother-in-law, Sara. She broke down and wept a few weeks after moving into the house built by that "very strong character," and told Franklin, ". . . I did not like to live in a house which was not in any way mine, one that I had done nothing about and which did not represent the way I wanted to live. . . . I was not developing any individual taste or initiative. I was simply absorbing the personalities of those about me and letting their tastes and interests dominate me."[7]

Aunt Edith was dealing with emotions of her own. On March 2, when, initiating a new First Lady custom, she invited her successor for a tour of the mansion, tensions rose dramatically. As they passed through one room, Nellie remarked in a loud whisper, "I would have put that table over there." Evidently, it was intended for Edith to hear, which she did.[8]

Mrs. Roosevelt nevertheless managed her placidly detached smile one more time, for a White House dinner honoring the Tafts, also invited as overnight guests, on Inauguration eve. The air was thick with more tension. Alice correctly decided not to do her now-famous bulging-eyed Nellie Taft "hippopotamus face" impersonation, complete with "Cin-cin-nasty" accent, but she secretly indulged her tastes for the occult by planting a voodoo doll of the new First Lady on the White House lawn. As dinner ended, Edith, dressed in black, took Nellie—in white—by the hand, and said, "I hope your first night here will be one of sweet sleep." And then the remote Edith Roosevelt cried openly.[9]

Nellie recorded tactfully that "neither Mrs. Roosevelt nor I would have suggested such an arrangement for this particular evening . . . Mrs. Roosevelt seemed depressed," but added "Presidents' wives are always given plenty of time to prepare themselves for that event . . ." Nellie felt "strange to spend my first night in the White House surrounded by such ghosts."[10]

By morning Alice's amulet had worked. A blizzard crippled the capital. Streets were immobilized with four inches of snow, railroad tracks were blocked, telephone lines were down. And Mrs. Taft's Inaugural gown was stuck on a train headed down from New York, with no word on its whereabouts. The swearing-in ceremony was rearranged to be held indoors.

After the swearing in, the new president delivered a short speech upon the advice of Nellie, who said "no audience can stand more than an hour." For herself, Nellie was anxious. She had complained that Will was usually "taken in charge by committees and escorted everywhere with honor, while I am usually sent with a lot of uninteresting women through some side street to wait for him at some tea or luncheon." Not this time. Since Roosevelt broke precedent by going directly to Union Station, where Edith had already gone, Nellie decided she, too, would break a rule: "I see no reason why the President's wife may not now come into some rights on that day also . . ." She rode back directly to the White House, seated next to her husband, later writing, "No President's wife had ever done it . . . Some of the Inaugural Committee expressed . . . disapproval, but I had my way . . . in

spite of protests . . ." The new tradition immediately illustrated her
power. The drive was her "proudest" moment. "I had," she reflected,
"secret elation in . . . doing something . . . no woman had ever
done . . ."

Her second-proudest moment came when she crossed the White
House threshold into the high north entrance hall, feeling like "Cinderella." She stood there briefly, staring down at the large brass presidential seal in the floor, and realized "now—that meant my
husband!"[11]

But Nellie began worrying again. "The suspense" of waiting for her
gown had made her "fearful," and after three failed attempts by her
hairdresser to get the new First Lady's coiffure the way she wanted it,
she said, the "process made me more nervous than anything else in the
whole course of the day." At the ball, she admitted to "frequent spasms
of anxiety" that people would step on her train. She even went to sleep
with "energy enough left to worry" about breakfast the next day. Nellie
said that her husband and children, Robert, Charles, and Helen, enjoyed teasing her "serious attitude toward my domestic responsibilities,
saying that I make them three times as difficult as they need to be by a
too positive insistence on my own methods." Even she confessed, "Perhaps I did make the process . . . to my own conceptions a bit too
strenuous."[12]

Nellie quickly became one of those few First Ladies utterly absorbed
in the daily politics of her husband, a "co-president." She admitted
with gingerly caution, "I had always had the satisfaction of knowing
almost as much as he about the politics and intricacies of any situation

in which he found himself, and my life was filled with interests of a most unusual kind."

With a manner described as "frank [and] direct," Nellie Taft could debate issues "with almost a masculine vigor." When asked who had first thought of Taft for president, she fired right back, "I did!" Absorbed in a Senate session, Nellie would skip lunch.[13]

"You are my dearest, and best critic, and are worth much to me in stirring me up to best endeavor," Will once wrote his wife. She calmed the president's insecurity as a poor public speaker. "Never mind if you cannot get off fireworks . . . that is not your style . . . we shall both be able to survive it." The casual president tended to forget things, and relied heavily upon Nellie's sharp memory for exact names, titles, and statistics. Sometimes his attitude exasperated her, but she once told him, "I know that I am very cross to you, but I love you just the same." The president occasionally acknowledged her power in public. On a trip to Mexico, President Taft asked President Díaz about his First Lady, adding that both of their wives played "an important part in the affairs of the public." Though she "kept pace with her husband on public affairs," Nellie "limited her discussions and expressions of opinion to the privacy of the family group . . ."[14]

In public, Nellie sometimes forgot that Will was the one elected. At their first reception, the First Lady stridently "bolted" in ahead of the president. The next day she admitted, "I was never so nervous . . . in my life . . . when I went ahead . . . and rather assumed his place . . ." She guarded her role, and was annoyed at even close friend Mabel Boardman's familiarity toward "Will," and "would show it when she was present." She lacked a good relationship with Fred Carpenter, the president's chief assistant. It was said that when "Mrs. Taft expressed disapproval of things in general or in particular, Carpenter's teeth chattered." Just fifteen months after being appointed, the assistant "fled," transferred to the position of minister to Morocco, because of the First Lady's power in personnel, a fact acknowledged by The New York Times.[15]

Ike Hoover left a vivid recollection of this most unusual First Lady's "prominent part . . . in official matters":

> It was no uncommon thing to see her taking part in political and official conferences . . . Speaker Cannon consulting jointly with the President and Mrs. Taft . . . [she] seemed always to be present and taking a leading part in the discussions. At large social gatherings a guest would often entice the President to a corner for a talk on some special subject. They would always be joined by Mrs. Taft as soon as she realized the situation. The conversation . . . would continue with her taking a full share in it . . . she attended almost every important conference that was held in the White House proper. She would even walk in on private confer-

ences, unheralded and unannounced. It was a familiar sight . . . her and
the President in a corner of the room with heads together talking to . . .
Senator Aldrich or . . . prominent politician[s]."[16]

Because the role of political partner was her priority, Nellie's very
specific ideas on managing the White House were given in her daily
meetings with housekeeper Jaffray. The social-secretary role was less
secure. Belle Hagner, still an official government employee, was transferred to a clerk position at State during the early part of the "honeymoon" period because Mrs. Taft wanted more of a subordinate than a
social lioness. Then came Alice Blech, who left after a year. Finally,
there was Mary Spiers, who was told that in the government "no
woman would be promoted to a higher salary than . . . $1400." She
lasted a total of sixteen days. Nellie was a terrifying boss—even from
security's viewpoint. "The secret service men, like the poor, we had
with us always," she said disdainfully. Though some sort of protective
escort had been acompanying First Ladies in public since Mary Lincoln,
Nellie saw no need for it.[17]
    Initially, she was insecure about her place among First Ladies, say-
ing the "house was haunted for me by memories of . . . charming
women . . . and I was unable to feel that such a commonplace person
as I had any real place there." But, with her classic understatement, she
added, "This feeling passed . . ." Nellie was shocked by the volume of
mail a First Lady received, especially the "petitions for assistance in
various forms," primarily from charity groups requesting "something
that could be sold as a souvenir of myself." To them, she sent auto-
graphed White House engravings. One particular request, however, and
her response to it, nearly caused an international controversy.
    When she received a "letter from a society of women engaged in
political and social reform work in one of the newer Balkan States,"
asking her to assist them by heading a similar organization of American
women, Nellie cordially replied that she could not do so but evidently
her response subtly indicated that she approved of the movement. The
women printed Nellie's response, and a flood of international press
broke proclaiming that she had "a personal interest . . . and . . . was
the warm friend of the young State and an enemy to all her enemies."
The press grabbed the attention of world leaders and "became the subject of an exchange of diplomatic notes." Finally, as she recorded, the
State Department had to "extricate me from . . . the trouble in
the Balkans . . ." Mrs. Taft wrote that, "It taught me a lesson."
But still, she used her power to help those she felt deserving. Sometimes citizens asked her to "shake the Political Tree" for a "Plum." One
newspaper headline announced PRESIDENT HEEDS MRS. TAFT'S PLEAS
FOR MERCY FOR CONDEMNED MAN, the story detailing how Taft was
hesitant to "interfere with the carrying out of the death penalty until

Mrs. Taft intervened." The convict's sentence was reduced to life imprisonment.

Pleas "for the sake of American Womanhood" appealed greatly to her. She rarely failed them. When one woman asked for a government position for her sister, the Civil Service Commission initially reported that an executive order, in this particular situation, could not be recommended, but a note was attached to Taft. "This is a case in which Mrs. Taft is interested . . . and . . . in view of Mrs. Taft's interest the President may wish to issue one." Another woman establishing a kindergarten in the South for blacks requested an appointment with the Tafts to discuss the issue. Her request was granted.

This First Lady was the first to display real sympathy with the tribulations of the millions of immigrants pouring into America. When an immigrant child was prohibited from entering America because officials deemed him an undesirable, the child's mother explained to Mrs. Taft that her son merely had a speech problem. The First Lady interceded, the ruling was reversed, and the child was allowed into the country. Later, during the controversial two-month Lawrence, Massachusetts, textile workers' strike, a thirteen-year-old Italian girl, Camella Teoli, who had been scalped by a cotton-twisting machine at a mill, came to testify before the House Rules Committee, a hearing prompted by socialist Margaret Sanger. There, sitting quite conspicuously, listening to the little girl's grisly details, was a moral supporter, the First Lady. Nellie Taft's presence was duly noted by the press, and young Camella's testimony was so shocking that it helped prompt investigation into working conditions throughout the nation.[18]

When someone wrote with hopes that she'd reinstate temperance policy, however, Nellie was unresponsive. She once wrote her daughter from Bermuda about a gift box of "three bottles of whiskey which your father says I can not bring home . . . I have only drunk one bottle of Scotch and have to begin on Rye and Bourbon as he sent me one of each . . . the way the Governor put away the champagne was a caution!" Liquor was served. "You should see Nellie's lip curl," wrote Taft, leaving no question as to his wife's view of abstainers, "at the suggestion of Sunday high teas and dinner parties without champagne."[19]

She couldn't understand all the press focused on her. "Accustomed as I had been for years to publicity," Nellie wrote, "it came as a sort of shock to me that nearly everything I did . . . had what the reporters call 'news value.'" She was nevertheless responsive to the press, favoring certain women journalists, and became the first incumbent First Lady to permit direct quoting of an interview. She supported women's right to independent careers and said as First Lady she "would interest myself in anything that vitally affected . . . or absorbed" the president. She subtley defended her co-presidency by advancing mildly feminist views:

> "I do not believe in a woman meddling in politics or asserting herself along those lines, but I think any woman can discuss with her husband topics of national interest and, in many instances, she might give her opinion of questions with which, through study and contact, she has become familiar . . . in the Philippines . . . I became familiar with . . . more than politics . . . [it] involved real statesmanship. Mr. Taft always held his conferences at our home, and, naturally, I heard these matters discussed more freely . . .[20]

Nellie extended her feminism to others, supporting higher education for women: "I believe in the best and most thorough education for everyone, men and women . . . My idea about higher culture for women is that it makes them great in intellect and soul, develops the lofty conception of womanhood; not that it makes them a poor imitation of a man . . . woman is the complement of man . . . No fundamental superiority or inferiority between the two appears plain to me. The only superiority lies in the way in which the responsibilities of life are discharged. Viewed in this light, some wives are superior to their husbands, some . . . women to men in varying circumstances. Education for women, as much as is obtainable, possesses to my mind, far greater advantages than the commercial one of providing means for making a livelihood. This is a very great benefit, when necessary . . ."[21]

One contemporary reporter described the First Lady as having been "a suffragist all her life, though never of the aggressive type." She became the first presidential wife since Julia Grant to support suffrage, but with an odd stipulation: "I favour bestowing upon women every civic right, but I should like to put in a prohibitionory [sic] clause debarring them from running for office. If women should indulge in a scramble for office, I think that the natural scheme would become disjointed and the aim of the home destroyed. I can see nothing unfeminine in women casting the ballot, but it seems to me for the present that it is practical to dissociate the right to vote from the right to hold office." It was nevertheless a radical departure from past First Ladies.

It was likely that Nellie had a role in the appointment of an old friend, Mrs. LeRoy, to the non–civil service position of chief clerk in the Land Office, where, as the First Lady proudly recorded, "She is the only person in government who has the right and power, given by special act of Congress, to sign the President's name to a document." She also probably influenced the appointment of Julia Lathrop as director of the new Children's Bureau, the first woman appointed to a major federal position.[22]

Mrs. Taft forged ahead as hostess. Her linguistic skills were used to "converse with some of the diplomats in their own tongues." On the private floor, she decorated with an Oriental look, a style never before seen there. In the midst of a reception when the punch ran out, she herself ran down to the kitchens to oversee the immediate preparation of a new batch. She was "very particular" about her terrapin soup, popping down to the kitchen, and peeking into boiling pots to sample it. Behind her back, disgruntled cooks impersonated her high-pitched voice: "They don't do things in the White House the way we used to do them at the Malacanang Palace."

Nellie relished "holding court" in the Red Room after events, before a warming fire, conversing with women activists. She looked every inch the First Lady, complete with her diamond tiara, dressed in starched grand pearl-embroidered whites with silver trim, her hair done up in the Japanese upsweep of the Edwardian Era. When, one evening before a dinner, Mrs. Jaffray eyed the First Lady in a scarlet and gold gown, she remarked, "My goodness, you look like a queen." The president patted his consort and quipped, "She is a queen."[23]

Mrs. Taft determined to exert influence in a civic role, too, and for the first time in history, a First Lady was to play a major role in the evolution of Washington. West Potomac Park, an area running along the river, had a paved road nicknamed "the Speedway." Nellie loved the drive, but the region was a "mosquito-infested swamp, rendezvous of tramps, and hiding place of criminals . . ." Mrs. Taft conceived a park modeled after the famous Luneta in Manila for what became the first truly public project of a First Lady, and it was credited as such in the press and by the public.

Just weeks after the Inaugural, with Archie Butt at her side, the First Lady summoned the Public Buildings Commissioner to an outdoor meeting in the muddy area, where she chose a site for a bandstand from which the Marine Band would play for the public. Government carpenters got to work immediately, and the White House announced that the citizenry was invited to hear the concerts beginning April 17, continuing on Wednesdays and Saturdays from three to five in the afternoon. Meanwhile, the First Lady had the "Speedway" renamed "Potomac Drive." She fretted herself "almost sick" that something would go awry. To her delight, it was a sensation.

On opening day, cars, carriages, and the common man on foot converged on West Potomac Park. Nearly ten thousand showed up. The band serenaded, lovers strolled, children frolicked as their parents laid picnics, social folk stopped to gossip. Grand Nellie, in large hat, cocked parasol, and white gloves, surveying it all from her cobalt Pierce-Arrow, boasted of the "exchange of friendly greetings . . . I felt quite sure that the venture was going to succeed and that Potomac Drive was going to acquire the special character I so much wished it to have." But the First Lady wasn't finished with West Potomac Park. She self-assuredly began plans for what would become her legacy, and generate millions of dollars for the city's tourist trade—planting the cherry blossom trees.

Mrs. Taft, a member of the National Geographic Society, was friendly with one of its only women board members, Miss Eliza Scidmore, American expert on Japanese culture. Among their mutual interests was the cultivation and ornamental use of the delicate cherry blossom trees, indigenous to Nippon. Bursting for a short time in early spring, they formed a romantic hue of varying shades from white to deep pink. Though Scidmore evidently suggested it, the First Lady determined to bring the Japanese Cherry Blossom trees to Washington, because "both the soil and climate encouraged such an ambition." Her first move was a drive to have all such trees in America transplanted to the Tidal Basin area, flanking Potomac Drive. When only a hundred trees were to be found, the First Lady's dream seemed to fade.

In Tokyo, Dr. Jakicki Takamine, who isolated adrenaline, learned of her interest in his nation's trees, and contacted the mayor, liberal leader Yukio Ozaki. Ozaki, upon hearing of, as Nellie put it, "our attempt to bestow the high flattery of imitation upon his country," donated two thousand native trees. Yukio had a purpose, too. Japan had been looking for an expression of thanks to America for T.R.'s mediation in terminating the 1905 Russo-Japanese War. The trees arrived in Seattle later in the year as a personal gift to the First Lady, who in turn donated the trees to the government. Unfortunately, it was soon discovered that the trees were infected with a rare disease, and had to be destroyed. Mrs. Taft, of course, was undaunted.

She began lobbying her effort on Secretary of State Philander C. Knox. He owed her a big favor. Knox had been appointed partly through Nellie's influence. In several months' time, he would confer with Japanese ambassador Yasuya Uchida, who immediately wrote his government, suggesting a new crop be sent. The Japanese took to the idea and increased the number from two thousand to three thousand. This time, however, the trees were kept in Japan, slowly cultivated and carefully watched by botanists for two years before they were sent.[24]

Less than a month after Nellie's opening day at West Potomac Park, on a beautiful May afternoon, the Tafts and a small party of friends headed down the Potomac on the presidential yacht, for what was hoped would be a respite from the severe stress the First Lady had experienced earlier in the day, as she saw her son Charlie through the difficult surgery of having his adenoids removed. As the boat slipped from the dock, Attorney General George Wickersham chatted with her on the outdoor deck. Suddenly, he realized that she was not responding. She was still and deathly pale. He screamed out that she had fainted.

Mrs. Taft was immediately carried to an inside room and revived, but could not move her right arm and leg.

The boat was rushed back to shore, and a closed motorcar raced her to the White House. She had to be carried in and brought upstairs. The president's face filled with suffering. He forced himself to host a scheduled event that night, alluding to Nellie's absence only by saying she had had a trying day and needed rest.

Upstairs lay his beloved partner, whom he respected before all people and all ambitions. In just two months, this First Lady had proved herself a political activist who promised to be one of the toughest but most caring and powerful women in the first ladyship, a woman who spoke out against racial and sexist injustice, a woman who never held her tongue just for the sake of being a lady.

Now, she could not even speak. Nellie Taft had suffered a stroke.[25]

- 36 -

Behind the Screen

AT NO POINT did the White House ever confirm Mrs. Taft's stroke to the press or public, but the sudden disappearance of her presence had an immediate impact.

Though she was not kept completely out of public view, Nellie's appearances were carefully controlled. She was seen in her car, but only from a distance, with her face covered in veiling. At the Taft summer home in Beverly, Massachusetts, she no longer would speak with the press or even executive staff members. Everyone except family was banned from the house. This seemed unusual in light of her earlier willingness to speak with reporters, but under the guise of separating her public role from private life, it was not questioned.

Pride wouldn't permit her to let the stroke become public knowledge, but having always been honest with the press, Mrs. Taft was frustrated by polite society's dictum to never reveal personal ills. "I do not like this thing of being silent," she scribbled to Will, "but I don't know what to do about it . . ."[1]

President Taft wrote a carefully worded note to "Miss Belle" Hagner about "the matter," saying "I believe the change to Beverly will do her good. She is getting stronger each day, and while she is by no means

out of the woods, I feel great encouragement in respect to her condition." He was more candid to his brother, Horace, writing that the First Lady "is quite disposed to sit as pope and direct me as of yore which is an indication of the restoration of normal conditions." For her to pass time, the president suggested to Ambassador Reid in England that he write to Mrs. Taft as he had to Mrs. Roosevelt. Reid's letters to the First Lady helped her spirits, keeping her informed of private diplomatic conversations and chronicling of political events particularly of interest to her, like the demonstrations of the British suffragists.[2]

During her absence in the summer of 1909, Nellie missed the thrilling sight of Orville and Wilbur Wright's flying exhibitions in their "aeroplane." Alice Longworth, who ran "a popular lunch wagon" with Tom Collins Thermoses, drove out daily to watch the flying from her open electric car. Women drivers were quickly becoming a common sight in America, but Alice wasn't the first to own and drive a car in Washington. That credit went to none other than Edith Galt, now a rich widow. Norman had died in January 1908, and left the jewelry store to her—debts and all. Edith was faced with the decision of liquidating or holding on. She held on. With her lawyer and a hired manager, Mrs. Galt ran the store, learning the business through experience. With Edith at the helm, Galt's was sustained, and the widow prospered. She enjoyed her independent life, and living alone in a comfortable home. She refused her brothers' offers to move in with her, and was evidently unbothered that her indigent mother would be forced to sell her small house and move into a residential hotel. Yet when the moment called for it, Mrs. Galt could still play belle in peril. Whenever she drove her car near the White House, a policeman she called her "special protector" held up traffic so she could drive by.[3]

In Denver, Colorado, the fourteen-year-old daughter of meatpacker John Doud sometimes borrowed his latest car to drive herself to Miss Wolcott's finishing school. Neither a good driver nor one who enjoyed it, she soon relinquished the privilege willingly. An outrageous flirt who loved dressing in pink, she was superficially feminine, but under the frills, steeliness could already be detected. Whenever she went to the amusement park's carousel, she insisted on always riding in her favorite chariot, which had emblazoned on its front the same famous female figure of Columbia that crowned the U.S. Capitol Building. Iowa natives, the Douds had moved to Denver at the turn of the century, and would begin wintering in San Antonio, Texas, that next year. Though they were wealthy and had servants, Elvira Doud, daughter of Swedish immigrants, instilled a strict frugality in her daughter. The girl began keeping her own financial accounts, and joked that she squeezed a dollar so tight that "you could hear the eagle scream." Her name was Mamie.[4]

When Nellie returned to the White House for the fall season, the "cover-up" of her stroke was more difficult to maintain, the White House only vaguely confirming a "nervous disorder." Her face was slightly disfigured, her speech slurred, her movement uncertain. Though she was still able to plan her superb state dinners, she had to settle for dining near the pantry, hidden from sight behind a screen. There, Nellie ate the same meal, alone, listening longingly to the laughter and conversation in the State Dining Room.

Though she described her stroke only as "a serious attack of illness," and "temporary retirement," Nellie was forced to ask her daughter and sisters, Eleanor More, Maria Herron, and Jennie Anderson "to represent me . . . whenever it was necessary for me to be represented." As he personally taught her to speak again, the president tried to keep upsetting political news from Nellie. His most real fear was that she might suffer a subsequent and more devastating relapse. Consequently, the president maintained a blissful facade about his growing political problems. Her handicap was to have terrible repercussions on the administration, Ike Hoover writing that she was prevented from consulting legislators because "her speech was visibly affected," and that the embarrassment the Tafts felt was a "severe burden."[5]

Without Nellie's knowledge, the president wrote a revealing letter to her bête noire, Theodore Roosevelt, admitting his duties were "heavier to bear because of Mrs. Taft's condition. A nervous collapse, with apparent symptoms of paralysis that soon disappeared . . . made it necessary for me to be as careful as possible to prevent another attack.

Mrs. Taft is not an easy patient and an attempt to control her only increased the nervous strain. Gradually she has gained in strength and she has taken part in receptions where she could speak a formula of greeting, but dinners and social reunions where she has had to talk she has avoided." With that letter, Nellie was now unwittingly made vulnerable before her enemy. Perhaps unconsciously, it was one reason to strengthen Roosevelt's feelings that by 1912, he might have to step into the ring again on behalf of his party.[6]

One of the rare events that the disabled First Lady did make a point of attending was a unique conference on American Jewry addressed by the president. Leading rabbis, social reformers, and attorneys attended, and at the formal luncheon held for the conferees, Mrs. Taft joined the men. In a speech before B'nai B'rith, President Taft made reference to his wife's work with Jews in forming the Cincinnati Orchestra, and sustaining an annual thirty-thousand-dollar fund-raising level. Taft came to know the Jewish families because of her: "[S]he found the leading Jewish members . . . with her and supporting every concert and every effort that she made, and I have never ceased to be grateful to them." Simon Wolf, one of America's most distinguished Jewish leaders, had been befriended by Nellie many years before it might appear politically expedient to court an ethnic leader. Nellie was already conscious of the presidential election, looming two years away, and the Jewish leaders' support could only help. She was not the only political wife then practicing religious tolerance. Ellen Wilson, now the newly elected New Jersey governor's wife, worked closely with Joseph Tumulty, Woodrow's Irish Catholic assistant.

Ellen began conferring on the national political scene with Tumulty, who considered her a better politician than her husband. She kept providing literary quotes for Woodrow's speeches, and made tours of state institutions, from a school for delinquents to an insane asylum. When powerful Democratic leader William Jennings Bryan came to speak in Princeton, Ellen immediately wired her husband to return from Atlanta, and organized a meeting between the two, who became allies. Tumulty told Ellen, "[Y]ou have nominated your husband." Wilson was attracting national focus. In 1909, even a wealthy widow uninterested in politics had peeked in on a speech of his in Philadelphia. It was Edith Bolling Galt's first glimpse of Woodrow Wilson.[7]

Wilson may not have alarmed Nellie Taft, but Roosevelt did, and her mistrust extended to his wife and daughters, all of whom she ostracized from the courtesy of White House invitations. T.R. wrote of this slight to Senator Henry Cabot Lodge, who replied that both he and Nick Longworth were "hurt and galled," but Nick wrote to his father-in-law that the culprit "was not a gentleman at all, but is Mrs. T." Archie Butt—who was being sent as Taft's personal emissary to welcome back the Roosevelts from Europe, strongly suggested that Nellie write a letter to Edith, making it clear that they were welcome at their old home. Only grudgingly did she do so. With a "shallow excuse," they turned her down.[8]

Nellie met the enemy head-on when Roosevelt visited the Tafts in Beverly that summer. She was not at all gregarious, unlike the president. ". . . I was glad . . . to find the old . . . comradeship . . . and myself . . . to be unwarrantedly suspicious . . . I was not destined to enjoy this . . . assurance for very long." For most of the meeting, Nellie remained silently self-conscious of her speech impediment. But when T.R. suggested that industrialist Andrew Carnegie be appointed to lead the American delegation of an International Peace Conference, the First Lady barked, "I don't think that Mr. Carnegie would do at all." That was that. Mrs. Taft had an innate sense of whom to distance from Taft, and with the increasingly evil perceptions of industrialists, she prevented Will from what he saw as innocent golf games with the wily John D. Rockefeller. She was unable to stop the president's game, however, with "bad name" Henry Frick, "reactionary lord of the steel industry."[9]

On another summer day, Nellie visited another Roosevelt—the kindly Eleanor. The First Lady took a trip to Campobello Island in Canadian territory, and ended the afternoon with Franklin and Eleanor; although they were Democrats, it proved to be an amicable visit. Nellie knew the importance of entertaining party enemies, and became increasingly ruthless in her political expediency. When the president planned a dinner honoring Speaker Cannon, with the purpose of cajoling him into supporting the administration's Canadian Reciprocity Treaty, Mrs. Taft became testy as she learned that the number of seventy-two guests were invited. But when Cannon refused to be twisted by Taft's gentle arm, Nellie wagged her finger. "I could have told you that nothing will move that old Cannon when he gets his head set . . ." The night of the dinner, from the recently completed Oval Office, in the new West Wing, the president phoned the First Lady, and Archie Butt captured one side of the unique Taft marriage:

"Is that you, my darling? . . . Come a little closer to the phone dear . . . Nellie? . . . It would be a little more grammatical to say, 'It's I' but I don't care what pronoun you use . . . Yes, 'me' does sound more natural, but we can't change the English grammar. I couldn't, at least; but I don't feel so sure about you . . . Don't hurry me so . . . I thought you might be interested in the good news. They have got the Reciprocity bill up in the House and are now voting on it . . . Yes, I thought it would interest you . . . I'm afraid it will make some . . . late . . . Would you mind having dinner a little later, say at a quarter to nine? . . . Too late, is it? Well, I don't want to upset your plans . . . All right, then, we will say half-past eight . . . Better tell the cook . . .

Of course, I might have known that you would think of that . . .
Goodbye . . . You are a trump all right."[10]

By late spring of 1911, the First Lady was back in fighting spirit.
With rest, expert medical care, and her own tenacious willfullness, she
was able to overcome even a minor relapse. By June, Nellie was up to
grandstanding at the event that proved to be her crowning moment
amid the bitter disappointments of the career she had so long coveted.
The Tafts were celebrating their silver wedding anniversary, and so was
the country. So it seemed.

In her own rather democratic gesture, Mrs. Taft issued four thousand invitations, to everyone across the United States whom she
deemed useful, including major American rabbis and bishops. Like so
many of Nellie's seemingly social forays, it served important political
purposes.

Congressional wife Ellen Slayden recalled the muggy air, the thick
throng, and the president and First Lady standing beneath a huge
electric sign with the dates "1886–1911." Searchlights on the nearby
State, War and Navy Building "made the lawn as bright as day, but
it was crude like a fair or a circus." The wet ground gave women the
opportunity to lift their dresses, and reveal a variety of colored calf
hose, a sight she found "grotesque." Alice Longworth, holding her blue
satin just a bit higher than dampness required, believed the party afforded Nellie the opportunity "to play the great lady" and "be admired," but more important it ". . . was a perfect excuse to gather
delegates" for next year's election. Going almost unnoticed was Taft
ally and former Ohio lieutenant governor Warren Harding and his wife,
Florence.

Everyone from government workers to Supreme Court justices was
encouraged to give silver gifts, and there were many sotto voce whispers
of "How much did you put up?" and "Did you get your money's worth?"
Rockefeller sent a cabinet full of silver tea caddies, and Elbert Gary of
the U.S. Steel Corporation, then under Senate committee investigation for its acquisition of Tennessee Coal and Iron Company, sent a
two-hundred-year-old silver tureen said to be worth eight thousand dollars. The Tafts did not return the questionable gifts, but prohibited
these particular pieces from becoming prominent. The president told
Nellie to "let no one see them, at least until certain ones have been
secreted in cold storage." She would be giving silver gifts to others
celebrating weddings and twenty-fifth anniversaries for many generations. With the Taft initials removed first, of course.[11]

The absence of invitees Theodore and Edith Roosevelt, however,
gave clear indication that a prediction Nellie made might indeed come
true. Edith and T.R. were making a western tour, on which the former
president was sounding like a candidate for reelection. After the Roosevelts had accepted an invitation to her home, and after her doctors

permitted her to travel into downtown Los Angeles to hear a rousing speech by "Teddy," the feeble but spry Lucretia Garfield wrote T.R., "[H]ow glad I was to see you and Mrs. Roosevelt," and how "thoroughly" she enjoyed his speech. Signing herself "your devoted adherent," the former First Lady had also pointed out, "It is not necessary to tell you more." At eighty, the rock-ribbed Republican Crete was converting to Roosevelt "progressivism."[12]

Even the Tafts' marriage was strained by the threat. "I have not asked him anything," Nellie confided to Butt one day about Taft, "and he has not talked to me. But this Roosevelt business is perfectly dreadful. I lay awake all last night thinking about it, and I don't see what is going to be the outcome." Turning to leave, Butt noticed tears in Mrs. Taft's eyes. Few ever saw such emotions displayed. "When she allows herself to be loved," he wrote poignantly, "she is very lovable, but as a rule she keeps herself buried down deep within herself."[13]

Discontent over Roosevelt momentarily invigorated Nellie's advisory role, Will consulting her on everything from Canadian trade issues to Mexican military affairs, to the controversial firing of Roosevelt's chief of the forest service, Gifford Pinchot. The First Lady fully comprehended the most complicated economic issues, like the Payne-Aldrich Tariff, which reduced 650 tariff schedules, increased 220, and maintained 1,150.[14]

She reproached Taft for approving what advisers suggested. He laughingly responded, "Well, my dear, if I approve everything, you disapprove everything, so we even up on the world at any rate." The First Lady unamusedly retorted, "It is no laughing matter." Nellie raised the issue of Interior Secretary Ballinger, accused of impropriety but defended by the president. She had advised Ballinger's dismissal because he was generating severe criticism of the administration. "You don't want to fire Ballinger, and yet you approve of Senator Crane and Mr. Norton [presidential assistant] trying to get him out. I don't approve of letting people run your business for you." The president defended himself: "I don't either, my dear, but if you will notice, I usually have my way in the long run." Nellie had the final word. "No, you don't. You think you do, but you don't."[15]

Amid these tensions was Archie Butt, who could bridge the widening Roosevelt-Taft chasm and still calm the First Lady. But when his companion, Frank Millet, had left for Rome in the winter of 1912, Archie found himself without an objective confidant as he struggled with the political situation. His health broke. At the Tafts' urging, Archie left for Europe, to join Frank in March, planning on a two-month vacation. By April, however, when the chance came to book two reservations on a new, elegant oceanliner, Archie wired the president to say that he and Frank were coming home on the SS *Titanic*.[16]

– 37 –

1912

ON APRIL 16, the White Star Line wired a response to the president's inquiry of the list of *Titanic* survivors. Neither Archie Butt nor Frank Millet was on it. Gentlemen to the end, they changed into white tie when they realized the *Titanic* was sinking into the icy North Atlantic. Nellie said that "our close and dearly loved friend" drowned, "facing death like a soldier, after the lives of nearly all the women and children had been saved . . . we felt that he belonged to us . . . nothing in all our experience ever touched us as deeply as the tragedy of his death."[1]

The First Lady immediately assumed leadership of a fund-raising drive to raise a memorial to the *Titanic* casualties, contributing the first dollar and issuing a public statement that the one-dollar donations being sought were reasonable enough to permit every American woman to contribute. It was built on the riverbank across from her own beloved cherry-blossom project, now in its final stages as the three thousand trees that were carefully nurtured for two years were ready for planting. On March 27, 1912, with spades and parasols in hand, the First Lady and Viscountess Chinda, the Japanese ambassador's wife, planted the first two trees.[2]

Mrs. Taft was not the only woman who would revel in nature. By the end of the year, a little daughter was born to a rich Texas businessman, T. J. Taylor. She would find her childhood's tranquillity among the hanging moss of Alabama, the native state of her mother, where she was raised. Like Eleanor Roosevelt, who lost her mother as a child, the girl matured into a lonely but extremely bright "wallflower." Dances and fine clothes never would equal the fulfillment she was finding in the "drifts of magnolia all through the woods in the Spring—and the daffodils in the yard. When the first one bloomed," she later recalled, "I'd have a little ceremony, all by myself, and name it the queen." Though christened Claudia, the infant was declared by a black maid to be as "purty as a lady bird," and the nickname stuck. Another little girl, the baby daughter of an Irish silver miner and his German immigrant wife, was also given a lifelong nickname. In a Nevada tent just eleven days before Mrs. Taft planted the first cherry tree, Thelma

Catherine Ryan was born on the eve of St. Patrick's Day. Her father nicknamed her Pat.[3]

That spring in Washington, the streams of annual tourists saw Nellie's cherry blossoms bloom for the first time. Many were groups of graduating classes, like the one from Northampton High School led by chaperone Grace Coolidge. At the White House, she became transfixed before Nellie Taft's piano in the Blue Room. Spontaneously, she sat down and ran her fingers over the keys, warming up to play. A guard quickly came over, tapped her shoulder, and prohibited her. "Some day," she reportedly said, "I will come back here and open that piano and play on it, too, and he won't put me out."[4]

While in town, Mrs. Coolidge undoubtedly read in the social column about the most talked-about women's event being held that season. A mammoth 140th birthday brunch was being held on May 20, in honor of none other than Dolley Madison, a century after the War of 1812. Someone suggested that the Democratic congressional wives gather for a formal breakfast, and the wife of the new speaker of the House, Mrs. Champ Clark, a history student, chose Dolley as "patron saint." Then the invitation list was opened to all women, and four hundred accepted. Held at Rauscher's catering hall, at five dollars a plate, it lasted from noon until five, and featured a rambling speech on Mrs. Madison's life, enough "raiment" noted Mrs. Slayden "to dim the luster of the Queen of Sheba . . ." The favor, a Dolley snuffbox, recalled her addiction.[5]

The Dolley revival inspired Allen C. Clark's authorship of *The Life and Letters of Dolley Madison,* the first thorough biography of a First Lady, which finally portrayed Dolley as more than merely a happy hostess. The momentary Dolley revival had infiltrated even Broadway, where one of the hits of the 1911 season was *First Lady of the Land,* a comedy written by Charles Nirdlinger. Not only did it keep Dolley Madison's legend alive, but it greatly added to the popular usage in the press of the title "First Lady," now developing semiofficial permanence.[6]

The true legacy of the birthday, however, was what would prove to be Washington's most popular exhibit, a Smithsonian First Ladies' gown collection. Prominent Washington women Rose Hoes and Cassie James began the movement, inspired by Hoe's gown collection of her ancestor Elizabeth Monroe. Before earnest collecting began, Mrs. Taft was approached for her support. Nellie was so enthusiastic that she donated her own Inaugural gown, giving legitimacy to the drive. Older gowns were more difficult to find. One of Martha Washington's was located in Baltimore. In Springfield, Illinois, a rich purple velvet hoopskirt of Mary Lincoln's was discovered. Both Nellie Taft and Frances Cleveland showed up at the brunch to announce their donations. The First Lady descendants present were equally responsive. One of Dolley's

relatives pledged a yellow gown and turban of the great lady herself, and children of the two Julias, "Mrs. Ex" and "Mrs. G.," promised clothes of First Ladies Tyler and Grant. Within a decade, nearly all administrations were represented by a gown, subsequent incumbents sending theirs directly to the museum.[7]

The event proved to be Nellie Taft's last public pleasure. That next month, at the Republican Convention, Roosevelt was not only a full-fledged candidate fighting Taft for the nomination, but planning to deliver a speech blistering his old friend. "Well," the First Lady told the shocked president, "I suppose you will have to fight Mr. Roosevelt for the nomination, and if you get it he will defeat you. But it can't be helped." She wouldn't let up. "I told you so four years ago and you would not believe me." Not without a slight trace of bitterness, President Taft replied, "I know you did, my dear, and I think you are perfectly happy now. You would have preferred the colonel to come out against me than to have been wrong yourself."[8]

Edith Roosevelt was equally disgusted, and wrote, "Politics are seething abominably." She was blunter with her husband: "You can put it out of your mind, Theodore, you will never be President of the United States again." Roosevelt thought otherwise, and it seemed that the couple had a heated disagreement. When the press had officially announced he was running, Edith was nowhere to be seen, having left for South America. Still, she went to the convention, and helped edit Theodore's speech, wisely suggesting the deletion of exaggerated passages, but knowing instinctively to retain the most stirring. Also there were Florence Harding and her husband, Warren, the Ohio Republican who nominated Taft. When Harding approached Nick and

Alice Longworth's box, trying to make a deal in offering support for Longworth as governor, Alice cut him off to say they'd "not accept favors from crooks." Her "active distaste" for him equaled the sentiment she held for the gray-haired and pince-nez-bespectacled Florence. Alice had first noticed her at the 1910 Gubernatorial Convention in Columbus, sitting near her in the spectators' gallery. She was called "Duchess."[9]

When Taft was renominated, an elated Edith Roosevelt told a friend, "Oh, I'm so glad my husband escaped; you cannot know how happy I am that the White House is not ahead of us." The First Lady, however, was more disturbed by the fact that Roosevelt accepted his following's nomination of the Progressive party, splintering the Republicans. The president claimed that his wife never "expected me to be re-elected," and was "gratified" in the "more important purpose of defeating Roosevelt." Nellie denied that, but admitted to not having "slightest expectation" of reelection and "longed for the end of the turmoil." She would not even mention Roosevelt by name: ". . . when the Republican party was divided . . . I stopped reading the accounts of the bitter political contest because . . . the opposition . . . made so much more impression on me . . . that I was in a state of constant rage which could do me no possible good."[10]

When Democrat Woodrow Wilson won his party's presidential nomination at their Baltimore convention, his wife told reporters frankly that she had full faith of winning in November. Also there, at her first convention, which she found boring, was Eleanor Roosevelt, who was facing a conflict. She believed in Uncle Ted, but could not support him since Franklin was a Democrat. Eleanor felt Franklin was pursuing his political career with "the glamour of Uncle Ted's example." By 1912, Franklin had already served one two-year term as New York state senator, and Eleanor had given birth to four children: Anna in 1906, James in 1907, Franklin, Jr., in 1909 (he died at seven months), and Elliott in 1910. Though exposed to Albany politics, she said, "It never occurred to me that I had any part to play. I felt I must acquiesce in whatever he might decide . . ." With meetings taking place in her home at night, Eleanor listened, attempting to understand issues because, she said, "It was a wife's duty to be interested in whatever interested her husband . . ." She was also confronted with political reporters like the *Herald*'s Louis Howe. He impressed her only as an odd, chain-smoking gnome in disheveled suits, but she also noted Howe was in FDR's corner.

As she became accustomed to politics, Eleanor began to act as a sounding board, and paid social calls to the wives of both Albany politicians and journalists. The fight for suffrage "shocked her," however, and she "took it for granted that men were superior creatures and knew more about politics than women did, and while I realized that if my husband was a suffragist I probably must be, too, I cannot claim to have been a feminist . . ."

Eleanor's aunt Edith believed it was wrong to split the Republican party, but publicly supported the Progressives. ". . . Theodore is whacking at Wilson," she wrote, "who deserves all he gets." T.R. did not "whack" when letters supporting the gossip of the Mary Peck–Woodrow Wilson love affair were brought to him. He said that nobody could believe that Wilson, "cast so perfectly as the apothecary's clerk, could ever play Romeo!"[11]

Ellen Wilson proved to be the public campaign wife, used in one political cartoon as a bonus to the South because she was Georgian, a prominent figure on a "whistle-stop" campaign train trip through her native state, touring women's universities like Wesleyan College in Macon, where Woodrow said that "the most significant thing in modern life is the larger and larger role women are playing in it. She is taking up now as she never took up before the things which concern the welfare of society." None of the candidates took a strong stand on suffrage, but, privately, Ellen supported it. She compared her campaign role to Lady Macbeth, who "wanted MacBeth to have the crown because he wanted it, not because she wanted to become Queen . . ." When she became a minor issue by the printed story that she approved of women smoking, however, Mrs. Wilson personally handed out her denial to reporters, stating that she disliked smoking by all people.[12]

Others watched with interest from the sidelines. Frances Cleveland supported her friends the Wilsons, but did not do so publicly. Lucretia Garfield, staunch member of the National Christian League for the Promotion of Purity, was "awakened by the Progressivism of . . . Roosevelt," but she made no public appearances for him. Even after Roosevelt was shot, but not killed, he did not pick up the support he'd hoped he might. Sympathy came in the way of telegrams—even one from Ellen Wilson to Edith Roosevelt—but not votes. The Democrats won.[13]

Americans in Europe that season heard of the election results the next day. In Paris, Edith Galt learned that Wilson won. That night she had dinner with a former Princeton professor who had taught there while Wilson was president, and spoke severely of him. Mrs. Galt was "interested," in the dissection of Wilson, but admitted that she could not understand her own fascination.[14]

Ellen Wilson now contemplated her new role as "a different kind of woman—in *some* respects—not *all*, thank Heaven." It was *her* persistence that influenced Wilson into choosing William Jennings Bryan as secretary of state, as well as retaining Joe Tumulty as press secretary in the face of anti-Catholicism. She wrote Tumulty on a patronage matter; she wanted another Catholic, Dudley Field Malone, appointed as the collector of the port of New York. Malone was appointed.[15]

The year 1912 marked changes for another candidate's wife. When Franklin developed typhoid during the campaign, he asked Eleanor to ask Louis Howe to manage it. Calling herself a "Puritan," she did so, but barely overcame her condescension toward Howe, even in light of the fact that he was the force that had Franklin reelected. She grudgingly began a working relationship with the man who was increasingly becoming her husband's confidant.

As Nellie packed, Ellen prepared. She had no interest in being a social leader, and to this end sent out feelers for a social secretary who would take greater command. For Belle Hagner, now a State Department clerk earning half the salary of her male peers, that meant opportunity. Evidently, Ellen Wilson had contacted Edith Roosevelt for advice, and the former First Lady recommended Belle. Mrs. Wilson, ever sensitive to party loyalties, knew how close Belle had been to Edith Roosevelt. Ellen asked a Washington Wilson supporter to address this issue to Belle, who responded strongly, almost defensively, and outlined the now-important staff role of First Lady's social secretary: ". . . I feel the principal value of a social secretary is to help in furthering the individual ideas of her chief . . . I do not want Mrs. Wilson . . . to be under any misapprehension." Belle was rehired.[16]

Before Mrs. Wilson took over, however, her Princeton neighbor visited the White House. On January 11, 1913, Frances Cleveland came back, marking her first return, but the visit also seriously defined just who was a president's wife and who was not. It was serious because it involved government money.

Also invited to the dinner honoring Frances was Mary Lord Harrison, the fifty-four-year-old widow of former president Benjamin Harrison. Mrs. Harrison had never been a First Lady, but rather secretary to the First Lady, Caroline Harrison, as well as her niece. When, four years after Aunt Caroline's death, Mary married Uncle Benjamin, twenty-five years her senior, she caused a scandal in the family, and a permanent breach between him and his two children, Mary McKee and Russell Harrison, her own first cousins. Ten months after the wedding, Mary had a child by her uncle, who was then sixty-three years old. He died four years later.

In 1909, both Mrs. Cleveland and Mrs. Harrison were granted the franking privilege, and a year later, the Committee on Pensions recommended that both women receive the now-automatic five-thousand-dollar-a-year stipend because of the "public sentiment that the widow of . . . President . . . should at all times be enabled to occupy a social position which, if not commensurate with that which she held before, at least shall be one which will be free from the necessities of a life of rigid economy," even though "[U]pon the death of a President or ex-

President, the widow retires practically from public life." Because of Mrs. Harrison, however, the bill did not pass.

Some in Congress resented Mary's posturing as a "presidential widow," for she was merely the widow of a man who *had* been president. To most in Congress, she was unequal to someone like Frances Cleveland. So, while the stated purpose of the pension was to keep presidential widows from financial distress, in fact only the woman who actually "worked" in the first ladyship was really qualified for a congressional pension—a belated sort of "salary" to First Ladies. Since First Lady was not an official government job with specifically stated requirements and duties, the only legitimate way to pay her was if she became a widow. The controversy of awarding Mary Lincoln a pension years before had been in part because of a questioning of how well—or poorly—she had conducted her role. Mary Harrison's very existence seemed a bane to many, a sentiment illustrated during her White House visit. Nellie, wanting to make Frances's visit a special evening, thought inviting Mary would bring historic association, but she knew that making too much of her might provoke criticism. Consequently, Mrs. Harrison was invited but barely acknowledged.

Ike Hoover, expert on unwritten protocol, about to assume the full duties of chief usher, felt that though Mrs. Harrison had a "standing of no consequence," she nevertheless deserved some special treatment. Yet, while Frances was given the seat of honor, at the right of the president, Mary Harrison was seated in Siberia, down the table two places to the left of the First Lady, probably on the Protocol Office's suggestion.

Frances was making her own news at the moment, for in less than a month she was to marry Princeton professor Thomas Jex Preston, Jr. No previous presidential widow had ever remarried. Hoover recalled that all the old employees were on their toes with excitement over "Frankie's" return, polishing up the house extra hard so "she might see things at their best." Since Frances hadn't seen the changes made in 1902, her car was directed to the new East Terrace entrance so she could walk past the First Ladies' portrait gallery. Upstairs, as she entered the Blue Room, where she had been married twenty-six years before, Mrs. Cleveland was deeply affected. "No eye present but was turned on her as she entered this room, and it was plainly evident that her inward feelings were profound," wrote Hoover.

At dinner, she marveled at the expanded State Dining Room, while eating off of the red-bordered china she had purchased for the White House. Hoover observed that she took "little interest" in the after-dinner musicale, and left the moment it was tactfully possible with "the queenly air so characteristic of her . . . She had come again, had conquered once more, had gone."[17]

Less than two months later, another First Lady who had also conquered was wistfully departing.

After her husband left for the Wilson Inauguration, Nellie Taft lingered, and "taking a last look . . . wandered around the second floor hardly knowing what to do with herself . . ." The staff nervously eyed their watches as the endless minutes of Mrs. Taft's last moments ticked by. They usually used this short limbo of time—after the outgoing First Lady left and before the new one arrived—to make halfway habitable the private rooms of the incoming family. Nobody dared move even a chair while Nellie postponed her departure by half-hour increments. She sat down to write some letters to her sons for one last time on White House stationery.

Trying gently to coax her out, the ushers offered to Mrs. Taft the guest register of the administration, saying that a similar book was given Mrs. Cleveland, and that when she returned for a second term, the book was continued.

The notion of someday returning "brought a real smile to her sad and forlorn face."

Finally, at eleven-thirty, Nellie put on her furs and hat and headed downstairs, with her letters, an orchid bouquet, and an armful of magazines for reading on the train. When she entered the usher's office, just inside the front door, Nellie was "deeply affected" and, as she attempted to hand her letters to Hoover to mail, dropped her load of magazines. Moved to silence, almost none of the staff dared to wish her good-bye. The grand Nellie Taft who had buoyantly sailed over the large presidential seal inside the entrance just four years ago to the day now shuffled sadly over the same spot again, in the other direction. [18]

Meanwhile, at the other end of Pennsylvania Avenue, the new president read his speech before the gathered crowds at the Capitol. Evidently, it was difficult to hear from behind him, so the new First Lady left her seat and stood underneath the speaker's podium to hear it better, unconscious of the crowds watching her. None of the speech was a surprise. Woodrow had read it to her several days before.

Mr. and Mrs. Franklin Delano Roosevelt were there, too. Within weeks, FDR, following in the footsteps of T.R., would be given the plum he coveted, assistant secretary of the navy. For his first few months on the job, he would live in town alone, taking rooms in the Powhatan Hotel. Also in residence there was Sally Bolling, genteel southern widow of reduced circumstances. Her daughter, Edith Galt, decided to pass up the chance to see the Inaugural Parade from Galt's store balcony, but she did buy a volume of Wilson's speeches, read through it, and wonder how he would achieve all he hoped to. The next night she went to the National Theater performance of Billie Burke with a relative who was an ardent Wilson supporter. Mrs. Galt frankly admitted that they went not to see Miss Burke, but President Wilson, who, it had been announced, would be attending the show. Mrs. Galt may not have been part of Washington's social or political circles, but she knew tradespeople in town. The old man at the National's box office gave her two tickets, right below the president and Mrs. Wilson's box. From her vantage point, Mrs. Galt watched Woodrow Wilson, and thought he was bored with the performance, as he yawned several times.

Ellen Wilson made no particular impression on Edith Galt.

At least, Edith Galt chose not to record any.[19]

PART VIII

The Great War
1913–1921

We did not labor in suffrage just to bring the vote
to women but to allow women to express their
opinions and become effective in government . . . Men and women are like right and left
hands; it doesn't make sense not to use both.
—JEANETTE RANKIN
First elected congresswoman (1916)

The Artist

OF HER FIRST ladyship, Ellen Wilson said, "A person would be a fool who lets his head to be turned by externals, they simply go with the position." To many, it was apparent that Mrs. Wilson, self-described as "unambitious," would turn no heads. Ellen Slayden found her "short, round-faced, round-pompadoured, red-cheeked and not becomingly dressed" as she gave each person "a limp hand and passed us on . . ."[1]

On Inauguration Day, a new, unexpected face was welcomed into the family circle. When the president's sister gashed her head, Cary Grayson, a naval doctor, came to the rescue, gaining the confidence of the Wilsons. He became their official doctor and a great influence on the president, coaxing him into regular exercise to relieve the nervous tensions from which he suffered. Grayson was then pursuing Miss Altrude Gordon, who sometimes feared that the middle-aged widow friend who introduced them was also sweet on him. Altrude's late father, a widowed Scottish millionaire, had evidently manifested affection toward the very same widow, and on his deathbed asked her to look after Altrude. It was none other than Edith Galt. She, of course, had known Cary since the loss of her own child, a fact almost nobody knew. Whatever might once have flared, by 1913 it was over, for Edith had brought Altrude to Cary. But now, Mrs. Galt had a connection to Woodrow Wilson.[2]

Though Ellen Wilson had given up her promising career, explaining that "three daughters take more time than three canvases," art was still her love. She reclaimed the nude "Love and Life," which Lucy had banned, Edith had reclaimed, and Nellie had banned again. Ellen had a studio installed for her use in an attic room. Some of her colleagues formed the core of the first American impressionists. Her work was professional, not amateur, and she had even had an exhibit just before assuming her public role.

As First Lady, Ellen focused public attention on art. As honorary president of the Southern Industrial Association, she assisted the group by using the White House to have mountain crafts like quilts, rugs, and counterpanes displayed for sale. The mountain women who made these crafts didn't want charity but opportunity. The First Lady provided it, by inviting both congressional and Cabinet wives to the showing,

which resulted in a large sale. Ellen herself made purchases. Her concern for those less fortunate was genuine. She was particularly gentle
and kind toward the little newsboys around the White House, going out
to buy their papers and "laugh away their return change." The black
staff called her "the Great and Good Lady."[3]

Though she made no attempt to stage a co-presidency like Nellie
Taft, Mrs. Wilson had considerable political power over her husband,
who once mused to her that he hoped "you don't know much about the
Constitution of the United States, for I know marvelously little about
art and if you know both subjects how am I to be head of the house?"
Their private life helped nurture their political relationship. Passionate
Woodrow's letters to Ellen were the most ardent ever exchanged between a presidential couple. Before returning to her from a trip, he had
written, "I tremble with a deep excitement . . . I never quivered so
before with eager impatience and anticipation. I know that I was not
half so much excited on the eve of our marriage." On another occasion,
he called himself the "intemperate lover," and asked Ellen, "Are you
prepared for the storm of love making with which you will be assailed?"
Age had not dimmed the "power" of his "queen."[4]

Secretary of the Treasury William McAdoo had nothing but praise
for the First Lady who "supplied" Wilson with "a calm excellence of
judgement . . . [and] with an extraordinary understanding that might

be truthfully characterized as a prescience, or intuition, [and] was keenly alive to . . . subtle influences in political life . . . Her knowledge of human nature was remarkable. The President had an enduring confidence in her estimates of men and their ideas . . . she was the soundest and most influential of them all [his advisers.] Yet she did not abuse her power; nor did she thrust herself into situations and try to run affairs."[5]

The navy secretary portrayed her as a woman conscious of power who "shared . . . fostered . . . and gave . . . momentum" to Wilson's political aspirations, "and was the more ambitious of the two . . . She kept up with every incident and move and I came to lean upon her wisdom as much as did Wilson . . . she spoke her own mind, agreeing or not agreeing. She sensed, with both woman's intuition and her knowledge of politics, situations better than . . . men . . . Though always behind the scenes, she knew the political situations and outlined them with grasp and judgement. Wilson often followed her suggestions . . . And she was generally right."[6]

The public sent the powerful First Lady their pleas, at least three advising her to block the appointment of Catholics to positions in the new administration—advice Ellen ignored. Public mail was routed to her through her staff, consisting of both a "personal secretary," filled by the president's delicate cousin Helen Bones, who ran the private side of the First Lady's life, and a public "social secretary," Belle Hagner. Hagner was quite shocked, and dismayed, at her boss's boldest gesture, Ellen's main project, which held highly political implications.[7]

Only eighteen days after the Inauguration, Mrs. Wilson met with Charlotte Hopkins, chairman of a Washington women's division of the National Civic Federation. Hopkins came to seek the First Lady's help on an ignored, worsening problem, the deplorable housing of the city's poor in alley dwellings. Built specifically for poor black laborers, they were tiny residences either converted from stables, or hastily erected from cheap materials. By 1913, they occupied every cranny near the Capitol, and were filthy firetraps, overrun by rats, often without plumbing, overcrowded by poor families, unsightly, unhealthy, and unsafe.

Mrs. Wilson was shaken by the briefing, and three days later became the first First Lady to enter the slums, touring the worst, looking in on ideal "sanitary" models, never letting the occupants know her identity. She became a stockholder in an improved housing company that raised eighty-five hundred dollars, assumed honorary chair of the National Civic Federation, and popped up at Associated Charities meetings.[8]

One chronicler said that the First Lady explained that her "upbringing" taught her that to "accept work in behalf of the Negroes" was her "Christian duty," an attitude that was "a point of view Negroes themselves found objectionably condescending," and "patronizing." Her daughter Jessie admitted that Ellen felt "strongly about the color line . . . [and] had far more of the old southern feeling . . . warm personal liking for the negroes, combined with an instinctive hostility to certain assumptions of equality."[9]

Whatever the unfortunate repercussions, Ellen Wilson's only motivation was to help, for she was troubled by the lack of openly public social work in the First Lady role. Behind her back, her project was condescendingly dubbed "slumming parties" by her own social secretary. Ellen Slayden recalled "sardonic laughter" at the joke that the First Lady had joined "the Society for the Prevention of Useless Giving." But to someone like Ellen Wilson, that attitude was inhumane. Ideally, she believed that if the dwellings were demolished, the poor would leave the city for other, healthier neighborhoods. Some read racism into that, but not once in any of her statements or letters was there substance for such a charge.[10]

Her plans took shape. A "Committee of Fifty" was formed to draft a congressional bill, with the First Lady's moral support. Secretary of State William Jennings Bryan spoke publicly of Ellen's leadership: "The fact that the wife of the President is with her presence here . . . lending support of the movement is enough . . . if she can find time out of her busy days to be here and go to work for this cause, I can too." There were problems with initiating Mrs. Wilson's bill. The Senate discovered that most of the alleys were owned by some who lived in the alleys themselves, not large real estate companies. The bill called for the alley conversion into parks and small streets without mention of providing housing for those to be displaced. Still, it went to Congress.[11]

Next the eager First Lady explored working conditions. Particularly distressed at the limited restroom and lunchroom facilities of government offices, as well as the poor lighting and ventilation and the lack of "little branch hospitals" for first-aid service, Ellen Wilson began pressing individual Cabinet members to improve these deficiencies in their departments. The demands were met, but when the departments' new dining and rest room facilities were opened, they were segregated.[12]

In fact, three southern Cabinet members, Postmaster Burleson, Treasury Secretary McAdoo, and Navy Secretary Daniel all prevailed in bringing "Jim Crow" to their departments. Legend began to circulate in the black community that it was the First Lady who instigated segregation, specifically using the example of the Post Office Department in late July 1913. One chronicler recorded that Ellen displayed "shocked disapproval . . . at seeing colored men and white women working in the same room." Yes, she was shocked, but at the working conditions, not integration. This was a woman who had lived and worked in New York, and was used to integration. And there was the glaring fact, which many ignored, that her lobbying for improvement occurred three months *after* segregation had been initiated. In fact, the *Bee*, a local black newspaper, praised Ellen's work.[13]

Mrs. Wilson's interests extended into truancy laws, child labor, care of the mentally ill and drug addicts, dependent and neglected children, adult education, open-air recreation facilities at schools, public baths and comfort stations, and community recreation centers. Previous First Ladies had assumed humane projects, but none had ever been so public-spirited. Trusting her instincts, Woodrow never stopped Ellen, to whom he'd write, "No president but myself ever had *exactly* the right sort of wife!"[14]

What troubled Ellen politically was the situation of General Victoriano Huerta, a military dictator who had assumed power in Mexico and controlled a government the United States did not recognize. "Perhaps it would save us the trouble in the long run," the First Lady wrote the president during one of their separations in the summer of 1914, "to give them [the Mexican insurgents] arms and let them exterminate each other if they so prefer." She later said Mexico was "a plague on the Monroe Doctrine! Let[']s throw it overboard! All the European nations have interests and citizens there as well as we, and if we could all unite in bringing pressure upon Huerta we could bring even that mad brute to hear reason."[15]

The First Lady also comprehended the details of tariff, a subject some of the public wrote about to her often, and it was the issue that provoked Wilson to break a historic precedent. On April 8, 1913, he became the first president since John Adams to speak before a joint session of Congress. Ellen beamed with pride over the speech, saying it was just "the kind of thing that Theodore Roosevelt would have liked to do—in fact would have done if he had thought of it."[16]

Another proud southern woman also there had to fight the crowds to hear the president. A police guard had allowed Edith Galt to pass into the House chamber without the required ticket. After "a definite effort on my part," Edith took a front-row seat in the visitors' gallery, where, directly above the speaker's rostrum, she had a close-up view of Woodrow Wilson. Mrs. Galt had attended the first big public reception of the Wilsons, but said she felt nothing special when she first shook hands with Woodrow.[17]

Just months after Wilson's appearance on Capitol Hill, an announcement came from the White House: "Upon the advice of her physician, Mrs. Wilson has decided to abandon active participation in the philanthropic movements which have commanded much of her attention . . ." Though not seriously ill, she found herself increasingly tired. It was hoped that her summer at a New Hampshire artists' colony, Harlakenden, would revive her spirits.[18]

Washington was like a ghost town in summer. Even tradespeople fled. In 1913, Edith Galt went to Europe with Altrude, who was still being romantically pursued by Dr. Grayson. Political wives began their exodus just after the social season ended, removing their children, nurses, drivers, cooks, and maids to the cool North. Husbands managed to steal away for long weekends.

That summer, suffrage became an increasingly serious subject of debate. In England, the suffrage fight was much more strident—and violent. Edith Galt was amused at a British policeman's suspicion that she might be one of the suffragettes. In Madrid, Mrs. Galt did something she never did in Washington—attended formal social affairs. In Tangiers, Edith watched women wrap "awful snakes" around their bodies, and declared native dancing "vulgar and uninteresting." When she witnessed a bride being transported to her future husband's home and was told the woman had probably never seen her groom, Mrs. Galt thought it a "horrible . . . fate" for a woman to marry a man she had not loved, let alone not seen. There was no mourning for Norman, but she admitted that she was "lonely."[19]

At Harlakenden, Ellen Wilson reveled in the intellectual discussion among the artists gathered there, including Maxfield Parrish. When someone suggested a government department promoting art, the First Lady responded, "[T]he Congressmen who would take that view . . . [are] not yet born." Her own art was progressing, and she entered several canvases under an assumed name for various shows and exhibitions. The work was highly praised, and she was invited to join the prestigious Association of Women Painters and Sculptors. She herself said as First Lady that no spouse could "rest on the laurels of another person [and] must grow to the limits of [her] own spirit, mind, and ability." The summer of 1913 was one of the happiest moments of her life. The possibility existed that Ellen Wilson might become in a short time the first First Lady to also maintain a professional career.[20]

However, she set no particular example for sub-Cabinet wife Eleanor Roosevelt, who followed convention, making her formal calls, receiving guests for tea, and putting in her appearance at White House receptions. But Mrs. Roosevelt also joined Ellen Wilson in the inspection tours of slums. After hearing a speech of FDR's before a group of North Carolina farmers, she wrote to a cousin, "There seems to be so much to see and know and to learn and understand in this big country of ours . . ." On her honeymoon, Eleanor had vowed to herself to learn more about government. Slowly, her world *was* opening. When she was invited to climb a battleship's mast, she accepted. When Franklin's half-brother announced his engagement to a woman from the lower-middle class, Sara was shocked, and called upon Eleanor to help her stop the impending union. Eleanor refused to. Still, tradition prevailed in her life. It was no longer possible to raise a growing family of children, as well as maintain an exacting social schedule, without assistance. She hired a social secretary. By early fall, 1913, an efficient, bright, and strikingly sensuous twenty-one-year-old was working in the household three mornings a week. When Eleanor was away, Franklin was comfortable with her. Even Sara liked Lucy Mercer.[21]

Ellen Wilson returned to the White House preoccupied with two of her daughters' weddings, but had a serious fall before Nell's marriage to Secretary McAdoo. ". . . I am still far from well," she wrote a relative, but tried to blame it on the role. "Nobody who has not tried can have the least idea of the exactions of life here and of the constant nervous strain of it all . . ." Her public appearances were limited, but her visibility at Woodrow's April 20 address to Congress on the Mexican situation seemed to indicate that the First Lady was on the mend.[22]

Something, however, was terribly wrong.

In June, Ellen was ordered to bed by Dr. Grayson, staying there through July when, finally, she learned the diagnosis. She had incurable kidney tuberculosis. Grayson canceled his summer plans in order to stay nearby. That meant his sweetheart, Altrude Gordon, did, too, and with Altrude in town, Edith Galt also decided to remain in the oppressively hot capital until August, when the women would go to Maine.[23]

While Ellen Wilson lay dying in Washington, across the Atlantic, the last days of La Belle Epoque flourished in Europe, where Alice Longworth was then summering. Through the dense crowd of aristocrats at the Longchamps Grand Prix rippled the unsettling news that Austria's archduke Francis Ferdinand and his wife had been shot by a student, protesting the nation's invasion of Serbia. Germany allied with Austria, although that meant fighting Serbia's ally Russia.

Wilson gave strict orders that news of the European war be kept from his wife. At her bedside, while she slept, he quietly drafted a letter to the warring nations that the United States would act as mediator, and scribbled instructions on official papers brought to him, but Wilson found work frustrating. "I can think of nothing—nothing, when my dear one is suffering." She never asked what he was doing, but she did inquire about the status of "my bill." Word went out to the Capitol of her last request.

By the next day, August 7, the alley-clearance bill was passed without question, or closer examination. The dying First Lady was told. She looked at her family, one by one. Moments before she slipped into unconsciousness, Mrs. Wilson whispered to Grayson to "promise me that you will take good care of my husband." At 5:00 P.M., with Woodrow holding her hand, Ellen died with a "divine smile on her face." A shaken Wilson turned to Grayson: "Is it all over?" The doctor nodded silently.

At that, the president of the United States, with war breaking out in Europe, looked out the window, burst into heavy sobbing, and cried out, piercingly, into the heavy, still air, "Oh my God, what am I going to do?"[24]

– 39 –

The Merry Widow

THE PRESIDENT OF the United States was spied arranging a shawl around the corpse of his wife, laid first on a sofa, not in a coffin. A servant heard him talking to the body: "Never, never, never." One maid believed he meant never to marry again.[1]

Ellen's 1914 death was more than just the loss of a wife. Woodrow had lost a political and spiritual partner. He found himself stripped of the will to shoulder the presidency. His closest unofficial adviser, Colonel Edward M. House, visiting his friend, recorded that the president "said he felt like a machine that had run down, and there was nothing left in him worth while . . ."

At a luncheon, conversation focused on how the president would resolve his condition. Just as a congressional wife casually remarked, "When the President marries again," she was cut off by a State Department official's wife: "Oh . . . how can you speak of such a thing! . . . he wouldn't dare to marry again while he is in the White House; public opinion would not permit it."

The president's depression remained severe. By late fall, he concluded, said House, that he "was not fit to be President because he did not think straight any longer, and had no heart in the things he was doing." Helen Bones, the only woman in the house with him, tried to shore up Woodrow's despondency by suggesting that the late First Lady's life be the subject of a book. Others tried to offer comfort in the knowledge that Ellen's slum-clearance bill would continue her legacy. In October, the "curiously unrealistic measure" had become law, prohibiting residence in alleys as of July 1, 1918. An Ellen Wilson Homes Association was formed and promised to someday provide low-cost rental homes in the converted alleys, but it was never to be. Those closest to the president were alarmed by his state of mind, especially Dr. Grayson, who'd been at his side since the summer. Grayson confided this to a lady friend.[2]

When Grayson visited Edith Galt at her Washington home, he told her of the "graver and graver" possibility America would enter the European war, as well as "the heartbreaking loneliness of the President . . ." To himself, Grayson recalled Ellen's dying request that he look after Woodrow, and he began taking the president out for exercise.

He asked Edith to spend some time with the rather lonely Helen Bones. Grayson thought exercise and companionship were also what Helen needed. Mrs. Galt hesitated.

Grayson persisted, spontaneously arriving at her home one day in a White House car with Nell McAdoo and Helen Bones. They asked Mrs. Galt to join them for a ride. She accepted, and shortly found herself cultivating a friendship with Helen, who effusively spoke of her cousin the president. Mrs. Galt listened closely, but cautiously refrained from asking questions that might make her appear overinterested. She did admit that "my imagination was fired by the picture Helen gave me of a lonely man . . ."

When Edith mentioned Helen to her lawyer, he appealed to her sense of the occult. "You have a destiny, but what it is I cannot determine; you should be preparing yourself for something that is to come." Edith consulted Washington's most prominent seeress, Madame Marcia, who predicted she'd be the next Mrs. Woodrow Wilson. If so, Edith told Marcia, she'd consult her as First Lady. A devotee of astrology, Edith, like Julia Tyler, Mary Lincoln, and Julia Grant, believed in dream messages and spiritualism.

After a jaunt in the park, Helen invited Edith back to the White House. When she protested that her shoes were muddy, Helen reassured her that nobody was there to see her anyway. As luck would have it, the president and Grayson were also returning from golf, and ran into the women. Edith reassured herself with the thought that she was at least dressed in a Worth. "Turn a corner, and meet your fate," she would say in the following weeks.[3]

The foursome took tea, and Helen Bones was amazed that Mrs. Galt had made her cousin laugh twice. "I can't say that I foresaw in the first minute what was going to happen," she said. "It may have taken ten minutes." Edith accepted the ensuing dinner invitations. By the evening of May 4, the president told Edith that he loved her. "Oh, you can't love me," Mrs. Galt responded, "You don't really know me. And it's less than a year since your wife died." Woodrow looked at her seriously. "But, little girl, in this place, time is not measured by weeks, or months, or years, but by deep human experience; and since her death I have lived a lifetime of loneliness and heartache. I was afraid, knowing you, I would shock you but I would be less than a gentleman if I continued to make opportunities to see you without telling you . . . that I want you to be my wife."

Edith was stunned silent after this soliloquy. They would maintain their romance secretly, with Helen posing as escort to a friend. To the marriage proposal, Edith could not yet say yes.

But she couldn't say no, either.

It was easy to see why he was swept away. Edith had a "soft, cultivated beauty . . ." With black hair, hazel eyes, and broad rosy cheeks, the mature Edith looked like a Rubens figure swathed by Worth in purple satin hobble skirts. The romance flourished also through letters. "A man," he wrote her, "is maimed and incomplete without his mate . . . to whom he is lover and comrade." In another, he said, "If you can not give me all that I want . . . it is because I am not worthy . . . Here stands your friend . . . in the midst of a world's affairs . . . Can you love him? . . . Will you come to him . . . without reserve and make his strength complete? . . . [S]erve I will to the utmost, and demand nothing in return."

Politics was also the subject of their love letters. At first Edith questioned, "Why should I be chosen to help you?" The president responded that "I know that no one can help me as you can . . ." That was all Edith needed to hear. She was already beginning to think of Woodrow's word as gospel.[4]

Not long after Wilson's courtship of Edith began, the Germans sank the Lusitania in spring 1915, killing American passengers on board. It was the first sign that America would be drawn into the war. Secretary Bryan felt aggression must be avoided at all costs. He strongly disagreed with Wilson's warning message to the agitators now at war with the European Allies. The president told Edith of Secretary Bryan's stance, and asked her what he should do if the secretary offered his resignation. "Take it, sir, and thank God for the chance," she responded, adding, "you can replace him with someone who is able . . ."

Edith hesitated about being intimate with the president, feeling her capacity for emotional and physical love was "dead." Yet she told Woodrow, "We both deserve the right to try . . ." But on May 27, when he made some advances in the back of a car, she was unable to respond.[5]

Meanwhile, Edith Galt, the woman with no thorough education and no interest in government, now burst forth on politics. She advised the president not to see German ambassador Johann von Bernstorff without other witnesses present. She suggested he rewrite "for her" his note of reply to the Germans on the Lusitania. She was happy that Bryan had resigned, but considered his replacement, Robert Lansing, a mere State clerk. "Much as I enjoy your delicious love letters," she told him, "I enjoy even more the ones in which you tell me . . . of what you are working on . . . for then I feel I am sharing your work and being taken into partnership as it were."[6]

Mrs. Galt now seemed bitten with the intrigue of love. And political power. The two became inextricably intertwined.

At the end of June, Edith joined Helen and Wilson's daughter Margaret at the family's summer spot in Cornish, New Hampshire. Woodrow followed later with Grayson, stopping first to see his confidant Colonel House, just returned from Europe, whom he boyishly told of his love for Mrs. Galt. When Woodrow joined Edith, it was obvious they were lovers.

Visitors to the president's cottage were strictly limited to close friends; reporters were nowhere to be seen. Here, on the porch, the couple held hands as the president toiled on his daily dispatches of work folders. President Wilson shared all his work—even classified information—with Edith Galt.

On June 29, they consummated their love. During their first separation after that day, he called her his "ideal companion . . . perfect *playmate* . . . sweetest *lover,* " and recalled ". . . the time when the real marriage of our hearts was consummated . . . all the wonder of intimate self-revelation . . . Those wonderful mornings when our minds grew to be intimate friends . . . those never-to-be-forgotten evenings when our hearts were opened to one another without reserve and with the joys of young lovers . . ."

At night, he found himself suddenly awake, alone in his bed, calling out, "Edith, my darling, *where are you?*" In the letters he wrote her during the day, the president shared even more state secrets—diplomatic relations between America and England and Germany, army defense plans, starvation in Russia, friction with Mexico, the difficult position of Haiti's relationship with America. "Don't you see," he wrote, "how comparatively easy it is to keep . . . a very complicated public matter in your head when some despatch or memorandum about it turns up every day? . . . You no doubt think it easy to do so yourself by this time."

Woodrow didn't want to keep his love a national secret for much longer. He wrote of "the loneliness of the power, which no one *can* share . . ." No immediate wedding plans were made, but Edith promised to marry him after the 1916 election. Public and press gossips knew he was courting someone. Just who remained secret.[7]

Meanwhile, Mrs. Galt had become so quickly comfortable with giving Woodrow her political judgments that she offered her *unsolicited* advice on his closest advisers. Edith disliked Tumulty, the middle-class Irish Catholic from Jersey City, adding "my idea may be colored by his commonness." She made her first attack on House as well, saying he was "not a very *strong* character . . . I know what a comfort and a staff Colonel House is to you . . . but he does look like a weak vessel and I think he writes like one . . . but . . . you are so sweet in your judgements of people and I am so radical." Her harsh attack on House rather shocked Woodrow, who gently chastised her, "He is a counsellor, not a statesman . . . You must remember, dear little critic, that sweetness and *power* do not often happen together." Privately, Edith resented Tumulty's warning to Woodrow not to marry her as much as she did House's suggestion to her that she keep out of politics.

Edith increasingly made it clear that she would assume a partnership in the presidency, writing ". . . I will come and hold those dear strong hands that steer the ship in both my own, and . . . carry out your orders . . ." Her motivation was love, but she considered situations with the calculation of a businesswoman. When Galt's had suffered financially a few years before, she'd fired several employees. Even with her tendency to see situations personally, she could discern them clinically. If she were to be around, she believed that Tumulty and House would have to go.

House was particularly distressed over the "infatuation." He advised postponing a wedding until after the 1916 election, and recorded, "It seems the President is wholly absorbed in this love affair and is neglecting practically everything else . . . I am sorry the President has fallen in love at this time . . ."

The Cabinet and leading Democrats met secretly to consider the political ramifications of remarriage, unanimously deciding that the president must wait until after 1916, otherwise it might alienate voters. Secretary McAdoo, upon learning of Wilson's recent seventy-five-hundred-dollar loan to Mary Peck, fabricated a "letter" from someone who claimed to have seen the Wilson-Peck "love letters," which Mrs. Peck was showing to people, implying that the loan was a payoff to keep quiet. If Wilson married Edith, McAdoo claimed that Peck would publish the "love" letters. House was in on the scam, and thought it might be a good way to get rid of Edith. McAdoo approached the president with the situation, and Wilson immediately became stricken with fear. He sadly wrote Edith that he would not think of embarrassing her, and he broke the engagement. McAdoo and House's scheme backfired. Mrs. Galt was determined to become Mrs. Wilson.[8]

Edith told Woodrow that she was unafraid of "gossip or threat . . . whether the wine be bitter or sweet we will share . . . the comradeship." Woodrow acknowledged that the Peck relationship had been more than platonic, as he might have first told Edith. "Surely no man was ever more deeply punished for a folly long ago loathed and repented of—but the bitterness of it ought to not fall on you, in the prime of your glorious, radiant womanhood." She didn't care, she would still marry him. Suspiciously, she would take no more risks by postponing the marriage, telling Woodrow that "I have never had to ask permission to do things in my whole life, I have always just done them, and that ended it. And I have seldom even discussed what I was going to do. Now, while I know it must be different, when things are all discussed and consulted over I get impatient and restless . . ." The wedding was announced immediately.[9]

If anyone doubted Edith's possession, they need only have read the announcement Woodrow himself punched out on his typewriter on October 6: "In the circle of cultivated and interesting people who have had the privilege of knowing her Mrs. Galt has enjoyed an enviable distinction, not only because of her unusual beauty and natural charm, but also because of her very unusual character and gifts . . . her thoughtfulness and quick capacity for anything she chose to undertake have made her friendship invaluable to those who were fortunate enough to win it." Wilson's concession to those fearing damage to his reelection plans was to state that when the widow had visited the widower at his isolated New Hampshire summer retreat, it was "as Miss Wilson's guest." Reporters discreetly left out any reference to those summer visits.[10]

Though photographers were forbidden by the Secret Service to snap pictures of Wilson leaving Mrs. Galt's home in the wee hours of the morning, it was impossible to halt the burst of fresh gossip about the premarital state of affairs. Rumors circulated that Edith had once been mistress to Ambassador von Bernstorff. The most popular Mrs. Galt joke was spread at dinner parties by wits like British embassy attaché Charles Crauford-Stuart, who asked, "What did Mrs. Galt do when the President asked her to marry him?"

The answer was, "She fell out of bed."[11]

And then there was the *Washington Post* "mistake," craftwork of publisher Ned McLean's wife, Evalyn, who often suggested items for the society column. "The President," ran a *Post* social note, "spent much of the evening entering Mrs. Galt." Alice Longworth said the deletion of "tain" from "entertaining" was no mistake.[12]

The most vicious gossip claimed that the couple had secretly been involved while Ellen was alive, and that, with Dr. Grayson's participation, Ellen had been poisoned, or pushed down a flight of stairs. Citizens, mostly women, were outraged that the new marriage came within a period far from acceptable protocol as an appropriate mourning. The first Mrs. Wilson's tombstone had not yet even been erected, a fact duly reported by the Hearst newspapers. The chairman of the Union Pacific Railroad reported to Colonel House that the engagement caused "unpopular" feelings in the West, even with men. Not everyone was scandalized. Cartoons appeared showing Edith and Woodrow in hearts, with Cupid's arrows shot through them. Another showed a smiling Uncle Sam, bouquet in hand, ringing the doorbell of the "Galt" door.

The actual December 18 ceremony was quite understated, taking place at Edith's home, where crowds were kept at bay behind police barricades. As the honeymoon train headed to a country resort, Secret Service chief Edmund S. Starling watched the president dance down the aisle, as he howled like an aroused boy, "Oh, you beautiful doll! You great big beautiful doll!"

One later friend of Edith's frankly admitted that at the very least she "gave Wilson a very good sex life."[13] Some thought that the Widow Galt had been akin to the scandalous Mesdames du Barry and de Pompadour. But unlike those courtesans, this woman led her king to the altar, and was given her own scepter.

— 40 —

Mrs. Woodrow Wilson

THE PUBLIC RESPONDED to their new First Lady with curiosity. Much was made of the fact that she was a direct ninth-generation descendant of Pocahontas, a point she was quite proud of, and which was reflected in many of the public's wedding presents to her—from statue to painting to furs—from Indians or with an Indian theme. So many gifts arrived requiring acknowledgment that Edith Benham, the new social secretary, had to abandon the task and turn it over to the executive staff.[1]

Among the most unusual letters relating to this first First Lady of "minority" identity since Quaker Dolley Madison was one directed to Interior Secretary Franklin K. Lane claiming that it was illegal for the president to serve liquor to his new wife, because of her Indian ancestry. Edith responded to Lane that "the law . . . applies only to those of my tribe living on a Reservation & is not applicable to *us* when we are at large," adding coyly that she and Lane should remember the president's technical law-breaking "for future use should he become irresponsible."[2]

Although issues like congressional appropriations for the Seminole tribe were frequently directed to her, Edith would not make Indians, or alley dwellings, or cherry blossoms, her concern. Her only cause was working with the president. Even her hostess role was secondary. Personally, she found the title of "First Lady" to be "disagreeable." She rarely referred to herself as Edith Wilson. It was always Mrs. Woodrow Wilson.[3]

Incredibly, there was barely an hour that she left his side. They slept, breakfasted, golfed, walked, lunched, motored, and dined together. In his private office, while stenographer Charles Swen took dictation, Edith listened to everything. After Swen left, the Wilsons went to work on the daily pile of "the Drawer," a large drawer in the president's desk where important documents were placed for his immediate attention. She walked him to the West Wing every late morning and kissed him at the door to his office. In the afternoons, she would stay with him in the office, sitting silently through his afternoon appointments. They worked late into the night from "the Drawer." As unofficial presidential assistant, Edith screened his mail, and limited callers

who she thought might be annoying to him. This situation became quite apparent to Colonel House upon his return from Europe. Expecting to brief the president alone, he was shocked to find himself sandwiched in the presidential limousine with both Wilsons, and that Edith was fully aware of all top-secret war information, having been given the responsibility of decoding House's messages.

One matter House acquiesced to Edith on was her determination to get rid of Tumulty, Ellen Wilson's confidant. Helen Bones now also ceased to serve a purpose, and Edith purposefully kept her at a distance, which was easier to do with more subtlety once her "friend" moved to New York, and took an editorial job at Scribner's, living "hand to mouth." Edith, "extremely bright and shrewd," took it upon herself to "get rid of all rivals" for Woodrow's affections, even platonic, according to one who knew her. She was never to leave him in the company of other women, except for one quick trip to New York, "obviously knowing this side of him."[4]

Edith's friend Altrude, who married Dr. Grayson in May 1916, complimented the First Lady by saying, "Those latent powers, abilities, and charms of yours have found their opportunity." The Graysons stayed Edith's intimates, but save for Altrude, Mrs. Wilson had no close women friends. In fact, she had enemies.

Alice Longworth's growing circle of Republican women like Ruth Hanna McCormick and Evalyn McLean, whose Mrs. Galt jokes were not to be quieted, were becoming quite involved in anti-Wilson politics and journalism. That circle now included the new Ohio senator's wife,

Florence "Duchess" Harding. Anyone who had bothered to get to know her would have learned that she was an extremely political woman in the tradition of fellow Buckeye native Nellie Taft. Florence had turned her husband's little newspaper, the *Marion Star*, into a financial success, and one of the state's leading Republican dailies. She understood modern journalism, and was one of the few political wives at ease with the press. Just as Eleanor Roosevelt and Louis Howe were beginning to actively interest themselves in Franklin's career, an Ohio attorney, Harry M. Daugherty, worked with "Duchess" in managing Warren's career. Meanwhile, her husband was having an affair with one of her best friends from home, Carrie Phillips. The lovestruck attentions to him of high school girl Nan Britton also raised suspicions. But Warren Harding wasn't the only secret adulterer in town.

Though others, like her cousin Alice, used birth control, Eleanor Roosevelt's "essentially secretive nature," prevented her from seeking advice on the subject. After the March 1916 birth of her son, Franklin, Jr. (her second son so named, the first having died as an infant), she decided she wanted no more children, and relations with FDR ceased. Meanwhile, with Eleanor's increased family responsibilities and demanding social duties, Lucy Mercer became more of a presence in the household. Franklin's increased attraction to Lucy was immediately noticed. Though she made no mention of it to anyone, the physical and emotional attachment of her husband and secretary frustrated Eleanor, resigned to play the role of wife, mother, and hostess.[5]

It was possible to be both dutiful wife and independent woman. Grace Coolidge, for example, still made the roles of wife and mother her priority but now served as the recently elected regional president of the international university women's sorority, Pi Beta Phi. At the moment she was celebrating this victory, however, her obligation as political wife suddenly increasesd. Her husband was running for lieutenant-governor.

In 1910, Calvin Coolidge had been home for a year, having been elected mayor of Northampton, but his role as husband and father became in absentia once again when he was elected to the state senate in 1911, serving as its president in 1914. Grace rarely took part in the public events of her husband's career in Boston, the exceptions being political rather than social events, like a 1914 speech of former president Taft, and, later, one of her own husband's addresses to the state senate.

As much as she sublimated her own interests in favor of Calvin's, Grace nevertheless insisted on remaining active in Pi Beta Phi, having helped found the Vermont branch. She traveled to annual national conventions, from New York in 1901 to Illinois in 1912. In 1915, without male escort, she traversed the country to the national convention in California, and was elected president of the Alpha Province, covering the eastern United States and Canada. While in the midst of a trip including tours of San Francisco, Stanford University, and the Pan-American Exposition, Mrs. Coolidge received a telegram from home that her husband was running for the Massachusetts lieutenant-governorship. She rushed back to be with him.[6]

Grace Coolidge, like Eleanor Roosevelt, was no suffragette, but neither woman quite so vehemently opposed granting women the vote as Edith Wilson. The very mention of female suffrage during Wilson's 1916 campaign made her uncomfortable. She hated only one speech of her husband's, because the subject, of "acute agony" to her, was suffrage. Suffragettes placed themselves and their banners in a permanent vigil in front of the White House on January 1, 1917, planning to stay until Wilson supported their cause, and Edith became "indignant" at those "detestable suffragettes." When some were thrown into prison, Edith called them "those devils in the workhouse," and advised her husband against his decision to pardon them. She said public mail asking her to help support the suffrage cause was her most unpleasant. Dudley Malone—appointed to the New York collectorship by Ellen Wilson's power—and his wife tried to persuade the Wilsons to consider the cause; Edith considered him a traitor. He was soon asked to resign. She labeled all suffragettes "disgusting creatures."[7]

Curiously, however, Ira Smith of the mail office revealed that Mrs. Wilson exercised a degree of feminism by influencing her husband to hire Galt employee Maude Rogers as an executive clerk. Some male staffers "resented the appointment and looked forward to trouble." The First Lady's choice proved capable. Everyone sensed Edith's power over the president. She even jokingly belittled Woodrow to Edward Bok, publisher and peace advocate: "Don't mind what he says. Upstairs here he is just like anyone else of us, and we pay no attention to him."[8]

Edith played no role in the campaign. It may have seemed odd not to use the crowd-pleasing woman, but advisers realized her presence could also remind voters of Wilson's weakness. A rumor spread that the financier Bernard Baruch, a loyal Wilson adviser, had paid Mrs. Peck seventy-five thousand dollars to keep quiet, and an affidavit circulated claiming witness to the president and Mrs. Peck's congresses. Wilson won only by a slim margin.

All the while, the First Lady had busied herself with decoding war messages. The ambassadors to Germany and England were both startled at her access and inside knowledge.

At the 1917 Inaugural, Edith Wilson broke precedent by becoming the first First Lady to ride with her president *to* and *from* his swearing in. The event was overcast with tension, coming just weeks before the president formally entered America into the war, but not just because of the European situation. As part of second term housecleaning, the First Lady again attempted to get rid of Tumulty, by urging the president to ask his loyal assistant to resign. With House backing her on this, the president, though his heart was not in it, offered Tumulty another, lesser appointment. Shocked, Tumulty emotionally wrote his chief that he would resign but refuse the new offer. Wilson backed down, Tumulty stayed, but Edith now no longer hid her contempt for the Irish Catholic.

Edith hadn't forgotten how both House and McAdoo opposed her marriage, and the latter's name, according to Dr. Grayson, was rarely mentioned around her. Because he was the president's son-in-law, however, she rather grudgingly accepted his presence. House was another matter. She was extremely angry with him when, after arguing a point with her that she then presented to Wilson, he changed his mind in front of the president. It made Edith appear foolish. She called House the "yes, yes man," and wanted his influence removed, arrogantly suggesting to him that he take the recently vacated ambassadorship to England. He stonewalled her, but his influence over Wilson waned as Edith's power increased.

With Wilson's April war declaration, America became an ally to France, England, Italy, and Belgium fighting Germany, Austria-Hungary, Turkey, and Bulgaria. Washington bustled. Only those with official appointments were permitted in the White House, the gates to which were now closed. There were no more public tours, no more Easter Egg Roll, no more New Year's Day Reception.

One day, though the president was sick in bed, he still managed to get word to Secretary Daniels that an old anti-piracy law permitted merchantmen to be armed. He informed the Cabinet member through a designated intermediary—the First Lady.[9]

With women doing their part for the war, it was a sign of the times, and of the times to come.

— 41 —

"The Shepherdess"

THE WAR COMPLETELY absorbed Edith Wilson.

If the president's schedule did not permit him to receive visitors, the First Lady substituted, at a simple tea. Visible to the public, Mrs. Wilson initiated the gesture of having twenty sheep, borrowed from Bel Air Farm in Maryland, graze on the lawn, foregoing the need for an extensive gardening crew. The shorn "White House Wool" produced a remarkable ninety pounds, and Mrs. Wilson directed that two pounds be sent to each state, where it was then auctioned, proceeds going to the Red Cross. Over fifty thousand dollars was raised. The next shearing yielded nearly as much for the Salvation Army, although some press comments and cartoons parodied Edith as "the Shepherdess." Mrs. Wilson personally made hundreds of pajamas, pillowcases, and blankets on her Wilcox & Gibbs sewing machine, and knitted trench helmets. She helped Mary Pickford and Charlie Chaplin in the promotion of war bonds, and the First Lady joined Mabel Normand on stage for the war-bond benefit premier of her silent *Joan of Plattsburg*. She responded to mail from soldiers' mothers. She even penned an open letter asking Allied women to help prevent the spread of venereal diseases, amid "temptations . . . [and] abnormal conditions."[1]

The War Department asked the First Lady to name the hundreds of sea transports, ships, and destroyers, and she often chose Indian names. On August 5, 1917, she became the first First Lady to christen a ship headed for active duty, the *Quistconck*. On the ship's bow, bedecked with large American flags, was a four-foot medallion photograph of Mrs. Wilson, larger than that of the president. The press praised her activity, and Secretary Daniels wrote her, "When women decide to become Cabinet officers, the Secretary of the Navy's portfolio should be assigned to you." At night, she decoded top-secret messages from Colonel House, Wilson's European representative, and then coded the president's communiqués back. Her only relaxations were playing billiards, trying to bicycle, and riding, though she was thrown.[2]

Other administration wives were doing their part in an even more public manner. Lou Henry Hoover, wife of Herbert, the chief of the newly created Food Administration, assumed leadership in handling the housing shortage due to the sudden tripling of the capital's population by war workers. Lou diligently sought and converted empty spaces into women's dormitories, personally financed low-cost rental housing, and organized an inexpensive government cafeteria. Even though Mrs. Wilson "Hooverized" the White House by initiating gasless, fuelless, meatless, and wheatless days, and signed a public pledge to strictly ration, as an act of public example for other American housewives, it was Lou Hoover who became the most visible woman in America in the cause of food conservation. Eleanor Roosevelt foolishly told a reporter that she had "Hooverized" by instructing her ten servants to cut back on food and utilities. A momentary laughingstock, she was mortified at the publicity that ensued. ". . . I'd like to crawl away from shame," she told Franklin.

The Hoovers felt that voluntary efforts to conserve food were more effective than rationing, and that women must lead the way. In October 1917, with conservation as the catalyst, Lou Hoover commenced her public-speaking career with her first speech, in New York. "No letup in food saving must be allowed," she said. "There is some individual who is unknowingly dependent upon you for life; maybe a soldier in the trenches . . . or a peasant woman. They will not have anything to eat next spring if we do not think of them now." Her patriotic appeal to housewives, restaurants, food wholesalers, and retailers not only succeeded, but it gave her self-confidence as a public speaker and women's leader.[3]

Washington was not the only place women did their part. At eighty-five, Lucretia Garfield became the first to join the Pasadena Red Cross war committee, for which she did daily volunteer work. Most surprising of all was her political support of a Democrat. Listening to the views of both candidates in 1916, Crete supported and voted for Wilson. She died peacefully in 1918.

In Switzerland, when fighting broke out, Frances Cleveland Preston managed to come home through Italy. With none of her previous aversion to publicity, she willingly accepted the visible position of director of the National Security League's Speakers' Bureau. Though she had never delivered a public speech, she began to do so frequently, sometimes making several a month. She traveled across the country, maintaining a hectic schedule, firing up citizens to do their duty. She pulled rank only once, to get a bunk on an overnight train. To the booking agent who evidently assumed her to be her own secretary, Frances said she thought it awful that a First Lady would be denied a sleeper. She also assumed the national presidency of the Needlework Guild, directing hundreds of its regional division presidents, like Edith Roosevelt of the Oyster Bay chapter, to oversee the knitting of soldiers' socks, scull helmets, and sweaters.[4]

On January 22, 1918, Edith and Theodore visited Washington for a four-day visit, with Alice, who brought the former First Lady to Franklin and Eleanor's for their weekly late Sunday night supper. While affectionate toward her Democratic hosts, Edith called Wilson a "vile and hypocritical charlatan."

Like Edith, Nellie Taft did war work and sent her sons to fight. Mrs. Taft now lived in Connecticut as the wife of a Yale law professor. Though she supported the idea of equality for women, she was disturbed by the hue and cry made by suffragettes' protests, particularly when her own daughter was involved in the radical fight. Mrs. Taft had little regard for the new Mrs. Wilson. The only way the Tafts might return to the city she loved was if Will finally got a seat on the Supreme Court. That would only happen under Republicans.

In Washington, cavernous Union Station became a focal point. In her striped Red Cross uniform, Edith Wilson spent afternoons there, distributing sandwiches, coffee, candy, and cigarettes to the soldiers heading out to training camps or ports to Europe, joined by Florence Harding and Eleanor Roosevelt, among others. Being exposed to the

different backgrounds of the enlisted men was a new experience for Eleanor, who called blacks "darkies," considered Jews vulgar, and felt uncomfortable with Catholics.

The trains pulling into Union Station were not carrying just military men. One young officer's wife carrying a seven-month-old baby in her arms was making the extremely arduous four-day trip from San Antonio, Texas, in April 1918. Now, she managed several hours' rest in the crowded station before she made the final trek to Gettysburg, where her husband had been relocated. Miss Mamie Doud was now Mrs. Dwight David Eisenhower.

In 1916, during her family's annual winter season in "San Antone," she was swept off her feet by the Kansan Eisenhower. The same day that they married, with Mamie in a pink sash, "Ike," as he was called, was promoted to first lieutenant. Mamie devoted herself to army life, which meant making a home from post to post. In September 1917, while her husband, now a captain, was one thousand miles away training men, she gave birth to her first son, Doud, at Fort Sam Houston, Texas. Nicknamed "Icky," for his father, the child brought tremendous joy to the couple as they lived with the possibility that Ike might next be assigned overseas.

Gettysburg proved to be a friendly town for Mamie, who was use to close family life and material comforts. Here, with other army wives, she passed time learning and playing bridge. She even had a chance to ride in a French tank. Mrs. Eisenhower considered Herbert Hoover the greatest war hero because of his efforts to get food to all people, American or European. When Ike had to leave, often for weeks at a time, Mamie stayed at home. Though he supported his Commander in Chief, Eisenhower was apolitical. His ambition was to advance in the military, and as he bluntly told Mamie, the army came before even his family. Nevertheless, whenever separated, he wrote her at least a daily postcard, if not a full letter.

At Union Station, all outgoing postcards were read and censored by Eleanor Roosevelt and other women working in a tin-shed canteen, as paranoia of spies and sabotage seeped through the capital. Even Mrs. Harding, the former Miss Kling, told people she was of "Pennsylvania Dutch" ancestry, not German. She feared anything that could stunt her political ambitions for Warren.[5]

Still other women clung to their plans for husbands who were not necessarily their own. During the summer of 1917, Lucy Mercer enlisted as a yeoman and was conveniently assigned to the Navy Department, working directly for her amour, Franklin Roosevelt. Eleanor openly confronted him about rumors of the affair. She said she would leave him, and warned, "My threat was no idle one." When Franklin had gone overseas to inspect naval stations, he received letters from Lucy that Eleanor discovered while unpacking his luggage. She flatly offered him a divorce, and his freedom to marry Lucy. At this point, his mother, Sara, entered the fray as mediator, explaining that she would completely cut him off financially if he left Eleanor. Without Sara's money, it was impossible for Franklin to support two families. Besides, his career would be ruined if he were divorced because of adultery. A deal was struck: Franklin must stop seeing Lucy, the couple would stay married, and Sara would continue providing monetary support. Eleanor said that though her own particular world was "shattered," she faced herself "honestly for the first time."[6]

At the eleventh hour of the eleventh day of the eleventh month, 1918, an armistice was declared. Talk focused on the terms of the peace-treaty negotiations to be held in Paris. Wilson surprised the world when he announced his own membership on the American commission at the talks, along with Colonel House, Secretary of State Lansing, former ambassador to France Henry White, and Army Chief of Staff Tasker Bliss. Wilson's "Fourteen Points" for peace included his dream, a League of Nations, which he wanted to present personally. Though most of his advisers urged against his going, Edith made a strong case

for Woodrow's participation. Her influence evidently weighed in the decision. That same month, she had vigorously warned Woodrow not to issue a statement that said a Republican victory in Congress in the 1918 elections threatened to split the nation's leadership. He went against her judgment, and the Democrats had lost substantially. Edith said it was "one of the greatest mistakes Woodrow ever made." He also ignored her sound advice to appoint more than just the one Republican member—former ambassador White—to the American commission.[7]

To some, the First Lady's presence in Europe with Woodrow would be an encumbrance. Her knowledge of the League proposal, Woodrow's demands, and the personalities of the diplomats, combined with Edith's unquestioning loyalty to everything the president said, would negate others who urged him to consider different concepts. To Colonel House, the news that Edith Wilson was coming over was calamitous.

She arrived on the Continent on December 13, becoming the first incumbent First Lady to travel overseas.

"Here," she soon wrote home, "the *world* seemed to be waiting to welcome and acclaim my wonderful husband." Her myopia was turning into blindness.

Markedly different since her last visit to Europe, Edith, now in a "Cinderella role," decked herself in "wine-tinted velvets" and "purple-shaded brocades," with an entourage of a black maid and social secretary Edith Benham, who was mistakenly identified as "lady-in-waiting." An amused First Lady made no attempt to correct the confusion.

The *only* reason she did not wear a tiara, Edith matter-of-factly told a British noble, was because she didn't own one.[8]

– 42 –

Queen Edith

IN FACT, EVERYWHERE she went, the American First Lady was treated with the status of a European queen. The Wilsons stayed at the Prince Murat Palace and Buckingham Palace. They traveled in trains of the king of England, the king of Italy, and the president of France. In turn, the people of Europe, who lined the promenades cheering and showering violets into Woodrow and Edith's open carriage, acknowledged the First Lady as the Yankee queen. In the European consciousness, it was the first widely public recognition of an American First Lady. And back home, it was reported that Edith was treated "as the consort of a reigning sovereign and been welcomed by queens on a footing of equality." First Lady was peer to queen.

Though she stuck to shopping and appearances with Woodrow, Mrs. Wilson was reported on by the press, one reporter gushing about the "all smiles and new clothes" Edith in her "very . . . League of Nationy . . . big blowsy all-tulle hat" and "coquettishly" wound scarf. Such reports infuriated those who believed the press should focus only on the critical peace talks.[1]

Edith did tour hospitals, now overflowing with seriously wounded soldiers, some missing limbs or, worse, parts of their faces. In one such ward, the First Lady said, "The room seemed to be turning upside down, and through a mist I saw human forms with faces so distorted and mutilated that the place seemed an inferno." She said she nearly fainted. But she didn't.

Eleanor Roosevelt, also on the trip with FDR, accompanied Edith on hospital tours, and was more familiar with the harsh realities, having inspected, on Franklin's behalf, Washington's St. Elizabeth's, where shell-shocked soldiers had been herded into deplorable, shocking conditions.

Edith also brought her bigotry to Europe. She called Signor Sonnino of the Italian commission "A shrewd, calculating Jew . . . [who] suspected everybody and took nothing for face value." After a trying

fitting at Worth's, she sniffed that she was glad to be "neither French nor an artist." She was uncomfortable with Queen Marie of Romania's earthy discussion of "new Russian laws concerning sexual relations . . ." Edith was even patronizing to her maid, whose "popping" eyes were permitted to see the British throne room: "With true Southern darky genius for getting words wrong, she called it the 'thorn' room." The First Lady wrote privately that "the three countries— France, England and Italy—are so different in customs, race, and expression there is no danger of confusing the events which marked our stay in each."

Perhaps because some Europeans perceived her provincialism, Edith was not treated warmly everywhere. Some resented that she was the only leader's wife who demanded to accompany her husband. At the Buckingham Palace dinner, John Singer Sargent, who had painted Wilson in the White House, snubbed her.[2]

Edith determined to be part of Woodrow's work, keeping abreast of the peace talks by sitting in on his daily briefings to his press representative, Ray Stannard Baker. From Commissioner White, she learned that Secretary of State Lansing, "a small man," was being ignored by House. She reported this to the president. The First Lady made arrangements for photographer Edward Jackson to capture on film the Wilsons' appearances, though she insisted that she not be photographed if possible. Dr. Grayson served as Edith's confidant when the president was in meetings at which she could not be present, during which time they began building a political camaraderie upon their friendship.[3]

Word reached the Wilsons in Europe that Theodore Roosevelt had died in his sleep, and as Edith watched Woodrow compose a letter of condolence to Mrs. Roosevelt, she blurted out reflectively, "Another White House widow." Besides a public funeral that she did not attend, Edith Roosevelt arranged an exclusive service at the house, for family and the very closest of friends, from which former President Taft was excluded.[4]

The crowning moment of the Wilsons' first leg of the European trip was to be Wilson's presentation of the League of Nations to the peace conference for acceptance as part of the treaty, a session closed to everyone except the commission members. Edith determined to witness it. Though Wilson jokingly called her a "Willful woman," she went ahead and made the request of the conference president, M. Georges Clemenceau. In the back of the vast Hall of Mirrors, she was the only woman present, hidden behind heavy curtains, standing for nearly five hours, and proudly watching Woodrow make history as the treaty was approved and signed, League intact.[5]

In basic definition, the League would create an international organization among member nations to ensure peace. To American conservatives, however, it meant a financial and military burden. Wilson led the fight for the League, which, because of personal animosities, made his enemies all the more against it. Wilson felt so assured of its acceptance, however, that he virtually ignored even slight dissent. The Wilsons left Europe briefly in February, arriving in Boston on the twenty-fourth with Franklin and Eleanor Roosevelt, whom Edith pronounced "delightful companions." Both couples were greeted by Massachusetts's new governor, Calvin Coolidge, and his wife.

Grace Coolidge, Eleanor Roosevelt, and Edith Wilson had much in common when it came to their activities of the last two years. Mrs. Coolidge had worked through the Red Cross in organizing entertainment and fund-raising efforts for the soldiers coming out of Massachusetts, co-chaired the Northampton Women's War Committee, and headed Victory Loan drives. Grace was now more of a public figure, the guest of honor at a Women's Republican Club of Massachusetts banquet in Washington, with Eleanor Roosevelt's aunt, Corinne Robinson, as speaker. The governor's closest political adviser, millionaire merchant Frank Stearns, wrote privately to another operative, "One of his [Coolidge's] greatest assets is Mrs. Coolidge. She will make friends wherever she goes, and she will not meddle with his conduct of the office." At a Boston College Club luncheon, Grace was given a can of "White House" brand coffee, with an attached card reading, "Eventually, why not now?"[6]

Nevertheless, the press focused on Wilson and Governor Coolidge, who, though a fellow Republican of Senator Henry Cabot Lodge, made a vague statement of support for the League. Lodge was already leading the opposition—the League required a two-thirds' majority vote in the Senate for ratification.

Wilson's relationship with Congress had never been close, but it became even more aloof after Edith became First Lady. One senator wrote that it was impossible to speak with Wilson at dinners because the president sat next to the First Lady and virtually ignored their guests across the table.

Wilson, while momentarily away from the peace talks, left Lansing in charge as his representative. But Colonel House believed that more problems would arise the longer the talks went on, and he compromised with many allies' requests. Edith legitimately used this to further unravel the Wilson-House relationship. When the Wilsons returned to Europe in May, she personally chastised House after a series of newspaper articles appeared claiming that the best work done by the Americans occurred when Wilson was gone and House was in charge. Still, Woodrow chided her, "Oh, I am sorry you hurt House, I would as soon doubt your loyalty as his." Mrs. Wilson would bide her time.

During the Wilsons' second absence from America, Lodge's anti-League movement strengthened. In Europe, the treaty was signed on June 28, and the Wilsons headed back to Washington. After submitting the League as part of the treaty to the Senate for ratification on July 10, Wilson determined to take the issue to the voters in a lengthy, strenuous national speaking tour by train. Edith was seriously concerned for his exhausted health, but had herself become imbued with the utopian promise of the League. To the Wilsons, there was no alternative.[7]

They departed Union Station for the 9,981-mile train tour of twenty-six stops in twenty-seven days along with twenty-four reporters, seven Secret Service agents, aides, a presidential valet, the First Lady's maid, Dr. Grayson, Joseph Tumulty, and a cook. On the seven-car train, they stopped in nearly every state west of the Mississippi with innumerable platform speeches along the way, northwest to Canada nearly, southwest toward Mexico. Along the way, it became alarmingly apparent that Wilson's health was failing. He suffered severe headaches, stumbled over words, and could not sleep peacefully. Smoky halls, stifling heat, and merciless scheduling wreaked havoc with him. Against the advice of Edith, Grayson, and Tumulty, he refused to rest.

Edith became so popular that she was often called for when she didn't first appear, but she made no solo appearances. The president told a crowd that Edith was the "best part of this travelling show." When photographers shouted to him to have the First Lady turn their way, he retorted, "I have no control over that little lady."

She laughed at a suffrage banner, and a "coloured messenger" putting on an oversized chef's cap and showing "his white teeth in a pleased smile." But there were ominous signs on the trip as well, which must have preyed on her superstitious mind, such as the automobile accident that killed a reporter following the presidential party. She was also exposed to a diverse slice of America, from "Happy Hooligan" hoboes to little boys running after the train, handing her whatever gifts they had for the president, to unruly farmers at the Indiana State Fair to a Western rodeo circus. In Los Angeles, she squared off, face-to-face, with none other than the famous Mrs. Peck, whom Edith called "sweet but faded." Mary thought the full-bosomed First Lady "junoesque," and remarked that she "played well the most difficult role of being the third party . . ." When Mary complained of being hounded by the press because of Woodrow, the First Lady startlingly interrupted, "Where there's so much smoke, there must be some fire." In California, however, Mary had heard various rumors, too. "Then perhaps you were von Bernstorff's mistress!"[8]

If Mary Peck proved stressful, the evening of September 25 became the moment to test all of Edith's strength. At eleven-thirty that night, the president broke down in nervous exhaustion, unable even to sleep. The next morning, Edith realized that she would "have to wear a mask . . . for he must never know how ill he was, and I must carry on." As the president argued against Grayson and Tumulty's assertion that the trip must be canceled, they noticed he was salivating from the left side of his mouth, the entire left side of his face was drooping, and his words were mumbled. Edith interceded. The remaining trip was canceled, and the train sped back, arriving in Washington on Sunday, the twenty-eighth. The official statement said Wilson had collapsed and needed rest.

In the White House on Monday, Edith met with reporters, making them laugh when she told of one stop on the tour where she bowed to what sounded like a cheer, only to turn around and see a cow. The little press conference served her purpose of dispelling any suspicions about Wilson's illness, which, she reassured reporters, was from exhaustion. On Tuesday, the First Lady met with House's friend William Wiseman of British intelligence, telling him flatly that his "important information" was not important enough for her to trouble the president.

Early Wednesday morning, she awoke to find Woodrow attempting, unsuccessfully, to reach for a water bottle. His left hand was limp. When she moved him, sharp spasms ran down his side. She bolted out to have Dr. Grayson called. When she returned, Woodrow lay unconscious on the bathroom floor.

Grayson immediately arrived and examined his patient. Suddenly—in front of Ike Hoover and the First Lady—he blurted out, "My God, the president is paralyzed."

President Woodrow Wilson had suffered a stroke.[9]

– 43 –

"Our Regent"

WITH GRAYSON AND other experts hovering around the incapacitated president, the First Lady asserted that his "brain was clear and untouched," an assessment made with the intent of immediately maintaining the impression of a White House in control. Grayson's strongest statement for the press was, "The President is a very sick man . . . absolute rest is essential for some time."

Ike Hoover thought Wilson already looked dead.

As the press and public were kept in the dark, uncertainty led to speculation. Traffic was diverted away from the White House, and a nearby hotel band was requested not to play loud music. Some said that Wilson had lost his mind or had contracted venereal disease in Paris. Even the pro-Wilson *New York World* gently criticized the White House for the "vague generalities" they released. In the Lincoln Bed, the stricken man lay, speaking only in gruff whispers. His entire left side was completely paralyzed, so he could not walk. He was blinded in his left eye. After the first critical days passed, however, it became apparent that there was indeed a living spirit in him, the spirit of his envisioned League of Nations. It was also apparent that only one person could keep him, and therefore the League, spiritually alive: The First Lady.[1]

She made an immediate decision to become a sole conduit to the president. The First Lady would be the only person through whom anyone could reach the president. As this unparalleled system evolved, she developed a power that many judged to be an assumption of the executive branch. Edith stonewalled any evidence of this, saying her only ambition was to protect Wilson and the League. In her notes, Edith left her own version of her unprecedented role:

Of course the burning question was how best to serve the country—and yet protect the President. Many people—among them some I counted as friends—have written much since of my own overwhelming ambition to act as President, of my exclusion of all advice—etc. etc. . . . I talked with the Drs. and asked them to be brutally frank with me—that I must know what the outcome would probably be—so as to be honest with the people. All of them said as the brain was clear as ever—that with the progress made in the past few days there was every reason to think recovery possible . . . But with this assurance on their part there was urged the utmost relief possible from any disturbing problems during these days of Nature[']s effort to repair the damage done.

"How can that be?" I asked the Drs.—"when everything that comes to an Executive is a problem, how can I protect him from them when the Country looks to the Pres. as the Leader?"

Dr. D. leaned toward me & said, "Madame it is a grave situation but I think you can save it[.] Have everything come to you—weigh the importance of them & see if it is possible by consultations with the respective Heads of each Dept. to solve them without the guidance of your husband. If not they of course must go to him—In this way you can save him a great deal . . . His nerves are crying out for rest—and any excitement is torture to them." Then—I said—["]Had he better not resign—let the V.P. act. . . ?" The answer again was—"No—Not if you feel equal to what I suggest—for to resign would have a bad affect on the country—& a serious affect on the Pres. He has staked his life & his promise to the World to do all in his power to ratify the Treaty to make the League of Nations complete[.] If he resigns—all incentive to recover is gone . . . He has utmost confidence in you & Dr. G[rayson] tells me he has always discussed public affairs with you—so you will not come to them uninformed—"

—So—I began my stewardship—I studied every paper & sent for the different Secretaries or Senators—. . . I never made a single decision regarding public affairs myself—the only decision that was mine was what was important & what not—and the *very* important decission [sic] of when to present them to my husband—

Naturally he asked thousands of questions & insisted upon knowing everything particularly about the Treaty—He would dictate notes to me to send to Sen. Hitchcock [sic] who was leading the fight for the Treaty in the Senate—or he would tell me what Senators to send for & what suggestions he had to make to them—Even these I made notes of—so, in transmitting his views I would make no mistake—& I would read them to him before going to the interviews . . .

This of course was the way the mith [sic] grew that I did not permit anyone to see the Pres . . .

Fortunately at that time my whole mind was so absorbed in working out my problems that I did not even hear these things . . . Every moment was filled & I worked way into the night.[2]

When her husband had been ill, Dolley Madison had acted as his "secretary" for a few days, and the only decision she made was in forestalling a congressional committee requesting to see her sick husband. Edith Wilson, however, made the conscious decision to act as her husband's personal representative. Though she claimed only to relay the president's decisions from him, that was her subjective word. Except for the First Lady and doctors, Woodrow Wilson was completely isolated from the world and his closest advisers.

Edith handled the crisis with calm confidence. Only Grayson was her consultant, and if her abilities were questioned, she pointed out that the president himself had been training her as political partner ever since their courtship. As she said when told the country was in trouble, "I am not thinking of the country now, I am thinking of my husband." Only when it came to the League did she become irrational.[3]

Edith's personal opinions began to dictate the League battle. She dealt not in percentage charts but in personalities, and had already made her own appraisal of Wilson's advisers. If she judged those men loyal, they could be of help to her. If she deemed them enemies, their ties were to be severed. That was not a minor decision of a mere conduit.

She did not make specific decisions on questions of government, only how to run it. Edith claimed that if a Cabinet member made a decision in his department, it was upon Woodrow's approval—through her. In this way, Edith exercised the power of influence over what he should approve. She herself provided the example of Interior Secretary Lane, who asked the president to approve a plan leasing government oil reserves to private interests. Since, as Edith admitted, "it was my habit to acquaint myself with the context of each thing" every government department put before Wilson for his signature, she recalled how Woodrow had previously been uncertain about approving the leases. So, when the leases were again brought to the now-stricken Wilson, Edith "explained what it was," and claimed that the president said "that will not be signed . . ."[4]

In censoring certain documents from her husband, the First Lady was also thereby emphasizing the importance of those she did bring to him. When later asked how she decided what issues to bring to the president, Edith said, "I just decided. I had talked with him so much that I knew pretty well what he thought of things." But she was also to admit that on many occasions she had disagreed with the president on issues, and said, "No two people ever think exactly alike." Matters she deemed "unimportant" were simply not dealt with.[5]

Within days of the stroke, however, government business was routinely piling up for presidential action. Questions on official statements, decisions, appointments—all were directed to Edith for approval. Her immediate reaction was to ignore anything that *she* did not consider the very most crucial to the maintenance of the nation, and she returned most of the papers to the Cabinet members who had sent the material to her. It was up to them to decide what they wanted to act on, and how to act.

Four days after the illness was announced, Secretary Daniels came
to the White House and was told honestly by Grayson that Wilson had
suffered a stroke. Agriculture Secretary Houston was told the same by
Tumulty, in great confidence. When Vice President Thomas Marshall
asked Houston what he had been told, the secretary refused to say.
Marshall was in a panic. When the attorney general was publicly asked
if the Cabinet knew more than what was printed in the newspapers, he
told reporters, "No." Finally, Secretary of State Lansing took it upon
himself in the emergency to call a Cabinet meeting five days after the
stroke, though Tumulty told him doing so was nothing less than dis-
loyal. Grayson, though still not revealing that Wilson had had a stroke,
refused to back Tumulty's claim that the president was not disabled. He
merely reiterated that excitement or pressures could kill him. Grayson
was evidently following Edith's orders.[6]

Though Grayson advised her on medical decisions, Edith had the
final say. When Wilson's bladder became inflamed, blocking elimina-
tion, which threatened to poison his body, it was the First Lady who
went against the experts' advice and refused to permit surgery. The
inflammation subsided naturally. At no time did Grayson cross her.
When Tumulty's appeals to see the president were ignored or denied by
Edith, he finally turned to Grayson, who liked him. Grayson gently
made attempts to convince Edith to permit Tumulty into the sickroom.

The First Lady denied even the doctor's requests, and as Ike Hoover observed in his unpublished notes, "Grayson could not insist."[7] When Tumulty slipped a note to Edith that his daughters were offering their Communion for Wilson, there was no response. If she could not fire him, she could ignore him as an adviser but use him as a buffer to the outside world.[8]

Outside the gates, accusations mounted that Wilson's mind was gone. Anti-League Republican Senator Albert Fall vigorously stated what many were already whispering. In a meeting of the Senate Foreign Relations Committee, he pounded his fist, shouting, "We have petticoat Government! Mrs. Wilson is President!"

The initial public charge that Edith was running the government had been prompted by her decision that the first outsiders to see Wilson would be the visiting king and queen of Belgium, unimportant in terms of government, but recently befriended by the First Lady. The queen's misquoted remark about seeing Wilson in a "torn" sweater (she had said "worn") was twisted to imply that Edith was preoccupied with the *presidency*, and neglecting the president.

Secretary Daniels pleaded with Grayson to release a statement admitting the stroke, believing it might provoke sympathetic League support. Senator Lodge had attached reservations to Wilson's version of the League, and was gathering strength. "I think you are right," Grayson admitted. "I wish I could do so. But I am forbidden. The President and Mrs. Wilson have made me promise to that effect." Edith's rationale was that saying nothing was better than admitting the truth, for if Wilson was portrayed as weak, League support would lessen. She did, however, permit her liaison, pro-League Senator Hitchcock, to see Woodrow briefly, though his plea of accepting the Lodge compromises met with obstinance from the isolated but rallying president.[9]

A new spate of controversy arose when, on October 22, a shaky Woodrow Wilson signature appeared on the veto of the Volstead Act, prohibiting liquor sale, trade, and consumption. Though the act was passed anyway over his veto, it was his signature that raised suspicion. Senators familiar with the Wilson handwriting claimed it was not the president's. Some said it was the First Lady's. Edith's response was to secure a steady writing board for Woodrow's weak hand. Nevertheless, many documents returned to Cabinet members and other government officials bore the president's "instructions" with the initials, "E.B.W.," and her unmistakable scrawl written all along the borders, which was her shorthand of what she claimed were the president's verbal instructions to her. But after Secretary of State Lansing's very simple questions were answered with what he said were "answers communicated through Mrs. Wilson so confused that no one could interpret them," many still wondered just who decided what.[10]

And so, with Edith Bolling Galt Wilson at the helm, the federal government limped along, with most business receiving no action. Under the circumstances, that seemed permissible when it was a matter of Navy Department dismissal of midshipmen requests, or acknowledgment of Herbert Hoover's resignation, or even recognition of the new government of Costa Rica. But as Tumulty was realizing, very serious matters demanded decisions. He wrote the First Lady about the railroads (controlled by the government during wartime), which needed to be turned back to owners, and the positions of interior and treasury secretaries, which required replacements, as did diplomatic posts for major European and South American nations. Edith steadfastly maintained that, in the long run, these matters were trivial compared to President Wilson's rallying but precarious health.

Nevertheless, the First Lady realized that a half-filled Cabinet could wreak havoc with her "stewardship" system. Consequently, she took it upon herself to get the president's advice on filling the vacant posts, and then ordered conferences with various individuals. Over teacups, she individually offered Agriculture Secretary Houston the treasury position, Edward Meredith, agriculture, shipping board chairman John Payne the interior, and Admiral Benson the shipping board. All four men accepted, and the "stewardship" system was maintained as a smooth process. Eventually, she held private meetings with individual secretaries, relaying what she claimed were verbatim responses from the president to their problems. If they had questions, she might go to the sickroom, shut the door, then reemerge and either clarify with new information, or expound upon her own message.

Meanwhile, Colonel House had returned from Paris and become sick during the passage. He immediately wrote Edith a series of letters, asking to see the president about serious diplomatic matters, including consideration of a League compromise, for the sake of ratifying it in some form. He got nowhere. The First Lady made no attempt to hide the fact from House that she did not tell all this to the president, but rather censored what she deemed as unimportant. It must have driven him mad. In one note, she indicated that she had told Wilson of House's recent illness, but not that he had returned to America, smugly teasing but subtley revealing her unspoken powers: ". . . I fancy he still thinks you are in Paris."

House directed an aide of his to go to Lodge directly and obtain in writing exactly what the senator wanted in terms of compromise. Then the colonel directed this information to the president via the First Lady. With this note, Edith finally had the justification to cut off House from the president without being accused of jealousy. She equated House's willingness to compromise with disloyalty to Wilson, and interpreted his letters as such—whether or not she truly believed it. Senator Carter Glass, peace commissioner White, journalist H. H.

Kohlsaat—all had appealed to Edith to support compromise and persuade the president to accept it. Though their appeals fell on deaf ears, she did not make them into hated enemies.

In truth, she, too, felt the desperation of the fight. She broke when, on November 17, loyal Senator Hitchcock returned to see her and made a final plea for acceptance of a compromised League, pointing out that some form of it would be closer to Wilson's dream than none at all. She went in to see Woodrow.

"For my sake," she questioned her husband, "won't you accept these reservations and get this awful thing settled?"

The president turned his head, and took her hand in his. "Little girl, don't you desert me; that I cannot stand . . ." Edith called Hitchcock in, and Wilson told him to convey the message that anyone loyal to him would vote nay to a League with reservations. That afternoon the loyal men followed his order, and defeated Lodge's concept of the League. Then Lodge's pack defeated Wilson's entire treaty. Both Wilsons were devastated.[11]

The League's November 19 rejection was a moment of rejoicing for Florence Harding, who "cooked the eggs" at a Republican victory supper that night at Alice Longworth's house. The Duchess was already known as a strong anti-Leaguer, and kept her husband in check when he expressed private thoughts of an eventual World Court. Florence, however, was less successful in managing Warren's extramarital affairs. Unbeknown to her was his fathering of a daughter by Nan Britton. Mrs. Harding was more concerned about his affair with her friend Carrie Phillips. Her fears, however, were based less on personal hurt and more on the damage it could do to her ambitions. By the time Wilson's League was voted down a second time in the new session of Congress, the Duchess was on the road to the first ladyship.

Mrs. Harding had grown even closer to Evalyn McLean, and became impassioned with Evalyn's devotion to the wounded veterans. Evalyn also led her to the town house of Madame Marcia, the same soothsayer who had predicted that Mrs. Galt would be First Lady. Now, Marcia read the same fortune for the Duchess.[12]

Though she unequivocally supported the League, Mrs. Wilson had purposely blocked the president from receiving a man who had come from England specifically to help Wilson in his fight for Senate acceptance of it. Her decision was based entirely on emotions, dating to her 1915 courtship. The early September 1919 arrival of the new British ambassador, Lord Grey, raised a fresh spate of controversy over Edith's "stewardship." The White House had refused even to acknowledge Grey, the first time such a slight had occurred. The news was passed to Grey—from Lansing from Grayson from Edith—that as long as the ambassador had one Charles Crauford-Stuart as his attaché, he would not be welcomed.

Crauford-Stuart had been part of the previous ambassador's staff at the embassy. An urbane wit who composed sarcastic ditties at social gatherings when he took to the ivories, his joke about Mrs. Galt falling out of the president's bed had been reported back to the Wilsons by their friend Daisy Harriman. Crauford-Stuart also sneered that Edith had gone to the peace talks only to attain the social status she was denied in Washington.

At first, Grey had no intentions of releasing his attaché, and to the seasoned diplomat it seemed absurd that a nonofficial like the First Lady could insult the British government by refusing their designated ambassador. Edith, however, would not back down, and was further insulted by the Franklin Roosevelts when they entertained Grey at Christmas, 1919, along with Alice Longworth. Grey finally had Crauford-Stuart demoted, changing his status to mere embassy employee, but Mrs. Wilson was still not placated. To her, Grey's refusal to obey her order to send Crauford-Stuart home seemed to indicate that the ambassador approved of his assistant's wisecracks. Had she the foresight to see the significance of Grey's appointment, she would have realized he was chosen by the British government to help get the Wilson League ratified.

Secretary Lansing was extremely disturbed about Edith's actions, and gingerly approached her to reconsider. Mrs. Wilson retorted by asking if Crauford-Stuart had been sent home. Lansing hedged, and told her that guests at the dinner where Crauford-Stuart had supposedly made his remarks had refused to legally support the claim, and based on lack of real evidence, Grey had refused to send his attaché home. The First Lady crisply retorted that Grey would not be seen by the president. Grey, of course, had come to America largely upon House's recommendations. It was Edith's final blow to House's relationship with Wilson. In a "Confidential Memorandum" of December 9, 1919, Secretary Lansing discerned that someone had obviously distanced House. That person was Edith. Grey wired home to England that he was returning there, disgusted with the "aspects of the situation . . . which cannot be adequately explained by telegram or letter."[13]

Edith's next victim was Lansing. Her hatred toward him was undoubtedly capped when, testifying under oath before the Senate Foreign Relations Committee, he admitted that he hadn't consulted with the president before issuing an official protest to Mexico over a supposed kidnapping. This prompted committee Republicans to send Senator Albert Fall as their representative to the White House and meet with the president over the issue. The real purpose was to finally determine Wilson's true mental condition. Edith made careful arrangements for the meeting, making herself a stern presence, taking verbatim dictation so Fall couldn't misrepresent anything. Wilson managed to hold his own. The "interview" successfully ended Republican hopes of having him removed from office, a fate that Edith now dealt out to Lansing.

The First Lady had considered Lansing's convening of the October emergency Cabinet meeting as a usurpation of President Wilson's power, failing to realize that this simple act actually strengthened her desired illusion that the government was under control and running normally. Lansing held subsequent Cabinet meetings, which kept Congress at bay. Still, Edith viewed his actions as disloyalty to the president.

It was only after Lansing had received Grey and testified before the Senate committee that a signed letter was sent from President Wilson to the secretary, chastising him for holding Cabinet meetings. A second letter followed, requesting Lansing to resign. Something seemed amiss. Why, suddenly, four months after Lansing had held the first Cabinet meeting, did Wilson reprimand the secretary, and ask him to resign?

Lansing quit, but released Wilson's letters to the press. The *New York Evening Post* raised the fact that while America had been reassured that Wilson was "in perfect mental condition and in touch with what was going on," these letters indicated that he was not at all aware of the fact that the country had been running only because of the work accomplished at the Lansing Cabinet meetings. The press again asked the question, if the president and his Cabinet were not in charge, then who was? The *Baltimore Sun* editorialized, "They ask in stage whispers at the Capitol . . . must we look for the woman in the case?"

To even loyal Cabinet members, it seemed clear that in the controlled environment she had created, Edith had turned the president against Lansing. Secretary Daniels was stupefied at her bitter remark, "I hate Lansing." Privately, even her social secretary thought Mrs. Wilson had "presented Lansing's efforts in a false light." A far less qualified man, Bainbridge Colby, was appointed, and as an almost sycophantic Wilson devotee, he initially became a favorite of the First Lady's.[14]

The Lansing firing provoked the public question of just how much liberty the First Lady had taken in this "stewardship." In the past, the power of Abigail Adams, Dolley Madison, Julia Tyler, Mary Lincoln, Julia Grant, and Helen Taft had been acknowledged by the press and public, but what made Edith Wilson's power completely different was the fact that her president was incapacitated. With all the secrecy involving his illness, it appeared that the First Lady had fully assumed the presidency.

The press acknowledged her power, the March 1920 issue of *Collier's* saying that she proved herself "the finest argument for suffrage . . ." Veteran White House correspondent Charles Willis Thompson referred to the period between October 1919 and April 1920 as "the Mrs. Wilson regency." Even Republican activist Dolly Gann praised the First Lady by saying, "All the more credit to her! I am glad there was a woman in the White House who knew how to take the reins and use authority when it was pressed upon her." The president called her "Strong" and "great" in her "stewardship" role.

Some European newspapers, like the *London Daily Mail,* praised Edith's "stewardship," saying she was a "buffer—and a very effective one . . . no suggestion is heard that Mrs. Wilson is not proving a capable 'President.'" Mistakenly, some Republican newspapers actually credited Edith with the defeat of the League—as if her isolation of Wilson had been conducted with the intention of doing so. Preferring her over Woodrow, they offered backhand compliments. One editorial, headed "Our Regent," sarcastically said Edith made a good "Mrs. President Wilson," and that "if the president does not interfere too much she will strengthen the government." While she complained to a maid that "I don't know how much more criticism I can take," the First Lady had the editorial clipped and saved, evidently tickled at the notion that she made a good regent.[15]

Sometimes, however, no matter how much Edith did for him, Woodrow's thoughts turned to his first wife. While resting in bed, Wilson was visited by daughter Nell. In Edith's absence, he spoke of Ellen. "Do you remember our picnics, and your mother reading poetry under the pines? I wish I could hear her voice . . . I owe everything to your mother. You know that, don't you?" Nell was quite moved, and told her father, "I wish I could have her touch on my children." He gently replied, "You can—tell them about her. That is enough."[16]

As winter turned into spring, Woodrow improved: He went out for drives, he finally held a short Cabinet meeting, he managed to shuffle along with the help of a cane. Daily, Edith arranged for him to see the most current silent moving pictures. Her routine now consisted of breakfast with Woodrow, during which she read newspaper headlines and sometimes full stories to him. She broke only to attend to domestic decisions that demanded attention. In March, her social secretary, Edith Benham, had a nervous collapse, and Mrs. Wilson handled her own correspondence with the help of a lone stenographer, Ralph McGee, in the afternoon. She then returned to Woodrow, and together they worked on pardon requests and departmental reports. Sometimes she took dictation. During the spring, in the afternoons, she now began to go out for air, outside the padlocked gates of the silent mansion. Evenings, she still worked on official papers, a lonely lady in the night.

To Wilson daughter Jessie, Edith asserted that she was still in charge: ". . . I will be less and less necessary—but now I never leave except for an hour . . . he gets nervous if alone and allowed to think . . . so many things in the conduct of affairs . . . worry him that I try not to let him have time to think." Slowly, her need to "steward" abated. Had a serious national crisis developed, it is uncertain what she would have done. She strongly believed that keeping her husband as president was what kept him alive. That was all she cared about. At times, she seemed to patronize him, humoring his alarming belief that he could not only be nominated for, but elected to and serve, a third term. She now spent time around town looking at homes to which she and Woodrow would retire. The Democrats nominated Ohio governor James Cox for president, with Eleanor's husband, Franklin, as vice president.[17]

Meanwhile, at the June Republican Convention in Chicago, Florence Harding shocked the press corps by seeking them out, answering all questions, permitting direct quotes, and actually discussing details of the deadlocked convention. Asked if she supported women's equality, she beamed, "Yes, I'm a suffragist." In private, the Duchess proved to be a tough boss. During the primaries, she had refused to permit Warren to pull out when returns proved less than favorable. With Harry Daugherty coaxing her on, Florence cajoled undecided delegates. Nevertheless, this bundle of energy had her fears. Madame Marcia had not only told her that Warren had "many clandestine affairs," but that if elected president, he would not live out his term.

Though other candidates' wives were not present at the convention, their interest in it was just as strong. After Harding received the presidential nomination, focus shifted to the vice-presidential candidate. Early in her husband's career, Grace Coolidge attempted to stagger his steady rise, realizing he could fall just as quickly. When Governor Coolidge received word of his nomination as vice president, she asked him, "You're not going to accept it, are you?" The remark was widely quoted to illustrate her supposed disinterest in politics. The truth of the matter was that Grace protested because she wanted him to be nominated as *president*, not vice president. Still, he accepted.

The 1920 election marked the first presidential race in which women were granted the right to vote, a fact that was extremely important to the Harding forces, particularly Florence. When Harding delivered his acceptance speech and mentioned the women, a reporter leaned over and asked Florence, "A mark, no doubt, of your influence, Mrs. Harding?" She smiled and nodded. The Hardings realized he could win with the support of women. With the campaign conducted largely from their Marion, Ohio, home, the Duchess was always introduced, often making impromptu remarks suggesting that all women join a political party first, then work for a local club. No candidate's wife had ever done so.

Unlike Florence, Eleanor Roosevelt thought that being photographed for and active in one's husband's campaign was improper, and resisted attempts by FDR's manager, Louis Howe, to involve her. As she wrote her "Dearest Honey" Franklin, "I hate politics!" But Howe persisted, and Eleanor began to make appearances from the rear platform of the train with Franklin. Gradually, she became confident.

When Franklin's speeches became a little too long-winded, she would "yank at his coat-tails." Louis told reporters to stand at the back of crowds and make funny faces at her, to prompt a broad Roosevelt smile. Howe began calling on Eleanor, to coax out her opinions and discuss FDR's speeches. She began to trust Louis, though she didn't see "that I'm of the least use on this trip." While away, Eleanor began to permit her willing mother-in-law to take care of the children. She became comfortable with the others who entered FDR's camp, from advance man Steve Early to secretary Marguerite "Missy" LeHand. Her jealously was aroused, however, at the sight of women who "crowded around him [FDR] and exclaimed over his good looks and charm."

Eleanor wasn't the only candidate's wife troubled by the sight of women. Candidate Harding vaguely referred to the "arrangement"— Florence's freedom to exercise power if she could endure his occasional dalliances—when he publicly introduced her as "a good scout who knows all my faults and yet has stuck with me all the way." Nevertheless, the presence in Marion of Carrie Phillips was trouble for the campaign. The Duchess had managed to chase the bold woman away one afternoon by finally hurling a piano stool at her, but it was only after the National Republican Committee paid off Carrie that she left the country. The printed handbills claiming that Harding had black blood proved a more persistent threat. Advisers panicked and pressed Warren to issue an open denial, but the emphatic Duchess, in her flat Ohio accent, declared, "I'm telling all you people that Warren Harding is not going to make any statement." No denial was issued.

When reporters began looking into her own background, Florence Harding fretted. Though she and Warren had no children, the Duchess had two grandchildren by a son, Marshall, from her first marriage. To questions about her first husband, Henry de Wolfe, she responded vaguely, saying only that he died before she married Harding, implying that she had been widowed. The truth was that he was an alcoholic ne'er-do-well whom she—pregnant—had had to marry at nineteen against her father's orders. After de Wolfe abandoned her and the baby, she gave the son to her parents to raise, obtained a divorce from Henry, and supported herself as a piano teacher. After she met Harding but before she married him, Henry de Wolfe died. That was how she justified being a "widow." Despite all the rumors, Harding won the election.[18]

As the "Second Lady," Grace Coolidge knew little about the new First Lady, though she traveled to Ohio with her husband to get acquainted with the Hardings. After following newspaper accounts of Florence's New York shopping trip with Evalyn McLean and Daugherty's assistant, the flamboyant dandy Jess Smith, Grace courteously wrote to her, consulting on colors she should avoid wearing at the Inaugural so as to not clash with Florence.

Through the press, Mrs. Coolidge also learned that it was Florence who supported the appointment of Albert Fall—Edith Wilson's bête noire—as interior secretary, Harry Daugherty as attorney general, and loyal Harding supporter jovial Charlie Forbes as chief of the Veterans' Bureau. Like Edith Wilson, Florence Harding made a doctor her confidant—hers was her hometown homeopath, Charles "Doc" Sawyer. Upon Florence's insistence, "Doc" was awarded an official position in the army medical corps, ostensibly so he could be at her beck and call, for she suffered from nephritis, a serious kidney ailment. These men formed the core of the "Ohio Gang."

Between her preparations for moving to their new S Street home in Washington, outgoing Mrs. Wilson had to contend with incoming Mrs. Harding in the now-traditional tour of the White House. The Duchess appeared in a large feathered hat, covering her face with mesh veil, upon which she planted her pince-nez glasses. Her cheeks were highly rouged, and she spoke so loudly and quickly that, after thirty minutes, Edith "could hardly stem the torrent of words," and left with relief for an appointment.

They next saw each other on Inauguration Day. Edith managed to repress her bitterness toward the Republicans, and wished Florence and Grace "all the luck in the world." Though she disliked Florence, she had "already warmed" to Grace, as did many others. Women reporters paid great notice to the beaming, youthful forty-two-year-old Mrs. Coolidge in the bright red dress, a conspicuously delightful sight at the Capitol. She was nearly twenty years the junior of the new First Lady, a fact not lost on the wrinkled Duchess.

Grace's oversized "picture" hat, in the most current style, seemed particularly appropriate for March 4, 1921. Overnight, things seemed metamorphosed. Before the ceremony, instead of ragtime, the Marine Band played a light jazz tune, to which the Duchess did a little two-step. It was the first Inaugural in which automobiles were used. Harding's Inaugural Address was the first to be carried by radio. In the stand were many of the new "movie stars," among them Al Jolson, Blanche Ring, and Ring Lardner, who had campaigned for their friends the Hardings. Once considered "vulgar," the actors of the orange grove known as Hollywood were suddenly respectable in the "new" Washington. Warren's first draft of his Inaugural speech had referred to the League of Nations; the Duchess had blue-penciled that out.

Edith Wilson would remain a presence in town now that an equally powerful woman was in the first ladyship, but she wasn't the only former First Lady of a determined nature to sit in the capital. Or even in her Kalorama neighborhood. One of President Harding's first appointments would be to former president Taft as Chief Justice. Nellie Taft was coming out of political exile at New Haven and returning to the city that so suited her nervous activity. Living on Wyoming Avenue,

Nellie would be within walking distance of Edith, and down the block from the Wilsons lived Lou Hoover, whose husband was the new commerce secretary.

In 1914, Nellie had made history by becoming the first First Lady to publish her memoirs. In them, she mentioned her cherry-blossom project, and wondered if the trees would "ever attain the magnificent growth" of those in Japan. Now, after eight years' exile, Nellie Taft would see for herself.

Before the Harding Inaugural, the official party had left together from the White House. As Edith and Florence broke another precedent by becoming the first outgoing and incoming First Ladies to ride together to the Inaugural, Mrs. Harding leaned over the mufflered and shocked Edith to wave wildly at the male reporters. "They're my boys!" the Duchess bragged.[19]

Florence Harding had many "boys." Besides the glib boys of the press, there were her maimed boys of the war, whom she planned to do something about.

And there were her overgrown boys of the "Ohio Gang."

PART IX

The Jazz Age
1921–1929

No wonder she has a power she can yield on occasions when necessary, and it is . . . unfortunate
that more women do not realize the influence
they possess . . . She may feel independent, but
no intelligent woman flaunts conventions, wisely
keeping within the general rule.

—*Etiquette: An Encyclopedia of Good
Manners* (1923)

The Duchess

WITHIN WEEKS, FLORENCE Harding revived the Easter Egg Roll and weekly Marine Band concerts. She reopened the house to tourists, and came down from the private quarters, surprising the elated visitors by guiding them through the rooms as if she truly were the housewife. In large crowds, Florence made a point of seeking out and hugging blacks. As a political force, they were Republican, and the Duchess made a point of their warm welcome under Harding.

Florence revolutionized the public first ladyship, the most dramatic change being her availability to the press. Having been a woman in the man's world of journalism, she had particular sympathy with women reporters, and for them she held informal press conferences before her public events, briefing them on the details. Though these were billed as "social calls," and though the "girls," as she called them, were not to quote her directly, Mrs. Harding answered their political questions. She became the first First Lady in most reporters' memory to make public speeches, though, like the campaign, they were spontaneous responses to gathered crowds, not political rhetoric. Compared to the Machiavellian days of "Madame Regent," everything seemed breezy.

Amid her activity, Florence visited Evalyn McLean's estate, Friendship, which sat on several dozen acres of manicured lawn dotted with sculptured trees, flower gardens, lily ponds, and a golf course. Here, the Duchess often chattered about and hatched ambitious plans. With Evalyn, she planned her trademark garden party, and the first one Mrs. Harding hosted was for wounded veterans, a symbolic sign of things to come. Unlike past lawn affairs, however, no liquor was served, since Prohibition was now in effect. But it was served upstairs, in the private study, where weekly poker games of the "Ohio Gang" took place. Though she didn't imbibe, the First Lady mixed the drinks. It would prove to be an apt metaphor.

Politics mingled informally with pleasure at the Harding poker games. The Hardings considered these Cabinet members and advisers their personal friends. The liquor was easily obtainable through Jess Smith, now the Duchess's personal fashion consultant, who though not a government employee was given an office next to the attorney general's at Justice. Nobody asked how Jess was able to get the liquor, and

when it was finally learned that he did so through Justice Department "B" permits, allowing for the purchase of liquor for "medical" purposes, that remained unquestioned also. When, several weeks into the administration, Interior Secretary Fall requested that the president sign an order transferring the navy's oil reserves at Elk Hills, California, and Teapot Dome, Wyoming, to his department, Warren did so easily, never questioning his friend's motives.

When the First Lady began her "project," the welfare of wounded veterans, she never questioned the demands of affable Charlie Forbes of the Veterans' Bureau. Forbes's budget for new supplies was running extremely high, but he declared that most of the warehouse items were broken, soiled, and unusable. Though her confidant "Doc" Sawyer mistrusted Forbes, the Duchess loved him.

Not all Cabinet members were part of the "Gang." The Hoovers attended one session, and never returned. Vice President and Mrs. Coolidge were never even invited. Though Harding was kind toward them, Florence had trouble hiding her jealousy of Grace.[1]

When the Coolidges arrived in town, they took a suite on the top floor of the Willard Hotel. They relinquished their rented rooms in the two-family Northampton house, and planned on spending vacations at his father's Plymouth Notch, Vermont, farmhouse. The "cheap Veep," as Florence called Coolidge, didn't think his position required a large home, and at the Willard he wouldn't have to pay for summer months. Here, the Coolidge boys, when visiting from their boarding schools, made popcorn over a hot plate. Calvin's one extravagance was buying clothes for his wife. Picture hats, waistless day dresses, red, gold, and white gowns with exaggerated trains, were all modeled about town by the Second Lady, who, except for light makeup, had no adornment. Grace made no protests to any of "Poppa's" decisions. Few women were as dissimilar as Florence and Grace. While the Duchess openly bragged about writing and editing Warren's speeches, the vice president's wife said she "never disturbed" Calvin "when he was preparing a speech, nor did I know what was going into it."[2]

Alice Longworth preferred the Second to the First Lady, writing that Grace, with "simplicity and charm," was "amused by all the official functions and attentions, yet was always absolutely natural and unimpressed by it all." However much she disliked the Duchess, however, Alice—who made alcohol in her own basement—approved of the First Lady serving liquor. Many women who protested Prohibition did so.[3]

As one visitor to S Street recalled, Edith Wilson "loved her bourbon" and, appropriately enough, her brand was Virginia Gentleman. Though Frances Cleveland had taken a childhood pledge not to drink, this did not necessarily reflect her attitude on Prohibition. Sometime after her remarriage, when she was told an evening's glass of wine would be good for her health, she imbibed, sipping from a glass with the Democratic donkey insignia. Nellie Taft's husband admitted that she was "an ardent although publicly silent wet . . . The truth is that Nellie and I differ on prohibition. We might as well face that, because I am utterly out of sympathy with her and she with me." On one occasion, in England, Nellie Taft and the American ambassador "took some bottles of beer" back to the embassy. Edith Roosevelt was sympatico. Alice watched with amazement as her stepmother "began serving the most extraordinary range of hideously colored cocktails at Sagamore. I don't think she knew what the word meant—let alone what went into them. She was just against Prohibition and being told what not to do." As the daughter of an alcoholic, however, Edith didn't drink herself. It was a painful memory, and her consequential self-denial was shared by niece Eleanor, with her own painful memories of her father's drinking.[4]

Eleanor Roosevelt found liquor consumption so distasteful that with Prohibition she now had a perfect excuse not to offer it to guests at her home in New York City, where Franklin had joined a law firm. They also stayed for long stretches at Sara's estate, Hyde Park, and summered on Campobello Island.

Louis Howe encouraged Eleanor to keep Franklin in politics by herself taking a more active role in political and social reform activities. With the motivation of being a concerned wife, she joined organizations like the League of Women Voters, the Women's Trade Union

League, the New York State Democratic party's Women's Division, and a diverse variety of consumer-protection and public-housing movements. In these circles, she began meeting different sorts of women, like lawyer Elizabeth Read and scholar Esther Lape, who lived together in "relations of intimacy described by the nineteenth-century term 'Boston Marriage,'" as a friend of Eleanor's delicately described it. A similar relationship existed between Eleanor's new friends designer Nancy Cook and educator Marion Dickerman, both Democratic activists. Eleanor contended with and befriended "militant socialist" Rose Schneiderman. Unlike the past, Eleanor passed no judgments on individuals' private lives. It was one's public life that improved society.

That first summer of the Harding administration at "Campo," Franklin and the children were sailing when they saw a small brushfire, and he helped beat it out. Soon after, he took a swim in the ice-cold water. The next morning, Franklin could not move his left leg. Soon his right leg was also immobilized. Doctors first thought a blood clot had formed—because of the sharp temperature change from hot flames to cold water—and settled in the lower spinal cord. Eleanor summoned Howe, who immediately arrived and assumed the role of spokesman for the alerted reporters. He became Eleanor's ally and supporter in this period, which she called perhaps "the most trying of my entire life."

Sara vigorously protested against the painful treatments that were attempted to rehabilitate Franklin's legs. She wanted him to retire to Hyde Park. With Howe behind her, Eleanor Roosevelt nervously but boldly told her mother-in-law that she would never accept such a life for Franklin. The treatments continued.[5]

Just seven months before FDR developed polio, at Camp Meade, Maryland, outside of Washington, Mamie Eisenhower and her husband, Lieutenant Colonel Eisenhower, were making arrangements for the transportation to Denver of the little white coffin holding their beloved child, Icky. Both Mamie and Icky had become seriously ill with scarlet fever during what was at first hoped to be a joyous Christmastime. Icky never recovered; he died a day after the new year began. Mamie's recovery was slow, and she had to recuperate in Walter Reed Hospital. When she was released and returned to the empty home, her grief was so deep that she was unable to cry. Ike would admit that he was on the verge of a "nervous breakdown." Mamie blamed herself and Ike himself for the death, but they didn't share their sorrow. To some, the marriage appeared to be on the verge of breaking up.[6]

The Roosevelts' tragedy, on the other hand, seemed to bring them closer emotionally. As Eleanor took control of her husband's transportation, as well as the continued care of her family, she began to gain a confidence she never knew she had. She wrote that the polio "made me stand on my own two feet," by going against Sara's demands. Had she sublimated herself this time, she feared she would have become "a completely colorless echo" of FDR and Sara, and "torn between them, I might have stayed a weak character forever if I had not found that out."

With Louis's and Franklin's moral support, Mrs. Roosevelt threw herself into politics, leading the Dutchess County delegation to the 1922 state Democratic Convention. "It is always disagreeable to take stands," she told the convention in her first speech, "it is always easier to compromise, always easier to let things go. To many women, and I am one of them, it is extremely difficult to care about anything enough to cause disagreement or unpleasant feelings, but I have come to the conclusion that this must be done for a time until we can prove our strength and demand respect for our wishes." The New York Times dubbed her a "highly intelligent and capable politician." Eleanor blanched at the thought of herself as such. She was just filling in for Franklin.[7]

In Washington, the man most thought of as "the political invalid" was still Woodrow Wilson. Edith had lost none of her possessiveness of him. When Tumulty visited, urging Wilson to give him a political statement regarding upcoming elections, the former president refused to speak on the record, but he did discuss politics with his old friend. When Tumulty paraphrased his comments at a public dinner and the press released them as quotes, Wilson was agitated. Edith was more than agitated, she was furious, and now she had the long-sought justification to cut Tumulty off from Woodrow once and for all. She rejected Tumulty's apologies as "sob stuff." His short visit was the last time he was permitted to see Woodrow.

Although Edith didn't like Florence Harding, she privately clung to the prestige associated with the first ladyship, regardless of who filled it. Edith surreptitiously wrote to Florence with a "suggestion" that they have tea at the White House, and the Duchess gregariously responded that the "personal pleasure in a call is very cordially reciprocated . . ." In private, Edith took tea with Florence on a March afternoon, back at her old house. One interest they shared was the care of veterans.[8]

Wobbling on her bloated ankles, the First Lady spent several hours each week going up and down the aisles at the Walter Reed wards, to which Evalyn McLean had first introduced her. Here, the Duchess sat at the individual bedsides of the several dozen boys who came to know her personally, writing letters for blind and disabled men, distributing cigarettes and food gifts, trying to cheer them up. The hospitalized vets at Walter Reed were the First Lady's guests at her annual garden party, a tradition she continued from the first one held by Edith in 1919. Only rarely did she go out to the hospital at Perryville, Maryland, which was near the Veterans' Bureau's warehouses for which Charlie Forbes was constantly purchasing new supplies to stockpile.

In the public's mind, the cause of veterans was linked to Mrs. Harding, and she shortly began receiving a steady stream of letters from vets

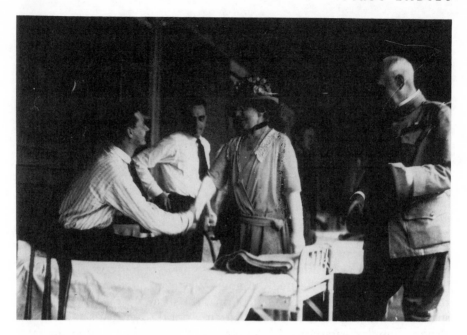

and their families asking for jobs, requesting financial assistance, reporting conditions at hospitals, complaining about pension delays, and requesting transfers to institutions closer to home. The Duchess alerted
both the war and navy secretaries that this was her "project," and requested their cooperation. Secretary Denby responded that "in the case
of your special interest in matters pertaining to the Navy, I hope you
will express to me what you would like to have done." When black
nurses at one hospital wrote to her with reports of abusive treatment,
the First Lady ordered an investigation through Sawyer. When she
learned of incompetent doctors at another institution, she ordered their
transfer. Unfortunately, there was only so much time for her to stop
inequities, and she had to rely heavily upon Forbes and Sawyer.
Sawyer, who still had misgivings about Forbes, privately had his bee-
hive of activity at the warehouses carefully watched.

Mrs. Harding, with social secretary Laura Harlan and her assistant,
Coranelle Mattern, read through each vet letter, making every effort to
meet every request. In addition to this growing First Lady's staff, Mrs.
Harding became the first First Lady to request, and receive, her own
Secret Service agent, Harry Barker. To the Duchess, there was nothing
unusual about an unelected woman having a funded staff working for
her. She saw her role as an opportunity to help those she felt needed
assistance. Besides the "boys" in the wards, there were the "girls." Florence Harding minced no words and hid no emotions on the subject of
women having complete equality in politics, the home, and the workplace.

Though neither Harding nor his advisers asked the First Lady to stop making her feminist public remarks, Florence was herself conscious of how far she could go before prompting criticism. In one letter, which she decided against sending, she wrote, "If the career is the husband's, the wife can merge her own with it, if it is to be the wife's as it undoubtedly will be in an increasing proportion of cases, then the husband may, with no sacrifice of self respect or of recognition . . . permit himself to be the less prominent and distinguished member of the combination." But Mrs. Harding accepted honorary membership in the progressive National Women's party, and not only invited women's political groups to meet her, but permitted her letters to such groups to be printed in the press.

Florence Harding's confidence in the promise of equality for American women emerged directly from her own unique marriage. "I know what's best for the President, I put him in the White House," the Duchess declared, unfazed. "He does well when he listens to me and poorly when he does not." For his part, Warren Harding depended heavily upon his wife's shrewd advice, once admitting that she "is too busy directing the affairs of government . . . she is full fledged in expressing her opinion as to how the Executive should perform his duties." Indeed she was. From the draft of his 1921 State of the Union Address, she edited out paragraphs implying eventual acceptance of the League of Nations. On another occasion, she steadfastly refused to allow the president to propose a one-term, six-year presidency. In one press cartoon, she and Warren were parodied as "The Chief Executive and Mr. Harding." A joke ran that immigrants, asked who was president, replied, "Mrs. Harding."

But the nation focused on the Duchess in a more sudden way in the fall of 1922, when it learned that she suffered a severe recurrence of her nephritis that resulted in her kidneys blocking, refusing to expel poisons. For days, Mrs. Harding's life hung in the balance. The president was literally immobilized by the thought of her death. For the first time ever, the White House made no proprietous attempt to hide a First Lady's illness, and the country responded with moments of group prayer, from a New York lawyers' club to a newsboys' association. Frances Cleveland, Nellie Taft, and even Edith Wilson sent telegrams.

Slowly, miraculously, through "sheer will," as she told her niece, Florence "fought" to keep alive, and her kidneys unblocked naturally. She had survived largely because "Doc" Sawyer fought against specialists who had said surgery was necessary. Incapacitated for six months, Mrs. Harding had to cancel her public appearances. Second Lady Grace Coolidge was asked to assume most of them, besides her duties as president of the Senate Wives Club, formed during the war, which continued doing Red Cross work. She even joined dancing classes in the new swinging steps of the twenties, being given at the famous "Castle" of former Senate wife Mrs. John Henderson, a mansion on Meridian Hill with a view of downtown.

One of the most respected authors of the day, Frances Parkinson Keyes, herself a Senate wife, said that she doubted "if any Vice-Presidential hostess has ever wrung so much pleasure out of Washington or given so much in return . . . She is the only woman in official life of whom I have never heard a single disparaging remark in the course of nearly twenty years." It was unusual for a Second Lady to be so popular. She was even evoking comparisons to Dolley Madison. In fact, it seemed that Grace had become the most famous vice president's wife in history, emerging with a distinction all her own.

Vice President Coolidge wanted Grace to say or do nothing that would have repercussions on his career. Consequently, he forbade Grace to try her new dances in public, to be quoted by the press, or to offer opinions. But even under such strict guidelines, she managed to smile knowingly without betraying her knowledge. As the proud vice president wrote a friend, "Grace is . . . wonderfully popular here. I don't know what I would do without her." Mrs. Coolidge would explain, "My training had been in the direction of avoiding subjects which dealt with matters in which public men were professionally engaged." It was classic "Coolidgian"—simple words, vague generality, subtle qualifiers.

Journalists termed Grace "the college type of woman," but more telling was a wise reporter's closer examination. It wasn't that Mrs. Coolidge wasn't privy to her husband's decisions, but that she "kept her wits at the end of her tongue."

Warren Harding remarked that "Mrs. Harding wants to be the drum major in every band that passes." All of the speculation and fame of her subordinate irked the Duchess, but she had subtle ways of proving her own powers. When word reached her that Mrs. Henderson was so taken with Mrs. Coolidge that she offered to donate outright her "Castle" to Congress as the official vice-presidential mansion, the First Lady began lobbying some of her old friends in the Senate against the bill, the government's cost of maintenance being her convenient reason. "Do you think I am going to have those Coolidges living in a house like that? A hotel apartment is plenty good for them."9

Grace continued living at the Willard.

As Mrs. Harding strengthened, she reemerged only to meet startling new troubles. Doc Sawyer's early instincts about Charlie Forbes had proved accurate, resulting in the first major scandal of the Harding administration.

After Sawyer prompted an investigation, it was revealed that Forbes had been receiving millions of dollars in bribes from building contractors, and had been selling new supplies he had falsely deemed "damaged" at ridiculously low prices to pharmaceutical-supply companies. To the First Lady, it was an insult to the "boys" in the wards, and a betrayal from which she never recovered. When Forbes's legal counsel, Charles Cramer, shot himself in the Hardings' rented home, the superstitious Duchess took it as a dark omen.

Just three months later, the Hardings learned that their crony Jess Smith had been part of the largest bootlegging ring in the city. When Smith was told by Attorney General Daugherty, who was also implicated, that he could not accompany the presidential entourage on a scheduled trip to the West and Alaska, Smith seemed to crack. Shortly thereafter, he was found shot in the head, apparently a suicide.

Then there was Albert Fall of the Department of the Interior, one of Florence's allies on the League issue. By late spring, 1923, word had reached the president that the naval oil reserves at Teapot Dome and Elks Hill, which he had transferred to the Department of the Interior at Fall's request, were being leased to private oil companies. A Senate committee investigation was inevitable.

Dispirited, the Hardings began their trip to Alaska in June 1923. Florence was filled with the fear of Madame Marcia's predictions of Warren's death before leaving office. When the president became ill and Sawyer diagnosed his ailment as ptomaine poisoning, the Duchess believed her fears were real. The party rushed to the Palace Hotel in San Francisco. When Attorney General Daugherty flew to the West Coast, he refused to see Harding, but instead dined with the Duchess on August 2. Several insiders claimed that he informed her of the impending Teapot Dome investigation. After dinner, the First Lady went upstairs to read to the ailing president.

Back in Washington, on S Street, having gone to bed with the sense of "something ominous . . . hanging over us," Edith Wilson awakened to the cries of newsboys shouting "Extra! Extra! . . . Death of President Harding!" She sent for a paper, and immediately wired her and Woodrow's sympathies to Florence. But, she also had a "queer feeling," and suddenly wondered "if I myself should have been so receptive to an unknown voice." Like Florence, Edith had not lost her belief in the spiritual world.[10]

Warren Harding died alone in the presence of his wife; her casual reactions and odd comments immediately following made many whisper that she might have poisoned him, a claim never proven, because Florence Harding refused to permit an autopsy.

At the Palace Hotel, the Duchess asked Lou Hoover, who was also on the trip, to act as her press spokeswoman. "Mrs. Harding is perfectly well," Mrs. Hoover told clamoring reporters. "Of course she cried, but . . . [s]he is going to be terribly upset if she sees in the newspapers that she collapsed."[11]

In Vermont, the household of an elderly farmer and notary public were roused at midnight by a messenger carrying the news. There was no telephone at the small white clapboard Plymouth Notch home of John Coolidge. He woke his son and daughter-in-law, who fetched an oil lamp. Before the ceremony, Calvin prepared a statement, several copies of which were typed up by a stenographer. Grace then went out to the waiting press, handing one out to each reporter. The vice president placed his hand on the family Bible, and repeated the presidential oath of office after his father. Grace stood by weeping, later commenting that Mrs. Harding "bears up wonderfully well under difficulties . . ."

When the funeral train reached Washington, Evalyn McLean was there to comfort Florence. The Coolidges greeted Florence and the late president's coffin at Union Station. Mrs. Harding refused to return to the White House in the new president's limousine, going instead with Evalyn. In the early morning, the Duchess suddenly wanted to see Warren. Walking down to the ghostly East Room, with the cloying smell of large floral arrangements hanging in the heavy muggy August night air, she told the president's corpse, "No one can hurt you now." After the Ohio burial, she returned to the White House and began furiously sorting through the late president's papers, private and official, while the Coolidges remained in their Willard suite.

While in their bedroom there, as Mrs. Coolidge slept, a burglar sneaked in through an open window from the outside ledge. It was a college student who needed money because he had overspent while on vacation. President Coolidge awoke, and gently confronted the fellow. Only by chance had the young man entered the Coolidges' room. Calvin added up the boy's expenses, gave him a "loan," and asked if the student could return to his room by the ledge to avoid security in the hall. The president never reported it, but he did tell Mrs. Coolidge and two Northhampton friends, one of whom, Frank McCarthy, was a journalist.

McCarthy promised not to report the tale, and Grace Coolidge typically restrained herself from repeating the story that would have greatly helped dispel the false public impression of her husband as a dour, cheap Yankee. To Grace, it was more important not to provoke other young people into using crime as a means to an end. As she wrote to McCarthy, who would twice request permission to print the story, "In my judgement this is not the time to release that story for I feel that there is already too much publicity given to acts of vandalism and violence in our papers and over our radios." She herself would never reveal it.

A few days later, Grace Coolidge prepared to enter her new home, two blocks away. In the early dusk, after a treacherous August rainstorm, Florence Harding walked out of the White House, stepped into a McLean limousine, which slipped through the black iron gates, and headed to Friendship. Several other cars followed her, with large wooden crates of Executive Office documents in their backseats.

The Duchess's final task of honoring her husband's memory lasted through the summer as she burned hundreds of Warren's papers that she believed could be misconstrued: entire document files, parts of letters torn at sections, the contents of a bank vault one day, an entire suitcase the next. After Evalyn left for holiday in Maine, Florence wrote to her from Friendship that she did "manage to do a lot of work in *that way* out of doors . . ."

Evalyn received a letter from another woman who came to visit Friendship one day, and witnessing the deed of the Duchess, calmly observed that the widow was "just as fine as she had been all along."

This woman would never betray any knowledge of Mrs. Harding's technically illegal destruction of government documents. This woman had no desire to provoke gossip, criticism, or debate about a woman who had not always been kind to her.

As the curls of black smoke rose from Friendship, the former First Lady was destroying history.

And the new First Lady watched.[12]

– 45 –

A Sunny Disposish

GRACE COOLIDGE ENTERED the White House in the middle of the steamy afternoon of August 21, 1923, and always liked to recall her first impressions of it, as she smelled the scent of flowers and eyed the cool white crispness of the rooms' interiors in their starched summer coverings.[1] "I wish," she wrote a group of friends, "I could describe my varied sensations as we came in . . ." She had learned to see, to hear, and to sense nuances in the air more than most people did, for she was a teacher of the deaf, and partner to an emotionally unexpressive man.

People spoke of sensing an aura of warmth near her. She was a woman thoroughly at peace with herself, and her lack of political ambition was refreshing. Her unabashed excitement at being in the White House was delightfully joyous, almost naive with childlike wonder. "I wish I could tell you all that is in my heart—but there is so much that even I am bewildered," she wrote, then cracked, in her dry humor, which always seemed to leaven self-importance, "Alice in Wonderland or Babes in the Woods—however you wish to regard me."[2]

Judging by the comments of the household staff, who nicknamed her "Sunshine," the press, and even Washington society, Mrs. Coolidge was the most natural woman in the first ladyship since "Frankie" Cleveland. Though she initially admitted, "I have been somewhat doubtful of my own ability," Grace inherently perceived that the intensification of press focus on the first ladyship meant that the public persona did not always reflect accurately the private person, but that the persona often had more impact than the person. She took to the role with, as a song of the era went, "A Sunny Disposish."

One of the possessions Grace Coolidge brought into the White House was her cherished radio, the first First Lady to use such a contraption. And use it she did. While working upstairs at her desk, she kept the radio blaring all day, though she could not bear the sound of a woman's singing voice. Between the dramatic "operas" sponsored by soap companies, she also heard the smooth voices boasting a product.[3]

Advertising abounded. With the need to sell was a need to promote to the public, whether it was a new moving picture or a prizefight, or the "stars" that made those events. Such industries contracted "public relations" men. A few termed it "image," but there was a consensus that in any role in the public eye, one now had to put forth a certain impression that kept in context the "profession."

Grace Coolidge proved to be "modern," by examining her role before plunging into it. She later wrote, "When I reflect upon my Washington career I wonder how I ever faced it . . . There was a sense of detachment. This was I, and yet not I—this was the wife of the President and she took precedence over me; my personal likes and dislikes must be subordinated to the consideration of those things which were required of her . . ." No First Lady had ever understood that quite so clearly or expressed it so simply.[4]

And yet paradoxically, from the onset, this First Lady remained traditional. She refused to be something she was not. "We New England women cling to the old way," she revealed, "and being the President's wife isn't going to make me think less about the domestic duties I've always loved . . ." She made no bones about the fact that she enjoying knitting and baking.[5]

As 1923 gave way to 1924, startling revelations of the assorted Harding scandals, collectively known as Teapot Dome, began unfolding. Though she had consciously distanced herself from that crowd, Mrs. Coolidge never once commented, either publicly or privately, about the stories. Neither did she discuss a book that implied Mrs. Harding had poisoned the president, or the one by Nan Britton, claiming he fathered her child. Grace's silence only helped the nation to dissociate Coolidge from Harding. Never pushing, never contrived, Mrs. Coolidge, consciously and unconsciously, played a major public-relations role for the administration by being herself. And, by being apolitical, she was actually beneficial to politics. In the first ladyship, Grace was unique. The public and press had come to expect a politically powerful First Lady, having had that type since Nellie Taft. Grace

Coolidge expressed a lack of interest in politics, and yet had so much power over the public and press that she even affected the international impression of the administration.

Breakfast with Calvin began her day. Sometimes they read the paper silently, sometimes they chatted. After her favorite repast of doughnuts and coffee, she had a second cup with her social secretary, Polly Randolph, who would arrive in time for them to begin work by nine, in the First Lady's office, established in a sitting room. With the hum of Grace's radio or a cranked phonograph, they worked together until noon on correspondence, and press releases of menus, flowers, clothes, and social schedules. Mrs. Coolidge, behind her small business desk, often typed out her own letters. At noon, she had her photo taken with a multitude of public groups, invariably in front of the white stone steps of the South Portico.

After lunch, which ranged from a sandwich upstairs to a public luncheon at the Mayflower Hotel tearoom, she went for a hike or walked her large collection of energetic dogs on the lawn. Late afternoons, she returned to work. On the month's last Wednesday, Grace conducted her Cabinet wives' "meeting." On Mondays and Fridays, she held her Red Room high teas before a roaring fire for both men and women who had managed to previously arrange an invitation through Polly Randolph. Several times a week, Grace also walked to the beauty salon. She had a variety of hairdressers, from Belle Pretty to Anna Bute, and "Leon and Jules," who had a salon on H Street. She desperately wanted to bob her hair, but wouldn't because the "President has his own ideas."[6]

Coolidge highly valued his wife, and admitted that she bore his "infirmities and I rejoiced in her graces." He was the first president to appreciate the growing task of being First Lady. "The public little understands," he wrote, "the very exacting duties she must perform, and the restrictive life she must lead." As president, he said, "I don't know what I would do without her." Gamaliel Bradford, social observer of women during the twenties, stated that the First Lady "was at the heart of Coolidge's life . . . the man would not have been what he was without the woman . . ." He relied heavily upon her presence, and when she was away, he lacked the support he needed and became depressed. While away, she wrote him daily. In the White House, he'd go down to the mail room, wait patiently for the mail to arrive, rummage through the stacks himself, pull her letter, and immediately read it in a corner. This bonding was noticed by others. "The whole union," noticed writer William Allen White, "seemed cabalistic . . . She is a vital part of his success . . ."[7]

She matched him when it came to wit as well, and had her own routine of one-liners. Grace capably did an impersonation of her husband's laconic speaking style and Vermont nasal twang. When he once used a whistle to call her pet raccoon, Rebecca, she saw the opportunity to give him a little of his own medicine. "What's the matter, Papa," she asked straight-faced, "don't your teeth fit tonight?" One story of a trip they made to a Maryland chicken farm illustrated her sense of humor and earthiness, as well as the teasing repartee between husband and wife. As the farmer took the First Lady through the henhouse, they came upon a rooster on top of a hen. "Does the rooster do that often?" Grace asked the farmer in mock-surprise. "Several times a day," responded the farmer. "Tell that to the President," the First Lady said, smiling. The embarrassed farmer did as he was told. "Mr. President, Mrs. Coolidge asked me to tell you that that rooster does that several times a day." Without missing a beat, the president asked, "With the same hen?" The farmer answered, "No, Mr. President." With as straight a face as his wife, Coolidge got in the final touché. "Tell *that* to Mrs. Coolidge."[8]

Though her personality was the single strongest influence over him, the president often attempted to repress Grace's exuberance by making her the butt of his rapier wit. "Don't you think," he told a friend after they sampled the proud First Lady's homemade pastry, "the road commissioner would be willing to pay for my wife's piecrust recipe?" He demanded that she follow *his* interpretation of the role. Her attempt to learn horseback riding was nixed by the president when the press reported it. "I think," he told her flatly, "you will find you will get along at this job fully as well, if you don't try anything new." Sometimes playing her role as Calvin saw it bothered her. A friend of the First Lady's, the prominent women's issues writer Mary Rinehart, claimed that she detected a strain in Grace's attempts always to keep things amicable in her relationship with the president. Although a feature article said that the first ladyship had freed her from "considerable repression," Grace's witty understatement sometimes illustrated her frustration. "Being wife to a government worker," she wrote a friend, "is a very confining position."

It was Calvin's strict interpretation of the role that dictated the limitation on Grace's political involvement, and which she followed. She herself raised the subject: "I know nothing of the conducting of affairs in the Executive Offices or in the Executive Departments considering they lay outside my province . . . If I had manifested any particular interest, I feel sure that I should have been properly put in my place." Almost wistfully, she examined why this was. "Sometimes I wonder if Mr. Coolidge would have talked with me more freely if I had been of a more serious turn of mind . . ."[9]

However, Mrs. Coolidge's public removal from politics was a result of *Calvin* being close-minded, not Grace. One of the First Lady's closest confidantes, outspoken feminist Florence Adams, commented that if Grace "had been trained politically she would have been quite astute. I don't believe that anyone encouraged her[,] for Calvin felt that woman's place was at the sink." One morning at breakfast, Grace needed to know his official schedule so she could make social arrangements. His thin lips cracked, "Grace, we don't give out that information promiscuously."[10]

Nevertheless, as a woman journalist of the period wrote, "while she does not talk politics . . . the impression that she is not interested in politics is wrong." Another woman writer claimed that the First Lady was "[n]either politically inept . . . nor politically uninformed . . ." It was Grace's doctor who later remembered discussing matters with her, and how she "went to the heart of an issue," and "could take a strong stand and often did . . . ."

The fact that she wouldn't discuss what private knowledge she might have, or even controversial public issues like Teapot Dome, proved in fact that she was astutely sensitive to politics as an art. She could often be seen in the visitors' section while the Senate was meeting, listening to political speeches. Mrs. Coolidge was careful not to say that politics didn't interest her, just that President Coolidge thought it best for her not to manifest any interest. The fact that Calvin forbade her any political role bothered her not in the least. Characteristically tongue-in-cheek, she remarked, "At any rate, I had my hands full discharging the duties of the position to which I had not been elected." As a free spirit, she found other outlets.[11]

Ironically, as dissociated with political power as she was by the public, two of Mrs. Coolidge's greatest admirers were her Washington sorority sisters Edith Wilson and Nellie Taft. It was a sudden but not unexpected occasion that joined the three of them, Florence Harding, and Lou Hoover together.

Woodrow Wilson had died.

Grace Coolidge had always liked Edith Wilson, and throughout Woodrow's final illness had expressed concern for them. Upon hearing news of Wilson's death on Sunday, February 3, the president and Mrs. Coolidge went directly from church to Edith. The president offered the widow the government's help in planning the funeral. Grace wrote to her, "I cannot refrain from sending you this personal word of sympathy for I want you to know that I am thinking of you in your great sorrow . . . your friend, Grace Coolidge." Grace and Calvin also visited Edith with an official party before departing for the Washington Cathedral funeral.

Edith's "queenly dignity and appropriate modesty" were praised in one editorial, saying they would give her "lasting fame," but behind the scenes of the funeral she was tyrannical, refusing to permit Tumulty into the formal procession and snapping at Wilson's daughter Nell McAdoo to the point of permanently alienating her. Though Edith pointedly wrote Senator Lodge that she would find his presence at the funeral unpleasant, her anti-League sorority sister Florence Harding was welcomed, and made a rare public appearance there. Some who wished to come couldn't make it. In New York, Eleanor Roosevelt attended the Wilson memorial service at Madison Square Garden. Whenever Eleanor went to Washington, she always called on Edith, and the two struck up an odd friendship. Though the latter retained her bigotry, the former was becoming increasingly liberal. Still, as she wrote Franklin, "I wired Mrs. Wilson today for both of us."

Chief Justice Taft's doctors wouldn't permit him to attend, but Nellie would, and when Edith learned this, she instructed John Randolph, her correspondence secretary, to respond to Taft that she was "glad that Mrs. Taft would come."[12]

As usual, Nellie Taft marched to the beat of her own drum. As a former First Lady, she preferred a geology lecture to a ladies' luncheon. In her role as First Lady of the Supreme Court, however, she frequently saw Grace Coolidge, and the two women got along marvelously, frequently discussing the history of the house. Annually, she and Will were honored by the Coolidges at the Supreme Court dinner, and also attended many state dinners. On one occasion, Mrs. Coolidge wrote to the Chief Justice, "We shall miss you and Mrs. Taft at the dinner . . . The early magnolia of which you wrote in a note last spring flourishes— it was a joy this year. Perhaps you would come over and have a look at it when it blooms again I shall let you know. I am looking forward to seeing Mrs. Taft when she is settled and ready to take up her social plans again." She signed off with her "friendly greetings to you both."[13]

Nellie had missed the unusual gathering of the sorority that past December when, along with Lou Hoover, Grace Coolidge, Edith Roosevelt, and Edith Wilson sat together to hear the president's first Congressional Address. It was the only time the politically polarized Ediths were together, and a chill pervaded.[14]

Like both Mrs. Roosevelt and Mrs. Taft, Grace never permitted her role to get in the way of her friendship with her children, John, who was to start at Amherst, and Calvin, Jr., sixteen, at Mercersburg Academy, both of whom visited the White House during their parents' first Christmas there. Seven months later, they returned for part of the summer, and a tragedy struck the family, suddenly and shockingly, and took the nation's attention off that summer's presidential campaign.

Calvin, Jr., had developed a blister on his toe while playing tennis on the White House courts. Not until the blister became infected did he tell his parents. By then, it was too late to save his life. The infection signaled blood poisoning, and the teenager's life ebbed away. On July 7, the boy died.

Though he was running for his own term as president, Coolidge would write, "When he died, the power and the glory of the Presidency went with him." FDR, addressing the Democratic Convention, called for a silent prayer for the Coolidges.[15]

That summer, it was *Mrs.* FDR who was the political activist, pushing herself further into politics, but not from altruism alone. Her cousin
Theodore Roosevelt, Jr., unjustly implicated in Teapot Dome, was running for the governorship of New York. When his brother-in-law Nick
Longworth called Franklin a "denatured Roosevelt," Eleanor was deeply
offended. She campaigned for Democratic incumbent Al Smith by campaigning against her cousin.

Eleanor began touring the cities and hamlets of New York as her
own uncertain driver, with a large teapot attached to the top of the car,
following campaign cars for Ted. (Alice said she should have done the
same—with Lucy Mercer strapped to the top of *her* car).

When a newspaper article stated that Franklin was heading the
Smith campaign but showed a picture of Eleanor, a friend joked to
FDR, wondering "how the newspapermen knew so well who was at the
head of the family." Without intending to do so, Eleanor was becoming
her own public figure. Newspapers frequently called for quotes, and she
managed to quell her fears of her shrill voice, and began speaking on
the radio. Sensitive to the fact that she seemed more active than her
husband, she wrote to him, "You need not be proud of me, dear . . .
I'm only being active till you can be again—it isn't such a great desire
on my part to serve the world and I'll fall back into habits of sloth quite
easily! Hurry up for as you know my ever present uselessness of all
things will overwhelm me sooner or later!"[16]

Through her husband's campaign, Grace Coolidge remained inactive, but not for want of interest in seeing him win. Very much in

private, she was in mourning, overcoming the shock of her son's death. Publicly, she would donate a portrait of him to Walter Reed Hospital. She would serve as a representative of American mothers who had lost a son during the war at a special Mother's Day ceremony held at the Tomb of the Unknown Soldier, which had been dedicated by Harding. Through it all, she retained her equanimity in the face of grief.

Months before her own sudden death, the Duchess dropped her grudge against the Coolidges and wrote to Grace, "No matter how many loving hands may be stretched out to help us, some paths we tread alone." Many wondered how Grace was able to withstand such a personal tragedy in such a public role. One outlet she found was poetry. But when Edith Wilson wrote movingly to her, Grace's response revealed spirituality as the source of her power: "Your note of sympathy and understanding helps the President and me and I am writing to tell you so. We had great hope that Calvin would recover up to the very last for he fought valiantly. It was not for our human understanding to comprehend His plan. I can only bow my head and thank Him for having loaned him to me for 16 years and ask Him for strength equal to his faith."[17]

The Coolidges had returned to Vermont for the burial, remaining there for most of the summer. Grace was removed from the daily grind of the campaign. On September 19, she made her first and only solo campaign appearance at a "political gathering" of the Montgomery County Maryland Women's Republican Club, where she listened to several speeches made on behalf of Coolidge, but made no remarks herself. That didn't mean she—or more precisely, her public persona— wasn't an integral part of the campaign.

Speaking before the Women's Universal Alliance, Vera Bloom, a friend of the First Lady's and a congressman's daughter, would pronounce Grace to be "worth $1,000,000 a year to the Republican party," and state that her "grace and charm are real assets . . . and contribute much to the prestige of the Administration." Labor Secretary James J. Davis said Mrs. Coolidge's skill with the public could be utilized as a campaign manager. One observer said, "She did the front door job." Ike Hoover put it succinctly, saying she was "ninety percent of the Administration." This was true, but Coolidge was firm about limiting the information the White House released about her to only domestic "news," like the fact that the First Lady gardened on the lawn and sometimes did her own dusting. The reality was, of course, that so did most women. That was the point of releasing such tidbits—it made the Coolidges all the more down-to-earth, and appealing.

During 1920, when the Harding campaign released the Duchess's famous waffle recipe, the Coolidge forces had released copies of Grace's baked-goods specialties. One exasperated woman wrote, "During the campaign don't you remember how we had Mrs. Coolidge's blueberry pie and mincemeat and doughnut recipes until I wondered if the poor girl was ever out of a bungalow apron." Nevertheless, the Coolidge campaign managers were not about to pass up another chance to extol Grace's domestic skills as part of their public-relations efforts.

Press releases including her "fine biscuits" recipe and the fact that she could construct "shirtwaists . . . for $1.69" were sent out. And when press photographers were gathered at the Coolidge homestead, they were invited to snap pictures of the president milking his cows as well as an obviously staged one of him pitching hay—in shining business shoes. Soon after, the entire public-relations attempt was referred to as "advertisement" by Elisabeth Marbury, National Democratic committeewoman from New York, at a meeting of women. She sweepingly dismissed it all as "milkpail stuff."

Immediately, there was an adverse reaction. The *New York Herald Tribune*, for example, received a flood of letters defending the First Lady and harshly criticizing Marbury, which they printed. Marbury then clarified that she faulted not Grace's abilities, but rather their exploitation by the Coolidge campaign "to seduce the vapid vote." Even a *New York Times* editorial criticized Marbury, pointing out that the same promotional tactics were used by "press agents" and that the public "will continue to say that Mrs. Coolidge had no part in the exploitation of her doughnut prowess."[18]

As Elisabeth Marbury had discovered, this First Lady could do no wrong in the public eye, simply because she did no wrong. Shortly after Coolidge won reelection, even Alice Longworth appreciated both the First Lady's genuineness and discretion.

Grace told journalist William Allen White that while she was entertaining some women, Alice popped in to share the news that she was pregnant, but that the president knew before she did. Mrs. Longworth, however, would affirm that the *first* nonfamily person she told was the First Lady. When the subject was raised, Mrs. Coolidge gently turned it into a joke about the president's taciturnity. "Imagine a man having a bit of gossip as choice as that, and keeping it a secret!" It was another of her seemingly offhand remarks, for Grace Coolidge discreetly avoided clarifying whether the "gossip" was that Mrs. Longworth was pregnant, or, the evidently accurate "gossip" that Senator Borah, not House Speaker Longworth, was the father.[19]

Ida McKinley had been petitioned by the Audubon Society to stop wearing egret feathers, but there was no public or press criticism when Grace Coolidge accepted a luxurious coat from Vermont fur dealers. When the Duchess's illness forced her to cancel all appearances, Mrs. Coolidge had herself substituted. Now, as First Lady, when she canceled her public schedule because she caught a cold, the Coolidge Second Lady, Caroline Dawes, did no such thing. In fact, one newspaper editorial praised Grace's belief that colds were contagious. The press was consistently kind to her.

As late as April 1924, Grace Coolidge had been able to go to New York City completely unrecognized, and indulge in a fashion shopping spree—a Boston paper later learned and reported that she spent one thousand dollars one day on such purchases. Now, she would not even be able to buy a hair comb in a Wisconsin department store without being mobbed.

On Sunday morning in America, before turning to the Katzenjammer kids in the funny pages, the public could page through the rotogravure section and see the First Lady in her activities. That was not new. Florence Harding was the first to willingly and frequently have her picture in the paper. But now, between the cameo shots of Clara Bow at a baseball game, Gloria Swanson in the new fashions, Tex Guinan walking her dogs, and Theda Bara window-shopping, was Grace Coolidge in front of the White House.

It wasn't always easy to tell the difference between the "moving-picture stars" and the First Lady.[20]

– 46 –

The Lady in Red

THE CHANGE IN the public's perception of the role that developed during Grace Coolidge's tenure began innocently enough with little press stories on her. In her first few months were reports that she had received honorable mention for a baby robe that she made and entered in a national knitting contest. She accepted a dog, a canary, and a five-foot bag of Girl Scout cookies. A rose was named for her. By 1925, when she looked at rooms at the Metropolitan Musem of Art for her "project" of restoring the White House rooms with historic integrity, *The New York Times* devoted an entire editorial column lauding her for coming right to the source, and told readers to follow her example.[1]

Few, even in the press, perceived that all the while very little about the real person of Grace Coolidge was pursued in stories. Nor did she ever willingly reveal anything about herself. Her sole attempt at writing as First Lady was on knitting, so she could donate the $250 earnings to the Home for Needy Confederate Women. An embarrassing situation arose when Grace consented to cooperate with a friend and Cabinet wife who was also a writer. Though she decided against writing it herself, Mrs. Coolidge permitted the commerce secretary's wife, Lou Hoover, to write several articles on the First Lady's girlhood for the Girl Scout magazine. The Girl Scouts, however, without consulting either woman, went ahead and offered serial rights free to the North American Newspaper Alliance for their wire-service publications. When Grace heard that her childhood story would soon be available in the *Washington Star*, a stern communication was sent from the White House. Soon after, in the third person, the *Star* reported, "It developed yesterday that their action was displeasing to Mrs. Coolidge. Therefore, as a matter of course, newspaper publication of the story was abandoned."[2]

Personally, Mrs. Coolidge was as comfortable with reporters as Mrs. Harding had been, and in fact she entertained a group of women writers at the White House and was herself feted twice by the recently formed Women's National Press Club, the first First Lady to be so honored. Still, there was a subtle determination to control her press. Silent Grace was conscious of the radio microphone that was now more the rule than the exception even at the ladies' luncheon affairs she attended. The technicians present switched the microphone on every time Mrs. Coolidge was near the dais and might murmur a thank you or crack a joke. She loved her own radio; she presented the Atwater Kent National Radio Audition Award; her husband created the Federal Radio Commission, setting radio regulations and license guides—but she didn't want her voice to be heard on it.[3]

She was simply admired for being Mrs. Coolidge. So publicly acclaimed was she that Grace became the first First lady to be bestowed with an honorary degree. At Boston University, she was cited as having "gained the confidence, admiration and love of America." She even earned that rare prize, a comparison to Dolley Madison. It wasn't just the masses, however, who responded to her. The era's most successful but cynical humorist, Will Rogers, dubbed her "Public Female Favorite No. 1," after a visit, and assessed:

> We have been particularly blessed with the types of Ladies who have graced our Executive Mansion. But this one there now has the reputation, given her by everyone who has met her, of being the most friendly and having the most charming personality of any one of them all. She is chuck plump full of magnetism, and you feel right at home from the minute you get near her. She has a great sense of humor, and is live and tight up and pleasant every minute.[4]

All this was not lost on her husband, a president who perhaps more than any of his predecessors understood the value of public relations. Though there was no organized effort or confidential memo planning it, the First Lady played a vital role in projecting the administration's image, and it permanently affixed a new dimension to the role of First Lady.

If the president thought that his wife's personal popularity had gained him a positive edge in the election, there was nothing to be lost in permitting her to be highly visible throughout his term. Many thought that Grace was the *only* thing exciting about the administration. That was the way the president liked it.

Increasingly, the president had found the social side of his duties taking too much time away from business, but since both Coolidges realized the importance of newspaper pictures at goodwill events or with charity leaders, it was reported that "President Coolidge is throwing more of the social side upon Mrs. Coolidge." She was a very willing subject, and probably met more of the general citizenry at public events and ceremonies than any of her predecessors, except perhaps for Mrs. Madison. She loved crowds so much that she herself snapped photos and took moving pictures of them, with her own camera.[5]

Perhaps with this in mind, she stepped up the traditionally limited solo interaction between First Lady and the public, appearing for photographs with nearly every group that requested a greeting at the White House. It was far more agreeable to make pictures available to the public than to give interviews that might delve into privacy.

Grace rarely refused to pose, even in the most ludicrous of situations, like handling flowers at the Amaryllis show under a large sign, DO NOT HANDLE THE FLOWERS.

She was seen in vignettes in which she helped establish traditional First Lady "duties"—receiving May Day flower bouquets, slicing anniversary cakes for the Visiting Nurses Association, planting a tree at the Lincoln Memorial, laying a cornerstone at a boys' school, kissing children at the Easter Egg Roll, posing in a Girl Scout uniform with the group's officers, cutting a ribbon to open a homemakers' exhibit. Her signed photograph, donated to a Long Island church fair, fetched a remarkable one hundred dollars. With newspapers throughout the country printing the "goodwill" pictures, the public came to view such events as First Lady events, and though Florence Harding began this "duty," Grace Coolidge doubled the number of appearances and made them a permanent part of the obligation of the first ladyship. No longer could a First Lady retreat into the Red Room and merely shake hands. The option of an Edith Wilson to make a rare surprise appearance with the president was no longer a matter of choice.[6] It was expected.

Photos were one thing; interviews, however, were another matter. Early in the term, while Grace was dressing, Coolidge entered their bedroom and asked what she had scheduled. She nonchalantly told him that she was about to be interviewed. Immediately, the president ordered her to cancel. "It has been by unbroken policy," the First Lady would explain, "not to see newspaper writers or give interviews to anyone. At the word interview spoken or written my ears go up and my chin out." Reporters tried to persuade the First Lady to change her mind, though she was steadfast. The situation became so frustrating that, one day at a luncheon, the fey Mrs. Coolidge rose before gathered women reporters as if she were going to speak. Then, raising her hands expressively, she delivered a speech in sign language. Witnesses there for the rare moment were amused by her unique acquiescing.[7]

Calvin's refusal to allow his press liaison to refute the constant rumors that had become part of the First Lady's public role also had repercussions. Whispered rumor, when allowed to grow undenied, often found its way into print. In 1925, packages started arriving at the White House addressed to Grace. They were baby clothes and sundries. No word of denial was forthcoming from the White House. The deluge of diapers and rattles stopped only after the better part of nine months had passed.

More disturbing was the persistent rumor that Grace planned to divorce the president. The story stayed strong for well over a year, but the Coolidges refused to publicly deny the gossip, which only fueled the fires. Finally, it was noticed that they began making conspicuous appearances together. This was their subtle response to the rumor, which eventually faded.[8]

Like thousands of other citizens, Grace watched the 1925 partial solar eclipse and became excited when she spotted the Graf Zeppelin. It was the release of such mundane news of her common touch that endeared Mrs. Coolidge to the public and personalized the role. The middle class felt comfortable with her. She was one of them. No more evident was this than in her influence on mainstream fashion.[9]

Her social secretary said that Grace became even more sensitive to fashion trends after becoming First Lady. Seeing the potential for setting the standard of contemporary but balanced taste, she seemed to combine the zaniest qualities of twenties women's fashion with pragmatic restraint. She was modern without being vulgar. Her skirt lengths were not as high as the more radical designs of the time, but she used bright primary colors, white cottons, and light pastels in flat-chested, low-hipped dresses. She could even carry off the daring man-tailored suit redesigned for women, with white shirt and black tie. Her hats were always "the last word"—from tight-fitting cloche to widebrim. Evenings, she preferred long-trained brocades of gold, silver, white, and red. Sparkled belts and fans, fur pieces, rhinestone shoe buckles—each meticulous detail of her clothing took on the quality of theatrical costumes, and the nation's "women's page" editors gave considerable space to her clothes. She was a woman who liked to shop, and the Retail Dry Goods Association cited her as an excellent example of the ideal "early Christmas shopper." On one occasion, some speculated that Coolidge was coming early to New York for a scheduled chamber of commerce speech so his wife could shop.

In this way, Grace helped firmly establish the role of fashion leader as the role of First Lady. First Ladies' clothing came under close scrutiny, first by women, eventually by everyone, and sometimes was criticized by haute couture houses and traditionalists alike.

One little girl, Elizabeth Bloomer of Grand Rapids, Michigan, remembered that her mother looked to the First Lady each fall before buying her clothes for the next season. As a little girl of the twenties, she, her friends, and their mothers all paid attention to the First Lady. As a matter of fact, her first impressions of the role related to fashion:

> When I first was aware of it [the term "First Lady"] . . . I thought it more "Perfect Lady." Because somehow . . . it was the hat and gloves and the proper accessories . . . "perfect." We . . . talked, as I recall, [when we were] quite young, about dress codes and First Ladies, and . . . a First Lady probably did have a lot to do with what fashion was going to be popular that year because of their selections, and certainly if they wore hats—but of course everyone wore hats then—they set a pace for fashion."

Miss Bloomer, known to her family and friends as Betty, was already thinking about a career in fashion.

Whereas there had been a cobalt "Harding Blue" for her predecessor, red became identified with Grace Coolidge. The Associated Press reported that "Mrs. Coolidge has started a new vogue for red which promises to grow as the season advances." She donated a ruby-colored dress to the Smithsonian collection, and her White House portrait by Howard Chandler Christy, also showing her dressed in bright red, became legendary. It pictured a "sensual" Grace, with white collie at her side and blue sky above, giving the life-size canvas a patriotic color theme. The First Lady's style was even recognized in Paris, and she was given a gold locket by Monsieur Worth and by Monsieur Cartier, on behalf of the workers in the French garment industries.[10]

Women were beginning to wear pants, particularly for their increased sports activity, but when Mrs. Coolidge appeared in riding togs, and later in culottes for a hike, Calvin forbade her to wear them again. Still, as one of the most physically fit First Ladies, Grace managed not only to exercise but to maintain her increased devotion to sports. The era marked a surge of interest in golf, tennis, swimming, boxing, and baseball, and Grace was the first First Lady to so genuinely reflect the nation's public obsession with sports. She was perhaps Babe "the Bambino" Ruth's most famous fan. At a time when Gertrude Ederle swam the English Channel, Mrs. Coolidge had an instructor teach her the new Australian "crawl" stroke. She presented the championship cup to a marine football team, and accepted the honorary chair of a fine-arts exhibit benefiting the U.S. Olympic team. In Georgia, the First Lady

awoke at three in the morning to go pheasant hunting. And long an avid baseball fan, with scorecard always in hand, Mrs. Coolidge had a front-row seat for a 1925 World Series game, staying, as she did for all Washington Senators games, to the end. In Boston, she sometimes sat in the dugout with the Red Sox.[11]

There was no exercise Mrs. Coolidge enjoyed more than her vigorous "hikes." She was a familiar sight on Washington streets, always walking if weather permitted. Though the Duchess had been the first to have a Secret Service agent, there was little concern for a First Lady's security. Still, as she strolled the avenues, there was always a tall, young, and handsome man by her side, Jim Haley of the Secret Service. At her hiking average of four miles an hour, Grace had "a gait that makes rangy James Haley . . . stretch his long legs."[12]

Grace genuinely preferred mixing with ordinary people to formal occasions, and she was inevitably surrounded by throngs. She loved people. As she told a friend, ". . . I have been fortunate in being placed where I had an opportunity to gratify my taste by meeting great numbers of them." On another occasion, when asked about her favorite reading, she responded, "People are my books." She particularly shone at the annual Easter Egg Roll on the South Lawn of the White House.[13]

At one such event, she stood smiling in white dress and yellow picture hat, surrounded by hundreds of children in their pinks, whites, and blues, straw bonnets and cotton knickers. A shy girl, on the edge of the crowd, Anne Frances Robbins, remembered the Egg Roll as her first visit to the White House, but had no lingering memory of Grace

Coolidge. She recalled, ". . . I had the fun of rolling Easter eggs on the south lawn."[14]

Anne Frances had a lonely childhood. By the time of her birth in July 1921, her father, Kenneth Robbins, had left her mother, Edie, who was an actress performing on Broadway. To stars like ZaSu Pitts, Alla Nazimova, Spencer Tracy, Walter Huston, Josh Logan, Jimmy Stewart, and George M. Cohan, the native Virginian Edie was friendly, funny, and affable, and she was known as "Lucky." As far as her daughter was concerned, Edie had always called her "Nancy." From the age of two until eight, she was left to Edie's sister and brother-in-law, who took her lovingly into their "tiny, tiny house." Nancy had to sleep in a makeshift room, in an enclosed porch.

As far as her natural father was concerned, his infrequent visits left her unsatisfied, and though she was his daughter in fact, he was never a father emotionally to her. Occasionally, Lucky had her daughter live with her when she had a long run in New York. Living in temporary residential apartments made Nancy feel desolate and insecure, but she recalled that "visits with Mother were wonderful. I loved to dress up in her stage clothes, put on her makeup, and pretend that I was playing her parts." When she watched her mother on stage in one play in which Edie played a character who was treated badly by the other characters, Nancy took it hard. She emulated her mother and announced, "I'm going to be an actress."[15]

On the "Great White Way," vaudeville was being given a run for its money as the Ziegfeld and many other follies' feathered costumes got scantier with each season. There were lavish musicals, intense dramas, even lascivious "sex" plays by young playwright Mae West. Then Hollywood burgeoned with vamps and gangsters, on and off the "silver" screen. And for the first time, professional actors were welcomed as guests in the White House.

When a favorite of the First Lady's, actor Tom Mix, visited her, he posed on his horse before the South Balcony with his trademark white cowboy hat for the press. Grace Coolidge was there, on the balcony, looking down on him. She breakfasted and even sang with Al Jolson in the White House. The Dolly Sisters, Jane Cowl, Mary Pickford, and Douglas Fairbanks accepted Grace's White House invitation. She caught a showing of *Rio Rita*. She went to see live performances: Groucho Marx in *Animal Crackers;* opera diva Rosa Ponselle in *Norma;* and Ethel Barrymore in *The Kingdom of God*. "Miss Barrymore was not convincing in the part," she wrote a friend. "It seems to me she is unsuited for it." The First Lady was a regular theatergoer, keeping a season seat at the National for matinees, but was just as avid a "moving-picture" fan. Grace liked *Gentleman Prefer Blondes*, and, like many women, Rudolph Valentino in *The Sheik*. She even saw a filmed Dempsey fight.[16]

The First Lady's cultural interests extended to the classic performing arts as well. She braved a snowstorm to see Pavlova dance. The great Sergey Rachmaninoff played for her and several hundred guests in the East Room. She was honorary chair of the World Fellowship through Music Convention, attended the performances of the Washington Opera Company, and lent support to the National Symphony and New York Philharmonic.[17]

Like Nellie Taft, who enjoyed ragtime disks on her Edison phonograph, Grace Coolidge was attuned to the music and entertainment of the era, but no First Lady had ever been so closely associated with popular culture and yet so thoroughly divorced from the permissive element of it all.

Native intolerance, the most shocking manifestation being a rise in Ku Klux Klan violence, marked the decade, but never once during her first ladyship—or her life, for that matter—did Grace express even subtly any prejudices. She treated the blacks on the domestic staff with open warmth, taking genuine concern in their lives and their families' well-being, and counted Jews and Catholics among her friends. The president had Indian ancestors, and while many laughed at his posing in a feathered headdress and accepting membership in the Sioux tribe, the Coolidges took it seriously and considered it a solemn honor. Though he signed an act authorizing the interior secretary to issue citizen certification to all American Indians, President Coolidge also signed the Immigration Bill, which further limited the quotas of those coming from southern and western Europe.

The First Lady, perhaps again playing a public-relations role, to alleviate some criticism of the bill, frequently greeted groups of immigrant women at the White House. From Boston, an Italian immigrant "Mothers' Club" traveled to Washington to present Grace with a white dress its members made "in the pattern . . . judged to be the type most becoming to the President's wife." Most of the women had never been outside of Boston, and had been saving money for this trip for two years. The First Lady went to a Norwegian centennial, and welcomed a group of Hungarian "Americanization" women students from Cleveland, Ohio, who came to visit her and present her with handmade lace.[18]

Though most of her peers served liquor at home during Prohibition, Mrs. Coolidge would not, because, as her son wrote, "she was against law-breaking of any kind." Privately, however, Grace concurred in Calvin's opinion that "any law which inspires disrespect for the other laws—is a bad law." In her own wry way, Mrs. Coolidge poked fun at Prohibition when she named her white collie dog "Rob Roy," the name of a popular drink.[19]

Grace Coolidge was America's most visible woman. It was now the rule rather than the exception for a First Lady to travel with her president, and wherever Grace went, she was the Coolidge who most often got the ovation, especially if there were members of her Pi Beta Phi sorority in the crowds. When University of Ohio Pi Phis made their presence known to the First Lady, she spontaneously led a sorority chant from the presidential train as it stopped briefly in Athens. The national organization had commissioned her Christy portrait, and a group of thirteen hundred Pi Phis presented it to the White House. Grace later mused how she was now ensconced with "the other White House dames," but didn't want the painting lighted, since "the other ladies must remain in outer darkness."

Because of her successful pursuit of a full college education and degree, she was held as an example for young American women, along with Frances Cleveland, to whom she was compared. "What the one gave and the other is giving could hardly have been possible without the contribution of college, which is happily now for women," ran one editorial. At the 1926 University of Vermont commencement, where another portrait of her was unveiled, Mrs. Coolidge was cited as being "the model of American womanhood," and her "tact" and "simple dignity" earned her comparison to Portia, who was nevertheless "not as comely as the picture of Grace Goodhue . . ."[20]

The decade was bringing sweeping changes for women. Now, armed with the right to vote, many took a more personal interest in politics—though there was no radical change in established voting trends. While more career girls entered in the workplace, postponing or foregoing motherhood, and flappers without escorts drank illegal "hooch" in urban speakeasy nightclubs, there remained a stable majority. Perhaps better than anyone else could, Grace Coolidge personified this element, balancing the changes in her own life with traditional wifely duties. When it came to the drastic social changes of women smoking, working, and wearing pants, her son John says, "She was very broad-minded about these things." Ike Hoover claimed that, in private, Grace herself tried cigarette smoking, the first First Lady to do so.[21]

The First Lady was conscious of women and their achievements. When her husband was to deliver his first congressional address, she made seating arrangements so the Cabinet wives would appear as a prominent and unified group. She accepted the invitation to receive her Boston University degree just at the time that Lucy Jenkins Franklyn became the first woman dean there. During the 1925 Inaugural ceremonies, Grace took time out of a busy day to seek out the nation's first woman governor, Nellie Tayloe Ross, and personally speak with her. When she heard that the famous conductor Elizabeth Kuyper was in town, Grace asked the Dutch woman to visit her in the White House, and it brought visibility to Kuyper, whose purpose in coming to the United States was to found the Professional Woman's Symphony Orchestra of America. On April 18, 1925, the First Lady accepted the invitation to symbolically press the button that officially opened the Woman's World Fair, in Chicago. Billed by an organizer as "an exhibition of the progress made by women in the commercial field through their own efforts and within their own ranks," it included booths of women lawyers, artists, bankers, inventors, farmers, oil-well owners, and cold-cream promoters.[22]

Though President Coolidge publicly stated, "Women can never escape the responsibility of home and children, and the working woman as a mother and potential mother challenges universal interest," First Lady Coolidge, with uncharacteristic bluntness, defended working women. "Everyone talks of the restlessness of women since the war, of their dissatisfaction to return to the old kinds of life. Of course they are restless. Soon there will not be an intelligent woman who is content to do nothing but live a social life."

The president also felt that women as a group were not fully using their right to vote. On this issue, Grace felt she could be a persuasive power over American women, and again played a public-relations role. In 1925, she gamely posed for a press photo session, as she filled out her absentee ballot on the White House lawn where her desk had been moved, thereby "setting an example for the millions of women voters of the country." The press caption noted that the First Lady "intends her ballot be secret as she carefully shields her vote from view."[23]

During the Coolidge administration, Edna Coleman wrote that the First Lady "holds that women have a very definite obligation and responsibility as citizens, and it is their duty and privilege to do serious and effective work towards an intelligent discharge of public duties." When the president of the Republican Women of Pennsylvania wrote to Grace about a program to educate women about politics, the First Lady publicly explained her own view of the importance of women understanding politics:

> I have been pleased to learn of the general movement to organize . . . the women . . . with a view to developing the widest interest in and understanding of the public questions before the country. It is always gratifying to know of such organized movements for more efficient citizenship, whether among men or women . . . and whether of one party or the other. The women have lately come into new, and, to most of them, rather unexpected responsibilities in their relations as citizens. It is altogether desirable that these be taken seriously, and effective work is undoubtedly needed among them, precisely as is also needed among a great section of the male voters whose preoccupation with other interests too often interferes with the most intelligent discharge of public duties.[24]

Well into her fourth year as First Lady, however, Mrs. Coolidge still kept her distance from public politics. Privately, there was evidence that the president made Grace privy to subjects she claimed to eschew. Earlier in her first ladyship, she had sat through a government-budget meeting with the president, as well as Senate hearings on the Teapot Dome investigation. It was not merely perfunctory, for she stayed at these events long past the opening remarks. She was present at more than one private political meeting of Calvin's, and in one instance she casually revealed herself during their 1926 summer respite at White Pines Camp in the Adirondacks, New York. Though there as "private person," Grace accepted invitations and made appearances in her public role. Whether visiting Marines who were guarding White Pine Camp or a silver-fox farm, the press were there to cover the event. Like the president, the First Lady kept "working."

At White Pines Camp, the Coolidges had a stream of guests, from the Cabinet to senators, leaders in the private sector, government, and labor. Mrs. Coolidge got along particularly well with the Democratic governor of New York, Alfred E. Smith. Mrs. Smith and Mrs. Coolidge were not sequestered when the president and the governor got down to business. On the contrary, perhaps because of Mrs. Smith's frank admission that she was involved in her husband's work, Grace wrote that she thought they had all "discussed problems of common interest and experience," and that "minds ran along parallel lines in many instances." Later in the day, Grace was present, with her husband, for a discussion about New York State utilities, waterways, and their cost to the state, potential sale of the Erie Canal to the federal government, and the possibility of the state's reservoir supply diminishing. Smith cited "Mrs. Coolidge and her ability to make guests feel at home" as a helpful factor in relaxing the atmosphere for his discussion of conservation issues with the man many thought he'd be running against in 1928.[25]

One journalist who covered Mrs. Coolidge closely thought the First Lady was "a shrewd judge of people," and that she was confident of the president's advisers. The president's closest assistants, Everett Sanders, an Indiana congressman, and Ted Clark, were both friends of Mrs. Coolidge, and when Assistant C. Bascom Slemp retired, he insisted that his stag farewell party include the First Lady. Only twice was the First Lady known to have exercised political power by intercessions. When she learned that veteran Emmett Rogers, son of a White House black maid, had been gassed in the war and suffered from breathing troubles, Mrs. Coolidge interceded with routine Veterans' Bureau procedures, and arranged for his transfer to a federal veterans' hospital out West, where the air was dry and more conducive to his recovery.[26]

On another occasion, the Commission on Battle Monuments chairman, General John Pershing, was presenting blueprints for a war memorial to President Coolidge when the First Lady arrived. She asked if she could look the plans over herself. Without being asked—but without being stopped by her husband—Grace vetoed the design outright, considering it unaesthetic, and the architect was directed to come up with another proposal.[27]

Another woman had an indirect influence on the success of Pershing's Battle Monuments Commission. Whereas Grace Coolidge liked Pershing as chairman, Mamie Eisenhower liked the idea of her husband, Ike, as Pershing's assistant, to do most of the actual research. The commission's final report, which came out in the form of a guidebook, *The American Battlefields in France*, was written by Eisenhower. Ike had first considered turning down the offer. Mamie prevailed. "I told him not to protest but to take it." After a short stint at the War College in Washington, Ike was given the opportunity to continue work on the battlefield project, this time in France. Mamie saw it as a chance to see Europe free, "on the eagle." Again, she persuaded him to accept the offer. He did so. They sailed for France and settled in Paris. While there, they toured the major European nations, and Mamie often went with her husband to search out the battle markers, and record them for history. In many respects, it had brought new direction to the marriage.[28]

After their son's death, there had been a breach in the marriage. Both parents painfully blamed themselves for the loss, and shared few of their emotions over it. In 1922, when Ike had been assigned to the Panama Canal Zone, the situation became even more depressing, as the couple was assigned to live in a rotting wood house ("a double-decked shanty, only twice as disreputable," Mamie recalled) in the middle of the jungle, infested with insects, bats, and snakes. On her own, however, bold Mamie enjoyed the new culture she found herself living in. She had written her parents in November 1923 that she went to the cockfights—"The people were so fascinating I couldn't pay much attention to the cocks"—and she won eight out of nine bets. She went to a cathedral "with the only bamboo organ in the world—was allowed to play it which was quite an experience . . . at dusk millions of bats fly from this cave . . . you can't imagine the sight of it." She was enjoying the native food as well. "I'll have to do some exercises or I'll be Miss Corn for sure."

The wife of Ike's superior, Mrs. General Fox Conner, proved to be of vital importance to the estranged Eisenhowers. Virginia Conner was a tough yet gentle army wife to emulate. She and Mamie spent much time together—from games of charades to getting costumes together for a joke "wedding" staged by some of the men at the base. Virginia later said that the Eisenhowers "were drifting apart." She counseled Mamie to use a subtle power. "You mean I should vamp him?" the surprised Mrs. Ike asked. "That's just what I mean," Virginia suggested. "Vamp him!"

Mamie altered her appearance. She cut her hair, and in the current rage of the "bob," included something new: bangs. Though many would deride what seemed like a childish coiffure, Mamie would keep her bangs, a sentimental symbol to both her and Ike. In less than a year, she gave birth to her second son, John.

While in Panama, Mamie helped found a children's and postmaternity hospital for the many Puerto Rican families there. As fund-raising chair, she ingeniously devised events that would trickle money in from military families on limited budgets, and arranged to get moving-picture stars Lila Lee and Thomas Meighan, then filming in Panama, to make appearances for a benefit. With Mrs. Eisenhower's leadership, over a thousand dollars was raised, and a hospital was established.[29]

As the years went on, Mamie was in charge of running her own tight ship. Ike turned over all his money to her, and she controlled their accounts, balancing their limited funds, and writing the checks. In Washington, when she returned by taxi from shopping at the military commissary, Mamie got out at the bottom of the Connecticut Avenue hill where the rate zone went up, and carried her bags up the incline to save pocket change. She and Ike took John to the White House, in April 1927, to join in the Easter Egg Roll festivities and see Grace Coolidge. Though it was not the first time Nancy Robbins was at the White House, it was the first time the Eisenhowers went to the White House, and the first time Mamie saw a First Lady.[30]

Though she presided at the 1927 Egg Roll, Grace was not in residence at the time. In March, the Coolidges had temporarily moved out of the White House while its roof was strengthened and its upper level expanded into another floor. They lived in a white marble mansion, lent by publisher Cissy Patterson, on Dupont Circle. Some days Grace made her hike with Rob Roy and Jim Haley down to check on the renovating. She had a deep reverence for the place. To a tour group, she meticulously explained the historic details of the gardens. She requested photographs of the rooms from before, and after, the 1902 renovation. Whenever she spoke about the Lincoln Bed, in which she and the president slept, Grace always pointed out that there was no evidence that Lincoln ever used it. "In the months that I have lived here in the great white house," she had written in 1925, "I have become greatly attached to it and there is much that is sacred about the associations connected with it." Like Julia Tyler, Mary Lincoln, Julia Grant, and Edith Wilson, Grace had a sense of the "other side," claiming to have felt Lincoln's ghost when she was alone, writing upstairs in a closed room.

In regard to the mansion, the First Lady could be quite political. Just after the election, she had decided to redecorate the family quarters, and then expanded her plan to include the historic staterooms, but she let Congress know she didn't want the renovations paid for with a government appropriation. Mrs. Coolidge planned a restoration based solely upon private donations of funds and furnishings. In 1925, Grace's project had gone public and legal as a joint resolution in Congress was passed, allowing the White House to accept such gifts. The First Lady formed an advisory committee, composed of antique experts and architects. Shortly thereafter, a battle raged when members of the committee were publicly confronted by the American Institute of Architects.

Prior to departing for summer holiday, Mrs. Coolidge had left some simple instructions for minor work to be done. Some members of the committee were incensed when they heard this, because they had not been consulted. Without permission of either the president or First Lady, they issued statements on *their* plans, which would now include the Green Room. This sparked a feud with the architects, who felt the Roosevelt beaux-arts restoration of 1901 would be "museumized Colonially" by a bunch of antiquarians.

Throughout the decorating war, carried out on the pages of the daily newspapers during the slow-news month of August, Mrs. Coolidge never made a single public utterance. It was wise and political, for if she took one side, she would inevitably be criticized in print by the other, and the president would have been angered. Coolidge had finally declared that there would be no redecorating at all on the state floor. Now, in the spring of '27, the First Lady was quietly continuing her plan to redecorate. She let the committee know, two years after she had formed her resolution, that she wanted to restore the Green Room, on the condition that "she would have a chance to act on the general scheme proposed and on individual pieces of furniture to be purchased" with the fund money. She made the decisions according to her own taste, with advice of the committee but without being told by antiquarians or architects how to do it. Through quiet tenacity, she finally managed to have the room completed with the donated antiques, as well as some she herself discovered in the attic.[31]

Neither the White House project nor her continued support to the cause of the deaf were thoroughly associated with Grace by the press and public, because she was linked to so many other goodwill movements. The impact became diffused. Even she admitted that it was "terrible to have to spread out so thin."

Early on, Grace had realized her own potential power, and reveled in the goodwill influence the first ladyship afforded her. "Daily I am impressed anew with the responsibility and opportunity which has been given me," she wrote. "In no sense does it overwhelm me, rather does it inspire me and increase my energy and I am so filled with the desire to measure up . . ."[32]

The cause of children's welfare became permanently ingrained in the first ladyship with Grace. For a drive to promote proper moving pictures for children, the First Lady attended a special showing. She became the first First Lady to open a benefit fair for the Association for the Aid of Crippled Children, send flowers to the children at the Hospital for Joint Diseases, visit Children's Hospital, and christen the annual Christmas Seals drive. The Campfire Girls named her "Aikayi, First Lady of the Land," the Girl Scouts sent her their annual report in the form of a valentine, and she headed the national honorary committees of both the Red Cross and American Legion Endowment Fund. Her Red Cross work was quite visible as she donned the nunlike "Grey Lady" uniform, reading to blinded veterans, buying their wares, and assisting in membership and fund-raising drives. On her own, Grace had already been working, long before she became famous, for the education and public understanding to the deaf, the cause dearest to her heart.[33]

She approached the issue from several perspectives. As a mother and herself a former teacher, the First Lady had "studied educational problems with minuteness, visiting all sorts of institutions of learning," and viewed "a close personal relation between the parent, the school and the child, as a solution for many difficulties that beset both pupil and instructors." Lawrence E. Wikander, who would help organize her papers, said that Grace's "interest in deaf children was a *professional* interest; she was a trained teacher of the deaf, wrote on the subject, and assisted understanding of the deaf person's problems. She was constantly in touch with the latest scientific developments." This was quite apart from most of her predecessors, whose causes were acquired interests.

Mrs. Coolidge frequently invited groups of students from the Clarke School for the Deaf to tour the White House and visit with her. Later on, she wrote to a host of prominent Americans in her efforts to publicize the cause and "educate the general public about the enormous problems which face a deaf child." Her work had a ripple effect for the handicapped in general, her husband giving his sensitive attention to those few national programs that assisted the disabled. How to best help the deaf in a hearing world was, as it would continue to be, a matter of divided opinions, and Mrs. Coolidge sided with the faction that advocated lip-reading.

Clarke's former president George Pratt recalled a conversation with Mrs. Coolidge in which she said "teaching the deaf was a vocation one could give one's whole being." Pratt felt she "had an instinctive understanding of their needs as well as a very practical knowledge of what was required," and that her greatest strength was "informing, and educating the public on the issue." Pratt believed her project was effective "because she was who she was and large numbers of Americans took her and her work seriously. Anyone she appealed to help the cause of the deaf answered the request of the First Lady."

Occasionally, there was something in the press about a deaf group

that visited the First Lady. On one occasion, she was given artificial flowers made by the girls of a special public school for the deaf in New York City. She also invited prominent deaf people to visit the mansion, and endeared herself to Chief Justice Taft by seeking out and conversing with his half-brother Charles and his wife, Annie, both of whom were deaf.

Helen Keller, who was both deaf and blind, was one of Grace's cherished personal guests, and the visit was captured in a photograph as Keller listened to Grace by placing her hands around the First Lady's neck and fingertips on her lips, to "hear" her. Helen Keller told Mrs. Coolidge, "I am so glad you have a place in your heart for the blind as well as the deaf. I have long anticipated meeting you because my deaf friends have told me such lovely things about you. They remember when you taught in the Clarke school." The two women exchanged flowers, and when she returned to her hotel, Keller praised the "so warm" Grace: "She gives out sweet thoughts freely and is so responsive to every human need and every sorrow that she is able to save our country in the spirit of . . . 'bear one another's burdens.'"

Keller's senses on first meeting "Silent Cal," were also perceptive, and Grace told her, "The President thought I was the only woman in the world who knew he had a warm heart." Keller responded, "I feel in the hand what the eye cannot see . . . your dear husband thinks many things he doesn't tell to every one and there are wonder-

ful things in his heart." With that, Grace Coolidge filled with genuine emotion. "Helen," she gently replied, "you have made me very
happy."

Though her interest in the deaf was generally known, it was never
billed, or covered by the press, as a singular "project." With her natural
modesty, Mrs. Coolidge seemed to feel that vigorously promoting a
cause that benefited an issue and institution that was so important to
her might be interpreted as self-interest. So she continued her work
quietly and subtly. That was proven toward the end of her first-
ladyship, when she headed a major fund-raising effort for the Clarke
School. Under Grace Coolidge's sponsorship of the "capital campaign,"
over $2 million was collected. No previous First Lady had raised such
substantial amounts for her cause.[34]

In the late spring of '27, while still in the Dupont Circle house, the
Coolidges entertained the celebrity of the hour, shy Colonel Charles A.
Lindbergh, who had just made his historic solo transatlantic flight. He
took to the motherly First Lady, as she guided him around town and
stood by his side on the balcony, waving at thousands gathered in the
circle. She introduced him to her friends the Dwight Morrows, and he
later married their daughter Anne. Impulsively, he offered to take the
First Lady for an airplane ride. She pointed out, "I'm not afraid [but] I
promised my husband that I would never fly."

Coolidge had signed an act creating the Army Air Corps, the Air
Mail Act, and the Air Commerce Act, putting civil aviation under
Commerce's control. He appointed the National Air Board to investigate the government's possible role in aeronautics, and approved its
suggestion of permitting individual air-service companies. Once again,
Mrs. Coolidge had skillfully played the public-relations role for his administration, by promoting aeronautics. She christened a dirigible air-
ship, a U.S.-West Indies route mailplane, and a commercial Pan-
American Airways Services plane. But Calvin still would not allow his
wife to fly in one.[35]

Lindbergh was the international hero of a nation then topspinning
at full speed with an economic, technological, and cultural boom that
was permitting leisure time not just for the rich but for the middle class
as well. Resorts for all classes and races flourished. Never before had
there been such a national preoccupation with leisure, and once again
the First Lady mirrored the age as the press highlighted her summer
sports. In 1925, when they summered at Swampscott, Massachusetts,
she was swimming daily in her black stockings and bathing suit. In
1926, she had paddled a canoe and rowed a boat in Lake Saranac. This
summer, the Coolidges were headed to the Black Hills of South Dakota, and besides housekeeper Ellen Riley, the Secret Service aide detailed to the First Lady was also going.

Even though the First Lady was always escorted by Jim Haley, the president's fear of harm coming to her bordered on the irrational, and he kept very close tabs on her movements. Her social secretary said Grace "was the sunshine and the joy in his life," and "solace in time of trouble." Coolidge could write his hometown cobbler that he loved him, and express emotion to his father, but he repressed his emotions about Grace. In public, he might demeaningly tease her, but he never kissed or hugged her. Yet he was so deeply in love with her that he was occasionally jealous of other men.

Grace was just the opposite. She could buss the public, and even joke about being the "National Hugger." Obviously, she had grown close to Jim Haley, coming to know him through their long hours alone together during her hikes through the city. Haley liked Mrs. Coolidge and what he called her "million dollar smile." But their relationship was more mother and son; the First Lady was friendly with his new wife, Joan, and exchanged gifts and letters with her.[36]

Just days before they all left for South Dakota, some gossip was bubbling about Haley. Reporter Dorothy Dayton stated that the First Lady's man Haley was "one of the handsomest and most distinguished men" one could see in Washington. A sarcastic editorial then appeared, saying that the young men of the Secret Service were "the most decorative," and that certain unnamed government leaders "might not take kindly to the presence of remarkably fine looking Secret Service men." It questioned the use of a "Secret" Service since the appearance of the men was as obvious "as if they were stage detectives wearing derby hats and chewing fat cigars."

Since the president became angry about harmless press coverage of his wife, his feelings concerning publicity over her Secret Service agent were predictable enough. He sarcastically referred to the agent as only that "long-legged Haley man."[37]

Like their era, the Coolidges were at their peak in 1927, and there seemed to be no hint that would change. Everyone was beginning to talk about the president running again in '28. Will Rogers asked the First Lady if her husband was going to run. She lightly responded, "You find out if you can and let me know."

Just before she left the Dupont Circle house, the First Lady finally completed a two-year personal project. Believing that First Ladies should leave something of themselves behind, she had been crocheting a Lincoln Bed afghan, sewing "Grace Coolidge" and the dates of her first-ladyship years into the design.

The dates read, "August 8, 1923 to March 4, 1929."

Did that mean Coolidge wouldn't run in '28? When a friend asked her why "1929" instead of "1933," Grace tersely replied, "I know what I'm doing."[38]

− 47 −

Mammy

THE BRACING COOL air of the Black Hills enhanced an upbeat but relaxed summer for both the First Lady and the press corps, watching her every move. "Grace Coolidge Creek" was dedicated. She would bake a cake and record a party with her own "moving picture" camera. She panned for gold and was given a baby coyote. A preacher said her smile helped him deliver a sermon, and a Sioux tribe gave her moccasins. She received a loud ovation at a national park, and a group of Montana women gave her a brooch. When her housekeeper became ill and had to be operated upon, Grace assumed her role, picking wildflowers for the tables, and going into Rapid City "to replenish the larder." She went to the rodeo and visited a school for Indian children. She was given a fishing permit, and hooked a trout on her first try, the press noting how her technique was better than the president's, a fact that irritated him.[1]

For the president, things were different. Personally, though still not politically, Calvin was becoming increasingly reliant upon Grace's nurturing encouragement, frequently calling her by his affectionate nickname for her, "Mammy." He looked forward to their early morning coffee on the wide, rustic porch, afternoon fishing in a rowboat, and dusks in the high-beamed living room with buffalo rug, stone fireplace, and antlers on the wall. But he had to travel to a local closed school every day where the executive offices were set up. "Mammy" noticed how easily "Papa" became petulant at the slightest irritation. The National Women's party was then mounting the first large-scale public effort to get the Equal Rights Amendment ratified, and badgered Coolidge for support. He withheld his own views, but said women would have equity only when "the majority" of them joined the fight for it, and added his hope that the male press would "give them good publicity." Grace never expressed support for the ERA, privately or publicly.[2]

While her husband was in his office, Grace reveled in the natural wilderness, hiking every day. She began her morning with a jaunt into the woods. Her routine hike one June morning, however, ended up making headlines.

When Calvin left at nine o'clock that morning for the office,

Grace, in black boots and white sweater and sports skirt, was just heading out along a new trail that went deep in the woods. For one hour, she said. She was accompanied by Jim Haley, as usual.

Ten o'clock came and went, but they didn't return.

The president had returned from his office at noon, expecting to have lunch with his wife. There was still no sign of her. She had never taken so long a hike before. Coolidge was perturbed. Lunch came and went, and no First Lady. Yet another hour passed, and the president became visibly tense. Fearful that she might have been bitten by a snake, he finally ordered a search party sent out. A reporter noted that he "took a post on the front porch leading to the lodge and did not leave it until after she had returned." The search party came upon Grace and Haley just as they were about to reappear.

It was 2:15 P.M.—over five hours for a hike of fifteen miles, somewhat longer than her average rate of four miles an hour.

This was both the First Lady's and Secret Service agent's first time to have "ventured over" that particular mountain trail. It was, as they stated, a misjudgment of time, and they had lost their way. As she got back to the cabin, Grace avoided reporters.

A five-hour walk in the woods, a seemingly breezy First Lady and her young Secret Service agent, and a visibly angered president were just what the slow headlines of summer needed. On the morning of June 28, many woke up to an Associated Press story, one of whose headlines ran: MRS. COOLIDGE'S HIKE CAUSES LATE LUNCHEON: FIF-TEEN-MILE WALK IN HILLS CAUSES PRESIDENT ANXIETY AS HE WAITS AN HOUR. The lead paragraph reported, "Returning long after regular luncheon time from her first extended hike in the Black Hills, Mrs. Coolidge today found the president anxiously awaiting her as well as his mid-day meal." That was an understatement.

The usually unemotional president was livid. "She went immediately to the President on the porch and as she sipped water told of her . . . walk over the hills. Mr. Coolidge paced up and down the porch . . . just a little vexed over the long time he had sat anxiously waiting . . ." The report delicately concluded that the couple went inside together, "everything apparently adjusted." Coolidge was still angry. But his reaction only caused more trouble. Calvin had only been worried about her. He had always thought it improper to keep the president waiting. And he was hungry. He remained sore at "Mammy," but took it out on Haley.

On June 29, the Associated Press broke the story that Haley was "recalled today to Washington to assume a new post there." In announcing Grace's new agent, John J. Fitzgerald, it claimed that Haley's "departure from here was described as due to a recent promotion." The real story was that Coolidge had immediately ordered Haley's transfer, away from his wife. Edmund Starling, chief of the Secret Service, felt it was extremely unfair, especially since Haley had earned his prestigious assignment. His wife would long respond to the president's name with discomfort, and would refuse to discuss him. The first report had been innocent enough, but Coolidge's order, hyped in the press, immediately set tongues wagging, the mildest innuendo being that he was a jealous husband, the worst being that he had reason to be. The publicity made him even angrier.

Grace herself "showed some resentment" at the implication of the stories, but was also dealing with her irate husband. Seething, he refused to speak with "Mammy," for several days. Amid all this were correspondents watching every one of the Coolidges' interactions with each other. It was ironic that this intensely private presidential couple was the first to have a marital spat reported in the press. Though a First Lady's fame could serve a public-relations purpose, it could also victimize.

Mrs. Coolidge was also concerned about the incident's effect on Haley's marriage. In the summer of 1926, when Haley had taken off with the First Lady for the Adirondacks just three days after his wedding, Grace had written sympathetically to his wife, Joan, of the "severe test" his role placed on the new marriage, "in which I am interested. . . ." Weeks after the Black Hill incident, the First Lady admitted, "I certainly miss Mr. Haley and the many, many thoughtful things he did for me daily." Some months later, Mrs. Coolidge—without her husband's knowledge—privately resumed contact with the Haleys. When Joan opened a restaurant, Grace came to dine as one of her first customers. After Haley died, she revealed to Joan, "When he bade me good-bye in the Black Hills he said that his one consolation was that he had you to go home to. I shall always be grateful that he was assigned to me and never cease to regret the unfortunate circumstance which terminated that assignment." Though she did not mention the president by name, Grace Coolidge added, "An injustice was done [to] Jim. . . ."[3]

Just weeks later, the president shocked the nation with his vague but firm announcement, "I do not choose to run for President in 1928." The Coolidges had both become irritated by the Haley "scandal," and sought to avoid any further press. It made the decision not to seek a second term easier.

After the president made the announcement, Kansas senator Arthur Capper joined the Coolidges for lunch, during which Grace said nothing about the peculiar statement. After lunch, Capper questioned Grace as she knitted in a large chair. All she volunteered was, "Isn't that just like the man! He never gave me the slightest intimation of his intention. I had no idea!" Typically, she did not clarify whether she meant she had no idea that he wasn't going to run, or that he would announce it when he did. She later offered, "I am rather proud of the fact that after nearly a quarter of a century of marriage my husband feels free to make his decisions without consulting me or giving me advance information concerning them." Again, she blurred what she meant. Was the "decision" she spoke of the statement's release, or that he wasn't running? Even when friends questioned her, "Does he really mean it?," Grace remained ambiguous, claiming no knowledge. Nobody ever called her bluff, and no matter how hard she was scrutinized, Grace Coolidge never cracked the facade.

At least, *almost* never. Several months after the announcement, as reported in the *New York Herald Tribune* on February 28, 1928, Mrs. Coolidge wrote that she had completed the Lincoln Bed coverlet in June 1927, and it identified 1929 as the end of her first ladyship. That was two months before Coolidge's announcement. He had either told her he wouldn't run months before he publicly announced it, or she felt that she could be persuasive enough to convince him not to. But Grace had made a second slip. In March of 1927, she had written a friend that the president had joked to her that she "would soon be walking, riding in the street cars and taxicabs." To the end, she would steadfastly maintain her image as an uninformed First Lady, but there was a thorough report in *The New York Times* that gave details that she had exerted some power over the decision.[4]

"Mrs. Coolidge had been informed of the President's plans . . . some time ago. It is known that she counseled her husband not to undergo the ordeal of another four years in an office of great responsibility and one that is such a strain on physical strength." At the Dupont Circle house, Grace had evidently made a point to "a friend"— who was the source that claimed she "desired President Coolidge to retire at the end of this term . . . [But] . . . It is not known whether Mrs. Coolidge's counsel . . . induced him to reach his decision." Precisely when Coolidge had reached his decision remained unknown by all, "except perhaps Mrs. Coolidge." The report further revealed that, Grace was "an instrument in reaching the decision," who ". . . aided and encouraged the President in reaching that state of mind . . ."[5]

Many thought the president's statement was open, that he would accept the nomination if drafted. It was Calvin who often cracked that Grace "has kept me running for public office ever since I married her." As the fall of '27 gave way to the winter preceding the election, however, there were signs that Grace had an increasing influence over the president's private life, and wanted desperately to get out of the White House. She was finding the role too repressive. When some letters sent her by friends were accidently pulled by the Secret Service as "seemingly silly letters," she recorded her reprimand to an agent: "I explained to him that I was a human being before I was the wife of a President . . ." When a friend asked her to go to a football game, Grace responded, "Of course, if I went I should have to go with 'bells on' and there's no fun in that. Couldn't get permission anyhow. I guess nobody but you has any real idea of how shut in and hemmed about I feel." As summer approached, her view of public life further dimmed. She was felled with severe sinus attacks, and her mother was dying.[6]

Although the public, through the press, learned something of the First Lady's serious bronchial troubles, another health problem of even more dramatic consequence was evidently being dealt with, in complete secrecy. Whether it was an irregular heartbeat, some form of palpitations, high blood pressure, or even a mild heart attack, what struck the First Lady through the winter, spring, and early summer of 1928 was serious enough to warrant the president to confide to a friend, "I'm afraid that Mammy will die." For some time, naval doctor Joel Boone limited Mrs. Coolidge's walking about the house, and as the First Lady herself wrote privately to a friend, "I guess my heart will last as long as my disposition and I know that would go to smash if I did not get some exercise. I am still going without coffee . . ." When she later indulged in "a few good swigs of perfectly poisonous coffee," the effect "set me up higher than a kite. . . ."

The president had told Starling of the Secret Service that "in all things Mrs. Coolidge comes first." It was, wrote Starling, "something I found to be true without exception." If his ambiguous "I do not choose to run" from the previous summer had permitted Coolidge the chance to reconsider renomination, his priority would not allow it. "Four years more in the White House," he wrote, "would kill Mrs. Coolidge."

"Papa" made no attempts to stop "Mammy" when she became involved in monitoring his schedule and health. By his last year in office, Coolidge suffered from severe asthma, and was often weak and listless. Those around him noticed this, and there was perhaps fear that press attention drawn to it might exaggerate the condition. And the president was not in good health, suffering from a bad heart, a fact unknown to all but his doctors, and Grace. The First Lady exerted considerable influence as part of an inner circle that made a concerted effort to keep private the true nature of his health.

In the summer of 1928, Grace wrote to Coolidge confidant and adviser Frank Stearns that Calvin's condition was "not known outside." She conferred privately with the president's physician, Dr. James C. Coupal, over her concern that Calvin took an inordinate amount of medication, which she felt was unnecessary. She feared that a heavy speaking schedule could break Calvin, and she guarded against this. Without his knowledge, she monitored his planned schedule, making certain that it was not overtaxing. Mrs. Coolidge even went so far as to direct Secret Service chief Starling that if the president took sick, and they had to leave a public appearance before its conclusion, the press should be told that it was she who was ill.[7]

During this stressful period, Mrs. Coolidge closely followed the conventions of both parties. She kept her radio blaring while the Republicans nominated Herbert Hoover, the husband of her friend Lou and Coolidge's commerce secretary. Mrs. Hoover was a thoroughly independent woman. Whereas Grace was not permitted by the president to drive her own car, Lou drove everywhere. So did Edith Wilson, who continued to drive even after colliding with a streetcar; she emerged "suffering from slight shock." In 1927, she had been urged as a vice-presidential candidate by some Iowa Democratic women. A year later, a group of Pennsylvania women suggested the same, but she wasn't interested.

Mrs. Wilson was particularly friendly with the Republican administration. When she asked for the White House flags that had been flown during her first ladyship, President Coolidge had them hand-delivered. When she was planning to travel by train to summer in Saratoga, the Coolidge White House made all the arrangements for her. Grace Coolidge sent a presidential aide to Edith's house to find out if she wanted to attend a state dinner. On March 5, Edith returned to the White House, commencing a reign as Queen Mother.[8]

Like Julia Tyler before her, Edith hadn't received a widow's pension immediately. At that point, neither had Frances Cleveland Preston. But unlike Edith, Frances supported a candidate. In New York, her daughter Marion, chairman of the New York League of Women Voters, backed Al Smith, who was nominated. It evidently sparked a latent political interest in her mother. Frances came out publicly for Smith, the first and only time she did so for any candidate since her husband's own election. She felt strongly about the election after meeting the Smiths, and considered the anti-Catholic smears against them "a great injustice."[9]

At the Democratic Convention in Houston, however, Mrs. Wilson shocked herself by delivering a speech. She hadn't planned on it, but millionaire Jesse Jones maneuvered her up on the speaker's platform, introduced her to the crowds, and announced that she would speak to them. Caught off guard, Edith had only a moment during the thunderous applause to compose a brief greeting. She delivered her words in her low-pitched "Shenandoah twist" voice. Still, it was historic. No president's wife had ever spoken before a convention. Though Bernie Baruch managed to get her to meet Al Smith over oysters, she called him "crude" and refused to support him publicly. As Eleanor Roosevelt discovered, Edith wouldn't support her party in even the most perfunctory role.[10]

Franklin had been nominated for the governorship, but Eleanor was at the center of the Smith campaign. Though the anti-Catholic smears offended her, she said it was a lesson in "what prejudice can do to the intelligence of human beings . . ." By now, she was self-employed, having established Val-Kill Industries, which turned out wood furniture, and she had learned how to inspire workers and package a marketing presentation to stores. Still, she felt inadequate. "If I had to go out and earn my own living, I doubt if I'd even make a very good cleaning woman . . . I have no talents, no experience, no training for anything." She got her chance when, with her friend Marion Dickerman, she became part-owner of the Todhunter School for girls. She taught a course in current events in which she took the girls into "the worst type of old-time tenement" housing, to courtroom hearings, and to police-station lineups of suspected criminals. In her history class, she asked students to submit essays on "your reason for or against allowing women to actively participate in the control of government . . . through the vote, as well as . . . holding office . . ." and "How are Negroes excluded from voting in the South?"

Eleanor was more conservative in her literature class. When Esther Lape sent her Gide's Les Faux-Monnayeurs, with its homosexual theme, she "read it in terms of a forbidden subject. She couldn't bring herself even to consider homosexuality. Generally, her reaction was not so final, but in this case it was."

Val-Kill and Todhunter, however, increasingly took a backseat to her work with the League of Women Voters, Women's Trade Union League, Women's City Club, and the women's division of the Democratic State Committee, as she lectured, wrote, and did radio broadcasts urging women to get into politics. "Women should not be afraid to soil their hands . . . Those who are not [afraid] make the best politicians." Her publication of the monthly Democratic News gave her a professional sense of journalism as she wrote editorials, laid out copy, sought advertisers, and composed headlines. Her teacher in all this was, of course, Louis Howe, Franklin's most devoted backer. He told FDR that his "Missus" was becoming more filled with "political wisdom every day." A New York Times Magazine article said Eleanor was "the strongest argument against the charge that being involved in politics would make a woman "lose her womanliness and charm."

She was not confined to state issues, either. Mrs. Roosevelt had promoted a national contest for an American Peace Award. As she testified at a Senate hearing, Eleanor's photograph made the front of the New York Herald.

Between lobbying Albany for a reduced hourly workweek for women and children, being elected to the Leslie Commission advancing the cause of equal rights for women, and vigorously opposing the repeal of Prohibition—against her own husband's views—Mrs. Roosevelt had little time to dwell upon the lack of a physical relationship with Franklin. "More than anything else," she wrote in the May 1927 issue of Success magazine, political activity "may serve to guard against the emptiness and loneliness that enter some women's lives after their children are grown."

Sometimes politics consumed her so much that other particulars, like fashion, seemed ignored. She attracted attention at one appearance in a purple satin ankle-length dress, with brown tweed coat and shiny flat tan oxfords. She no longer had the time to argue with cantankerous Sara, who attempted not only to control her son's life but her grand-children's as well.

Eleanor had as much trouble with Edith Wilson. In July, she asked the former First Lady to serve on her women's committee. Edith replied that "plans made several weeks ago for rest" prevented her accepting, but assured her of "deep interest." Eleanor persisted, telling Edith she probably felt it "meant a great deal more work than it really does," and admitted, "I am most anxious to have your name simply to show your interest and willingness to cooperate with us . . . you would be most valuable to me if you would just let me know what you think [,] as time goes on [,] should be our line of work with the women in general and what you hear from different parts of the country."

This time Edith had her brother-secretary John answer that her "plans for the next months are so uncertain [that] she still feels it is better not to serve . . . even in the indirect way you suggest, as she would only be a name . . ." Eleanor was undaunted. She thanked Edith for "having taken the trouble even to listen," but wrote John rather firmly to please send her "a dozen photographs of Mrs. Wilson and a short biography . . . to use for publicity . . ." Just as firmly, Edith tersely scribbled, "Regret I cannot comply with your request as Mrs. W. objects to such publicity," but wouldn't sign it. Instead, John had to do so. At the end of August, Edith did write to say she hoped Eleanor was "not working too hard, and getting some recreation."[11]

Eleanor would be getting no rest. On election day, she learned that she was going to Albany as the new governor's wife. And Lou Hoover, her old friend from wartime Washington with whom she had played cards and entertained, was going to the White House. Few political wives were as alike as Lou and Eleanor. Both addressed controversial issues, did magazine writing, vigorously advocated that women become active in politics, and were political advisers to their husbands. Lou was actually better traveled, and conversant in a multitude of languages, unquestionably the most worldly woman to become First Lady. None but Mrs. Hoover had surpassed Mrs. Roosevelt's superior successes in public-welfare projects, and few had such a personal grasp of the diver-gent cultures and races of the world as the new First Lady.

While meeting a group of women reporters who gathered in her home after the election, Mrs. Hoover noticed how they stared at her signed Grace Coolidge photograph. Lou and Grace were close, the lat-ter calling the former "Lily of the Valley," who called her "Bleeding Heart." "If, four years from now," Lou told the group, "even one of you looks at my picture as you all seem to look at Mrs. Coolidge's, I shall feel I haven't lived in vain."[12]

On Inauguration Day, the two First Ladies laughed at an usher's joke as they exited the front door of the White House. They rode together up to the Capitol, where, in the rush of gathering officials walking the labyrinth of corridors, they became lost, and literally held up the ceremony. In the confusion, Hoover's choice of a Bible passage to place his hand upon as he took the oath was lost. Instead, it rested on another randomly chosen page, Proverbs II 9:18, which read, "Where there is no vision the people perish; but he that keepeth the law, happy is he." It foreshadowed something ominous.[13]

Though Mrs. Coolidge had made a little speech in the Black Hills about their similarity to Vermont's Green Hills, she had resisted making one for public audiences while First Lady. Now, appropriately enough, Grace spoke her first words into a microphone at Union Station, just as she was leaving. "Good-bye, folks," she piped into radioland, waved farewell, and turned away into the pullman. Tranquillity restored, she "suddenly realized I had come back to myself."[14]

She was headed home, to her old two-family rental unit in Northampton. Many were sad to see her go. And many were still confounded at just how much power she might have exercised. William Allen White expressed succinctly the frustration of many reporters: "To what extent Mrs. Coolidge has influenced her husband's judgement only two persons may testify. One is too silent to say, even if he realized it; and the other too smart!"

To the public, Grace would maintain, "We seldom discussed current events, history, [and] government . . ." But once again, she used a Coolidge clarifier. She said "seldom"—not "never." One issue "Mammy" had indeed discussed with "Papa" was the national economy, and she privately admitted that they deliberated on how it required increased federal spending activity, not saving, as he had done. After conceding that she had talked about it with the president, Grace Coolidge dropped a secret so devastating that it would have sent Wall Street reeling.

"Papa says there's going to be a depression."[15]

PART X

The Great Depression and World War II
1929–1945

In all the women's services the women are governed by exactly the same regulations as are the men . . . Rank, not sex, determines all questions of precedence . . . But with all this, it is hoped that the gallantry will not disappear permanently because many pleasant ways of life were given up "for the duration."

—EMILY POST
Wartime Edition (1945)

Scouting

MRS. HOOVER WAS in a bit of a quandary. Like Elizabeth Monroe, Lucy Hayes, and Caroline Harrison, she had the misfortune to follow a darling of the press into the first ladyship. Public-spirited Lou, with her impressive record, seemed uncertain. She was qualified to lead serious causes, understand international political nuances, and serve as a role model for American women of all ages. Was she to continue as a reformist leader as private person Lou Henry Hoover, or now to assume the more remote traditional public persona that the successful Grace had, with no interviews, no public discussion of politics, no involvement in controversial subjects?

Though most thought of her as a quintessentially progressive Californian, Lou was born in Iowa, but because of her mother's poor health, the family settled in Monterey. Her father, a banker, had taken her hunting, fishing, camping, hiking, and riding, and she became conscious of the mental benefit of physical exercise. Initially, she planned to become a teacher, but her life changed completely when she attended a geology lecture by a Stanford professor. She transferred to the university, and became the first woman in America to earn a degree in geology. In that department, she met Herbert Hoover. He courted her, and proposed by wire. She back responded with a one-word telegram: "Yes."

Married in 1899, Lou and "Bert" honeymooned en route to China, where he was to serve as a mining consultant to the emperor. They were caught in Tientsin when the Boxer Rebellion broke out, and Lou cycled daily to the hospitals, where she personally attended to the wounded. She refused to leave until the patients were also removed. In London, during the First World War, she organized the American Women's Committee for Economic Relief, to help get Americans stranded in Europe back home, as well as to provide help to those Americans who found themselves destitute overseas. In Belgium, she established the American Women's Hospital, and was later awarded the Cross of the Chevalier, Order of Leopold, by King Albert. Always working with Bert, she'd explored and lived in China, Burma, Tasmania, the Suez, Egypt, New Zealand, France, Italy, Japan, Australia, Russia, England, and Belgium.

She wrote scholarly articles on the dowager empress of China, seis-mologist John Milne, and the economic needs of Belgium, as well as translating from Latin, with her husband, the 1556 bible of geology and mining, *De Re Metallica* by Agricola. She had plans to write a history of Chinese culture, but her whirlwind activities prevented her from com-pleting it.[1]

Her Girl Scout work was her most visible endeavor. Having been sworn in as a troop leader by founder Juliette Low in 1917, Lou found the group appealed to her support of physical activity for women. Dur-ing the war, she had won universal praise for the vegetable gardens that she initiated through the scouts. In 1922, she had been elected national president of the Girl Scouts, holding that role for three years. Now, as First Lady, she was honorary president. To scouts, she preached pro-gressivism on issues like working mothers (". . . even after marriage it is possible for a woman to have a career"), the importance of woman's self-esteem (". . . [it] helps her develop initiative and personality"), and leadership (". . . more important to us than money are lead-ers . . ."). As First Lady, Lou managed to make her scouting role more than honorary. She conceived and financed their "Little House," a home built in Washington as a demonstration center, and initiated wildlife sanctuaries and, animal, botany, and geological studies.[2]

Her belief in women's physical power had led Lou to organize the

National Women's Athletic Association, and she had served as vice president—and only woman officer—of the National Amateur Athletic Federation. She espoused equal opportunity for women in competitive sports, and even thought sports might help stop teenage "spooning." The only woman to receive honorary degrees *before* entering the first-ladyship, and collect them rapidly once she was in the role, Mrs. Hoover was recognized by Mills, Whittier, Swarthmore, Elmira, Goucher, Wooster, and Tufts, honored as doctor of law to doctor of letters. She was an active member of the American Association of University Women and the National Geographic Society. So modern a Cabinet wife had she been that she told the DAR that short women's skirts were "sensible."[3]

Perhaps her most political work for women had been her founding of the National Women's Conference on Law Enforcement, in the aftermath of Teapot Dome. "Women of the country," she boldly said, "are tired of seeing the laws of our land ignored . . . We must arouse the whole country to an understanding of the dangerous significance of continued evasion of the law." That was radical stuff for the Republican wife of a Cabinet member of the Harding administration. Five hundred women had come to Washington from thirty-six states, and membership of all the clubs represented at the conference totaled ten million. It was no ladies' lunch.[4]

Lou was liberal in her public expression stating, "Women should get into politics. They should take a more active part in civic affairs, give up some of their time . . . for their duty as citizens. Whether we are wanted in politics or not, we are here to stay and [the] only force that can put us out is that which gave us the vote. The vote itself is not a perfect utility. It is only perfected in the way in which it is used." She equally advocated involvement in the League of Women Voters: "As a strictly nonpartisan organization the League can be and will be more of a power behind the throne than were it to enter the field as a third party . . . We need women as well as men in politics. To make a party whole there should be as many feminine as masculine minds."[5]

Working toward a political alliance with South American women, Lou had addressed the Pan-American International Women's Committee in perfect Spanish, and personally arranged for women speakers from thirteen Latin nations. Her egalitarian values extended to the public education system as well, believing that if it was less than exemplary, wealthy families would send their children to private schools, and society would eventually separate into an aristocratic elite and poorly educated underclass.[6]

The motives of Mrs. Hoover's whirlwind of public works were unquestioned. She wanted to contribute as much as she could to create a world of decency. But there was an obvious need to be politically cautious. In England, her support was restrained for the often violent British suffrage movement. "I never can feel I can play the 'Progress of Women,' against the 'Abstract Right For Humanity." A close friend, Mary Austin, who was jailed for her suffrage work, pressed Lou into become involved in the rights of American Indians and Mexicans. She resisted.[7]

Her public work, of course, preceded her first ladyship. When she assumed the role that could most benefit women, Lou Hoover spoke more generally. It was unquestioned that she believed in equality free of sexism in all phases of life. She hadn't changed her mind, only her willingness to express it. Three months after she became First Lady, Lou timidly expressed her belief that women should be afforded equal opportunity and that men must share in traditional women's work, by veiling it in terms of children. She advised little boys to "remember you are just as great factors in the home making of the family as are the girls."[8]

Paradoxically, she retained a sense of traditionalism. "Few girls," she said in one speech, "receive domestic training these days. A girl may be a good stenographer, bookkeeper, law clerk or politician, but few know how to bake a cake . . ." She said that women who used motherhood as an excuse for not working were "lazy." She didn't mention that most didn't have nursemaids.[9]

During the campaign, she had told a reporter, "Women in politics do not seem any different than men in politics. They are both human and voters, and frankly I don't think they are very different . . . I never thought that women were downtrodden by the men before they had the vote." She began to retreat. "I enjoy campaigning because my husband makes the speeches," she explained, "and I receive the roses."[10]

Less than eight months after the Inauguration, the news of October 29, 1929, with the newspaper headline that screamed WALL STREET LAYS AN EGG, did not alarm the First Lady. On "Black Friday," the stock market, sliding for several days, crashed to its lowest point.

The president reassured the nation that staying financially optimistic was the best way to avert what he judged to be a momentary panic. But as the following weeks, and then months, proved, this was no panic. Within fifteen months, as small and large businesses closed, five million Americans were unemployed. Food, clothes, even housing, were at a premium. The indigent ate in soup kitchens, or waited in "breadlines." Homeless families built paper, wood, and tin houses on the outskirts of towns, bitterly—and unfairly—calling them "Hoovervilles." Moderate and wealthy investors alike lost life savings.

As Lou Hoover saw it, this fleeting setback was the sort of challenge she could tackle with Bert, as she had a score of other volunteer efforts. Without cooperation from Congress, many of Hoover's visions for some government action couldn't be enacted. In the meanwhile, the First

Lady could rally the nation, as she had so successfully done during the war. But that was a war.

This was a "Great Depression."

— 49 —

Charity

WITH SNOW-WHITE hair, a plump figure, gentle, understanding blue eyes, and a beautiful, soothing voice, the fifty-nine-year-old grandmother was a First Lady who cared. The press knew that the private Lou Hoover was a compassionate woman, and her first months indicated that she might deftly play both traditionalist and activist. Publicly, however, she became more subdued, steadfastly refusing to publicly acknowledge the total bleakness the Depression was wreaking. Privately, she was well aware of it. She would not support the notion of radical government programs that might possibly alleviate some situations. There was no need to break precedents and invite criticism at a time when her husband was already being unfairly blamed for all the nation's ills. Charity had long been part of the traditional first ladyship. Now, it would have to become its main focus.

As reporter Bess Furman wrote, some of the efforts on behalf of the impoverished were embarrassingly silly. She covered a meeting of the board of the Red Cross, which resembled a ladies' tea rather than an emergency planning session. The socially prominent women, waiting for Mrs. Hoover to arrive, debated whether coat-lapel pins worn by one group of volunteers would offend others. "And the canteen women," as Furman wrote, "who toiled over hot stoves—could they not be provided with a striped uniform instead of the light blue that shows—with a visible effort they brought up the indelicate subject out in open meeting—perspiration stains?" When the First Lady entered the room, she smiled and shook hands but was genuinely appalled, particularly in light of the stated purpose to mobilize help for the indigent. "This is more like a kindergarten circle game than a dignified official board meeting," she chastised.

At that very meeting, Edith Wilson and Nellie Taft were making a rare appearance together. Six months following the crash, Chief Justice Taft died, and shortly afterward Nellie took off for Europe alone, beginning an annual tradition. Spring meant an annual trip to Charleston, summer to Murry Bay, Canada. During her months in Washington, she

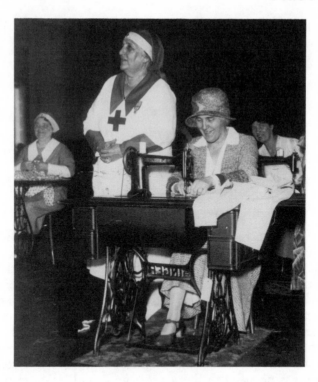

lived alone in her large brick house. Edith resisted committing herself to even bipartisan relief associations. Though she accepted the First Lady's invitation to join Nellie, Grace, Frances, and Edith Roosevelt as the Girl Scouts' honorary vice presidents, she refused Mrs. Hoover's request to join the National Women's Welfare and Relief Mobilization Committee.[1]

Upon returning to Northampton, Grace Coolidge joked to a friend to "kick me about a bit so I'll realize I'm human," but the crowds of the curious forced her and Calvin to buy a more secluded home, the Beeches. Here, she began typing out what amounted to a mini-memoir. "I sewed and wrote in turn until I became rather more interested in the paper than in the cloth . . . for several weeks, I wrote on in spare moments, unknown to anyone . . . not even my husband knew I was entering his 'field.'" Her series of articles were published in *American Magazine.* Grace remained popular, and was voted one of the nation's greatest women. But she didn't miss the trappings. On a trip to Washington, she visited the Hoovers, and when they came to visit Boston, the Coolidges paid a call on them. Mrs. Coolidge admitted that while "[i]t was interesting to see all the old guard," she was relieved "to walk out a free man and woman leaving them to their misery."

Now, Grace journeyed with Calvin to California, staying at William Randolph Hearst's gargantuan estate. She got stuck in an elevator, and told Hearst all he needed to do to improve the place was to import a cathedral. In Hollywood, she was guided through the studios by Mary Pickford and Douglas Fairbanks. But Grace was making a little "moving picture" of her own.

Now that she was out of the first-ladyship, Grace Coolidge surprised everyone when she accepted an offer to make a "talkie" short on behalf of the Christmas Seals drive. She appeared in a movie newsreel, ringing the Northampton Memorial Hall bell, and had her voice recorded. "I take great pleasure in the ringing of this bell to symbolize the opening on Thanksgiving Day of the twenty-second annual sale of Christmas Seals for the prevention of tuberculosis throughout the United States."

It was the first time a woman who would be, was, or had been a First Lady spoke for the movies.[2]

Because of the Depression, Mrs. Hoover initiated a bold new aspect to the first-ladyship, as she made one radio speech after another, advising the nation, particularly women and children, on how to help solve some of the welfare problems, insisting that there was "ample food and clothing for us all" if only people shared. Lou was a successful speaker. One staff member said she was "an interesting and intelligent talker, and spoke very rapidly, especially when she seemed to be a little more intent than usual." On the private floor of the White House, the First Lady even established a practice studio to rehearse her "talkie technique."[3]

On March 7, 1931, for example, she addressed the nation's children on NBC:

Don't neglect your plans for your future joy hours as well as for your . . . work . . . take concern for the welfare of others' lives . . . This year is one giving special opportunity for the consideration of others' problems of helpfulness. For this year more than usual there are more people in need of special care. More than usual in need of your care. There is something for each one of you to do in this emergency. A special achievement awaiting you. You have all read or heard so much of these times of Depression . . . prices are bad and unemployment has existed in industrial sections of our country. Indeed some of us will find the greatest problem is the problem of our family. Some of us are going to find actual need there. Perhaps the greatest need to be seen anywhere is our neighborhood. To know how to do without, cheerfully—how to decide what must be done this year for the ultimate good and what can wait until next year—how best to help the other members . . . how to help make a winter's campaign for achievement instead of submitting to an aimless day to day worry . . . We want to face it confidently, courageously . . . the attitude of the children . . . is going to help or hamper many families in pulling through these next months. There is nothing more discouraging than a moody, complaining child . . .

She used an example from her own childhood when a family of nine in her area had no money and limited food.

> The children of our neighborhood might have been more helpful in many little ways that winter if we had only noticed more carefully and realized that those children had absolutely nothing that cost money. We might have been more charitable . . . I think I have indicated indirectly here the fact that in daily friendliness, you can be a very essential help to all about you. But of course there are other and far more practical ways that you can find to be of more material assistance . . . to families . . . in actual want.[4]

Although the Hoovers spent their own money lavishly on imported foods for their sumptuous dinners, they also paid for the daily breakfasts, lunches, and dinners of nearly all of the fifty-eight-person White House staff. Lou was extremely generous in providing cash to anyone of them who needed assistance. She threatened a health-care director that she would have him fired if he didn't start giving proper care to a White House butler suffering from tuberculosis. Another, who had ulcers, couldn't afford the necessary cream and milk. Lou took care of it. She also offered to pay a maid's college tuition. Lou did not buy the innovative refrigerator because she didn't want the iceman to lose a client. Such private charity, however, was never used for public relations. Consequently, a misimpression set in deep.[5]

To Lou, housekeeping was a science, with daily meetings on the proper balance of food on menus, deliberations on furniture and fabrics, and even conferring after a reception to see how it could have been improved. She moved Martha and George Washington's paintings into the East Room. She personally paid for reproductions of some Monroe furniture, grouped them together, and established a Monroe Room. She did the same with Lincoln-era furniture when she moved the Lincoln Bedroom. She ordered a friend to compile the first historical survey of objects in the house. Lou was also a cinematographer of sorts. In the house, she established a room for editing the movies she took from her own camera, often showing guests the results.[6]

Privately, there was an unpretentiousness to her, a side the public never saw. She was bothered by having to have a Secret Service agent with her. Though she had been trained to use a gun in China, she never used or carried one in the White House. Grudgingly, she accepted the protection. She still insisted on driving her secretary's Ford V-8, in the nearby countryside. Protocol was of little consequence to her. She dressed less in fashion than Grace, and wore almost no jewelry or makeup. "It isn't so important what others think of you," she once remarked, "as what you feel inside."[7]

Doris Goss, Ruth Fessler, Mildred Hall, and Philippi Butler composed her First Lady staff—the largest to that time. Goss took over the job of social secretary from Polly Randolph, who served Lou into the first year. Ruth Fessler was in charge of Mrs. Hoover's organization and association work, except for the Girl Scouts. Mildred Hall was the First Lady's indispensable personal secretary, as well as her Girl Scout liaison, having worked with Lou since before the presidency. Additionally, she served as a press secretary and scheduling secretary. Hall paid the bills, opened the mail, and traveled with the First Lady. Sometimes she stayed until six in the evening, sometimes all night.

Philippi Butler had the most interesting of positions. She was personally assigned by the First Lady to take care of all her requests for help from those needing material assistance. Every single one of these letters received a response, and if a relief agency couldn't directly help, then one of her contacts in the private sector might. If this failed, Mrs. Hoover undertook the overwhelming responsibility of helping personally. From her own private monies, the First Lady sent a check, sometimes small, sometimes quite large. Whether it was for a pair of shoes or monthly groceries, Lou Hoover paid for it. If, down the road, someone paid back her "loan," she left the check uncashed, putting it in a large basket. Butler recalled that the contributions were sometimes made anonymously to the individuals "after receiving a report that the appeal was perfectly genuine and special help was deserved." Hoover was never to know of his wife's one-woman relief clearinghouse. Except for the official government social secretary, Lou paid all her staff's salaries.[8]

Mrs. Hoover maintained her office in a sitting room connected to her bedroom, while her staff worked out of offices upstairs. In her office, the First Lady's bed was covered with papers, and daily she read through all her public mail, passing it on to the appropriate secretary for response. None of the staff had ever seen a First Lady so dedicated to public issues in private. Lou was "so busy making decisions and selections that she worked like a day laborer." She would often lock herself in her room, working in bed, unavailable to anyone.[9]

In her public role, Mrs. Hoover assumed an admirable policy of refusing to lend her name to or join groups in which she couldn't be active. "I try to insist on not belonging to boards or committees on which I can not really work," she wrote.[10]

And yet, once again paradoxically, her press policy was less than warm. During the campaign, she had refused to talk to reporters, even on a supposedly sentimental trip back to Hoover's Iowa birthplace. She walked past the gathered public and press. When reporters caught up with her, resting in the train, she was curt. When asked if it were true that she spoke eight languages, she wondered why "the number had not been set at twenty-three." So uncooperative was she that reporter Bess Furman had to disguise herself as a Girl Scout in order to enter the house during a Christmas party, sing with the choir, hold a lantern, and then return to write her story.[11]

And yet, Lou liked the press to cover her Depression speeches. At a Buffalo Girl Scout convention, in August 1931, the First Lady addressed the role of women in the crisis: "The women of the country are half the people in it. The ones who are not in trouble will have to help the ones who are. One way is to keep on living a normal life. We should not curtail too many activities that are essential, because otherwise we throw the whole machine out of gear. If we stop buying things we need, employment will drop tremendously." Lou's timing was no accident. That month, economic indicators showed that, psychologically, consumer spending might enjoy an upswing. "There is no reason at all," she continued, "for just feeling sorry for ourselves over our present economic social problems. But there is every reason for each one of us to help solve the problem near us."

The *Chattanooga Times* found wisdom in the speech. "These few sentences spoken by Mrs. Hoover might well be framed and hung up in our homes, shops, banks, and factories for they have had particular sanity that the world itself holds to." To a group of magazine editors, Lou expressed the unquotable opinion that no single individual could be held responsible for the Depression, that other nations after the war had suffered economic collapse, which had an effect on America, and that citizens should initiate co-op stores and farms, as well as developing a barter-exchange system within the community.[12]

For the public, she also set examples. When the president ordered the Federal Farm Board to release five hundred thousand bales of cotton to the Red Cross for public relief, the First Lady directed a campaign toward supporting American industry by wearing homegrown cotton clothing, woven with modern rayon, as a sort of faux silk, which was imported from Japan. Editorials, like the one in the *San Francisco Chronicle*, praised her role after newsreels shown at the movies and newspapers carried the picture: ". . . Mrs. Hoover's original idea . . . is now receiving impetus by American women everywhere as an economic slap at the depression." The British *Manchester Guardian*, however, predicted "grave international complications" with Japan.[13]

The First Lady also sponsored a fund-raising effort conceived by the famous Polish pianist Ignacy Jan Paderewski, by hosting his Washington concert and arranging further ones in New York, Boston, Philadelphia, and Chicago, to benefit the Red Cross. She sent a personal check for nearly twelve thousand dollars, a monumental sum in the deflated value of the Depression dollar. With it, she issued a public appeal that "Mr. Paderewski very especially wishes it to purchase food for Americans hungry and in distress, so if you can see that it quite certainly goes for that purpose we will be carrying out the wishes of the generous donor [Paderewski]."[14]

During the tense administration, the Hoovers remained close and supportive. He would silently smooth her hair, and she "never missed an opportunity" to walk him, arm in arm, over to the Oval Office, where she would stay for a while "for a special conference that she would not otherwise have had an opportunity to enjoy." After every speech he made when they were apart, Lou sent him a supportive telegram. Her comprehension of some of the president's most complicated issues made her a valuable adviser. In time, she was even compared to Madame Chiang Kai-shek, the powerful wife of China's leader. The Hoovers did disagree on at least one issue, Prohibition. Lou Hoover thought the Volstead Act worthwhile, and it was she who got rid of the president's fine collection of California wines. "I don't have to live with the American people," the president sighed, "but I do have to live with Lou." She let it be known that she would leave any party where illegal alcohol was served, and Eleanor Roosevelt, for one, considered Lou's Prohibition stance "a very wise thing."[15]

The chief usher thought that the First Lady "occupied a peculiar position in her husband's official life. The president, moreover, was quite willing to have her do so, but he simply did not have time to share his responsibilities with her. She could, however, discuss official matters with anybody."[16]

She provided balm, too, surrounding him with friends and advisers, introducing him to young journalists, though they were often yes-men rather than individuals who could bring different perspectives. Early on, she realized that the White House was not the place to relax. But neither Hoover wanted to take vacations, which might appear callous during the Depression. So the First Lady created "Camp Rapidan," a solace away from statistical reports and market readings. Though unschooled in architecture, Lou was quite skilled in transferring her modern designs to paper. She had sketched and planned the stunning Spanish-style Hoover home in Stanford, with terraces for pools and musical concerts. She pulled out her sketchpads and got to work after discovering an isolated spot, inaccessible by cars, less than one hundred miles from the capital, twenty-five-hundred feet high, on the edge of the cool Blue Ridge Mountains, close to the Rapidan River. It became the first official presidential retreat.

A rustic sylvan setting, high in the sky, with mountain air wafting through the cabins, and the mist rising from rushing streams and waterfalls, it was a haven for the president. Here, in summer whites or warm wools, seated in blocky Mission-style chairs, the Hoovers flourished. Lou worked on projects and correspondence, met with political and Girl Scout leaders on the sprawling outdoor decks with thick green forestry framing her, giving the illusion of sitting in the trees.

But Rapidan was not confined to leisure. When Mrs. Hoover learned that neighboring mountain children had no school, she met with architects to plan a two-room school, hired a superb teacher, and paid for the entire endeavor, giving an education to children who would not otherwise have received one.

Impressed by the local Clore furniture plant, she made purchases and gave the firm a two-hundred-dollar loan on "the-five-year-without-interest-plan," after its factory was destroyed by fire. A local newspaper added that "as a result of widespread publicity following and amplifying our recent item about Mrs. Hoover," the Clore factory was getting a flood of orders.[17]

The president spoke proudly of the "loyalty and tender affection of an indomitable soul" that was Lou and her "gentle consideration for the rights and needs of others, no matter who." Lou proved this even as hostess. She felt that pregnancy was a ridiculous excuse for women to absent themselves from life, and encouraged expectant mothers to remain active and be seen as long as they could. At one affair, she gregariously welcomed an eight months' pregnant woman who'd followed her advice.[18]

As one who'd lived with peoples of the world, Mrs. Hoover believed in equality of the races. She once said that she could "lick the depression" with the help of a corps of organized blacks, who'd long suffered through other deprivations. It was in this vein of justice that she stood firmly on what was perhaps the most controversial decision of her first ladyship. She would welcome the black wife of black congressman Oscar DePriest, an Illinois Republican.

The decision was not made lightly. Both Hoovers, as well as his advisers, very carefully considered what to do. Entertaining a black could prove to be a political liability. During her first full social season as First Lady Mrs. Hoover had invited all other congressional wives to a series of teas, but the decision on what to do about inviting Mrs. DePriest was postponed. That season she was not invited, but that troubled the First Lady. Throughout the winter of 1930, the issue was discussed in the White House. Ike Hoover said Lou "seemed to have an open mind and was willing to be guided by whatever course was mapped out for her."

When President Hoover decided that the invitation was to be extended, Lou then "seemed hesitant and began to figure how it could be done," wanting to make sure that neither southerners nor blacks were offended. The First Lady decided to invite for one particular reception in her series, a group of congressional wives, who would not mind mixing with a black. The actual event, on June 12, was routine. Mrs. DePriest was received by the First Lady, spoke awhile with her and other wives, and was served tea, then departed with the group.[19]

What followed was the first national press controversy about a First Lady's racial views. For the first time in history, a state government officially reprimanded a First Lady, as the Texas legislature's House and Senate passed a resolution chastising Mrs. Hoover.

Southern newspapers took the same line. Editorials in the *Houston Chronicle, Austin Times, Montgomery (Alabama) Advertiser*, the *Memphis Commercial Appeal*, and the *Jackson (Mississippi) Daily News* vilified Lou. In the North, *The New York Times*, the *Boston Journal*, the *New York World*, the *Chicago Daily Tribune*, the *Cleveland Gazette*, the *Boston Evening Transcript*, and the *Topeka Plain Dealer* praised her, one editorial saying, "she put into practice the brotherhood of man . . ."

But the *Mobile Press* unmercifully said Lou "offered to the South and to the nation an arrogant insult yesterday when she entertained a Negro woman at a White House tea. She has harmed Mr. Hoover to a serious extent. Social admixture of the Negro and the white is sought by neither race. The Negro is entitled to a social life, but that the two races should intermingle at afternoon teas or other functions is inadmissible."[20]

Mrs. Hoover become even warier of the press, just as upset at the display of racism as the repercussions the issue might have had on her husband's hopes for reelection in 1932. The Hoovers didn't want to do anything that would further aggravate the South, and it led to another first. Lou became the first First Lady to make a public regional tour without a president. Originally, she had planned to join the president on an itinerary leading to Florida, but in the end he canceled. Mrs. Hoover made the tour of the coastal South alone in March 1932.

Through Georgia and Florida, the First Lady attended lily-white "ladies'" teas. Black groups were avoided. There were no tours of depressed areas. It was termed "unofficial," and like all their trips, "official" or not, the Hoovers paid for it. But it had a political purpose, as a *Washington Star* editorial noticed: "The First Lady of the land has furnished the best possible example of the indirect method of fostering the success of the Republicans in the South . . . Mrs. Hoover is exactly the type of womanhood to enlist the interests of Southern women.[21]

While Lou Hoover took tea, a serious and fearful problem was unfolding at home. In the winter of 1932, thousands of veterans began converging on Washington with their families, in hopes of convincing Congress to redeem the bonds they had received as bonuses, not scheduled for maturity until 1945. They became known as the "Bonus Army," and the sight of the nearly twenty thousand protesting veterans panicked security. With threats of imminent violence, police and Secret Service agents saturated the city. Congress refused to redeem the bonds, and by summer the disgruntled "army" set up its camps along the Anacostia River and in town, on military property. President Hoover sympathized, ordering medical supplies for the "army," and suggesting Congress issue them complimentary train passes back home. When a permit for protest in front of the White House was denied, a small group attempted to storm the property. Confronted by police, they were unsuccessful, and driven back. The White House became a fortress.

Mrs. Hoover was extremely upset on behalf of the "Bonus Army."

On one occasion, she ordered sandwiches and coffee sent out to them. It was kindly, but it did nothing to alleviate the gravity of their needs. The next day, she delivered a radio speech, avoiding direct reference to the marchers. "My plea is that our most important duty is to find when, how, and where people need help. We cannot be warm, in the house or out . . . if we do not know that it is possible for every child, woman, and man in the United States also to be sufficiently warmed and fed." At this point, the First Lady's voice cracked, but she continued, "We must give not only a helping hand, but a willing ear and an understanding heart to those about us in little or great need through no fault of their own." But she expressed her hopes from her safe radio room. She was not out at the desolate camps several miles away. [22]

Meanwhile, when some bonus huts had to be moved to begin a federal building project, a violent fight broke out. Security wanted the vets removed. Though the president ordered General Douglas MacArthur to move them with care, conscious of human dignity, the general ignored him. The huts were burned and the veterans' families treated brutally. Hoover was blamed for the scandal. [23]

MacArthur's most reliable assistant was Dwight Eisenhower, who privately detested his superior's cruel directive. Ike had to keep his opinion about MacArthur's actions to himself, but his emotions on another issue were different. His marriage was flourishing, and on his fifteenth anniversary he wrote Mamie praisefully ". . . that you have stood me for fifteen years is only another proof that you are the outstanding woman in the world. And since you love me—you are all the world to me." [24]

Herbert felt the same way about "my good lady who already knows all about a thing or else finds it out." He was open to all her plans. Had there not been a depression, Mrs. Hoover might have lobbied on behalf of projects that lay dormant. She believed that wilderness areas not considered national parks should still remain undeveloped, and had hoped to initiate some environmental protection. She had also wanted to begin a program that would bring Shakespeare to American schoolchildren. Still, the public associated her with administration endeavors, and she was even introduced at a ship launching as "the President's Chief of Staff." But that was becoming a dubious distinction. [25]

The Depression was worsening, and both Hoovers appeared woefully out of touch with the reality of the situation. A friend compared Lou to a garden "in that it seems so beautifully out of the rush and noise of the city, yet is in the heart of it. She is so seemingly untouched by all that is going on around her, yet is so vitally and keenly interested and involved in everything worthwhile." It was an ironic description. Though she grasped the fact that one reason the economy remained collapsed was due to loss of buying power, her wellintended response was naive. She bought new curtains for the White House. [26]

Had the First Lady visited a "Hooverville" and seen the vast extent of deterioration that the Depression had caused, her frustration might have reactivated her activism. Not everyone had time to sit and compose a letter to her, asking for money. Some had to sell apples on corners, scout for odd jobs, migrate each season for work, and give their children away to relatives who could afford to feed them. While the farmer and city worker alike woke up with desperation on their faces and hunger in their stomachs, the traditional symbol of benevolence on the marble steps, the motherly woman with a snowy head and a heart of gold, stood passively hesitant in the storm, a corsage pinned on her gray coat as the only public badge of courage. If Lou had continued to break barriers, people might have seen her humanity, but she retreated from public recognition. Perhaps she saw public role and true self as entirely separate beings—the "person" and the "personage," as the governor of New York's wife, Eleanor Roosevelt, named the two entities.

— 50 —

"... Overwhelmed at the Mere Possibility..."

THE REPUBLICANS RENOMINATED Hoover. Governor Roosevelt got the Democratic nomination. Associated Press reporter Lorena Hickok noticed that Mrs. Roosevelt seemed indifferent to it all. But Eleanor was glad for the chance to try to turn unemployment around and help the indigent, not just through private largess but government assistance. As she wrote Edith Wilson, it was "a great honor but such a great responsibility if by chance he wins that I feel rather overwhelmed at the mere possibility."

Eleanor had valiantly continued to try to lure Edith into politics. She gently wrote to get Mrs. Wilson's statement of support for a woman running for Congress. Edith responded that "having been in public life [you] know how essential it is to be consistent—and I have had to decline several similar requests." Eleanor responded, "I understand your position perfectly and rather expected you would say just what you have said." But when FDR won the nomination, Edith wired "congratulations to you, Mrs. Roosevelt and our Party." "Apolitical" Edith hadn't missed the convention, relishing the proceedings while fanning herself with a palm leaf and eating a cheese sandwich.[1]

The election was the impetus for Eleanor's reactivation in politics.

Upon Franklin's gubernatorial inauguration, she had publicly removed herself, fearing conflict-of-interest charges, resigning from her political groups, halting her lobbying and speeches, assuring him that "you see I'm being most discreet." Privately, she kept active. Though she removed her name from the masthead of the *Democratic News*, she wrote anonymous editorials. When asked if women running for office could be elected, she suggested they concentrate on "being of service." As governor's wife, she supported various groups she had worked with when they came to Franklin with their issues. She insisted on keeping her job as teacher at Todhunter, commuting from Albany a few days a week.

Nevertheless, with FDR's polio preventing him from much traveling or getting out of cars when he did visit an institution, Eleanor began playing a new role. She felt that "the ideal type of modern wife" was a partner, before mother or homemaker. Described by many as his "eyes and ears," she began to assume this role under his tutelage. He wanted to know about medical care, overcrowding, food quality, and assigned his wife to these inspections. At first, she wrote, "my reports were highly unsatisfactory to him. I would tell him what was on the menu for the day and he would ask: 'Did you look to see whether the inmates were actually getting that food?' I learned to look into the cooking pots on the stove and to find out if the contents corresponded to the menu. I learned to notice whether the beds were close together . . . I learned to watch the patients' attitude towards the staff, and before the end of our years in Albany I had become a fairly expert reporter on state conditions."

Her campaign role was vital. Jim Farley, a close adviser of Franklin's, called her "a strong and influential public figure in her own right," and a *New York Times* article referred to her as the "advance agent." She assisted in the writing of FDR's campaign biographies, and permitted herself to be photographed. She helped the women's division write and print the highly successful "Rainbow Fliers," Roosevelt campaign literature aimed at women, on various pastel-colored paper. Some joked that the campaign's only problem was "getting the pants off Eleanor and onto Franklin," and to the circle of men surrounding FDR during the campaign, known as the Brain Trust, Mrs. Roosevelt's "well-meant probings" could cause trouble with the Middle American voter. So public, so political, a candidate's wife could be a serious liability. This, combined with her own sense of propriety about promoting one's own husband, meant that she consequently was not out on the hustings during the campaign.[2]

As the campaign began, the Hoovers faced a hostile American public, even in their beloved midwestern plains. In Kansas, on his whistle-stop, the president's campaign train was pummeled with tomatoes. Disheartened, he turned to Lou: "I can't go on with it anymore." She put her arm around her husband, and gave him the strength to continue. But he wasn't the only Hoover to suffer under malicious smears and tactics. When Lou Hoover was addressing a Girl Scout convention, someone cut the radio wires that were to carry her speech. As a result of the DePriest criticism, a photograph of a fake Hoover home with a sign, NO WHITE MEN WANTED, was recirculated by enemies.[3]

Toward the end of the campaign, the First Lady belatedly realized the usefulness of the press. After Lorena Hickok of the New York AP had been churning out complimentary stories on Eleanor, Lou called in Bess Furman of the Washington office, saying she thought Furman would be interested in some facts of the First Lady's life. Still, she insisted that she not be directly quoted, to make it appear as if no interview had been given, as if the reporter had gathered information from another source. Lou Hoover, the woman who had made speeches calling for women's equality, made her one and only campaign speech in Iowa. Students called not for the president, but the First Lady. From the back of the train, she uttered, "I'm so glad to have my husband know you too."[4]

After receiving over three hundred congratulatory letters from the public who thought Franklin was her grandson or son, or worse, her husband, Edith Roosevelt decided the time was ripe to go public. She bought envelopes with Hoover's image, and then signed her frank on them. And the former First Lady took a very uncharacteristic step. She headed to the airport, spoke to the press, and even made a little speech "for the movies," as she put it. "I'm on my way to Washington." She still refused to be interviewed. "I haven't talked to the press, not in seventy-one years, and it's too late to begin now." As Edith Roosevelt flew into Washington, she was met by reporters, one of whom said the "fragile-looking little lady" sailed "strong as steel, through a tumultuous airport welcome, a White House garden party of large proportions, and a long political mass meeting in Constitution Hall that night." Soon after, Edith made her first public speech. On October 31, Mrs. Roosevelt addressed a vast political assemblage in Madison Square Garden, praising Hoover and urging voters not to vote for her nephew-in-law. After that, she slipped back to her less public Needlework Guild work.[5]

The national president of the Needlework Guild, however, was thrilled by the emergence of FDR, for whom she proudly voted. The Depression had mobilized Frances Cleveland Preston into public action. Though not political, Frances also did a great amount of public speaking, rallying local Needlework Guilds to continue their work as feverishly as possible, making warm clothing for the "ill-clad" of the Depression. While traveling to make a Chicago speech, she kept her needles clicking, creating white wool leg warmers. The former First Lady also participated in a most unique public-speaking endeavor "via radio from station WOR to the Girl Scouts of America . . . the first of a series of half-hour talks to be delivered by the wives of the ex-Presidents." Likely prompted by Mrs. Hoover, most of the sorority—Edith Roosevelt, Nellie Taft, Grace Coolidge—participated in this historic occasion. As a group, First Ladies had never done such a thing.[6]

Eleanor Roosevelt hoped campaign work might make her marriage closer. She emphasized "unselfishness" in an article, "Ten Rules for Success in Marriage," and said selfishness sometimes comes "through the desire of either husband or wife to be the dominating person in the household." Her closeness with handsome state trooper Earl Miller had not been romantic, though rumors were thick to the contrary, and even Sara sarcastically impersonated Eleanor's "Earl dear!" Franklin's intimacy with Missy LeHand, his secretary, was loving, but evidently confined to friendship.

Eleanor's campaign work was made efficient by her secretary, Malvina "Tommy" Thompson, and other people had begun entering her sphere, like Lorena "Hick" Hickok. The intense, almost radical social worker Harry L. Hopkins, serving as the governor's chief of unemployment relief, had been brought to FDR's attention by Eleanor's persistence, and he proved doggedly devoted to both.

These were the people who celebrated the Roosevelt victory, and would become part of Eleanor's own "New Deal"—a deal with FDR, the press, her family, Cabinet members, and social workers, with the impoverished and the willing, to help her forge her own radical interpretation of a powerful first ladyship.[7]

With "superhuman kindness," Mrs. Hoover gave a tour to the press "girls" of the White House rooms. With them, she hid well her bitterness, but she told a maid that her husband would live to do great things for America. She also said she wouldn't have voted for him, either, if she believed the lies circulated about him—that Camp Rapidan had been paid for by the government, that he ordered the bloody attack on the "Bonus Army," that he was somehow part of the kidnapping and murder of the Lindbergh baby.[8]

Meanwhile, Mrs. Roosevelt was trying to decide how she'd balance her public and private lives. She wrote that "for myself I was deeply troubled. As I saw it, this meant the end of any personal life of my own. I knew what traditionally should lie before me; I had watched Mrs. Theodore Roosevelt and had seen what it meant to be the wife of the president, and I cannot say that I was pleased at the prospect. By earning my own money, I had recently enjoyed a certain amount of financial independence and had been able to do things in which I was personally interested. The turmoil in my heart and mind was rather great . . . and the next few months were not to make any clearer what the road ahead would be."

In her first public act as "First Lady-elect," Eleanor came face-to-face with the woman she had "defeated," and a member of the new sorority she was about to enter. Along with her son James, Eleanor attended the funeral of Calvin Coolidge, who had died of a sudden heart attack, meeting briefly with her unpretentious predecessor, Grace Coolidge, with whom she struck a chord. Edith Wilson couldn't attend, but sent a sympathy letter. Eleanor had already written to Edith that she was "looking forward to seeing you often in Washington." Given an inch, Edith would take a mile.

With characteristic calm, Grace Coolidge ordered a simple New England funeral. Though incumbents Lou and Herbert Hoover attended, Eleanor's presence was unexpected, and Grace was warmed by the thought that Mrs. Roosevelt felt the Coolidge funeral important. Franklin's letter would have sufficed, but Eleanor's decision to attend was a sign of respect to Grace. Though they played utterly different roles, Eleanor and Grace shared a calm optimism that bonded them. After the ceremony, the two women chatted briefly, as Mrs. Roosevelt offered her formal sympathies. Frances Keyes felt that though Coolidge had "relied" on Grace, "completely and comprehensively, in a different way she leaned on him." Now, in a different way, she would be freer than ever.[9]

Eleanor was in quite a different position. She next saw Lou Hoover at the traditional changing of the guard, the tour of the White House by the outgoing First Lady for her successor. In spite of political animosities, they made a good go at it.

At the time, Eleanor was being criticized in the press for continuing her lucrative radio show, as well as editing a magazine, *Babies, Just Babies,* parodied by *Harvard Lampoon* magazine in an issue called "Tutors, Just Tutors." The *Hartford Courant* warned Eleanor that "being the first lady of the land is a full-time job in itself and that the dignity of the President and the country cannot but suffer when his name is used for commercial purposes." On a national radio show, with the commercial backing of a cosmetics company, Eleanor had made an argument that Prohibition failed to stop heavy drinking among the young. Unfortunately, she illustrated her point by saying young girls had to learn their liquor tolerance by trying "whiskey and gin, and sticking to the proper quantity." She raised a furor.[10]

Whatever Mrs. Hoover thought about all this, or the fact that Mrs. Roosevelt had refused her kind offer of a government car and military aide to escort her to the White House from the Mayflower Hotel, she kept to herself. Eleanor walked down Connecticut Avenue to the White House with no guard or escort.

After touring the public rooms and living quarters, Eleanor asked Lou to take her into the kitchen. As they neared it, Lou stopped, and pulled herself up. In four years, she'd never entered that territory.

"I'm sorry," she explained to Eleanor, "but the housekeeper will have to show you the kitchens. *I* never go into the kitchens." Embarrassed, the looming five-foot, nine-inch Mrs. Roosevelt thanked her profusely for the tour. Mrs. Hoover shook her hand. With that done, the kitchen doors swung open. And Eleanor Roosevelt walked in.[11]

– 51 –

". . . In with the Radical!"

THERE WAS A tiny rosebud vase in Lou Hoover's Monroe Room that Eleanor accidently broke as she lifted the delicate furniture out of the room to make way for her more durable Val-Kill factory pieces. While the chief usher was visibly startled to see a First Lady actually moving furniture, she was upset over the little vase incident, and secretively whispered the tale later to Cousin Alice. Eleanor had been worried that she had broken a delicate historic object. She had stared at the porcelain slivers a few moments. Then she swept them up and continued rearranging.

Alice teased her, "'Out with the old, in with the radical!'"[1]

Eleanor gave directions as she took flight down the halls, up the stairs—she disliked waiting for elevators—on her way to conferences, or in between dictation to her loyal personal secretary, Malvina "Tommy" Thompson, as she ran to catch a plane across the country, or a bus across town. Instead of taking the large First Lady's bedroom, she installed a narrow single bed in the dressing room, and used the grander room to work in when she was there. Which was not often.[2]

When Franklin told her to stop worrying about not having cash on hand because he ordered a bank holiday as his first economic-recovery move, she had an epiphany. She was now in a unique position during unique times. The intangible concept that clinical "New Deal" economists failed to grasp was the crippling malaise of spirit—something that could not be solved by a program. But Eleanor instinctively understood. When Louis Howe motored a timid First Lady over to the Bonus Army's camp, she didn't bring pension checks, just spirit. Lou Hoover had sent coffee and sandwiches from the safety of the White House; now, the First Lady was *in their camp*.

In all of this was a paradox. What some saw as radicalism, Eleanor Roosevelt cherished as a traditional value—the noblesse oblige or duty of the affluent to serve those less fortunate. Even her unusual marital arrangement retained that tradition. Whatever private tensions existed between Eleanor and Franklin, it was perfectly natural that they remained committed partners, helping each other help others. "... those who are not employed will need more than they have needed before . . . their courage is not as high as it was a year ago," Eleanor said over the radio in 1933. "So there is no reason for letting up in our sense of responsibility."

The severity of the Depression, the nature of her relationship with the president, and his dependence upon her to make his inspection tours all gave Eleanor Roosevelt the opportunity to break barriers. Having nearly two decades of professional experience with politics, organized labor, the press, rural issues, as well as careers in lecturing, teaching, and writing, she was superbly qualified to spur the changes she had been long spiritually motivated to make. Had the times been different, she might not have been able to expand the first ladyship to its limits.

Although admirers credited her with it, Eleanor hadn't consciously invented a "modern" first ladyship; it had been evolving. What she did was mobilize traditional components of a volunteer role into a "job," and though it may have sounded condescending to the ears of twentieth-century activists, she was the modern Dolley Madison. First Ladies would no longer be judged against Mrs. Madison. The new ideal would be Mrs. Roosevelt.

"I truly believe," she said, "that I understand what faces the great masses of people in the country today. I have no illusions that anyone can change the world in a short time . . . Yet I do believe that even a few people, who want to understand, to help and to do the right thing for the great numbers of people instead of for the few can help."[3]

She had never suffered from malnutrition or discrimination, never felt the terror of poverty, but Eleanor's experiences of psychological alienation and pangs of inferiority gave her a kinship with the neglected, and she instinctively saw the first ladyship as her springboard, a woman's version of the bully pulpit, as Uncle Ted had described the presidency. "I think in some of us there is an urge to do certain things and, if we did not do them, we would feel that we were not fulfilling the job which we had been given opportunities and talents to do." As she told civil-rights activist Gladys Duncan, "I am in a position where I can do the most good to help the most people."[4]

Mrs. Roosevelt's first decision proved her most enduring. Just forty-eight hours after the Inauguration, she conducted the first First Lady press conference, permitting direct quotes.

The press conferences had been arranged before the Inauguration, in New York, upon the advice of AP reporters Lorena "Hick" Hickok and Bess Furman. Just after the swearing in, as she took off her gloves, the new First Lady was interviewed by Hick.

She was somber, due to the "extremely critical times," but revealed her unique view of her role: "No woman entering the White House, if she accepts the fact that it belongs to the people and therefore must be representative of whatever conditions the people are facing, can light-heartedly take up residence here . . . It must be willingness to accept and share with others whatever may come and to meet the future coura-geously, with a cheerful spirit." She would be FDR's "eyes and ears."5

Mrs. Roosevelt cultivated her friendship with Furman, sending her flowers, permitting her to ride in White House cars and lunch in the mansion. Such kindnesses evolved casually, "on a basis of day-to-day camaraderie." Hick was already feeling her journalistic objectivity com-promised as an avid fan of Eleanor's, and Bess was equally admiring, but not as personally attached. Nevertheless, in the very inside track of the Washington press corps, what these two women were doing was en-hancing public relations. In turn, it helped sustain their careers, as well as those of sister journalists. Hick would prompt a pro-Eleanor story lead to Bess, who in turn tipped off the other women reporters, and suddenly, out in the far reaches of the country, Mrs. Roosevelt was being praised in the local papers. To those outside of this circle, of course, this chummy arrangement was not common knowledge. Nor was it common journalism.6

The press conferences were held in the Green Room, and the re-porters became known as "the Green Room girls." Shortly, politics slipped into the weekly events. When she talked about fashion, the First Lady remarked that she always thought there should be some sort of government label to indicate for women shoppers whether or not the dresses they bought were made under conditions of decent wages and working hours.7

When she was asked about Europe, the First Lady spoke with a premonitory sense: "We ought to be able to realize what people are up against in Europe . . . We've got to find a basis for a more stabilized world . . . Only a few years are left to work in. Everywhere over there is the dread of this war that may come."8

Across the globe, however, there were other dreads for other women. Mamie Eisenhower and son John would shortly join Ike in the Philippines, where he served on McArthur's staff. Walter Trohan, the bureau chief of the Chicago Tribune, said he knew "for an absolute fact . . . that Mamie had a high opinion of MacArthur and convinced her husband to go to the Philippines with him . . . Ike told me that and she prevailed." In Manila, during FDR's first term Mamie was confined to her hotel rooms because of health problems, from a stomach hemor-rhage to a near-fatal coma. She recuperated, propped up in bed, pink bow binding her bangs, writing, reading, or playing solitaire. As she strengthened, Mamie began inviting other women in for mah-jongg games, and like Nellie Taft, ignored the unwritten code of segregation between Caucasians and Filipinos, asking native women to attend. One night, after a bridge game with other army wives and their husbands, she invited Madame Hebibi, Manila's most famous Gypsy fortune-teller, to read their cards. Hebibi predicted that Ike would someday "be president . . ." and he retorted that perhaps he'd soon head an officer's club. Mamie's reaction went unrecorded, but even her star was rising. When they later left the Philippines, President Quezon awarded Ike the Distinguished Service Medal, and asked Mamie to pin it on her husband. A battery of cameras flashed, and for the first time her picture was in newspapers.[9]

Having her picture and quotes in the paper was commonplace to Eleanor. In fact, a woman's comments seemed no longer confined to recipes and parties. Mrs. Roosevelt's press conferences held professional implications. In one fell swoop, "the Green Room girls" had their level of importance—as well as their own consciousness—raised. The "girls" became invaluable to their male editors, and since Eleanor specifically banned male reporters, to ensure these women's jobs, they were often-times scooped on news the President's Office had not yet announced. One Furman AP story read, "Give Mrs. Roosevelt a roomful of newspaper women, and she conducts classes on scores of subjects, always seeing beyond her immediate hearers to the 'women of this country' with whom she would share the quickening thought-streams that pour over a President's wife."[10]

At the conference, she welcomed "girls" visiting Washington, thereby ensuring herself good press when she toured the country. She asked experts—like Mary Anderson of the U.S. Women's Bureau—to address timely issues, and invited guests visiting the White House—Ishbel MacDonald, the Canadian prime minister's daughter—to speak with reporters. The First Lady's personal secretary and social secretary were always there, the latter with social news, the former taking rapid-fire dictation.[11]

Some "girls" also traveled with her on public trips. When she thought their presence might be unwelcome by the group she would be meeting, Eleanor acted as journalist herself, providing news and quotes. Her fostering of women in journalism permeated society. After receiving her history degree from the University of Texas in 1933, Lady Bird Taylor studied for another year to earn her journalism degree because she thought "that people in the press went more places and met more interesting people, and had more exciting things happen to them." As a reporter for the Daily Texan, Miss Taylor forced herself to become more public.

She was not meek, however, and one beau surrendered when he realized "it would take a strong man to be the boss . . . she would not marry a man who did not have the potentiality of becoming somebody." Another called her "determined . . . ambitious and able." She took more courses to develop business savvy that could ". . . get you inside the door," so "with a little skill and a great deal of industry, you can go on and take over the business—or else marry the boss." Considering her ambition, it was understandable that she thought it "some kind of joke" when, on her first date with the secretary to U.S. Congressman Kleberg, he asked her to marry him. Almost as surprising was her acceptance shortly after the proposal. "I knew I had met something remarkable, but I didn't know quite what . . ."

Suddenly, in 1935, Lady Bird found herself in Washington, guiding herself alone through the city because her demanding and often insensitive husband defaulted on his promise to do so. When he refused to read important sections of government reports that she had underlined for him, she followed this six-foot, three-inch man consumed with political ambition, reciting them to him. But Mrs. Lyndon Baines Johnson was as self-reliant as Mrs. Roosevelt.[12]

Amazingly, Mrs. Roosevelt had a staff of only two. At an annual salary of thirty-five hundred dollars, Tommy was the first member of a First Lady's staff to be paid as personal secretary, but when she worked on Eleanor's personal business, she was paid by her. A former employee of Edith Wilson, Edith Benham Helm, first volunteered to help Eleanor as a part-time social secretary, and her role quickly evolved into a full-time job. Her role was not politically superfluous, for Mrs. Helm briefed her boss with important background details on guests. At first, they were headquartered in two small rooms that—phone ringing, First Lady dictating, aides running—the chief of protocol dubbed "The Girls of the Second Floor Front." In time, the distaff as well the military social aides who helped at functions were stationed in the newly built East Wing.[13]

Tommy's role as stenographer became particularly significant when the First Lady signed a contract with a syndicate to do a daily newspaper column, "My Day." Like the press conferences, "My Day" was originally intended to focus on facets of the First Lady's day that appealed to traditional women—family, housekeeping, and entertaining—but they, too, became infused with politics. Each morning, nearly every American citizen could read the paper and learn what Eleanor was doing, thinking, and saying. The whole notion of a president's wife going so public was astounding, and "My Day," along with the press conferences, made the First Lady all the more a part of American life. Admitting it served as FDR's "trial balloon," she said, "If some idea I expressed strongly—and with which he might agree—caused a violent reaction, he could honestly say that he had no responsibility in the matter and that the thoughts were my own."[14]

At five hundred dollars a minute, Eleanor also contracted to do weekly radio speeches sponsored in different years by mattress, typewriter, shoe, and soap companies, turning over her income to charities. Then, at a thousand dollars per appearance, Eleanor contracted with a professional lecture service, making a national tour twice a year, dis-

cussing topics like "Mail of a First Lady" and "A Typical White House Day." Hundreds turned out for her speeches. In time, she was earning $100,000 a year, and the charge that she was exploiting the presidency for personal profit provoked the initial wave of severe criticism against her. For the first time, the personal tax returns of a First Lady were examined by request of a suspicious Congress wary of her activism. Her earnings all went to charity.

Besides the radio, lecture, and newspaper work, Mrs. Roosevelt penned a column for *Woman's Home Companion* magazine, and later a Q-and-A page for *Ladies' Home Journal.* In her August 1933 *Companion* column, she implored citizens, "I Want You to Write to Me." It provoked an avalanche. In 1933, she received 300,000 pieces of mail, and though it would dip to 90,000, it rose again to 150,000. She sometimes got 600 to 700 letters a day, and though there were twelve correspondence-division employees to help, Tommy handled all of Eleanor's personal correspondence, which was substantial. Sometimes the public wrote to her as they had to her predecessors—to get to the president— but the vast majority addressed her because she was emerging as a symbol. When she discovered form letters from Frances Cleveland's day still in use, Eleanor redrafted them, and every one of the tens of thousands of citizens received a response, often from a New Deal government agency established to help solve their particular problem.

In one letter, an Italian immigrant complained that he did not qualify for relief aid because he didn't have children. So he asked Mrs. Roosevelt to send money so he could bring his progeny over from Italy. Such letters frustrated her. "I do not think," she wrote, "we have done a very good job in publicizing the various functions of the government agencies, because people write me, and we find the address of the nearest place for them to apply, and often it is practically around the corner from where they live." Still, she considered it part of the job. "I think I have been asked to do something about everything in the world except change the weather!" Mrs. Roosevelt admitted that the majority of her mail criticized her for jeopardizing the role's dignity. Undaunted, she would respond that they had a right to their opinion, but "I answer and tell them why I do it . . . Everyone must live his own life in his own way."[15]

Mrs. Roosevelt broke a second precedent when she traveled to the Caribbean without Franklin on what would become her trademark "eyes and ears" inspection tours. Her justification was simply to investigate personally "what really was the condition of people in Puerto Rico," whom she was told bore witness to "three generations of poverty." It was also at the specific bidding of FDR, who wanted an investigative report on the feasibility of federal revivification of the antiquated rum industries as a means of economic restoration to combat poverty, illiteracy, and overpopulation. She was accompanied by the press, and Hick.

Months earlier, the First Lady had chastised the agriculture secretary when surplus pork was used as fertilizer instead of food donations for the poor, and she exerted her power to have the latter task carried out for the Puerto Ricans. Even though the natives gathered at a San Juan relief office were unaware of this, they cheered her as the symbol of America, waving bundles of "NRA pork." In San Juan, the poverty-stricken children greeted her as a saint, as she traipsed undisturbed past human refuse and muddy pools, and they clustered about screaming, "¡La Presidenta!" In St. Thomas, she told the first-ever mass gathering of native women, "No matter how little you have done in the past, reach out for influence and try to use it to make your government respond to what is best for your homes." The American First Lady was greeted by the Dominican Republic's president's wife, who evidently liked the Yankee title and had her own limousine engraved with brass plate, "Primera Dama de la República."[16]

As Hick watched Eleanor, she realized that the First Lady was never to be the exclusive companion she had first hoped. Having developed a deep emotional bond, they exchanged what some described as passionate letters, and Hick even gave her a ring. Unquestionably, Eleanor loved Hick, but she also loved many other people, men and women alike, and her letters to this circle were all effusive. Much was read into these friendships. With respect to Hick, a granddaughter, for one, thought that Eleanor had "difficulty being intimate with her husband, let alone others."[17]

To rest from the trip, Eleanor took a coast-to-coast auto trip, popping up everywhere—from a bucket crane carrying her over the Norris Dam to the Blackfeet Indian Reservation, where she was named "Medicine Pipe Woman." In a small Canadian hamlet, she was thrilled when introduced to an old-timer who asked if she was related to the great Teddy. He seemed to be one of the few in North America who had not heard of Eleanor Roosevelt. The absolutely fearless First Lady's travels endeared her to a vast cross-section of the citizenry. Even after a dreaded respite with relatives in Newport, where it was feared society would ignore a dinner party in her honor, there was an eager turnout of swells. By fall, she had logged twenty-five thousand miles. By the end of a full year, she had traveled thirty-eight thousand miles, her second year—forty-two thousand, her third year—thirty-five thousand. Soon after, it was impossible to track.[18]

Mrs. Roosevelt preferred flying, and in her attempts to lend public support to the industry, she accepted her friend Amelia Earhart's invitation to make a night flight to Baltimore, along with some "girls." When given the co-pilot's seat and offered the controls, however, she hesitated, at least for the moment. She also went down in the coal mines. On a West Virginia trip, Eleanor delighted the nation when she put on a helmet and descended into a mine, as she did elsewhere across the country, resulting in a famous New Yorker cartoon showing two miners looking toward the entrance, one exclaiming, "For gosh sakes! Here comes Mrs. Roosevelt." The press forgot that Julia Grant and Lucy Hayes had also descended into the mines.[19]

Not everybody took her activities lightly.

One critic was a woman by the name of Pauline Pierce, daughter of a judge. Her husband was a native Ohioan like herself, and while they lived in toney Rye, Marvin Pierce was a self-made man. He had worked his way up in the publishing business to become president of the McCall Corporation, which owned not only the women's magazine by that name but dress-pattern publications as well. Their adolescent daughter Barbara, a student of public grammar school, believed that her parents "probably had an influence" on her own interest in reading, both being "great readers," yet stated frankly, "I was not a great student, but I had many good teachers."

The last of four children, Barbara recalled vividly her mother's dislike of Mrs. Roosevelt, Eleanor having been "the First Lady from my seventh year on." Barbara's own memory of Eleanor was that she'd been "very visible," and "highly praised and highly criticized." Of the First Lady's earnings for "My Day" and her radio work, Barbara would reflect, "I guess that opens one to more criticism." She noted that her father "respected" Mrs. Roosevelt, and he, along with Pauline, was invited to the White House to meet the First Lady at an event for publishers. Barbara recalled that after her Republican mother personally spoke with Mrs. Roosevelt, she "then raved over her."[20]

Sometimes Democrats were Eleanor's harshest critics. Interior Secretary Harold Ickes was particularly annoyed at her, "the most outspoken critic," of his bailiwick, and he wished she would "stick to her

knitting and keep out of the affairs connected with my department."
When she refused, he eventually resigned because "a constant repeti-
tion of these groundless charges on her part is bound to have an effect
. . . on the President." Paul Pearson, governor of the Virgin Islands,
said she "handicaps him [FDR] politically . . ." When, on the radio,
she called on Congress to support FDR's request that America join the
World Court, many legislators criticized her, and rejected the proposal.

If such men disapproved of the First Lady's visibility, there was little
they could do, for she had the complete support and encouragement of
the president. "Lady, it's a free country," he once told her, "if you get
me in hot water, I'll manage to save myself." To outsiders, he defended
her travels, saying, "My missus goes where she wants to, talks to everybody, and does she learn something!" Her "eyes and ears" role proved
itself successful early on, after the Caribbean trip. FDR used her reports
as background material, and proudly wrote her, "Everywhere, they
spoke of your visit." If experts came to him with information that contradicted her more honest investigations—often left as reports on his
night table—he contradicted their rosier versions by opening with,
"Yes, but my missus tells me . . ."[21]

Eleanor claimed that the "political influence . . . attributed to me
was nil, where my husband was concerned. However, one cannot live
in a political atmosphere and study the actions of a good politician . . .
without absorbing . . . politics . . . though Franklin always said I was
far too impatient to be a good politician . . ."[22] While she publicly
maintained that stance, many others disclaimed it. Her son Elliott recalled a typical parental exchange:

"I know I shouldn't bother you with these things, but it's the only
chance I have to talk with you nowadays," the First Lady pressed the
president at dinner.

"Let's fix a time in the morning," came the response.

"I would prefer to talk now, Franklin."

"Fire when ready," he resignedly sighed.[23]

– 52 –

Power and Influence

SHE WOULD ADMIT that "I felt sure I would be able to use the opportunity which came to me to help Franklin gain the objectives he cared
about . . . I think I acted as a spur even though the spurring was not

always wanted or welcome." She said he "might have been happier with a wife who was completely uncritical," and conceded, "I was one of them who served his purposes."[1]

But his purposes were sometimes hers. She was indirectly responsible for the National Youth Administration's creation. After being approached by Harry Hopkins—head of the National Relief Administration—and Aubrey Williams, who were unable to get FDR's time to discuss their program to keep youths in school as well as work, the First Lady went to him. Along with some of her own suggestions, she detailed the entire proposal. "If it is the right thing to do for the young people," he agreed, "it should be done." FDR adviser Rexford Tugwell called her "keeper of and constant spokesman for her husband's conscience." Upon Franklin's suggestion, speechwriter Sam Rosenman often sought her "helpful" advice on speeches. As Harry Hopkins explained, "She continually impressed . . . that we must not be satisfied with merely making campaign pledges, the President being under moral obligation to see his domestic reforms through . . . she hoped neither the President nor I thought it was settled in any way by making speeches."[2]

Others came to perceive that moral influence over FDR. When economist John Kenneth Galbraith was planning munitions plant sites, and wanted them built in the impoverished South, he asked textile manufacturer Donald Comer if he could get him into see the president to approve the sites chosen. Comer replied that it was "far more important to get to Mrs. Roosevelt." He did so, the First Lady backed him, *and,* in a few weeks, Galbraith learned that "we had the support of the President." The economist later dubbed her "Eleanor the Good."[3]

Few were more loyal to New Deal ideals than the First Lady. Morally, she believed "that the government had an obligation to give its people security as well as freedom in a world which could shift suddenly from prosperity to depression." This commitment led her into acting as an unofficial administration spokesperson, not so much for FDR as for herself, and she made that clear. "As time went by," she thought, "I found that people no longer considered me a mouthpiece for my husband but I realized that I had a point of view of my own with which he might not at all agree. Then I felt freer to state my views."[4]

Stumping for the New Deal, she debated so disarmingly that critics were often left confounded. Subtly pushing her liberalism, she told one group of law students, "The code of ethics is changing. The things that were all right ten years ago are not now, because people as a whole are changing in their standards, I believe for the better. You are for what is good not only for you but for your fellow citizens. This is the new social-minded code. You do not wish special privileges. You wish privileges for all. With this code goes an open mind—a real inquiry into how to use that mind to best advantage. With it goes a real determination that what you have gained you are going to give back to your country and its people, not only looking to your own gain, but to the gain of others. You will never get the greatest joy of living until you feel you are one with a great many people—a whole country perhaps." What made the speeches all the more convincing was that almost none were ever read from prepared texts. Her words sprang from her heart and mind.[5]

An occasional "Green Room girl," Liz Carpenter of Texas, examined the First Lady's politics, and later commented, "She was willing to be the catalyst and the trial balloon for liberal causes. She was intensely interested in them, and probably much truer to them. She had that whole coterie of women who were out of the Department of Labor— the women's bureau—which was really the cutting edge of liberalism in the New Deal . . . Eleanor would bring those people into her press conferences." Carpenter was impressed, and never forgot the ability it afforded for a network of political women.[6]

Son Elliott felt that Eleanor "did want power and influence, provided it was in her own right and her own name," and as a sort of "evangelist" quickly developed her own following. Whether she did so consciously, Eleanor exuded power. As John Kenneth Galbraith recalled, he never saw her "without a certain sense of trepidation . . . That sense of anxiety, tension, is the feeling anyone exercising power must induce. This she did."[7]

White House staff member J. B. West described how Eleanor worked politics for herself as well as the president: "There would be at least three or four or five sometimes for breakfast . . . government people . . . lower, not Cabinet rank . . . but people who wanted things done by the President, and they worked through her . . . it was never really out in the open . . . she was more . . . well, smart about it . . . She was strictly a politician." To get the best sources on any number of issues, she frequently summoned people—"from the trashman to the president of a motor company."[8]

Whether it was to a Cabinet member or labor leader, her granddaughter Ellie Seagraves recalled, "She was terrific at writing letters, she'd dash off dozens of notes or dictate, or send stuff from her mail to other people—with recommendations . . . It wasn't her job to make recommendations, but sometimes she'd say 'I'd like a report or a follow-up,' but she never ordered anybody to do something." West recalled that the only time she expressed anger was if interrupted while toiling on her correspondence.[9]

"Eleanor's people," however, were rarely "Franklin's people," said West, who "never" saw the couple alone together in the same room. Publicly, when the occasion called for it, they appeared together, even bussing each other for photographs, but the understanding they had reached years before about maintaining separate lives, interests, and friends remained intact. Still, West said, it was also "completely equal."[10]

Ironically, it was their estranged personal relationship that afforded their close political one, but those who believed the couple devoid of emotional attachment were mistaken. On their first wedding anniversary in the White House, Franklin penned an affectionate note to his "Babs," attached with a check:

"After a fruitless week of thinking and lying awake to find whether you need or want undies, dresses, hats, shoes, sheets, towels, rouge, soup plates, candy, flowers, lamps, laxation pills, whiskey, beer, etchings or caviar I GIVE IT UP! And yet I know you lack some necessity of life—so go to it with my love and many happy returns of the day."[11]

Still, it seemed obvious that Eleanor's complete involvement in other people's lives was, in part, a substitution. Her sense of daring also added a degree of adventure that was missing at home.

The First Lady remained adamant that she not be shadowed by Secret Service agents. As granddaughter "Sistie" recalled, she was "a fatalist." She did accede to the Service's request that she learn how to use a gun. "I am a better shot each day," she wrote Bess Furman, "I'm practicing daily . . . taught like a prison guard, and I am making as many as four bull's-eyes out of six shots!" Practice did not mean use. "Sistie" said the First Lady considered carrying the gun to be "pointless."[12]

Eleanor was more fearless than Franklin. Behind his laughing élan lurked a terror of fire, because of his disability, and he was less lax about security, having nearly been shot before his Inaugural. Bullets intended for him killed Chicago Mayor Cermak.

Anton Cermak was replaced by Ed Kelly, loyal Democrat, Roosevelt ally, and friend of Edie Robbins, the new wife of conservative Republican Chicago neurosurgeon Loyal Davis. Daughter Nancy was thrilled with Edie's 1929 remarriage, and her new home in a luxurious Lake Shore Drive apartment. She attended the Girl's Latin School, and became president of the dramatic club, starring in George S. Kaufman's *First Lady*. With Dr. Davis, she said she "grew up" as she emulated his conservative "principles." At fourteen, upon her own initiative, Nancy asked her natural father to legally relinquish her. In fact and name, she was Dr. Davis's daughter, and unflinchingly enjoyed watching him perform brain surgery. Edie Davis, however, remained a Democrat, involved in city politics and helping the mayor with voice lessons.[13]

If Mrs. Davis maintained a busy schedule, the First Lady kept a frantic one. After an invigorating 7:00 A.M. ride in Rock Creek, it was breakfast—which meant discussions with everyone from house guests to congressmen circling around her on chintz-printed chairs before the fan-shaped window. Afterward she headed to her little office and dictated "My Day" to Tommy. If it was a Monday, then it was time for the press conference. Throughout the day, if she was in the mansion working, she popped in and out of the Chief Usher's Office with lists of people who would be coming to see her at odd hours. As J. B. West recalled, the First Lady "never took a meal alone . . ." Lunch was merely more worktime, with bank presidents, social workers, labor leaders, congressmen, and a person she might meet on the street. She arranged the seating.

After lunch, it was correspondence work, after which she quickly met with several large groups of callers, rapid-fire, one after the other, while serving tea. Some afternoons she hosted East Room conferences on New Deal welfare issues, listening from the front row, occasionally voicing an opinion, otherwise following the proceedings while her hands furiously knitted away, the needles clicking as the conferees debated. Dinner often meant heated banter with government-agency chiefs whose work she was specifically interested in—subsistence housing, WPA's art program, NYA. Franklin was rarely present, though Eleanor always reported the information she had gathered. Through her entire tenure, she would never waste meal time by eating alone. Eleanor told a reporter, "I have trouble going to bed when all these night conferences are going on—I am so curious I have to stay up and see what happens." Her days lasted often until 3:00 A.M., when she finished her handwritten letters to friends and family.[14]

Sistie's remark that her grandmother had "extraordinary good health, energy, and drive" seemed a monumental understatement. Occasionally, she took ten-minute catnaps, and would "later wake up and resume her conversation."[15]

When in town, Mrs. Roosevelt made her presence felt. In time, the city's welfare became her concern, and using the Democratic party's Discover Your Home Town Project, she began a series of unannounced tours to a multitude of public institutions, taking congressional wives with her. At one school, she marched them from basement to attic, and with the expertise of a handyman, pointed out leaky plumbing, poor ventilation, and bad lighting. Of the District government, she said, "I never knew a place where things moved more slowly." Eleanor's interest led her to testify in Congress before the House District of Columbia Committee. Chairman Jennings Randolph proudly told her before a packed committee room full of spectators and press, "Mrs. Roosevelt you are the first First Lady of the land who has appeared before a Congressional Committee. I can assure you that we are deeply appreciative of your presence . . . would you please tell the Committee about the conditions as you found them on your visits to the various welfare institutions." She restrained her anger, but began by criticizing a retirement home: "Mr. Chairman, if this is our conception of how to care for the aged, we are at a pretty low ebb of civilization . . ." and then a children's home: ". . . the story should be told, and told and told!"[16]

In Washington, Mrs. Roosevelt also revived Ellen Wilson's alley-clearance work. Driving over in her own blue Buick to inspect the slums, she toured unannounced. Through the city's Park and Planning Commission, she instigated slum-clearance legislation, eventually brought before Congress again, recalling Eleanor's days as a sub-Cabinet wife with Mrs. Wilson.

Mrs. Roosevelt was also making an indelible impression on the young congressional wives. Lyndon Johnson won a House seat of his own—campaigning with ten thousand dollars his wife borrowed from her father against her inheritance. Lady Bird didn't have "the vaguest" idea of what a First Lady was supposed to do, but she was avidly pro-Roosevelt, and cast her first vote for him. She never expected to see Eleanor, "except from the street as she went by in the car." That changed after a meeting of the Congressional Wives' Club.

"We got together once a month, and we decided, 'Gee, wouldn't it be wonderful if we could get Mrs. Roosevelt to be our honored guest?' One member of the club . . . said . . . 'I know of a real deserving fine young man who is crippled and cannot afford a wheelchair . . . I bet if we charge for the luncheon tickets, everyone would love to bring some guests. And if Mrs. Roosevelt would just come, we could make enough to buy that wheelchair.' It was presented to her [Mrs. Roosevelt], and what do you know—she accepted! Because helping an individual—or a whole segment of the population—was her role in her eyes." When the First Lady "got out of that big black car," Lady Bird took some short movies of her walking in.

Soon, Mrs. Johnson was to have "a very interesting hour" with the First Lady, who invited congressional wives to join her in the alley inspections. Lady Bird, among them, recalled, ". . . I remember a smallish group, twenty of us, let us say, sort of trooping along behind her long, purposeful stride, and it was an eye-opener. We had never been there, we really didn't know what it was like." Mrs. Johnson never forgot the urban blight. She also savored one particular evening: "Tonight," she recalled in her diary, "I went to my first (will it be my last and only!?!) Dinner at the White House!"

The Alley Dwelling Act received only $500,000 in funding, with a presidential public-works-fund addition of $365,000. That fell far short of the necessary $3 million. Though forty-four alleys from forty-one squares were cleared, only about a quarter of the actual dwelling units were demolished. As the administration shifted its goals, the hope for new low-cost housing fell by the wayside. Perhaps some future First Lady would revive the Wilson-Roosevelt dream.[17]

Although Mrs. Roosevelt had no "special project" because everything was a special project, she did focus on issues close to her heart, like homestead subsistence, specifically Arthurdale, for unemployed West Virginia coal miners.

The whole notion of the government's purchase of land and the building of homesteads in planned utopian communities—which the miners would pay back over several years—was perhaps the most intangible project of the administration, but it was exactly the challenge Eleanor wanted. Told of the area's poverty, she made unannounced inspections. She conferred with the Subsistence Homesteads Division chief, Interior Secretary Ickes, and Harry Hopkins. She hired architect Eric Gugler to design a post office, a factory to produce postal boxes, motel, church, theater, and three prototype homes, and personally paid for Elsie Clapp to devise a workable education system and teach in a school there.

On one typical Arthurdale trip, Mrs. Roosevelt, "the girls," and Bernard Baruch—who donated vast sums to pick up any slack in Arthurdale funding—left Washington at 11:00 P.M., and arrived in Arthurdale at 6:30 A.M. Immediately, the First Lady made a fifty-mile motor tour, delivering three speeches—all before a 9:00 A.M. breakfast. Then it was a college commencement, inspection of two farming communities, a battlefield tour, and eight more speeches, covering another 150 miles by car. All in a routine nineteen-hour Eleanor day.

From its inception, Arthurdale seemed doomed. Conservatives balked at Mrs. Roosevelt's "socialism." The Indiana firm contracted by the government to provide the postal boxes successfully exerted pressure on that state's congressman, Louis Ludlow, to stop funding for the Arthurdale factory. Criticism reduced funding necessary to a successful project, and financially Arthurdale proved a failure. But, as one Arthurdale teacher said, "In spite of all the mistakes . . . Mrs. Roosevelt's ultimate aim, that of providing children with more desirable surroundings and better opportunities for all-around development, has been realized." Dozens of girls named after Eleanor attended the school there.[18]

Women responded spontaneously to Mrs. Roosevelt, and perhaps because she did not mind discussing her role as wife and mother, she did not threaten such traditionalists. In small ways, she strove for women's equality, even in breaking the taboo against cigarette smoking, which she enjoyed after White House dinners.

As much as the First Lady liked the ideals of the Civilian Conservation Corps, she was bothered that it was all-male, and conceived a special division for young women to do lighter reforestation, presenting the plan to Labor Secretary Frances Perkins, the first woman Cabinet member. The initial camp was established at Bear Mountain, New York.

While Perkins helped Eleanor's goals to have women appointed to government positions, it was Mollie Dewson who remained the First

Lady's liaison on women's issues. As the National Democratic Committee's women's division chief, Mollie wedged qualified women into every possible administration vacancy, and some joked that her initials stood for "More Women." Molly increased women's participation in the party and, in time, had 109,000 women campaigning for FDR.

Eleanor herself was directly responsible for appointments of women to government jobs. If a list of appointee candidates didn't include women, the First Lady went directly to the president. On one occasion, he even apologized, "Of course, I thought a woman's name had been put on the list. Have someone call up and say I feel a woman should be recognized." Eleanor suggested personal choices, and though not all were appointed, this forced FDR to realize women were qualified for federal jobs. To Eleanor, inspiring hope was as valuable an investment for women's futures as government jobs, and she quickly became a symbol of emulation to young, ambitious American women.[19]

During the depths of the Depression, in the small farming community of Artesia, California, on the outskirts of Los Angeles, young Thelma Catherine Ryan graduated from high school, determined to get ahead by going to college. In the summer of 1929, Thelma had taken a shorthand class in the daytime while nursing her widowed tubercular father, who had moved the family from Nevada and started a small farm. After he died, she formally changed her name to Pat, and with personal savings enrolled at Fullerton Junior College.

For tuition money, Pat worked as a janitor in a local bank, starting at 6:00 A.M. It was embarrassing work for the redhead with the high cheekbones, thin lips, and wide eyes of a Hollywood model. However, with nothing less than a steel determination, she excelled in school, one teacher evaluating, "In any type of occupation requiring the meeting of the public, Pat will be a great success." Nevertheless, Pat accepted an offer to drive a couple cross-country, seeing America and settling in New York as a secretary and X-ray technician in a tuberculosis ward. She forged an emotional bond to many young terminally ill patients. At night she helped a few of them sneak out to go sledding, describing those dark evenings on the snowy hills near the hospital as "among the most haunting of my life."

During Mrs. Roosevelt's first summer as First Lady, Pat had traveled to Washington, and toured the White House. But just a few months later, while attending a hospital conference, she found herself in the presence of Eleanor herself. As she wrote her brothers, "Last night Al Smith, Mrs. and President Roosevelt, etc. attended the formal dinner and the latter gave the main speech of the evening." Catholic Miss Ryan voted Democratic, even campaigning for Smith in 1928, but was a registered Independent. However, completing her education, not politics, was her goal. Pat didn't want to marry because she felt she "had not lived yet . . ." As she wrote her brothers, "The world is just what we make it—so let's make ours a grand one."[20]

Other young women had to observe the First Lady in newsreels only. One Georgia schoolgirl, named Eleanor Rosalynn, eyed portraits of Martha Washington and Dolley Madison, and "pictured them as women who sat in the White House with their hands clasped in front of them . . ." As the girl matured, however, Mrs. Roosevelt made her "aware that there was more to being the wife of the President than sitting back in the White House and enjoying the nice life. We admired and looked up to the First Ladies, liked to know what they wore and . . . what their interests were," but it wasn't until Eleanor that she first "thought about what a First Lady could do." In a small white house, "secure and isolated from the outside world," surrounded by a rainbow of flowers and fruit and nut trees, on the red soil of Plains—population six hundred—lived the Edgar Smith family. But after Rosalynn's seventh-grade teacher brought in a world map one day, the girl recalled that she "began to realize that the boundaries of the world extended beyond our sheltered and isolated community . . ."[21]

Other independent women used Mrs. Roosevelt as an unconscious role model. Fourteen-year-old Betty Bloomer of Grand Rapids, for example, was earning her own money. She had started taking dancing lessons in 1926, and explored all forms of dance, but "the freedom of movement" that modern dance offered was her "happiness." After her Saturday morning job as a department-store fashion model, she toiled in her own small business. Renting a neighbor's basement and hiring a pianist, Betty organized her own "school," teaching children the foxtrot and the Big Apple.

At home, Betty heard her father talk enthusiastically of FDR and the New Deal. Mrs. Roosevelt had a "strong impact" on her as she "matured," and Betty admitted that Eleanor "became a role model for me because . . . I liked her strange charisma . . . that independence . . . I really liked the idea that a woman finally was speaking out and expressing herself rather than just expressing the views of her husband. That seemed healthy to me. I'm not sure why I liked that . . . but it appealed to me. I never really thought about why I so much admired Eleanor Roosevelt . . . it was sort of her trend. A very new trend."

Miss Bloomer had a "sunny childhood" and "a wonderful girlhood," marred only by the sudden death of her father. At his funeral, she learned that he had suffered from alcoholism.

Betty spent two full summers studying modern dance under Martha Graham at Bennington College, and even tried cigarettes and a "few beers," which made her "giddy." Betty considered Graham "a goddess," and became determined to study under her in New York. Graham had another devotee—the First Lady. In between Betty Bloomer's summers with Martha Graham, the latter performed, at Mrs. Roosevelt's request, in the White House.[22]

If Eleanor's public persona was avant-garde, the private person was traditional. Initially, Eleanor was bothered by the ancient hostess role, considering it a "useless burden," "utterly futile," and "not an inspiring occupation." Because of the Depression, she considered it wrong "to think very seriously about purely social matters." Under Mrs. Helm's coaxing, however, Eleanor realized being hostess "had real meaning and value," because she discovered "the White House has a deep significance," as a form of "the people's hospitality . . . to representatives of other countries," and to citizens who had "a sense of ownership . . ." and to whom it "symbolized the government." It marked the first time a member of a First Lady's staff played an important role in influencing her boss behind the scenes, for Eleanor discovered that she could shape an old role with new interpretations.[23]

As Mrs. Helm foresaw, Eleanor was able to use the hostess position to her political advantage. The First Lady began sponsoring East Room conferences, the first one being "the Cause and Cure of War," chaired by feminist Carrie Catt. For every single woman employed in clerical government jobs, she initiated an annual garden party. For most of these women, employed for years by the government, it was their first White House invitation. Mrs. Roosevelt also began hosting special luncheons for women of great achievement, in government, labor, social welfare, and the arts and sciences. Also invited for the first time were the lonely adolescent congressional pages, as well as all members of the press corps, photographers, and their spouses.[24]

The First Lady took an avid interest, too, in the more traditional sphere of historical preservation. Considering the cause important, and prompted by preservationists, she took the press on visits to Monticello, Mount Vernon, Stratford Hall, and Oatlands. Familiar with Monticello, she herself guided a tour for reporters, adding to their "education." When the opportunity arose, Eleanor wanted to see the Red Room restored, because she used it as her personal reception area.[25]

The traditional role of mother to her children—Anna, Elliott, James, John, and Franklin, Jr.—was also important to her. For her grandchildren, she established a nursery, and had sandboxes, slides, and a rope swing—which the First Lady herself tested out one evening. Having family with her during the summer in the country, winter in the city, Thanksgiving, and Christmas, provided continuity to Eleanor's otherwise unpredictable lifestyle. She sympathized deeply when her children became subject to false as well as justified criticism in the press and public, and though required to make appointments to see her, "whenever they became seriously ill," J. B. West recalled, "she was right there with them, wherever they were, anywhere in the country. Flew out immediately!"

If their mother was sometimes remote, Grandmother Sara overindulged them to defy Eleanor. At Hyde Park, Eleanor regressed, but in the White House, as maid Lillian Parks said, ". . . there is only *one* Mrs. Roosevelt." When Sara complained to Eleanor about her decision to have a full black household staff, the First Lady *finally* gave her mother-in-law a terse piece of her mind. "Mother, you run your house. And I'll run mine."[26]

Though she had opposed Franklin in the election, the First Lady's aunt, Edith Roosevelt, believed he would succeed, being "a shrewd politician." Edith thankfully responded to a letter "full of things I wanted to know" from Eleanor about White House life, remarking, ". . . such conditions met me in the White House, and I am quite sure that I did not deal with them as efficiently as you have done." But whereas Edith had departmentalized the role, Eleanor scrambled it. Personal friends were often political contacts called in for public business in private settings like teatime. Though she and Franklin had mutual friends, both had their own orbits. Harry Hopkins, for example, had been brought to Franklin's attention by Eleanor. When he became increasingly closer to the president, the First Lady shared few confidences with him. Hopkins became an extension of Franklin, first heading the NRA, eventually the WPA, and in time becoming commerce secretary. Then there was Missy LeHand, the president's secretary, who was the undisputed "first lady" of the Executive Offices. Louis Howe, the only person whose advice both Roosevelts jointly sought and trusted, was now a proud behind-the-scenes public-relations manager, though rapidly declining in health.

In the early years, "Hick" remained Eleanor's closest friend, leaving journalism to work first for Harry Hopkins and later for Molly Dewson. She kept to herself in a small corner bedroom, directly across the hall from Eleanor. Other confidants, like Joseph Lash, the young executive secretary of the American Student Union, didn't live in Washington but made their home in the White House when they stayed in town. Lash, once suspected of being a communist, was so close to the First Lady that the FBI actually spied on them when he visited Mrs. Roosevelt's hotel room in Chicago, by secretly placing recording devices under her bed. When the president learned of this, he was enraged not at his wife, but at the FBI.

There were many government and private-sector officials whom she counted on as her allies. In Washington, Eleanor Roosevelt had the ultimate—and perhaps first—power network, the ranks of which included Walter Reuther of the United Auto Workers, Congresswoman Caroline O'Day, publisher Cissie Patterson, Treasury Secretary Morgenthau, philanthropist Mary Lasker, and public-welfare authority Lillian Wald. The First Lady gently persuaded them to help her with projects or problems, and when she needed their public support. More often, however, she sought their help to assist a single, unknown individual, who, for Eleanor, always served as an almost experimental device. "Out of my response to an individual develops an awareness of a problem to the community, then to the country, and finally to the world." As different as she was from her predecessors, however, it was some of their support that provided even more encouragement.[27]

Eleanor's earthiness appealed to Frances Cleveland Preston. A month after the Inaugural, she wrote Eleanor, ostensibly extending an invitation to the Needlework Guild's convention:

You must know that I am especially happy and proud this year to invite you to be our guest . . . I am going to take advantage of this occasion to enclose personal words of my joy and enthusiasm that you are reigning in the dear old house—and my gratification at the way everything is going. And to tell you of my hearty and I may say affectionate good wishes for the President and your self in all the fine things you are both doing. I have wanted to write you many times, but dreaded to add to the burden of your mail. Now that my duty requires me to demand your attention for a moment, I take advantage to slip in my own words of greeting.

An enthused Mrs. Roosevelt responded that it was "indeed a joy" to hear from her, and invited Frances to "come to Washington" and "give me the pleasure of showing you the White House again."[28]

Another member of the sorority *did* come to Washington, but conspicuously avoided the White House. In December 1934, widowed Grace Coolidge made her one and only trip back to Washington, examining the WPA's construction of new government buildings, the Smithsonian's First Ladies' gowns collection, and even drove up to the White House—but she did not go in. She saw herself now only as a private citizen, and there were no honorary luncheons or reunions. "I thought it was a great lark to spend a night there undiscovered," she wrote her son John, "but I am glad I did not have to stay."

Grace had emerged from her widow's weeds. Though she had loved Calvin, she enjoyed doing all the things he'd forbidden—wearing hiking shorts, bobbing her hair, and, shortly thereafter, flying in an airplane to Europe. Son John said she was ". . . game to try anything and she loved something new, something different." With her liberal feminist friend Florence Adams, she traveled, read, and discussed current events. Though Grace remained a registered Republican, some of the New Deal ideas appealed to her, and when Mrs. Adams defended Roosevelt policies, she said Grace would "always listen . . . and sometimes she'd agree with me." Mrs. Coolidge found Eleanor appealing, and never once even hinted at being anti-Roosevelt. Only once—when Roosevelt's Congress awarded her the franking privilege in 1934—did she jest about the New Deal's "alphabet soup" programs: "I wonder if I come under XYZ or KLM or what . . ."

Though identified as a Republican in public, she refused not only to criticize FDR but to express any opinion. "Well, we all are interested in politics—we should be," she told reporters after her incognito twelve-thousand-mile European road tour. "But I am not actively interested." Grace guarded her new independence with a vengeance—even turning down a marriage proposal from her husband's former executive assistant, joking that she was "safe and sound and single and . . . in her right mind."

When Claude Fuess began researching his definitive biography of Calvin Coolidge, he interviewed Grace and noted that she listened intently but remained a knowing, silent Cheshire cat. "You could almost see her thinking, 'I wonder if I dare tell him,'" he recalled. ". . . she knew how to deal with people." To those who knew, Grace remained the silent Coolidge.[29]

Lou Hoover, based in New York, made no public remarks about her successor, but as Girl Scout president still concentrated on volunteerism to fight the Depression. Curiously, independent Nellie Taft found little common ground with Eleanor, and removed herself even further from public notice. When in town, she played cards, attended concerts, and appeared at Supreme Court functions. She did not frequent the White House. To her, the New Deal was anathema.

Mrs. Woodrow Wilson presented a more complicated matter. If Sara Roosevelt held sway as American Mother, her friend Edith Wilson was visibly crowned Queen Mother, witnessing the first FDR Inaugural seated next to her escort, Bernard Baruch. Through the twenties, Edith couldn't be bothered by Eleanor's political pleas, but now that Eleanor was a First Lady, Edith saw the obvious advantages to having her own star resurrected. She quickly attached herself to the Roosevelts through Sara and Baruch, getting high visibility by often sharing the spotlight with Eleanor, and her publicity far outran that of Dolley Madison, Julia Tyler, and Julia Grant when they reigned as Queen Mothers. In Japan at the time of FDR's election, she clipped the newspaper announcing it in Japanese and gave it to Sara, who gave it to her son. A thrilled president, who was an avid memorabilia collector, put the clipping in his scrapbook. Suddenly, Edith Wilson was very much "in," though privately she disapproved of the "new buildings, new methods, New Deals."

At state functions, Queen Mother Wilson was awarded the highest-ranking spot in protocol after the Roosevelts, the visiting foreign delegation, the vice president, and Chief Justice—another benchmark of the government's recognition of the public status of the "nonofficial" role of First Lady. Though Edith still ignored Eleanor's political invitations, she rarely turned down a chance to party at the White House. Only Franklin dared to razz Edith. She was miffed when, after a long series of letters to FDR beginning in 1934, she was unable to remove from the White House a portrait of her late Woodrow that she considered less grand than another she had in mind. She went over his head to attempt to get congressional approval, but was unsuccessful. When she learned that FDR owned a desk intended for Wilson, she rudely told him, "You're nothing but a common thief." FDR retorted that he bought it out of admiration for Wilson. She sniffed, "All the same, it's my desk."

Edith's direct link to the First Lady was strengthened by her "special friend" Barnard Baruch. Edith took to "Bernie's" daughter Belle like her own, and traveled and socialized frequently with her. Bernie made marked overtures to Edith. Millionaire, gentleman, rapt devotee of Wilson, he appealed to Edith. He rented a Scottish castle for her pleasure. They yachted and went to the Kentucky Derby together. At Christmas, he gave her an expensive silver fox cape; on financial matters he advised her wisely. Presented with memorial plans for Woodrow, she turned instinctively to Bernie. When a woman inquired of one of Edith's acquaintances why Mrs. Wilson hadn't married Baruch, since they seemed to care for one another, the questioner pressed, "Is it because he is Jewish?" The response was affirmative. Edith, however, kept her opinions from Eleanor.[30]

If some of the sorority disapproved of Eleanor, they had eminent company. Among their society peers, the Roosevelts were considered betrayers of their class. The appointment of millionaire movie mogul Joseph P. Kennedy, to head the Securities and Exchange Commission particularly enraged Wall Street broker and Republican John Vernou Bouvier. Bouvier was a French Catholic, from a distinguished New York family, who summered in Southhampton, Long Island, where the first of his two daughters, Jacqueline Lee, had been born just three months before the Crash.

Her mother, Janet, an accomplished horsewoman, taught Jacqueline to ride, and, at five, the child astonished spectators as she deftly managed her horse over jumps, winning several ribbons. But it was her paternal grandfather who instilled a reverence for history, a study with which "Jackie" became preoccupied. Confident and independent, she favored the Bouviers, with high cheekbones, dark hair, and wide-set hazel eyes. An intenseness and curiosity marked a discernable difference between Jackie and her peers. Janet described her as "original," adding, "She was brilliant, with strong feelings about things, gifted artistically and always good in her studies." The headmistress of the Chapin School, where Jacqueline was enrolled and made a lifelong friend, Nancy Tuckerman, pronounced Miss Bouvier "the most inquiring mind we'd had in the school in thirty-five years."

Jackie was obsessed with books, even devouring adult fiction. Writing became another passion, as she turned out stories and poems. There was no denying that this was a child more like a miniature adult. But she was also a loner. Part of her aloofness stemmed from an intense shyness, along with a need for privacy, even from her sister and cousins. She preferred walking on the beach in autumn alone, by herself. The sea inspired her poetry.

> I love the Autumn,
> And yet I cannot say
> All the thoughts and things
> That make one feel this way.
>
> I love walking on the angry shore,
> To watch the angry sea;
> Where summer people were
> before,
> But now there's only me.[31]

Other creative writers chose one of the nation's most controversial topics as their subject. In the process, Eleanor Roosevelt unwittingly expanded the first ladyship into a completely new role—pop-culture figure. She became a female folk hero of the thirties. Eleanor anecdotes, many apocryphal, began making the rounds. A true story had her leaving the house to inspect a penitentiary. When FDR asked where she was, Tommy Thompson said, "In prison." "I'm not surprised," FDR retorted. "What's she in for?" The story spread, with variations posing Sara Roosevelt calling her son in a horrified state, informing him that Eleanor was in prison, as well as other versions attributing Tommy's response to Edith Helm, Anna Roosevelt, and even a butler. Like the henpecked husband, the battle-ax mother-in-law, the farmer's daughter, and the traveling salesman, there was now this larger-than-life caricature known as the First Lady, and the image permanently entered legendary American mythology.

Mrs. Roosevelt came onto the stage just as sound technology was being refined. This wasn't lost on Hollywood. For the first time, a First Lady became a public figure to lampoon in film and theater. Impersonations sprang up at parties, her image was alluded to in a Popeye cartoon, she was even a character in a play in a movie, *Babes in Arms*, played by Judy Garland. It opened up the role of First Lady to permanent burlesque.

The power of Hollywood, enjoying its golden age during the New Deal years, was not lost on the Roosevelts, who realized the public appeal of movie stars and regularly invited them to the mansion, nicknamed "Little Hollywood." The First Lady was a theater devotee—often a first-nighter—who caught matinees between appointments. After the show, she often invited the cast back to the mansion, sometimes to perform for guests.

Though Edith Wilson had sold bonds with Chaplin, Florence Harding was a friend of Lillian Russell's, and Grace Coolidge enjoyed being photographed with Tom Mix, none had aggressively pursued actors for political causes as Mrs. Roosevelt had. It was a shrewd move, particularly for FDR's cause, the March of Dimes.

Jean Harlow, Robert Taylor, Tyrone Power, Marie Dressler, Errol Flynn, Ralph Bellamy, George Raft, Gene Kelly, Clark Gable, Dorothy Lamour, Eve Arden, Bob Hope, Bing Crosby, Myrna Loy, Deanna Durbin, Elizabeth Taylor, Shirley Temple, Bette Davis, Dinah Shore, Abbott and Costello, James Cagney, Irene Dunne, Hedy Lamarr, Kay Kayser, Greer Garson, Lana Turner, Charlie McCarthy, John Barrymore, and Jane Wyman all came to meet—and be photographed with—America's most legendary lady. When Red Skelton, upstairs on the family floor, spotted that familiar beat-up packed suitcase in the hallway, he joked, "Eleanor is off again!" The First Lady even appeared in one film short, promoting a charity with Jack Benny by purchasing one 25-cent ticket. Gamely playing along with the gag on herself, she offered him a dollar. Benny joked, "Well, I haven't the change with me just now, but I'll be glad to send it to you . . . if you'll stay in one place."

Hollywood and Washington became inextricably connected during Mrs. Roosevelt's tenure. When Alice Longworth told Mae West that she had fans in the White House, the actress replied that she admired "jus' two" women in history, "Catherine the Great and Ela'na the Good." One of Franklin Roosevelt's favorite White House maids, Lizzie McDuffie, took a leave of absence to audition for the Mammy role in Gone With the Wind, and nearly got it.

In newsreels, FDR was posed, usually stilted. It was Eleanor who spontaneously moved as the visual embodiment of the New Deal's vitality. Never before had the world seen so much of a First Lady. And never before was a First Lady literally turning up at every corner of the nation, in the most unlikely scenarios, being filmed and photographed. Up on the silver screen, audiences watched Eleanor Roosevelt grinning as she sailed in a pitchfork over a New Deal dam project, her ratty fur piece swaying in the wind of the dustbowl, or her large frame bopping to a Virginia reel in a coal miners' community center. At home, after the movies, several generations of the family gathered around the radio, and between Fibber McGee and Charlie McCarthy, there was Mrs. Roosevelt again, broadcasting her Sunday night speeches.

With the era's popular music, she was equally comfortable, enjoying the music of Benny Goodman and Glenn Miller's "swing," played in the mansion and danced to in the East Room. She was herself immortalized in modern dance, with three pieces—the "Eleanor Glide," the "Eleanor Walk," and the "Eleanor Waltz–Tea for Two"—performed for her in the mansion. When one lyricist submitted a song praising "How she clum up White Top Mountain," however, his request to perform was turned down.[32]

Two annual events at which the First Lady was the subject of parody were parties that she attended and participated in, gamely spoofing her role. At the annual Women's National Press Club party, an Eleanor skit was always staged, after which she gave her traditional comic rebuttal, delivered straight-faced. The other event, "Gridiron Widows," was for reporters' wives and "the girls," conceived by the First Lady after the male press did not invite Secretary Perkins with the rest of the Cabinet to their annual "Gridiron Club" spoof dinner. Eleanor was mistress of ceremonies at the White House "widows" party, and again parodied her role. Once, she appeared as an indigent "Apple Mary," who is changed by the devil into the First Lady in three vignettes: a scene with her attempting to knit while mobbed by fans on a train; another showed her arriving at an airport, weighted down by several dozen rose bouquets and a literally impossible schedule for the day; finally, "driving" a car as an angry motorist followed her and shouted criticisms. Another year's skit had the First Lady visiting West Virginia, with Mrs. "Arthur Dale," actually played by Eleanor and Tommy in a cameo. At yet another Gridiron Widows' party, the First Lady even planned on singing "I've Been Working on the Railroad," but realized her voice was so flat that she talked the lyrics through.[33]

Mrs. Roosevelt was not seemingly conscious of creating a pop-culture persona, but as time went on, she did indeed sustain it. And, ironically, it provided a surge of confidence as 1936 approached. Franklin was running for reelection, and the campaign signaled another four years of sacrificing her personal life. Unlike in previous campaigns, she would have to stand on her own, for Louis Howe was to die before the election. He seriously told Eleanor that if *she* wanted to be president in 1940, she should soon let him know, so he could begin the public relations necessary. She honestly admitted that she had no interest in elected government, but now, "running" as First Lady, Eleanor was confidently in charge of her own ability to exert power.

At the convention, Secretary Perkins spoke directly to the women: "There is a woman Democrat who is not at this political convention because she is detained by social conventions. But she has not shown herself to be restricted by the usual conventions . . . Her talent was an unusual ability and capacity to love the human race, and to hear, learn, and understand its troubles, miseries, wants and aspirations. She has therefore gone out through the length and breadth of the land, in the face of unfavorable criticism, not only to meet the people of the country personally as a friend, but also to utilize that contact, and make herself a channel through which their needs, their hopes, their desires could be carried directly to places where solutions could be found . . . Many women in this country when they vote for Franklin D. Roosevelt will also be thinking with a choke in the throat of Eleanor Roosevelt!"[34]

Eleanor disliked the self-effacement she felt necessary to campaigning. As she told Bess Furman, a successful candidate's wife should always be on schedule, offer no personal opinions, remain undisturbed at commotion, limit personal appearances, and lean back when in an open car so the crowds can see *him*. Toward the end of the campaign, she joined FDR on whistle-stops, but was now furiously at work on a new, satisfying personal project—her memoirs. Entitled *This Is My Story*, it covered her life up through the White House years.[35]

Eleanor wasn't the only sorority member writing a book. Once again Edith Wilson joined Eleanor for the ponies. On FDR's Second Inaugural day—the first to take place on January 20—Mrs. Wilson gleamed from the official stand. Edith Wilson was angry when her former social secretary published her own letters from Europe during the Treaty of Versailles talks. She was angry when Wilson biographer Edith Gittings Reid "studiedly ignored" her, and was outraged when a spate of Wilson books by Tumulty, House, Lansing, and Lodge came out with their versions of her "stewardship." So Edith Wilson—guided by Baruch, encouraged by Eleanor—wrote her own book.

Published by Bobbs-Merrill, Edith's *My Memoir* was extremely vague about her early years, as if life began when she met Woodrow. Ellen Wilson was virtually ignored, except to clarify Edith's timeline. Reviews were mixed, the *Chicago Herald Tribune* saying, "There is nothing half-way . . . about the lady's punches . . ." and one Washington columnist calling Edith a "smudge pot" of a First Lady next to Eleanor, but Mrs. Roosevelt herself commented favorably upon the book in "My Day," and even Grace Coolidge defended it. With all the publicity, Edith still refused to be interviewed, affirming that First Ladies "should not speak in public." It was an indirect way of stating disapproval of Mrs. Roosevelt.[36]

If Edith was bewildered by Eleanor's public activism, one could only imagine what she said behind closed doors of the First Lady's public defense of blacks.

Amid increasing stories of German Führer Adolf Hitler's anti-Semitism, Eleanor Roosevelt's most famous antiracist action occurred. In 1939, the DAR refused to permit black singer Marian Anderson to perform in their Constitution Hall. Swiftly, Eleanor turned a private decision into a public issue, resigning from the group, because "to remain a member implies approval of that action . . ." She then helped arrange for Anderson to hold her concert, which was attended by thousands, on the steps of the Lincoln Memorial. Now, all across the world, minorities rallied behind Eleanor, and though there were some disapproving editorials, she was overwhelmingly commended. As one black newspaper wrote, "She broke another shackle in the chain which binds so much of our country in intolerance and bigotry."

Though she still retained some anti-Catholicism, Eleanor had overcome her earlier bigotry against blacks and Jews. She may have taken gentler positions on other issues, but when it came to American blacks, she had no apologies about her work, explaining, ". . . we must not just accept things that are wrong and placidly sit back and say, 'Well, people have stood that for a long while, they'll probably live through it some time longer,' and be content with things as they are. You've got to want to change the things that are not satisfactory. You have got to want to do it so much that you will take some trouble about it."[37]

Gladys Duncan, wife of internationally acclaimed dancer Todd Duncan and herself a civil-rights activist, said blacks needed more than economic recovery from the Depression, they wanted "social reform." Dorothy Height of the National Council of Black Women said that her people "came to think Eleanor Roosevelt could do anything." Eleanor had no formalized "project" to help blacks, Height said. "It was simply to see where people were hurting and what needed to be done about it." Once she started, however, Height said, the First Lady "was willing to use her power without fear . . . Whether it was popular or not was never a consideration. She repeated that 'no one can make you feel inferior unless you give them your consent.'"[38]

Mrs. Roosevelt invited black educators, reformers, and activists to dine regularly at the White House as her guests. Only T.R. and the Hoovers had done so in this century. This challenged the rigid segregationist views of many Americans, and though the hate mail and editorials never stopped, neither did Eleanor. As First Lady, it was her prerogative to invite and confer with whomever she wanted.[39]

Her basic philosophy on civil rights went far beyond the earlier reformist attitude of "separate but equal." She believed full integration was the only way to achieve real equality. This extended beyond blacks to all races and socioeconomic backgrounds. Gladys Duncan said the First Lady always attempted to overcome the notion of treating blacks as a race apart, and thought of "people as people." Sistie Roosevelt concurred that "she did not select them out particularly as her responsibility when she became president's wife. It just naturally evolved because she felt an obligation to do what she could to make life better to a lot of people . . . But, when she was presented with their real conditions, she adopted it as her cause."[40]

There was one person in particular who seemed to lead the First Lady gently by the hand into the open battlefield of civil rights. Her name was Mary McLeod Bethune, daughter of slaves, eminent educator, and chief of the National Youth Administration's Division of Negro Affairs. Quickly, the two women formed not only a close working relationship but a warm friendship, and Mrs. Bethune became the

First Lady's government contact on black issues. Joyously, Mrs. Bethune boasted that, with Eleanor, "never in American history has the
Negroes' future seemed so secure." Eleanor said when she was able to
greet Mary with a kiss without first thinking about it, her racism was
really gone.[41]

Immediately, the First Lady practiced what she preached. Early on,
she received black sharecroppers in the White House, and later visited
them in their tar-paper shacks. At a segregated Birmingham, Alabama,
meeting, she and Mrs. Bethune sat together in the black section. When
officials asked the First Lady to move to the white side, she shifted her
chair into the middle of the aisle. At the leading black college, Howard
University, she attended meetings and made a speech, escorted by two
black men. When photographers approached, she slowed down with
her escorts. When the NAACP informed her of the NRA approving
wage differences based on race, she immediately responded to black
leaders that they must not accept such terms. When a mid-level official
threatened to fire some black women from their jobs at the Census
Bureau, a superior gasped, "If Eleanor hears about this, there'll be hell
to pay." As Gladys Duncan said, the First Lady "strived to open federal
jobs" for blacks.[42]

With Walter White of the NAACP keeping her informed of specific
cases of bigotry in all phases of American life, the First Lady's cham-

pioning of civil rights touched every one of her other causes. To those who believed that "Jim Crow" was a permanent part of American life, it was nothing short of social revolution. Southern Democrats frequently expressed their outrage to the president, but as Eleanor wrote, he "never never tried to discourage me and was undisturbed by anything I wanted to say or do . . ." She did say, however, that presidential advisers Steve Early and Marvin McIntyre had "grave concern" over "many of my racial beliefs and activities in the field of social work . . . afraid that I would hurt my husband politically and socially."

FDR did warn her, however, "You can't get too far in front. You don't just pass a law and that's it. Only gradually can you create the impact that will get people to recognize that more has to be done for the downtrodden and for the education of the Negro."[43]

J. B. West observed that the First Lady's speeches on civil rights were unequal to the force she exerted "behind the scenes." Gladys Duncan concurred, believing Mrs. Roosevelt did influence several loyal congressmen into at least considering civil rights. And blacks knew that their representative was not Franklin but Eleanor. One black woman wrote first to FDR about discrimination, but told him that if she didn't hear from him soon enough, "I'll write to Mrs. Roosevelt!" To Gladys Duncan, she emphasized that "integration will never become . . . legislation until housing is equalized . . ." With that in mind, she sent Harry Hopkins lists of suggestions to insure equal subsistence housing for blacks under NRA programs. She also focused on equal education, telling a civil-rights leader she couldn't "help but think how stupid we are for not realizing how important to our race, that you should have the best educational opportunities."

Duncan said Mrs. Roosevelt never emphasized her own work but rather focused on "what we should do and were accomplishing . . . and she never made you feel that you were inferior in any way . . ." Her granddaughter said Eleanor didn't think of herself as "a martyr" who had "turned a new life . . . she just thought it was a process of long, hard work . . . but a process of educating people and making them consider the idea of equality."[44]

Nevertheless, she was hailed as a savior in the black press. "For the very first time," one journal announced, "Negro men and women have reason to believe that this government really does care . . ." Another gave credit where it was more precisely due: "[N]ever before has a First Lady made a plea in behalf of fair play and equal opportunity for Negro citizens." If there was praise, however, there was twice as much hateful criticism.[45]

The photograph of her being escorted by two black men to her Howard University speech was copied and distributed on handbills in the South. A nasty ditty spread in some segments of the press, supposedly quoting FDR speaking to Eleanor about staying in the presidency:

> You kiss the niggers,
> I'll kiss the Jews.
> We'll stay in the
> White House as long as we
> choose.[46]

One team of scurrilous chroniclers, Jack Lait and Lee Mortimer, blamed Mrs. Roosevelt directly for the disintegration of society ". . . with certain homely and all-wooly virtues by the worship of millions . . . with her Negro friends, her boondoggling, sweaty indigents, her professional Socialists, her dedicated slum-house guardians of gutter garbage, and her antics as the militant apostle of democracy and equality. The bedrock of Society is inequality, the existence and recognition of an aristocracy . . . No female in American history had ever been so despised in the drawing-rooms and so venerated in the kitchens and furnished rooms." Indeed, after she encouraged Washington's black maids to form their own union and demand higher wages, the First Lady was resented by many rich white women who complained about the lack of "good help," even though no union was formed. Some charged that Eleanor was a mere "chief propagandist" and her alley clearance was bogus, and that one slum always photographed was actually surrounded by fine housing. "But this slum is permitted to remain behind the Capitol only so the lefties will have something to breast-beat over."[47]

Eleanor's civil-rights views surfaced during 1939's dramatic visit by England's King George and Queen Elizabeth to the White House. Eleanor got along well enough with the queen, though she found her "a little too self-consciously regal." When the royals visited Hyde Park, the First Lady served American hot dogs, and received some rebuke for it, but it was mild compared to criticism like that of "a staunch Democrat from Miami," who said she was insulting the British "who are caucasians to present a Negro vocalist for their entertainment. Do you want to engender racial hatred which might lead to serious consequences in the entire South?" The First Lady instructed Edith Helm to reply that she only wished to present the full spectrum of American culture, and that included blacks.[48]

Mrs. Roosevelt was still determined to fight racism, sexism, and poverty, while her husband concentrated on the serious situation in Europe. The unstated purpose of the king's visit had been to secure American military support for the inevitable English-German war.

Eleanor was troubled by one particular leader. As she wrote an old friend, now a reactionary living in Europe, "Although we do not hate the German people, there is only an inability here to understand how people of spirit can be terrified by one man and his storm troops to the point of countenancing the kind of horrors which seem to have come on in Germany not only where the Jews are concerned, but in the case of the Catholics and some of the liberal German Protestants . . . no country can exist free and unoppressed while a man like Hitler remains in power."[49]

Her views on world governments became more pronounced at the end of the second term. After the Spanish civil war, she argued vehemently with Franklin about his neutrality toward the struggle. Wagging her finger at him, she told a guest, "We should have pushed him harder!" Her support of the Spanish democrats provoked criticism from the reactionary Catholic priest Father Charles Coughlin, who had an extremely influential weekly radio broadcasting of his sermons.

She also believed America should be prepared to fight tyranny: "All of us have an equal responsibility in the one great country that is free . . . to the rest of the world wherever there may be people who are not free to become free again . . ."[50]

Nevertheless, she defended the freedom of political choice, and supported the right of communism to exist as inherently American, and even said she could understand how disillusioned Depression youth could find hope in it, which she said was "closer to Democracy than Nazism." Most, however, questioned her close association with the American Youth Congress, the ranks of which had been infiltrated by communists. She appeared publicly as a supporter of Joe Lash, a former AYC official, as he testified before the Red-baiting Dies Committee, and invited him and friends to lunch and dinner at the mansion, between testimony.

Not long after her appearance with the AYC, her name appeared in The Red Network, which listed those suspected of being communists. FBI Director J. Edgar Hoover presented the president with evidence that she had given money to charitable organizations that served as communist fronts, and some right-wing journalists said she had "tie-lines" to Washington's "white collar Communist underground."

When, however, the AYC defended the Russians in their invasion of Finland in November 1939, she questioned their motives. She even gave the leaders a second chance to explain themselves privately to her and FDR after they booed his initial speech. But when they again shouted him down, she fired back, "How dare you be so rude to the President of the United States? Even if you disagree with him, you should show more respect. The President of the United States should not be insulted in such a disgraceful fashion." After that tongue-lashing, the First Lady was booed in her own house. There was no more AYC work. She now knew it was controlled by communists.[51]

Another of the sorority involved herself in interesting "foreign affairs." On September 1, 1939, while promoting My Memoirs, Edith Wilson came in close contact with another Bobbs-Merrill author.

Italian laborer and writer Pietro Di Donato, whose book Christ in Concrete had been published that same year, joined Mrs. Wilson at the Librarians' Convention at beautiful Lake Mohonk, where a large Vic-

torian hotel overlooked a placid lake. After a swim, the twenty-seven-
year-old noticed grand Edith, whom he recalled as a "womanly
woman—designed like the succulent matron models of the early Sears-
Roebuck winter-underwear ads," eyeing him.

"Mr. di Donato, you are a vigorous swimmer," the former First Lady
said, coming up to him. "I was enjoying watching you in the water. Do
you ever tire? Ah, youth." Di Donato invited her to join him in a
rowboat excursion across the lake. She accepted.

Shortly after, Di Donato recalled "the lovely-fleshed . . . Lillian
Russell" making her move, and found himself interested. They shored
the boat in a cove.

There, hidden in the brush, the sixty-six-year-old Edith demonstrated
a rather startling sexual prowess, impressing the young man as a sensuous
woman in control of the encounter. The genteel matron who had a history
of disdaining commoners, blacks, Catholics, and Jews exercised dexterous
muscles with a such an abandon of inhibitions that the experienced Italian
was happily surprised. When, however, after they returned to the boat and
he shouted obscenities at the radio news of Hitler's invasion of Poland,
Mrs. Wilson was unseated by the verbal vulgarity.[52]

The news brought more serious reasons for shock. France and England declared war on Germany. Hirohito aligned Japan with Germany,
while America, remaining out of the war, provided England with reserve American weaponry and naval destroyers. Italy's Mussolini, leader
of that nation's Facism, became allied with Hitler and Hirohito, forming the Axis. In their criticism of America, the dictators attacked Eleanor, Mussolini calling for an "embargo" on the First Lady, and Nazi
propaganda claimed, "While President Roosevelt is trying to keep the
United States out of war, his wife is trying to drag it in." It was the first
time the international press had criticized America's First Lady.

"Eleanor Roosevelt," said Adolf Hitler, "is America's real ruler."
The self-described "agitator" was nonplussed.

"I love a fight," quipped the First Lady.[53]

– 53 –

1940

IF ELEANOR WAS committed to the larger, public issue of world har-
mony, the smaller facets of her personal life were neglected. To her,
"food was just something to nourish energy . . . an antique sofa was

only valuable if it could hold three labor negotiators at one time . . ."
She was "amused" when named to the national best-dressed women's
list, because "she usually ordered the same dress in five colors." The
house, lacking a dedicated mistress, fell into seediness, a condition noticed by tourists.[1]

During the 1940 spring tourist season, one New York woman
brought her daughters to visit the capital at Easter break, and they
joined the lines of tourists snaking through the White House. The elder
girl felt "strangely let down by the White House. It seemed rather
bleak; there was nothing in the way of a booklet to take away, nothing
to teach one more about that great house and the Presidents who had
lived there." To disappointed eleven-year-old Jacqueline Bouvier, the
mansion lacked a sense of history.[2]

Nineteen-forty was a trying year for the Bouvier sisters. Just three
months after the White House visit, their parents divorced. During
their visits with their father, there were excursions to Belmont Park
races, art galleries, fine clothing stores, and a multitude of museums.
Jacqueline recalled her most "thrilling moment," when Jack Bouvier
took her to the New York Stock Exchange, where he worked. In between ballet and writing, Jackie began painting watercolors. When she
boarded at Miss Porter's School in Farmington, Connecticut, Jacqueline
emerged somewhat from her shyness, and like all students there, served
duty as waitress in the dining room. The momentous occasion was a
visit from Jack Bouvier, whom she called "a most devastating figure . . ." Her days with her father became even fewer when, less than
two years later, her mother married Hugh D. Auchincloss. It meant
summers at his Hammersmith Farm in Newport, instead of the
Bouviers' house in Southhampton, and home base was now a Washington suburb.[3]

Miss Bouvier was not alone in preferring New York over Washington. After she gave up her apartment on Eleventh Street, which she
used for trips back to New York, Mrs. Roosevelt took a Washington
Square Park brownstone. Here, without even guards at the door, she
found complete refuge from public life. Right past the First Lady's new
home, another independent woman trudged daily from her apartment
to her dance classes at Martha Graham's nearby school. A fearless
"strong-willed" twenty-year-old Betty Bloomer believed "I had my place
in this world . . . and my place [was] . . . New York City." She marveled at the kosher delis, the Automat, and the subway. She also
blacked out when she drank a grain-alcohol concoction at a party.

In the afternoons, dressed in a silver fox cape draped over a gown,
Betty began marching through skyscraper lobbies to all the top model-
ing agencies, looking for work. "You could tell," she later related, "I
was straight from the sticks." Though she got work with the best agencies and fashion houses, it was when she first danced as part of the

Graham troupe at Carnegie Hall that she thought, finally, "I had arrived." Her mother, disturbed that Betty would pursue a career instead
of marrying and having a family, coaxed her daughter back to Michigan. Almost regretfully, Betty would belatedly realize, "I had made my
choice."[4]

As retirement from the first ladyship loomed with the 1940 election, Eleanor planned to resume her career. Franklin, however, wanted
a third term.

He would not attend the convention, but he was certain about
whom he wanted as his vice president—Henry Wallace. A depressed
Eleanor tersely told FDR, of the third term notion, "I do not believe in
it."[5]

Privately, Eleanor was angry at Franklin's growing disinterest in
New Deal programs and principles. She refused to stop provoking him
into supporting a congressional antilynching bill, which would have
protected blacks from being taunted and killed in the South. FDR
didn't want to alienate southern Democrats, and refused her. Sounding
more and more like a candidate, he expressed the belief that the Depression's malaise had dissipated. To a great degree, he was right.

By now, Pat Ryan had earned her degree from the University of
Southern California, while working as a makeup model, department-
store gift-service assistant, movie extra, and professor's assistant. Miss
Ryan accumulated enough credits to be accredited with the equivalent
of a Masters' degree. She now taught high school in Whittier, on the
Los Angeles outskirts, particularly sensitive to students who had to
work as she did, especially Mexican-Americans. Meanwhile, a young
local lawyer pursued her, writing love letters, saying Pat was "destined
to be a great lady . . ." He wanted to marry her because ". . . [i]t is our
job to go forth together and accomplish great ends and we shall do it
too." Pat told friends, "He's going to be President someday." Though
she remained fiercely independent, unwilling to open her scarred life to
him, he strove to break her coolness, and thought her smile to be
"strangely sad but lovely . . ." In his car, at dusk on the beach at San
Clemente, she finally accepted. They married on the first day of summer, 1940, at the Mission Inn in Riverside, California. Thelma Ryan
was now Mrs. Richard Nixon.[6]

Summer found Mrs. Roosevelt at her Val-Kill cottage, along with
Tommy and an extra secretary, Dorothy Dow. Between diving lessons,
cooking and cleaning for an ill friend, and hosting a tea for eight hundred—"just a little afternoon's diversion!"—she listened to the radio
broadcast of the Chicago convention nominating FDR to a third term.
She was not to sit long. Most delegates were stonewalling his vice-
presidential choice of Wallace. Franklin knew they needed to be unified.

He sent Eleanor.

In a flash, she was flown to New York, joined by Franklin, Jr., and proceeded to Chicago. Before they landed, however, Eleanor fulfilled a dream. Up in the sky, over American farmlands, the First Lady of the United States took over the controls of the airplane. Though she piloted for just a short while, the simple act was not just another goal achieved but as an apt metaphor of the role she was to now play.

Mrs. Roosevelt found an embattled convention of factions. Both Frances Perkins and Hick, who had urged her to come, now panicked. Chicago Mayor Ed Kelley came up to speak with the First Lady as she approached the podium. Kelley temporarily left his personal guests, Edie Davis and her daughter, Smith College student Nancy, now engaged to Princeton student Frank Birney. Also watching Mrs. Roosevelt, from the special seating section not far from Nancy, was Edith Wilson, who supported her friend Jesse Jones for vice president. The First Lady was about to speak before the convention.

Eleanor approached the microphone before the loud mob, nervous at the thought of what her nastiest critics would now write, but before the hushed and rapt convention, she spoke with confidence: "You cannot treat it as you would an ordinary nomination in an ordinary time . . . rise above . . . partisan[ship]. This is a time when it is the United States we fight for." Immediately, it seemed, the scolded delegates quieted and nominated Wallace. One newspaper headline yelped MRS. ROOSEVELT STILLS THE TUMULT OF 50,000.

Within eighteen hours, she had left with a frightening mission, flown a plane, addressed a national convention, and was back home knitting and answering mail.[7]

When a story was printed that rock-ribbed Republican Nellie Taft had given an interview during a trip to Mexico and stated her support for Roosevelt, she went to great lengths to see that it was denied. The third-term notion shocked even Roosevelt supporters like Frances Cleveland Preston, who decided not to vote at all. But as her nephew Jack Cadman recalled, "Mrs. C. admired Mrs. Roosevelt." When Eleanor had come to Princeton to deliver an address in the late thirties, Frances took Jack with her to hear the First Lady speak at Alexander Hall. "Afterwards," Cadman remarked, "we went to a little room off the podium where Mrs. Roosevelt, all alone, was packing her single piece of luggage." The First Lady "visited" for a short while with her elder predecessor of nearly a half-century before.[8]

Although Eleanor again did not campaign, she found herself made an issue by the opposition. "We Don't Want Eleanor Either" buttons appeared along with "innuendos of all kinds," as she wrote. It was "as bad in personal bitterness," she admitted, "as any I have ever been in." She was evidently unaware that Franklin was ready to use Republican candidate Willkie's own estranged marriage as a campaign issue. On secret White House tape recordings, FDR referred to a recent joint

public appearance of the couple, saying, "Mrs. Willkie may not have been *hired*, but in effect she's been hired to return to Wendell and smile and make this campaign with him." FDR ignored the fact that he himself was in the same situation, though no money had been paid Eleanor to stay with him. As they headed to victory, she admitted. "Frankly I hate the next four years . . ."9

As a sense of war preparedness pervaded the White House, Tommy wrote that Eleanor was "quite uncontented . . . She has wanted desperately to be given something really concrete and worthwhile to do in this emergency, and no one has found anything for her. They are all afraid of political implications, etc., and I think she is discouraged and a bit annoyed about it."10

Meanwhile, some women refused to consider doing anything for any cause. NBC, in it's attempt to present "all viewpoints" on the issue of "paramount interest," sent an urgent request to Edith Wilson for her "present views, in the light of your intimate knowledge of what happened during the last war, on the subject of American neutrality." Any time or place convenient to her was fine, and NBC even offered to set up equipment in her home, and if she didn't want to make a bona fide speech, she could give a short five-minute "address."

Edith didn't reply.11

In September 1941, however, Edith responded immediately to the news of her friend Sara Roosevelt's death. Knowing how disagreeable Sara had been to Eleanor, Edith wrote to the president that his "distinguished" mother "was one of my ideals, and those of us who were privileged to know her are poorer since she fell asleep." To *that*, it was the First Lady who tersely responded that Sara "would not have enjoyed living an invalid's life." Three months earlier, another rival had been rendered powerless. Missy LeHand, the president's secretary, suffered a stroke, and was replaced with Grace Tully. Just days after Sara's funeral, Eleanor rushed to Walter Reed Hospital, where, for ten days, she watched her brother Hall slowly die of a disintegrated liver, the result of severe alcoholism.[12]

Hall's death was painfully emotional for Eleanor, and at a rare moment like this, when she broke down, Franklin responded to her with gentle love. As son James recalled poignantly, "Father struggled to her side and put his arm around her. 'Sit down,' he said, so tenderly . . . And he sank down beside her and hugged her and kissed her and held her head to his chest . . ."[13]

But if some black clouds dissipated, others gathered. The year before, France had fallen to Germany, Greece to Italy. In June, Adolf Hitler's Third Reich had invaded Russia. FDR was certain America would have to assist the Allies, and that autumn Eleanor made yet another unprecedented decision. She took a job outside of the First Ladyship, happy to find a niche.

At first, she had hoped to visit European Red Cross units, but there was a real fear that she might be captured by Nazis. After pleas from Albert Einstein and others, the First Lady helped some refugee groups to emigrate. She influenced Franklin to ask Herbert Hoover to lead a national relief organization for European refugees with her. Hoover wasn't interested. For the moment, he retained a grudge against the Roosevelts. Mrs. Hoover's secretary would later write that Mrs. Roosevelt told and wrote many things that "were not only unkind but untrue" about Lou. When Eleanor invited Lou to join her as co-chair of the Women's Committee on Mobilization for Human Needs, Mrs. Hoover refused, politely explaining, "I feel that the spirit of effective mobilization demands me to be at my post of duty here."

But only after arm-twisting Franklin into establishing a volunteer organization calling upon "women power," which she herself helped structure, did the First Lady get her job, the unsalaried deputy director of the Office of Civilian Defense (OCD). Two days after Hall's October burial, the first First Lady in history to be "employed" in a government job went to work.[14]

Nellie Taft, like her son Robert, a U.S. senator, was adamantly opposed to American intervention in the war. She even took part in a raucous protest against the Land-Lease Bill.

One sorority member was doing her part. Grace Coolidge had begun work two years before, raising money to bring Germany refugee children to America, and leading the local "Queen Wilhelmina Fund" for Dutch refugees, after Hitler invaded Holland. Then, publicity-shy Grace joined her first politically active organization, the National Fight for Freedom Committee, which opposed the isolationist America First. On her own, Mrs. Coolidge now shifted to apparently liberal philosophies. After an argument with a "Firster," Grace recounted, "I told her a few things and asked her to let me know when she saw the light." The once-conservative wife who never dared express political viewpoints now asked, "Shall we never grow up as individuals or as a nation?"

In between all this, Grace, like Eleanor, had taken a full-time "job," the classic case of an independent woman who abdicated her profession for a family, and in maturity resumed her work. Former teacher Grace was now president of the board and trustee of the twenty-acre Clarke School for the Deaf, on Round Hill. A visible and strong presence because of the office she kept there, Mrs. Coolidge studied electronic equipment, visited classrooms to chart progress, monitored the efficiency of experimental hearing aids, marked professional studies she considered helpful, commissioned reports, and kept abreast of the research department's latest studies. The elderly woman studying electronical equipment belied the former image of a red-dressed lady with a white collie. But Grace hadn't lost her youthful quality, admitting to a friend that she still kept a pair of her garish twenties red shoes, ". . . and, worse, I do sometimes wear them when I am feeling unsixtyish." She moved into a new home, Road Forks, which she herself designed.[15]

During her few hours on a trip to Smith College in February 1941, Mrs. Roosevelt found flowers and a note apologizing "that I cannot be in Northampton to-day to greet you in person. I hear that the women of Smith will give you cordial welcome and I hope that you will enjoy them half as much as they will enjoy you." Adding "my own welcome, in absentia," it was signed "Grace Coolidge." Eleanor responded that she was "sorry not to . . . see you . . . as I would have enjoyed telling you how much affection there is for you in the White House and among your many friends in Washington." She reported to Grace on the Smith trip, and when Eleanor returned for commencement sixteen months later, the two conferred on war preparedness. Mrs. Coolidge held a tea at her home in honor of her fellow First Lady.[16]

One Smith junior that year said she was unaware of Eleanor's visits to campus or even that Grace Coolidge lived in town. "The students were much less serious," Nancy Davis claimed, and "much less politically involved." She admitted that she "knew nothing about politics . . . but it didn't seem important then." Majoring in drama, Nancy planned for an acting career *and* marriage to Frank Birney. Fate, how-

ever, intervened, when he crossed an oncoming train's tracks and was killed.[17]

In Washington, Mrs. Roosevelt strode up Connecticut Avenue in the blue-gray coverall uniform she herself had designed for OCD female workers, to her office in the Dupont Circle Building. Her duties involved organizing a national volunteer network of women, but behind the scenes she infused the OCD with many of the New Deal principles. One afternoon, when she learned that the restaurant in the building refused to seat blacks in the "Whites Only" section, Eleanor reacted: "Very well, we'll all eat together in the lobby," which for several days they did, thereby integrating the restaurant.[18]

Her reaction to the sudden news of Sunday morning, December 7, 1941, a date that, FDR would say, "will live in infamy," would also spring her into action. Hawaii's Pearl Harbor base was "suddenly and deliberately attacked by the naval and air forces of the Empire of Japan."

The First Lady went ahead with her scheduled Sunday afternoon broadcast. "We know what we have to face," she told a stunned nation, "and we know that we are ready to face it."[19]

The next day, Edith Wilson sat prominently in the senate gallery next to Eleanor as FDR read his declaration of war on Japan. Jonathan Daniels thought that "well-preserved" Edith was far from a "symbol for the continuity of times and causes," but in "My Day" Eleanor said her presence was a reminder of the first war.[20]

Three days later, Germany and Italy declared war on America.

And amid rumors that San Francisco had been bombed and that "Jap subs" were in the Bay, a fearless First Lady flew there directly, for a prescheduled civilian-defense inspection tour.

"If I feel depressed," Mrs. Roosevelt said, "I go to work."[21]

– 54 –

"Our Eleanor"

UPSTAIRS, AMID HER chintz-covered chairs in the Sitting Hall, the First Lady sat on the edge of her desk, lecturing the household staff that they must now eat half of what they used to. In the house, change was immediate. Tours were stopped, blackout curtains ordered, GIs with machine guns stationed on the roof, a bomb shelter built. There were air-raid drills, and everyone—including Eleanor—had a gas mask ready at hand.[1]

All four of her sons, as well as Anna's husband, went off to war, placing an extra level of anxiety on Eleanor.

The First Lady's OCD job still stirred curiosity. Even the duchess of Windsor came with her little dog to see Eleanor in the office. Though Wallis wanted to visit privately, photographers turned out in droves, waiting outside the Dupont Circle Building lobby. Upstairs in her office, Eleanor met with harsh criticism as she persisted in emphasizing welfare, educational, and health issues. But when she hired her friend dancer Mayris Chaney at forty-six hundred dollars a year to initiate an exercise program—and conducted classes on the roof of the building—the First Lady was reprimanded by Congress for putting "a fan dancer" on the federal payroll, and the House voted to stop the funding of OCD's teaching of "physical fitness by dancing." The issue seemed to hit the public nerve, resulting in a tremendous flood of "more or less abusive" mail. Because Eleanor suspected the nastiness was indirectly aimed at FDR, and "in wartime it is not politically wise to attack the President," she resigned. Eleanor concluded it was "unwise" for a woman in the role of First Lady "to try a government job."[2]

Once again confounded by the role, the First Lady retreated, momentarily enjoying afternoon teas with those, like Gertrude Stein and Alice B. Toklas, whom she thought interesting. As the Axis invaded smaller nations, however, displaced royalty seeking refuge in America became frequent guests. In 1942, for example, the kings of Greece and of Yugoslavia, Holland's Wilhelmina, and the crown prince and princess of Norway all came. A frequent secret guest was British prime minister Winston Churchill, whose morning tray of liquor wheeled into the "Queen's Bedroom," announced his presence. The suite, fashioned in lady's pink, was reserved for ranking females, and was used by a succession of visiting queens, but Churchill liked it. The most intriguing guest in that suite, however, was Eleanor's personal guest, Nationalist China's Madame Chiang Kai-shek.[3]

As the generalissimo's powerful political partner, Madame's role paralleled the American First Lady, which fascinated Mrs. Roosevelt. Because Mrs. Roosevelt so championed her peer's activism, she rather naively overlooked the delicate lady's tyranny. FDR didn't, and teased Eleanor about Madame Chiang's ruthlessness when she demonstrated how she would deal with labor leaders, sliding an imaginary knife across her throat.

In town, the First Lady headed up to Union Station, where the ceremonial rooms were being used by the Community Chest's Travelers' Aid Society for soldiers. She also visited GI rest centers—for both blacks and whites—throughout the city, including the USO, and managed by volunteers like Missouri senator Harry Truman's wife. Never using elevators, she usually left all others panting as she vaulted up stairwells.[4]

War hadn't dimmed her feelings on civil rights, but it left her frustrated. She was unable to do anything directly about rumors whispered to her concerning Hitler's "final solution" for Jews. She became enraged when Japanese-Americans were evacuated to relocation camps from the West Coast, and though unable to halt the order, she boldly visited one Arizona camp as public defiance against the government's tactics. The First Lady wanted to "adopt" a family, but her husband was strongly urged to not permit her to do so. She was equally frustrated with the segregation of the armed forces, and the placement of blacks in menial jobs at the front. Of the black GIs, she wrote, "I don't wonder they are resentful & [I] will of course tell FDR but I wonder if he can do anything." FDR was unmotivated. But she never let up.[5]

Evenings were the only moments away from war pressures, but whenever Eleanor was around, she pressed Franklin with unceasing demands. "Mother," Anna curtly told her at one dinner, "can't you see you are giving Father indigestion." As Roosevelt aide Rexford Tugwell recalled, "Really serious talk at table was avoided if Roosevelt could manage it. Eleanor, so humorless and so weighed down with responsibility, made this difficult."[6]

Franklin shared almost no top-secret military affairs with her, and his military chiefs planned maneuvers from a ground floor, heavily guarded "Map Room" on a large world map, with colored pins indicating troop movement. That didn't stop Eleanor. Once, when she wanted to see where her sons were located—as indicated by special pins—she sailed in, past flustered guards.[7]

After some initial training-camp tours, the First Lady bitterly told Franklin, "We spend now to send them to die for a 'way of life' . . ." Suddenly, the young GIs, like the poor, the women, and the blacks, began to see her as their voice, and once again her mail swelled. Each GI who wrote her received a personal Eleanor letter, and she looked after their welfare: She reprimanded General Osborne when a soldier wrote that the top brass took the good seats at USO shows; helped get a soldier's poem published; had FDR's form letter of condolence rewritten with warmth; suggested to Navy Secretary Knox that overseas broadcasts include hometown news for the men; persuaded the National Gallery to open on Sundays, and helped fund National Symphony concerts for GIs visiting Washington; and got resting cots placed in Union Station. She put her earnings into war bonds, donated to war charities, and visited hospitals. Yet, she lamented, "I do not seem to be doing anything useful."[8]

Franklin had, in the meantime, paved the way for Eleanor to break yet another precedent. Leaving with Tommy for the British Isles in October of 1942, she became the first First Lady to fly the Atlantic, and though Edith Wilson had been to Europe during her tenure, Eleanor became the first to make a solo trip there. When her plane landed in Ireland, the secret was out. Now, instead of a miner, it was an Irishman who repeated the familiar, astonished, "Why, there's Mrs. Roosevelt."

Staying part of the time with the royal family at Windsor, Eleanor spent every moment inspecting—bombed London, American Red Cross units, women's training centers and voluntary services, the defense grottoes beneath the white cliffs of Dover, a Spitfire factory. She emphasized her role as the GIs' link to home, and took down their names and families' addresses as she toured a parachute battalion, a bomber squadron, a photo reconnaissance unit, a tank corps—and the Liverpool barracks of segregated black troops. At a shipyard, in the cold drizzle, she addressed fifteen thousand workers. She spoke on the BBC. She lunched with women members of Parliament. Churchill wired FDR that she was "a great success," and Foreign Secretary Anthony Eden toasted her, "first, as the first lady of the United States; second, as the wife of a great President . . ." In America, a Gallup Poll gave her an approval rate of three out of five, stating that she was the most criticized and praised woman in American history.

When she heard grievances from servicemen about the lack of durable socks in the freezing British Isles, Eleanor informed a general, who responded by formal letter, as if to the Commander in Chief, that he would see to it "that no man needs to march without proper footgear."[9]

If the general had his hands full with this visiting lady, there was another equally annoyed one back home—his wife, Mrs. Dwight Eisenhower. After three-star general Ike was sent to the front, Mamie moved to the residential Wardman Park Hotel, entrenched there while Ike rose in rank, eventually becoming Supreme Commander of the Allied Expeditionary Forces in Europe. Though Elliott Roosevelt recalled seeing Mamie at the White House when Ike was appointed assistant chief of staff of the War Plans Division, Mrs. Ike's contact with Eleanor Roosevelt was limited to the annual Army-Navy Reception. But, during her regular stint as lunch waitress at the Airmans, Sailors and Soldiers Club, Mamie was serving coffee when one day Mrs. Roosevelt swept in. Mamie did not go up to introduce herself. "She was there to do her job, and so was I," Mamie told brother-in-law Milton, ". . . that wasn't the place to make a show . . ." Mamie continued pouring coffee, including a cup for the First Lady. At her apartment, however, Mamie prominently displayed a photograph of FDR, simply because she "liked Mrs. Roosevelt." She exhibited it for years, despite criticism from some of Ike's military aides.

Mrs. Ike's public appearances, however, became less anonymous. She placed a wreath at an Armistice Day ceremony at the Tomb of the Unknown Soldier. On another occasion, Mamie joined Edith Wilson in the Red Cross uniform, pulling numbers from bin to choose blood donors. Besides writing to Ike, who wrote or telegrammed almost daily, Mamie was asked to answer her elderly mother-in-law's public mail, as well as the hundreds of fan letters that came to her. Besides all this, she was lobbied by military personnel asking her to influence Ike in getting them higher positions. While the general scorned those who saw the army as a mere job, her son said Mamie "exhibited little sympathy with her husband's point of view."[10]

Mamie appeared happy in public, but privately she was suffering. With the quite real fear that Ike would be killed, she was physically unable to hold down food. She lost twenty pounds, had a serious bout of pneumonia, and strained her heart condition even further. Besides this, she suffered from severe vertigo attacks, nausea, visual blurriness, all the result of Ménière's disease, which affected her inner ear. There was also mental anxiety over the rumors that Ike was in love with another woman. She was so uncertain that she felt it important enough to raise the question of infidelity in letters to him.

Ike detailed each individual of his wartime "family," and described an Irishwoman in the British Army, Kay Summersby, as "my driver and secretary," adding, "All are nice—and I think all personally devoted to me." Life magazine thought so, too, and when Eisenhower moved headquarters to Algiers, it printed a photo of him with Kay, described as his "pretty Irish driver." Mamie asked Ike about Kay's being sent down to him. He responded, "So Life says my old driver came down! so she did—but the big reason she wanted to serve in this theater is that she is terribly in love with a young American Colonel and is to be married to him come June—assuming both are alive. I doubt that Life told that. But I tell you only so that if anyone is banal and foolish enough to lift an eyebrow at an old duffer such as I am in connection with the

Waacs—Red Cross workers—nurses and drivers—you will know that I've no emotional involvements and will have none."[11]

If Kay Summersby—later Morgan—told friends that she and Ike were in love, there were few who knew whether it was true. His own son—who saw much of Kay when later assigned to work with his father—said, "No one alive can say that isolated incidents as described by Mrs. Morgan positively did not happen."[12]

Evidently, Mamie believed the rumors, because she continued to ask Ike about Kay. As early as August 1942, the question of other women near the general was raised. "Darling," Ike wrote her, "stop worrying about me. The few women I've met are nothing—absolutely nothing compared to you, and besides I've neither the time nor the youth to worry about them. I love you—always." The day before, he had written that he wished she were a Red Cross official, because "[t]hen you might be ordered here. How I'd like that—you're good for me, and I do much better work when you're around." Still, more than twenty-four months later, he wrote," "I assure you again—you are my only girl. I love you and can say no more than that." And, yet again, after writing about his attempt to have her permitted to come to his European headquarters once fighting ceased, he responded with exasperation, "I'm not even going to argue about the coming over business; apparently you don't choose to believe anything I say so that's that."[13]

In July 1943, Mamie wrote Ike back, telling him she was "following your success closely." On their anniversary, he responded, "After twenty-seven years my only regret is that we cannot begin once more and live them all over again. Much love always." Sometimes, when Mamie asked, he gave her privileged information. On April 24, 1943, he wired that a friend, Lieutenant Campbell, was captured, and to relay this news that she had requested on him to his family.[14]

Mamie questioned Ike's letter, which said that if she came to Europe to see him, he suggested doing so away from his headquarters. As he explained to her in a typed letter, "The only reason that I have always suggested meeting me somewhere else in the event I could get away for a day or so is because I cannot allow, as a matter of policy, wives of soldiers to come into this theater. Consequently, I couldn't allow you to come because it would be taking advantage of my own position." He thanked her for a photo of herself and John, adding that "you look almost as young as he does. When I come home everybody will assume that I am the father of you both."[15]

Before Ike would come home, Mrs. Roosevelt would leave home again. Now nicknamed "Rover" by Franklin, Eleanor undertook an even riskier trip in 1943, without Tommy. In an uncomfortable military plane, dubbed "Our Eleanor," the First Lady made a grueling flight to the South Pacific, touring New Zealand, Australia, and nearly every

small island where American troops were stationed, as the Red Cross's "special delegate."[16]

Waking up at 6:00 A.M. so she could breakfast with the boys, Mrs. Roosevelt found that her days proved more exhausting than any previous schedule. GIs were told not to shower naked in the rain because Eleanor might pop up at any moment. When the boys shouted, "How's Eleanor?" to USO entertainer Gary Cooper, he yelled back, "Well, we saw her tracks in the sand at one of the islands where we stopped, but we couldn't tell which way they were headed." In Australia, she rubbed the nose of a native Maori tribeswoman.

Her escort, Admiral William F. Halsey, who had initially balked at the waste of time the First Lady's visit would entail, "marvelled at her hardihood, both physical and mental . . . she went into every ward, stopped at every bed, and spoke to every patient: What was his name? How did he feel? Was there anything he needed? Could she take a message home for him?" She "walked for miles, and she saw patients who were grievously and gruesomely wounded. But I marvelled most at their expressions as she leaned over them. It was a sight I will never forget."

As the *Pacific Times* wrote, she symbolized "some boy's mother back home, [more] than the wife of the President . . ." One GI wrote that her motherly voice and questions had an extremely emotional effect. "Maybe it sounds funny," wrote Captain Robert M. White, "but she left behind her many a tough battletorn GI blowing his nose and swearing at the cold he had recently picked up." As men prepared to head out for open combat, she insisted on walking through the jungle to wish each truckload of boys good luck. Joe Lash said it was the first time her voice quavered.

From the moment of her arrival, Eleanor was determined to visit the famous Guadalcanal island, where Americans had defeated the Japanese in perhaps the bloodiest battle of the war. Halsey had stalled that decision, hoping to dissuade her, but after spending time with her, he concurred, saying, "She alone had accomplished more good than any other person, or any group of civilians, who had passed through my area."

At Guadalcanal, as she passed a carload of Seabees, the First Lady leaned out of her passing jeep and waved. "Gosh, there's Eleanor," shouted one shocked GI. When fifty marines passed in a bus, the driver did a double take and drove into a ditch. Though the Japanese had bombed the island the night before her arrival, she remained calm. By trip's end, it was estimated that she had personally seen four hundred thousand men, about 10 percent of the entire armed forces. She also kept writing "My Day"—typing it out after teaching herself on a battered typewriter.[17]

Shortly before Eleanor had begun her South Pacific trip, in May of 1943, Nellie Taft died. Before becoming ill, however, Nellie Taft had sailed back to the White House one last time. This woman, who'd first determined to live in this house when she visited Lucy Hayes there nearly seventy years before, was now welcomed by a woman Nellie had known as the insecure niece of President Teddy Roosevelt. Early in 1941, Eleanor Roosevelt warmly welcomed back Nellie Taft as her "honored guest," for a luncheon honoring Supreme Court justices' wives. The women gathered in the Blue Room. The former First Lady stood and "surveyed with many memories of the past."

Her grandson William, while teaching in Maryland, had provided her company when he lived with her temporarily in the early forties. He recalled how there was still a perceptible trace in Nellie's voice of the stroke she had suffered long before. During the war, she had seen the beginning of the building of the Jefferson Memorial encircled by her cherry blossoms, but also, because of the war, the suspension of the annual Japanese Cherry Blossom Festival. Just before she died, Mrs. Taft was memorialized by a small, impersonal plaque that simply marked the first tree, which she had planted.[18]

"How incredible it all seems," Grace Coolidge had written just after Pearl Harbor, "it will be a long hard conflict which will call for the utmost effort upon the part of every one of us but we cannot doubt that the forces which have truth and right and justice on their side will win." She prayed for leaders who would "establish the new peace upon foundations which will uphold it for long, long years to come." Grace had immediately thrown herself into war work: Red Cross bandage-rolling, serving as a civilian-defense monitor, selling bonds, joining the Victory Book campaign, following food and utility conservation, and pulling her own wheeled cart into the grocery, instead of using her car.

Women of all ages were doing their part. The summer before starting Smith College, teenager Barbara Pierce worked at a nut-and-bolt factory near her home in Rye, joining other young women sorting the pieces that would eventually find a place in America's defense. Six months before, while on Christmas break from her South Carolina boarding school, Ashley Hall, Miss Pierce had attended a society dance in Greenwich, Connecticut. There, she met George Herbert Walker Bush, a recent Andover Academy graduate. He asked her to dance, and he became the first man she kissed. By that summer, they became quietly engaged before he took off as a naval aviator, but since she was notoriously bad at keeping a secret, he cracked that only the "German and Japanese high command weren't aware of it."

Barbara began Smith in the fall of 1943, but didn't meet Nancy there. The two students missed being at Smith together by one year. Miss Pierce started just three months after Miss Davis graduated. Although Barbara lived on campus in Northampton, not far from Grace Coolidge's home, she never got to meet or see her, and after reading about the former First Lady, said she was "very sorry" not to have, "as I would have loved knowing her."

When the navy chose Smith College as a training ground for Women Appointed for Voluntary Emergency Service (WAVES), Mrs. Coolidge became their foster mother, entertaining them, hosting parties, attending ceremonies. For a nominal rent, she gave them her home, and moved in with friends. After work, Grace often treated WAVES and friends to dinner at the local hot spot, Wiggins Tavern, where students, like Nancy Davis, flocked, "many, many times," as she recalled.

After her 1943 graduation, Nancy returned to Chicago, working at the Marshall Field department store, and as a Cook County Hospital nurse's aide. The sight of wounded men didn't disturb her, and she worked diligently as the only woman in a ward of forty men, since most professional nurses were at the front. On her very first day, she even bathed a man who turned out to be dead. "Science," she admitted, "was never a strong subject for me in school." Acting was her passion, so she soon made the switch from hospital to Chicago USO center, entertaining troops.

When her mother's friend ZaSu Pitts asked a thrilled Nancy to take a nonspeaking role in a Broadway show, *Ramshackle Inn*, she accepted, moving to New York. It opened in January 1944, and closed quickly with bad reviews, but Nancy's role was so small, it didn't appear in the

program. When she played a Chinese woman in *Lute Song*, director John Houseman dismissed her as an "awkward and amateurish virgin." His critique didn't deter the tenacious actress.

Nancy also had her mother's friends Walter Huston and Spencer Tracy, both in New York, looking after her. Through Tracy, Clark Gable got Nancy's number, and called her for dates. She had a crush on him, and when they went to the Stork Club, all eyes focused on them. "It was my first experience going anywhere with a star of that magnitude," she said. "He made me feel important, and I must say it gave my ego a boost."[19]

Back in Washington, women were working overtime for the war. On Capitol Hill, when Congressman Johnson enlisted in the navy, he left Lady Bird in charge of his office as his proxy. "I learned I could handle things if I tried hard enough . . . [and] I could Make A Living. It was a good thing to know, and it gave me an increasing sense of self-reliance and self-esteem." Not long after, she risked her sixty-seven-thousand-dollar inheritance by buying a "small, down at heels, no-nighttime, low-wattage, in-debt-to-everybody radio station in Austin with absentee owners who were glad to sell."[20]

With the images of toiling "Rosie the Riveter" and "Rover" Roosevelt, there seemed a new chance to pass an Equal Rights Amendment to the Constitution, a move initiated two decades previous. Edith

Wilson was doing her part for the war. She mowed her own lawn and stopped using her car, giving way to the rather odd sight of the grand lady riding city buses and hiking rides in a friend's work truck. But she was uncooperative with the National Women's party's plea:

> . . . we who worked side by side with our husbands and realize . . . the power of equality . . . should stand for that equality which must come after this terrible war is over . . . you, being a Virginia gentlewoman . . . have rarely allowed the use of your name in any political move-ment, but for the sake of peace of the future . . . I feel now is the time above all other times for you to come forth and speak.

They asked Edith for "a letter endorsing the ERA." Across the re-quest was written Edith's response: "No reply." Eleanor opposed the ERA, but "on the ground that until female workers were better orga-nized, they needed the protective legislation for which a generation of social reformers had worked so hard."[21]

As Edith joined Mamie at events sponsored by the Red Cross, the organization got a new volunteer secretary in 1942—Pat Nixon—who arrived in town after successfully urging Dick to take a position at the Office of Price Administration. Pat got a paying job at the OPA also, reviewing businesses that claimed price freezes would ruin them. Within a year, however, Dick was fighting in the Pacific—where he glimpsed Mrs. Roosevelt—and Pat worked as an OPA price analyst in San Francisco, enjoying her renewed independence and choosing books to send him—from Karl Marx to Guy de Maupassant.[22]

American women of all ages and classes were exercising all types of independence. When wartime restrictions created a servant shortage at Hammersmith Farm, Jacqueline Bouvier worked in the gardens, learned housecleaning, and cooked for her family. Like Eleanor Roosevelt, she was disturbed at even small signs of bigotry. To the straight-A student, it was clear that blacks and Jews were specifically excluded from Farm-ington. She determined someday to change that.[23]

A similar realization was being made in Georgia. Rosalynn Smith was shocked when a black girl she knew came to the back door seeking her help on a school paper, full of errors. Rosalynn realized standards were lower in black schools, but said that "challenging the status quo was inconceivable." The only white person who crossed into the black section was Lillian Carter, a nurse and mother of Rosalynn's friend Ruth. During the war, Miss Smith earned her own money by giving shampoos in a beauty parlor. By the time she graduated, the studious young woman was class valedictorian and, though trembling, delivered her first speech. She wanted to leave little Plains, but financial con-straints permitted her only to commute by Greyhound bus to Georgia Southwestern, a junior college.[24]

Yet another woman, this one in the Midwest, was disturbed at the poor education that segregation caused. But the dance teacher ignored the color line, and weekly traveled to teach young, enthusiastic, talented blacks. Though her family voiced disapproval, she kept teaching, and in her own way helped to break the racial barriers. Betty Bloomer wasn't trying to cause trouble, it was just that there were no black dance teachers in Grand Rapids.

The "Martha Graham of Grand Rapids," started the town's first modern-dance troups, staging one avant-garde performance on the cement steps of a Baptist church, leading up to the altar, using a voice choir and unusual instruments. But in Grand Rapids, free spirits were not the norm, and Betty soon found herself caving in to societal pressures. Against her better judgment, she became engaged to a conservative lawyer, but handed back his ring because he wanted her "to change my ways . . ." Amid uncertainty, she rushed into marriage with one Bill Warren, following him to Toledo, where she taught dance at the university, and to Syracuse, where she worked in a frozen-food factory on a production line, inspecting and boxing vegetables on a conveyor belt. Returning to Grand Rapids, Betty was hired as the executive fashion coordinator for a large store, dealing with buyers, advertisers, and models for shows. She wearied of Bill's drinking, and as the war neared its end, so did Betty's marriage.[25]

If the *Our Eleanor* flew the South Pacific, the *Barbara* was shot down. Barbara Pierce, as it developed, was not to be in Northhampton for long. When she learned that her fiancé, navy pilot George Bush, had been downed in his torpedo bomber, which he named and had painted in her honor, they had a wartime wedding upon his return. Barbara began keeping a family scrapbook.[26]

Meanwhile, another wife separated from her husband by war, Mamie Eisenhower, was showing her scrapbooks full of stories to reporters coming to see her, curious about Ike. Her brother-in-law said she was "just naturally comfortable" with people, "even reporters," and the press found her a "witty" woman of "remarkable self-control, for never by word or sign does she indicate that there is any strain for her in the separation." In referring to the scrapbooks, however, she admitted, "One or two articles which have recently been written are conspicuously missing . . . because she herself has such a deep respect for her husband . . . and . . . resents deeply any inference of flippancy." The "flippancy" consisted of stories on Ike and Kay.

For the many reporters and a group of army wives she regularly invited to her apartment, Mamie always kept a roast or ham on hand for sandwiches. And though never for herself, she also kept a well-stocked liquor cabinet for them.[27]

Mamie *never* drank much. When she used Barclay bourbon, "her preferred blend" for her favorite cocktail, an old-fashioned, she always insisted that it be made very "light and with plenty of fruit." But a few of the women she spent her evenings with playing mah-jongg did tend to drink heavily. One, in fact, was an alcoholic. It was Mamie's best friend, and the wife of Ike's chief assistant.[28]

An Abilene, Kansas, newspaper editor and acquaintance of Ike's, Henry Jameson, later offered the opinion, "It was an old, old story, one that happened many times during the war. It was tied to a whirl which led many officers' wives during that period of stress and loneliness to drink too much. For a year or even two, Mamie was part of that whirl, worrying too much, drinking a little too much. There is not much doubt that the Summersby story was a significant factor. It reached a point where members of the family became seriously concerned about her, afraid that she might be approaching an alcohol problem. I must emphasize that it had not reached that point. Still, one close family member talked seriously to her and Mamie quickly understood what was happening and where she would be drifting. She stopped at once. And after that, she took only a single drink."[29]

The one family member who saw Mamie regularly at this time, and whose advice she took seriously, was Milton. "She drank no more than anyone did in those days—which, for a 'lady' was only one. But, she did think some of the others had a little too much . . . I only told her to be careful not to drink too freely in front of strangers. You could have a ginger ale in your hands and people can say whatever they want. I heard those stories, and I told her to be careful. Not about drinking too much—because she didn't—but about drinking in front of those miserable . . . gals."[30]

One of the "gals" Mamie befriended was fellow Wardman Park apartment resident Perle Mesta. Trusting Perle, Mamie frankly shared her personal emotions, saying of herself and Ike, "Neither of us really knew what the other went through." Perle viewed the revelation out of context, and though she knew nothing of Mamie's serious illnesses— Ménière's disease and a heart condition—drew observations about the army wives and their drinking. She reserved comment, at least for the moment.[31]

In some households, the separation of wife and husband had become a matter of convenience. In December 1943, FDR had refused Eleanor's request to join him in meetings with Stalin and Churchill in Tehran. But in the spring of 1944, Eleanor undertook her third tour, this time to the noncombat military bases in the Caribbean and Central and South America, a total of thirteen thousand miles, which Franklin himself planned. She hadn't wanted to make this trip, but went "because my husband insisted . . ."[32]

Overcoming a serious influenza bout in the winter, FDR relaxed away from Washington, at his Warm Springs, Georgia, cottage, Bernie Baruch's South Carolina estate, or at the rustic cabins of Shangri-La, the newly established presidential retreat in the nearby Maryland mountains. He never lacked for female presence. Since Missy LeHand's stroke, he had relished the company of his daughter, Anna, as well as Norway's Princess Martha, who even substituted as White House hostess when Eleanor was away, which seemed outrageous to some—an actual monarch in the democratic first ladyship. Eleanor was less than pleased when Harry Hopkins's new wife, Louise Macy, was invited by Franklin to come live in the White House, and left strict rules for the bride, making clear that though in absentia often, this president's wife was still *the* mistress of the house. Unknown to her, there was a mistress of the heart.[33]

In the winter of 1944, just six weeks after her husband, "Winnie" Rutherford, died, Lucy Mercer Rutherford was with FDR, lunching at Baruch's. On July 7, she came for the first time to the White House, dining with Franklin and Anna. The next day, she returned for another dinner, and the next day they drove together to Shangri-La. On the twenty-fourth, Franklin and Anna drove to the airport to see Lucy during a "stopover." A month later, it was tea at the White House. A week after that, Franklin and Lucy reunited when his Hyde Park–bound train stopped at Allamuchy, New Jersey, Mrs. Rutherford's home. Two months later, it was lunch together at Warm Springs.[34]

Publicly, the president seemed resigned to serve yet another four years. He wanted to lead the country in the postwar era, particularly in deciding Europe's fate. On the morning of June 6, those prospects became inevitable.

"What invasion?" a shocked Mamie Eisenhower responded. A reporter had called to ask what she thought about her husband's successful staging of the largest military invasion in world history as American troops stormed onto the beaches of Normandy, France. Having herself broadcast two Christmas messages over the radio, Mamie permitted the Office of War Information to release a statement reflecting for the public "the great strain" she had privately been living through:

> We know that our men . . . have many trying hours ahead. Hours in which we will . . . be restless and unnerved . . . And yet if we ask our fighting men what they would have us do, they would tell us ". . . remaining as cheerful and busy as possible." So let's have faith . . . and work a little harder than ever before . . .[35]

Mrs. Roosevelt was somber about D-Day. During the Normandy invasion, the First Lady made a speech expressing hope for speedy victory, but adding "It is not enough to win the fight. We must win *that for which we fight*—the triumph of all people who believe that the people of this world are worthy of freedom."[36]

- 55 -

Unprecedented

"SOMETIMES," ELEANOR ROOSEVELT wearily admitted, "I feel like I am dressing the Washington Monument."

In the course of redefining her unprecedented first ladyship, Eleanor had created an overpowering paean, which some of the public elevated to sainthood. Without the crises of depression and world war, could the First Lady continue breaking barriers? Now, facing yet another four-year term—but this one in a prosperous postwar era—could even Eleanor emulate and improve upon her decade of accomplishments? And what of the women who would someday follow her? Would the legend of "Eleanor the Good" prove unrealistic to endure for a woman of less lofty motivations?

By summer, when FDR was renominated for a fourth term, even Eleanor wanted out of the role. Only when she thought of the United Nations and its goal of world peace as her new project did she resign herself to another term.

Some Democratic ladies did not approve of a fourth term. In August, Edith Wilson, disapproving of Eleanor's nose-rubbing with Maori natives, secretly delighted in sending a nasty anti-FDR poem to a friend with the warning not to "dare tell" who sent it. The poem concluded with the thoughts of a Maori: ". . . A thought has just occurred to me, which I find rather stunning. Since my nose rubbed a Roosevelt nose, will it, too, keep on running?" Still Edith accepted Eleanor's continued invitations.[1]

Other women did support Roosevelt. Frances Cleveland didn't vote for FDR in 1940 because, as she told her son, "Your father did not believe in third terms," but she *did* in 1944, because Grover had "never said anything about a fourth term!" Mamie Eisenhower also evidently voted for Roosevelt, but out of military loyalty, not politics. "She viewed Roosevelt from the distaff side," her daughter-in-law Barbara later explained. "In the Army, you don't actively support a political party . . ."[2]

Mamie was slightly "upset," however, when FDR failed to invite her along to the White House when he conferred with Ike, secretly back in the States in the winter of 1944–45. Although the Eisenhowers spent six isolated days together, Ike was "only in for a very short time, and she wanted to be with him every minute—even if just for the car ride down to the White House." The secretiveness of Ike's return furthered pressures and gossip. When the general was smuggled into Wardman Park through a back entrance to see her, rumors spread among residents that *she* had an unidentified lover, but because his trip was secret, Mamie couldn't deny the rumors by confirming it was Ike.[3]

Sadly, she also realized, "He belonged to the world and not to me anymore." Though she'd admit, "There were a lot of times when Ike broke my heart," he reassured her that "there is no 'problem' separating us . . ." Mamie was displeased with the 1944 visit of the "problem," treating Kay "with cool disdain," and asking Ike's biographer, Kenneth Davis, not to mention her.[4]

Regardless of the precise nature of his relationship with Kay Summersby, General Eisenhower used this time with Mamie to verbally renew his filial devotion to her. As one discreet woman writer would put it, Mamie "gained new strength and awareness of her importance as a wife by talking through their mutual problems during the days she and the General were together." One night, after Ike impulsively rounded up cold cuts and onions, he and Mamie stayed up talking until dawn. And there were other unspoken signs of Ike's affection for his wife. One morning, he slipped a package onto her breakfast tray. It was a platinum watch with diamonds. Instead of building his collection of golf clubs and trout rods, the general of the United States Army had pinched his weekly paycheck—save for cigarette money and petty cash—to get this for Mamie.

Albeit unwittingly, Mrs. Eisenhower was no longer some routine army wife. She also made her presence felt in the U.S. armed forces. While at Fort Sam Houston she demanded that a passageway from the dining room be closed off so she could have a wall long enough for her sideboard. "It almost took an act of Congress—government property is supposed to remain intact until it falls apart," said Mamie, "but I got my way. I think they gave in to shut me up, so other wives wouldn't get the same idea."[5]

Other women also resisted having their husbands in the limelight. Under pressure from FDR's operative James Byrnes a the Democratic Convention, Senator Truman finally accepted the vice-presidential nomination, which he won after the balloting. Already, however, the scrappy bespectacled fellow with the double-breasted jacket, bow tie, and pocket-square had made a grave error. He had forgotten to clear his decision with the Boss. This Boss didn't run a political district, but rather held sway over the senator's decisions, and could stop his cusswords with a single glance. The Boss worked daily in the Senate office, and long into the night with him, alone at home. *This* Boss was his wife.

After the nomination, as Bess Truman and her husband left the floor, she wore her stone face, indicating a rising temper, which she usually held. Not this time. She tersely turned on Harry: "Are we going to have to go through this all the rest of our lives?" Eating crow, he said nothing. "What would happen if he should die?" she badgered. "You'd be President."

During the war, Bess had rolled bandages for the Red Cross and cut carrots for the USO, but she despised publicity. Behind-the-scenes strategies, issues, and policy were her forte. As one party leader said, Bess was "a shrewd politician." Daily, she read the Congressional Record cover to cover. She understood tax bills, mistrusted the wiliness of FDR, was a source for pro-Truman newspaper editors, and ran Harry's office when he was out of town. Unlike Mrs. Roosevelt, whom she admired, Bess kept her politics secret. She did not want to appear powerful.[6]

Mrs. Truman feared "this awful public life" for many reasons. Privately, she worried that the press might discover that her father had committed suicide, and that her brother was an alcoholic. Just after the convention, she had her first press encounter as the notorious "Payroll Bess." Republican congresswoman Clare Boothe Luce charged the senator with nepotism, and had so-dubbed his wife because Truman hired her at forty-five hundred dollars annually to work in his Capitol Hill office. The senator shot right back, "She earns every cent of it. She helps me with my personal mail, helps me with my speeches and with my committee work. I don't know where I could get a more efficient or willing worker . . . I never make a speech . . . and . . . decision unless she is in on it. Not one of these reports has been issued without going through her hands."

Bess remained publicly mute on the subject. As she said, "A woman's place in public is to sit beside her husband, be silent and be sure her hat is on straight."[7]

Neither Bess nor Eleanor made many campaign appearances. Rumors circulated that Democratic leaders were quieting the First Lady because of her views on desegregating the army forces, which she denied. "You can't live in the White House for eleven years and not have made friends and foes. But if, because you have certain convictions, you have made foes, would those people, on Election Day, let their feelings toward you influence their vote? I doubt it, doubt it very much. When they vote they will consider the person who really matters, and they will say to themselves: 'What she thinks and feels doesn't make a pin's difference.' . . ."[8]

Her lack of involvement reflected her attitude toward politically active women at the time, and she broached a subject that many thought might have personal implications for her—the exciting but distant notion of the first woman president. The First Lady said that "women have not reached enough political maturity for a woman to become

President. Any elected official in a democracy must have a sense of being backed by as great a proportion of the people as possible, and I doubt if women have held enough public offices to have acquired that sense." But, she concluded, "[t]he time will come . . . when a woman can be elected . . ." After FDR won, Eleanor was asked how she felt about four more years for herself. She searched carefully for words to express her private emotions: ". . . everyone should be glad for opportunity even if they are not glad for responsibility."[9]

As she had been for the last three Inaugurals, Queen Mother Wilson was an honored guest at the fourth Roosevelt swearing-in, though momentarily insulted when the Inaugural Office didn't mail her invitation to the White House ceremony until two days before the event. Only after Mrs. Roosevelt "then insisted" did Edith accept, escorted by Baruch. As Eleanor greeted the two thousand people invited for a postceremony lunch in the dilapidated house, the crowd was sprinkled with familiar faces who'd weathered the Depression and war. There was Mary Bethune. Harry Hopkins and Grace Tully brought memories of the late Louis Howe and Missy LeHand, respectively. There were new faces, too. Bess Truman stood beside the First Lady, who'd also invited busloads of wounded GIs.[10]

Even Edith Wilson comprehended the toll of war. "I think we all feel solemn this year," she wrote Eleanor, offering hope "that the world may rise again from . . . suffering and horror through which we have lived . . ." Edith would be seeing Eleanor, having accepted the invitation to an annual event:

The Thrift Shop
cordially invites you to a
White Elephant Tea
at the Sulgrave Club
on April Twelfth from four to six
our guest of honor
Mrs. Franklin Delano Roosevelt[11]

While Eleanor kept to her typically ambitious schedule, the president kept seeing Lucy Mercer Rutherford. On March 12, with Anna and her husband, FDR and Lucy went motoring before dinner. The next night, it was dinner at the White House again, this time with the Canadian prime minister. The day after, it was lunch *and* dinner. Days later, it was another motoring trip and dinner, alone together. The following afternoon there was tea, just for two.[12]

At the White House, Lucy seemed more familiar than the new Second Lady. When the latter made her first appearance there in that role, attending one of Eleanor's "women in government" luncheons, assistant usher J. B. West hadn't a clue who the sturdy-looking woman was. "Mrs. Truman," replied Mrs. Truman.[13]

Nevertheless, around town, Bess Truman was being feted as guest of honor at dinners, like the one hosted by Chicago socialite Gussie Goodwin, at which invitee Mamie Eisenhower made a rare appearance. By now, Mrs. Ike was a celebrity in her own right, but she tended to befriend those who, like Bess, shared her own midwestern values and propriety. Bess and Mamie's backgrounds were remarkably parallel, as daughters of domineering matriarchs to whom they were deeply attached, as well as being mothers of only one child. Both had grown up wealthy by the standards of their small-town roots, and both were addicted to that most popular of ladies' table games, bridge. There were some obvious differences. Mamie was a chatty extrovert in bright, flamboyant dresses. Bess's own daughter, twenty-year-old Margaret, called her mother a "pessimist," and in a severe uniform of navy blue, open-toe shoes, boxy hats, and shoulder pads, Mrs. Truman appeared forbidding. As differently they viewed their sudden fame, neither "lady" liked being a public woman.

To the few who knew them well, folksy Bess and Mamie were thoughtful women with a sense of spontaneous humor, who also shared a fascination with Latin American culture. Together they joined Gussie's Spanish Speaking Society language classes, along with other women, mostly Democrats. As a founder, Mamie signed an incorporation certificate, and cooked her share of the Latin luncheons that the women served each other after class.[14]

Though she claimed to have no political ambitions, Mamie became excited when someone told her that General Eisenhower was considered future presidential material. "Oh! Oh! *Me in the White House!* . . . .I'll put it on the teletype right away."[15]

Mamie was *in* the White House now, at "several occasions," as a regularly "invited guest" of Mrs. Roosevelt's. If the First Lady knew anything about Mamie's personal life, it was only that she was not in robust health. Others, however, jealously twisted that into gossip. When one "friend" revealed that Mamie sometimes stumbled, she conveniently left out the fact that Mrs. Eisenhower suffered from severe vertigo attacks, and implied that she drank. As UPI White House correspondent Merriman Smith said, she "sometimes found it necessary to touch somebody to get a point of reference or cross a room" because of her vertigo. Mamie would state clearly, "I don't think there's anybody that drinks less than I."[16]

As early as November 1943, when she sponsored an East Room conference on United Nations relief and rehabilitation, Mrs. Roosevelt had been interested in the organization. Now, at her April 12 press conference, she told the "Green Room girls," that she would join FDR at the San Francisco UN conference later in the month. That must have come as a unspoken surprise to the "girls," because independent Eleanor had never traveled with the autonomous Franklin to a political, let alone international, conference. Perhaps the couple would draw closer as they aged.[17]

"You know," the president confided to an astonished Elliott, "I think that your mother and I might be able to get together now and do things together, take some trips maybe, learn to know each other again . . . I only wish she wasn't so darned busy. I could have her with me so much more if she didn't have so many other engagements." Delighted, Elliott went to his mother with this promising change of heart. Eleanor's response was equally encouraging: "I hope this will come to pass."

"You know that I do," the son told his mother.[18]

After the press conference, Mrs. Roosevelt hurried over to the Sulgrave, where she listened to a concert, took tea, and sat next to Mrs. Wilson as the speakers began.

At that very moment, in Warm Springs, President Roosevelt put his hand to his head, remarking, "I have a terrific headache." He was having his portrait painted, surrounded by the artist, Madame Shoumatoff, Grace Tully, who replaced Missy LeHand as FDR's secretary, his cousins Laura Delano and Margaret Suckley. And Lucy Mercer Rutherford. Lucy, like the others, was there to provide fawning female company for FDR.

At the Sulgrave, the First Lady was called to the telephone. She took the call, then returned to Edith, whispering her apology that she had to leave. As her car sped down the avenue, she clenched her fists. "In my heart of hearts I knew what had happened . . ." In the house that suddenly was no longer her home, Eleanor was gently told that FDR had died of a cerebral hemorrhage.

Down South, moments after he died, Grace Tully snapped at Lucy rather sternly, "You better get out of here fast. Mrs. Roosevelt has just been called." Lucy fled immediately.[19]

Up North, returning from a People's Institute meeting, Grace Coolidge clicked on her radio and heard the news. She quietly slipped into a memorial service in the local auditorium. She said her "mind turned back to 1923 when another President had died," and immediately thought not of Eleanor, but another, new sorority member: "I am more sorry for Mrs. Truman than for anybody else." At Oyster Bay, old Edith Roosevelt was shocked. "Could he but have lived until Peace," she wrote sadly in her diary. She wired her widowed niece, "Love and sympathy." When Lou Hoover had died just a year before, Eleanor ignored partisanship, and impulsively wrote a moving letter to the former president. Now, he wrote her, "With Mrs. Hoover's passing I know the great vacancy that has come into your life, and I cannot forget your fine courtesy in writing to me at that time."[20]

In her modest apartment, Bess Truman, a woman known for her composure, had burst out sobbing after getting the phone call from Harry. Her mother and daughter were stunned and asked what was wrong. Through her crying, she told them. That one phone call had instantly and dramatically shaken her entire private life.

Before watching Harry take the oath in the West Wing, Bess Truman called on Eleanor, who remained in the mansion. Mrs. Truman wanted to be sure Mrs. Roosevelt remained as long as she liked, but already Eleanor had ordered the organizing, boxing, and removal of twelve years' accumulations, between her planning of the Hyde Park burial after a White House funeral.

Just prior to the funeral, however, came Anna's unpleasant revelation that Lucy Mercer Rutherford had been with the president when he died, and many times in the last year. Anna's daughter, Ellie, learned that her grandmother was at first "surprised and perhaps hurt. But by that time had become so understanding of what loyalty meant that she didn't hold it against my mother, nor [Lucy]. She was less surprised at her [Lucy's] presence, and more surprised that my mother had arranged it. But that sort of thing no longer conflicted with her ethics on loyalty. It was a matter of my mother [Anna] being loyal to FDR." Lucy's presence as an entertaining cocktail companion, Eleanor realized, could never diminish the far deeper spiritual commitment that she and Franklin had fashioned for themselves. As her friend Esther Lape said, "I don't think she ever stopped loving someone she loved." Not long afterward, Lucy wrote her sympathies to Eleanor, who responded in kind.[21]

While packing, Eleanor reminisced about FDR, "He was a very lonesome man. I wish I had been able to be closer to him, to comfort him sometimes, but I suppose that could not be."[22]

After the funeral, a forlorn Mrs. Helm and Tommy sat with their heads down. Suddenly, a hand reached into Mrs. Helm's as the guests filed out. It was the new First Lady. Here was a woman who loathed what life was now to offer, and her first impulse was to soothe a staff member.[23]

With all of her other responsibilities, Mrs. Roosevelt felt Mrs. Truman's smooth transition into the first ladyship to be important enough for her to help. She gave a guided tour of the second and third floors. After FDR's funeral but before his burial, Mrs. Roosevelt said her last press conference could be Bess's first, and she would introduce the new First Lady to the "girls."

Graciously, the midwestern matriarch accepted this offer. Inwardly, she trembled with fear.

Not only was she shy, but Mrs. Truman did not want to be First Lady—especially one who attracted publicity. On the train going back to Washington, Mrs. Truman asked Frances Perkins if it was all right if she did not hold press conferences. Perkins assured her that they had only begun with Mrs. Roosevelt.[24]

A row behind Bess at the funeral had sat one of her predecessors, Edith Wilson. Perhaps thinking of Woodrow's slow demise, she was emotionally shaken by FDR's death and quite sympathetic to Eleanor, writing the latter that she hoped the world's empathy would "sustain and strengthen you." But it was as Mrs. Roosevelt prepared to leave Washington forever that Mrs. Wilson dropped all pretense, opening up to this sorority sister who'd made every attempt to include Edith in White House events, where she magnanimously shared the limelight. Neither seemed to ever really understand the other, but they had grown to respect each other. "Washington will miss you, but wherever you are, you will carry with you the assurance of a welcome back and the earnest hope that the many interests you have will fill the void in your life that fell with such crushing suddenness."[25]

Eleanor seemed to doubt that. With all of her accomplishments, she still felt "lost deep down inside myself," troubled by the old question of whether she had achieved because she was the wife of a powerful president, or as a power in and of herself.

When she met waiting reporters in New York, where she'd now live, they asked what she would do next. Eleanor Roosevelt stopped in her tracks, and turned around with a single response.

"The story is over."[26]

PART XI

The Atomic Age and Fabulous Fifties 1945–1961

As a result of successful careers in many lines where they compete with men, women are learning their own strength. Unintentionally they now frequently take the dominant role in marriage . . . Every marriage has a delicate balance of power. More and more today it is tipped toward the woman. But our research shows that the happiest marriages are still those where the male wears the britches.

—JAMES F. BENDER, Ph.D.
"The Trouble with Most Brides . . ."
American Magazine (1948)

"I Have Nothing to Say to the Public"

AFTER MRS. ROOSEVELT'S farewell April 19 press conference, some of the "girls" rushed to a radio station to do a broadcast evaluating Eleanor's first ladyship, calling it "one of the most important aspects of this passing chapter in American history."[1]

For the new First Lady, that was the handwriting on the wall.

"The country was used to Eleanor Roosevelt," Bess Wallace Truman reflected. "I couldn't possibly be anything like her." And then she added one of those delightfully starch Bess Trumanisms.

"I wasn't going down in any coal mines."[2]

Margaret Truman wrote that her mother, "whose public facade has been unvaryingly sedate and whose public utterances have been . . . cryptic, is the least understood of our family."

Bess didn't mind being misunderstood. She didn't even mind not moving into "*that* place."—the White House. "I just dread moving over there."

Unfortunately for Mrs. Truman, many others dreaded it, too.

Journalist Helen Brown said Bess Truman had caught the "girls" with "their pencils down." Bess and Margaret did host a tea for them, but the most revealing thing they learned was the First Lady's favorite color: gray. When an exasperated reporter finally had the audacity to ask the First Lady how she expected them to write about her if she wouldn't talk to them, Bess did respond: "You don't need to know me. I'm only the president's wife and the mother of his daughter." One sarcastic reporter noted that while Eleanor had been no social lioness, "surely, Bess Truman was not sent from above for the Restoration."[3]

Mrs. Truman finally made a concession to the reporters clamoring for news to keep their careers going. Bess directed her two secretaries to brief the press weekly with mimeographed information about her public schedule. For Edith Helm, staying on as social secretary, the terror of such an unexpected duty was frightening: "Whatever is made public about a President's wife is matter for vital concern to her husband and his administration . . . I knew that when I was brought face to face with press women who had asked Mrs. Roosevelt searching questions, I might easily make one of those disastrous errors of judgement." Elderly Mrs. Helm pronounced her boss as "made of equal parts of goodness and granite." Only a discreet woman could work for Bess, and Mrs. Helm would handle everything, including press, always first consulting the president's press secretary before her conferences. It was the first working relationship of the West and East Wing staffs.[4]

The reporters' attempts to learn something interesting by submitting written questions to Bess failed miserably. When asked if she thought there would ever be a woman president, if she would want a son to become president, or if she ever wanted to be president, her response was simply, "No." To the questions of what her concept of the role of First Lady was, and what special training she recommended for a woman preparing to become First Lady, her answer was, "No comment." She did offer, "Skill in public speaking would be very helpful," to the question of what professional training was good preparation for the first ladyship. Asked what character traits helped in the role, she responded, "Good health and a well-developed sense of humor."

Privately, Bess bristled at even the written questions. To one reporter's inquiry, she scribbled to her personal secretary, Reathel Odum, "Better tell her. God only knows what they might be saying. I'd prefer telling her it's none of their d———business." When she responded the same way to a question about a gown she planned to wear, Reathel sanitized it as "Mrs. Truman hasn't quite made up her mind."[5]

The First Lady's instincts were best put to use on West Wing press. To friend and feminist Mary Paxton Keeley, Bess dismissed rumors that the *Kansas City Star*'s Washington correspondent, Duke Shoop, who had penned many uncomplimentary stories about the Trumans, was to be appointed as the president's press secretary. "He's made an ass of himself," Bess wrote Mary, "the way he broadcast the fact that he was going to be H's Press Sec'y. Even went down to the Press Club & spread it there of all places. If there is anybody on earth that H. has absolutely *no* use for it's D.S." Mrs. Truman instead urged the appointment of old schoolmate and Washington editor of the *St. Louis Post-Dispatch*, Charlie Ross. Mr. Truman made the appointment. And although the First Lady herself never held a formal press conference, she was interested enough in them to attend two of the president's.[6]

Though she became an honorary member of the American Newspaper Women's Club, and attended most of their functions, the First Lady refused to address them. Liz Carpenter, onetime club president, recalled that Bess not only "never made a speech," but "never even said thank you—to the point of almost being rude. You yearned for her to say, 'Thank you for the luncheon in my honor.' She wouldn't even do that. I resented that . . ." One member of the Women's National Press Club did, in time, befriend Bess. Active member Katie Louchheim, who'd later serve as director of women's activities for the Democratic National Committee, observed Mrs. Truman carefully, and concluded that the First Lady had both "greatness and magnanimity," and was "real . . . natural, and . . . pleasant." When she met Bess, she was "so overwhelmed because she seemed so grim and almost forbidding from her photographs and what little we knew about her in the press."[7]

Other women in Washington *wanted* to like Bess Truman, but had difficulty adjusting to her. There were even those of the First Lady's secretariat who found her dull. Dorothy Dow wrote confidentially that Bess would "be just nothing after Mrs. Roosevelt . . . the activities that Mrs. Roosevelt was always engaged in were interesting . . ." Shortly after, her prediction became true: "Things have settled down here into a dead calm. And I do mean *dead*! . . . Mrs. Truman apparently meant what she said when she stated that she was going to do *nothing* . . . we [typing pool] shall all go stark raving crazy if something doesn't happen."[8]

Reathel Odum was a former secretary to Senator Truman, and she and Mrs. Truman worked in the tiny office used by Malvina Thomson and Mrs. Roosevelt. Miss Odum recalled that "Mrs. Truman was a most considerate 'boss.' Although she was a no-nonsense type of woman, she was fun to be with and our relationship was pleasant . . . We shared a small office together, and were on good terms with each other. I was never treated . . . 'as a second-class employee' by any of the President's staff . . . I do not remember any bias toward the First Lady's staff coming from the West Wing."[9]

Though she wasn't a daily physical presence in the East Wing, Bess controlled her bailiwick, resenting the presence there of military aide Jake Vardaman, and his attempt to reorganize her staff. She talked to Harry. Vardaman was transferred to the West Wing.[10]

Bess was acutely aware of the fact that people still cared about and were writing to Eleanor. She made no attempt to change that. In fact, when she learned that several secretaries were ordered to stop working on Eleanor's behalf because she was no longer First Lady, Mrs. Truman rescinded the order, perhaps not realizing it was her first exercise of her new power. The president was equally self-effacing with Eleanor.

Truman's first executive order was to name Mrs. Roosevelt as United States delegate to the UN Charter Conference in San Francisco. "Eleanor no longer lives in the White House," wrote one reporter. "But she is still a potent force in Washington, where her kitchen cabinet continues to rule the nation that President Truman thinks he rules." In some respects, it was true. A month after becoming president, Truman penned an eight-page letter to Eleanor, seeking her advice on how to treat Churchill. She first chastised him for wasting time writing in longhand, then gave her advice.[11]

If Eleanor's new, independent life was now taking flight along the course *she* charted, she suddenly faced its drawbacks, regardless of her claim that she disliked privileged treatment. As Dorothy Dow wrote,

"Mrs. R still hasn't bumped up against the facts of life, but I think it won't be long now. She can't get the pump for the pool repaired and is having seven fits all at once. They simply can't get the parts, but she can't understand that. She is also going to come a cropper on the gas situation if she doesn't slow up a bit on driving the car. It would be good for her to . . . find out what other people have been going through, as she doesn't know what it is all about." There were other pedestrian worlds that Eleanor also now explored. Like a subway.

After a meeting in the Bronx, the former First Lady decided that a taxi was too expensive, so she paid for a token, descended into the grimy subway, and jostled into the steamy mass of humanity, "another old lady," she said, hanging on to an overhead strap, "trying to stay on my feet." Casually, one seated passenger looked from above his newspaper, and recognized Eleanor Roosevelt. He blurted out her name, offered her his seat, and the entire subway car suddenly enlivened. Eleanor told her friend, "A path opened for me like the Red Sea parting; everybody gathering around." With absolute naiveté, she remarked in afterthought, "It made me feel so good that people remember Franklin!"

She was equally humble when it came to cleaning bathrooms. One day she brought the famous lawyer Fanny Holtzmann through the rooms of the Wiltwyck School for problem boys, an institution to which she dedicated not only money but her time. On this visit, before the housekeeper had come through, Eleanor chatted with Fannie as they walked through. After nonchalantly changing the bed linens, she headed to a broom closet, gathered pail and brush, went into the lavatory, and casually began scrubbing the floor. Said Holtzmann, "There, in that washroom for forgotten little boys, I felt in the presence of greatness."[12]

Mrs. Roosevelt realized the war's end was in sight when, on May 8, all European hostilities ceased. It was declared V-E Day. Eleanor wrote her congratulations to a returned General Eisenhower on June 20, 1945, after his victorious acceptance of the German Army's surrender. At the bottom of the page, she scribbled a handwritten P.S.: "My congratulations and affectionate thoughts have been with Mrs. Eisenhower too. I hope it is some compensation for the years of anxiety."[13]

Mamie saw Eleanor when she accompanied Ike to Hyde Park, where he placed a wreath at FDR's grave. Mamie and Ike were earlier feted by Bess and Harry Truman at a White House victory dinner, but the male Ike-Truman connection seemed rather tenuous.

Rumors had circulated through the capital that the Eisenhower marriage had been on the brink of permanent separation. Truman later suggested that Ike wanted to divorce Mamie and marry Kay, and had written a letter to General Marshall asking permission to do so. Eisenhower did write a letter to Marshall regarding Mamie, and also requesting permission for an official action.

The letter had requested that Mamie be permitted to sail to Europe ahead of other military wives, in 1945, when it was clear the war would shortly end. He requested the "special favor to see her" because he had been separated from her "for so long."[14]

Mamie, however, was not unaware of the romances the war did forge. Divorce became a reality right in her own home, but not personally. Her best friend, with whom she shared an adjoining apartment, Ruth Butcher, was the wife of Ike's naval aide and confidant Captain Harry Butcher. Upon return from the war, Butcher divorced Ruth and married Mollie Ford, a Red Cross worker. "Mamie held Butch responsible for the breakup of his marriage and for Ike's friendship with Kay," Mollie recalled, "and she discouraged contact between the two men." It was not implausible that the letter to Marshall that Truman claimed Ike wrote was indeed written by him, but on Butcher's behalf.[15]

There was, however, no greater documentary proof that Ike was *not* planning to divorce Mamie, and wanted her to come to Europe and be at his side, than her reapplication for a passport. She hadn't left America in over a decade, and the only reason she would have reapplied in 1945 was because Ike wanted her with him. The only monkey business involved was her fibbing about her age on the application. Mamie cut off one year.[16]

When Ike did return for good at the end of the year, Mamie met him in Boston, then visited Boone, Iowa, where she collapsed from exhaustion. She was transported to Walter Reed Hospital. No statement of any kind was given to the press, since the Eisenhowers insisted that Mamie's health was a private matter. That gave people like Perle Mesta the opportunity to create their own fanciful reasons. And spread them.[17]

The press and public still had not quite decided what to make of Bess Truman. Mrs. Truman at first failed to acknowledge her public persona. She resisted the notion that she was now important, historical, or in any way different from other women of her age, class, and background. Initially, to her, there was no role outside of hostess, and even that held little appeal.

"I don't know what I am going to do," Bess Truman confided to Frances Perkins. "I'm not used to this awful public life." To Mary Keeley, Bess admitted that she was unhappy "to be where we are but there's nothing to be done about it except to do our best and forget about the sacrifices and many unpleasant things that bob up." Her only similarity to Eleanor was equally messy closets, about which Bess said, "Well, I'm pleased that I resemble Mrs. Roosevelt in at least one respect."[18]

So anonymous was she that during her first Christmas as First Lady, Mrs. Truman was able to shop in Washington stores unrecognized, without guards, walking through the aisles and picking out gifts. She called the Secret Service "understanding but underfoot," resenting the agents' presence. She refused to be trailed in Independence, and proudly claimed that the agents "didn't bother me" because she lost them "[e]arly in the game."[19]

She particularly detested the public's attentions to her. Lunching at the Mayflower with friends, she asked to have her chair positioned so she could face the wall. "I've developed a distaste for being stared at," she explained. Her view of the public was manifested in occasional malevolent wit. As she watched Ray Bolger in *Where's Charley?*, pouring scalding tea and missing several dozen teacups on a table, the First Lady suggested to Reathel, "Why don't we do that at the White House someday?"[20]

"Perhaps unconsciously," Margaret's college friend Jane Lingo admitted, "Mrs. Truman placed her family and friends before her public responsibilities as First Lady." When Margaret thought that being a president's daughter meant she could order breakfast in bed, however, Bess nixed that notion immediately. If there was one vestige of normality that Bess was determined to maintain, it was that their fame would not alter the family's private lifestyle. Though she did not express it directly to her daughter, Bess took great pride in Margaret's equally independent decision to have a singing career upon her college graduation. As she wrote Mary Keeley, ". . . Of course we were very proud of her—really more because she had nerve enough to do it than of her performance . . . Thank goodness she is really *interested* in *something* & is not content to sit around in Wash for the next two years. It becomes very deadly in a hurry."[21]

The Truman partnership extended back to just after World War I. While Harry was fighting overseas, Bess momentarily considered a career as a teacher, though she had only a finishing-school education. After her wedding in 1919, she worked in Harry's Kansas City haberdashery shop as an unsalaried bookkeeper, store manager, and saleswoman. A co-venture, the store eventually failed, but as Truman made his way through local, state, and national politics, Bess remained his partner.

Harry had been in love with Bess ever since he first saw her as a child in Sunday School, though they came from different classes. The Trumans were poor dirt farmers—"clodhoppers," he called them. Bess was Independence aristocracy, living in the Victorian mansion built by her grandfather, owner of one of the most successful flour mills in the Midwest. When her father suddenly shot himself, her mother, the intolerant Madge Gates Wallace, immediately developed a complicated psychological co-dependency with Bess, and at times seemed to have drained her emotionally. Madge was narrow-minded, imperious, and censorious of those she considered beneath her socioeconomic station—including Harry. Bess remained impervious to her mother's worst qualities, but did develop a pessimism, the most negative, and challenging, aspect being stone-stubbornness. No person—husband, mother, or daughter—could move her to do anything she didn't want to.

Physically, Bess was stout, and by the late forties her wavy blond hair was turning gray. As a youth, she'd been an expert tennis player and shot-putter, and could cast with a fishing rod farther than boys. She was still strong-armed. Her daughter said she was "extremely suspicious" of those who paid her compliments, and was "a very combative person. There is nothing mean or vindictive about her. She just likes to argue." Because of Bess's controlled, unemotional personality, many thought her "harsh and uncaring." Margaret said Bess was "unintentionally cruel" to her. Clifton Daniel, who later married Margaret, recalled how Bess "loved to argue."[22]

But within her most private self, there lurked a warm and gentle spirit. Her wide, sparkling light blue eyes twinkled with a mischievous humor, and she had one of the driest wits ever to pepper the first ladyship. She compared her voice to a "dying crow," impersonated Jimmy Durante, and once wrote a friend while, "[i]mmobilized under a dryer." Sometimes she did things just to belie her image as a "square" matron. Knowing it would shock her friends, she relished the idea of lighting up a cigarette and smoking in the Kansas City Club. Bess liked her old-fashioneds just as stiff as Harry's. When a butler made one that tasted like "fruit punch," the First Lady sent it back. Another was made. Again, it was too weak. Finally, the miffed bartender cascaded a glass full of straight bourbon over ice. "Now that's what I call an old-fashioned," she cracked. She was also unpretentious, proud of her ability to cook and to park her boatlike Chrysler.[23]

The Trumans depended upon each other, and were even nicknamed "the Three Musketeers" by the staff. But according to Margaret, even with her family, Bess remained emotionally unexpressive. Harry was the only human being to whom Bess sometimes opened up. When he caught her burning letters she had written him, he tried to stop her with a reminder to "think of history." As she threw the rest of the stack into the flames, she responded, "I am." While she didn't think her letters worthy of preservation, she preserved Harry's to her. Throughout his negotiations with the Soviet Union's Joseph Stalin and England's Churchill at the Potsdam Conference, the president kept the First Lady fully informed of all intricacies.

To what extent President Truman actually consulted the First Lady about dropping the atomic bomb was uncertain. When questioned specifically on it, he said he had. Margaret claimed he had merely informed Bess. Mrs. Truman later defended the decision by saying, "Harry always placed high value on the life of a single American boy. If the war with Japan had been allowed to continue, it would have claimed the lives of perhaps a quarter-million American soldiers, and twice that number would have been maimed for life. It's difficult to calculate the number of Japanese lives that would have been lost . . . as many or more, undoubtedly, as died at Hiroshima and Nagasaki. So the atom bomb was the lesser weapon, although it's hard to look at it that way." Presidential counsel Clark Clifford believed that Bess "wouldn't pretend to make a final approval of such a decision . . . She left that to experts . . ."

Bess was still in Missouri when the first bomb exploded, but was back in Washington just before the second was dropped. Evidently, Truman *did* seek her advice on the latter, targeted on Nagasaki. The night before he issued the order, White House butler Charles Ficklin said the Trumans were in their nightly meeting in the president's office longer than usual. When they emerged, "both looked real serious. Usually, they'd joke or kid around before going to bed. Now they didn't say a word, just looked straight ahead . . ."[24]

For some, the bomb was a good omen.

Rosalynn Smith had begun dating her friend Ruth's brother, Jimmy Carter, an Annapolis Naval Academy student, who would now not have to fight in a war. The couple married in less than a year, Jimmy joking that she did so only to get away from Plains. They moved from base to base, seeing a vast variety of American cities and cultures. Her time as a navy wife was not unlike Mamie Eisenhower's early years. And just like Mamie, Rosalynn's cooking skills were limited to fudge. She learned to be "the total wife," but also took art courses and language classes. Her three sons, Jack, Chip, and Jeff, were born at two-year intervals. Rosalynn enjoyed "the independence I had finally achieved" by careful management. When her father-in-law suddenly died, however, his diverse agricultural businesses, which included a peanut farm, were assumed by Jimmy. Rosalynn was devastated. "I argued. I cried. I even screamed at him." But she returned to Plains, living in a miserable government-project apartment.[25]

When she was asked about the atomic bomb, Edith Wilson's face went blank with disapproval, and she once remarked pointedly, when asked about the Trumans, "I do think *she* has been wonderful." Edith admired Bess's ladylike restraint and "felt sorry" for her. Mrs. Wilson accepted an invitation to a victory service at the White House, but since Bess Truman did not seek the spotlight for herself, there was none for Edith to bask in. She was barely noticed at the San Francisco UN Charter conference, especially in Mrs. Roosevelt's presence. Edith still refused to help in public efforts. In its last bond drive, the Treasury Department begged her to support its cause because she'd been requested so frequently. Her brother responded that since "she has never appeared on any radio programme," she wouldn't help.

Edith did continue her devotion to the cause of Woodrow Wilson, assisting any organization honoring him. During the "Atomic Age," Hollywood was making several romanticized films about presidential

couples, miscasting slim Susan Hayward as obese Rachel Jackson, and blond Ginger Rogers as black-haired Dolley Madison. In *Woodrow Wilson,* Geraldine Fitzgerald had appeared as an unrealistically youthful Edith. When Mrs. Wilson received fifty thousand dollars from the film, she turned it over to the Wilson Foundation, a trust that financed the restoration of his birthplace at Staunton, Virginia, of which she was honorary president. But Edith's devotion was also selective. Having created a profession as Mrs. Woodrow Wilson, she dexterously avoided raising Ellen Wilson's memory. Just before leaving the White House, Edith had discreetly given Ellen's paint pallette, brushes, parasol, and other personal items to an auction house. It was some time before the items were recovered and brought to Staunton, lying in storage while Edith was alive.[26]

Ironically, it was a widow of a conservative Republican who raised doubts about the use of nuclear weapons to end a war. "It gives one cold shivers," Grace Coolidge wrote, "and makes one question our justification for dropping a bomb on a thickly populated section." The progressive former First Lady favored the United Nations charter, and publicly signed a petition supporting it, even posing for a photograph as she did so. When a group of United Nations guests visited Northampton with Eleanor Roosevelt several years later, it was Grace who entertained.[27]

When she visited Hiroshima, U.S. delegate to the UN Eleanor Roosevelt said, "I know we were justified in dropping the bomb but you can't help feeling sorry when you see suffering . . . if there is another Pearl Harbor, there will be undoubtedly another Hiroshima." Eleanor respected Bess Truman's decision to remain inactive, simply saying, "I liked her."[28]

The dean of First Ladies, Frances Cleveland Preston, now in her eighties, did not express her opinions on nuclear weaponry, but was a strong Truman supporter. When the Trumans traveled to Princeton to take part in a ceremony, along with Edith Wilson and Herbert Hoover, they were warmly welcomed by the tall, unassuming grande dame of the college town. The Eisenhowers, also present, didn't know the old woman. When Frances turned to Ike and told him that she had once lived in Washington, he responded, "Oh really? Where?" When she told him, "Sixteen hundred Pennsylvania Avenue," Frances added, "Why else would they put me next to you?"

President Truman told her how his mother, as a young woman, traveled from her farm to Kansas City just to catch a glimpse of the beautiful Frances Cleveland, and had a yellowed clipping about the First Lady in her scrapbook. "And I am grateful to have met you since now I can tell my mother that the real person surpasses even the person whom she imagined."

Age never dimmed Frances. When blindness seemed imminent, her calm reaction was to learn Braille. Shortly afterward, she began a correspondence with a blind Indian boy, typing stories for him in Braille. He looked forward to her stories. Though an operation corrected her sight, she continued typing his tales.

Before her eyesight gave out, Frances still drove her "sedate and careful brown station wagon." Though she hated "jukeboxes," she loved theater, and had a circle of actor friends. She took particular interest in the summer theater her son Francis founded, the Barnstormers, which derived its name from a schedule of presenting plays on an eighty-mile circuit. Frances would follow the troupe, driving sometimes until two or three in the morning. After one performance, Frances wrote whimsically, "I was . . . surrounded by people . . . who I am sure did not know me, and I was interested in hearing [their comments about the play]." Indeed, there were few left who would know the college girl who had married a president in the White House over sixty years before. A month after she penned the letter, Frances died peacefully in her sleep, at age eighty-three. Edith Roosevelt, whose opinion on the bomb went unstated, survived her by only eleven months.[29]

The manner in which President Truman had shared with Bess his decision to drop the bombs was indicative of the new dynamics of their marriage. In her first months as First Lady, her advisory role had been reduced to that of an observer. According to Margaret, her parents were verging on "an emotional separation."

Harry was becoming frustrated with Bess's refusal to play a public role. He was perhaps the first president to take an active interest in the first ladyship's history, stating that Abigail Adams would have made a better president than her husband, and that Mary Lincoln was unjustly criticized. He later wrote that "I hope someday someone will take time to evaluate the true role of the wife of the President, and to assess the many burdens she has to bear and the contributions she makes." Attempting to coax Bess into an active role, he wrote her several months before FDR died, "The President told me that Mrs. R was a very timid woman and wouldn't go to political meetings or make any speeches when he first ran for governor of N.Y. Then he said 'Now she talks all the time.'" It didn't work. Bess knew her First Lady history, too.[30]

"I am not the one elected," she snapped. "I have nothing to say to the public." Asked which predecessor she most identified with, Bess chose the obscure and extremely private Elizabeth Monroe, who of course followed directly the legendary Dolley Madison.[31]

If Mrs. Truman thought she would remain untroubled by merely playing a social role, she was mistaken. That first fall, when she casually accepted an invitation to a DAR tea, she was blasted by black congressman Adam Clayton Powell, because the group still barred blacks from performing at Constitution Hall. The First Lady responded to the congressman with a public statement explaining that she regretted that "a conflict has arisen for which I am in no wise responsible. In my opinion my acceptance of the hospitality is not related to the merits of the issue which has arisen . . . I deplore any action which denied artistic talent an opportunity to express itself because of prejudice against race or origin." Powell was unsatisfied, and called her "the Last Lady in the Land." He was barred from the White House, but privately even the president considered his wife's decision a bad one.

Bess still considered herself a private citizen, not a symbol, but the DAR incident forced her to reconsider. Her attendance, however, was also an act of defiance. As she wrote Mary Keeley, "I agree with you that the DAR is dynamite at present and I'm not 'having any' just now. But I was plenty burned up with the wire I had from that————in N.Y."[32]

The issue sparked debate on the question of desegregation, and stirred comparisons to her predecessor. One Pennsylvania segregationist praised Bess by writing, "You are a Greater First Lady in every way, than Eleanor Roosevelt ever thought of being, and much more to be admired." It also raised unwarranted speculation about the First Lady's racial views. Bluma Jacobson, the widow of Harry's former haberdashery partner, recalled that the Trumans "never had us at their home" because "[t]he Wallaces were aristocracy in these parts, and under the circumstances the Trumans couldn't afford to have Jews at their house." Though Harry Truman and her mother had both expressed racial and religious slurs in earlier years, there was never even a hint that Bess shared their bigotry or spoke, even in private, against any minority. When the First Lady worried about the controversy that might ensue when Margaret planned to travel through the South with the family's black servant, her concern was for the maid, not the political consequence.[33]

Unfortunately, the public at large was never given the opportunity to know the real Bess Truman on the issue. Asked if she'd continue to attend DAR events, the First Lady replied, "Why not?" It sparked Walter White to comment in the black journal The Crisis that Bess Truman "is most disappointing, particularly in contrast with the action of her distinguished predecessor."

The DAR incident only deepened Bess's resentment of the role thrust upon her. When Harry came home to Missouri to celebrate Christmas two months later, she exploded, "So you've finally arrived. I guess you couldn't think of any more reasons to stay away. As far as I'm concerned, you might as well have stayed in Washington." He remained only a few days. "I guess I'm a damn fool," he wrote her after a rough scene, "but I'm happier when I can see you—even when you give me hell I'd rather have you around than not."[34]

By early 1946, however, the relationship rebounded and an ease developed. An ease with and for Bess, too. The nation accepted the fact that she was not Mrs. Roosevelt, and Bess accepted her public role. After eight o'clock breakfast with Harry and Margaret, she held household meetings and dealt with public mail in her little office. She lunched with the president or her mother. At two, when the president napped, the First Lady declared that she would keep working, but J. B. West said "many times" he'd find her "sitting upright in her chair, sound asleep." By three, Mrs. Truman made public appearances at charity teas, or greeted visiting groups. After cocktails and dinner, sometimes taken on the back "porch" south balcony—which Harry ordered built—bowling, bridge or Ping-Pong followed. It was, however, at nine in the evening that Bess Wallace Truman played her most crucial, and clandestine, role as advisor to the president.

At that hour, President Truman took his briefcase and his wife and marched into his private study. The door was shut behind them. The First Lady went to work, according to West, "editing his speeches . . . and designing his policies . . . [with] more influence on political decisions than Mrs. Roosevelt had on social issues . . . Although it went unsuspected by nearly everybody in government, Bess Truman entered into nearly every decision the President made . . . [she] applied . . . her analytical thinking to every action of the President's.[35]

Some knew of her power. India Edwards, vice chair of the Democratic National Committee and Women's Division chief, called the First Lady "a shrewd politician." Press Secretary Ross said, "Whenever Bess felt changes should be made, she would offer her recommendations to Harry. . . . Invariably, he'd act on them." Special Counsel Charles Murphy recalled that Truman wouldn't postpone a decision to get Bess's advice, but that "she had a lot to do with the shape of his attitude about things and people."

President Truman admitted, "She never made a suggestion that wasn't for the welfare and benefit of the country and what I was trying to do. She looks at things objectively, and I can't always . . ." He said it was Bess on "whose counsel and judgement I frequently called," and named her his "chief advisor" and "full partner in all transactions—politically and otherwise . . . a wonderful influence and help. A President is in a bad way if he doesn't have a First Lady that knows her job and is a full support to him. She's the greatest help a President can have."[36]

Family friend Jane Lingo pointed out that Bess's silence in the presence of political figures was a front, since she was "actually watching them very closely—their . . . enthusiasm or hesitancy to something the President might be saying . . ." Later, in private, "she'd carefully report it back to him." Lingo said that few were ever able to provoke Bess to discuss issues. "People would come and see her, and . . . hint to hear her political views. When they told her some inside information or their opinion as a way to get her to talk, she'd just say, 'Uhm-hm! Uhm-hm!' But no politics." Clark Clifford added that Mrs. Truman was "a valuable in-house adviser . . . [but] at no time did the President or Mrs. Truman ever make a public statement on that particular role while he was in the White House."[37]

The president revealed, "Whenever a controversial subject came up, I'd usually consult Bess because she has a pretty good idea of what the everyday person is thinking and would do under the circumstances." Clifford believed that the First Lady's judgment was also vital in personnel, for both domestic political appointments and diplomatic assignments. Truman later told Liz Carpenter that Bess was his "best warning signal . . . She could smell out . . . somebody trying to use him."[38]

Bess mistrusted Harry's second secretary of state, James Byrnes, an FDR man, fingered him as a self-promoter, and suggested he be replaced by Dean Acheson, which he was. She was also familiar with each individual of the president's executive staff. When he was out of town, she marched down to the West Wing to ascertain that they were working just as diligently as if he were there, and reported back to Harry.[39]

As a speechwriting assistant, Bess was rather adept with midwestern colloquialisms. Harry's two best lines during a Senate primary against Missouri governor Lloyd Stark, who owned apple farms, and District Attorney Maurice Milligan, were written by Bess. First she hit on Stark: "Any farmer who is dang fool enough to vote for another farmer who's losing money farming ought to have his head examined!" Then she trounced Milligan: "And any farmer who's dang fool enough to vote for a lawyer who never sees a farm ought to have his head examined twice!" Bess told Treasury Secretary John Synder that Harry's speeches "were far too verbose," and wrote Katie Louchheim about one that Harry was working on: "If he gives me a chance to see it before he leaves, I solemnly promise to cut out *plenty* of it."[40]

When it came to Harry's impromptu remarks, Bess had less control of censorship. A famous story had him using the word "manure" in a speech, and one of Bess's friends disapproving.

"Good Lord," the First Lady shot back, "it's taken me years to get him to say 'manure.'"

Her brother admitted that cusswords didn't shock her because Bess Truman "knew how to use them herself."[41]

– 57 –

The Boss

IT WAS THE era of "Don't Fence Me In," wide cars in pastel colors, the exodus to "sub-urban" areas developed with split-level houses, a high marriage and birthrate, and streamlined kitchenware created to provide

relief for women, who were now returned from the tedium of the war effort. Eleanor Roosevelt's stridency seemed out of synch. The public didn't mind that a First Lady would no longer make speeches, adopt social "projects," and foster independence for women.

As a public speaker, Bess was silent. Her first First Lady appearance was the dedication of two Navy hospital evacuation airplanes. She stepped up to the microphone and spoke: "In sending forth these planes we send them with out love and sincere desire that the wounded whom they carry will be brought safely home." Then she tried to smash an unscored champagne bottle against one of the planes. She hit, and hit and hit, but the bottle wouldn't break. It was an embarrassing scene for the shy woman. She may have decided at that moment never to permit herself to be caught in such circumstances again. When goaded into rising before the speaker's stand at a Prevention of Cruelty to Animals gathering, Bess did manage her second, and last, public speech as First Lady. "Thank you for asking me here. I wish you good luck." She later admitted, "I have no desire to have my voice recorded for posterity."[1]

Bess refused to adopt a cause. Instead, she emphasized her role as hostess, making herself available to most women's groups requesting an audience. Mrs. Truman seemed an almost professional club lady. She belonged to the Daughters of Colonial Wars, the Red Cross Motor Club, and the Women's National Farm and Garden Association, but though she was honorary president of the Women's National Democratic Club, she disliked openly political women. To Katie Louchheim, who told her about greeting several hundred of the committeewoman, Mrs. Truman wrote in a private letter, "I wouldn't want that many women on my hands for anything under heaven. Women en masse don't appeal to me." In another letter, she amplified, "Don't let the Committee Women wear you out. I take a dim view of them . . . Have you ever found one of them different from the rest of them [?] . . ."[2]

Edith Helm said that Bess continued Eleanor's "get together" luncheons for women, though they were soon phased out. Still, the First Lady worked behind the scenes on pressing the case for equality. India Edwards said, "In many ways Bess Truman was an early advocate of female rights. She was instrumental in her husband appointing more women to top jobs than any previous President. There were nineteen women in key national posts and more than two hundred others as delegates, alternates or advisers to international conferences. Bess Truman earnestly believed that a woman is as good as a man—and she's the living proof."[3]

After arranging a stag dinner for the prince of Iraq, Bess remarked, "The American system which calls for equality of women is undoubtedly superior." When she thought of "the many things" that the wives of men in public service had to sacrifice for their husbands' careers, Bess told Katie Louchheim that "All of those things should pay needed dividends." And though she had no personal ambitions, she was sensitive to women of achievement, once passing a note down to the president at a Women's Press Club dinner to remind him that he was seated next to Dr. Lise Meitner, a nuclear-fission scientist.[4]

If Mrs. Truman's social conscience seemed uninspired, at least it had the effect of reducing criticism to equal mildness. When she had her controversial "poodle cut" styled at Jill's Beauty Shop on Connecticut Avenue, the hairdo became a point of detraction by some petty women in the press. On another occasion, Drew Pearson tried to stir a great deal of attention over the boring fact that Bess traveled in a private Pullman car, while "GI's had to travel in day coaches." Nobody cared.[5]

Edith Helm thought of Bess Truman's social schedule symbolic of the postwar era. The visit of Bess's Independence "Tuesday Bridge Club," an institution familiar to most Middle American women, reflected the reactivation of leisure pursuits, and the press had a heydey chronicling the matrons' week-long stay. Dior's "New Look" ballgowns seen in abundance in Washington's revived social whirl in 1947 was a sign that wartime frugality and food rationing were over. Mrs. Truman's favorite movie stars were Bob Hope and Bing Crosby in their road-picture series. When Hope came to see her in the White House, a starstruck Bess considered it one of the few "exceptional compensations" of her job.[6]

The Latin craze was then sweeping the nation, with dance-floor conga lines, loud tropical shirts and ties, and bamboo chairs and home bars. On Mondays at eleven, starting in October 1945, Bess began hosting her Spanish classes at the White House, for a thirty-two-week

course. Mamie Eisenhower was again one of the students, and several months later, at a White House luncheon held at the conclusion of "Pan-American Week," Mrs. Ike dressed in a white apron and served the guests. "You make a marvelous waitress," Bess joked to Mamie. When later asked if she learned how to speak Spanish, Mamie admitted, "Heavens, no! We just talked." At the end of the thirty-two weeks, Bess's class broke up, her daughter claiming that the First Lady was frustrated by those who hadn't learned. [7]

Mamie remained ambiguous about being a public figure. In private, she was not above pulling rank, as in her unsuccessful attempt to get a civilian friend living quarters at Fort Myer. She very willingly made a radio appeal for Mrs. Roosevelt's March of Dimes charity, but when asked to participate in a fund-raiser for postwar European children, Mamie scribbled to a secretary, "Will you be kind enough to write this person a nice note and tell her I will be away or something? Better, [that] my father and mother are arriving. Ho Hum. I'm a rotten liar!" [8]

She became a sponsor of the United Services to China, and responded to a plea for support of an educational program with a letter saying that "efforts to promote peace, understanding and security for the people of the world must begin with the school children." Mamie was so besieged with requests that, as she explained to the National Council on American:Soviet Friendship, "Because of my husband's position, I find it impractical to participate in activities which are not service connected." One activity proved embarrassing. When it was learned that the Nurses National Memorial began illegally sending lottery tickets through the mail, violating postal laws, she resigned her sponsorship. [9]

Mamie resisted an offer from *The Woman* magazine to write her own story because she didn't want any press "just now." She was just then getting a small stream of letters attempting to prompt her to influence Ike into the '48 presidential race. "You cannot," one writer pleaded, "refuse to use your influence at a time like this." To another, Mamie responded, "I am indeed flattered by your suggestion, but it revolves around one question which I would never presume to advise him about. I feel certain that you will agree it is a subject on which he alone should make a decision." Coyly, she did approach Ike with the growing speculation. "You could probably be President if you wanted to." He tersely responded, "I don't."[10]

Mamie seemed somewhat intrigued with the notion, and while considering herself a private citizen, she strove to maintain a faultless public life. When she first planned to serve a beef roast for a small private dinner but realized it was on a "meatless Tuesday" she served turkey instead. If Mrs. Truman was following the new food-conservation laws, so, too, was Mrs. Ike.[11]

Mamie's last Washington appearance before Ike took over as president of Columbia University was at Bess Truman's Army-Navy Reception. With son John's 1947 marriage to the bright Barbara Thompson, and the birth of their grandchildren, David in 1948, Anne in 1949, and Susan two years later, and the Eisenhowers' purchase, expansion, and renovation of an old farmhouse in Gettysburg, Pennsylvania, Mamie's time was full. The "farm" was just under two hours from New York. And Washington.[12]

While the Eisenhowers were in New York, they were courted by none other than the unofficial woman's leader of the Democratic party, former First Lady Roosevelt. In 1948, Eleanor invited Ike and Mamie up to stay with her at Hyde Park, but he, not she, responded that they were too busy. Mamie would later accept Mrs. Roosevelt's supper invitation in New York after the latter's radio broadcast on education. When, however, just two months after the broadcast, Eleanor again invited them to stay with her, the general once again turned it down. There were no further invitations. If Ike was distancing himself from the liberal Eleanor, Mamie still liked her, according to Milton Eisenhower, who called them both "genuine."[13]

If Mamie wasn't "running" in '48, a displeased Bess was. Some Democrats had wanted to run Ike, and at the Democratic Convention that nominated Truman, there was serious discussion of nominating Eleanor Roosevelt as vice president. Republican Clare Luce first publicly suggested that if Eleanor was nominated, it would ". . . raise the woman issue . . . challenge the loyalty of women everywhere to their sex, because it would be made to seem that the defeat of the ticket meant the defeat for a hundred years of women's chance to be truly equal with men in politics."

The drive that motivated Mrs. Roosevelt, and made her feel that she was finally making a real contribution, was her work at the United Nations. Selected as chairman of the Commission on Human Rights, she would be hailed as "the First Lady of the World" for her drafting of the Declaration of Human Rights. It stood as a brave document demanding an answer from all the world. As she prepared to sail to Europe for the first session of the UN General Assembly, Mrs. Roosevelt bubbled, "For the first time in my life I can say what I want." She told reporters, off-the-record, "For your information it is wonderful to feel free."[14]

During the election year, Eleanor and her son Elliott were in Luxembourg, where they were entertained by the American ambassador there, Perle Mesta, Mamie Eisenhower's old "friend" from Wardman Park. Knowing that Mamie and Perle were acquainted, Mrs. Roosevelt asked Mrs. Mesta how Mrs. Eisenhower's health was, as she "understood she had been ill," referring to Mamie's near-fatal attack of pneumonia in the winter of '46. Perle said that Mamie was "much better," but went on to state that "Mrs. Eisenhower had been in a drying-out clinic for alcoholics." Eleanor was shocked at such a statement, particularly from an ambassador, and never believed that such a problem had existed.[15]

Meanwhile, as the summer turned to fall, the polls showed that Truman would lose. Bess thought so, too, her daughter claiming, "Not once throughout . . . the campaign . . . did I hear her express any confidence in Harry Truman's reelection." When friends reassured the president that he would win, despite the polls, the First Lady remained silent.[16]

In the beginning of the whistle-stop campaign, Harry introduced Bess to the crowds as "the Boss." They roared with affectionate laughter as the plump lady with the shoulder pads and square hats came out and waved. At one stop, as he called out, "And here comes the Boss," Bess's voice was picked up by a mike as she audibly murmured, "You better believe that one!"[17]

The controversy over civil rights became apparent at some stops. When Truman was booed for shaking hands with a black in Waco, Texas, the First Lady "whispered" to him, "Don't mind them, Harry! You did the right thing!" in a voice heard ten feet away. She reasserted her point just as the train was pulling out of Waco by waving to a small black girl in a wheelchair.[18]

Every night Bess was part of a small circle of advisers, scrutinizing schedules and evaluating appearances. At one stop, a reporter noticed her in a window as she penciled remarks on one of Truman's speeches. The First Lady also monitored the president's health and diet. On one occasion, when Bess learned that a governor who had earlier criticized her husband was planning to join the train when it stopped in his state, she put a dead stop to it. Though Bess Furman wrote that she wouldn't "oblige by saying a few words," Mrs. Truman did make one speech: "Good morning, and thank you for this wonderful greeting."

The Trumans didn't openly court Hollywood as had the Roosevelts, but they did get support from "stars." If Mrs. Truman was angered several years earlier at Lauren Bacall's leggy presence on top of a piano Harry was playing, the First Lady welcomed the campaign help of what seemed like an odd friend for her, the liberal actress Tallulah Bankhead.[19]

That season Grace Coolidge attended most of the Boston Red Sox games. She was a familiar sight at Fenway Park, following innings carefully, a graying former First Lady with a slight widow's hump, leaning on a hot-dog stand, frankfurter and scorecard in hand. Politically, Mrs. Coolidge remained a loyal Republican. So, on election morning, she expressed bemused surprise when Republican candidate Thomas E. Dewey lost to Truman .[20]

That year's Inaugural was the first such integrated event, and at the parade, when segregationalist Strom Thurmond walked by the grandstand, he was loudly booed by Tallulah Bankhead. "I wish," said the First Lady to a nearby friend, "I had nerve enough to do that." At the Inaugural Ball, popular bandleader Xavier Cugat played some of Bess Truman's favorite Latin rhumbas. Shaking hands with crowds until after 2:00 A.M., she deadpanned, "I wonder if Martha Washington's feet ached so much."[21]

The new term was marked by renewed austerity, ordered by Mrs. Truman because of hunger in postwar Europe and America's donations of staples. It prompted her to issue the first of her only two public statements, "The Pledge of the American Housewife," which read, "I will do my utmost to conserve any and all foodstuffs which the starving millions of the world need today so desperately . . . buy only the food my family actually needs . . . neither waste nor hoard . . . be particularly watchful in the use of Wheat and Cereals . . . and Fats and Oils . . ."[22]

There were other domestic changes as well. A structural investigation of the White House proved that the old mansion, embedded in nothing more than soft clay, was ready to collapse. The family moved to Blair House, and Edith Helm moved her mansion office to the East Wing, where she continued working through the rest of the term, walking over to meet with the First Lady. Helm's stay thereafter established the East Wing as the permanent headquarters of the first ladyship.[23]

Of the several proposals offered for the renovation of the crumbling White House, Mrs. Truman favored the costlier version, which planned to save the original walls of the mansion and rebuild the rooms within a steel skeleton. Many in Congress, the press, and public supported the cheaper plan, to tear down the old and build a new house. Bess didn't agree, and it became the only issue for which she exercised political power over legislators. She personally lobbied senators and representatives, and no less a person than House Speaker Sam Rayburn. She telephoned the wives of influential congressional leaders, even Martha

Taft, wife of Truman's foe Robert Taft, who recalled, "Browbeating was not her style, but she let it be known that the building had to be saved at all costs." Mrs. Truman issued her second, and last, public statement, calling for public support of renovating the original White House. Among her backers was Mrs. Roosevelt, who issued the statement, "No new design or new house could possibly have the historic interest of this old one." In the end, Bess was successful, and Congress voted nearly 85.5 million dollars for the job, which commenced in 1949.[24]

In many ways, the move to Blair House made the First Lady's role easier. As a staid private home offering no public tours, the residence suited her. But because of its limitations, Mrs. Truman had to break up the traditional congressional wives' reception into several smaller ones by the alphabet. On the day that the wives with last names beginning with "F" were invited, the bride of a new congressman made her way into the complex. On the day of her marriage just a few months before, in October 1948, her groom appeared at the church with dusty shoes, squeezing in the ceremony between campaigning. Although she kept her own job for a while, the new Mrs. Gerald R. Ford had campaigned vigorously for "Jerry." Although married to a Republican, Betty admired Bess Truman, with whom she continued to speak at subsequent receptions at Blair House during her "training."

"My whole focus," Mrs. Ford remembered, "was pretty much learning about government and politics, because I had not been aware of how the government really operated in depth to any extent. This was my husband's new career, and I thought I should find out about it . . . Mrs. Truman . . . came across as a very strong lady as far as influencing her husband [went], but . . . she did what she pleased . . . What she wanted was her family life . . ."

The world of Washington opened up for the bright Mrs. Ford, and she absorbed all the color and activity of the postwar capital. "I did all the things that a political wife should participate in. I went to speakers' clubs to learn how to speak—it was almost the chic thing to do. And I was—as far as the Republican wives were concerned—instigating some of their activities." Betty was also befriended by one congressional wife who, that year, became a Senate wife, Lady Bird Johnson.[25]

Johnson's election to the Senate was due in no small part to his friendship with Speaker Rayburn, and that was partly due to Lady Bird. Rayburn was very fond of her, lavishing attention on her and little daughter Lynda, born in 1944, but also sharing many serious evenings of political discussion. Mrs. Johnson furthered her already extensive knowledge of domestic and international issues under the tutelage of "Mr. Sam." He wrote to her at the time, "Your friendship for me is one of the most heartening things in my life."

Lady Bird fondly recalled Betty: "Once a month the Eighty-first

[Congress] Club would have a party. I almost always went, because I liked to get to know the wives of Lyndon's colleagues. She almost always went. And she was young and pretty and just as terrifically busy with raising a family. Ever so likable."[26]

If Betty Ford saw Lady Bird Johnson occasionally, she saw much of one woman whose husband was reelected to the House in '48, Pat Nixon. Both Betty and Pat worked in their husbands' offices, overseeing administrative duties. They saw each other once a month at the meetings of the social-political "Chowder Marching Club," and Pat recalled "having a lot of fun and exchanging ideas" with Betty. The Fords and the Nixons even lived at the same suburban Virginia complex for several years.[27]

Dick had won his first race for Congress in 1946 largely because of Pat. Several thousand dollars that she had carefully saved for a home went directly into the campaign. Just six hours after the birth of their first child, Tricia, Mrs. Nixon was doing research, studying stacks of Congressional Records to familiarize herself and Dick with their incumbent opponent. She not only helped write and edit campaign literature, she typed it, had it printed, and hand-distributed it. In very conservative Whittier, she became that extreme rarity, an openly political woman. She stopped smoking in public. She persuaded dozens of women to volunteer for the campaign, made short "remarks," and was capable of addressing the issues. Pat Nixon sold her only inheritance of several small acres of her father's farm to raise three thousand dollars to cover the expensive cost of illustrated pamphlets. When the campaign office was broken into, the pamphlets were stolen.

Almost exactly a year after Lady Bird gave birth to her second daughter, Lucy, Pat had her second girl, Julie, on July 5, 1948—once again during Dick's campaign. The Nixon star rose quickly. He was appointed chairman of the Subcommittee on Un-American Activities and charged with investigating claims of journalist Whittaker Chambers that a communist underground existed in the government. When harsh criticism was leveled at Dick, Pat perceived that his political independence could bring permanent enemies.

Just two years later, he would be elected senator, with Pat again playing a public role in the campaign. Literature described her as "well-informed, intelligent and . . . seriously interested in national affairs and problems of government." But Mrs. Nixon's guarded attitude about her private life was now for the first time challenged, when an issue was made of the fact that her father had been a Roman Catholic. Pat did not deny it, but because it was personal, she ignored it. Throughout California, she made hundreds of appearances, attending "coffee" meetings with women supporters. She kept a record of where she wore what dress, trying never to reappear in the same suit, striving, in a word, to be "perfect" in public. The woman in newspaper pictures, however, was entirely different from the spontaneously effusive person who hugged, kissed, and warmly delved into massive crowds.

As a Senate wife, Mrs. Nixon continued working in Dick's office, even drafting responses for him, working side by side with his new secretary, Rose Mary Woods. Lady Bird Johnson knew Pat as both a congressional and Senate wife, and remembered the Nixons' second home, large but "modest," in Washington, with a "California look" of aqua walls. "I remember they had a sequoia [tree] in their front yard . . . they had planted . . . In taking constituents around town, I would always point it out . . ."[28]

If Democrat Lady Bird thought highly of Republican Pat, the latter's husband spoke well of the First Lady. Richard Nixon said Bess was "strong," and "salty. She is right down to earth . . . a good strong character. I imagine when Harry Truman has had to handle some of the hard, hard ones, he would go home and I am sure Bess Truman stood there, like a rock with him."[29]

Bess may have been popular with Republicans, but Harry wasn't, as his administration became plagued with a shooting war, an assassination attempt, a defiant general, "witch hunts," and a cold war.

Jane Lingo recalled Mrs. Truman's "great concern" for the wounded men coming back from Korea, where, in June 1950, the president had ordered military forces to help the South Koreans against their northern invaders. Bess held special afternoon receptions for them, "making sure she talked with each . . ." In November, the sounds of crackling gunfire broke the sleepiness of afternoon. Outside Blair House lay a policeman killed by Puerto Rican nationalists, one of whom was also killed while trying to get into the house and shoot the president. When Bess heard the sounds, she bolted downstairs. "What's happening?" she quizzed Mr. West. When she was told, her eyes popped, and she rushed back up. As Edith Helm said, "Mrs. Truman is a very self-contained person, but . . . the assassination attempt was a great shock to her and she probably was more affected by it than she would acknowledge."[30]

The incident that touched the nation's nerve, however, was Truman's dismissal of General MacArthur due to his insubordination during the Korean War. When Mrs. Wallace snidely asked Bess, "Why did your husband have to fire that nice man?," the First Lady shot back. "My husband, Mother, happens to be commander-in-chief! And that outranks a general! My husband does what he believes best for the country!" There were some who claimed that Mrs. Truman had actually advised the president to dismiss MacArthur.[31]

Increasing diplomatic disagreements between the United States and Soviet Union began to manifest themselves even in the first ladyship. When the Soviet ambassador refused Bess's invitation to the Diplomatic Corps dinner because the Lithuanian envoy, living in exile in America, was also invited, the president considered it an insult to the

First Lady. He wanted the ambassador recalled by the Soviets. This alarmed Dean Acheson, who knew it could deepen the "Cold War," and he attempted unsuccessfully to reason with the president in the Oval Office. Just then, the phone rang. It was the First Lady, calling from her office. She gave hell to the man who gave hell. Chastised, he sheepishly changed his mind.[32]

When Truman's popularity sagged, he turned to the First Lady for bolstering. "The general trend," he wrote her, "is that I'm a very small man in a very large place and when someone I trust joins the critical side—well it hurts. I'm much older and very tired and I need support as no man ever did." He admitted, "The Boss is not only my good right arm, but the left one as well."[33]

After Margaret moved to New York, "the Three Musketeers" were now reduced to the two "lovebirds" by the staff. One morning, after Bess's return to the White House from her annual Missouri retreat, the passion of the relationship became clear to J. B. West. The night before, the Trumans retired early, sending the maid downstairs after a short dinner was served. In a "small, uncomfortable voice," the First Lady told West that "we have a little problem." Clearing her throat, she explained, "It's the President's bed. Do you think you can get it fixed today? . . . Two of the slats broke down during the night."[34]

Mrs. Truman disapproved of easy divorce, feeling that some spouses treated "a sanctified union much too lightly . . ." She believed in birth control. When her daughter bore several children, Bess bluntly remarked, "Well, you're not a Catholic, so I can only conclude you're careless."[35]

Columnist Drew Pearson, who attacked Truman, praised his wife as "one of the most influential people around," but she herself did not escape a taint of scandal. In 1949, Bess was implicated in a controversy when it became known that Harry Vaughan, chief military aide to the president, had accepted a deep freezer worth $375 as a gift for Mrs. Truman in 1945, from a Chicago firm interested in federal contracts. Senator Clyde Hoey began an investigation, but learned that Mrs. Truman was innocent. "In the future," she told a friend, "if someone offers me a tray of ice cubes, I'll refuse." Clark Clifford said that Bess "followed a strict code of ethical conduct in every move she made."[36]

Even right-wing Senator Joseph McCarthy rushed to the First Lady's defense in the freezer question. "I am sure that she did not know anything about this matter," he told reporters. "She just graciously accepted a gift and knew nothing of the background . . . She's the only good thing about the White House." McCarthy was already among the leaders of various "witch hunts" to rid reputed communists from government, and eventually from motion pictures. A pervasive fear swept Hollywood even among the innocent, like actress Nancy Davis of Chicago. Since she she had some stage and television acting experience, MGM gave her a screen test and offered her a contract in 1949.

In her studio press biography, Nancy cut off two years from her age, said she disliked "superficiality," particularly "in women," and listed her greatest ambition as to have "a successful marriage." She got her own little house. She modeled at a fashion show with Carmen Miranda. She began shopping at the expensive clothing boutique Amelia Gray's. As an actress, Nancy never became a glamour girl, but she did learn to smile or cry on cue and maintain a perfect appearance. She developed an instinct for dramatic visual poses, but found Hollywood "self-centered."

When Miss Davis started getting communist literature at home, however, she understandably feared being blackballed by the industry, and told director Mervyn LeRoy about the mailings. He asked the Screen Actor's Guild president to call her about it. The president told LeRoy there was another actress by the same name who was a communist, and Miss Davis's name would be cleared. The president and Nancy talked, and began to date. His name was Ronald Reagan. Among other attractions, they shared the same Hollywood society astrologer, Carroll Righter, who had even printed Nancy's star patterns in his horoscope column.[37]

The woman many once accused of being communist, Eleanor Roosevelt, was not battling communists at the UN, demanding that they acknowledge the debate on human rights. She eventually traveled to the Soviet Union, and most Far East and Middle East nations. In Holland, in 1948, she received a degree of Doctor of Laws at the University of Utrecht. She retained her interest in American issues as well, serving as vice chairman of the Committee on the Mid-Century White House Conference on Children and Youth.

Besides continuing "My Day" and radio shows, Eleanor forayed into television, doing an NBC Sunday afternoon interview program, with a country-house set, as she poured tea. Her guests were as diverse as Albert Einstein and the duke and duchess of Windsor, but when an invitation went out without her permission to Bess Truman, Eleanor was "appalled," because "I know she does not do anything of this kind and that I should not have asked her."[38]

Eleanor wasn't the only woman exploring postwar Europe. In 1951, the Eisenhowers had arrived in France as he began his role as chief of NATO's European forces, on leave from Columbia. France proved to have its difficult moments. Mamie and Ike listened in silent horror to an insulting radio skit about their arrival in Paris, on time bought by a communist group. Mamie turned down an offer to stay at the fussy estate of the late Elsie DeWolfe, society decorator, and the insulted French press made a headline issue of her decision. When she accepted a more suitable mansion, she learned to live with contemporary art but had corn planted in the French fields, a sentimental reminder of her beloved Midwest.[39]

Another American in Paris sensed hostile sentiments. College stu-

dent Jacqueline Bouvier was "galled at the patronizing attitude towards America, annoyed by the compliment 'but no one would think you were American,' if one showed a knowledge of literature or history." Upon graduating from Farmington in 1947, she had gone to Vassar College, during which time she was dubbed "Deb of the Year" and appeared in *Life* magazine. Jackie spent her junior year in France, first studying in an intense language program at the University of Grenoble. Then she moved to Paris, as a student at the Sorbonne, boarding with the widow of a concentration-camp victim. While in Europe, Jacqueline made a special pilgrimage to the Nazi camp Dachau. This was her second European trip. As a teenager there, she'd met Churchill.

Jackie finished college at George Washington University in the capital, earning a degree in French history. After a brief introduction to a New England congressman, with her sister, Lee, she returned to Europe, where they visited art scholar Bernard Berenson. He advised them, "The only way to exist happily is to love your work . . . Anything you want, you must make enemies and suffer for . . . marry American boys, they wear better." As a remembrance, they wrote and illustrated a self-satirizing book, *One Special Summer*. Later that year, Jacqueline entered a *Vogue* writing and couture-design contest, the prize being a year in Paris as an editor. Out of 1,280 entries, she won, though she decided to stay in America and pursue a writing career. Her high school ambition, "[n]ot to be a housewife," seemed to be proving successful.[40]

During her European stay, Mamie came to know world leaders and royalty while touring several countries. It was in Luxembourg that the Eisenhowers learned of some shocking news, at least the way it was told to them at the American embassy by chatty ambassador Perle Mesta. Recalling Eleanor Roosevelt's 1948 visit and inquiry about Mamie's health, Perle twisted her own statements into a story that implied that Eleanor "had inquired as to the state of Mamie's health and whether she had recovered from her stay at the [alcoholism] clinic." Understandably, the story enraged Ike, and hurt Mamie. It was not forgotten.

If such gossip bothered Ike, the stories of Kay Summersby didn't disturb Mamie in the least. Discussing General Montgomery, she joked to her doctor that "if I had one thought that there was an iota of truth in the Kay Summersby affair, I would have gone after Monty. And believe you me, my friend, I could have gotten him!" When a speaker at a public banquet told the audience that "General Marshall wants nothing more than to retire to his . . . home with Mrs. Eisenhower" the crowd broke out in roaring laughter. The mortified speaker blurted out, "My apologies to the general!" Mamie piped up in mock insult, "Which general?"[41]

As the 1952 election approached, however, there were draft movements to make Ike a nominee—in both parties. When it finally became known that he was a Republican, a full-blown campaign was under way, even though he was across the ocean and not actively participating. Privately, Mamie fearfully confided to friends, "I think if Ike should become President, it would kill him."[42]

During the months when Ike was courted, invitations overwhelmed Mamie. In March 1952, she received one from a friend whose husband had come to know Ike during the war: "Dr. and Mrs. Loyal Davis announce the marriage of their daughter Nancy to Mr. Ronald Reagan . . . Will be at home after the fifteenth of March . . ." A telegram was sent to Mr. and Mrs. Ronald Reagan, 94-1/2 Hildgard Avenue, Los Angeles: "The announcement of your recent wedding has just reached here. This message brings Mrs. Eisenhower's and my heartiest congratulations and best wishes."

Nancy Davis hadn't hidden her eagerness to marry Ronnie. Feeling "a little in awe" in the home and presence of Ronnie's first wife, Jane Wyman, when she joined him in visiting his children, Nancy nevertheless felt that Jane "had convinced him that he shouldn't get married again until she did. It took me a little time, but I managed to unconvince him." By February 1952 Nancy said, "We felt we were already married, and it was time to make it official."

Nancy made only two more movies after her marriage, saying, "I had no desire to continue as an actress once I became a wife . . . I had seen

too many marriages fall apart when the wife continued her career. I knew it wouldn't be possible for me to have the kind of marriage I wanted—and Ronnie wanted, though he never asked me to give it up—if I continued my acting career." Mrs. Reagan said that after marriage she "immediately wanted to have children." At the time of her wedding, she was two months' pregnant already. Her daughter, Patricia, would be born in October.[43]

In May, knowing that Harry wasn't running in '52, a happy Bess Truman conducted a tour for reporters of the renovated mansion. She took little interest in decorating, because "I'm only going to be around for a year. It would be unfair to the next First Lady to impose too many of my ideas upon the house." Consequently, the decorators of the New York department store B. Altman's outfitted it with showroom reproductions, giving it a dismally fake atmosphere.[44]

During the '52 election, Eleanor and Bess were both attracted to the sophisticated nominee of their party, Adlai Stevenson of Illinois. It was through Mrs. Truman that Eleanor came in regular contact again with Edith Wilson. All three attended many Democratic party events that year. The UN reminded Eleanor of Wilson's League, and she wrote Edith, "It must be a help to you to feel that your husband's ideals are being translated into action now."

Edith came to know another woman whose life would change with the election. At "an absolutely fascinating luncheon," Lady Bird Johnson remembered her first time "in a small group" with Edith Wilson. "It must be that some very seemly person got sick and couldn't come, because they asked me! There was a fabulous group there. Mrs. Wilson in her black-belted cartwheel sort of a hat . . . And Lady Astor from England. It was really big-time stuff for a youngish congressional wife! They were talking about the triumphal tour through Europe . . . of President and Mrs. Wilson, after the war, before he had the stroke."

During the campaign, when Stevenson planned a stop at Hyde Park, Eleanor invited Edith to come up, hear the speech, and stay at Val-Kill, particularly since "as far as I know you have never been to Hyde Park . . ." Edith didn't make the trip, but she no longer disapproved of Eleanor's activities, having gladly accepted the Women's Joint Congressional Committee's invitation to a dinner honoring Mrs. Roosevelt as a UN delegate.[45]

At the Chicago Republican Convention, nominee Ike spent much time in Mamie's room, "reporting to her briefly on the proceedings." At a nearby sandwich shop, a TV news flash informed Pat Nixon that Ike had chosen Dick as his running mate. Shortly thereafter, she found herself on the speaker's podium with the world watching her, seated next to Mrs. Eisenhower, whom she had never met. The first thing Mamie blurted out to Pat was, "You're the prettiest thing," and amid the drama, chatted about her toothache. With Kansas senator Frank Carlson as her "mentor in political nuances," Mamie followed rule changes, delegate-block shifting, and power brokerage.[46]

The first tour of the nineteen-car "Eisenhower Special" train with the theme "Look Ahead, Neighbor" included about eighty whistle-stops. Covering 45 states, it carried 163 people, but one was especially popular and sought-after—not Ike but Mamie.

— 58 —

Look Ahead, Neighbor

IT BECAME STANDARD routine for crowds to call out, "Where's Mamie?" Then a guttural voice warbled, "Here I am!," and she popped out from behind a curtain to the roar of voter applause. James Reston of *The New York Times* wrote that Mamie was worth "50 electoral votes." There were campaign tape dispensers with Mamie's face on them. Two

of the official campaign songs were "Mamie" and "I Want Mamie." It was the first time a candidate's wife was so honored. Even Ike wore an "I Like Mamie" button.[1]

Passing out buttons from the back of the train, she shrugged her shoulders, kidding the crowds, "I've been working on the railroad!" At every stop, recalled her daughter-in-law, "there'd be flowers for her," but at regular interwals, reported Bess Furman, Mamie ordered the bouquets turned over to local old-age homes. Her army years, Mamie boasted, gave her "personal knowledge of all sections of the USA" that she now traveled.[2]

Though her spontaneity was genuine, Mamie was conscious of the benefit of her appearances. On one occasion, she willingly dressed in curlers and robe to restage a photograph some photographers had missed. Along for part of the whistle-stop was Mamie's mother, "Min." At first, whenever Mamie's photo appeared in newspapers, Min considered it improper. But when women delegates began coming onto the train at stops, and were photographed with Ike, Min told Mamie, "You should be the lady in the pictures!" The lounge car used by the press, known as "the playroom," was "decorated with spicy undraped cheesecake." One afternoon when reporters were off on assignment, Mrs. Sherman Adams, wife of the campaign manager, and a friend, came into the car and "pasted red paper panties and matching accessories" over the girlie pictures. Merriman Smith joked that "the accomplice" was Mamie.[3]

Milton Eisenhower said that Ike's speeches were Mamie's first real exposure to rhetoric. "After a while she got to where she would make suggestions—say, less statistics, talk more about farming to farmers— that kind of . . . sensible advice that the advisers knew, but didn't always remember . . ." Once, while Ike rehearsed a speech, she interrupted, "Ike you can't say that, it's not in character." Angry, he continued. She stopped him again. "Ike, that simply isn't you." For twenty minutes, she continued with suggestions. Finally, according to aide Kevin McCann, Ike threw the speech down. But he never delivered it. Barbara Eisenhower said, "If there were people who appealed to her . . . she might talk him into seeing them . . . They conferred."[4]

And if Ike's campaign manager, former New Hampshire governor Sherman Adams, thought he could manipulate Mrs. Eisenhower, he was in for a surprise. At the first stop during the campaign tour in Philadelphia, Adams instructed aides that he would always have the adjoining suite next to the candidate, for immediate access and consultation, and Mamie was to be given a room on another floor, at the far end of a hall. Mrs. Eisenhower was surprised, but made no comment. The arrangement was repeated in Chicago, the second stop, over protests from Senator Seaton and Governor Carlson. Adams even wrote a memo affirming that the order was to remain through the entire campaign. Then they got to Los Angeles. One aide protested, "We have a man with a wife. Let's use her! The Democratic candidate doesn't have a wife. We have a ready-made appeal for the family vote." Adams persisted—until he opened the door to his suite, connecting to Ike's.

There, "uncompromisingly ensconced" was Mamie. When Adams left and sought out the aide who made hotel arrangements, he bawled him out. "I couldn't help it, Sherm," the aide helplessly responded. "Mrs. Eisenhower just moved in and said that was where she intended to stay. Moreover, she announced she's going to insist upon the connecting room everywhere from now on."[5]

Mrs. Eisenhower exercised her independence off the trail as well. On a stay in Denver, when her family's cook, Jerusha, asked Mamie to attend a meeting of her black Republican women's club, Mrs. Eisenhower impulsively accepted without even notifying the local managers of the campaign headquarters. It infuriated those more exclusive white women's clubs whose invitations Mamie had turned down. When Ike left Denver for some speeches and the Nixons arrived in town, Mamie organized her own political reception for them, with the help of Governor Thornton. When a St. Louis ladies' reception got out of hand, the honoree chortled with authority, "Form a line! If you form a line, I'll be glad to shake hands with all of you." In a private letter, Mamie instructed Thorton's mother-in-law, "Keep working on those

Taft people and I will try to take your advice about keeping my sense of humor." Ike understated, "She is a better campaigner than I am."[6]

Mamie was acutely aware of the alcoholism rumors about her, according to Katherine Howard, secretary of the National Republican Committee. When once Mrs. Ike was drinking water, she eyed a photographer snapping her picture, and sharply called out that she wanted the film destroyed. It was. The gossip turned up in print only in crude "smear brochures." In Europe when he had been asked point-blank by one Nebraska delegation, Ike had frankly told them that "the truth of the matter is that I don't think Mamie has had a drink for something like eighteen months." But Milton Eisenhower said that it wasn't those charges that hurt her the most. What really upset her "was hearing [gossip] that he [Ike] was anti-Semitic. That really shocked her, so completely an untrue thing."[7]

The campaign produced another scandal. Some reporters created a story about a fund they termed "secret," which they charged Senator Nixon was using to personal advantage. Nixon thought of quitting the ticket, but it was Pat who firmly told him, "We both know what you have to do, Dick. You have to fight it all the way to the end, no matter what happens." He followed her advice. Pat agreed to appear on TV with him in a public defense, a silent but visibly strong image, sitting behind him. She was nevertheless devastated by his decision to publicly reveal all their private finances, bursting out at him, "Why do we have to tell people how little we have and how much we owe? Aren't we entitled to have at least some privacy?"

When they got to the TV station and up on the set, Dick suddenly said he couldn't go through with it. "Of course you can," she told him. Among his other defenses—the most famous being acceptance of "Checkers" the dog—Nixon told a viewing audience of several million that Pat wasn't on the government payroll like many of her Senate wife peers, that as a woman of Irish heritage, she was a fighter, and that she "doesn't have a mink coat. But she does have a respectable cloth coat." The supportive response kept Nixon on the ticket.

Mamie and Min wept as they watched Nixon's speech, but the ordeal had angered Mrs. Ike. Not long after, when she and Pat were riding together in a motorcade one dark night, she broke their strained silence, complaining that the Nixon issues had "hurt the campaign, adding, "I don't know why all this happened when we were getting along so well."

"But you just don't realize what *we've* been through," came the quick but polite retort. Pat was restrained, but the tone of her voice let Mamie know how she felt.

Mamie and Pat campaigned separately, with their husbands, but did make a joint TV appearance on a national call-in show in which the candidates answered questions.[8]

At the White House, after the Eisenhower victory, Mrs. Truman was happily planning her departure. During the campaign, she had been spending an increasing amount of time with her dying mother, while the president traveled. He continued to write her about everything, including news of the fun she was missing, like one night in Missouri when "Ronald Reagan and his wife Nancy Davis . . . gave us a half hour of grand entertainment." Her mother's death that fall left Bess deeply affected. She told Katie Louchheim that she was a daughter "tyrannized by a love that sometimes overwhelmed," and confided that she had "imaginary conversations" with the recently departed Madge.[9]

Though she would leave no particular legacy, Bess fostered the State Department's program of exporting American theatrical productions overseas, and influenced the president to increase substantially the funding for the National Institutes of Health, in hopes of increasing advances in cancer research. After the election, Bess hosted a special luncheon not only for the wives of White House executive staff, but also "for the women who held such positions on their own." She insisted on also including her East Wing staff, "even though they were not division heads."[10]

On December 1, Bess gave Mamie the traditional tour of the White House. Reporters eyed Mamie's expensive coat, asking about it and attempting to draw a comment akin to Nixon's remark about Pat's cloth coat. She saucily shot back, "Mink, of course." The congenial tour was marked by a cartoon showing the two women shaking hands in the White House. Both women liked each other, and Mrs. Truman's only offhand comment was a warning to the house staff that they would be seeing a "lot of pink." *Life* reported that Mamie would be like Bess, "with a touch of Ethel Merman on the side." Their husbands were a different story.[11]

Mamie resented Truman's campaigning against Ike, and while he claimed that Ike refused to come into the mansion and escort him out on Inauguration morning, Mamie privately revealed to her cousin James Shaaf that Truman hadn't invited her and Ike in.[12]

That morning, the president-elect impulsively decided to write an Inaugural prayer, consulting only Mamie, who backed the innovation. The moment after he took the oath of office, Ike turned and kissed her. It was the first time in history that such an open expression of emotion was shown between a president and his wife. The *Washington Times-Herald* account of the Inaugural focused on the First Ladies. "Mamie's lively laughter could be heard far back in the crowd," wrote the paper's new reporter, "while Mrs. Truman sat stolidly with her gaze glued on the blimp overhead through most of the ceremony."[13]

Just two months before, the same reporter had raised the ire of "Mike," Mamie's sister, because she had interviewed the new First Lady's school-age niece, and did a newspaper story on the girl and Aunt

Mamie, along with her own artful drawings. The article caught the attention of Eleanor Roosevelt's old friend "Green Room girl" Bess Furman, who suggested in a note to her young colleague that she write a children's book covering history from a younger perspective on her own highly acclaimed *White House Profile,* though she warned that "trying to write anything original about the White House is like asking for the moon."

The reporter joked that Mamie's niece "just might turn out to be my meal ticket." Then she wrote, "That is the most wonderful idea—the children's book . . . I would so love to meet you . . . I'm so in love with all that world now—I think I look up to newspaper people—the way you join movie star fan clubs when you're ten years old." It was signed, "Jacqueline Bouvier."[14]

Jackie was diverted momentarily from writing history and kept pursuing journalism, recalling, "Being a journalist seemed the ideal way of both having a job and experiencing the world, especially for anyone with a sense of adventure . . ." She said its virtue was, "You never know where it's going to take you . . ."[15]

For a cub reporter, Miss Bouvier got some impressive interviews with outgoing Cabinet members, Richard *and* Julie Nixon, even the congressman she had met a year before, who was now elected to the Senate, John F. Kennedy. She called him Jack.

Most of Jacqueline's interviews were for her column, "The Inquiring Camera Girl," for which she also took her subjects' photographs. Frequently her column questions were fey twists on the battle between the sexes. She asked if "marriages have a better chance of survival when the spouses don't breakfast together. . . ? "Are men braver than women. . . ?"; "Is your marriage a fifty-fifty partnership. . . ?"; "Can you give any reason why a contented bachelor should get married?" Personally, Jackie told a friend that there was a "combination of good and evil" in men.

That night at the Inaugural Ball, First Lady Mamie's gown shimmered with 2,000 pink rhinestones, accompanied by pink gloves, pink high heels, and a pink purse encrusted with 3,456 pink pearls and beads. Amid all the attention focused on her, Mrs. Eisenhower typically thought of others. She insisted on paying all costs for her two black maids to attend the Inaugural, and went to much personal trouble helping arrange their accommodations. The city was still segregated. Republicans Pat Nixon and Betty Ford and their husbands were there. Among the revelers was the loyal opposition, Senator Kennedy, and his date for the night, Miss Bouvier.[16]

The next morning White House chief usher Howell Crim and his assistant, J. B. West, were summoned upstairs to see Mrs. Eisenhower. When they entered the First Lady's bedroom, West said that they "stopped dead in our tracks." There, smoking a cigarette, sat the First Lady of the United States.

In bed.

If Eleanor Roosevelt's most enduring advice had been the responsibility of women for world peace, the new First Lady's was markedly different.

"Every woman over fifty," said Mamie Geneva Doud Eisenhower, "should stay in bed until noon."[17]

The Fabulous Fifties had begun.

– 59 –

In the Pink

HER COMMAND-POST bedroom was a garishly delightful tribute to her increasingly legendary trademark: pink.

She ordered a massive king-sized bed with a pink pincushioned headboard, pink sheets and covers, a monogrammed pink wastebasket, pink slipcovered furniture, with rare touches of her almost-as-famous green. There was a large bowl of orchids, and a bowl of pink carnations and mums. Her bathroom replicated the one at Gettysburg: pink ceramics, pink fluffy rug, pink hamper, monogrammed pink towels, pink paper, pink soap, and pink-white Elizabeth Arden cream jars. She even had a pink cloth cover for her case of pink lipstick.[1]

Mamie's morning uniform was pink bow in hair, pink satin breakfast jacket, pink nightgown, and—when she rose—pink housecoat and spike-heeled feathered pink bedroom mules. She was breezy, warm, and folksy. Her blue eyes "puddled" at anything sentimental. But, J. B. West said, under the frills was "a spine of steel . . . She knew exactly what she wanted . . . exactly how it should be done. And she could give orders, staccato crisp, detailed, and final, as if it were she who had been a five-star general."[2]

She forbade the staff to use nicknames. She lost her temper if there were footprints on "my" carpet. She announced to members of the president's staff making their way from West to East Wing, "You are not to use the mansion as a passageway." She was to be escorted leaving and entering the house. No staffers were to use the elevator. And yet, despite her demands, Mamie took an intensely genuine interest in the well-being of the entire house staff. On birthdays, everyone got a cake; at Christmas, gifts even for their families. She was the only First Lady to invite every employee to her private home, in Gettysburg, for barbecues.

Besides Gettysburg, Mrs. Eisenhower paid detailed attention to "Mamie's Cabin," a modern pink-interior, white-pillared house on the private golf club at Augusta, Georgia. Besides working vacations there, the Eisenhowers made winter golf sojourns to Palm Desert, California, where they often saw the Loyal Davises, and their daughter and son-in-law, Nancy and Ronald Reagan. Mamie lavished her homemaker's touch mostly on the White House, but when she learned there were no funds for antiques, she resolved, "Well, I guess I'll have to make do!"

With both the household and her personal accounts, Mamie was cautious. She was not above buying costume jewelry at C. C. Murphy and dresses at J. C. Penney. She was scrupulous about never putting personal items "on the eagle," her army phrase for government funds, yet feared an old age on limited money, because the "world outside is pretty cold and impersonal."[3]

Budgeting didn't mean she was flippant about fashion. To the editors attending the opening session of 1953 "Fashion Press Week," she wrote, "As a soldier's wife I learned early in life that pride in personal appearance is not a superficial thing. . . . Knowing . . . how to tell . . . fashion from . . . fad . . . always helped me to shop intelligently." When she popped backstage at a fashion show to see dresses she liked, one shocked model in brassiere responded to Mamie, "Gosh, I never dreamt I met Mrs. Eisenhower in my Maidenform bra." The public-relations head of Garfinkel's Department Store prophesied that Mamie's "flair for fashion will give new impetus to fashion in Washington." But when complimented on a hat assumed to be a Paris original, Mamie cut through the gush, "I got it by mail order . . . $9.95."[4]

Merchants were quick to capitalize on her favorite color. She proudly endorsed the Textile Color Institute's request for her permission to come out with "First Lady Pink." Also called "Mamie Pink," it catapulted pink paint, cloth, draperies, rubber and plastic goods, tiles, pottery, and linoleum into American households, making it the most popular color of the fifties. Even the State Department caught "Mamie Pink" fever, redecorating U.S. embassies around the world with at least one pink bedroom, in case Mamie was coming. Mr. West chuckled in recalling Mamie's excitement at getting complimentary pink cigarettes.[5]

If pink was her insignia, bangs were her trademark, and they provoked not a small amount of controversy. By the time Mamie was in the White House, Elizabeth Arden was using her most famous customer as a means of promotion. Not everyone thought bangs flattered Mamie, and they let her know it. A Life magazine editor suggested a change in hairstyle by presenting a retouched photo to reflect the new do. Mamie responded that she had "great resect for the judgement of photographers," but the bangs stayed. When Jolie Gabor tried to change Mamie's bangs, she protested no, because "the whole nation is imitating me . . ."

Mamie loved theme parties. At a Halloween lunch she put goblins, autumn leaves, cornstalks, and "disembodied witch heads" in the state rooms, orange lights in a chandelier, dessert in pumpkin molds, and decked herself in gold dress and shoes. On St. Patrick's Day, she dressed in green, had green ribbons wrapped around the columns, and dyed-green carnations hung from the Green Room chandelier. At Easter, she had bunnies popping out of eggs on mantelpieces, butterfly nets hanging from the celling, pink daisies in a pink flowercart, a running-water fountain in the dining room, fake roses wrapped around the columns, and the sound of singing birds. Mamie, however, sabotaged the last touch when she audibly orderred a servant to "turn down the birds."[6]

Her public example as fifties housewife was amplified by her line "Ike runs the country, I turn the porkchops." This First Lady had her cakes made from "the new cake mixes" in a box. On her wrist, she jangled a charm bracelet. Like other housewives of the era, she favored full-petticoated print dresses by Mollie Parnis, and little Sally Victor hats with matching gloves and dyed spike-heel shoes, as sharp as her manicured fingernails.[7]

Even the First Lady's cultural tastes were popular. She played the electric organ by ear. Her favorite movies included Gigi, The King and I, and, *Never Wave at a Wac.* Her formal entertainment was often provided by the bubbly sounds of her favored music makers—Fred Waring and Lawrence Welk, but she did host the first White House evening of musical theater, including songs from *The Pajama Game, West Side Story, My Fair Lady,* and her favorite, *The Music Man.* Her tastes were mainstream, but Mamie was enthusiastic about Ike's signing of the National Cultural Center Act, laying groundwork for one in the capital. As for the new sounds of "rock and roll," Mamie, according to her grandson, "didn't mind it . . . [and] knew it was . . . benign." Milton said the First Lady "wasn't as bewildered by it as he [Ike] was . . . but she thought that music was just right for the generations who played it." Mr. West recalled her tapping a toe to "Jingle Bell Rock."

For the middle-class Middle American, whom Mamie epitomized in the fullest sense, it was a time of the cha-cha, Hula-Hoops, three-button gray flannel suits, poodle skirts, saddle shoes, western ties and western movies, and barbecue grills at the kidney-shaped poolside. Even "beatnik" leader Jack Kerouac liked Ike and Mamie. The average man related to her better than stoic Bess, liberal Eleanor, or erudite Lou.[8]

Remnants of Eleanor's "Green Room Girls," among other new, younger faces representing both the print and radio media, were thrilled as they gathered in the ground floor "Broadcast Room" of the White House on March 11, 1953, for Mamie's first press conference. Greeted with "Good morning teacher," Mamie had as her purpose to discuss her public schedule, after which questions were asked. It proceeded well, the First Lady's breeziness pervading. But when asked to comment on the controversial marriage of a Norwegian prince to a commoner, She responded, "I haven't thought about it." When a reporter insisted, Mamie clarified, "I haven't thought about *making any comment* about it."

Mamie concluded with reference to Eleanor's having barred male reporters by teasing those standing in the back, hoping to get a political scoop, who outnumbered the women in attendance, "I didn't hear a thing from the gentlemen." Still, her first press conference proved to be her last. All others were canceled.[9]

It was a bewildering decision, for she was comfortable with even political reporters. Sitting in the front seat of her black Chrysler with the driver, as usual, she once ordered the car pulled up to a streetcar stop, rolled down the window, and called out to *U.S. News and World Report* reporter Jack Sutherland, "Can we give you a lift?" After she made a speech at the dedication of a Denver park named in her honor, Ike joked to political journalist that he "warned" Mamie that "hereafter I'm going to relinquish as much speech making activity as possible to her!" Reporter Liz Carpenter said she "was a considerate, nice woman to the press. . . ."[10]

Being interviewed, declared presidential press secretary Jim Hagerty,

indicated that an "exclusive" had been granted. The cancellation of Mamie's conferences was *his* decision. He feared an unmanageable number of reporters requesting credentials to cover them, increasing the risk of controversial questions being asked. Hagerty acted as Mamie's "protective shield." In the *Life* magazine that featured rare color pictures of "The First Lady at Home," Mamie was shown in pink, arranging flowers, checking the pantry, greeting matrons in spaghetti-strap gowns, and watching her grandson play in his aqua toy car. The text avoided issues.[11]

Hagerty even told Mary Jane McCaffree, who ran the entire East Wing operation, to "shy away" from an educational television station's request that Mamie accept honorary chairmanship of its advisory council, because of "controversy as to whether by using such programs Government is not going into the education and propaganda field." The First Lady didn't mind her staff going to the president's staff for advice, but resented West Wingers making unsolicited edicts affecting her domain. "That's my side!" she'd snap.[12]

Some West Wingers thought it their job to search for some sort of First Lady project for her. Adviser Charles F. Willis, Jr., for example, was considering a proposal to "hire" an old army wife friend of the First Lady to serve "as liaison between Mrs. Eisenhower and the various women's clubs of the United States, with an office in the Executive Office Building." It would formalize Mamie's work with women's clubs into a bona fide "project," with public-relations benefit. Chief of Staff Sherman Adams dourly retorted, "I don't think this is any of our business." He had no desire to again stir the hornet's nest. [13]

It was no secret that Mrs. Eisenhower "did not get along" with the president's secretary, Anne Whitman, though they maintained a polite truce. From the campaign on, the First Lady would unsuccessfully attempt to oust her. Mamie kept East-West Wing relations formal. She didn't even approve of Ike calling her secretary "Mary Jane," herself addressing her always as "Mrs. McCaffree."

When Mrs. McCaffree and her crew first arrived, there was not so much as a folder available to tell them how to run things. She was later told by the chief of calligraphy, "You *are* the policy office—we are administrative." When Edith Helm offered advice on running the East Wing, Mamie nixed it: "If we make mistakes, they will be *our* mistakes." The First Lady managed the household, and trusted the administration implicitly to McCaffree. Mamie visited the East Wing only once. In her bedroom, she used Eleanor's old desk, but mostly she read and wrote from bed, on a tray, viewing work on her public correspondence with utmost importance. [14]

The First Lady received an average of seven hundred letters a month, and said she was "determined to answer each one in a personal way." Pat Nixon reported that her local deli owner bragged about a friend who got a Mamie letter. "People are marvelling," wrote Second Lady to First, "that you have personally signed so much mail, and they are filled with admiration and appreciation." Because of the letters, Senator Stu Symington wrote to Mrs. Eisenhower that she had the nation "in the palm of your hand."

Through her mail, Mamie exercised a small degree of political power. If she approved an appeal, the First Lady forwarded the letter to "Sherm" Adams. In one case, for example, Adams sent to the Selective Service, "for immediate consideration and acknowledgement" a request for deferment of one young man whose mother had written Mamie. The First Lady forwarded a suggestion to tattoo blood type on servicemen, for the Defense Department's consideration. In another case, an unemployed Missourian was given consideration for a government job. She reviewed requests for military transfers, federal housing, pensions, civil-service employment, even "suggestions" on government reform. When a blind musician sent her an original composition, Mamie facilitated an audition with the National Symphony Orchestra. [15]

But if she used her power to affect small decisions, Mrs. Eisenhower did not view such activity as political. For her there was no soul-searching about a role. She said she was "perfectly satisfied to be known as a housewife" and "homemaker." When a little girl boldly asked, "Why don't you do any work around here?," Mamie, "stopped cold for a moment," laughingly responded, "Oh, honey, but I do—who told you I didn't?" When *The Washington Post* criticized her "inactivism," an angry Ike told her not to read the paper anymore. She was nonplussed, and secretly kept reading the *Post*. Political cartoons had usually satirized First Ladies' involvement, but now it was a beaming Ike with a sheaf of "Problems," grinning about the news, "Mamie Heads List of 'Best Chapeaued Women,'" over the cartoon First Lady.

Barbara Eisenhower recalled that Mamie "had very definite ideas about what she thought was the right thing for her to do," and within her role definition, Mamie relished the first ladyship. She loved "girl talking" to every single woman guest in a reception line, chatting about hats, jewelry, grandchildren, or flowers. One woman's club leader gushed to Mamie that her "enchanted" group "spoke of your warmth, your youthfulness, your unhurried hospitality." There was never any mistaking her role. At Gettysburg, her canvas chair was clearly marked FIRST LADY.[16]

Though she stayed in the pink bed until noon, Mamie actually awoke about seven, read national newspapers, breakfasted, tackled correspondence, and held meetings. There was one moment that never interfered with the First Lady's schedule, her favorite soap opera, *As the World Turns*. The staff learned not to schedule meetings with her at that time slot, because she invariably made them sit through the entire show—even commercials—before getting down to business. She found soap operas "true to life." In the late afternoon, after greeting groups, she indulged in her favorite pastime of all, bridge, or canasta, or bolivia or Scrabble.[17]

Mamie's table games became legendary. When Congressman Gerald Ford's wife was invited to a canasta luncheon with the First Lady, Betty was bewildered, since "I didn't play canasta! I wasn't socializing much in the middle of the afternoon in the city. I was living in the suburbs raising a family. Not playing cards, but driving to Cub Scouts." When Jerry returned home to their newly built house after occasional White House meetings, he told Betty that Mamie had been present and listening to his political deliberations with the president. Ike and Mamie helped the congressman in his campaigns, making appearances with the Fords in Grand Rapids, and Betty felt that Mamie "could not be exposed to the complexities of the nation's and world's problems as the wife of a leader without absorbing most everything—whether or not she discussed them with people besides Ike." Often, the eldest Ford sons played with Mamie's grandchildren.[18]

A life revolving around family was the common denominator for most wives of the fifties across the country. Three years after their 1945 wedding, the Bushes had moved to Odessa, Texas, living in a one-bedroom apartment and having to share a hallway lavatory with a mother and daughter also in residence, who both happened to be prostitutes. From there, the Bushes had gone to Midland, where George's

oil business burgeoned, and permitted them to sell his small company for $1 million. From there, they'd settle in Houston, with Barbara, like Betty Ford, Rosalynn Carter, and Nancy Reagan, concentrating on the chores of being mother and housewife. The Bushes would have six children, George, Jr., Jeb, Neil, Marvin, Dorothy, and Robin. But in Texas three-year-old Robin developed leukemia.

The Bushes suffered for eight long months as their daughter's life ebbed, Barbara remaining at the child's side in a New York hospital. She would later recall a statistic that stated that 70 percent of those couples who experience the death of a child either divorce or suffer strained relations, as Mamie and Ike had. For the Bushes, however, the emotionally traumatic period drew them closer because they freely opened all their emotions to each other. Curiously enough, Mamie's haircut to bangs, which she styled during her marital rapprochement, had remained a private symbol of another time. Now, Barbara Bush's rich brown hair began to turn white, emblematic of the trauma she had lived through with George. She would momentarily try to color it, but then decided to keep it as it really was.

With her active brood of now five children, Mrs. Bush ruled with discipline but was also acutely attentive. Through the traditional role, however, her consciousness was raised in spheres outside the home. She began to notice that her son Neil had great difficulty reading. After learning that he suffered from dyslexia, she began to investigate the wider variety of reading problems confronting both adults and children. An interest in literacy was stirred in her, as was an awareness about civil rights when a "white only" hotel refused to permit her children's black sitter to stay with them, as Barbara drove through the South, up to Maine.[19]

In the White House, the First Family included mother Min, son John, his wife, Barbara, and their four grandchildren, of whom a doting Mamie said, "Every moment I spend with my grandchildren is the best moment of my life." When Min visited for a rest, she would chat on the phone with Mamie—from her bedroom across the hall. She sometimes joined the president and his wife for dinner served on TV trays, as they sat glued in front of the special television sets built into large wall consoles. Mamie was so devoted to *I Love Lucy* that she invited Lucille Ball, Desi Arnaz, Vivian Vance, and William Frawley to a reception in November 1953, marking the first time television actors were welcomed at the White House. The First Lady was even worked into the script of an *I Love Lucy* episode, which made much of the fact that women like Lucy and Mamie did not play golf. The Eisenhowers watched TV sometimes as late as ten thirty, after which they retired, together, to the same room.[20]

Mamie was thrilled because, as she told a friend, "I can reach over and pat Ike on his old bald head anytime I want to!" For her, the White House meant a full marriage, and she happily bragged, "I've got *my* man right here, where I want him!" They were one of the few openly affectionate presidential couples, kissing and hugging in front of the public. Every Valentine's Day, Ike surprised her with his "lovebug" undershorts. Each morning, the president brought her a "Mamie Pink" carnation. One morning, however, Mamie made an exasperated call to the chief usher. The night before, in the dark, she had been reaching for what she thought was a jar of Vicks ointment. When they awoke, they realized it was ink, and they were covered with it. An amused J. B. West wrote, "Not since Harry Truman's four-poster bed broke down had I heard such a good bedtime story."[21]

The First Lady wanted home to be a sanctuary from work, and fumed if she perceived that politics was infringing on Ike's personal time. Nevertheless, it was during those very private moments that she also served as his confidante. Kansas editor Henry Jameson said Mamie told him that "Ike confided in her on many subjects of business, government, military and otherwise. She kept well any secrets he may have disclosed."[22]

It was President Eisenhower himself who once publicly introduced Mamie as "my invaluable, my indispensable, but publicly inarticulate lifelong partner." In later reflection, he said that Mamie had "intelligence [and] . . . was always helpful and ready to do anything." Mamie later explained, "It wasn't that I didn't have my own ideas, but in my own era, the man was the head of the household. Ike was strong enough to make his own speeches." But if she chose not to exert political opinions publicly, she certainly did so in private.[23]

One of the greatest liabilities posed to the administration was the increasingly reactionary Republican Senator McCarthy's continued hearings on alleged communists. Though Barbara "never heard it dis-

cussed," she recalled that the First Lady did "show disgust," knowing that he was "drinking all during those hearings. His glass of water was gin."

David Eisenhower said that during the McCarthy hearings his grandmother "was no babe in the woods. She recognized that things were getting serious with McCarthy." With a clear concept of Ike's popularity, she "knew that it was best that he didn't associate himself by saying anything about McCarthy." Mrs. Eisenhower disliked McCarthy intensely, and followed administration policy by considering him persona non grata. Interestingly enough, Mamie had invited Lucille Ball to the White House before the actress had been cleared of the ridiculous charge by McCarthy that she was a rabid communist. At an official dinner for Vice President Nixon in 1953, McCarthy was the only United States senator specifically left off Mamie's guest list. It was the president who made that decision, but publicly, as reported in the press, it was believed that Mamie had withheld the invitation, and there wasn't an attempt to deny that.[24]

Mamie told reporters that she was "interested in the tax reduction" to exempt working mothers, proposed in a congressional bill, and had been following it "over the television." She hoped the Korean War would end, but not with "peace at any price." During an economic conference, Ike said in seriousness, "Let me try this out on Mamie. She's a pretty darn good judge of things." The president also admitted of his wife, "She is a very shrewd observer. I frequently asked her impression of someone, and found her intuition good. Women who know the same individual as a man do give a different slant . . . I got it into my head that I'd better listen when she talked about someone brought in close to me."[25]

Mamie went into the Oval Office only four times, and emphasized that "each time I was invited," but she did make her presence felt in the West Wing, according to later Cabinet Secretary Bob Gray: "[She was] not a woman without opinions and not a woman averse to expressing them [though] . . . seldom . . . one to call a Cabinet officer or an Administration official . . . If she had input to make, she did it through Eisenhower, or . . . Milton . . . it's hard for me to recall any specific conversation in which she didn't refer to the General half a dozen times . . ." Gray recalled that "one of her major roles . . . [was] administration morale . . . keep the staff morale high, keep the staff happy. She knew names of those at the switchboard. She'd stop and talk to the secretaries in the office, knew them by name . . . she was very mindful of her role to keep . . . efforts high on the part of those who worked for her husband, those in the Cabinet as well as those on the staff." Mamie relayed information Ike wanted the executive staff to know by dashing off a note to the staff member's *wife*, once opening with "Just between us girls, the President told me your husband did a great job . . ." As Steve Neal, who interviewed Mamie, noted, "It had done Treasury Secretary George Humphrey no harm that Mamie liked his wife . . ."[26]

The First Lady was protective of Ike's position to the point of mistrusting the political jockeying of even friends like General Al Gruenther. She didn't appreciate his decision to appear on the television program *What's My Line?*, particularly when Bennett Cerf said many in the country hoped Gruenther would eventually "take an important place in government." Ellis Slater asked Mamie whether that meant secretary of state or of defense.

"No," she dryly retorted. "President."[27]

Merriman Smith, dean of the White House press corps, wrote that "behind the scenes she can cut loose in highly precise terms about what she thinks of an event or a personality . . ." If the First Lady had a strong sense of personnel, she also viewed global events in a perspective of how they affected Ike. From the U-2 American reconnaissance plane shot down in the Soviet Union, to the end of the Korean war, Gray said, they "were crises for her too. She's bound to have talked with him [Ike] on it . . ." Mrs. Eisenhower often displayed her sensitivity to foreign affairs. When asked to receive a Jewish group, she sought out the advice of Maxwell Rabb, presidential adviser on minority issues. Among other Jewish groups, it was recommended that Mamie entertain the National Jewish Welfare Board, because they were not, in Rabb's words, "concerned with the Israel question . . ." Much to the disapproval of CIA director Allen Dulles, Mamie did attend a White House briefing on Ike's controversial Guatemalan policy, attended only by the Cabinet and ranking staff.[28]

The entire West Wing—and that included the president—learned that Mamie had the final word on event scheduling in her domain. While Gruenther was on the president's staff, he sent a memo to Max Rabb, also then serving as Cabinet secretary, stating that "Mrs. Eisenhower is very anxious to have all department heads know that it is important that clearance must be made with her Secretary . . . whenever arrangements are made at any time for groups to visit the White House . . . I will discuss this at the next Staff meeting—or perhaps you would like to suggest that Governor Adams comment on it. Mrs. Eisenhower says that even when the President approves luncheon dates she would like to have contact be made with her office to be sure that she has not made previous arrangements." As a result, when the president was asked to attend even a stag affair, he responded, "You know, I have a wife—I'll have to see what Mamie is planning." Often, she didn't approve his scheduling, once dismissing a dinner suggestion: "Now look here, Ike, I'm doing everything I can to make this thing go. Don't push me any harder because I won't be able to take it."[29]

When she visited the dismal presidential retreat, Shangri-La, the First Lady learned a redecoration could be ordered on Navy Department funds. She went to Ike; the funds were allocated. She redecorated in "1950's modern," and Ike rechristened it "Camp David" in honor of their grandson.[30]

Mamie later joked, "I did all the things that ladies do when they want their little way. I cried, and I argued . . . finally got m'way." That sounded innocuous, but Mamie did exert some power over the president. David recalled his grandmother as "an uninhibited freewheeling spirit, with a strong will of her own." Her son, John, said, "She could more than hold her own with him in private—her frail health belied the strength of her will . . ." Kevin McCann claimed that Mamie "was a determined woman," and even "shield" Jim Hagerty admitted that Mamie's opinions extended into the actions of the administration: "She'd argue with him plenty of times about his policies . . ." Her friend Mrs. Arthur Nevins said Mamie was "the boss" of the marriage.[31]

Priscilla Slater perfectly captured Mamie's paradoxical quality. She had "great concentration powers, a good memory, and is sharp and alert." Though "feminine . . . dainty and loveable, appealing in an almost childlike way . . . no individual would impose upon her more than once. She has a forceful personality, but her warmth . . . more than makes up for her decisiveness."[32]

Mamie avoided even a hint of assuming any aspect of Ike's responsibilities. When asked if "it will be your purpose to take off the shoulders of the President as much as possible such duties?" she understated that she didn't "know anything about that," but didn't deny it. Five months later, on June 26, 1953, she was Ike's "stand-in" at a stag group of Shriners. Half-hour sessions of groups queuing up for pictures with the president were a thing of the past. But if she sometimes substituted for the president, her own "groups" held priority.[33]

When inquiring cameragirl Bouvier questioned Second Lady Nixon, "Who will be Washington's Number One Hostess now that the Republicans are back in power?" Pat responded, "Why, Mrs. Eisenhower, of course. I think her friendly manner and sparkling personality captivate all who see or meet her . . . she has the knack of getting acquainted with each person instead of merely shaking hands with the usual phrase, 'How do you do?' . . ."

In one typical week, Mamie welcomed the National War College Officers' Wives Club, the Association Nationale des Medailles de la Résistance Française, National Federation of Business and Professional Womens Clubs, Women's Group of the American Savings and Loan Institute, National Council of Catholic Women, wives of the male members of the National Association of Real Estate Boards, and the Women's Forum on National Security. In one three-day period, she shook hands with fifty-five hundred individuals.[34]

So many organizations wanted to be received by Mamie that she began combining them, but some were incensed at being shuffled en masse. One group of navy wives was insulted at being combined with dentists' wives. Larger gatherings created new problems. Girl-talking with thousands, one by one, every single day turned into a First Lady's nightmare. Mamie's first DAR reception, for over three thousand, was too large for anyone to handle, and shouldn't have been scheduled. Some women lined up three hours ahead of time, and immediately there was serious traffic trouble as the Daughters jammed up Pennsylvania Avenue, and one side street had to be closed off. The reception lasted until 7:00 P.M., several hours longer than planned, and there was many an irate Daughter. Since Mamie sometimes had to take a breather, a Cabinet wife would fill in, an act that angered the already grumbling women. "Who are you?" asked one Daughter. "I didn't come to see you. I came to see Mrs. Eisenhower." Finally, Mamie decided that rather than shake individual hands, she'd stand on a raised platform, and later on the staircase landing, smiling and waving, as groups were snaked through the rooms and out the door.[35]

A by-product of popularity was commercial exploitation, and not since Frances Cleveland had a First Lady been so widely used. Just after the Inaugural, Macy's immediately had its milliner copy Mamie's hat, and named it "Elected." As time went on, so did the boldness of advertisers using Mamie. There were $2.50 "Ike & Mamie" plates sold at a Gettysburg souvenir stand near their home. General Foods advertised its German's Sweet Chocolate in magazines featuring the recipe for "Mamie's Million Dollar Fudge." The Town Hosiery Company advertised that "Mrs. Ike Likes Topaz," the trade name of one of its color-tinted ladies' stockings. Sunshine Bakeries had enough propriety to *tell* the White House that they were planning on naming their new Augusta, Georgia, public grocery store "Mamie's Cabin." When she accepted the complimentary subscription to a magazine, it quickly advertised that the First Lady was one of its readers.[36]

Ever since the campaign, Mamie realized how her popularity could influence mature, conservative women. Writing to one during the campaign, she had said that "we Republicans" would win, in part due to "the hard work of Republican women," though she realized "how busy you must all be with your homes and families." Only subtly did her public statements carry a political message, reflecting heartfelt issues of the moment—the Korean War, the fight against cancer and polio, supporting the UN, and "duck and cover" protection from the bomb. The popular mass causes of fifties housewives became a theme of Mamie's role.[37]

As National Honorary Chairman of the "1953 Crusade" against cancer, she praised women volunteers for their increasing of the drive's annual donations. She was appalled at the low blood donations to the Red Cross, and reminded women to think of "a wounded son in Korea," and that "next summer when polio strikes there will be a new weapon, gamma globulin, a blood derivative, to prevent the crippling and deformity that so often follows a polio attack." The First Lady called on "American clubwomen" to join the government's "Bond-a-Month Plan"; she praised the American Women's Clubs Overseas for participating in an international convention, and wired USO Mothers, hoping that all "will soon be free from the fear of war." She asked "women of this country" to observe UN Week, since they knew "too well the anxiety and anguish that war brings . . ."

In her Civil Defense statement, Mamie said that, "any housewife may be tomorrow's heroine . . . women of the nation . . . from girls to grandmothers, must do our part . . . This is America's spirit of neighborliness . . . It is difficult in the midst of our present day lives, filled with so many home and community activities, to believe that an atomic attack could happen here. *It can happen.* We must be prepared . . ."[38]

Mamie felt that she must be an example to young women too, but felt more comfortable entertaining the winners of the Betty Crocker

Homemakers of Tomorrow contest than women law students. She frankly felt women should primarily be domestic. For *Today's Woman* magazine, Mamie "wrote" an as-told-to article, "If I Were a Bride Today," revealing her idea of feminism:

". . . Let's face it. Our lives revolve around our men, and that is the way it should be. What real satisfaction is there without them? Being a wife is the best career that life has to offer a woman, but . . . It takes wit and straight thinking . . . I can speak as strongly as I like about the dreadful mistakes . . . I was a spoiled brat when I married . . ." Mrs. Eisenhower addressed the question of women's professional careers: "Your husband is the boss—and don't forget it. I am very sorry for the young wife who . . . has in the back of her head the idea, I can always get a divorce, or who thinks, There is no future in all of this housework—I'll get a job . . . The endless routine of a house sometimes seems like a meager, futile little job—especially when your husband comes home full of important news . . . Those are the moments when a job that will take you out among people and give you extra money seems very desirable. But life will be far more rewarding if you do not yield to that temptation. If you do, you may find yourself with nothing but a job twenty years from now . . ." And yet, paradoxically, she added, "Your independence . . . depend[s] on you," warning that the only way "to avoid debt . . . is for the husband to give his wife the paycheck and let her be responsible for it . . . If he sets up charge accounts and pays the bills . . . things are almost certain to get out of hand . . ."39

Mamie didn't travel with Ike. At her press conference, a reporter had told her, "It has been reported several times that you are going to be in Europe along about Coronation [of Queen Elizabeth] time." Mamie bantered back, "No truth to that. Not that anyone wouldn't like to go." Jacqueline Bouvier of the *Times-Herald* was assigned to cover the historic event. In London, she received two wires from Jack Kennedy, the first asking her to get him some books unavailable in America. The second told her, "Articles excellent but you are missed." Upon her return, he proposed marriage, and Jackie accepted.

Many friends had long perceived that under his detached harriedness, the senator was very much in love. Kennedy's closest intimate, Lem Billings, said, "They were so much alike. Even the names—Jack and Jackie: two halves of a single whole." Another friend, Chuck Spalding, recalled that "he really brightened when she appeared. You could see it in his eyes; he'd follow her around the room watching to see what she'd do next. Jackie *interested* him, which was not true of many women." Betty Ford, who'd noticed the "young and handsome congressman" whose office was across the hall's from Jerry's, recalled the delighted surprise in Congress over the news.

Superficially, many focused on the difference of Jackie's background with that of the clannish, hyperathletic, and very political Boston Irish-Catholic Kennedys. But if one examined the spirits that moved them, one could understand their bond. Both had been loners as children, and were inexplicably drawn to the mesmerizing rhythms of the sea. Both had a deep, aesthetic response to history and the arts and were voracious readers. The wedding took place in September 1953, attracting enormous national attention. Though unable to attend, Vice President and Mrs. Nixon were invited. On their honeymoon, Jackie penned a telling poem, in the style of Stephen Vincent Benét, part of the verse reading, "He would find love, He would never find peace, For he must go seeking, The Golden Fleece." Mrs. John F. Kennedy realized early on where her husband's ambitions lay.[40]

Pat Nixon did not associate the young reporter who had interviewed her several months before with "Senator Kennedy's fiancée," whom she met at a performance of Guys and Dolls and called "a darling girl." As the most active Second Lady since Grace Coolidge, Mrs. Nixon balanced a frantic schedule, between her family life and public demands. Sometimes the two roles conflicted. At a Cabinet wives' luncheon, before Mamie had officially signaled its end, Pat simply told her, "I hope you don't mind, but I have to leave to pick up my children at school." On politics, she continued to have strong opinions. Though she mistrusted McCarthy, she felt that his investigation into the State Department was warranted. She wasn't fooled by Ike's public gregariousness, and considered the vice presidency "a dead end."

When Ike sent the Nixons "as a team" as his international representatives, Pat broke precedents. She visited not only orphanages, but a leper colony. In Vietnam, she witnessed none of the communists fighting the government, but she did see the severely wounded. Dick compared her to "a great actress—always being her best on stage," but her presence also raised the visibility of women in some nations where they'd not been acknowledged as individuals. "Everywhere I went," she would admit, "it helped women."[41]

Mamie's view on that differed drastically. She had nothing to do with Ike's appointment, for example, of Oveta Culp Hobby, a colleague of Mrs. Roosevelt, to the Cabinet as secretary of health, education and welfare, and avoided mentioning her to intimates. Barbara Eisenhower said Mamie "thought that women who had jobs like that were very unfeminine." The First Lady was more interested in "the wives of." When Omar Bradley married, she piped up, "Well, he sure picked a chicken!"

Mamie was uncomfortable making a decision as to whether or not she should invite congresswomen to a "congressional wives' tea." A presidential adviser recommended that "lady members of Congress not be invited to this function. It has been the policy to avoid placing the First Lady in any position that would be political and having this group could be misinterpreted. (After all, a Congresswoman is a politician and will make political capital of any situation even if it is a social call.)"

And yet, paradoxically, without any provocation from the GOP, she impulsively decided to assist Denver Republican Ellen Harris in her 1954 campaign for Congress. A bus was rented, and Mrs. Harris and Mrs. Eisenhower toured through neighborhoods, making stops where housewives boarded the bus to "have coffee with Mamie." The First Lady admonished them, "I hope you'll all vote for her. We women have to have a voice in things."[42]

On the surface, it seemed that Mamie retained her apolitical military beliefs. She quoted Ike in a letter after the election, saying, "Democrats, Republicans, Independents—we all love our country . . . and desire to see it realize its enormous potential . . ." In truth, Mamie seemed more partisan than even Ike. Before sending a support message to Republican women, she let Ike look at the final draft, and he changed his First Lady's wording to "take your letter a little bit more out of the partisan and put it a little more in the 'public service' level." Ike understated that Mamie "is quite clear in her own mind on the differences of the Democratic stand and the Republican." When she later entertained some Democrats, and they discussed a recent election, Mamie presented partisan views, and at evening's end asked, "Well, are you still happy with your votes?" According to Kevin McCann, because she was a moderate Republican, Ike considered her opinions as being "a counterbalance to the Dewey influence." When the Eisenhower campaign forces in 1952 snubbed Everett Dirksen, Mamie had gone out of her way to give him a prominent and warm reception. "I'm a Republican," she later said, "so I support Republican candidates." So loyal was Mamie that she resented deeply a friend who had been a longtime Democrat who campaigned for Stevenson, and briefly stopped talking to her. And again, paradoxically, if Mrs. Eisenhower personally liked someone, she dropped her partisanship. "She made a point of emphasizing people's positive qualities and highlighting friendships," her grandson pointed out, "like that with Averell Harriman, which went beyond partisanship. She respected him."[43]

When it came to the "sorority," Mamie drew no lines. After the election, a Northampton woman wrote Mamie that Grace Coolidge wanted to see the renovated White House, and Mrs. Eisenhower invited the former First Lady to come. Mrs. Coolidge was "extremely touched," but "[a]t the present time I am living under rather strict limitations and cannot go so far afield as Washington. I shall be . . . hoping that you will enjoy your occupancy of the White House . . . as much as I did." Mamie wrote Grace that she hoped "when you are feeling better, you will visit us." She invited her to a state dinner that fall, and at Christmas sent her a print of the president's painting of George Washington.[44]

At a 1954 dinner honoring the vice president, Mamie hoped to have both Grace and Edith Wilson present, but the former regretted. During dinner, Vice President Nixon spilled chili on his white dinner shirt, and Edith and Mamie tried to wash the stain off his shirt with soda water.

Edith was liked by the Republicans. Pat Nixon first met Mrs. Wilson at the 1953 reception for wounded vets, and found her "very personable." Edith even agreed to lend her name, along with Mamie, Grace, Eleanor, and Bess, to the Girl Scouts' honorary board. Mamie called Edith "a great friend of mine [whom] I had known through the years [since the war.]" The two commiserated on many mutual complaints, not the least of which was money. Mamie recalled that Edith "told me one day that all she received from the government was a frank for her mail. Now I thought that was *pretty*—after all being in government is pretty hard—they should do more than that. There aren't that many of us living."

Over a century had passed since old Dolley Madison had played whist with Louisa Adams. Now, in the fifties, Edith had Min and Mamie over for a long lunch and bridge games. Mamie sent Edith her "Mamie Pink" carnations; Edith invited Mamie to drive down to a Virginia girl's boarding school, in her own car, but added, "knowing the Secret Service I hardly dare think I can." Edith had bought herself a new black Buick and an RCA Victor television set, but unlike Mamie's, her viewing wasn't limited to soap operas and westerns. "Don't you think that McCarthy investigation is awful?" she wrote a friend.[45]

Edith Wilson, Mamie Eisenhower, Lady Bird Johnson, and Pat Nixon were joined at the 1954 Senate wives' luncheon by Bess Truman, but Eleanor Roosevelt "never visited Mamie in the White House," according to son Elliott. It was an invitation withheld not by the First Lady, but by the president. Some felt that Ike didn't reappoint Mrs. Roosevelt to the UN for two personal reasons. First, there was the fallacy that Perle Mesta had told Ike about Eleanor hinting that Mamie was an alcoholic, but there was also the old FBI dossier prepared by J. Edgar Hoover falsely implying that Eleanor and Joe Lash had been romantically involved in the forties. The file was shown to Eisenhower, and it was reported to Hoover that Ike "has a thorough distrust, distaste and dislike for Eleanor and told Dulles several times to get her out of the picture." Her searing campaign speech in Harlem against Ike in the campaign hadn't helped matters.

Both publicly and privately, the fifties brought dramatic change to Eleanor's life, marked by "Tommy" Thompson's death, and Eleanor wrote that she "learned for the first time what being alone was like."

Tommy died just prior to a seventieth-birthday tribute to Mrs. Roosevelt, who willingly allowed herself to be "commercialized" to raise funds for the American Association for the UN, where she now worked as board chairman. When asked what she considered her greatest accomplishment, she responded, "I just did what I had to do as things came along." No Eisenhower administration UN representatives attended the tribute.

Eleanor stayed in the public eye; in her new job, she continued globe-trotting. She did a TV commercial, and gave her earnings to charity. She doggedly rallied against McCarthyism, fought New York Cardinal Spellman on public funding of parochial schools, and helped found the liberal Americans for Democratic Action. She also registered three black friends at Washington's Willard Hotel under her name. When the hotel, having initially accepted the reservation, later refused it, there was much embarrassment. Eleanor made her point, and they went to another hotel.[46]

Although Eleanor maintained written contact with Edith Wilson, they now rarely saw each other. On one occasion, the two were joined by Bess Truman at a tribute to Edith Helm, social secretary to the trio.

The longer she was out of the first ladyship, Eleanor Roosevelt was less America's Queen Mother and more its liberal godmother. And, the more Eleanor was partisan, the less Mamie Eisenhower felt a pressure to match her. When Ike declined to take on FDR's projects, David said Mamie "perhaps had less of a feeling to emulate his wife." Only once did she express disapproval of Eleanor. In turning down the offer to pen a daily column, Mamie said, "It sounds like a terrible chore and smacks of 'My Day' column, of which I have a perfect horror!"[47]

Unlike Eleanor, Mamie disliked flying, but came to enjoy its speed, eventually wearing a pair of pilot's wings, engraved with the insignia of the *Columbine*, the presidential plane named by her for Colorado's state flower. In July 1955, Mamie flew to Geneva to join Ike at the historic conference with Soviet Premier Bulganin, British Prime Minister Eden, and French Premier Faure. She made it clear to Mrs. McCaffree, however, that her presence was for "vacation only, not official. I didn't come over here to entertain."[48]

Regarding the politics involved at Geneva, Mamie didn't "want to be put on the spot" with press questions. So, reporter Betty Beale sent over a list of questions for Mamie's responses. The First Lady dictated, but never sent, the answers. Before she began, Mamie said, "I do not even want you to hint that this came from the First Lady [directly]." She further told Mary Jane to tell Miss Beale, "For your private information, the First Lady has never intruded in government affairs or politics and doesn't plan to start now." Along those lines, when asked if Ike had first discussed with her his "electrifying proposal for mutual inspection of armaments," Mamie responded, "Please do not even ask

this question!" She told Mary Jane: "Say something nice about Lady Eden because he said some nice things about Ike."[49]

Just two months after their return from Geneva, the Eisenhowers made their annual trip to Min's house in Denver. As early as their visit in the summer of 1954, Min stirred a bit of controversy telling everyone from cabdrivers to grocery clerks that Ike would not run in '56 because of the strain on his and Mamie's health. But in Denver, that early autumn of 1955, their life did indeed drastically change without any warning.[50]

On September 24, sometime around two in the morning, Ike awoke and came over to Mamie's bedside, complaining of chest pains that wouldn't go away.

She gave him some milk of magnesia, but he remained ill. She called their doctor, Howard Snyder, whose diary recorded that Mamie had "summoned" him "many times about midnight to minister to the President," but this time, "the tone of Mamie's voice contained a particular note of alarm."

A few minutes after 4:00 A.M., he instructed her "to slip into bed and wrap herself around the President to see if this would quiet him and assist in warming his body. This had the desired effect almost immediately. The President settled down and went to sleep quietly. Mamie remained in bed with him until about 0600 when she, without disturbing him, returned to her own bed."

"I was really shaken," recorded Snyder. Apparently, he had reason to be.

The next morning, from Fitzsimmons Hospital, to which Ike was rushed shortly after he awoke, it was announced that the American president had suffered a heart attack.

Had it not been for Mamie, the president might have died.

And in the period that was to follow, had it not been for her, he might not have survived.[51]

– 60 –

Sweetheart of the GOP

THE FIRST LADY took charge of the personal side of the presidency in a suite adjoining Ike's hospital room. Her only request was a pink toilet seat. One was airmailed from Washington.[1]

Throughout, Mamie phoned the White House regularly, reporting on Ike and keeping tabs on the staff. Ike said Mamie "conversed daily on a wide range of subjects, but on none that might encourage emotional outbursts . . . Mamie, above all others, never accepted the assumption that I had incurred a disabling illness. She told John, and I'm sure she told others, too, that she could not reconcile herself to the idea that efforts on behalf of what I believed in had come to an end. While solicitous above all for my health and welfare, she perhaps more than any other retained the conviction that my job as President was not yet finished."[2]

Meanwhile, she was spending hours on an incredible self-imposed task, personally responding to over eleven thousand get-well letters, signing every single response. There were no prepared cards, no stamp signatures, no secretary's forgery. Hourly, daily, weekly, the First Lady worked. It was motivated purely by her "neighborliness," but at the same time it was a genius stroke of public relations—particularly if Ike decided to run for a second term the next year. She had form-letter replies prepared for three categories: "Governors, Congressmen, Senators," "Friends and Administration Officials," and "Miscellaneous." Each day, she read Ike a few of the most encouraging letters, like one from a hundred-year-old man who had survived a similar attack, and many wrote complimentary letters to her, one praising "the way that you have handled the whole situation . . ."[3]

But Mamie wasn't the only Washington wife occupying a hospital suite next to her husband. Just before Ike had left for Geneva, the new

Senate majority leader had suffered a massive heart attack, and nearly died. The tough side of gentle Lady Bird Johnson emerged as she asked Lyndon's doctor, "Do you think that his staying in the Senate will shorten his life in any way?" They concluded that though political life could kill him, the challenge of it could keep him going. At Bethesda Naval Hospital, Mrs. Johnson "turned her room into an office," abuzz with LBJ's key staff members.

Lady Bird had already earned a niche on Capitol Hill. She listened to Senate debates from the gallery, and took public-speaking and foreign-language classes. To the Senate Wives' Club meeting, she brought Texas-shaped sugar cookies, and fondly recalled one particular First Lady's luncheon for the group because she sat at Mamie's table, and that "was big stuff . . . none of us would have missed it short of being *real* sick."

Mrs. Leverett Saltonstall recalled "one little happening" that brought a "smile to . . . all" of the Senate wives. She and a fellow wife escorted a new, young member down to the Red Cross unit, where she was given her veil. "Then she vanished. We could not imagine where she had gone, when we found that she had hurried all the way back to her husband's office to show him how she looked in her veil. It must have pleased him too." Mrs. Johnson had her own recollection of the new Senate wife. "I remember distinctly . . . this beautiful young woman coming to my *very* simple house . . . I'd taken the garage and made it into a recreation room for the children, but also if I had a luncheon for more than about ten people we had the table stand there. So that's where I took all the new Senate wives . . . and she was one of the new ones. I thought how *young* she was, and how *different* from all the rest of us!" It was Jacqueline Kennedy.[4]

That year, Jackie also nearly lost her husband. Senator Kennedy's injured back required risky spinal surgery, and like Mamie and Lady Bird, Mrs. Kennedy also assumed some of his correspondence work, even writing one letter to the majority leader:

"I just wanted to tell you how terribly much your kind letter meant to Jack . . . I never realized how much letters from friends who are thinking about you mean to people who are sick—they give you so much strength and courage for the long weeks when you have to lie in that horrible dark hospital room . . . I've just realized that here I have been scribbling away about my husband's illness and never told you how wonderfully thrilled we are for you being Majority Leader—You must be so happy and proud—and I know that you will absolutely make history in it—Please remember me to Mrs. Johnson—and so many many thanks from Jack and me."[5]

As Jack recuperated and began working on his book *Profiles in Courage*, Jackie served as an assistant, reading, editing, and providing sources. Just as the book appeared on the market, Ike and Mamie were facing the important question of another term. Min had provoked more speculation by her statement that "Mamie can't stand another four years in the White House."

None realized just how delicate indeed the First Lady's health had been. Dr. Snyder's diary entries for 1945–46 revealed that "Mrs. Eisenhower always became very alarmed when she had a pulmonary attack which often was complicated by an asthmatic shortness of breath . . . On many occasions I had listened to the adventitious sounds in her chest provided by lesions in the mitral and aortic valves in her heart . . . the Cardiac Consultant said he would like to prescribe a moderate sedative such as phenobarbital for her. I informed him that phenobarbital was a drug against which Mrs. Eisenhower had a phobia but that I had found that she showed no incompatibility when I had given it to her in an elixir of which she did not seem to know the contents."

Mamie's behavior was unaltered by the elixir. Snyder's diary further recorded that Ike had had a "hard time getting Mrs. Eisenhower even interested to go out to inspect the Chief of Staff's quarters at Fort Myer . . . We had almost to take her physically and transport her to Fort Myer before we could persuade her that she could be very happy in the home that was provided for them there . . ."[6]

Besides her serious heart condition and asthma, Mamie still suffered from Ménière's disease, which disturbed her balance. She frankly explained, "I never know when it's going to hit me. Doctors tell me there's no assurance that an operation would do any good. I'll probably walk down this hall and hit the wall. I'm black and blue from walking around the house."[7]

Unfortunately, though details on Ike's health were released to the press, such personal information on the First Lady was not. Two years later, when Mamie entered the hospital for a hysterectomy, the West Wing vaguely responded to inquiries that it was merely some problem typical of women her age. What some criticized as inactivism was actually an effort to reserve her strength and not overwork her heart, but since that wasn't public knowledge, the old rumors gained credence through the fifties. Mamie later told an interviewer, "I couldn't walk a straight line. Everybody thought I was inebriated. This would happen nine o'clock in the morning . . ." Her claims were substantiated by medical records. There was never a hint of evidence, even in Snyder's diaries, to confirm the rumors.[8]

In the White House, Mamie hadn't stopped having her cocktails with guests because of the gossip. In thanking the Slaters for a gift of "the generous bottle of 'liquid refreshment' . . . and the chrome jigger," she said they were both "useful" and "welcome." Most often, however, rather than a light cocktail, she had none. It was on Mamie's orders that their guests were offered only one cocktail. At state dinners, wine was served, and at receptions no alcoholic beverage was offered. At her bridge games with army wife friends, she had just coffee and soda available. But Mamie was less concerned about rumors than she was about Ike.[9]

When a reporter asked in December 1955 if he would run for a second term, she uncharacteristically snapped, "Oh come now. This is Christmas—isn't it?" She was torn by the decision that had to be made. She claimed that she wouldn't offer unsolicited opinions, but in the diary of her friends the Ellis Slaters Mamie was quoted as having told Dr. Snyder, "He isn't going to run again, and I'm going to take him to Gettysburg . . ." However, the president claimed that Mamie "insisted" retirement was "a mistaken notion . . . She thought idleness would be fatal for one of my temperament; consequently, she argued that I should listen to all my most trusted advisors, and then make my own decision. She said she was ready to accept and support me in that decision, no matter what its nature."[10]

The First Lady learned of his decision to run when she phoned Ann Whitman. It was indeed his own.[11]

On June 8, 1956, however, Ike suddenly suffered a serious inflammation of the small intestine—ileitis. Rushed to Walter Reed for surgery, a recuperating Ike established executive headquarters there. Again, the determined First Lady moved right in, guarding against any stressful scheduling, meeting with doctors, and eating all meals with Ike as a means of monitoring his diet. She wrote that she'd "put the 'slow me down Lord' prayer" in Ike's room, "as a daily reminder . . . I think . . . most appropos." When he watched a TV golf match, she asserted that "he is improving rapidly." Against the predictions of many, Ike stayed in the race.[12]

Many of Mamie's public duties devolved to Pat Nixon, who privately wrote, "I would like to do part-time work rather than all the useless gadding I am expected to do." After all the work the Nixons had done for him, Ike remained lukewarm about his veep. It was Pat who told Dick, "No one is going to push us off the ticket." But Mrs. Eisenhower had taken much notice of the Nixons' loyalty, and she supported them.

She praised Pat as her "rock of Gibraltar" and "helpmate," and "never hesitated to ask her to substitute." Privately, Mamie offered the political counsel, against brother-in-law Milton and other advisers, to keep Nixon. She said he had never upstaged Ike, and conducted himself as an able executive during the crisis following Ike's heart attack. Nixon stayed on the ticket.[13]

Although a new song, "Sweetheart of the GOP," was composed in Mamie's honor, her campaign role was minor compared to '52. For the first time, a First Lady was used by the medium of television in a campaign. At the convention, which Betty Ford also attended, Mamie jan-

gled a bracelet, the gift of Republican women, from the podium, for the
television audience. In October, she joined Ike on a TV stage set for a
show that had seven women pose seven affectionate questions to the
president. Aired nationally, the questions proved less important than
the vision of Mamie "chatting easily with women from everyday pursuits." The only issue she discussed was her voter-registration listing of
her occupation as "First Lady."[14]

Through the campaign year, she maintained public nonpar-
tisanship, successfully charming one woman, who, in a note to the First
Lady, wrote that she "could never find words to express how much I
enjoyed your luncheon for the Senate Ladies . . ." praising her "unbe-
lievable graciousness," and concluding, "I think it is so wonderful the
way you make everyone feel so much at home. Thank you so very much
for having made such a memorable occasion possible—I will never forget it." Other things also made an indelible impression on Jacqueline
Kennedy that May afternoon.

It was her first visit inside the White House since she had toured it
as a child. Again, she said she noticed its bleakness, with "reproduction
furniture and imitation Renaissance damask on the walls." The food
"was not very good," and she remembered reading in the newspaper
that for one state dinner the dessert was "'Betty Brune de Pommes'—
Apple Brown Betty." As for antiques, "There were two white pottery
Scottie dogs with philodendron coming out of them on the mantlepiece
in the East Room." They must have been at least ten years old.[15]

Although Mrs. Kennedy first met Edith Wilson at a Senate wives'
function, lunching was not Jackie's preoccupation. She may have
seemed apolitical, but she wasn't. Arthur M. Schlesinger, Jr., historian
and liberal supporter of JFK's, wrote upon first meeting her that "underneath a veil of lovely inconsequence, she concealed tremendous
awareness, an all-seeing eye and a ruthless judgment." Jacqueline called
politics "the most exciting life imaginable, always involved with the
news of the moment, meeting and working with people who are enormously alive, and every day you are caught up in something you really
care about . . ."

Jackie worked for Jack. She admitted to having "translated many
books on Indo-China for JFK," before they had married, "and before he
gave his Indo-China speech in the Senate." She continued researching
the issue of communist encroachment in Vietnam, and among those
works she translated were "lengthy excerpts" from the sophisticated defense analyses by French writer Paul Mus. Mus presented the complex
reasons for French defeat in Vietnam. To translate such studies, of
course, Jacqueline had to understand the subject.[16]

Schlesinger said JFK told him that "if I had anything I wanted to
get to him, I should communicate through Jacqueline—a channel designed, I assume, to simplify his relations with his immediate staff."

Jackie toiled as a speechwriting assistant. When she read passages of de Gaulle's *Mémoires* to him, the senator was inspired by the image of France, and used this concept in his own speeches about America. She attended some of Jack's committee hearings, and felt "strongly" in her opposition to the limitations outlined by the McCarran Immigration Act. "A bill that restrictive might not have let in the Bouviers or the Kennedys . . ." When Jack's opinions were attacked by Dean Acheson, she fiercely defended her husband's views in a fiery letter. Artist Bill Walton, a friend of both Kennedys, told of their private political banterings, and "there was nothing shy or quiet about Jackie. She was involved with all our conversations, and actively. She was very talkative. She had opinions on everything."[17]

"Politics was a challenge to her," affirmed Dave Powers, a staff member and longtime supporter. "Jackie is a perfectionist; anything she did, she wanted to do very, very well—and she became very, very good at it. That went for politics, too." She took more language classes so "she could help him with the ethnic mail," because Massachusetts was composed of a heavy immigrant constituency. On an official visit to Rome, when they dined at the American embassy, Jack wanted to communicate with George Bidault, who spoke only French. Jacqueline acted as interpreter.[18]

But if Jacqueline dressed Jack properly in impeccable suits, and had hot lunches delivered to him, they also teased each other unmercifully, something most outsiders misread. A friend recalled how Jack once said, "Jackie is superb in her personal life, but do you think she'll ever amount to anything in her political life?" Nonplussed, Jackie shot back, "Jack is superb in his political life, but do you think he'll ever amount to anything in his personal life?" The couple also had divergent literary tastes, Jackie reading Kerouac and *Connaissance* magazine, for example, but she explained, "We both have inquiring minds—that's the reason we chose each other. I have always felt so alive with him . . . I couldn't suggest anything he couldn't do . . ." Jack's brother Bobby described her as "poetic, whimsical, provocative, independent, and yet very feminine. Jackie has always kept her own identity and been different."[19]

Jacqueline frequently designed her own fashions, and it was no secret how much she appreciated haute couture, but she was conscientious about money. After she and Jack found themselves fifteen cents short at a movie-theater box office, they borrowed the ticket money from another customer. Much to his surprise, she sent him a thank you letter with three nickels taped to it.[20]

Schlesinger said that Adlai Stevenson, the leading candidate going into the Democratic Convention in Chicago, was "the first political voice" to whom Jacqueline "listened." That was an understatement. JFK asked her with great curiosity what it was about Adlai that made women devoted to him.[21] Rumors also floated about Kennedy's liaisons

with women, though many were rehashed stories from his days as a freshman congressman. There was indeed one special woman, however, whom he saw at least once a year, and with whom he made no bones about being photographed. She was a winsome Bay Stater he first met while serving with her on the board of trustees of the Clarke School. She had been chairman of the board. It was Grace Coolidge.

With her heart condition, life was circumscribed to Northampton for Mrs. Coolidge. That was the reason she was unable to escort the 1955 Clarke School graduating class to the White House, where they were greeted by Ike and Mamie. With the class, Grace sent along a film made by the school, which she wrote Mamie "gives a very good idea of the methods used in teaching deaf children." The elderly former First Lady had made a brief appearance in the movie.

In Washington, Grace Coolidge was legendary as the woman in the red dress, whether it was the one she wore in her White House portrait or gown on the Smithsonian mannequin. The style and color of the two were nearly exact, but the dress in the portrait wasn't as short as the gown. Most people confused the two, even Lady Bird Johnson. She took friends through the White House, eager to see the portrait, "and when we got there, that dress had grown six inches!"

Some of the sorority thought often of Mrs. Coolidge. "At the Senate Ladies luncheon," Mamie wrote her, "Mrs. Wilson and I were speaking of you, and we agreed that it would be wonderful if you could ever come to Washington and join us. Everyone would be so happy to see you." But Grace would never return. A year after Ike's ileitis, she died quietly, on July 8, in her home, at age seventy-eight. Senator Kennedy glowingly eulogized her. He had "a strong personal recollection of her untiring devotion and labors throughout her life to this most worthy cause [the deaf] . . . Since her days in the White House she continued to epitomize the qualities of graciousness, charm and modesty which marked her as an ideal First Lady of the Land."[22]

It was Jacqueline Kennedy, however, not the senator, who drafted his official support statement for another man:

"In recent months I have been questioned frequently as to the candidate of my choice for the Democratic Presidential nomination. My position can be stated simply. Adlai Stevenson was my choice for the Presidency in 1952 . . . his intelligence, farsightedness & reasonableness have neither diminished nor been matched by any other potential nominee. Consequently Adlai Stevenson remains in my opinion, the most outstanding choice for the Presidency in 1956.

"Some have accused him of being too liberal—others have charged him with being too conservative. But Adlai Stevenson is beholden to no man & to no section—only to the welfare of our nation at home and abroad (only to the welfare of the party and the Nation.)" JFK was so pleased with Jacqueline's writing that he deleted only the second paragraph and made minor word changes. He ordered her statement to be typed and released to the press.[23]

Jacqueline attended her first convention that August, but didn't see another Adlai supporter, Mrs. Roosevelt.

Eleanor had said in '52 that if Ike won, she doubted he could "stand a second term, and I doubt if the country can stand Nixon as President." She was equally wary of Democrats, calling LBJ "one of the ablest people at maneuvering that we have in the party." When Mary Lasker told Eleanor that he was a "secret liberal," she responded, "You're crazy."

Her energy never stopped. At seventy-five, Eleanor became a visiting lecturer at Brandeis University. During a testimonial dinner, the emcee suffered a stroke. She calmly took over. She narrated *Peter and the Wolf.* When she began a friendship with liberal Allard Lowenstein, she coyly told her secretary, "By now . . . you ought to know me well enough to know that I like young men." She calmly managed to continue a debate on the Democratic platform with Tallulah Bankhead as the actress seated herself, in the powder room and remained there with the door left open to hear Eleanor. And though Jacqueline, Rosalynn, and Nancy were all fans of Frank Sinatra, it was Eleanor who traveled to Hollywood and appeared as a guest on his TV show. She wrote that her part was "rather nice," and though "not very good at 'entertainment,'" she "found watching the mechanics amusing."

Bess Truman—who, like Eleanor Roosevelt and Jackie Kennedy, also supported Adlai Stevenson—was so concerned with Harry's steadfast support of Harriman, that she tearfully asked a friend, "Can't you do something to stop Harry? He's making a fool of himself." Eleanor was displeased with those urging her to support Kennedy for vice president. She begrudgingly met briefly with him, but left unsatisfied with his response to her question if, in retrospect, he didn't think that he should have come out stronger against Senator Joseph McCarthy.[24]

Meanwhile, a pregnant Jackie sat in her box, waving a Stevenson banner. When a *Chicago Sun-Times* reporter asked if she'd like Jack nominated for veep, she responded crisply, "I don't know whether I'll like it or not." But afterward, when Kennedy hadn't been nominated, Jackie cried. From her husband, she learned "that I must not take politics personally." The stop-Kennedy movement was a new offense with which she had to deal. Sister-in-law Ethel said Jackie "had an elephant's memory when somebody cut Jack."

After the convention, Jack rested in France. There, he learned that Jackie had suffered a miscarriage. Later, in the midst of his Senate campaign, when her father died, he changed his schedule to be at her side. Though again pregnant, she not only assumed responsibility for all of Jack Bouvier's funeral arrangements, but also looked after his long-term housekeeper Esther Linstrom's "well-being and provided for her comfort as much as possible." The Kennedys frequently traveled together. On a summer trip to Cannes with Jack, Jackie again met Winston Churchill, at a dinner they attended aboard the yacht *Christina*, owned by Greek shipping tycoon Aristotle Onassis.[25]

One familiar guest at Democratic conventions had missed the last one. After suffering a heart attack, Edith Wilson slowed down, writing to Bernie Baruch that year, "Darling, I Am Growing Old." In '56, Edith had still remained apolitical, but she did have a soft spot for Lyndon Johnson, who wrote to tell her that Congress had approved her long-overdue pension of five thousand dollars a year, which he guided through. She became an LBJ fan when she learned Woodrow Wilson was his childhood hero.

Subtly, however, Edith's Democratic loyalty manifested itself. After Ike's victory, Mamie invited her to all the Inaugural functions. Edith claimed she was "unwell," and thought it "unwise to accept as the weather may be inclement." Bad weather had *never* prevented her from going to an Inaugural party.

Mamie gently tried to coax Edith into becoming a sponsor of a committee raising funds to build a Washington residence hall for army widows, to which the First Lady even donated her pink hair dryer, pink curlers, pink washbasin, and pink beauty salon chair. Edith refused. But when the First Lady invited her once again to the Veterans' Garden Party, because it "would never be quite complete without you, its founder," Edith accepted. Mrs. Wilson still considered Mamie "the most thoughtful friend in the world," but she was clearly maneuvering herself away from Republicans. Across Edith's vague note, Mamie scribbled hastily, "Send her some Mamie carnations to-day." And, instead of her typically personal touch, she instructed that "Mr. Tolley can write—we missed her last night—on my personal card."[26]

There was one issue on which Mamie would have disagreed with Edith. None associated the First Lady with civil rights, but subtly, Mrs. Eisenhower displayed public support for the struggle. The administration's most historic blow to segregation was Ike's ordering of federal troops to Little Rock (Arkansas) Central High School, where there had been violent white protest against integration. Mamie fully supported the move.

In fact, the reason North Carolina congressman Charles Raper Jonas suggested that Mrs. Eisenhower accept an honorary degree from Queens College in his district was because "it would be a tremendous help to the friends of the Administration who are slowly overcoming the prejudices of Little Rock." Her trademark warmth had no color boundary. In Augusta, she made a point of thanking both the white and black help. When she learned that a ninety-four-year-old former slave ran a government greenhouse, she sent him a personally written Christmas card.[27]

In the beginning of the administration, the presence of E. Fred Morrow, the first black appointed to a nonclerical political role in the White House, almost gave the Eisenhowers' friend George Allen "a nervous breakdown." Morrow was barely acknowledged at the 1953 Inaugural church service. And yet, there was a public message of where the Eisenhowers stood. They approved of Marian Anderson singing the national anthem at the swearing-in ceremony, the first black to participate in such an event. Mamie's sympathy had evolved during her tenure, and emerged through her hostess role. In arranging the state dinner for the black president of Haiti, she requested that full protocol rights be given him. The most noticeable change in her revival of the Easter Egg Roll, abandoned since 1940, was its integration. Mamie invited Alice Dunnigan of the Association of Negro Press to her one press conference. She held a special reception for the one hundred members of the National Council of Negro Women in November 1953. At her birthday party, Mamie asked Mahalia Jackson to perform. When Dorothy Ferebee, president of the National Council of Negro Women, invited her to become an honorary member, Mamie immediately accepted.[28]

To a woman complaining about Mamie's letter to a little girl at "the Negro Mission School," Mary Jane McCaffree defended the First Lady by saying, "Mrs. Eisenhower has most carefully sought to avoid her personal involvement in matters of public policy," and had intended only "a very personal note praising the little girl for her strong faith." To another, McCaffree pointed out that Mamie supported the work of the Cerebral Palsy Association for both "white and Negro."

On the death of Mary Church Terrell, the first president of the National Association of Colored Women, Mamie wrote directly to the group that Terrell was "rarely endowed . . . her great gifts were dedicated to the betterment of humanity, and she left a truly inspiring record. Her life was the epitome of courage and of vision and of deep faith—an example worthy of emulation by all who love their fellow men." The First Lady was keenly aware of the capital's black community through her subscription to the *Washington Afro-American*. Sometimes, refrain made a statement as well. Min complained that the family's new color TV had a picture that made everyone look "like a bunch of niggers," in both Ike and Mamie's presence. The Eisenhowers stood by in disapproving silence.[29]

Mamie's opinion of Little Rock was significant enough to impress two family members. Barbara affirmed that her mother-in-law "agreed with him [Ike] sending troops in. I remember thinking one time that she never gave any of those things a thought. But every now and then I'd be amazed at her knowledge . . . She had a lot of common sense." Milton Eisenhower recalled Mamie's attitude toward the resistance at

Little Rock: "But it's the law," she said, "those folks have got to get an education. The law says that plain."[30]

The Supreme Court order that schools should be integrated met the most formidable resistance in the South. In Plains, Georgia, Rosalynn Carter was definitely in the minority. She accepted integration as "a foregone conclusion; the issue was not defiance, but, rather, how to go about integrating the public schools . . ."

Except for the growing animosities toward the Carter family from racist whites, life in Plains was full for Rosalynn. She joined the PTA, Garden Club, and Baptist church, became a Sunday school teacher, a Cub Scout den mother, and board member of a local theater. Her community activism paralleled Jimmy's own activities in Plains, and their peanut business prospered. Rosalynn was now controlling the books. "After a few years," she recalled, "I was explaining some things to him. I knew more about . . . the business on paper than Jimmy did. I knew which parts of the business were profitable, which were not, how much money we had, how much credit, and how much we owed on our debts." Proudly, she wrote, "We grew together—as full partners."[31]

Mamie's influence over Ike exercised itself more fully, too. November 25, 1957, evoked her power as another unexpected event threatened the president. That afternoon, he suffered a stroke.

After being rushed to bed and told to stay there, Ike shuffled into the First Lady's room, where she was deep in consultation with Dr. Snyder and son John, who were, he wrote, "appalled to see me." He told them that he planned to host the planned state dinner that night, which provoked "an argument" of "spirited opposition." Ike recalled that Mamie "asserted that if I insisted on going then she would not! . . . I went back to bed." She said to the chief usher, "Continue as planned, I'll call Vice President Nixon to act as host." A controlled Mamie explained, "The President has had a slight stroke . . ."

Her protectiveness of Ike's health extended to his diet and calendar, and she frequently called Ike's appointments secretary and secretary Ann Whitman to monitor and limit the president's schedule if she felt it to be strenuous. She gave strict attention to the most minute of changes in his health. Mamie was prepared for anything. She frankly asked Ellis Slater, while discussing plans for Ike's retirement, "What would I do if something did happen—he doesn't want to be buried in Arlington." She agreed that Gettysburg might be more accessible to visitors, and therefore best suited for an Eisenhower museum and mausoleum.

Mamie later revealed, "After 1955, whenever Ike gave a speech, I always sat there in utter dread that he would have a heart attack on the air." Meanwhile, Ike was just as worried about her. In the second term, it was he who urged that she abandon her hand-shaking of thousands at every reception, because "[s]he insists on talking to everyone. It's a strain on her."[32]

When Ike planned his 1959 eleven-nation international trip, it was decided that Barbara would be surrogate First Lady. Though "a little sad about not going herself," Mamie, because of Ménierè's disease, was unable to bear extended time at high-flying altitudes. Pat Nixon's role also increased. In Africa, with Dick, she was highly visible, touring public institutions in Liberia, attending the Ghana independence celebration alongside American civil-rights leader Martin Luther King, Jr., and his wife, Coretta. In Caracas, Venezuala, however, her powers of endurance were tested as anti-American protestors smashed her car window with rocks, and the foreign minister's wife became hysterical. It was Pat who serenely calmed her, seemingly removed from the the terror. When one girl spit and cursed her, Mrs. Nixon gently patted her shoulder, and the youth shrank in embarrassment. Upon Pat's return, newspaper columnist Betty Beale said none had known "just how much mettle was behind the fragile blonde."

On a trip to the Soviet Union, it appeared Pat would be the only woman of rank present at the political and social gatherings until she told Soviet leader Nikita Khrushchev that she'd like to meet the Russian representatives' wives. To her surprise, Khrushchev ordered it, and Pat came to know the Soviet "First Lady" Nina. But Mrs. Nixon was not above making a political retort of her own when Khrushchev refused to answer a question about solid fuel and missile production. "I'm surprised there is a subject that you're not prepared to discuss, Mr. Chairman. I thought that with your one-man government, you had to have everything firmly in your own hands."

As Second Lady, Pat also presided over the Senate Wives Club, and Lady Bird said, "She was probably the most faithful presiding officer . . . never missed a meeting, unless she was helping her husband on some trip . . ." Mrs. Johnson added that Pat's reports on foreign countries often had a subtle "new" aspect.

Mamie was friendly but formal with Pat: Almost twenty years separated them. Several officials had been trying to get Mamie to invite the Nixons to Gettysburg, and when finally Sherman Adams himself asked Mrs. McCaffree to ask her to do so, Mrs. Eisenhower retorted, "What on earth would we talk about? We don't have anything in common! She doesn't play bridge!" When later asked if she was "deeply fond" of Nixon, Mamie responded, "I wouldn't say I knew him that well . . ." Mamie felt indebted to the Nixons for their loyalty, but it didn't yet translate into public support for what was shaping up as Nixon's 1960 run for president.[33]

Pat and Mamie were often seen about town together, attending the gargantuan benefit luncheon-fashion shows that the First Lady liked. Mrs. Nixon's role rivaled Mamie's during the historic visit of Soviet premier Khrushchev to America in the fall of 1959, and Pat's travels with Dick were undoubtedly what prompted the Communist leader into bringing his wife Nina along. The "jet age" of the late fifties was a

period of cold war between the two superpowers, competing in the development of space technology and nuclear armaments. The closest the First Lady came to weaponry was dedicating America's first nuclear submarine and first atomic merchantship. She considered having a bomb shelter built at Gettysburg, but nixed it when she realized it would be the only one in the area. Mrs. Eisenhower was surprised at Nina's plain, unadorned appearance. Mamie gave Nina a little Sally Victor hat, but the Soviet First Lady wouldn't dare wear the symbol of capitalism, though she promised to "take it back to Russia so the millions can copy it."[34]

Style remained of utmost importance to Mamie, and she and Pat Nixon shared at least one devotion, Elizabeth Arden's. For both women, the association would have public consequences.

Besides her beauty salon–boutiques, Elizabeth Arden ran a tony Phoenix health spa, Maine Chance, where matronly woman went to lose weight. Mamie made her first extended stay there in 1958, arriving with a retinue of fifteen people, and Miss Arden spent twenty-five thousand dollars sprucing up a seven-room cottage for them, featuring a large, frilly pink bedroom for Mamie. The First Lady wore the traditional Maine Chance blue tank suit like everyone else, but avoided the "more strenuous treatments." Arden wrote Mamie that "You must not gain back a single ounce you have lost," and later reaffirmed that "we will always find a spot for you at Maine Chance. You have a permanent niche there, really . . . as befits a saint!"[35]

Mamie's trip sparked a fire of criticism when Ike rerouted the presidential airplane by nearly three thousand miles to pick her up from Phoenix, at government expense. The next year, when she decided to take the train, there was even harsher criticism from Drew Pearson, who pointed out that "Operation Mamie," still cost taxpayers several thousand dollars because of the staff, guards, and signalmen who traveled with her, as well as her two-day stopover in San Antonio, where a private phone line was installed in her sixty-dollars-a-day hotel suite, as was done at Maine Chance. More important to Pearson, however, was the indication that the First Lady was breaking the Railroad Act, forbidding the acceptance of free transportation by public officials. Also, there was a railroad workers' union threat to strike just then.[36]

The most unfortunate repercussion, however, was the vile claim that the First Lady had gone to Phoenix to "dry out." This time the slander was actually printed by columnist John J. Miller, who said that at 1959 cocktail party, an "unladylike" Mamie "boozed it up so much that the hostess tried to cut her off . . ." It claimed that Ike had left the room momentarily, returned to find a "soused spouse," and with the Secret Service, "tried to get her out as quietly as possible . . ." Because the White House would not dignify the charges by denying them, Mamie—who had successfully avoided saying anything that could possibly be misconstrued—was now maligned by dubious journalists.[37]

There had been minor criticism in the past. When she permitted a close male friend to greet her with a kiss, some harped that she was "setting a bad example" for youth. Pearson had falsely accused her brother-in-law, Gordon Moore, of attempting to influence an FCC ruling on a television station allocation in Miami. By 1958, censure became petty. She shopped at a chain store, and the National Federation of Independent Business angrily protested. She crossed a picket line at Bonwit Teller in New York, and raised a press brouhaha. The Labor Secretary's Office advised a clarification that Mamie had done so with "the understanding that this dispute involved only the shoe concession," but didn't "recommend that a substantive reply be made."[38]

When Mamie was offered a beaver coat by Maine furriers who said it would promote their sales, she initially refused it. But since she really wanted the coat, Ike drafted a careful letter for her, saying, "I would do anything feasible to help out," but the coat would be welcome only "on the condition that I may pay the actual cost," and she would be happy to have a Maine citizen present it and have publicity pictures taken. "A story that the Maine Fur Industry refused to make a profit on the transaction would be just as effective." The White House overlooked the fact that Mamie paid only $385 for a coat worth $1,800. For that innocent act, the First Lady was again unfairly criticized.[39]

Perhaps as a result of the backlash, Mrs. Eisenhower rather belatedly adopted a "project," but since it was toward the end of her term, and because there was no attempt on the part of the White House to use it for public relations, the press—and consequently the public—failed to give attention to the First Lady's promotion of the American Heart Association's efforts in the fifties.

The AHA wouldn't have been shocked to learn that the First Lady was actually a smoker, as were Jacqueline Kennedy, Pat Nixon, Betty Ford, and Nancy Reagan. Since the Depression, women had composed the majority of American smokers, even after experiments late in the decade concluded that cigarette use was linked to a variety of heart and lung diseases. Though she'd lent her name to AHA fund-raising projects since 1953, it was after Ike's heart attack, that Mamie focused her involvement. By February 1956, when she lighted the "torch of hope" for the annual fund-raising drive, the First Lady was leading not just the Washington but the national effort. The next year, she accepted the national honorary chair of the "Heart Campaign," until the end of her term. "The work of the Washington Heart Association," she wrote, "appeals to me in a very personal way. It's one area of service of such intimate concern to so many of us . . ." Grace Coolidge, before her death, and Eleanor Roosevelt, Pat Nixon, and Lady Bird Johnson had all joined Mamie as patrons of one fund-raiser.

In her last year as First Lady, Mamie was praised by the AHA president for having "stimulated public support . . . against heart and circulatory diseases," and pointed out that the Heart Association's years under her sponsorship were "the most fruitful," in its history: income increased by more than 70 percent, the number of volunteers rose by more than 750,000. Her "generosity," he continued, "has made possible many dramatic advances in the research . . . as well as in our supporting programs of education and community service." The lesson to be learned, however, was that a First Lady "project" should begin early and be well organized and publicized. In fact, Mamie Eisenhower would be the last First Lady not to have a separate staff position of Press Secretary."[40]

Mamie exercised even more influence over Ike toward the end of their term. In the summer of '59, when asked if he would take an apartment in town after retiring, Ike told reporters, "You had better . . . go and talk to her about it." By 1960, *Newsweek* magazine observed of Mamie, "She has a will before which any general would retreat. The President's famous temper holds no terrors for her." When Ike returned to America from his final European summit, he planned a Caribbean vacation. The First Lady preferred Georgia. They went to Georgia.

During their visits to Palm Desert's El Dorado Club for golf, Ike and Mamie socialized with Loyal and Edie Davis, Mamie also saw Edie in Phoenix, the Davis's hometown. Sometimes Nancy and Ronald Reagan were there as well. Nancy remembered that Mamie was a "very, very strong" woman who "had her opinions" on current events, and "power over Ike."

Ronnie, as his wife called him, had long been involved in film-industry politics, and now was an actor-spokesman for General Electric, hosting their TV program, episodes in which Nancy sometimes acted. She said acting was good training for politics.

In Pacific Palisades, the Reagans lived in a perfect home, completely outfitted with modern GE gadgets. Nancy was removed from "the Hollywood I often heard about—heavy drinking, pushing starlets in pools, etc. . . . If there was trouble brewing in other parts of town, I never saw it." Besides her own children, Patti and Ron, who was born in 1958, the family included Maureen and Michael, from Ronnie's previous marriage to actress Jane Wyman.

Michael and Maureen resented what they felt were Nancy's purposeful efforts to alienate them from their father. At the Reagans' ranch, Maureen named a wild, unridable horse "Nancy D." When Nancy's Lincoln Continental accidentally rolled off a hill and crashed, Michael said he wished she'd been in it. They nicknamed their step-mother "the Dragon Lady."[41]

Nancy and her father were in the conservative Republican camp, but her husband remained a Democrat, at least in registration. As the 1960 election approached, Ronnie was advised not to switch parties by those organizing Vice President Nixon's campaign for the presidency. He acceded to their wishes to head "Democrats for Nixon." Conversely, it was Jacqueline Kennedy, only thirty years old, who admitted that though "born and reared a Republican," she was happy to be so no longer. "You have to be a Republican," she added, "to realize how nice it is to be a Democrat." She learned that while maintaining a tight schedule in early 1960. Jack was running for president.

– 61 –

Race for the Ladyship

TWO YEARS PREVIOUS, in the Senator's reelection race, Jacqueline had proven herself in campaigning, as Dave Powers recalled, "in every single district of the state—from Cape Cod to the Berkshires." For the first time, she gave speeches, often in foreign languages. To the Worchester Cercle Français, she wryly explained that such public speaking wasn't "as frightening as it would have been in English . . ." Now, in the '60 primaries, she was just as effective, in her own very different way. In a Wisconsin parade, sitting between two political wives, she calmly read the second volume of de Gaulle's memoirs. Staffer Joseph Cerrell recalled how she caused "quite a stir" on the West Coast because it was "one of the few times Californians saw a hemline above the knee."

Powers credited Jacqueline's appearances as having helped win the West Virginia and Wisconsin primaries for JFK. "In Wisconsin, at one stop, when Jack's voice got hoarse, she took over for him . . ." At another stop, when Jack suddenly had to rush back to Washington to give his vote on civil-rights legislation, he left Jackie there, to serve as his representative. After making a spontaneous speech, Mrs. Kennedy toured a dairy farm, asking specific questions about the cows. She even milked one. She told shoppers over a supermarket intercom in her breathy voice of Jack's career, dramatically concluding, "He cares deeply about the welfare of his country—please vote for him."[1]

She went with Jack into poverty-stricken regions of West Virginia, and while she'd heard and read about poverty, Jackie had never witnessed it. It overwhelmed her, and she responded to the people, touring through the miners' shacks and staying to talk with the wives. Then, as she was being driven to another site, she asked her driver to stop the car near some railroad tracks. Jacqueline got out, and spent a half hour in deep discussion with a group of railroad workers about their lives.

Powers said that the senator was himself stupefied at her charm with the miners, "I just can't believe it. I am so proud of Jackie." It wasn't just marital admiration. West Virginia political figure Alfred Chapman said, "Mrs. Kennedy made such a wonderful impression upon the women of this valley and took them by surprise [with] her personality . . ."

Later, Jacqueline wrote a friend, "In all the places we campaigned . . . those are the people who touched me most—The poverty hit me more than it did in India—Maybe because I just didn't realize it existed in the U.S. . . ." There was much debate over the chance of a Catholic being able to get support in traditionally Protestant regions. But Jacqueline actually preferred going "into [Senator Hubert] Humphrey territory" instead of Catholic regions, because it was "more challenging."[2]

Whether or not Jackie discussed West Virginia poverty with the woman who'd had a career that once involved assisting the mining families couldn't be recalled, but in the spring of 1960, Mrs. Kennedy first met Mrs. Roosevelt at her Val-Kill cottage, joining JFK in a courtesy call there. Chatting outside in the warm weather, Jackie thought the political climate was considerably colder.

Mrs. Kennedy endured campaigning without complaint. She explained, "Not many people know how physically wearing [it] . . . can be . . . you catch yourself laughing and crying at the same time. But you pace yourself and you get through it. You just look at it as something you have to do . . . you knew it was worth it." In her case, however, the physical strain was actually dangerous, and she scrapped plans to attend the convention in Los Angeles. She was again pregnant, and had a history of difficulty with childbirth. Arthur Chapin of the Democratic National Committee staff vividly remembered her attendance at "a gathering of black women" that was a "successful affair and very unusual because Mrs. Kennedy . . . wasn't making public appearances at that time . . ." Although she wasn't present, she kept informed of the convention maneuverings, the proceedings of which she watched on TV. When someone had earlier suggested Stevenson might run in 1960 and make Jack his running mate, Jacqueline retorted knowingly, "Let Adlai get beaten alone." She wanted Jack to be nominated, and to win.[3]

When Eleanor Roosevelt, now noticeably old, swept into the Los Angeles convention hall, a spontaneous roar and standing ovation met her. She wouldn't acknowledge it because she felt it "impolite to the speaker." Mrs. Roosevelt continued to push for Adlai, bitterly opposing JFK's nomination, saying he showed "too much profile and not enough courage." Still, she joked that while Harry Truman resigned as a delegate because he felt the convention was rigged for Kennedy, "I got the feeling he wouldn't mind having it rigged for Lyndon Johnson." One of the things Mrs. Kennedy respected in her husband was his ability to not take political snippings personally. For her part, Jackie thought Eleanor was "spiteful."[4]

At the convention, Lady Bird Johnson was clearly disappointed that Lyndon didn't win the nomination. When the phone rang the next morning in their suite, she answered it. It was JFK asking to see LBJ. Mrs. Johnson told her husband, "Honey, I know he's going to offer the Vice Presidency, and I hope you won't take it." After much discussion with her and Speaker Rayburn, however, Johnson accepted, and Lady Bird supported the decision. Amid all the madness in the Johnson suite, someone noticed the beautiful fresh flowers that Lady Bird Johnson always managed to find.[5]

During the campaign, Eleanor remained unenthusiastic about Kennedy, partly because of the influence of his father and—thought her confidant, Dr. David Gurewitsch—"Catholicism." She agreed to see him, even though her granddaughter had been killed in a riding accident the day before. After the Val-Kill meeting, she said he had "a mind that is open to new ideas." Privately, there were other serious matters. According to Dr. Gurewitsch, Eleanor had ". . . some kind of blood disease."[6]

The year before, in the Midland Texas home of granddaughter Chandlor Lindsay, Eleanor Roosevelt met Barbara Bush. "I can't recall any conversation," Mrs. Bush later said, "I suspect I sat perfectly quiet. She had come to visit her granddaughter, a good friend of mine. I was impressed by her graciousness . . ." Not only social friendship, but family connection brought Barbara Bush in contact with political women. In 1953, just after Jacqueline Kennedy had married, she met Barbara Bush, who recalled, "Her mother and George's mother were friends." Bush was now beginning to plan the steps of following his father, a U.S. senator, in a political career. Although the Bushes had personally admired the Trumans, Barbara recalled proudly that Dewey was "our first vote." They were loyal Republicans. If Lady Bird was working Texas, so was Barbara Bush. She first met Pat Nixon while the candidate's wife was campaigning there.[7]

Before the Republicans even nominated Nixon, Pat was actually a part of some of the campaign's earliest strategy sessions. (Present at the convention, Betty Ford thought that if her husband had been nominated as vice president instead of Henry Cabot Lodge, Nixon would win in November.) Because newspapers had long emphasized Mrs. Nixon's domestic skills, some began sniping that she was too perfect, "Plastic Pat." The advice Pat gave Julie was directly applicable to her own attitude with critics: ". . . some people are not as friendly . . . as others. The main thing is to treat them in a friendly fashion and stay your own sweet self rather than becoming like them . . . they will change for the better. That is true all through life."

Time pronounced Mrs. Nixon "one of U.S.'s most remarkable

women—not just a showpiece Second Lady, not merely a part of the best-known team in contemporary politics, but a public figure in her own right." One columnist declared that "for the first time in American history one woman could conceivably swing a presidential election." The Republican National Committee had a "Pat Week," of rallies and "coffees," stating in their press release, "When you elect a President, you are also electing a First Lady . . . The First Lady has a working assignment. She represents America to all the world. Pat Nixon is . . . uniquely qualified . . ." There were "Pat for First Lady" buttons. Mrs. Nixon even defended herself against sexist charges that she was too active, saying her work was "reflective of women all over America taking an active part, not only in political life, but all activities. There was a day when they stayed at home . . . but they have emerged as volunteers for a cause they believe in."[8]

In no previous campaign had candidates' wives all played such active roles. Lady Bird began making public speeches, and called the Democrats "the party with heart," while Stevenson called her "beguiling and efficient." For seventy-one days, covering thirty-five thousand miles, Mrs. Johnson campaigned for the office of "Second Lady." *Time* magazine quoted Bobby Kennedy as saying, "Lady Bird carried Texas for us." With race and religion prominent issues, it would have been politically expedient to avoid them. Mrs. Johnson did not. It was a proud black newspaper, the *Austin Mirror*, that reported that at one of her receptions, there were in attendance "approximately 350 Negroes, many of whom had received special invitations." The *Mirror* said that Lady Bird ordered "that there was to be no racial discrimination at her party." As she received with prominent "Negro ladies," there was no attempt by anybody to draw the color line. The paper added, "Many of her friends predict that Lady Bird Johnson will be the nation's next Eleanor Roosevelt and carry the banner for equality . . ." But Mrs. Roosevelt had never been shuffled and *spit upon.* Through such tense moments, Mrs. Johnson never lashed back.[9]

Meanwhile, the press corps descended upon Jacqueline. A friend, Larry Newman, told of her making "an incredible little speech," and then inviting reporters to the family house with her, as she answered questions. Some had stopped in their tracks when they first caught a glimpse of Jackie in electric-orange pullover sweater and bright pink pedal pushers. As *The New York Times* wrote, many journalists "knew they were witnessing something of possible political consequence." Suddenly, Jackie and Pat found themselves in a press fashion war, focusing on how much they spent.

Mrs. Kennedy thought President Truman had put it best by saying, "The wives of these candidates are both wonderful ladies and that's the way they ought to be treated." Margaret Price, DNC vice chairman, told reporters that it was a nonissue: "I have been in thirteen states, and I have not had one question on Mrs. Kennedy's wardrobe." Candidate Kennedy made light of it, telling clothing manufacturers, "I know you'd rather have my wife here." Though she admitted, "I've gotten ruthless about what looks best on me," Jacqueline told reporters, "All the talk about what I wear and how I fix my hair has amused and puzzled me. What does my hairdo have to do with my husband's ability to be president?" Pat Nixon also considered the "feud" ludicrous.[10]

When she was asked about Jack's possible selection of a woman Cabinet member, Jackie responded, "He certainly could pick a good woman if he's looking for one." She offered that, politically, "Women are very idealistic and they respond to an idealistic person like my husband." She herself refused to "express any views that were not my husband's," but added, "not because I can't make up my mind on my own." She tried to shift focus to her abilities, and admitted, "People say I don't know anything about politics . . . But you learn an enormous amount just being around politicians." Though Jackie had to stay physically inactive during the campaign, her husband emphasized that she "plays a considerable part in it. What she does, what she does not do, really affects that struggle." He in no way diminished her role. In a private note to managers, Jack scribbled, "We need to promote her more." Jackie was quite capable of that herself.

Early on, Mrs. Kennedy exercised her power in changing the senator's campaign schedule. "When I saw his schedule," she explained, "I told him it was silly zigzagging back and forth, and he agreed. He told me to talk it over with Bob Wallace [a campaign aide]. I did, and things were changed." She also served as a means of reporting back to the candidate exactly what his audiences really thought of his views on issues. As she explained, "I give him reactions from people I talk to . . ."[11]

She was particularly helpful with speeches, providing literary quotes and allusions. "I thought of some lines from a poem I thought he ought to use and he told me to get the rest of it . . . I used to worry myself sick when Jack said to me that he didn't know what he was going to say in his next speech . . ." When once she provided a Tennyson quote, she thought he'd ignored it. Two days later, it popped up in a speech. Early in the campaign, when he lost notes for a speech in which he had planned on concluding with a quote from Tennyson's "Ulysses," Jackie came to the rescue by "quickly reciting the appropriate lines."

She played another crucial role as a liaison to important political allies. According to Arthur Schlesinger, Jr., Senator Kennedy "became delighted that he could remain aligned to Stevenson without liability" through Jackie. For his part, Adlai "felt the bond with her much more [important] than him [JFK]. It was a personal friendship which became a superb political alliance." The Kennedy forces had unsuccessfully attempted to get the support of theologian Reinhold Niebuhr. Jackie stepped in. At a Liberal party fund-raiser, they sat in deep conversation throughout the entire dinner. "She's read every book I ever wrote," bragged an amazed Niebuhr. He came out for Kennedy.[12]

In her Washington home, Jackie hosted women's meetings on political issues. Among the thirty members of the Women's Committee for the New Frontier that Mrs. Kennedy invited for a "conference meeting" were "four prominent Negro women," who included attorney Edith Sampson, Rosa Gragg, president of the National Association of Colored Women's Clubs, Anne Hedgeman, consultant to New York community church groups, and Dr. Jeanne Noble, president of the Delta Theta sorority. Civil rights was among the topics discussed, as it pertained to foreign policy.

Jackie began writing a newspaper column, with obvious political purposes since the DNC served as its syndicate. "Campaign Wife," was frank and observant, and interwove personal stories with politics, not unlike Eleanor's "My Day."

She made many observations about her husband, believing that "Jack shows such control under stress—more than I ever could; an absolute calm beforehand—then, when it is over, he relaxes and laughs and is happy to talk about it with me and with friends." As far as the hundreds of women working for the Kennedy campaign through the Democratic party went, Jackie expressed no jealousy, saying it was "gratifying" to have "so many eager and intelligent women ready to work for my husband," adding that she agreed with JFK's comment, "One woman is worth 10 men in a campaign!"

After receiving a large number of letters on the issue of education of young children, Mrs. Kennedy gave her views in another "Campaign Wife." Referring to a story she'd read that a suburban Washington school board was using trailers as temporary classrooms, to deal with an overflow, she wrote that it was "a resourceful and necessary solution" but emphasized "the urgent need all over the country for additional classrooms," and used an Office of Education's estimate that there was still a shortage of at least 140,000 classrooms. "Although I certainly agree that education is primarily a local responsibility . . . it does seem imperative that the Federal Government step in and do its share." She said that "more teachers must be trained, but . . . they must be paid more so they will enter the teaching profession."

"Campaign Wife" proved that this was not a woman consumed with fashion. In fact, Miss Bouvier's own newspaper stories had never focused on fashion. Still, the "women's page" reporters of the national press harped on that traditional topic in covering political wives. It was easy to see why Jackie began to resent many women reporters.

In one "Campaign Wife," she raised a controversial issue. "Several days ago," she wrote in the October 27 column, "the Sub-Committee on Medical Care for the Aged released its report for the Women's Committee for the New Frontier. So many people all over the country had written me about this problem that I was particularly interested in what they had to say. So often this is considered a problem affecting only older people, whereas actually it equally affects those younger people who take care of their parents and sometimes must choose between this and educating their children." Mrs. Kennedy believed that it was better to have the medical costs covered by Social Security, instead of "requiring older people to pass an income or means test . . . This way each person pays for his own medical care by contributing during his working years to a system which provides assistance in later years . . ." For readers, she also recalled a recent visit from pediatrics expert Dr. Spock, whose books she read and whom she "admired greatly." Spock told her about "his views on education and medical care for the aged . . ." She was "glad . . . he believes that Jack is the man best qualified to build on a realistic program in these fields."[13]

Meanwhile, Jacqueline sent a copy of the statement on medical aid to the aged to Lady Bird, because she "knew you would be interested . . ." When Mrs. Johnson received a golden donkey pin with sapphires and diamonds from Van Cleef & Arpels, it arrived anonymously. Lady Bird had no idea who had sent it. After writing the firm, she learned that it was a gift from Mrs. Kennedy.[14]

Though unable to deliver her speeches in public, Jacqueline still managed to deliver her message. In the September 24 "Campaign Wife," she wrote, "This week I made some radio tapes appealing to Puerto-Ricans, Mexican-Americans, Haitians and Poles to register and vote. I am grateful to my parents for the effort they made to teach us foreign languages. All these people have contributed so much to our country's culture; it seems a proper courtesy to address them in their own language . . ." Then she added a personal note: "Jack telephones late each night . . ."

In October, Mrs. Kennedy made a rare public appearance, to launch a national "Calling for Kennedy" week at an Arlington Holiday Inn, by telephoning the chairmen of eleven state programs in the nationwide drive aimed at housewives. They were asked what they considered to be the most serious issues facing the country. Then, the very pregnant Jacqueline appeared with her husband on television when he answered the solicited questions. In her next "Campaign Wife," she commented that "without exception the issue uppermost in every woman's mind is peace—not a single person put the budget first. Next came education, medical care for the aged, and the cost of living."[15]

Jackie hosted "listening parties" for the first two debates, inviting Lady Bird to one, but joined her husband in the New York studio for the third debate. After the first, she had difficulty expressing publicly "the pride" she felt in "watching that brave young man on the screen," but admitted that "my reaction [was] a wife's loyalty." What struck her

was Jack's tying the past to the future, when he said, "I do not want future historians to say, 'these were the years when the tide ran out for America . . .'"

Besides the broadcasts, "Campaign Wife," and answering about 250 letters a day, she held a series of teas in her home for women reporters, and defended her ability to be First Lady: "I have been married to one of the busiest men in the country for seven years. I ran three houses for him. I have entertained for large and small groups on long and short notice." She told them that she'd revive Mrs. Roosevelt's press conferences and daily column only "if Jack wanted me to," asserting, "I wouldn't put on a mask and pretend to be anything that I wasn't."

Just before election day, in her eighth month of pregnancy, Jackie gamely joined Jack in a New York trip, including a ticker-tape parade in which their car was rocked by overenthusiastic crowds. It wasn't just Jack they were drawn to. Before a Puerto Rican community gathering, with Eleanor Roosevelt also present, Jackie spoke in Spanish, telling them that her "knowledge of your history, culture and problems" would help "assure" them they'd have "a real friend in the White House," if they voted for JFK. Senator Kennedy later wisecracked, "I assure you that my wife can also speak English."[16]

The single most astonishing campaign "activity" of any woman, that season, however, came from one who had lived a lifetime remaining "unpolitical." It had been twelve long elections and forty-four years since her own husband had been reelected, but at age eighty-eight Edith Wilson showed the old mettle from her days as regent.

In her capacity as honorary president, Edith had annually attended the meeting of the Wilson Foundation at her late husband's Virginia birthplace. In 1960, Ike announced his planned attendance, accepting the foundation's invitation sent several months previous. Mrs. Wilson claimed that she did not know of this, and was extremely perturbed at not being consulted "in this crucial time." Since Ike was to be there, Edith canceled.

For the first time in her entire life, she admitted that she acted from purely political, not social, motives, and she let the world know it in her first and only statement to the press: "I like President Eisenhower very much, but I am for Mr. Kennedy. I think it would be politically unwise for me to go in the circumstances." She emphasized that though "fond" of Ike, she was an ardent Democrat, and that was where her first loyalty lay. Edith then clarified that since Virginia was "on the borderline," she feared that a picture of her with Ike just two weeks before the election might influence voters to vote Republican.

Edith Wilson, who had despised Irish-Catholic Tumulty for his "commonness," supporting Kennedy? The widow devoted only to causes of Wilson placing politics before his memory? The "Mrs. President" who long denied any political interests, matter-of-factly contacting the press to let them know of her politics? Ironically, almost sadly, Mrs. Wilson's "influence" existed more in her imagination than it did with Virginia voters. She did receive one letter, anonymously sent, from "A Virginia Democrat" who sniped that her husband had been "President of both the Democrats and Republicans," and that in the same capacity Ike had been invited. "Your action is so petty," he scolded her, "as to influence the voters to do just the opposite of what you think. Incidentally, this is so characteristic of the unwise actions taken by you while living in the White House." She saved the letter. When she saw a car parked in her driveway with a Nixon-Lodge bumper sticker, Mrs. Wilson angrily barked, "Don't you ever park a car with that thing on it in *my* driveway again!"[17]

Not far from Edith's home, the night before an important meeting in which Ike was going to offer his full schedule in campaigning for Dick, Pat Nixon's telephone rang. It was a rare call from Mamie. The First Lady was on the verge of tears, pleading with Pat to influence Dick not to accept Ike's offer. She feared that his health couldn't stand it. She asked Pat to cooperate further by never allowing Ike to know that she had called. The call was later followed up with one from Dr. Snyder to Dick. Nixon turned down Ike's help. Eisenhower was bewildered. As Barbara explained, Mamie "really wanted to see him get out of there in one piece and have a little time left."

One aspect of the campaign that had frightened Pat was what she considered the ruthless machinery of the Kennedy campaign. On election night, she argued with Dick's decision to concede before all votes were in, and when Kennedy won by the closest margin in history, she urged a recount. Dick rejected her suggestion. When he conceded, she was there, behind him. Suddenly, glistening tears swelled in her eyes. She contorted her face, in trying to hold back from openly crying. It was a flash of Pat's emotions that the TV set hadn't before caught. "I knew it would be close," she later said, "but I thought we would win."[18]

Across the country, facing the other ocean, Jacqueline Kennedy had slipped out of the Hyannisport house where friends and family were celebrating victory. Once again, she was seeking solace, drawn to the sea, a solitary figure along the shoreline, pondering her future. "I feel as though I had just turned into a piece of public property," she revealed. "It's really frightening to lose your anonymity at thirty-one." Later in the day, Jack also slipped away from the crowds, to walk alone on the beach.

Soon after, when the Johnsons visited, Jackie recalled how Lady Bird carried a spiral pad, "and when she'd hear a name mentioned she'd jot it down. Sometimes if Mr. Johnson wanted her, he'd say, 'Bird, do you know so-and-so's number?' And she'd always have it down. Yet she would sit talking with us, looking so calm. I was very impressed with that."[19]

Just after the election, reporter Maxine Cheshire claimed that women journalists turned against Mamie's "smalltown dowdiness," when contrasted with the sophisticated Francophile about to assume the first ladyship. During the transition, Mamie was torn. She was relieved to trade criticism and scrutiny for the security and promise of relaxation for Ike's health, but J. B. West wrote, "More than any of the others, Mamie Eisenhower hated to leave." Mrs. Eisenhower's tenure, however, had been a benchmark. In her eight years as First Lady, technology changed the role. With a fully air-conditioned house and nearby Camp David for relaxation, the First Lady no longer left town for the whole summer. Jet planes made it possible for her to make trips with—or without—the president to regions of the country for just a day. Even though she hated to fly, she got into the habit of using air travel. By her last year, Mamie had flown a total of about 590 hours, and traveled almost 32,000 miles. Finally, television beamed glimpses of her right into America's living rooms—a double-edge sword, with benefits and drawbacks. The first ladyship had taken wing with the "Jet Age." Now, it would soar.[20]

Mrs. Eisenhower had been planning a large victory party for Dick and Pat, and was clearly disappointed at the loss. She contented herself with a November 25 tea for her two nieces, Ellen and Mamie Moore— Mamie being the former schoolgirl whom reporter Bouvier had interviewed. Among those present were Pat Nixon, making "her first social appearance since the defeat of her husband," who "went through the receiving line and then left immediately." Two grande dames and famous archrivals, Alice Longworth and Edith Wilson, avoided each other. Once again Mamie had risen above politics to invite Edith, and once again she accepted, unembarrassed for her recent politicking. She strode into the entrance, passed through the receiving line and made a special request to be escorted to the Red Room. There, she stood, alone, staring at the portrait of her late husband.

If Democrat Edith had no trouble being feted by Republicans, Republican Alice was happy about the coming Democrats, dubbing Jacqueline "a charming child. I liked it when she said that she didn't think much of being the First Lady . . . That's marvelous, just as it should be." As the crowd dwindled, with the Marine Band still playing, a reflective Mrs. Eisenhower made her way up the first few steps of the marble staircase. She turned back and looked at the State Floor. "Youth is wonderful," she said.[21]

She was about to change her tune rather quickly.

When Mrs. Kennedy's newly appointed social secretary Letitia Baldridge told reporters that Jackie hadn't yet received Mamie's invitation for the traditional White House tour, the women's press created a headline story out of it, giving the impression that Jackie was insulted. Mrs. Eisenhower's invitation was sent, and Mrs. Kennedy accepted. Before the tour, however, she suddenly gave premature birth to her son, John, Jr., delivered by cesarean surgery on November 25.

About the only thing they had in common was that Jackie's father spent part of his childhood in Nutley, New Jersey, a block away from Mamie's cousin, who delivered newspapers at the Bouvier home—which was also near that of Nancy Reagan's natural father. Mamie was polite in her remarks about Jackie—guarded, but polite. Barbara recalled, "The only thing I ever heard her say right out about her was, 'My heavens, she's *younger* than Barbie!' I think she thought she [Jackie] was too young . . ."

When Mamie learned that Jackie's doctor had requested that his patient be taken through the house in a wheelchair because of her postsurgery condition, Mamie frowned: "Oh, dear, I wanted to take her around alone." She decided that a wheelchair should be placed behind a door and made ready—*if* Mrs. Kennedy requested it. On December 9, the day of the tour, J. B. West escorted a shy Jackie up to Mamie, standing in the middle of the hallway, "very much in command." Mrs. Kennedy took a deep breath. He announced her. Mrs. Eisenhower did not come forward. West took Mrs. Kennedy up to Mamie, "aware that neither lady had looked forward to this meeting." In what he called her "gracious meet-the-visitor pose" Mamie asked about the baby. Jackie didn't mention the wheelchair, admitting later, "I was too scared of Mrs. Eisenhower to ask."

The tour began, Jackie wearily tramping through uninspiring "historic" rooms filled with antique reproductions, later recalling its "interior remoteness," and comparing Mamie's "Pink House" to the Lubianka, the famous Russian prison. On the point of physical collapse, she went immediately to the Kennedy home in Palm Beach, but not entirely to rest.

In Palm Beach, amid the clamor of hyperactive in-laws, concern for her baby, approving Inaugural festivities, and designing her own Inaugural ensemble in collaboration with "official" designer Oleg Cassini, Jacqueline Kennedy isolated herself with the familiar comfort of history. She had ordered about forty books on White House architecture, history, and interiors from the Library of Congress, and read them all. She familiarized herself with each room, each hall, each storage area. She took copious notes from each book on her favorite "stationery" of yellow legal-pad paper.[22]

The morning after her tour, Mamie was in bed, finishing breakfast. With the wave of her manicured nails, she dismissed the housekeeper, telling her to make sure that her petticoated summer dresses were all packed for Gettysburg, and to substitute beef stew for lamb. She speared a bite of grapefruit. J. B. West sensed that she was suppressing her temper. He stood uncomfortably by as the First Lady tersely expressed herself, arching a disapproving eyebrow. "She's planning to redo every room in this house . . . You've got *quite* a project ahead of you. There certainly are going to be some changes made around here!"

On a morning just before the Inaugural, Mr. West noticed that the TV set was on, and that Mamie was annoyed at a special report on Mrs. Kennedy that interrupted her soap opera, which referred to herself as the last First Lady born in the nineteenth century, and Jackie as the first born in the twentieth century. But Mamie was intrigued by a news report that it would be the largest gathering ever of First Ladies.

Besides Jacqueline and Mamie, Edith Wilson, Eleanor Roosevelt, and Bess Truman were all expected. Scattered among them would be other official wives, ranging from Second Ladies Pat Nixon and Lady Bird Johnson to congressional wife Betty Ford.

Mrs. Eisenhower expressed her excitement to Mr. West.

"Won't that be lovely? All of us there together."[23]

– 62 –

Ladies' Day

BESS TRUMAN ARRIVED with Harry, by train. Eleanor Roosevelt was on the last plane permitted to land at National Airport. The snow was piling up rapidly. At the White House, Mamie Eisenhower was frantically packing. Pat Nixon was positively jovial, ready for a vacation after the official proceedings. Lady Bird Johnson was home, choosing a black dress with a yellow rose of Texas for the Distinguished Ladies' Reception. In Virginia, Betty Ford was getting ready for out-of-town guests from New York. Edith Wilson was snug at home, but dying to catch a glimpse of Jackie Kennedy at one of the several Inaugural events she planned to attend. This Queen Mother of the sorority was an unabashed "fan" of the woman about to become the third-youngest First Lady. After the election, Edith had sent a telegram to Jackie offering "warmest congratulations and personal gratitude for your great victory."

The press caught only a quick glimpse of Mrs. Kennedy as she returned from Florida. *The New York Times* appraised Jackie's "devil-may-care chic," adding that American women considered it their "constitutional right" to know all the details on a First Lady's clothes. It outlined the serious financial and political impact of a First Lady's fashion, considering American designers, manufacturers, the millinery industry, fur-trapping lobby, and magazines trying to get her design drawings to boost sales.

Jacqueline was more concerned about the press focus on her three-year-old daughter, Caroline, and infant son, John. "I don't want my young children brought up by nurses and Secret Service men," she told a reporter. She absolutely determined that her role as mother came before anything else, official or not. She hoped to emulate Bess Truman because she had kept her daughter "from being spoiled."

Though Mrs. Kennedy joined Lady Bird and their husbands at an Inaugural Concert at Constitution Hall, the precarious roads prevented Edith Wilson from getting there in time to see the Kennedys and Johnsons, who then headed to the Armory for an Inaugural Gala. At that performance, Eleanor Roosevelt was scheduled to appear onstage, reading excerpts from Lincoln's speeches. The snowy roads had also prevented her from appearing. Her absence the next morning, however, was more conspicious.

As Jackie and Lady Bird arrived at the White House for the traditional pre-Inaugural coffee, joining Mamie and Pat, the three elderly former First Ladies were arriving at the Capitol platform for the swearing-in ceremony. Edith had arrived early, with police escort heralding her ride up Pennsylvania Avenue. To ward off the 20-degree temperature, she took sips from her bourbon flask, and Alice Longworth thought she looked like a "tipsy Margaret Dumont." Bess had brought a more reliable plaid wool blanket. Though Eleanor had been assigned a seat of prominence in the third row, next to Mrs. Wilson and two behind Lady Bird, she refused it. She told reporters that she wanted to sit in the diplomatic section because "she couldn't hear sitting behind the speaker," but her real reasons were political: She still held a grudge against Joe Kennedy, the president-elect's father, and resented JFK for not appointing Adlai Stevenson as secretary of state. Edna Gurewitsch also recalled that Eleanor "was very happy not to be up there [on the stand] . . . To be displayed as a has-been First Lady was of no interest to her. She loved being free."

Focus, however, was not on Eleanor, but "her."

"I think Mrs. Kennedy will be a great asset to her husband—as she is cultivated and charming," Edith Wilson remarked. "She will find it not too difficult," said Bess Truman. "I think she will be a perfect First Lady. Her age is a tremendous asset." Eleanor told reporters, "I know she'll do very well."

Betty Ford sat in the congressional section. When she later learned that Mrs. Roosevelt, a woman she'd long admired, was at the ceremony, she said, "I really would have loved to meet her." Though sitting some distance from the other women, Mrs. Ford said that it was "pretty impressive to be there and take part in history." Dressed in a winter-white cloth coat and hat, Betty waited for the principals, who were in a holding room, watching the proceedings on TV. Before Jackie headed out, her three companions preceding her, Jack had arranged for them to "have a private word." Then she descended the platform, into the public.

The new First Lady stood out like a pearl amid the dark clothes and brown minks. Her outfit was a simple beige coat with a narrow sable collar, sable muff, and white gloves. But it was the beige pillbox hat that fascinated fashion editors and milliners. When a friend had told Mrs. Kennedy that she'd have to make concessions to the First Lady role, she responded, "I will. I'll wear hats!" Today, there was something different about her hat, quite apart from all the other women's headpieces. The large pillbox was actually *behind* her head so as not to crush the other unusual chic fashion statement, a bouffant hairstyle. The understated outfit was scrutinized by hundreds of reporters, one of whom noted that "everyone agreed that Jacqueline Kennedy's career as a major fashion influence was beginning impressively."

The "Jackie look" was born.

Jacqueline in beige, Mamie in "Chinese" red, Pat in "sapphire blue," Lady Bird in "parrot green," Edith in violet, Betty in white, Bess in black-white paisley, and Eleanor in gray all watched as John F. Kennedy, the first Roman Catholic and the youngest man elected to the office, repeated the presidential oath.

Throughout Kennedy's Inaugural Address, one reporter watched Jacqueline's "luminous eyes," which gave "rapt attention to every detail on the program." Mamie "warmly" applauded JFK, and suppressed tears as Marian Anderson sang. Through the powers of television, Jackie's influence was being felt that day by women married to men who worked at the state level—coast to coast. Rosalynn Carter of Plains watched it

all on TV, as did Barbara Bush in Houston, who particularly recalled "admiring the young, beautiful Mrs. Kennedy." In the sunny GE home of Pacific Palisades resident Nancy Reagan, however, the television was not turned on. Mrs. Reagan later said that she "did not watch the Kennedy Inaugural," but was drawn to "the Jackie look."

Seconds after the oath, the new president turned immediately to meet the eyes of his wife. *The New York Times* said she "gave him a 'you-did-all-right' smile." Jack did not kiss his wife before the millions watching, as Ike had done to Mamie.

The Kennedys were to maintain a very private relationship. Not only was Jacqueline disquieted by strangers dissecting her every little interaction with Jack, but he considered it improper to display emotion in front of the press. The reporters didn't know of the encounter before they came out, or the one after the ceremony as the couple stole a moment behind the walls, in the hallway of the Capitol's labyrinth.

"I was so proud of Jack," she recalled. "There was so much I wanted to say! But I could scarcely embrace him in front of all those people. So I remember I just put my hand on his cheek and said, 'Jack, you were so wonderful! And he was smiling in the most touching and most vulnerable way." Jacqueline characterized his speech as "soaring," and said she "knew I was hearing something great," ranking it with one of Lincoln's . . . and Pericles'.

The crowd dispersed: Jackie, Lady Bird, Bess, and Edith partook of the official Capitol luncheon; Eleanor headed to a private lunch; Mamie and Pat were feted at a farewell luncheon. As the parade began, with Mrs. Kennedy, Mrs. Johnson, Mrs. Wilson, and Mrs. Truman all riding in the official caravan, Mamie and Ike climbed into her Chrysler and left.

The Nixons headed home as private citizens. After a Bahamas vacation, Pat and her daughters would stay in Washington until summer. Then it was back to private life. They would live in Beverly Hills, where Nancy Reagan lunched and shopped, just up the coast from her Pacific Palisades home. A friend recalled, "I had never seen Pat Nixon so happy. She was so glad to be out of politics." In retrospect, she would wish she'd immediately moved to California instead of staying in Washington "limbo."

That night, as an Inaugural Ball chairman recalled, Jackie stopped "everybody dead in their tracks!" But rather than stand back in awe, the tuxedoed and gowned "crush" of "stampede proportions" shoved each other for "advantageous gawking" of Jackie, whose natural tallness was heightened by her white satin pumps, new bouffant coiffure, and a dramatic, sweeping white satin cape. Underneath lay a strapless white bodice with shimmering white brilliants, covered by a white chiffon sheath.

The Kennedys had gone first to the Mayflower Hotel Ball to see the Trumans, who were staying there. Dressed in a gold-white brocade gown, Eleanor Roosevelt appeared at the Armory in time to see Jackie, Lady Bird, and their husbands, but left soon after. Edith, wearied from the excitement of the afternoon, stayed home and watched on TV. By now, Mamie's car had slipped silently over the snowy dark Gettysburg fields, through the gates to the farmhouse. Bess, Eleanor, Edith, and Mamie would visit their old home and new successor, but they were reminiscent of past eras.

There were others now—Jacqueline, Lady Bird, Pat, and Betty— whose time had come.

Experience and time, not politics, separated the "ladies" born in the nineteenth century from this "new generation of Americans—born in this century," whom the new president addressed that afternoon. These women, coming of age during depression and war, had all pursued college educations and professional careers. Few realized what had happened, least of all the younger women.

But the torch had been passed.[1]

Notes

Because hundreds of sources—including all Library of Congress listings related to the Presidents, First Ladies, and White House—were utilized directly or as background, the author has found it more beneficial to combine the traditional bibliography within the Notes section. The full notation on a source is therefore given at its initial appearance.

PROLOGUE: MAY 1789

1. References for the Prologue include: Tom Tierney, *Great Empresses and Queens* (New York: Dover Publications, 1982); *Webster's New Biographical Dictionary* (Springfield, Massachusetts: Merriam-Webster, 1983); Abigail Adams letters from Ishbel Ross, *Daughters of Eve* (New York: Harper & Row, 1969), pp. 8–20 and Lynn Withey, *Dearest Friend: A Life of Abigail Adams* (New York: Free Press, 1981).

1. THE LADY IN THE COACH

1. References for Martha Washington's journey to New York are taken from Robert Lewis journal, May 13–20, 1789, William Heth to GW, May 3, 1789, and Gabriel Van Horne, May 12, 1789, courtesy of John P. Riley, archivist, Mount Vernon; *Maryland Journal and Baltimore Advertiser,* May 22, 1789; *Pennsylvania Packet,* May 26, 1789; *Pennsylvania and Daily Advertiser,* May 26 and 27, 1789; Martha Washington to Fanny Bassett Washington, June 8, 1789, Martha Washington Typescript Letters, Mount Vernon (hereafter MWMV); *Gazette of the United States,* May 30, 1789; Robert Lewis to GW, Mar. 18, 1789, W. W. Abbot, ed., *The Papers of George Washington,* Presidential Series 1, Sept. 1788–Mar. 1789 (Charlottesville, Va.: University of Virginia Press), p. 404; Mount Vernon Ladies Association, *Yesterday, Today and Tomorrow* special supplement, Spring 1989, p. 2; Anne Hollingsworth Wharton, *Martha Washington* (Boston: Scribners, 1897), pp. 184–93; Miriam Anne Bourne, *First Family: George Washington and His Intimate Relations* (New York: W. W. Norton, 1982), p. 128; Stephen Decatur, Jr., *Private Affairs of George Washington* (Boston: Houghton-Mifflin, 1883, pp. 20–21, 75; Alice Curtis Desmond, *Martha Washington: Our First Lady* (New York: Dodd, Mead, 1951), pp. 217–18; Mary Ormsbee Whitton, *First First Ladies* (New York: Hastings House, 1948), p. 16.

2. "A VERY GREAT SOME BODY"

1. Desmond, pp. 9, 33; Martha Dandridge Custis to Robert Cary Esq. & Company, Aug. 20, 1757, and to Messrs. John Hanbury & Co., Dec. 20, 1757, and June 1, 1758, Custis Papers, Virginia Historical Society.
2. GW to Francis Dandridge, Sept. 29, 1865, reprinted in Whitton, p. 6;

Arden Davis, *Wives of the Presidents* (Maplewood, New Jersey: Hammond, 1972), p. 9.

3. James Thomas Flexner, *George Washington: The Indispensable Man* (New York: New American Library, 1984), p. 372.

4. Desmond, p. 132; newspaper clipping, reprinted in Desmond, p. 142.

5. Bourne, p. 104; MW to Miss Betsy Ramsay, Dec. 30, 1775, reprinted in Desmond, pp. 145–46.

6. MWMV to Nancy Bassett, Aug. 20, 1976, reprinted in *Mary and Martha Washington: The Mother and the Wife of George Washington,* John Benson Lossing (New York: Harper & Bros., 1886), pp. 158–59; MW to [Miss Betsy Ramsay], Dec. 30, 1775, reprinted in Desmond, pp. 145–46.

7. Bourne, pp. 61–62.

8. MW to Miss Betsy Ramsay, Dec. 30, 1775, Desmond, p. 192.

9. MW to Fanny Bassett Washington, Oct. 22, 1789, MWMV.

10. MW to Mercy Warren, Dec. 26, 1789, MWMV.

11. George Washington Parke Custis, *Memoirs of Washington* (New York: Edgewood Publishing, 1859), p. 509; Mary Caroline Crawford, *Romantic Days in the Early Republic* (Boston: Little Brown, 1912), p. 79.

12. Wharton, pp. 210–11; Bourne, pp. 128–30, Desmond, pp. 227, 243, Decatur, pp. 38–39, 92, 96, 101, 105, 120, 181, 214, 222.

13. Desmond, pp. 227–28.

14. MW to Mercy Warren, June 12, 1790, Warren-Adams Letters, Vol. 2, p. 319; Wharton, p. 213, Decatur pp. 106–7.

15. Decatur, pp. 18–19, 29, 65, 194, 195, 290; Desmond, p. 208; Abigail Adams to Eliza Peabody, June 28, 1789, reprinted in Stewart Mitchell, ed., *New Letters of Abigail Adams,* p. 13; MW to "Mr. Whitelock," Apr. 17, 1794, University of Alabama, School of Dentistry.

16. Decatur, pp. 57, 104, 129.

17. Decatur, pp. 150, 194–95; Francis Watson, "Americans and French Eighteenth-Century Furniture in the Age of Jefferson," *Jefferson and the Arts,* p. 284.

18. Laura C. Holloway Langford, *The Ladies of the White House* (Philadelphia: A. Gorton & Co, 1882), pp. 57–58.

19. Custis p. 395; Decatur pp. 43–44.

20. Decatur, p. 51; Desmond, pp. 222–23.

21. Desmond p. 228; Meade Minnigerode, *Some American Ladies* (Freeport, N.Y.: Books for Libraries Press, 1969), p. 38.

22. Minnigerode, p. 34; Crawford, p. 87; Page Smith, *John Adams* (New York: Doubleday, 1962), Vol. 2, p. 878; *Gazette of the United States,* May 30, 1789, p. 3; Decatur, p. 173.

23. Ruthey Jones to MW, May 12, 1795, MWMV; countess of Buchan to MW, Jan. 8, 1794, MWMV; The Mount Vernon Ladies Association Annual Report 1981, pp. 3, 36.

24. *Daily Advertiser,* June 15, 1789; Douglas Southhall Freeman, *George Washington,* Vol. 6 (New York: Scribner's, 1954), pp. 212–13; Decatur, pp. 45–46.

25. Desmond, pp. 223–24, 230; James Thomas Flexner, *George Washington: Anguish and Farewell 1793–1799* (Boston: Little, Brown, 1972), p. 330; journal of Pennsylvania Senator William Maclay, reprinted in Crawford, p. 85.

26. Decatur, pp. 36–37; Edna M. Colman, *White House Gossip* (New York: Doubleday, 1926), pp. 21–22.

27. Elswyth Thane, *Washington's Lady* (New York: Dodd, Mead, 1960), p. 306.

28. MW to Fanny Bassett Washington, Feb. 25, 1788, MWMV.

29. Custis, p. 514; MW to Fanny Bassett Washington, Sept. 29, 1794, MWMV.

30. Bourne, p. 195; *The Writings of Thomas Jefferson,* Vol. XIX, Andrew A. Lipscomb and Albert E. Bergh, editors (Washington, D.C.: 1903), p. 130; MW to Annis Stockton Boudinot, Jan. 15, 1794, MWMV.

31. Thane, pp. 307–8; MW to Fanny Bassett Washington, Mar. 2, 1794, MWMV.

32. MW to unidentified person, Jan. 29, 1791, Boston Public Library; MW to Fanny Bassett Washington, Apr. 6, 1795, Oneida Historical Society; the Edward S. Harkness Collection, Bulletin of the New York Public Library, Dec. 1950, Vol. 54, No. 12, pp. 593–94; MW notes to and from Mrs. Clinton, n.d., circa 1790's, New York Historical Society; Decatur, pp. 184, 313.

33. James Thomas Flexner, *George Washington and the New Nation* (Boston: Little, Brown, 1970), p. 24; *Brieven en Gedenkschriften van Gijsbert Karel van Hogendorp*, Vol. 1, pp. 394–97.

34. Custis, p. 408; Though her grandson later disclaimed this quote, it is in absolute character with political statements Martha Washington made about the Democrats in retirement. Besides which, it would be unlikely that she would discuss politics with her young grandson.

35. William North to Ben Walker, Mar. 9, 1784, Pennsylvania Historical Society.

36. John Wallace to Matthew Carey, Nov. 22, 1784, MWMV.

3. "THIS ELEVATED STATION . . ."

1. Isaac Heston letter, catalog no. 2203, John Todd, Jr., letter, catalog no. 622, and Dolley Todd letter, catalog no. 638, W. Parsons Todd Collection, Independence National Historical Park Collection.

2. Custis, pp. 403, 503–8; Decatur, p. 136; Desmond, pp. 180–81, 173, 167; Martha Washington to unidentified person, MWMV, n.d. Dec. 1776.

3. Desmond, p. 251; Mary Beth Norton, *Liberty's Daughters: The Revolutionary Experience of American Women, 1750–1800* (Boston: Little, Brown, 1980), pp. 179, 184–85; editors of *The Ladies Magazine* to Martha Washington, May 18, 1793, Papers of GW, Vol. 260. No record survives of the magazine's patrons; Lossing, p. 281.

4. Elizabeth Monroe's background is taken from chapters on her in Holloway's *Ladies of the White House,* Mary Whitton's *First First Ladies,* Harry Ammon, *James Monroe* (New York: McGraw-Hill, 1971), W. P. Cresson, *James Monroe* (Chapel Hill, N.C.: University of N.C. Press, 1946); George Morgan, *The Life of James Monroe* (Boston: Little, Brown, 1921), pp. 143–47; Background on Dolley Madison: Lucia Cutts, ed., *Memoirs and Letters of Dolly Madison* (Boston: Houghton Mifflin, 1886), pp. 15–16; Dolley Madison (hereafter DPM) to Anna Payne Cutts, July 31, 1805, Cutts Papers, LC; W. W. Wilkins to Dolley Todd, Aug. 22, 1794, regarding investigation of Madison's wealth, reprinted in Allen Clark, *Life and Letters of Dolley Madison* (Washington, D.C.: W. F. Roberts, 1914); DPM to Eliza Collins Lee, Sept. 16, 1794,

Madison Papers, LC; Reverend Teunis S. Hamlin, "Historic Homes of Washington," *Scribner's Magazine,* Oct. 1893; regarding DPM holding on to her Philadelphia properties as personal income from rent, DPM to Mr. Jackson, Nov. 7, 1807, Cutts Papers, LC; Clark, p. 90; regarding Madison and snuff tax, Robert Heimann, *Tobacco in America* (New York: McGraw-Hill, 1960,) pp. 78–79; regarding John Adams (hereafter JA) meeting DPM, JA to Abigail Adams (hereafter AA), Feb. 27, 1796, Adams Papers, Massachusetts Historical Society; regarding Dexter incident, Virginia Moore, *The Madisons* (New York: McGraw-Hill, 1979), p. 57; Ethel Arnett, *Mrs. James Madison: The Incomparable Dolley* (Greenville, N.C.: Piedmont Press, 1972), p. 128; Martha gave Dolley a small china milk jug, part of a set given her by the Count de Custine and now owned by Mount Vernon; Dolley Madison, Martha Washington, and Elizabeth Monroe all traded recipes with each other: see Poppy Cannon and Patricia Brooks, *The Presidents' Cookbook* (New York: Bonanza Books, 1969), pp. 85, 100, 101, 102, 105.

5. MW to Mary Stillson Lear, MWMV, Nov. 4, 1796, letter of Dr. Cotton of Charleston, West Va., May 21, 1889, Eliza Powel to MW, Nov. 30, 1787, and MW to Fanny Bassett, Sept. 15, 1794, all from MWMV; George Washington to Charles Thompson, reprinted in James Thomas Flexner, *George Washington and the New Nation (1783–1793)* (Boston: Little, Brown, 1969), p. 33.

6. Quoted in Bourne, pp. 135–36; the story of Eliza Law dressing as a man to enter her soldier-lover's encampment is repeated in many books on the Washington family and the early city life of the Federal City, cited in Flexner, p. 492, among other references; for listing of Martha Washington's charitable contributions to women in need, see Decatur, pp. 22, 24, 64, 78, 182, 233, 250, 254, 321.

7. MW to Elizabeth Powel, May 20, 1797, and MW to Fanny Bassett Washington Lear, May 24, 1795, MWMV; regarding Martha Washington and her attitudes toward black Americans, slavery, and the Oney Judge incident, see Flexner's *George Washington: Anguish and Farewell (1793–1799),* chapter entitled "Black Mount Vernon," beginning on p. 432; Tobias Lear to George Long, Spring 1789, quoted in Decatur, pp. 314–15; Decatur, pp. 32, 39, 260.

8. Martha Washington on alcoholism, MW to Mrs. George A. Washington, Apr. 6, 1795, original at Oneida Historical Society.

9. AA to Eliza Shaw Peabody, Oct. 4, 1789, from Stewart Mitchell, ed., *New Letters of Abigail Adams, 1788–1801* (Boston: Houghton-Mifflin, 1947), pp. 25–29; AA to Mary Cranch, June 28, 1789, *New Letters,* p. 13; JA to AA, Jan. 11, 1797, Adams Papers; AA letter of May 30, 1790, quoted in Freeman, p. 260; Whitney, pp. 236–37, 241; AA letter, Dec. 23, 1796, quoted in Lynne Withey, *Dearest Friend: A Life of Abigail Adams* (New York: Free Press, 1981), p. 241.

10. MW to Mrs. Nathaniel Greene, Mar. 3, 1797, MWMV; Paul C. Nagel, *Descent from Glory: Four Generations of the John Adams Family* (New York: Oxford University Press, 1983), p. 23; AA to Mercy Warren, Mar. 4, 1797, quoted in Laura E. Richards, *Abigail Adams and Her Times* (New York: Appleton, 1917), pp. 248–49.

4. MRS. PRESIDENT

1. Withey, p. 249; Page Smith, p. 938; Jane Whitney, *Abigail Adams* (Boston: Little, Brown, 1947), pp. 264, 303.

2. Abigail Adams's early life and education is culled from several secondary sources, including the noted biographies of her by Lynne Withey, Laura Richards, Janet Whitney, and the JA biography by Page Smith; Charles Francis Adams, ed., *Familiar Letters of John Adams and His Wife Abigail Adams During the Revolution* (Boston: Little, Brown, 1876), p. 77.
3. *Familiar Letters*, p. 412; Charles Francis Adams, ed., *Letters of Mrs. Adams* (Boston: Little, Brown, 1848), pp. 266, 234; Adams Manuscript, Feb. 1788, quoted in Whitney, p. 217.
4. Smith, p. 839; AA to JA, Feb. 20, 1796, Adams Papers, Massachusetts Historical Society; Charles Akers, *Abigail Adams* (Boston: Little, Brown, 1980), p. 145; Nagel, p. 50, and JA to AA, May 31, 1797, Adams Papers, quoted in Smith, p. 923; Whitney, p. 269.
5. Whitney, p. 272; Withey, p. 246; Akers, pp. 153, 161; AA to JA, May 22, 1800, Adams Papers, quoted in Withey, p. 269; *New Letters*, AA to Mary Cranch, May 24, 1797, p. 91, and Apr. 16, 1801, quoted in Smith, p. 966.
6. *Letters of Mrs. Adams*, 1v, 1vi; Nagel, p. 22; AA quoted in Marianne Means, *The Woman in the White House* (New York: Random House, 1963), pp. 45–46.
7. Katherine Anthony, *Dolly Madison* (New York: Doubleday, 1949), p. 195; AA to Mary Cranch, Dec. 26, 1797, quoted in *New Letters*, pp. 119–20; Withey, p. 254; Smith, p. 937; *Charleston (South Carolina) City Gazette*, March 5, 1800.
8. Smith, p. 993; Withey, p. 253; Whitney, pp. 275–79; AA to Mary Cranch, Apr. 26, 1798, and May 10, 1798, quoted in *New Letters*, pp. 164, 172.

5. WARMONGER

1. Smith, pp. 955, 958, 965, 979; AA to John Quincy Adams, July 14, 1798, and July 20, 1798, quoted in Whitney, p. 280; AA to William Smith, Mar. 5, 1798, Whitney, pp. 274–76.
2. Charles Francis Adams, ed., *Works of John Adams* (Boston: 1856), Vol. 1, p. 547.
3. MW to Lucy Knox, 1797, Lossing, p. 313, MWMV; Rev. Louis G. V. Du Bourg to MW, July 20, 1798, MWMV, original in LC; MW to Eliza Powel, May 20, 1797, MWMV; MW to "Mrs. P," Apr. 20, 1799, MWMV; MW to JA, Dec. 31, 1799, MWMV; JA to Congress, Jan. 8, 1800, MWMV, Parke-Bernet Galleries, Sale Number 1385, Item 387, 1952; 2 Stat. L. 19, United States Congress, Apr. 3, 1800; MW to Governor Trumbull of Connecticut, Jan. 15, 1800, MWMV.
4. AA to Mary Cranch, Nov. 26, 1799, and Mar. 18, 1800, *New Letters*, pp. 218, 241–42.
5. Nagel, pp. 14, 24, 56; Smith, pp. 608–9, Withey, pp. 106, 123.
6. Withey, pp. 233–34; AA to Eliza Peabody, July 19, 1799, Smith Papers, LC; AA to Eliza Peabody Shaw, June 1809, quoted in Richards, p. 267; JA to Thomas Adams, Oct. 17, 1799, quoted in Smith, pp. 1016–1017; AA to Mary Cranch, Dec. 4, 1799, quoted in *New Letters*, pp. 217–19.
7. "Madame Doré" to Elizabeth Monroe, n.d., James Monroe Papers, LC; Morgan, pp. 192, 257; Cresson, pp. 154, 205, 309; Ammon, pp. 137–38.

8. Nagel, pp. 69, 73; Akers, pp. 150, 170; Jack Shepard, *Cannibals of the Heart* (New York: McGraw-Hill, 1980), pp. 64, 80–82.

9. "not teach" quote from Nagel; AA to Mary Cranch, Dec. 8, 1800, *New Letters*, pp. 261–62; Smith, pp. 993, 1037; Whitney, pp. 231, 299.

10. AA to JA, Feb. 13, 1797, quoted in Smith, p. 926; AA to Cotton Tufts, Dec. 28, 1800, Adams Papers; for AA's early convictions on civil rights, see *Familiar Letters*, pp. 41–42.

11. H. Cushing to Mrs. Margaret Bowers, Jan. 29, 1801, describing White House, Emnet Collection, #10184, Manuscript and Archive Division, New York Public Library.

12. Withey, pp. 271, 281; Smith, pp. 1054–1055, 1061; Akers, pp. 174–75; AA to Mary Cranch, May 26, 1800, *New Letters*, pp. 252–53.

13. AA to Mary Cranch, Dec. 21, 1800, MWMV; July 29, 1801, excerpt of Pintard Dines diary, MWMV; Bourne, p. 195.

14. Visit to Martha Washington by Dolley Payne Madison (hereafter DPM) and Jefferson, see Cutts, p. 25, and Jefferson note to DPM to serve as hostess for first entertainment of "females," p. 28; AA to Thomas Adams, Nov. 13, 1800, *New Letters*, pp. 430–31.

6. "THE TENDER BREASTS OF LADIES"

1. Opening quote of DPM, DPM to Mary Cutts, Aug. 1, 1833, quoted in Clark, pp. 259–60; background material on Martha Jefferson from entire chapter on her in Fawn Brodie, *Thomas Jefferson: An Intimate History* (W. W. Norton, 1974), pp. 80–89; and see Whitton chapter, "Thomas Jefferson and the Rights of Women," pp. 39–53; quoted in Julian P. Boyd, ed., *The Papers of Thomas Jefferson* (Princeton, N.J.: Princeton Univ. Press), Vol. XIII, Thomas Jefferson to Angelica Church, Sept. 21, 1788, p. 623, and to Anne Willing Bingham, May 11, 1788, p. 151; *Autobiography of Thomas Jefferson* (introductory essay by Dumas Malone, Boston, 1948), p. 110; Gordon Carruth, *What Happened When* (New York: Harper & Row, 1987), p. 44.

2. John Quincy Adams diary entry of Jan. 19, 1804, quoted in Anthony, p. 121; Noel Bertram Gerson, *The Velvet Glove* (Nashville: Thomas Nelson, Inc., 1975), p.158; Cutts, p. 33; DPM to Anna Cutts, July 8, 1805, quoted in Clark, p. 79; DPM to James Madison, Nov. 1, 1805, quoted in Cutts, p. 60; Clark, p. 83.

3. Hetty Ann Barton manuscript, May 1803, quoted in Conover Hunt-Jones, *Dolley and the Great Little Madison* (Washington, D.C.: AIA Foundation, 1977), p. 22; rules number 11 and 12 of the *Cannons of Etiquette to be Observed by the Executive*, Thomas Jefferson, Cutts Papers, LC.

4. Jan. 1802, diary of Massachusetts Congressman Manasseh Cutler, from an undated newspaper account of *The Star and the Chicago Record-Herald*, MWMV; Cutler diary, MWMV; diary of Mrs. William Thornton, the records of the Columbia Historical Society, Washington, D.C., Vol. X, 1907; Sally Foster Otis to Mrs. Charles W. Apthorp, Jan. 13, 1801, MWMV, original in Massachusetts Historical Society; assorted newspaper obituaries of MW, MWMV; newspaper clipping with portrait on MW's death, n.p., n.d., the Prints and Photo Division, LC; Louisa Adams visit to MW, Nagel, p. 83;

Margaret Smith, later Mrs. Zachary Taylor, reference from Margaret Klapthor, *The First Ladies Cookbook* (New York: *Parents* Magazine Press, 1965), p. 89; Smith, p. 1101; Withey, p. 296.

5. Ammons, p. 163; James Madison to James Monroe, Feb. 5, 1797, Madison Papers, LC; quote from JQA diary Mar. 13, 1806, Arnett, pp. 78, 95–97; Lucy Washington to Anna Cutts, July 20, 1811, and James Madison to Richard Cutts, Aug. 24, 1811, Cutts Papers, LC, quoted in Moore, pp. 250–51; Gerson, pp. 77, 119–21, 159–62, 179; Anthony, p. 186; the rumors romantically linking Jefferson and Dolley Madison may stem from his supposed affection for her mother, and pursuit of her as a wife when they were both young and single, see Maud Wilder Goodwin, *Dolly Madison* (New York: Scribner's, 1896), p. 76.

7. THE QUEEN OF HEARTS

1. Clark, pp. 101–3; Arnett, pp. 161–63; use of the term "presidentress" seems to have first appeared in the press in the Mar. 4, 1809, edition of the *National Intelligencer*. Senator Mitchell of New York, however, used it in a letter to his wife on Jan. 25, 1808. He also termed her "Lady President" in letter of Nov. 23, 1807—see Clark, pp. 91, 93.
2. General background on the household aspects of Dolley Madison's White House life is best presented in Moore, *The Madisons*, while Arnett provides specific facts and details.
3. Time-Life editors, *American Cooking* (New York: Time-Life Books, 1968), pp. 43, 159; Cannon and Brooks, p. 92; Hunt, p. 24. Later, at the home DPM owned in Philadelphia, its tenants started an ice-cream production business, gracing the company with her name.
4. Anthony, p. 196; Clark, pp. 40, 207–8, 226–28; *The Port Folio Magazine*, April 1818, Philadelphia.
5. Rebekah Hubbs to DPM, July 13, 1814, Cutts, pp. 123, 124–27; Bess Furman, *White House Profile* (New York: Bobbs, Merrill, 1951), p. 58; Hunt, pp. 42–43, Gerson, p. 104; Mrs. Seaton's diary entry of Jan. 2, 1814, Clark, pp. 157–58, 403.
6. Senator Mitchell quote from Crawford, pp. 178–79.
7. Phoebe Morris letter, Feb. 17, 1812, quoted in Clark, pp. 126, 143, 208, 467; Furman, p. 58; Hunt, pp. 12, 33–34; Arnett, pp. 156, 177, 181–83; *The Globe*, Aug. 12, 1836; Colman, p. 99.
8. Gerson, pp. 93–94; Anthony, p. 195.
9. DPM to Mrs. Isaac Winston, Apr. 9, 1804, quoted in Clark, p. 74; Crawford, p. 329; Theodosia Burr Alston to DPM June 24, 1809, see Clark, p. 106; Anthony, pp. 184–85; Moore, p. 161.
10. Moore, p. 217; Arnett, p. 103; Clark, pp. 92, 461; James Madison to DPM, Aug. 17, 1809, DPM to Anna Cutts, Dec. 20, 1811, quoted in Cutts, pp. 66, 73.
11. Arnett, pp. 14, 105, 114, 215; Moore, pp. 249–50, 263; DPM to Lucy H. Conway, Feb. 2, 1839, quoted in Clark, pp. 293, 459; Goodwin, p. 147; Anthony, p. 241; DPM letter of June 10, 1813 quoted in Cutts, p. 92.
12. Arnett, p. 274; Clark, p. 127; DPM to Anna Cutts, Dec. 20, 1811,

Moore, p. 269; Furman, p. 68; DPM to Mr. and Mrs. Joel Barlow, n.d., 1811, quoted in Cutts, pp. 86, 73.
13. Cutts, pp. 86, 73, Clark, p. 130; DPM to Edward Coles, May 13, 1813, Cutts Papers, LC.

8. LEGEND

1. John Jacob Astor to DPM, Nov. 29, 1812, quoted in Clark, pp. 145, 272; Cutts, p. 141; Moore, pp. 165, 215; Means, pp. 70–71.
2. Clark, p. 151; the anonymous letter from the British to Dolley Madison warning her that they'd take her hostage and/or burn down the White House is referred to by her niece, but the author has been unable to locate it—see Cutts, pp. 99–101.
3. Hunt, p. 13; Arnett, pp. 111, 215–16; Moore gives no source for this note—see Moore, p. 290.
4. Arnett, pp. 418, 421; DPM to Lucy Todd Washington, Aug. 23, 1814; Cutts, pp. 99–101; Moore, pp. 313–20; Clark, pp. 161–67; regarding DPM taking her own portrait miniature, see Hunt, p. 47.

9. "AN INFLUENCE"

1. William Seale, The President's House (Washington, D.C.: White House Historical Association, 1986), Vol. 1, pp. 135, 137; Hunt, p. 50; Arnett, pp. 240–49; Mrs. Thornton's diary entry for Aug. 29, 1814, quotes DPM; see Clark, p. 176, for the full eight verses of "The Bladensburg Races"; Clark, pp. 179, 184, 188, 190, 197; Cutts, pp. 114–17; Sarah Seaton's letter describes the flag presentation—see Josephine Seaton, William Winston Seaton: A Biographical Sketch (Boston: Osgood and Co., 1871), p. 99.
2. Seaton, pp. 131–32; in reference to Dolley Madison meeting Rachel Jackson, see Arnett, p. 195; regarding Rachel's presence in Washington, National Intelligencer, Dec. 9, 1815, and Dec. 28, 1815—see Mary French Caldwell, General Jackson's Lady (Nashville: Kingsport Press, 1936), pp. 339–43.
3. Moore, pp. 279–351; Gerston, p. 223; Arnett, pp. 422–23; Hunt, p. 48.
4. National Intelligencer Oct. 10, 1815; see Clark, p. 254–55; Colman, pp. 115–16; Lilly Page, an orphan in the Washington City Orphans Asylum, later sent DPM a Christmas basket of fruit from a group of orphans in Clarke County, Virginia, Lilly Page to DPM, Dec. 25, 1847; Goodwin, pp. 138–39; Phebe Hanaford, Daughters of America (Augusta, Me: True & Co., 1901), p. 75; Moore, p. 370.
5. Arnett, pp. 87, 113, 254; Clark, pp. 77–78, 92, 122, 124, 267, 439–40; Gerson, pp. 146–47; Hunt, p. 21; Furman, pp. 62–63; Moore, p. 418; Whitton, p. 65; Cutts, pp. 189–90; Anthony, pp. 312–15; for DPM's feelings on wife-beating, see her letter to Anna Cutts, June 4, 1804, in Clark, pp. 77–78; when Mellimelli came to the United States from Algiers, President Madison charged the State Department with "Georgia a Creek [Indian]" and listed her fee as "appropriations to foreign intercourse." (!)
6. Clark, pp. 107, 154–56; 211–12; Hunt, p. 35.
7. Hunt, pp. 13, 32; Clark, pp. 109–10, 407.

8. Means, p. 59; Brodie, p. 473; Moore, p. 375; Clark, pp. 76, 341, 477.

9. Anthony, p. 723; Clark, pp. 91, 363, 381.

10. Eliza Lee to DPM Mar. 4, 1817, quoted in Cutts, p. 145; Eliza Lee to DPM, Mar. 30, 1819, DPM Papers, LC; Clark, p. 238.

11. Margaret Byrd Bassett, *American Presidents and Their Wives* (Freeport, Me: Bond Wheelwright, 1969), p. 56.

10. QUEEN ELIZABETH

1. Ammon, pp. 134, 402; Sol Barzman, *The First Ladies* (New York: Cowles Book Co., 1970), pp. 45–46; some of the Louis XVI furniture is still extant, at the Monroe Law Office and Museum, Fredericksburg, Virginia; Bassett, p. 56; Ingrid W. Hoes to author, Apr. 2, 1976.

2. James Monroe to S. L. Gouverneur, Dec. 29, 1826, and Sept. 23, 1830, New York Public Library; see Owsel Tenkin, *The Falling Sickness: A History of Epilepsy* (Baltimore: Johns Hopkins Press, 1971); author conversation with Ann Scherer, National Epilepsy Foundation, Apr. 6, 1983; for symptoms of James Madison's epileptic condition, see Moore, pp. 38–39; Ammons, p. 673; Cresson, pp. 374–376; Whitton, p. 72; Mrs. Monroe had suffered in London from severe rheumatism, see Cresson, p. 205.

As late as nine months after she became the Lady, none of the Washington society women—except for Dolley Madison's sister, Anna Cutts—had even seen Elizabeth Monroe—see Margaret Bayard Smith, *The First Forty Years of Washington Society* (New York: F. Ungar, 1965), p. 141. As Lady, Mrs. Monroe was evidently hit by the yellow-fever outbreaks in Washington in Oct. 1820 and Oct. 1821. She was also absent from public view in the late spring of 1820 and Nov. 1820—see John Quincy Adams's diary, May 19, 1820, and Nov. 21, 1820, as cited in Esther Singleton, *The Story of the White House* (New York: McClure & Company, 1907), Vol. 1, p. 143. She was ill and out of public view in Dec. 1823—see Andrew Jackson to Rachel Jackson, Dec. 28, 1823, as cited in Mary French Caldwell, *General Jackson's Lady* (Nashville: Ladies Hermitage Association, 1936), p. 387, and also for part of the winter of 1824. Her "chronic disease" in fact prevented the Monroes' departure by two weeks, from the city to their relatively nearby home, at the end of the president's term, see Cresson, pp. 470–71.

3. Ammon, pp. 405–7; Burt and Jane McConnell, *Our First Ladies* (New York: Thomas Y. Crowell, 1964), p. 62; Morgan, p. 411; Gerson, p. 74; Smith, *Forty Years*, p. 141; Furman, p. 86; Louisa Adams to John Adams, Jan 1, 1818, and Mar. 2, 1818, Adams Papers, Massachusetts Historical Society, as cited in Ammon, p. 401; Harrison Gray Otis, Jan. 27, 1821, Otis Papers, Massachusetts Historical Society.

4. *Letters of Mrs. Adams* (1840), p. LXI; Moore, p. 468.

5. John Quincy Adams diary entries, as quoted in Singleton, pp. 133, 137, and Cresson, p. 358.

6. Mrs. Seaton diary entry of Dec. 18, 1819, quoted in Singleton, p. 141; John Quincy Adams's diary quoted in Cresson, pp. 362–63.

7. Richards, pp. 267–68, 276; AA to John Quincy Adams, Feb. 27, 1814 and Nov. 5, 1816, AA to Louisa Adams, Nov. 24, 1818, as quoted in Withey, p. 313.

8. Cresson, p. 356; Ammons, p. 542, quotes August Levasseur on Mrs. Monroe; Elizabeth Monroe and Rachel Jackson met in Dec. 1815—see Caldwell, pp. 378, 387–88, 396, 513.

9. Whitton, pp. 89–90; Barzman, p. 47; Ross, p. 29; George Hay to Elizabeth Monroe, Feb. 15, 1815, James Monroe Papers, LC. Except for her signature on some legal papers, now at the Monroe Law Office and Museum in Fredericksburg, Virginia, not one scrap of Elizabeth Monroe's handwriting is extant. Not one letter of hers survived. Like Jefferson, Monroe was left a widower, and he probably destroyed his wife's correspondence to protect her privacy. There is not even an extant direct quote of hers in any sources of the period.

10. Shepard, pp. 206–8, 211, 214, 226, 239; Andrew Jackson to Brig.-Gen. John Coffee, Dec. 27, 1824, and Jan. 23, 1825, as quoted in Caldwell, pp. 394–96; Nagel, p. 61.

11. ". . . SUCH EXPECTATIONS . . ."

1. Louisa Adams's letters, diary entries, and autobiographical notes are excerpted from passages in Shepard, pp. 56–57, 227, 257, 260, 267–69, 287–88, 292, 303–4; reference to Louisa Adams discovering pornographic book is from Nagel, p. 115; Louisa Adams quote on "popular governments . . ." cited in Perry Wolff, A Tour of the White House with Mrs. John F. Kennedy (New York: Doubleday, 1962), p. 171.

2. For background material used on Rachel Jackson, see Caldwell, pp. 8, 13, 24–25, 173, 288; excerpted quotes from Andrew and Rachel Jackson letters are from Caldwell, pp. 253, 279, 314, 379, 383, 414, 421, 433; on Rachel Jackson in New Orleans, pp. 328–31; pamphlet of speech delivered by attorney Thomas Kennedy at Jackson meeting, Aug. 4, 1827, quoted in Caldwell, pp. 411–12; for the most objective presentation of facts regarding Rachel Jackson's unwitting "bigamy," see Robert Vincent Remini, Andrew Jackson and the Cause of American Empire, 1767–1821 (New York: Harper & Row, 1977), pp. 41–45, 58–68; Julia Dent Grant, Memoirs (New York: G. P. Putnam's Sons, 1975), p. 47; Mary Clemmer (Ames), Ten Years In Washington (Hartford: Hartford Publishing Co., 1882), pp. 214, 216.

12. THE FEVER

1. The first record of DPM dining with Martin Van Buren is on Jan. 24, 1837, but he evidently called on her earlier—see Clark, pp. 283, 286–87, 371; Anthony, pp. 359, 384; Cutts, pp. 200–202; Arnett, p. 342.

2. John Niven, Martin Van Buren: The Romantic Age of American Politics (New York: Oxford University Press, 1983), p. 23, 479; The Albany Argus, Feb. 8, 1819; Angelica Van Buren to DPM, Mar. 8, 1839, cited in Clark, p. 292; Angelica Van Buren to Rebecca Coles Singleton, Mar. 4, 1839, and Angelica Van Buren envelope letter of Dec. 16, 1839, using presidential free frank, both from Angelica Van Buren letterpress book, LC; Langford, p. 340. Almost nothing was known of Hannah Van Buren—even by her children. When her son John's wife had a daughter, he wrote his father, ". . . we all agree to name it after my mother. Was her name Anna or Hannah?," Niven, p. 495.

3. Seale, p. 213; Langford, pp. 342–44; Christine Sadler, *Children in the White House* (New York: G. P. Putnam's Sons, 1967), p. 103.

4. Seale, p. 247; copy of the group engraving in files of Smithsonian Institution, Museum of American History, Division of Political History; Ogle speech was delivered on Apr. 4, 1840, and soon after printed and widely distributed in pamphlet form; Robert Seager, *And Tyler Too* (New York: McGraw-Hill, 1962), pp. 34–39.

5. Mary Todd to Mercy Ann Levering, Dec. 1840, *Journal of Rutgers University*, Apr. 1961, quoted in Justin and Linda Turner, eds., *Mary Todd Lincoln: Her Life and Letters* (New York: Alfred A. Knopf, 1972), p. 19; Langford, p. 354; Whitton, pp. 164–76; Seager, p. 40; Anna Harrison to "my dear Louisa . . ." Feb. 10, 1845, William Henry Harrison Papers, LC.

6. Langford, pp. 318–30, 374–75, 377, 385, 393, 395; Clark, pp. 308–9; Seager, pp. 41–45; Anthony, pp. 341, 365, 371; Arnett, p. 345; *The Cooper Papers* (University of Alabama Press, 1952), Vol. VII, p. 313ff; John Tyler quoted in Arden Davis, p. 31; Whitton, pp. 182, 186; Gordon, pp. 204, 206. Although Robert Tyler writes of his mother silently throwing her arms around his neck when he told her of his plans to marry, his wife, Priscilla, later writes of Letitia asking her questions, Langford, p. 378; for Priscilla Tyler's 1842 letter referring to Letitia Tyler in theater, see Clark, p. 311. The only other "Mrs. Tyler" in the family was Rochelle (Mrs. John Tyler, Jr.) Tyler, and she was estranged from her husband; for what apparently is one of the only extant quotes of Letita Tyler as Lady, see Willets, p. 150.

7. Seager, pp. 180, 182–89, 191–201; Arnett, pp. 347–48.

8. Seager, pp. 204–6; Arnett, p. 350.

9. Arnett, pp. 355–58, 371, 451.

10. Seager, pp. 1–4.

13. "THE LOVELY LADY PRESIDENTRESS"

1. Seager, pp. 207, 243–44, 6–7; photo of Mrs. Tyler became part of the private Rinehart Collection, now in LC; Gerson, p. 195.

2. Furman, p. 129; Ross, *Daughters*, p. 33; Jessie Benton Fremont, *Souvenirs of My Time* (Boston: D. Lothrop and Co., 1887), p. 99.

3. Seager, pp. 340, 244, 249; Margaret Gardiner to Julia Gardiner Tyler (hereafter cited as JGT), Oct. 31, 1844, and Feb. 27, 1845, JGT to Juliana Gardiner, Dec. 1844, Gardiner Papers, Yale University; Margaret Gardiner to JGT, May 16, 1845, Tyler Family Papers, LC; Martha Washington danced only when she was younger. There was no evidence that she danced at the many subscription minuets that President Washington did. Abigail Adams hosted a dance for her son in the presidential mansion in Philadelphia, but there was no record of her dancing. Some legends claimed that Dolley danced, but one account claims that she specifically stated that she enjoyed watching dancing. Louisa Adams danced in St. Petersburg and Berlin but did not do so while she was First Lady; Ruth Painter Randall, *Mary Todd Lincoln: Biography of a Marriage* (Boston: Little, Brown, 1953), pp. 15, 18, 22.

4. Seager, pp. 242, 245–46; JGT to Juliana Gardiner, Sept. 8, 1844, Tyler Family Papers, LC.

5. Lucy Marie Murphy to JGT, Feb. 14, 1845; Esther Gibbons to JGT, July 13, 1844; Mary Smith to JGT, July 21, 1845; Juliana Gardiner to JGT, n.d., N.Y. 1844, Tyler Family Papers; *New York Herald*, Jan. 31, 1845.

6. Sophy Burnham, *The Landed Gentry: Passions and Personalities: Inside America's Propertied Class* (New York: G. P. Putnam's Sons, 1968), pp. 75, 78; Seager, pp. 271–77.

7. JGT to Juliana Gardiner, Dec. 6, 1844, Lyon G. Tyler, *Life and Times of the Tylers*, Vol. II, p. 358; Seager, pp. 197, 246–47, 282; JGT, "Reminiscences," Lyon Tyler, *Life and Letters of the Tylers*, Vol. III, p. 198; the cartoon is now in the Tennessee State Archives.

8. Seager, pp. 283, 263–64, 333.

9. Arnett, p. 363; Anthony, pp. 355–56; Clark, pp. 360, 364; Seager, pp. 192, 282, 290–92.

14. PRIM MADONNA

1. Clark, p. 359; Arnett, p. 361; JQA diary entry for Mar. 4, 1845, cited in Louise Durbin, *Inaugural Cavalcade*, p. 57.

2. Anson and Fanny Nelson, *Memorials of Sarah Childress Polk* (New York: Anson D. F. Randolph & Co., 1892), pp. 16, 19, 66–68, 134, 206; Whitton, p. 203; Sarah Polk to James Polk, Apr. 17, 1843, Polk Papers, LC; Seale, pp. 256–57.

3. Nelson, pp. 43, 51.

4. George Ticknor Curtis, *Life of James Buchanan* (New York: Harper & Bros., 1883), Vol. 1, p. 21; Hannah Cochran letter of Dec. 14, 1819, cited in John Updike, *Buchanan Dying* (New York: Andrew Deutsch, 1974), p. 186; Leonora Clayton to Mary Ann Cobb, Aug. 9, 1856, Cobb Papers, University of Georgia, as cited in Updike, p. 190; Updike, pp. 191–92.

5. King was elected to the House of Representatives in 1811, initially from North Carolina, then Alabama, a position he held until 1820, when he was elected to the U.S. Senate, at which time he was thirty-four years old. Buchanan was elected to the House that same year, and they began living together about sixteen years later, in 1836, according to Philip Shriver Klein, *President James Buchanan* (University Park, Pa.: Pennsylvania State University Press, 1963), p. 111; Charles Sellars, *James K. Polk* (Princeton: Princeton University Press, 1966), p. 34; *Sketches of the Lives of Franklin Pierce and William Rufus Devane King*, Democratic party campaign pamphlet, 1852, Main Reading Room, LC.

6. Klein, p. 101; William Rufus Devane King to James Buchanan, April 2, 1837, James Buchanan to Thomas Elder, Nov. 7, 1836, both Buchanan Ms., Historical Society of Pennsylvania, cited in Klein, pp. 111, 119; Elbert Smith, *Francis Preston Blair* (New York: Free Press), p. 238.

7. William Rufus Devane King to James Buchanan, May 14, 1844, and July 1, 1844, James Buchanan Papers, LC.

8. Buell, *Jackson*, Vol. II, p. 384; Sellers, p. 34; A. V. Brown to Sarah Polk, Jan. 14, 1844, Polk Papers, LC (microfilm).

9. Leonard Jones to "President-Elect Lady," Dec. 26, 1844, Polk Papers, LC (microfilm); Nelson, pp. 49, 81, 92–93; Sellers, p. 308; Jimmie Lou Sparkman Claxton, *88 Years with Sarah Polk* (New York: Vantage Press, 1972), p. 182.

10. Whitton, p. 207; Seale, p. 265; Sellers, p. 307.

11. Unidentified and undated clipping in Polk Papers, LC (microfilm); Nelson, p. 93.

12. Seager, pp. 333, 337; JGT to Alex Gardiner, March 3, 1846, Tyler Family Papers.

13. Colman, pp. 214–15; Nelson, p. 105; Furman, p. 138; Claxton, p. 89; Seale, p. 263.

14. DPM to G. L. Depeyster, Feb. 11, 1848, cited in Clark, p. 407; Nelson, p. 251.

15. Nelson, pp. 48–49, 39.

16. James Buchanan to Sarah Polk, July 4, 1847, as cited in Nelson, p. 108; George Dallas to Mrs. Dallas, Feb. 16, 1845, Dallas Papers; Nelson, pp. 94–95, 96, 114; benefit ball, Feb. 12, 1846, Polk Papers, LC (microfilm); Sellers, p. 308.

17. Nelson, pp. 52, 54, 80, 94, 112, 162, 190, 199, 262; manuscript on Sarah Polk in possession of the Alumnae House, Salem College, prepared by Claudia Jack of Columbia, Tenn., n.d.—sent to author, early 1980's, p. 4.

18. Seale, pp. 260–63; Nelson, pp. 103, 116–17, 143, 199, 276, 259; Henry Gilpin to Martin Van Buren, Feb. 24, 1845, Van Buren Papers, LC.

19. *Recollections of Elizabeth Benton Fremont* (New York: Frederick Hitchcock, 1912), p. 15.

20. Nelson, pp. 51–52; Means, p. 80.

21. Ishbel Ross, *The President's Wife: Mary Lincoln* (New York, G. P. Putnam's Sons, 1973), pp. 61–62; Abraham Lincoln to Mary Todd Lincoln (hereafter cited as MTL), July 2, 1848, Abraham Lincoln Assoc., cited in Turner, p. 39.

22. Ishbel Ross, *The General's Wife* (New York: Dodd, Mead, 1959), pp. 29, 34; William S. McFeely, *Grant* (New York: W. W. Norton 1982), p. 24.

23. Furman, pp. 138, 141; Hunt, p. 114; Clark, pp. 258, 364, 370, 374, 389–90, 433; Arnett, title page, pp. 377–78; Anthony, p. 391, daguerreotype of Dolley Madison, Sarah Polk, and Harriet Lane, Eastman House Museum; Sarah Polk on James Buchanan, quoted in *Boston Herald*, Feb. 26, 1883.

24. Nelson, p. 99; Claxton, p. 84; regarding the Seneca Falls Convention and Mrs. Polk, see chapter on Sarah Polk in Betty Boyd Caroli, *First Ladies* (New York: Oxford University Press, 1987).

25. Claxton, p. 118; Clark, p. 427; Arnett, pp. 388, 390; Furman, pp. 142–43.

15. PHANTOM OF THE WHITE HOUSE

1. Seale, p. 282.

2. "poor-white of the wilds," quoted in Barzman, p. 116.

3. The portrait issue persisted well into the 1970's, during which time the White House Curator's Office was sent a reputed portrait of Mrs. Taylor. Author conversation with Bill Allman, White House Curator's Office, July 1982; Margaret Klapthor, political history curator at the Smithsonian, an expert on the portraiture question, resolved that it was not First Lady Taylor. Regarding photographs, Mrs. Klapthor deduced that several pictures of women of the Taylor family found in Winchester, Virginia, in the last home of Betty Taylor

Bliss Dandridge were not Margaret Taylor, judging from the period costumes and dating of the pictures, and Trist Wood of New Orleans, President Taylor's great-grandson, concurred with Mrs. Klapthor—author conversation with Margaret Klapthor, Mar. 30, 1983; Mrs. Taylor's daughter stated that the First Lady "never wished to sit for her portrait . . . and she [Mrs. Bliss] was sure that no likeness of her was extant"—cited in Whitton, p. 326. The engraving frequently used as her picture seems to have been drawn almost like a police composite sketch, drawing upon the facial details from photographs of her two daughters, Ann Wood and Betty Bliss, that don't resemble their father.

4. Holman Hamilton, *Zachary Taylor: Soldier of the Republic* and *Soldier in the White House* (Hamden, Conn.: Archon Books, 1966), Vol. 1, p. 135; Brainard Dyer, *Zachary Taylor* (Baton Rouge, La.: Louisiana State University Press, 1946), p. 284; Barzman, p. 116; Langford chapter on Margaret Taylor; Bassett, pp. 123–24; Arden Davis, p. 36; on Margaret Taylor's presence in Washington for her husband's Inaugural, arriving on Feb. 23, 1849, and staying at Willard Hotel, see Dyer, p. 304; Gerson, p. 245; Oliver Otis Howard, *Zachary Taylor* (New York: D. Appleton & Co., 1892), pp. 299–300.

5. Hamilton, Vol. 1, pp. 110, 116, Vol. 2, pp. 166, 171, 220, 223–24, 241; Furman, p. 149; McConnell, p. 137; Seale, p. 281; clipping, Vice President Millard Fillmore's social calendar record, with sample of listing of guests, including Margaret Taylor, showing that the First Lady dined with him, the president, and Reveredy Johnson, on Mar. 2, 1850—from Charles Hamilton autograph auction catalogue, n.d., ca. 1970's, author's collection; *Maryland* magazine, Winter 1980.

6. Arnett, p. 390; Gerson, p. 12; Gerson does not give a source, but it was evidently taken from an earlier biography of Dolley Madison that persists in the legend that the title "First Lady" was first used by President Taylor at Dolley Madison's 1849 funeral. In fact, in less than ten years, by early 1860, the first reference to the title in print appeared, in the *Leslie's Illustrated*, referring to Harriet Lane. It would become so widespread that within five years not only a western newspaper—the *Sacramento Union*—used it, but a German immigrant visitor referred to Mrs. Lincoln as First Lady in a letter to his wife; Anthony, pp. 402–04; Clark, p. 452.

16. IRON BELLES

1. Hamilton, Vol. 2, pp. 393, 396; Barzman, p. 118. It is not unreasonable to believe that Mrs. Taylor, as a widow, may have burned her personal papers as well as those of the late president.

2. Whitton, p. 236; Gordon, p. 264; Langford, p. 462; Barzman, p. 124.

3. Barzman, p. 124; Whitton, p. 245; for letter of Abigail Fillmore to Mary Abigail Fillmore, see Benson Lee Grayson, *The Unknown President: The Administration of Millard Fillmore* (Washington, D.C.: University Press of America, 1981), p. 31; Seale, pp. 291–92; Gladys Denny Shultz, *Jenny Lind* (New York: J. B. Lippincott, 1962), pp. 239–40; "Señor Spinetto" invitation to Millard and Abigail Fillmore, roll 13, Millard Fillmore Papers, LC (microfilm); Roger Butterfield, *The Camera Comes to the White House: A Portfolio of Historic Photographs, with Text*, p. 35, n.d., n.p., author's collection.

4. Abigail Fillmore to Millard Fillmore letters, see Charles M. Snyder, *The Lady and the President: The Letters of Dorothy Dix and Millard Fillmore* (Lexington: University Press of Kentucky, 1975), p. 30.

5. Container 75, file folder number 1, Bess Furman Papers, LC.

6. Whitton, p. 244; Furman, p. 155; William Elliot Griffiths, *Millard Fillmore* (Ithaca, N.Y.: Andrews & Church, 1915), pp. 61, 70.

7. *Richmond Enquirer*, Jan. 28, 1853; Seager, p. 405.

8. Paul Angle, ed., *Herndon's Life of Lincoln* (New York: World Publishing Co., 1949) pp. 246–47; Randall, p. 168.

9. David Powers to Abigail Fillmore, Feb. 2, 1849, David Powers to Millard Fillmore Feb. 19, 1849, Millard Fillmore Papers, roll 13, Buffalo Historical Society, LC (microfilm); Whitton, p. 245.

10. Franklin Pierce to James Buchanan, Dec. 7, 1852, see Curtis, Vol. 2, p. 69; Grayson, p. 55; Seale, p. 304; Millard Fillmore to Julia Hall, Apr. 12, 1853, Franklin Pierce to Millard Fillmore, Mar. 27, 1857, Millard Fillmore to Franklin Pierce Mar. 28, 1857, Hon. W. A. Graham, Greensboro, N.C., to Millard Fillmore, Apr. 3, 1858, roll 41, Millard Fillmore Papers, LC; Fillmore's second wife, wealthy widow Caroline McIntosh, had a running feud with her stepson Powers after the former president's death in 1874. Caroline became more bizarre as time went on, finally dying in 1881. One former coachman claimed that she was insane when she rewrote the will for the last time, Snyder, p. 363.

11. Whitton, p. 255; Roy Franklin Nichols, *Franklin Pierce: Young Hickory of the Granite Hills* (Philadelphia: University of Pennsylvania Press, 1958), p. 104; Jane Pierce letter, Summer 1852, clipping from autograph catalogue, n.p., n.d., late 1970's, author's collection.

12. Nichols, pp. 224–25, 230–34, 242; Ross, *President's Wife*, p. 182; Seager, p. 353.

13. Jane Pierce letter to Mary M. Aiken, October 1852, Concord, New Hampshire, clipping from Charles Hamilton Autograph Auction Catalogue, n.d., p. 60, author's collection; Nichols, pp. 242, 345–46, 360, 421; Amos Lawrence diary entry for Apr. 13 and Apr. 17, 1854, reprinted in Klapthor, *The First Ladies Cookbook* (New York: Parents Magazine Press, 1975), p. 101; Seale, p. 309; regarding visit to Lee house, author conversation with William Seale, Apr. 1985.

14. Nichols, pp. 416, 482–83; Arden Davis, p. 38.

15. Nichols, pp. 501, 508–9.

16. Updike, p. 219; Klein, p. 272.

17. VOLCANO DANCER

1. Klein, p. 274; Lloyd C. Taylor, Jr., "Harriet Lane: Mirror of an Age," *Pennsylvania History*, Vol. 30, Jan.-Oct. 1963, pp. 216–17.

2. Margaret Leech, *Reveille in Washington* (New York: Harper & Row, 1941), p. 17; Seale, pp. 337, 341, 348, 349; Updike, pp. 197–98.

3. Whitton, pp. 269, 271–72, 275.

4. James Buchanan to Harriet Lane, Nov. 4, 1851, George Plitt to James Buchanan, June 13, 1851, Harriet Lane to James Buchanan, Feb. 6, 1853,

James Buchanan–Harriet Lane Papers, (hereafter JB-HL Papers), LC; author conversation with Edie Mayo, curator of political history, Smithsonian Institution, June 10, 1984.

5. Sally Cahalan, *H. L. Johnston, First Lady of Wheatland* (James Buchanan Foundation for the Preservation of Wheatland, n.d., n.p.); Taylor, pp. 214, 217.

6. As quoted in Updike, pp. 191, 246; Klein, p. 156; Furman, p. 162; newspaper clipping about Sarah Polk, single column, n.d., n.p., Polk Papers, LC (microfilm).

7. Furman, pp. 164, 165; Klein, pp. 401, 426.

8. Furman, p. 164; Taylor, pp. 220, 221.

9. Taylor, pp. 214–20, 223; Wingematub to Harriet Lane, Sept. 1858, JB-HL Papers; JB to HL, May 14, 1858, JB-HL Papers, LC.

10. Whitton, p. 277; Colman, p. 253; *Lancaster Intelligencer*, Oct. 26, 1858; *Lancaster Evening Express*, Oct. 21, 1858; the battleship *Lancaster* was christened on Oct. 20, 1858; Historical Papers and Addresses of the Lancaster County Historical Society, 1929, Vol. 33, p. 107.

11. *Frank Leslie's Illustrated Newspaper*, Mar. 31, 1860, and Oct. 13, 1860; *Philadelphia Times*, Aug. 29, 1886; *New York Times*, Mar. 20, 1857.

12. Klein, p. 415; Seale, p. 349.

13. Klein, pp. 246, 332–33; Historic Papers and Addresses of Lancaster County Historical Society, Vol. 33, p. 101; author conversation with Charles Kelly, Library of Congress, Manuscript Division, in reference to Harriet Lane's beaux, Apr. 12, 1987; Howell Cobb Papers, University of Georgia, Kate Thompson to Mary Ann Cobb, June 8, 1859.

14. Klein, pp. 334, 276; Updike, pp. 231, 237–38.

15. Whitton, p. 279; *Harriet Lane: First Lady of the White House*, Mary Virginia Shelley and Sandra Harrison Munro (Lilitz, Pa.: Sutter House, 1980), p. 28; contemporary account of the prince from Margaret Leech, *Revelry in Washington*, p. 20.

16. Seale, p. 358; Updike, pp. 239, 240.

17. Anonymous letter to Edward McPherson, Philadelphia, Jan. 4, 1861, Manuscript Reading Room, LC, courtesy, Charles Kelly; Langford, pp. 519, 521, 524; Container 75, files 1,2,3, Bess Furman Papers, LC; Klein, pp. 282–83, 53, 401, 414; Whitton, p. 277.

18. Seager, p. 451, 453.

18. SECESSION!

1. Seager, p. 453; Furman, p. 169; Turner, p. 79.

2. Helm, p. 140; Randall, pp. 174, 178, 183, 185, 193; Turner, p. 66.

3. Turner, p. 71. Randall, pp. 196, 202–3; Ross, p. 99.

4. Klein, p. 402.

5. Ross, *President's Wife*, p. 79.

6. Randall, pp. 79, 332.

7. Randall, p. 221; Ross, *President's Wife*, p. 112.

8. Seale, pp. 385, 390; Randall, p. 262.

9. Seale pp. 377, 405; Ross, *President's Wife*, pp. 89, 105, 123.

10. Seale, pp. 380, 388, 409; Randall, pp. 213, 263.

19. MRS. PRESIDENT LINCOLN

1. Colonel W. H. Crook, *Memories of the White House: Personal Recollections of Colonel W. H. Crook* (Boston: Little, Brown, 1911), pp. 14, 16, 17, 19, 35, 37; Randall, p. 321.
2. Turner, pp. 82–83, 109; Randall, p. 249; Ross, *President's Wife*, p. 112; cartoon is in the Prints and Photographs Division of LC.
3. Keckley, p. 101; Randall, p. 221.
4. Randall, p. 346.
5. Seale, 383–84.
6. Ross, *President's Wife*, p. 154; Randall, pp. 244–48.
7. *New York Herald*, Aug. 8, 1861; *Sacramento Union*, Dec. 4, 1863; Carl Schurz to wife, Apr. 2, 1865, as quoted in Randall, p. 374.
8. Randall, pp. 305–8.
9. Turner, pp. 44, 46; Ross, pp. 98–99, 277, 340, 430.
10. Randall, pp. 228–29, 296, 313; Ross, *President's Wife*, p. 73, 337; Turner, p. 200.
11. Turner, p. 200; Randall, pp. 239, 241.
12. Turner, p. 81.
13. Turner, pp. 90, 102, 105, 117–18, 129, 194, 195, 199; Ross, *President's Wife*, pp. 142, 153; Randall, pp. 252–54.
14. Randall, pp. 360–61; Turner, pp. 152, 193, 146; Ross, *President's Wife*, p. 142.
15. Turner, pp. 70, 187; Randall, pp. 239, 250–51.
16. Randall, p. 250; Turner, pp. 128, 135.
17. Randall, p. 368; Turner, pp. 185–86.
18. Turner, p. 111.
19. Randall, pp. 283–84, 291; Ross, *President's Wife*, pp. 176, 297, 112; Turner, pp. 122, 128.

20. A CIVIL WAR

1. Turner, pp. 123, 134.
2. Seager, p. 468; war, regarding Angelica Van Buren's donation of blankets to Confederates in prison is from Emma Edwards Holmes's diary, South Carolinian Room, Library of the University of South Carolina, Columbia, S.C., and Duke University Library, Durham, N.C., Vol. 3, p. 374 (late 1864 or Jan./Feb. 1865); for James Buchanan's concern for Senator King's niece during the war ("*We must win again; God willing . . .*"), see Klein, p. 426; for Anna Harrison's encouragement of her sons and grandsons to fight for the Union, see Ames, p. 219; Sarah Polk information from Whitton, pp. 212–16.
3. John Y. Simon, ed., *The Personal Memoirs of Julia Dent Grant* (hereafter cited as JDG) (New York: G. P. Putnam's Sons, 1975), pp. 34–35, 45, 49, 78, 80, 83, 84, 87, 91, 93, 113, 125; Ross, *General's Wife*, pp. 11, 45, 81–82; McFeeley, p. 27, 92;
4. Ross, *President's Wife*, pp. 177, 221; Randall, pp. 152, 231–32, 298.

5. Randall, pp. 234, 300, 322–23, 327, 341; Turner, pp. xiv, 91, 107, 133.
6. Turner, p. 174; Ross, *President's Wife*, p. 180; Randall, pp. 299–301, 355–59, 362–63.
7. Seager, p. 481.
8. Randall, pp. 324–25, 359.
9. Seager, pp. 482–85; Turner, pp. 87, 341; Ross, *President's Wife*, p. 195; Mrs. Lincoln was away from Washington from late summer through early December, staying mostly in New York, at the Fifth Avenue Hotel, not far from Lord & Taylor. As evidenced by her receipts and mail-order requests, it was probably her favorite store in Gotham.
10. Randall, pp. 331–35.
11. Randall, pp. 343, 309, 332; A long-held legend claimed that a Congressional Committee on the Conduct of War questioned the loyalty of the First Lady, and that an indignant president came to Capitol Hill to defend his wife. Though apocryphal, the story illustrated the support Abraham gave his wife when her dignity was crossed; Rev. N. W. Miner, "Mrs. Abraham Lincoln, A Vindication," Ms., Illinois State Historical Society.
12. Ross, *General's Wife*, pp. 193, 162–66; JDG, p. 134.
13. Randall, p. 253.
14. Seager, pp. 490–91, 505.
15. Randall, pp. 222, 302, 312, 314, 347, 348; Turner, pp. 162–63, 174–75.
16. Randall, pp. 261, 314, 306, 317.
17. Seale, p. 414; Randall, pp. 317, 350, 352, 371; Turner, p. 189.

21. 1865

1. JDG, p. 142.
2. McFeely, pp. 81, 105, 195; Ross, *General's Wife*, p. 151.
3. JDG, p. 133; Ross, *General's Wife*, pp. 139, 140, 142, 156.
4. JDG, pp. 102, 136, Ross, *General's Wife*, pp. 156, 172; McFeely, p. 210.
5. JDG, pp. 104, 109; Ross, *General's Wife*, pp. 145, 168; McFeely, p. 164.
6. Randall, pp. 330, 359; Turner, pp. 142, 148–50.
7. JDG, pp. 137–38, 145.
8. McFeely, p. 211; Ross, *General's Wife*, pp. 178–82; Randall, pp. 372–74.
9. JDG, pp. 150–51; Ross, *General's Wife*, pp. 183–84.
10. Keckley, p. 178; Randall, p. 379; Ross, *President's Lady*, p. 236; Turner, p. 210; JDG, pp. 154–56.
11. Turner, pp. 211, 221–23; exhibition tags, Ford's Theatre Museum.
12. JDG, pp. 156–57; McFeely, p. 225; Seager, pp. 508–9.
13. Keckley, p. 247; Ross, *President's Wife*, p. 246–7.
14. Turner, p. 245.
15. Randall, p. 421; Turner, p. 583; Keckley, p. 208.

22. RECONSTRUCTIVE COUNSEL

1. Lately Thomas, *The First President Johnson* (New York: William Morrow, 1968), p. 319.
2. Furman, pp. 198–200.

3. Thomas, p. 21; Robert W. Winston, *Andrew Johnson: Plebian and Patriot* (New York: Henry Holt & Co., 1928), p. 20.

4. Thomas, pp. 170, 190; Eliza Johnson to Maj.-Gen. B. Kirby Smith, Apr. 24, 1862, Andrew Johnson Papers, microfilm edition, LC. When Eliza Johnson visited Washington in the winter of 1860–1861, it is highly likely that, as a congressional wife during the social season, she came to the White House at least once and met Harriet Lane or Mary Lincoln, or both.

5. Thomas, pp. 200, 223, 230, 234, 238, 242–48, 253, 338; Barzman, p. 156. Legend claims that during the Civil War period, when Eliza Johnson was safely settled in Nashville, former First Lady Sarah Polk came to visit her and her family. See Sadler, p. 166.

6. Winston, pp. 293–95; Thomas, pp. 355–56, 582; Crook, pp. 49, 60.

7. Winston, 293–95; Bassett, p. 166; Crook, pp. 50, 53, 55; the Reverend James Sawyer Jones, *Life of Andrew Johnson* (Greenville, Tenn.: East Tennessee Publishing Co., 1901), pp. 391–92; Howard Kennedy Beale, *The Critical Years: A Study of Andrew Johnson and Reconstruction* (New York: F. Ungar, 1958), pp. 22–23; Thomas, p. 245.

8. Seager, p. 515.

9. JDG, pp. 158, 164, 170; McFeely, p. 168.

10. Crook, pp. 198–99, Thomas, pp. 598, 606, 524; Jones, pp. 391–92.

11. Turner, pp. 268, 276, 295, 345, 348, 356.

12. Randall, p. 43, Turner, p. 415.

13. Turner, p. 418.

14. Turner, pp. 440–41, 447–88, 461.

15. Crook, pp. 66–68.

16. Thomas, pp. 478, 614–15; Crook, p. 69; Furman, p. 199.

17. JDG, p. 171; Ross, *General's Wife*, p. 204.

23. MRS. G.

1. JDG, p. 126; Ross, *General's Wife*, p. 225; McFeely, p. 238; Crook, p. 82.

2. Crook, pp. 81, 85, 88–91; Ross, *General's Wife*, p. 209.

3. Seale, p. 474.

4. Colman, p. 60; Willets, pp. 139–40; Ross, *General's Wife*, p. 208.

5. Willets, p. 138.

6. JDG, pp. 174, 182; Ross, *General's Wife*, pp. 235–56, 242; McFeely, pp. 324–29.

7. Turner, pp. 504–5, 519, 523–24, 533, 542, 544, 547, 548, 556.

8. Seager, pp. 516, 522–23, 536–38; Seale, p. 500; author conversation with Paynie Tyler, Apr. 1986.

9. JDG, p. 186; Ross, *General's Wife*, p. 245; for the matter of "Sylph," a fictional "lewd woman with whom the President of the United States had been in intimate association . . ." see McFeely, p. 409.

24. THE BUSTLE OF POWER

1. McFeely, pp. 296–97.

2. Ross, *General's Wife*, p. 205; McFeely, p. 293–94.

3. JDG, pp. 187, 199; *New York Herald*, Nov. 5, 1870.

4. McFeely, pp. 390–391; Ross, *General's Wife*, p. 241.

5. JDG, pp. 189–92, 199; Ross, *General's Wife*, p. 243.

6. JDG, pp. 183–84.

7. JDG, pp. 198, 193–94.

8. McFeely, pp. 400–401.

9. Ross, *General's Wife*, pp. 66, 225.

10. JDG, p. 173.

11. JDG, pp. 179, 185.

12. Ross, *General's Wife*, p. 210; Klapthor, p. 122; Seale, p. 455; JDG, pp. 175–76.

13. Ross, *General's Wife*, p. 226; Colman, pp. 70–71.

14. McFeely, pp. 375–79; JDG, pp. 107, 175; Crook, pp. 98–99; Seale, p. 456.

15. Turner, pp. 608–13, 617.

16. JDG, pp. 188–89.

17. JDG, p. 186.

18. JDG, p. 194.

19. Corinne R. Robinson, *My Brother Theodore Roosevelt* (New York: Scribner's, 1921), pp. 204–5.

20. JDG, pp. 195–97; Emily Apt Geer, *First Lady: The Life of Lucy Webb Hayes* (Kent, Ohio: Kent State University Press & Rutherford B. Hayes Presidential Center, 1984), p. 231.

25. SANTA LUCIA

1. Geer, pp. 138, 156; Mary Clemmer Ames openly admitted her dislike of Grant as president, and wrote with as much a touch of condescension of Julia Grant as she did of Mary Lincoln. It is no doubt that she liked the comparatively uncontroversial Lucy Hayes—see Ames, pp. 253, 257.

2. Geer, p. 63; Seale, p. 490; Mrs. Hayes was more moral than political. According to Simon Wolf, Kate Sprague—he wrote with droll understatement—"managed to secure Mr. Conkling's absence" from the Senate at the very moment that body was voting on Louisiana being able to vote on the disputed election between Hayes and Tilden. Conkling's absence gave the vote in Hayes's favor. Later, Mrs. Sprague said, "I got even with Mr. Tilden for defeating my father"—see Simon Wolf, *The Presidents I Have Known from 1860–1918* (Washington, D.C.: Byron S. Adams Press, 1918), p. 101.

3. Geer, p. 145; Crook, pp. 116, 121, 127.

4. Furman, p. 219; Margaret Leech, *In the Days of McKinley* (New York: Harper & Row, 1959), p. 20; Gilson Willets, *Inside History of the White House* (New York: Christian Herald, 1908), p. 478.

5. Lucy Hayes to Birch Hayes, May 19, 1877, Hayes Presidential Center; Margaret Harrington, "Lucy Webb Hayes as First Lady of the United States" (Master's thesis, Bowling Green State University, Ohio, 1956), p. 70; Geer, pp. 176, 181; typewriters were first brought into the White House in 1880, see Seale, p. 495.

6. Edith Bolling Wilson, *My Memoir* (New York: Bobbs-Merrill, 1938), pp. 1, 2, 5, 12.

7. Geer, pp. 159, 213–16. Lucy Hayes was especially benevolent toward the veterans of the Old Soldiers' Home, see Geer, pp. 141, 206; Geer's assessment of the liquor ban is excellent, pp. 127, 147–55.

8. Harrington, p. 48; *Chick Magazine*, Jan. 25, 1881; Geer, pp. 150–51.

9. George Tressler Scott, *Illinois' Testimonial to Mrs. Rutherford B. Hayes* (reprinted from *Journal of the Illinois State Historical Society*, Spring 1953), p. 7. The title page of the six-volume testimonial presented to "Mrs. President Hayes" read, "For God-Home-Native Land."

10. Bassett, p. 183; Wolf, pp. 101–2; Geer, pp. 238, 153–54. It was on Feb. 22, 1881—just two weeks before he left the White House—that President Hayes banned the sales of all intoxicating liquors at military installations, by presidential order.

11. *Lucy Webb Hayes: A Memorial Sketch*, (Cincinnati: Women's Home Missionary Society, 1890), pp. 37–38.

12. Allan Nevins, *Grover Cleveland: A Study in Courage* (New York: Dodd, Mead, 1933), pp. 75–76; Cleveland did not pay for Frances Folsom's education, as has been repeatedly written. Her grandfather Folsom—a relatively wealthy man—did—Jack Cadman to author, Sept. 4, 1987.

13. Geer, pp. 167, 169.

14. Geer, 162; Willets, p. 140; RBH diary, Mar. 27, 1878, Vol. III, p. 472, and Hayes family scrapbook news clippings, Vol. CXII, p. 40, Hayes Presidential Center; Crook, p. 239.

15. Geer, p. 175; Seager, p. 457.

16. Turner, p. 694.

17. JDG, pp. 231, 260; McFeely, pp. 472–73.

18. Geer, pp. 159, 185–86; Seale, p. 500.

19. Geer, p. 258; *Lucy Hayes: A Memorial Sketch*, pp. 81–101; Lucy Hayes to Lucy Cooke McCandless, July 19, 1880, Rutherford Hayes Presidential Center; it is perhaps not an irrelevant fact that Mrs. Hayes was the second-to-last First Lady who never left America. Caroline Harrison, who followed her eight years later and died "in office," was the last.

20. McFeely, p. 482.

21. JDG, pp. 321–22; JDG to Lucretia Rudolph Garfield (hereafter cited as LRG), "JDG" folder, container 55, and container 90 and Lucretia Garfield Comer's remembrances of her grandmother, LRG Papers, LC.

22. JDG, p. 323.

23. Seager, pp. 548–49.

24. Collection of the Division of Political History, National Museum of American History, Smithsonian; LRG Papers, container 90, Lucretia Garfield Comer's remembrances of her grandmother, LC.

26. DISCREET CRETE

1. Allan Peskin, *Garfield* (Kent, Ohio: Kent State University Press, 1978), pp. 298, 479.

2. Peskin, pp. 160, 279–80.

3. Margaret Leech and Harry J. Brown, *The Garfield Orbit* (New York: Harper & Row, 1978), p. 281; Furman, p. 226; Peskin, p. 514; that Garfield sought

Crete's political advice is evidenced by a letter of Apr. 21, 1875, when he wrote her of a rumor about Blaine and its effect on his chances of getting the 1876 nomination, "How does this story strike you? If it is true, should it have weight with the people in the Presidential Campaign? Please give me your thoughts on the subject . . ."

4. Biography and printed material, container 90, LRG Papers, LC; Robert W. Sawyer, "James A. Garfield and the Classics," *Hayes Historical Journal*, Vol. III, No. 4 (1981), p. 50.

5. "Rough Sketch of an Introduction to a Life of General Garfield" file, 1887, container 90, LRG Papers, LC.

6. Bassett, pp. 193, 196; "Mrs. Garfield and the Late President's Letters and Other Writings" file, box 90, LRG Papers, LC; Colman, p. 145.

7. Thomas C. Reeves, *Gentleman Boss: The Life of Chester Alan Arthur* (New York: Alfred A. Knopf, 1975), p. 211.

8. "Notes on artists and authors" file, Sept. 3, 1880, container 89, "Memorial Services, March 1918," printed matter in "Lucretia Garfield bio" files, both container 90, LRG Papers, LC; *New York City Telegram*, Mar. 13, 1918; Lake County Historical Society librarian Carl T. Angle to author, Sept. 5, 1983.

9. Peskin, p. 546; printed matter in "Lucretia Garfield bio" files, both container 90, LRG Papers, LC.

10. Typescripts of LRG diary, entries Mar. 17, 1881, and Mar. 19, 1881, LRG Papers, LC.

11. LRG diary entry, Apr. 2, 1881, LRG Papers, LC; Robert Granville Caldwell, *James A. Garfield: Party Chieftain* (New York: Dodd, Mead, 1931), p. 349.

12. LRG diary entries, Mar. 22, 1881, Mar. 23, 1881, Mar. 29, 1881, LRG Papers, LC.

13. LRG diary entries, Mar. 25, 1881, and Mar. 21, 1881, LRG Papers, LC.

14. LRG diary entry, Apr. 2, 1881, LRG Papers, LC.

15. LRG diary entries, Apr. 5, 1881, Apr. 1, 1881, Mar. 25, 1881, LRG Papers, LC.

16. James A. Garfield to Susan B. Anthony, Aug. 24, 1880, James A. Garfield Papers, LC; Scope and Content Note to LRG Papers, p. 4, LC; Allan Peskin to author, May 13, 1984; LRG diary entry, Mar. 25, 1881, LRG Papers, LC.

17. "Mrs. Garfield on Women's Duty," n.d., container 89, LRG Papers, LC.

18. LRG to James A. Garfield, June 5, 1877, LRG Papers, LC.

19. *Evening Transcript*, Mar. 13, 1918; LRG diary entries, Mar. 5, 1881, and Apr. 2, 1881, LRG Papers, LC.

20. LRG diary entries, Apr. 15, 1881, and Apr. 18, 1881, LRG Papers, LC.

21. Leech & Brown, p. 241; LRG diary entry, Apr. 20, 1881, LRG Papers, LC.

22. LRG diary entry, Mar. 11, 1881.

23. Printed matter in "Lucretia Garfield bio" file, container 90, LRG Papers, LC.

24. Caldwell, p. 349; Peskin, p. 573.

27. WIDOWS AND WIDOWER, SISTERS AND BACHELOR

1. Peskin, pp. 592–93.

2. Furman, p. 229.

3. Peskin, p. 598.

4. "Sarah Polk" file, container 60, "Julia Tyler" file, container 64, LRG Papers, LC.

5. Poem, "To the Poplar Tree Outside the President's Window," Aug. 1881, container 89, "Scope and Content Note," p. 5, assorted materials, container 63, LRG Papers, LC; Seale, p. 526.

6. Printed matter, LRG biography file, container 90, LRG Papers, LC.

7. "Julia Tyler" file, JGT to LRG, Sept. 21, 1881, container 64, LRG Papers, LC.

8. Turner, p. 713; Seager, p. 549; Furman, p. 236.

9. JDG, p. 327; Ross, General's Wife, pp. 276–81.

10. Turner, p. 452; Ross, pp. 331–32.

11. Crook, p. 160; Margaret Brown, The Dress of the First Ladies of the White House (Washington, D.C.: Smithsonian Institution, 1952), pp. 91–93; Furman, p. 236.

12. Reeves, pp. 32, 72, 84, 131; Barzman, pp. 193–95; Ellen Arthur's address book is in the Arthur Papers at the Library of Congress.

13. Reeves, p. 159; McConnell, p. 214–15; Peskin, p. 546.

14. Allan Nevins, Grover Cleveland: A Study in Courage (New York: Dodd, Mead, 1933), p. 175.

15. Ishbel Ross, Grace Coolidge and Her Era (New York: Dodd, Mead, 1962), pp. 1–2.

16. Colman, p. 136; Nevins, pp. 213, 300; Marius Risley, The Victorian Magazine, Oct. 1942, "The Yesteryears of a First Lady," p. 21.

17. See Rose Cleveland to JGT, Mar. 20, 1885, Tyler Papers, LC. Emma Folsom and Frances Folsom Cleveland visited Cleveland for a stay immediately following the March 4, 1885, Inaugural, and it is possible that Julia Tyler first met Frances Cleveland at that time, since the Folsom women were personal guests of the president. See Furman, p. 239, and Seale 559–60.

18. Robert McElroy, Grover Cleveland: The Man and the Statesman (New York: Harper & Row, 1923), p. 184.

19. The total amount of money earned by the two-volume Grant memoirs was over $470,000; U.S. Stats, Vol. 24, p. 819.

20. McElroy, p. 184; Denis Tilden Lynch, Grover Cleveland: A Man Four-Square (New York: Van Rees Press, 1932), p. 322.

28. "YUM-YUM!"

1. Grover Cleveland to Mary Hoyt, Mar. 21, 1886, as cited in Allan Nevins, ed., Letters of Grover Cleveland, 1850–1908 (Boston: Houghton Mifflin, 1933), pp. 104, 106, 112.

2. All accounts of events preceding, including, and following the wedding are taken from numerous newspaper articles published between May 25 and June 7, 1886, e.g., the Washington Post, the Evening Star, The New York Times, and the New York Tribune; Marius Risley, "The Yesteryears of a First Lady," Victorian Magazine, Oct. 1942, p. 22; "Frances Cleveland" file, container 54, LRG Papers, LC; McElroy, p. 187; Furman, pp. 241–43; Seale, pp. 562–66.

29. FRANKIE

1. Author conversation with Jack Cadman, Oct. 31, 1988; Gordon, pp. 443–44; Memorial Service of Frances Cleveland Preston; Prints and Photo Division, Cleveland file, LC.
2. Author interview with Jack Cadman, Dec. 28, 1982; Colman, p. 231; Nevins, *Study*, p. 311.
3. Kate Field to Lawrence Hutton, Lawrence Hutton Collection, Princeton Library; author interview with Jack Cadman, Dec. 28, 1982, and conversation, Mar. 2, 1988; Rose Elizabeth, who never did marry, eventually moved to Italy with a wealthy widow friend. The two women were buried beside each other, sharing a cemetery plot.
4. Author interview with Jack Cadman, Dec. 28, 1982; Ike Hoover, *Forty-two Years in the White House* (Boston: Houghton Mifflin, 1934), p. 15.
5. Prints and Photos Division, LC; Means, p. 268; Colman, p. 170; Memorial Service of Frances Folsom Cleveland; FFC to DSL, June 16, 1887, Series 3, Grover Cleveland Papers, LC. On at least one surviving letter that Minnie R. Alexander wrote out in dictation, she placed her own name with the notation "pen" under the First Lady's signature. It is not clear how long she was employed, or whether it was a part-time position or whether she was salaried.
6. Memorial Service for Frances Cleveland Preston; Nevins, *Letters*, pp. 151, 155, 166.
7. Frances Cleveland letter of Nov. 18, 1887, Cleveland Papers, LC; Elise Kirk, *Music in the White House* (Urbana and Chicago: University of Illinois Press, 1986), p. 144; Jack Cadman to author, Sept. 4, 1987.
8. HHT, pp. 5–10, 19–20, 30–31; William Howard Taft to HHT, May 1, 1885, May 10, 1885, Mar. 6, 1886, and to Alphonso Taft, July 12, 1884, both William Howard Taft Papers, LC.
9. Constance M. Green, *Washington: A History of the Capital, 1800–1950* (Princeton: Princeton University Press, 1976), p. 67; Frank Carpenter, *Carp's Washington* (New York: McGraw-Hill, 1960), p. 264.
10. Gordon, p. 448.
11. Crook, pp. 195–56.
12. Author conversation with Jack Cadman, Dec. 30, 1982, author interview with Jack Cadman, Dec. 28, 1982; the New Jersey College for Women is now Douglas College.
13. Anonymous to FFC, Jan. 27, 1887, Series 3, Grover Cleveland Papers, LC.
14. *New York Herald*, Oct. 17, 1887; Ross, *General's Wife*, pp. 319–20; Cannon, p. 176; Seager, p. 551; author conversation with Paynie Tyler, Dec. 1987; JGT to LRG, June 7, 1887, container 64, LRG Papers, LC.
15. Nevins, *Study*, pp. 309, 311; author conversation with Jack Cadman, Dec. 30, 1982, and author interview with Jack Cadman, Dec. 28, 1982; McElroy, p. 379; Crook, pp. 185–86.
16. Horace Samuel Merrill, *Bourbon Leader: Grover Cleveland and the Democratic Party* (Boston: Little, Brown, 1957), p. 91; Rexford Tugwell, *Grover Cleveland* (New York: Macmillan, 1968) pp. 146–47.
17. Willets, pp. 142–43; Gordon, p. 444; Nevins, *Study*, p. 312.
18. Nevins, *Study*, p. 393; Gordon, p. 444.

19. McElroy, p. 188; Gordon, p. 444; Nevins, p. 311; Lynch, p. 330.

20. Nevins, *Letters*, p. 129; S. Oppenheimer & Bros. to FFC, May 20, 1887, (she did not show up), and Caroline Harrison to FFC, Nov. 28, 1887, Series 3, Grover Cleveland Papers, LC.

21. Carp, pp. 47, 48–49, 101, 102; Colman, p. 195.

22. Nevins, *Letters*, p. 321.

23. Lynch, p. 343; Carp, pp. 48, 100.

24. Lynch, p. 338; Bassett, p. 215; Nevins, *Letters*, p. 117.

25. Nevins, *Letters*, p. 143; lettter of Governor Russell, July 9, 1892, quoted in Nevins, *Study*, p. 454).

26. Nevins, *Study*, p. 310; FFC to "DSL," June 16, 1887, Series 3, Grover Cleveland Papers, LC.

27. Gordon, p. 448.

28. Henry Watterson's *Marse Henry, an Autobiography*, reprinted in Roland Hugins, *Grover Cleveland: A Study in Political Courage* (Washington, D.C.: Anchor-Lee Publishing Co., 1922), pp. 89–90.

29. Colman, p. 194; Crook, pp. 188–89; Lynch, p. 721; Mae West to author, Aug. 28, 1976.

30. Lynch, pp. 359–40. Mrs. Cleveland's letter was carried in the June 6, 1888, issue of the *New York Evening Post*, then reprinted in other papers.

31. Collection of the Chicago Historical Society; Gordon, p. 448; Lyndon Baines Johnson Library campaign memorabilia collection display audiovisual film.

32. Author interview with Jack Cadman, Dec. 28, 1982; article by George W. Childs, *Philadelphia Public Ledger*, Mar. 6, 1887; Crook, p. 176.

30. THE PRESIDENT-GENERAL

1. Seale, pp. 581–91.

2. Crook, p. 215.

3. Constance Green, p. 86; Furman, p. 254; Ike Hoover, p. 109; Stephen, Gwynn, ed., *The Letters and Friendship of Sir Cecil Spring Rice* (Boston: Houghton Mifflin, 1929), Vol. I, p. 104.

4. *Indianapolis Sunday Star*, Aug. 20, 1933; Harry Joseph Sievers, *Benjamin Harrison: Hoosier Statesman* (New York, Indianapolis: Bobbs-Merrill, 1959), pp. 178, 399; *St. Paul Pioneer Press*, Oct. 16, 1888.

5. Willets, p. 141; Harry Joseph Sievers, *Benjamin Harrison: Hoosier President* (New York, Indianapolis: Bobbs-Merrill, 1968), p. 148.

6. Kirk, p. 142. One stanza ran: "For the place needs the boom that my presence will bring/ And my friends who belong to the real estate ring/ Have promised a cottage to which I shall cling/ Said he to himself, said he"; *New York Sun*, June 11, 1890; *Philadephia Record*, June 16, 1890.

7. Photocopy of advertisement, author's collection; Crook, p. 234.

8. Crook, p. 219; Seale, pp. 593–94.

9. Special Collection Pertaining to the History of the National Society of the Daughters of the American Revolution; Caroline Scott Harrison Collection, box 7, folder 23.

10. Author conversation with Paynie Tyler, Dec. 1987; EBW, pp. 13–15.

Whether Edith Bolling was intimate with her northern gentleman friend, or whether she had had an unwanted pregnancy as a teenager—by no means a dilemma confined to contemporary times—is unknown. There is no primary evidence to prove either. Several years later, when married to her first husband, Edith had difficulty becoming pregnant, and when she finally gave birth, there were great complications. Edith did not include her personal medical history in her very thorough papers. Alice Longworth would later privately speculate that there had been a previous pregnancy. She referred to a conversation with "a southern Senate wife" who knew Edith before she married Woodrow Wilson. It must also be remembered that it would be a gross understatement to say that Alice and Edith were not friendly—author conversation with Alice Longworth, March 1976.

11. Seager, p. 555.

12. EBW, pp. 17–18.

13. Julia Foraker, *I Would Live It Again: Memories of a Vivid Life* (New York: Harper & Bros., 1932), p. 135; R. Hal Williams, *Years of Decision: American Politics in the 1890's* (New York: John Wiley & Sons, 1978), p. 56.

14. Julia Grant to Frances Cleveland, Oct. 15, 1891, roll 133, Series 3, Grover Cleveland Papers, LC. In New York City, the Clevelands lived first at 816 Madison Avenue, and later at 12 West Fifty-first Street, not far from Julia Grant, who lived at 3 East Sixty-sixth; HHT to William Howard Taft, Aug. 22, 1891, Taft Papers, LC.

15. Nevins, *Letters,* p. 220; Grover Cleveland Papers, Frances Cleveland from J. B. Burwell, with clipping, June 18, 1889, Series 3, LC.

16. Nevins, *Letters,* pp. 291, 302; R. Hal Williams, p. 66.

17. GCLC, Julia Grant to Frances Cleveland, Dec. 3, 1892, reel 136, Series 3; *Memoirs,* p. 327; upon return to Washington in 1893, Julia Grant lived first at 2014 R Street, NW. Nellie Taft had lived nearby at 5 Dupont Circle when she and her husband were in Washington, 1890–91. Julia Grant moved to 2111 Massachusetts Avenue in 1895.

18. Grover Cleveland file, Prints & Photos Division, LC.

31. HOME AGAIN

1. Colman, p. 222; Memorial Service for Frances Cleveland Preston; Hoover, p. 12.

2. Lynch, p. 418; Hoover, p. 13; Jack Cadman collection of Cleveland family letters; Seale, p. 616.

3. Colman, pp. 228–29, 231–32.

4. Colman, p. 227; Hoover, p. 15; author interview with Jack Cadman, Dec. 28, 1982.

5. All Cleveland biographies written since the early twentieth century accurately detail the cancer operations—see Seale, pp. 604–6, for best summary.

6. Nevins, *Letters,* p. 329; R. Hal Williams, p. 79.

7. Colman, pp. 233, 238; Lynch, p. 465; though only a discreet two-sentence Associated Press story announced Marion's arrival, the Clevelands gave way to public curiosity enough to allow the two-month-old baby to press the electric button that opened the September "Cotton States and International Exhibition," setting in motion revolving wheels that opened the fair's gates.

8. Crook, p. 204; author interview with Jack Cadman, Dec. 30, 1982; Jack Cadman collection of family papers, Frances Cleveland letter from Fall 1896; Colman, p. 225.

9. Grover Cleveland Papers, Frances Cleveland to Grover Cleveland, June 9, 1894, reel 85, Series 2, LC.

10. Grover Cleveland Papers, Frances Cleveland to H. T. Thurber July 11, 1894, reel 139, Series 3, LC.

11. Colman, p. 234; Gilder, p. 213.

12. Telephone interview with Carl Angle, Lake County Historical Society (LCHS), May 1982, letters of LRG to Lide Rudolph, Jan. 12, 1896; Jan. 6, 1896; Jan. 24, 1896, LCHS; container 55, "Julia Grant" file and "Frances Cleveland" file, LRG Papers, LC; Mrs. Garfield lived at 1328 Massachusetts Avenue, Mrs. Grant at 2111 Massachusetts Avenue.

13. Grover Cleveland Papers, details of seating arrangements for Jan. 18, 1894, dinner, LC; Julia Grant to Grover Cleveland, Feb. 16, 1887, Series 2, Grover Cleveland Papers, LC; Harriet Lane Johnston lived at 1738 M Street; General's Wife, pp. 326–32.

14. Sylvia Morris, Edith Carow Roosevelt: Portrait of a First Lady (New York: Coward, McCann & Geoghegan, 1980), p. 149.

15. Eleanor Roosevelt (hereafter ER), Autobiography of Eleanor Roosevelt (New York: Barnes & Noble Books, 1978), pp. 5, 8, 9; Joseph P. Lash, Eleanor and Franklin (New York, W. W. Norton, 1971), p. 72; Morris, p. 142.

16. Hoover, p. 15, Carpenter, p. 295; telephone conversation with Bill Allman, White House Curator's Office, Oct. 12, 1987; U.S. Grant, Jr., to Galt & Company, Mar. 13, 1876, reel 4, Series 2, Vol. 3; U.S. Grant Papers, LC; Edith Wilson, pp. 17–18; note of Frances Cleveland to Mr. Galt, "March 11" (ca. 1890's), "Frances Cleveland file," EBW Papers, LC.

17. Grover Cleveland Papers, Edith Roosevelt to Frances Cleveland, Mar. 7, 1896, Series 2, LC.

18. Colman, p. 239.

19. Hoover, pp. 14–15.

20. Hoover, pp. 18–19.

32. USURPING CUCKOO

1. Crook, p. 242; Margaret Brown, Dresses of the First Ladies of the White House, p. 109.

2. H. Wayne Morgan, William McKinley and His America (Syracuse, N. Y.: Syracuse University Press, 1963), p. 236.

3. Crook, p. 246.

4. Morgan, pp. 47, 49, 82, 122–24, 310–13; Leech, pp. 30, 120, 432–64; John B. Moses and Wilbur Cross, Presidential Courage (New York: W. W. Norton, 1980), pp. 122–23; Ross, Daughters of Eve, p. 52; Willets, pp. 397, 417; Barzman, p. 220; Colman, p. 247.

5. Hartzell, Josiah, Sketches of the Life of Mrs. William McKinley (Washington, D.C.: Home Magazine Press, 1896), p. 11; Ishbel Ross, Grace Coolidge, pp. 1–10; author conversation with George and Violet Pratt, October 1985; Lash, Eleanor and Franklin, pp. 74–87.

6. Terrell Webb, ed., *Washington Wife: Journal of Ellen Maury Slayden from 1897–1919* (New York: Harper & Row, 1963), May 6, 1897, account, pp. 8–9.

7. Crook, p. 246; Leech, p. 444; Willets, p. 143.

8. Container 75, files 1, 2, and 3, Bess Furman Papers, LC; Leech, pp. 458, 459, 491; Morgan, p. 46.

9. Leech, pp. 31, 436, 456–57; Crook, p. 260; Willets, pp. 153–54; Morgan, p. 313.

10. Lewis L. Gould, *The Presidency of William McKinley* (Lawrence, Kan.: Regents Press of Kansas, 1980), p. 193; Leonard Wood appointment, Thomas Beer, *Hanna* (New York, Alfred A. Knopf, 1929), p. 104; William C. Beer to Thomas Beer, Oct. 23, 1898, as reprinted in Beer, p. 211; Crook, pp. 260, 262; Seale, p. 625; *The Christian Advocate*, June 22, 1903; Beer, p. 303; Peggy Anderson, *The Daughters: An Unconventional Look at America's Fan Club—The DAR* (New York: St. Martin's Press, 1974), p. 6.

11. HHT, pp. 50–51, 61–62, 68–69, 84, 125–28, 133, 183–84, 192–94, 197, 212, 221, 240, 393; William Howard Taft to HHT, July 8, 1900, William Howard Taft Papers, LC.

12. Crook, 248; Willets, pp. 416–18.

13. Furman 262; Seale, p. 638.

14. Morris, p. 208; Ross, *General's Wife*, pp. 327–32; Colman, p. 245.

15. EBW, p. 36; Leech, p. 467; Alice Longworth, *Crowded Hours* (New York: Scribner's, 1933), p. 36.

16. Leech, pp. 575–85; Furman, 263; Seale, p. 647; undated letter of Edith Roosevelt to Alice Roosevelt (Sept. 1901), in the Alice Longworth Papers (hereafter ARL), LC, indicates that Mrs. McKinley was not at the Capitol funeral, and that Mrs. Roosevelt visited her in the White House, but it is more likely that she missed seeing her. McKinley friend Charles Dawes recorded that he was with Ida at the funeral.

17. Crook, pp. 268–69.

18. Morris, pp. 220, 221, 224.

33. INSTITUTIONALIZING

1. Box 3, "Edith Roosevelt" file, Edith Roosevelt to ARL, (n.d., ca. Sept. 1901), ARL Papers, LC.

2. Longworth, pp. 42–47; author conversation with Alice Longworth, March 1976; ARL Papers, Box 3, "Edith Roosevelt" file, n.d.; Seale, p. 657.

3. Morris, p. 222.

4. Crook, p. 290; Hermann Hagedorn, *The Roosevelt Family of Sagamore Hill* (New York: Macmillan, 1954), p. 189; Hoover, p. 279; Michael Teague, *Conversations with Mrs. L* (New York: Doubleday, 1981), p. 36; Morris, p. 8.

5. Morris, p. 114; Bassett, p. 253.

6. Ross, *Daughters of Eve*, p. 58; Furman, p. 266; Will Manners, *T.R. & Will* (New York: Harcourt, Brace, Jovanovich, 1969), p. 8.

7. Crook, pp. 280–81; Colman, p. 278.

8. Ross, *Daughters of Eve*, pp. 53–56; James Brough, *Princess Alice* (Boston: Little, Brown, 1975), p. 43.

9. Ross, *Daughters of Eve,* p. 54; Morris, p. 226; Teague, p. 36.

10. Ross, *Daughters of Eve,* p. 54.

11. Crook, p. 287; Hoover, p. 276; Morris, p. 249; Manners, p. 168.

12. Morris, pp. 98, 194, 233.

13. Morris, pp. 259, 270; Ross, *Eve,* p. 58; Henry L. Stoddard, *It Costs to Be President* (New York: Harper & Row, 1927), p. 171; Howard Teichmann, *Alice: The Life and Times of Alice Roosevelt Longworth* (Englewood Cliffs, N.J.: Prentice-Hall, 1979), p. 15.

14. Seale, p. 697; Archibald Butt, *The Letters of Archie Butt, Personal Aide to President Roosevelt,* Lawrence Abbott, ed. (New York: Doubleday, 1924), p. 53; "H" file, box 3, ARL Papers, LC.

15. Morris, pp. 457–58; Mary Wolfskill, first draft of chapter manuscript on "Four Twentieth Century First Ladies," pp. 3, 4, 7 for *Modern First Ladies* (Washington, D.C.: National Archives, 1989); Seale, pp. 666, 694–98, 700–701.

16. Frances Cleveland to Theodore Roosevelt, Series 1, June 26, 1902, and July 12, 1902; Theodore Roosevelt to Frances Cleveland, July 16, 1902, Vol. 35, p. 417, and Oct. 13, 1902, Vol. 36, p. 329, Series 2, Theodore Roosevelt Papers, LC (microfilm); Manners, p. 86; author interview with Jack Cadman, Dec. 30, 1982; Frances Cleveland to Woodrow Wilson, Aug. 10, 1902, Series 2, Woodrow Wilson Papers, LC (microfilm); Frances Wright Saunders, *First Lady Between Two Worlds: Ellen Axson Wilson* (Chapel Hill, N.C.: University of North Carolina Press, 1985), p. 233.

17. Saunders, pp. 14–15, 44–45, 49–53, 70, 81, 85, 89, 94, 106, 114, 116, 126, 130–31, 151, 179, 188, 201–2; Furman, pp. 290–91.

18. Author conversation with Betty Monkman, White House Curator's Office, Jan. 1988; EBW, p. 20; Ross, *Power with Grace: The Life Story of Mrs. Woodrow Wilson* (New York: G. P. Putnam's Sons, 1975), p. 24; Tom Shachtman, *Edith and Woodrow* (New York: G. P. Putnam's Sons, 1981), p. 71.

19. Morris, pp. 242, 260; telephone interview with Betty Monkman, White House Curator's Office, Dec. 1987.

20. Author conversation with Alice Longworth, March 1976; Julia Grant to Theodore Roosevelt, June 26, 1902, Series 1, and Theodore Roosevelt to Julia Grant, June 28, 1902, series 2, T.R. Papers, microfilm edition, LC; Ross, *General's Wife,* pp. 330–35; McFeely, pp. 518–19; *New York Tribune,* Dec. 22, 1902; *New York Journal,* June 1, 1901. By the turn of the century, several other of the former First Ladies had also died: Angelica Van Buren in 1878, Sarah Polk in 1891, Eliza Johnson in 1876, Harriet Lane in 1903. Just fifteen days before Julia Tyler died, Lucy Hayes died, on June 25, 1889.

21. Telephone interview with Carl Angle, LCHS, May 1982; container 89, "children's essay" file, LRG Papers, LC; Jan. 22, 1988, tour of Union Station restoration project conducted by Brian Brady, "Union Station Venture."

22. Teague, pp. 69–70, 72; Longworth, p. 34; Brough, pp. 131–35, 158; Frances Benjamin Johnston collection, Alice Longworth and Theodore Roosevelt files, Prints and Photo Division, LC.

23. Morris, pp. 221, 239; Wolfskill, p. 5.

24. Morris, p. 237, 542; Colman, p. 299.

25. Seale, p. 709.

26. Seale, p. 711; Furman, p. 267; Morris, pp. 239–40; Brough, pp. 68, 103, 142; this has been frequently quoted in numerous profiles of Alice Longworth, in slight variances of phrase—author conversation with Alice Longworth, Mar. 1976.

27. Morris, p. 276; HHT, pp. 233, 269, 276–77, 281, 284.

28. Morris, pp. 4, 237–40, 250, 265; Saunders, p. 243; Brough, p. 142; Furman, p. 279; Seale, pp. 722–23; author conversation with Alice Longworth, Mar. 1976.

29. Ira Smith, *The Story of Fifty Years in the White House Mail Room* (New York: Julian Messner, 1949), pp. 61–62.

30. Brough, pp. 158, 162, 167; Henry Brandon, "A Talk with an 83-Year-Old Enfant Terrible," *New York Times Magazine,* Aug. 6, 1967.

34. THE CABINET WIFE

1. Lash, pp. 89–103; Teague, pp. 151, 154; ER, *Autobiography,* p. 37, 41, 43; Brough, p. 149.

2. Teague, p. 73; Morris, pp. 268, 280–81.

3. Morris, pp. 104, 313, 259, 285–87, 325; Wolfskill, p. 7.

4. Colman, p. 296; Wolfskill, p. 6; Teague, p. 72; EBW, p. 36; Lash, pp. 103, 137–41; ER, *Autobiography,* pp. 41, 48, 55; Brough, p. 56, 161; Teague, p. 157; Furman, p. 274.

5. Ross, *Grace Coolidge,* pp. 22, 27, 39.

6. HHT, 292–94; Manners, p. 11; Teague, pp. 57, 128; Lash, p. 156; see further accounts of the Roosevelt-Longworth wedding in Brough.

7. Morris, pp. 301–2, 311, 331–32.

8. Morris, pp. 4–5, 253, 294, 349, 376.

9. *Buffalo Evening News Magazine,* Nov. 27, 1977 p. 6; conversation with Wallace Dailey, Harvard University, Houghton Library, Jan. 1988; Frances Cleveland to Theodore Roosevelt, July 18, 1908, Series 1, Theodore Roosevelt Papers, LC (microfilm).

10. Manners, pp. 47; HHT, pp. 302–5, 312–13, 317, 323; HHT to William Howard Taft, Feb. 15, 1908, and "Easter Sunday" 1907, William Howard Taft Papers, LC; Willets, p. 480–81; photo identified as "1908 campaign from "Pictorial News Co.," n.d., n.p., author's collection.

35. NERVOUS NELLIE

1. Author conversation with Alice Longworth, Sept. 7, 1977; Hoover, p. 41.

2. Butt, p. 371; HHT, pp. 347–48.

3. Manners, p. 17; Brough, p. 12.

4. Longworth, p. 158; Ishbel Ross, *The Tafts: An American Family* (Cleveland, Ohio: World Publishing Co., 1964), p. 236.

5. William Howard Taft to HHT, Mar. 25, 1909, cited in Wolfskill, p. 12.

6. HHT, p. 324; Furman, p. 277.

7. ER, *Autobiography,* p. 61; Lash, *Eleanor and Franklin,* p. 168.

8. Manners, p. 9.

9. Manners, pp. 11–14.

10. HHT, pp. 325–27; Ross, *Daughters of Eve*, p. 59.

11. Brough, pp. 11–16; Ross, *Daughters of Eve*, p. 59; Manners, p. 16; HHT, 331–33.

12. HHT, pp. 343, 346–47.

13. HHT, pp. 365, 391; Willets, p. 481; Manners, pp. 6, 83.

14. William Howard Taft to HHT, July 8, 1895, HHT to William Howard Taft, Aug. 18, 1907, and June 9, 1890, William Howard Taft Papers, LC; Ross, *Daughters of Eve*, p. 62; Pringle, p. 464; Colman, p. 331.

15. Seale, p. 751; Hoover, p. 237; Manners, p. 168.

16. Hoover, pp. 41–42, 275.

17. *Prologue* (publication of the National Archives), Summer 1987, p. 73; Wolfskill manuscript, p. 14; HHT, p. 369.

18. HHT, p. 342, 380; Wolfskill manuscript, pp. 15–16; Paul Cowan, "Whose America Is This?" *Village Voice*, Apr. 2, 1979.

19. HHT to Helen Taft (Manning), marked as Jan. 14, 1910 (year was likely misdated by Mrs. Manning), box 2, Series 27, William Howard Taft Papers, LC; Manners, p.44.

20. HHT, p. 347; see Ishbel Ross, *Ladies of the Press*; Willets, pp. 479–80.

21. Colman, p. 324.

22. Colman, pp. 329–30; HHT, p. 139.

23. Colman, pp. 331, 334; Lillian Parks Rogers, *My Thirty Years Backstairs at the White House* (New York: Fleet Publishing Co., 1961), pp. 108–9, 111, 125; Elizabeth Jaffray, *Secrets of the White House* (New York: Cosmopolitan Book Corp., 1927), pp. 27–8.

24. HHT, p. 362; Archie Butt, *Taft and Roosevelt*, p. 40; Longworth, p. 167; *Washington Post*, Apr. 6, 1986; copy of letter from Yukinobu Ozaki to J. Roderick Heller, Apr. 15, 1986, sent to author; National Geographic Society Magazine, July 1965; HHT to [?] Copen, n.d., HHT to Yukio Ozaki, n.d., box 2, Series 27, William Howard Taft Papers, LC; in the draft to Ozaki, Mrs. Taft handwrote her memories of how the cherry-blossoms project began, but crossed out her credit to Scidmore.

25. Manners, pp. 86–88.

36. BEHIND THE SCREEN

1. Wolfskill, p. 14.

2. Series 8, Presidential Letterbook No. 5, p. 119, July 3, 1909; William Howard Taft to Horace Taft, Aug. 11, 1909, William Howard Taft Papers, LC; Wolfskill, p. 16.

3. Manners, p. 100; EBW, pp. 22–23, 38; Edith Galt lived at 1308 Twentieth Street, near Dupont Circle. The house has since been razed.

4. Dorothy Brandon, *Mamie Doud Eisenhower: a Portrait of A First Lady* (New York: Scribner's, 1954), pp. 31–32, 47–48; Lester and Irene David, *Ike and Mamie* (New York: G. P. Putnam's Sons, 1981), pp. 27–28, 30–34, 58.

5. HHT, pp. 365, 376, 391; Hoover, p. 42.

6. Henry Fowles Pringle, *The Life and Times of William Howard Taft* (New York: Farrar & Rinehart, 1939), two volumes, p. 543.

7. Wolf, pp. 294, 331, 352; Saunders, pp. 211, 213–218; EBW, pp. 34–35.

8. Manners, pp. 166–67.

9. Manners, pp. 172, 174.

10. HHT, pp. 383–85; Manners, pp. 194–96.

11. Manners, pp. 196–97; Slayden, pp. 156–57; Francis Russell, *The Shadow of Blooming Grove* (New York: McGraw-Hill, 1968), p. 218.

12. LRG to Theodore Roosevelt, Feb. 22, 1911, and Mar. 25, 1911, Series 1, Theodore Roosevelt to LRG, Apr. 19, 1911, Series 3A, Theodore Roosevelt Papers, microfilm edition, LC.

13. Manners, p. 177.

14. Wolfskill, p. 17; Manners, p. 98.

15. Manners, p. 175.

16. Manners, p. 221.

37. 1912

1. Seale, p. 763; HHT, pp. 333–34; Wyn Craig Wade, *The Titanic* (New York: Penguin Books, 1979), p. 432.

2. Colman, p. 332.

3. Robert A. Caro, *The Years of Lyndon Johnson: The Path to Power* (New York: Alfred A. Knopf, 1982), pp. 295–97.

4. Ross, *Grace Coolidge*, p. 34.

5. Slayden, pp. 174–75.

6. Allen C. Clark, *The Life and Letters of Dolley Madison* (Washington, D.C.: W. F. Roberts, 1914). Though two small books on her had been written—an 1886 collection of letters, and an 1896 life story drawn from them—the Clark book was the first thorough biography of a First Lady written to that time. Some of Abigail Adams's letters had also been published in the mid-nineteenth century, but no biography of depth had been written. Lydia Gordon's 1889 *From Lady Washington to Mrs. Cleveland* and Laura Holloway Langford's *Ladies of the White House* were both collective biographies drawn largely from legends and flowery reminiscences, focusing on First Ladies as hostesses. The Clark book broke the ground for more scholarly studies.

7. Conversation with Margaret Klapthor, Jan. 4, 1988. Others were uncooperative—Edith Roosevelt considered public display of her clothing as vulgar, and Nellie Taft's donation did nothing to influence her. She was "coaxed" into donating only after it was pointed out that she would seem "more conspicuous by its absence than by its presence." Lucretia Garfield was equally resistant, but finally gave in.

8. Pringle, pp. 562, 769.

9. Morris, pp. 367, 371, 376–79; Manners, p. 238; Stoddart, p. 21; Longworth, pp. 180–81, 202–3; Teague, p. 170.

10. Manners, pp. 270–71; William Howard Taft to HHT, July 14, 1912, William Howard Taft Papers, LC; HHT, pp. 392–93.

11. Lash, *Eleanor and Franklin*, pp. 168–79; ER, *Autobiography*, pp. 63, 66, 68; Brough, p. 222; Manners, p. 278.

12. Shachtman, p. 27; Saunders, pp. 221–28.

13. Scope and Content Note to Lucretia R. Garfield Papers, p. 4; Ellen Axson Wilson to Edith Kermit Roosevelt, n.d., 1912, Series 2, Breckinridge, O.C., Woodrow Wilson Papers, LC (microfilm); Morris, p.388.

14. EBW, p. 34.
15. Saunders, p. 232.
16. ER, *Autobiography*, p. 71; Seale, p. 769; Isabella Hagner to Mrs. Harriman, ca. 1912–1913, Woodrow Wilson Papers.
17. Sixty-first Congress; 2nd Session; Senate Report No. 506 to accompany S. 124; Jack Cadman to author, Sept. 4, 1987; Hoover, pp. 46–48.
18. Hoover, pp. 49, 52–53.
19. Saunders, pp. 232, 237, 239; Furman, p. 292; EBW, pp. 36–37.

38. THE ARTIST

1. Wolfskill, p. 19; Saunders, p. 244; Slayden, pp. 199–200.
2. Shactman, pp. 71–73; EBW, p. 51; Ross, *Power With Grace: Edith Wilson*, pp. 26–29, 31–33; author conversation with confidential source, April 4, 1986; author conversation with Alice Longworth, Sept. 7, 1977.
3. Parks, pp. 133–34; Saunders, pp. 192, 243; Colman, p. 352.
4. Wolfskill, p. 18; John M. Mulder, *Woodrow Wilson: The Years of Preparation* (Princeton N.J.,: Princeton University Press, 1979), p. 114.
5. William McAdoo, *Crowded Years* (Boston: Houghton Mifflin, 1931), p. 284.
6. Josephus Daniels, *The Wilson Era—Years of Peace* (Chapel Hill, N.C.: University of North Carolina Press, 1944), pp. 479–80, 482–83, 484.
7. Wolfskill, p. 20.
8. Saunders, p. 245; Green, *Washington*, Book 2, p. 161.
9. Green, *Washington*, Book 2, pp. 75, 169; memo of Jessie Sayre interview, Dec. 1, 1925 Ray Stannard Baker Collection, LC, p. 7; Saunders, p. 247; According to Lillian Parks, in the black community, Ellen Wilson was known as "an Angel in the White House"—Parks, p. 130.
10. Daniels, p. 480; Seale, pp. 784–85; Slayden, p. 225.
11. Green, 161–63; Saunders, p. 246.
12. Colman, p. 351; Shachtman, p. 16; Saunders, p. 246.
13. Green, p. 223; Saunders, p. 247.
14. Colman, p. 351; Shachtman, p. 30.
15. Saunders, pp. 253–54.
16. Daniels, p. 485.
17. EBW, pp. 40–41; *New York Sunday Times* Rotogravure section clipping files, EBW Papers, LC; Alden Hatch, *Edith Bolling Wilson: First Lady Extraordinary* (New York: Dodd, Mead, 1961), p. 59.
18. Saunders, pp. 248–49.
19. EBW, pp. 42, 48–50; Ross, *Edith Wilson*, p. 27.
20. Saunders, pp. 251, 257–59.
21. Lash, pp. 184–85, 192, 220–21; ER, *Autobiography* pp. 72, 75.
22. Arthur S. Link, *Wilson: The New Freedom* (Princeton, N.J.: Princeton University Press, 1956), pp. 460, 461.
23. Shachtman, p. 20.
24. Shachtman, pp. 37–38; Saunders, p. 276; Link, *New Freedom*, p. 462.

38. THE MERRY WIDOW

1. Parks, p. 139.

2. Furman, pp. 290–91; Slayden, p. 247; Link, *New Freedom*, pp. 463–64; see also William Howard Taft to Mabel Boardman, Aug. 10, 1914, William Howard Taft Papers, LC; Daniels, p. 487; Seale, p. 791; Green, p. 163.

3. Gene Smith, *When the Cheering Stopped* (New York: William Morrow, 1964), p. 10; EBW, pp. 51–56; the account of Edith Galt visiting Madame Marcia Champrey is from *Liberty*, Apr. 9, 1938; she did in fact use the Ouija board, and had one at home. When Warren Harding died, she had a presentiment of it beforehand—see EBW, pp. 131, 350–51.

4. EBW, p. 61; Gene Smith, pp. 15–17; Wolfskill, p. 22; Shachtman, pp. 81–82, 85; author conversation with Arthur S. Link, Feb. 17, 1988; Jonathan Daniels, *Washington Quadrille* (New York: Doubleday, 1968), p. 96; author conversation with Alice Longworth, March 1976.

5. Shachtman, pp. 86, 93; Frances W. Saunders, " 'Dearest Ones': Edith Bolling Wilson's Letters from Paris, 1918–1919" *Virginia Cavalcade*, Autumn 1987, p. 52; EBW, pp. 63–64.

6. Shachtman, pp. 94–95, 98.

7. Shachtman, pp. 98–106 (all letters quoted are from the EBW Papers, May, June, and July 1915).

8. Daniels, *Quadrille*, pp. 94–96; Arthur S. Link, ed., *The Papers of Woodrow Wilson* (Princeton: Princeton University Press, 1980), Vol. 33, Edith Galt to Woodrow Wilson, Aug. 26, 1915, p. 327, and Edith Galt to Woodrow Wilson, Aug. 26, 1915, p. 336; Shachtman, pp. 106, 107; John M. Blum, *Joe Tumulty and the Wilson Era* (Boston: Houghton Mifflin, 1951), p. 116; Patrick Devlin, *Too Proud to Fight: Woodrow Wilson's Neutrality* (New York: Oxford University Press, 1975), p. 598; Arthur S. Link, *Wilson: Confusions and Crises 1915–1916* (Princeton N.J.: Princeton University Press, 1964), p. 4; Gene Smith, p. 21.

9. EBW, pp. 76–77; Shachtman, pp. 112–113, 116.

10. Link, *Wilson: Confusions and Crises*, p. 9.

11. Shachtman, pp. 118, 121; Teague, p. 169; Daniels, *Quadrille*, p. 140.

12. *Parade* magazine, Jan. 5, 1986, p. 2; author conversation with Alice Longworth, Sept. 7, 1977.

13. Gene Smith, pp. 21–24; Link, *Wilson: Confusions and Crises 1915–1916*, p. 11; *Illustrated Weekly Newspaper*, Dec. 23, 1915; author conversation with confidential source.

40. MRS. WOODROW WILSON

1. Colman, pp. 356–57.

2. Wolfskill, pp. 24, 25.

3. EBW, pp. 124, 127.

4. Shachtman, pp. 130–31; author interview with Mrs. Mary Clark, childhood friend of Tumulty family, Mar. 20, 1988; author conversation with Frances Saunders, Mar. 14, 1988; author conversation with Arthur Link, Feb. 17, 1988; Seale, p. 825.

5. For Harding material, see references to Florence Harding in Francis Russell, *Shadow of Blooming Grove*, and Evalyn Walsh McLean, *Father Struck It Rich*; Teague, p. 169; Elliott Roosevelt, *An Untold Story* (New York: G. P. Putnam's Sons, 1973), pp. 73, 83–84.

6. Ross, *Grace Coolidge*, pp. 43–44.
7. Ross, *Edith Wilson*, pp. 309, 313, 314–15; Colman, pp. 61–62; Hatch, p. 80; Marianne Means, p. 154; EBW, p. 90.
8. Ira Smith, p. 98; Edward W. Bok, *Twice Thirty* (New York: Scribner's, 1925), pp. 346–50.
9. Shachtman, pp. 136, 139, 142–46, 153.

41. "THE SHEPHERDESS"

1. *Washington Sunday Star*, Oct. 20, 1918; Colman, pp. 366–67, 371; Furman, p. 297; EBW, p. 163; Shachtman, p. 158.
2. Photograph of *Quistconck* christening, photo files for "My Memoir," container 45, EBW Papers; Ross, *Power*, pp. 307–8; Wolfskill, p. 26.
3. Colman, p. 368; Helen Brenton Pryor, *Lou Henry Hoover: Gallant First Lady* (New York: Dodd, Mead, 1969), pp. 106–121; Elliott Roosevelt, p. 87.
4. *Baltimore News*, Mar. 13, 1918; *Pasadena Star News*, Mar. 14, 1918; *Kansas City Star*, Mar. 20, 1918; "Memorial Services" file, container 90, LRG Papers, LC; author interviews with Jack Cadman, Dec. 28, 1982 and Mar. 18, 1988.
5. Joseph P. Lash, *Life Was Meant to Be Lived* (New York: W. W. Norton, 1984), pp. 28–29, 33; Lash, *Eleanor and Franklin*, p. 215; author conversations with Alice Longworth, March 1976 and September 1977; Dorothy Brandon, pp. 91–100; "3 First Ladies Choose the 'Most Meaningful American,'" *Ladies' Home Journal*, interview by Lynda Johnson Robb, July 1976; Elliott Roosevelt, p. 85; Colman, p. 369; Teague, pp. 157, 163; Morris, pp. 409, 419; Longworth, p. 269; Shachtman, p. 164.
6. Elliott Roosevelt, pp. 89, 92–96; Teague, pp. 157–58; Lash, *Life Was Meant to Be Lived*, p. 34.
7. Shachtman, p. 171; Ross, *Edith Wilson*, pp. 117, 124.
8. Frances Wright Saunders, *Virginia Cavalcade*, Nov. 1987, p. 57; EBW, pp. 221, 195; Ross, *Edith Wilson*, pp. 140, 142, 137.

42. QUEEN EDITH

1. Colman, p. 372; Furman, p. 297; Wolfskill, p. 26; Professor Joyce Williams to author, Dec. 13, 1985, p. 134; Daniels, *Quadrille*, pp. 156, 175.
2. EBW, pp. 184, 186, 199, 200, 258, 270; Ross, *Edith Wilson*, p. 145; Saunders, *Virginia Cavalcade*, Nov. 1987, pp. 64, 66.
3. EBW, pp. 226, 227; Ross, *Edith Wilson*, pp. 127, 168.
4. Manners, pp. 310, 312.
5. Ross, *Edith Wilson*, p. 150; EBW, pp. 238.
6. EBW, pp. 240–41; Furman, p. 298; Jonathan Daniels, *Time Between the Wars* (New York: Doubleday, 1966), p. 65; Ross, *Grace Coolidge*, pp. 49–51.
7. EBW, pp. 250–52; Shachtman, p. 185; Williams, pp. 121, 125–26.
8. Gene Smith, pp. 60–79; EBW, pp. 275, 276, 278; Furman, p. 299; Shachtman, p. 202.
9. Gene Smith, pp. 81–95.

43. "OUR REGENT"

1. Gene Smith, p. 100.

2. Pencil draft of "My Memoirs," container 50, EBW Papers, LC.

3. Cary T. Grayson, *Woodrow Wilson: An Intimate Memoir* (New York: Holt, Rinehart & Winston, 1960), p. 53.

4. EBW Papers, pencil draft of "My Memoirs," container 50.

5. Hatch, pp. 226–27.

6. Gene Smith, pp. 97–101.

7. "Notes on President's Illness" file, containers I and II, Ike Hoover Papers, LC.

8. Link, *Papers of Woodrow Wilson,* Vol. 33, Edith Galt to WW, Aug. 25, 1915, p. 327; Hatch, p. 65; Gene Smith, p. 97.

9. Gene Smith, pp. 112–13, 119, 287.

10. Colman, p. 375; *The Southwest Virginian,* Oct. 5, 1987; Gene Smith, p. 125.

11. Judith L. Weaver, "Edith Bolling Wilson as First Lady: A Study in the Power of Personality, 1919–1920," *Presidential Studies Quarterly,* Vol. XV (Winter 1985), is the most excellent summarization of the details of Mrs. Wilson's power; Joyce Williams, *Colonel House and Sir Edward Grey,* is excellent on Edith's relationship with House; Gene Smith, pp. 119–25; R.S. Baker Papers, container 7, Series 1, EBW to House, Nov. 18, 1919, LC.

12. Russell, pp. 353–55; author conversation with Alice Longworth, Mar. 1976.

13. Williams, pp. 130, 142–3; Elliott Roosevelt, p. 104; Brough, p. 251; Alexander and Juliette George, *Woodrow Wilson and Colonel House* (New York: Dover Publications, 1964), pp. 185–87; "Confidential Memorandum," Dec. 9, 1919, Lansing Papers, LC.

14. Gene Smith, pp. 144–45; Williams, pp. 138, 152.

15. Ross, *Edith Wilson,* pp. 206, 218, 201, 204–5; Furman, p. 299; Wolfskill, pp. 28, 29; Hatch, p. 228; unidentified newspaper clipping (probably the *New York Herald Tribune*), n.d. (probably early 1920), EBW Papers, clipping files, container 65. Though her brother was doing the clipping at this point, it is unlikely he would have kept anything that Edith did not first read herself and approve of as being worthy of retaining; Gene Smith, pp. 140, 157.

16. Daniels, p. 488.

17. Gene Smith, pp. 136–40, 149, 159–65.

18. Florence Harding's role during the campaign is taken from Francis Russell, *The Shadow of Blooming Grove: Warren G. Harding in His Times* (New York: McGraw Hill, 1968); Samuel Hopkins Adams, *The Incredible Era* (Boston: Houghton Mifflin, 1929), Harry M. Daugherty, *Inside Story of the Harding Tragedy* (New York: the Churchill Company, 1932), pp. 37–38, 58; and scrapbooks of clippings in Florence Harding Papers of the Warren Harding Papers, Ohio Historical Society; Ross, *Grace Coolidge,* pp. 55–56; Elliott Roosevelt, pp. 119, 121–25.

19. Ross, *Edith Wilson,* p. 235; EBW, pp. 315–19; *Washington Evening Star,* Mar. 4–8, 1921; HHT, pp. 362–63.

44. THE DUCHESS

1. All notes for Mrs. Harding's chapter have been taken from the newspaper articles and interviews, and the correspondence in her papers, owned by the Ohio Historical Society, as well as *Washington Star* and *New York Times* stories on her from June 1920 through Nov. 1924. The material in this chapter is drawn from early drafts of a biography of Mrs. Harding that the author is now preparing. For general information, see Francis Russell, *The Shadow of Blooming Grove,* and Andrew Sinclair, *The Available Man: Warren Gamaliel Harding* (New York: Macmillan, 1968).

2. Ross, *Grace Coolidge,* p. 46.

3. Longworth, pp. 324–26.

4. Frances Saunders to author, quoting her conversation with Dr. Arthur S. Link, Mar. 19, 1988; Seale, p. 835; author conversation with Jack Cadman, Mar. 15, 1988; William Howard Taft to Horace Taft, Oct. 3, 1929, William Howard Taft Papers, LC; Pringle, p. 1001; Teague, p. 157; Ross, *The Tafts: An American Family,* p. 343.

5. Lash, *Life Was Meant to Be Lived,* pp. 40–41; Bassett, pp. 346, 11; Teague, p. 159.

6. David, pp. 73, 80–81; Brandon, pp. 121–22.

7. Lash, *Life Was Meant to Be Lived,* pp. 41–42.

8. Florence Harding to EBW (2 letters), 1921, container 20, EBW Papers, LC; Gene Smith, pp. 205–7.

9. Ross, *Grace Coolidge,* pp. 62–66, 70, 71.

10. EBW, pp. 350–51.

11. Pryor, p. 132.

12. Ross, *Grace Coolidge,* p. 79; Grace Coolidge to Frank McCarthy, Mar. 20, 1948, reprinted in *Washington Post,* Aug. 6, 1983, by Richard C. Garvey, Independent Press Service; Florence Harding to Evalyn McLean, Aug. 25, 1923; Grace Coolidge to Evalyn McLean, Aug. 1923, n.d.; "Friday morning, before breakfast," McLean Papers, LC.

45. A SUNNY DISPOSISH

1. General information on Grace Coolidge's White House years, and quotes from her about life there, are from several sources: Ishbel Ross's *Grace Coolidge and Her Era;* "Mrs. Coolidge's Own Story," a sort of mini-memoirs serialized in *American Magazine* (Sept. 1929–Jan. 1930); the memoirs of Mrs. Coolidge's social secretary, Polly Randolph, *Presidents and First Ladies* (New York: D. Appleton-Century Co., 1936); and Grace Coolidge's "Round-Robin" letters to a circle of close women friends, many of which are now in the Forbes Library in Northampton, Massachusetts, or quoted by Ross. Several Calvin Coolidge biographies are used as general sources, including: Edward Connery Lathem, *Meet Calvin Coolidge* (Brattleboro, Vt: Stephen Greene Press, 1960); Donald R. McCoy, *Calvin Coolidge: The Quiet President* (New York: Macmillan, 1967); Claude M. Fuess, *Calvin Coolidge* (Boston: Little, Brown, 1940); Duff Gilfond, *The Rise of Saint Calvin* (New York: Vanguard Press, 1932); and William Allen White, *Puritan In Babylon* (New York: Macmillan, 1938).

2. *American Magazine*, Sept. 1929; *Good Housekeeping*, Apr. 1935; Ross, *Grace Coolidge*, p. 100.

3. Parks, pp. 175, 182, 285; Ross, *Grace Coolidge*, p. 163.

4. *American Magazine*, Sept. 1929.

5. Ross, *Grace Coolidge*, p. 89.

6. See Polly Randolph, *Presidents and First Ladies* (New York: D. Appleton-Century Co., 1936); *New York Times*, Mar. 27, 1927; Ross, *Grace Coolidge*, p. 149.

7. See Calvin Coolidge, *The Autobiography of Calvin Coolidge* (New York: Cosmopolitan Book Corp., 1929); see Grace Coolidge reference in Gamaliel Bradford, *The Quick and the Dead* (Boston: Houghton Mifflin, 1931); Colonel Edmund Starling, *Starling of the White House* (Chicago: People's Book Club, 1946), p. 211; Ross, *Grace Coolidge*, pp. 69, 149, 188, 240.

8. Richard Norton Smith, *An Uncommon Man: The Triumph of Herbert Hoover* (New York: Simon and Schuster, 1984), p. 42; see Irving Wallace, *Intimate Sex Lives of Famous People* (New York: Dell Books, 1982). Mrs. Longworth, from whom the author first heard the story, had quoted it differently in author conversation with Alice Longworth, Mar. 1976.

9. Ross, *Grace Coolidge*, pp. 32, 93, 94, 100; *American Magazine*, Sept. 1929; *New York Times*, Mar. 27, 1927.

10. Ross, *Grace Coolidge*, p. 295; McCoy, p. 161.

11. Colman, pp. 414–15; Ross, pp. 74, 254; *New York Times*, Mar. 27, 1927; *American Magazine*, Sept. 1929.

12. John Randolph Bolling to Chief Justice Taft, Feb. 6, 1924, *Chillicothe, Missouri, Constitution*, Feb. 7, 1924; letters between Grace Coolidge and Edith Wilson, container 12, Coolidge file, EBW Papers, LC; Gene Smith, p. 251.

13. Grace Coolidge to William Howard Taft, n.d., William Howard Taft Papers, LC.

14. Ross, p. 111; Edith Roosevelt also visited Mrs. Coolidge in the White House on Jan. 5, 1926.

15. *Washington Star*, July 9, 1924, *Washington Post*, July 8, 1924; Ross, *Grace Coolidge*, pp. 120, 123, 161.

16. Morris, pp. 449, 458–60, 473; Lash, *Eleanor and Franklin*, pp. 287, 291–92, 282.

17. *New York Times*, Nov. 26, 1927, and May 4, 1925; Mary (Polly) Randolph, p. 87; GC to EBW, July 11, 1924 (on microfilm of her scrapbooks, in July 1924 section), EBW Papers, LC.

18. *New York Times*, Sept. 20, 1924, Oct. 5, 1924, Oct. 11, 1924; as quoted in *New York Times*, May 7, 1927; anonymous, *Boudoir Mirrors of Washington* (Philadelphia: John C. Winston Company, 1923), p. 85.

19. Brough, p. 268; William Allen White, *A Puritan in Babylon*, ixx; Carol Felsenthal, *Alice Roosevelt Longworth* (New York: G. P. Putnam's Sons, 1988), pp. 155–57.

20. *New York Times*, Feb. 25, 1926, Mar. 10, 1925, and Aug. 24, 1928; Ross, *Grace Coolidge*, p. 147; throughout the twenties, *The Sunday New York Times*, *Washington Star*, and *Boston Globe*, among many other daily newspapers, as well as the weekly illustrated magazines, carried photographs of Mrs. Coolidge.

46. THE LADY IN RED

1. *New York Times*, Aug. 17, 1923, Aug. 24, 1923, Sept. 21, 1923, Sept. 23, 1923, Dec. 15, 1923, Nov. 1, 1923, Dec. 6, 1923, Nov. 21, 1925.
2. *New York Times*, Oct. 16, 1926; as reprinted in *The New York Times*, Dec. 30, 1926.
3. *New York Times*, Oct. 27, 1928, Mar. 22, 1927, Nov. 21, 1928, Feb. 24, 1929, Feb. 13, 1929.
4. *Saturday Evening Post*, Jan. 8, 1927.
5. *New York Times*, May 20, 1925; Ross, *Grace Coolidge*, p. 238; Furman, p. 306; Mrs. Coolidge was also a "moving picture" photographer, owning her own camera. She was not only photographed taking moving pictures but filmed in a newsreel as she operated her camera, a sequence of which appeared in the episode on the 1920's "Between the Wars," as part of Alistaire Cooke's *America* series.
6. Coolidge file, Prints and Photo Division, LC.
7. On Grace Coolidge's press policy see Ross, *Grace Coolidge*, pp. 68, 107–8; *New York Times*, Oct. 27, 1928, Nov. 21, 1928; Regarding Grace Coolidge's use of sign language in place of a speech, there were many witnesses present, most of them women journalists. It evidently was the only time she used sign language, however, and she may have learned a few welcoming phrases for the occasion—an outdoor luncheon. As her son wrote, "Clarke [School for the Deaf, where she had taught and later worked] is strictly an oral school. The students are taught to speak and read lips. Sign language is not taught there. I am sure my mother did not know how to use it. . . ."—John Coolidge to author, Feb. 9, 1983.
8. Ross, pp. 187–88.
9. *New York Times*, Jan. 25, 1925 and Nov. 13, 1927.
10. Author interview with Betty Ford, Nov. 7, 1983, Rancho Mirage; *New York Times*, Nov. 6, 1927, Nov. 17, 1925, Nov. 19, 1925, and Nov. 9, 1926; Seale, p. 856.
11. Ross, *Grace Coolidge*, pp. 125, 137–38, 159, 177; *New York Times*, Nov. 21, 1926, Apr. 9, 1928, Oct. 13, 1925.
12. *New York Times*, Mar. 27, 1927, and June 29, 1927.
13. Furman, p. 306.
14. *The Living White House* (Washington, D.C.: White House Historical Association, rev. ed., 1982), p. 6.
15. Nancy Reagan, *Nancy* (New York: William Morrow, 1980), pp. 11–12; Frances Spatz Leighton, *The Search for the Real Nancy Reagan* (New York: Macmillan, 1987), p. 6.
16. Ross, pp. 65, 251, 160–65; Amy LaFollette Jensen, *The White House and Its Thirty-five Families* (New York: McGraw-Hill, 1970), p. 227; *The American Heritage History of the 1920s & 1930s* (New York: Bonanza Books, 1987), pp. 90–91.
17. Kirk, p. 208; Ross, p. 163.
18. *New York Times*, May 14, 1926, May 21, 1926, and June 10, 1925; John Coolidge to author, Feb. 9, 1983; New York congressman Sol Bloom, an Orthodox Jew, and his daughter Vera, were particularly close friends of Mrs. Coolidge's.

19. John Coolidge to author, Feb. 9, 1983; Ross, p. 205.
20. *New York Times,* Nov. 11, 1926, Nov. 12, 1926, Oct. 8, 1925, Mar. 28, 1927, June 21, 1926; Ross, p. 186; Grace Coolidge to "the Robins," May 14, 1924, reprinted in Ross, p. 154.
21. John Coolidge to author July 11, 1983; Ike Hoover, p. 290.
22. Kirk, p. 208; *New York Times,* Apr. 12, 1925, and Apr. 19, 1925; Colman, p. 419; Ross, p. 142.
23. Calvin and Grace Coolidge quoted on women's roles in the 1920's, see Ross, pp. 175–76; Coolidge file, Prints and Photographs Division, LC.
24. Colman, p. 415.
25. Ross, pp. 181–82; 254; *New York Times,* July 17, 1926; Ike Hoover, p. 158.
26. Ross, pp. 142, 225; Parks, pp. 192–93.
27. Ross, pp. 143–44.
28. Lester and Irene David, p. 96; Piers Brendon, *Ike: His Life and Times* (New York: Harper & Row, 1986), p. 56.
29. "Mamie Eisenhower file" MDE to Douds, Nov. 1923, box 173, Pre-Presidential Collection, Dwight D. Eisenhower Library (hereafter DDEL); Lester & Irene David, pp. 83, 92; Dorothy Brandon, pp. 146, 160; Steve Neal, *The Eisenhowers* (Lawrence, Kan: University of Kansas Press, 1984), pp. 66–67.
30. Brandon, p. 160; conversation with Nancy Reagan on Marine One, July 14, 1985.
31. Parks, p. 195; Ross, pp. 97, 110, 114, 143–44; Lathem, p. 93; Seale, pp. 864–81; John Alexander, *Ghosts: Washington's Most Famous Ghost Stories* (Washington, D.C.: Washington Book Trading Co., 1988), p. 63.
32. Ross, p. 110.
33. *New York Times,* Indexes for Oct.–Dec. 1925 and Jan.–Mar. 1926, and specifically, Nov. 1, 1925, and Nov. 25, 1924; Coolidge file, Prints and Photos Division, LC.
34. Ross, pp. 38, 92, 112, 239, 257, 311–14; Colman, pp. 409–10; Lawrence E. Wikander, director of the Calvin Coolidge Memorial Room at the Forbes Library in Northampton, Mass., Mar. 4, 1984; *New York Times,* Jan. 13, 1926, Jan. 29, 1926; author interview of George and Violet Pratt, Apr. 11, 1984.
35. *New York Times,* Nov. 26, 1924, Nov. 22, 1928; Ross, p. 219.
36. As quoted in Ross, pp. 188, 189, 232; author conversation with Joan Haley, Aug. 10, 1988.
37. *New York Times,* June 4, 1927; Ross, p. 109.
38. Seale, p. 879; *Time,* Dec. 26, 1927; Furman, p. 309; Ross, p. 192.

47. MAMMY

1. *New York Times* listings for Apr.–Sept. 1927.
2. *New York Times,* July 4, 1927, and July 16, 1927.
3. Ross, pp. 231–34; Associated Press reports, June 27, 1927, and June 29, 1927, Rapid City, S.D., byline; Grace Coolidge to Joan Haley, Aug, 1925, July 28, 1927, Oct. 5, 1927, Feb. 1, 1949, author's collection.
4. Seale, p. 879; *Time,* Dec. 26, 1927; Furman, p. 309; Ross, pp. 217, 222–23, 235.

5. *New York Times*, Aug. 3, 1927.

6. Ross, pp. 224, 236; Grace Coolidge to "the Robins," 1928 as quoted in Ross, p. 181; *New York Times*, June 1928 Index, and Jan. 16, 1929, Jan. 17, 1929, Jan. 20, 1929.

7. Ross, *Grace Coolidge*, pp. 241–42, 222, 226, 238, 244; Grace Coolidge to "Members of the Charmed Circle," Mar. 10, 1929, Forbes Library, Northampton, Mass.

8. Herbert Collins, *President on Wheels* (New York: Bonanza, 1971), p. 147; *New York Times*, Sept. 4, 1927; clipping files, box 65, EBW Papers, LC; Ross, *Edith Wilson*, pp. 257–61, 324, 263; EBW draft letter to Calvin Coolidge, Nov. 28, 1924, E. W. Smithers [White House] to Randolph Bolling, Aug. 10, 1927, EBW to Pierrepont Moffat [White House], Jan. 6, 1927, "Coolidge" file: container 12, EBW memoir draft, container 45, EBW Papers, LC.

9. New York *Post*, July 17, 1967; author interview with Jack Cadman, Dec. 28, 1982.

10. Ross, *Edith Wilson*, p. 281; Hatch, pp. 270–71.

11. Lash, *Eleanor and Franklin*, pp. 283–84, 306–7, 311–12; ER, *Autobiography*, p. 148; interview with Eleanor Roosevelt Seagraves, Apr. 18, 1980; Alice Longworth, Mar. 1976; Eleanor Roosevelt correspondence with Edith Wilson, July through Aug. 1928, Eleanor Roosevelt file, EBW Papers, LC.

12. Richard Norton Smith, p. 53; Ross, p. 253.

13. Ross, *Grace Coolidge*, p. 256; Glenn D. Kittler, *Hail to the Chief! The Inauguration Days of Our Presidents* (Philadelphia: Chilton Book Company, 1968), p. 176.

14. Ross, *Grace Coolidge*, pp. 230, 257.

15. Ross, *Grace Coolidge*, p. 253; McCoy, p. 389.

48. SCOUTING

1. The early biographical material is drawn from several routine sources on Lou Hoover, the most thorough of which is Dr. Helen Pryor's biography of her friend. Mrs. Hoover's vast papers were only opened in 1985.

2. Ross, *Grace Coolidge*, pp. 262, 269, 272–73; *New York Times*, Nov. 25, 1929; *Lou Henry Hoover: A Tribute from the Girl Scouts*, ca. 1944, p. 7; Pryor, pp. 111, 141, 144; Bess Furman, *Washington By-Line* (New York: Alfred A. Knopf, 1949), p. 48; container 44, "Lou Hoover file," Bess Furman Papers, LC.

3. Pryor, pp. 128–29, 148.

4. Pryor, pp. 136–37.

5. Pryor, p. 130.

6. Pryor, pp. 133; LHH to Frank B. Kellogg, Mar. 1, 1922, "Kellogg, Frank B.," Personal Correspondence Series, Lou Hoover Papers, Herbert Clark Hoover Presidential Library, quoted in *Prologue*, Summer 1987.

7. David Burner, *Herbert Hoover: A Public Life* (New York: Alfred A. Knopf, 1979), p. 45.

8. As quoted in *New York Times*, June 23, 1929.

9. Pryor, pp. 127, 144.

10. Pryor, pp. 149–50, 155.

49. CHARITY

1. Furman, *Washington By-Line*, p. 34; box 21, Lou Hoover file, EBW Papers, LC.

2. Ross, *Grace Coolidge*, pp. 259, 261, 269–70, 272–73; Grace Coolidge to "Dear Members of the Charmed Circle," Mar. 10, 1929, courtesy, the Coolidge collection, Forbes Library, Northampton, Mass.; *New York Times*, Nov. 25, 1929.

3. Ike Hoover, p. 186; regarding White House recording room, see Caroli, p. 184; *New York Times*, Nov. 6, 31.

4. Recording of Lou Hoover radio speech to 4-H Club, Nov. 7, 1931, Museum of Broadcasting, New York.

5. Seale, p. 900; Richard Norton Smith, pp. 94, 111; Ike Hoover, p. 184.

6. Ike Hoover, p. 197; Seale, pp. 887–88, 901, 911, 912.

7. Ike Hoover, p. 236; Burner, p. 37; Richard Norton Smith, pp. 71, 328; Seale, p. 908.

8. Ike Hoover, p. 258; Mildred Hall to author, Jan. 22, 1985; Darwin Lambert, *Herbert Hoover's Hideaway* (Luray, Va.: Shenandoah Natural History Association, 1971), p. 44.

9. Ike Hoover, pp. 182, 185, 187.

10. Excerpt of letter, Lou Henry Hoover to Mrs. Lothrop, Washington, D.C., n.d., 1923, in Charles Hamilton Autograph Catalogue, n.d. (late 1970's), clipping, author's collection.

11. Furman, *Washington By-Line*, pp. 8–9, 58.

12. Pryor, p. 198.

13. Pryor, p. 197.

14. Pryor, p. 195.

15. Hoover, p. 257; Burner, p. 218; Richard Norton Smith, pp. 32, 105.

16. Hoover, p. 276.

17. Richard Norton Smith, pp. 34, 71, 123, 328; Lambert, p. 50.

18. Burner, p. 21; Wilton Eckley, *Herbert Hoover* (Boston: Twayne Publishers, 1980); author telephone interview with Bob Wood, director of Herbert Hoover Library, May 15, 1884.

19. Ike Hoover, pp. 301–3.

20. All quoted in Pryor, pp. 179–80.

21. Pryor, p. 199.

22. Richard Norton Smith, p. 138; Pryor, p. 211.

23. Richard Norton Smith, p. 138.

24. Dwight D. Eisenhower (hereafter DDE) to Mamie Doud Eisenhower (hereafter MDE), note fragment, 1931, "Mamie Eisenhower file," box 173, Pre-Presidential Papers Collection, DDEL.

25. Richard Norton Smith, p. 328; conversation with Bob Wood, director of the Hoover Library, Apr. 4, 1982; Pryor, p. 189.

26. Pryor, p. 125.

50. ". . . OVERWHELMED AT THE MERE POSSIBILITY . . ."

1. Edith Wilson and Eleanor Roosevelt correspondence 1928 to 1932, EBW Papers, LC; Furman, *By-Line*, pp. 118–19.

2. Lash, *Eleanor and Franklin*, pp. 337–346, 351–55; ER, *Autobiography*, pp. 154–55; "getting the pants off Eleanor" remark is another famous and frequently quoted Alice Longworth witticism.

3. Richard Norton Smith, pp. 131, 147; Herbert Hoover, *The Memoirs of Herbert Hoover: The Great Depression 1929–1941* (New York: Macmillan, 1952), p. 225.

4. Furman, *By-Line*, pp. 133–34.

5. Sylvia Morris, pp. 476–77; Furman, *By-Line*, pp. 126–27.

6. Morris, p. 479; conversation with Jack Cadman, Dec. 28, 1982, and Sept. 4, 1987; the information on the broadcast is from an undated clipping with no publication, in a scrapbook kept by Frances Cleveland Preston, in the private collection of Mr. Cadman. Unfortunately, the broadcasts no longer exist, and no further information on what was said is extant.

7. Lash, pp. 337–45; ER, *Autobiography*, pp. 154–55.

8. Furman, *By-Line*, p. 138; Herbert Hoover, *Great Depression*, pp. 344–45; Richard Norton Smith, p. 28.

9. ER, *Autobiography*, p. 163; Coolidge funeral and ER: John Coolidge to author, July 11, 1983, James Roosevelt to author, April 19, 1988, ER to EBW, Nov. 14, 1932, EBW Paper, LC.

10. Lash, *Eleanor and Franklin*, pp. 355–56.

11. Eleanor Roosevelt, *This I Remember*, p. 75; Lillian Parks, p. 218; Oral History Interview with J. B. West, Apr. 5, 1980.

51. ". . . IN WITH THE RADICAL!"

1. Author conversation with Alice Longworth, Sept. 7, 1977.

2. J. B. West, *Upstairs at the White House: My Life with the First Ladies* (New York: Coward, McCann, Geoghegan: 1973), pp. 13, 27.

3. Lash, *Eleanor and Franklin*, p. 357.

4. Parks, pp. 238–39; author interview with J. B. West, Apr. 5, 1980; author interview with Gladys Duncan, Apr. 12, 1980.

5. Associated Press story, Mar. 4, 1933, New York correspondent Lorena Hickok.

6. Associated Press story, Mar. 4, 1933, Washington bureau reporter Bess Furman; Furman, *By-Line*, p. 153.

7. Furman, *By-Line*, p. 162.

8. Furman, *By-Line*, p. 169.

9. David, p. 98; Brandon, pp. 179, 183–84, 191–92, 201.

10. Furman, *By-Line*, p. 194.

11. Furman, *By-Line*, p. 166; Edith Benham Helm, *The Captains and the Kings* (New York: G. P. Putnam, 1954), pp. 170–71; ER, *Autobiography*, pp. 164–65.

12. Furman, *By-Line*, pp. 189, 170–71; Caro, pp. 297–300, 303–4.

13. Dorothy Dow, *Eleanor Roosevelt, an Eager Spirit: Selected Letters of Dorothy Dow, 1933–1945*, Ruth K. McClire, ed. (New York: W. W. Norton, 1984), p. 332; Helm, pp. 142, 144–45.

14. ER quoted in letter from Edward E. Purcell III to author, Sept. 27, 1988.

15. Lash, *Eleanor and Franklin*, pp. 418–24; Dow, pp. 24, 34; *Prologue*, Sum-

mer 1987, pp. 95–96; Furman, *By-Line* p. 173; Thomas A. Bailey, *Presidential Saints and Sinners* (New York: Free Press, 1981), p. 212.

16. Furman, *By-Line*, pp. 195–201.

17. Furman, *By-Line*, p. 199; for a view of the Lorena Hickok relationship, see Doris Faber, *The Life of Lorena Hickok: E.R.'s Friend* (New York: William Morrow, 1980); author interview with Eleanor Roosevelt Seagreaves, Apr. 18, 1980.

18. Furman, *By-Line*, pp. 211, 219, Furman, *White House Profile*, p. 320.

19. Furman, *By-Line*, pp. 158–59; Helm, p. 178; the famous *New Yorker* cartoon first appeared in the June 3, 1933, issue.

20. Barbara Bush to author, May 1989; *Time*, Jan. 23, 1989; *Life*, Oct. 1988.

21. Means, pp. 191, 201–2, 204–5; Bassett, p. 349; Elliott Roosevelt and James Brough, *A Rendezvous with Destiny* (New York: G. P. Putnam's Sons, 1975), p. 117; John Kenneth Galbraith, "Eleanor the Good," *Esquire: Fifty Who Made a Difference* (New York: Esquire Press Book, 1984), p. 475.

22. Means, p. 208.

23. Elliott Roosevelt, *Hyde Park*, p. 302.

52. POWER AND INFLUENCE

1. Means, p. 190; Archibald MacLeish, *The Eleanor Roosevelt Story* (Boston: Houghton Mifflin, 1965), p. 79.

2. Means, pp. 199–200, 204.

3. Galbraith, *Esquire*, pp. 472–73.

4. Program from Eleanor Roosevelt Centennial Conference, sponsored by Americans for Democratic Action, June 22, 1984.

5. Furman, *By-Line*, p. 176; author interview with Eleanor Roosevelt Seagraves, Apr. 19, 1980.

6. Author interview with Liz Carpenter, Oct. 4, 1987.

7. Elliott Roosevelt, *Hyde Park*, p. 299; Elliott Roosevelt and James Brough, *Rendezvous*, p. 238; Galbraith, *Esquire*, p. 474.

8. Author interview with J. B. West, Apr. 5, 1980.

9. Author interview with Eleanor Roosevelt Seagraves, Apr. 18, 1980; author interview with J. B. West, Apr. 5, 1980.

10. Author interview with J. B. West, Apr. 5, 1980.

11. Elliott Roosevelt and James Brough, *Rendezvous*, p. 46.

12. Eleanor Roosevelt letter is in Furman, *By-Line*; author conversation with Eleanor Roosevelt Seagraves, Apr. 28, 1988.

13. Galbraith, *Esquire*, p. 475; Frances Spatz Leighton, *The Search for the Real Nancy Reagan*, pp. 16, 18; Nancy Reagan (hereafter NR), *Nancy*, pp. 15, 20.

14. Author interview with J. B. West, Apr. 5, 1980; Furman, *By-Line*, p. 155.

15. Author conversation with Eleanor Roosevelt Seagraves, Apr. 28, 1988.

16. Furman, *By-Line*, pp. 278–79.

17. Furman, *By-Line*, pp. 157–58; author interview with Lady Bird Johnson, Oct. 2, 1987.

18. Furman, *By-Line*, pp. 206–10.

19. Seale, p. 931; Furman, *By-Line*, pp. 174, 228; Caroli, p. 192; Means, p. 203; Lash, *Eleanor and Franklin*, p. 471; Joseph P. Lash, *Love Eleanor: Eleanor Roosevelt and Her Friends* (New York: Doubleday, 1982), p. 157.

20. Julie Nixon Eisenhower, *Pat Nixon: The Untold Story* (New York: Simon and Schuster, 1986), pp. 35, 37, 39–41.

21. Author interview with Rosalynn Carter, Sept. 12, 1984; Rosalynn Carter, (hereafter RC), *First Lady from Plains* (Boston: Houghton Mifflin, 1984), pp. 10, 11, 12, 13, 15.

22. Betty Ford (hereafter BF) *The Times of My Life* (New York: Harper & Row, 1978), pp. 8, 13, 17, 18, 20, 23–24, 286; Kirk, p. 234; author interview with Betty Ford, Nov. 7, 1983; author phone interview with Betty Ford, Apr. 18, 1988.

23. ER, *Autobiography*, pp. 167–68.

24. Helm, pp. 151, 156, 162, 175.

25. Furman, *By-Line*, p. 176; Seale, p. 949.

26. Sylvia Morris, pp. 482–83; Parks, p. 251; Elliott Roosevelt and James Brough, *Rendezvous*, p. 68; author interview with J. B. West, Apr. 5, 1980.

27. West, pp. 19–20, 28–29; the full account of the FBI's suspicions that Mrs. Roosevelt and Mr. Lash were lovers, and the subsequent spying that took place, are recounted by the latter in the thorough appendix of *Love Eleanor*; ER, *Autobiography*, p. 413.

28. Author interview with Jack Cadman, Dec. 28, 1982; Frances Cleveland Preston to ER, Apr. 16, 1933, and ER to Frances Cleveland Preston May 6, 1933, box 1274, Franklin D. Roosevelt Library (hereafter FDRL).

29. Ross, *Grace Coolidge*, pp. 289–90, 293–96, 298, 300, 301, 304, 307; author telephone interview with James Roosevelt, Apr. 19, 1988. In 1937, Senator Carter Glass (D-Va.) successfully introduced the bill awarding Mrs. Coolidge her annual five-thousand-dollar pension.

30. Furman, *By-Line*, p. 149; Ross, *Edith Wilson*, pp. 263, 266–68, 272, 279, 300, 324; Hatch, pp. 267–68, 271–72; EBW to ER, May 16, 1935, and Mar. 23, 1940, EBW to FDR, Dec. 7, 1934, and Mar. 9, 1937, FDR to EBW, Mar. 25, 1933, Dec. 30, 1934, Mar. 11, 1937, and Mar. 6, 1939, Randolph Bolling to Rudolph Forster, Nov. 13, 1937, Rudolph Forster to Randolph Bolling, Nov. 17, 1937, box 30, EBW Papers, LC; after some prodding, Edith gave the White House permission to use *her* property. When Josephus Daniels wanted to obtain a letter in the Wilson Papers from suffragette Carrie Chapman to President Wilson recommending Mrs. Daniels as an American representative to a suffrage conference in 1920, he asked the White House to approach her. The subject of suffrage was so still repugnant to Mrs. Wilson that she removed herself from personal involvement, and let her brother handle it—see Randolph Bolling to Rudolph Forster, Jan. 22, 1940, Rudolph Forster to Randolph Bolling, Jan. 19, 1940, and January 22, 1940, box 30, EBW Papers, LC; confidential source, Mar. 14, 1988.

31. Gordon Langley Hall and Ann Pinchot, *Jacqueline Kennedy: A Biography* (New York: Frederick Fell, 1964), pp. 67–68; Kathleen Bouvier, *To Jack with Love: Black Jack Bouvier, a Remembrance* (New York: Zebra Books, 1979), pp. 163, 168–69.

32. Parks, pp, 254–55; Dow, pp. 35, 41; Margaret Truman, *Souvenir* (New York: McGraw-Hill, 1956), p. 81; MacLeish, p. 58; Mae West to author, Aug. 28, 1976; Kirk, pp. 232–3, 242, 252.

33. Furman, *By-Line*, pp. 161, 165, 226, 273; Helm, p. 174; Kirk, p. 250.

34. Lash, *Eleanor and Franklin*, p. 390; Furman, *By-Line*, p. 241.

35. Furman, *By-Line,* p. 253; Lash, *Eleanor and Franklin,* pp. 430–32.

36. Hatch, pp. 266, 272–74; ER to EBW, Sept. 26, 1938, and Mar. 6, 1939, EBW Papers, LC; Ross, *Edith Wilson,* pp. 289, 291–92, 329.

37. Eleanor Roosevelt, "My Day" column, Feb. 27, 1939; James R. Kearney, *Anna Eleanor Roosevelt: The Evolution of a Reformer* (Boston: Houghton Mifflin, 1968), pp. 91, 94; Elliott Roosevelt and James Brough, *Rendezvous,* p. 96.

38. Author interview with Gladys Duncan, Apr. 12, 1980; Americans for Democratic Action Conference and Tribute to Eleanor Roosevelt, June 22, 1984.

39. Author interview with J. B. West, Apr. 5, 1980.

40. Author interview with Gladys Duncan, Apr. 12, 1980; author interview with Eleanor Roosevelt Seagraves, Apr. 19, 1980.

41. Kearney, p. 83; author interview with J. B. West, Apr. 5, 1980; Joseph P. Lash, *Love Eleanor,* xi.

42. Lash, *Eleanor and Franklin,* pp. 520, 522, 526; Jack Lait and Lee Mortimer, *Washington Confidential* (New York: Crown Publishers, 1951), pp. 41, 43; author interview with Gladys Duncan, Apr. 12, 1980.

43. ER quoted in letter from Edward R. Purcell III, Sept. 27, 1988; Elliott Roosevelt, *Hyde Park,* p. 303.

44. Kearney, p. 93; Lash, *Eleanor and Franklin,* p. 513; author interview with J. B. West, Apr. 5, 1980; author interview with Gladys Duncan, Apr. 12, 1980; *Prologue,* Summer 1987, p. 100.

45. Kearney, p. 57; *Opportunity* magazine, Dec. 1935.

46. Kearney, p. 72; part of a copy of the contents and photo of the anti–Eleanor Roosevelt *Racial Distinction Abolished* booklet appears in Jess Flemion and Colleen M. O'Connor, eds., *Eleanor Roosevelt: An American Journey* (San Diego, Calif.: San Diego State University Press, 1987), pp. 130–31; for the offensive poem, see Elliott Roosevelt and James Brough, *Rendezvous,* p. 141.

47. Lait and Mortimer, pp. 38–39, 135; Lash, *Eleanor and Franklin,* pp. 672–73.

48. Lash, *Eleanor and Franklin,* p. 582; Kirk, p. 229.

49. *Prologue,* Summer 1987.

50. Lash, *Eleanor and Franklin,* p. 570; Means, p. 208; MacLeish, p. 65.

51. Lait and Mortimer, p. 104; Elliott Roosevelt and James Brough, *Rendezvous,* pp. 247, 250–52; also see Lash, *Eleanor and Franklin,* pp. 536–54.

52. Author conversation with Richard di Donato, Mar. 23, 1988, and through his courtesy, Pietro di Donato, "My Afternoon with Mrs. Woodrow Wilson."

53. Arden Davis, p. 72; Means, p. 204; author interview with J. B. West, Apr. 5, 1980.

53. 1940

1. Author interview with J. B. West, Apr. 5, 1980.

2. Jacqueline Kennedy Onassis to author, Dec. 3, 1987.

3. Hall and Pinchot, p. 70.

4. BF, *Times of My Life,* pp. 27–32; BF, *Glad Awakening,* p. 30.

5. *Rendezvous*, p. 194.

6. Means, p. 202; Eisenhower, *Pat Nixon*, pp. 42–43, 46–47, 52, 58, 63, 65, 68.

7. Furman, *By-Line*, p. 280; Dow, pp. 62, 66, 68, 104, 116; Ross, *Edith Wilson*, p. 299; Lash, *Eleanor and Franklin*, pp. 621–25; Alice Longworth—although present at the convention as a Republican news commentator—was also given a seat in the VIP boxes, near Mrs. Wilson, and among the list of others she noted was Mayor Kelley, but she would not have known Edie Davis—author conversation with Alice Longworth, Sept. 7, 1977; Nancy Reagan to author, through Mary Gordon, May 1988.

8. See Nellie Taft references in *New York Times Index, 1940*; Jack Cadman to author, Sept. 4, 1987.

9. Lash, *Eleanor and Franklin*, pp. 629, 631; *Washington Post*, Jan. 4, 1982.

10. Dow, p. 132.

11. NBC General Manager K. H. Berkeley to EBW, Sept. 27, 1939, "N" file, box 27, EBW Papers, LC.

12. EBW to ER, Sept. 7, 1941, ER to EBW, Sept. 19, 1941, box 1627, FDRL.

13. James Roosevelt, as quoted in Galbraith, *Esquire*, p. 475.

14. Lash, *Eleanor and Franklin*, pp. 636, 638, 640; Mildred Hall to author, Jan. 27, 1985; Pryor, p. 222; Richard Norton Smith, pp. 275, 287, 297.

15. See Nellie Taft references in *New York Times Index, 1940–1942*; Ross, *Grace Coolidge*, pp. 29, 308–9, 313–14, 317.

16. GC to ER, Feb. 4, 1941, ER to GC, Feb. 10, 1941, box 1595, FDRL; Ross, *Grace Coolidge*, p. 315.

17. NR, *Nancy*, pp. 41–42; Nancy Reagan to author through Mary Gordon, May 10, 1988.

18. J. B. West, p. 34; Stella K. Hershan, *A Woman of Quality* (New York: Crown Publishers, 1970), p. 166.

19. ER radio broadcast, Dec. 7, 1941, cited in Lash, *Eleanor and Franklin*, p. 647.

20. Ross, *Edith Wilson*, p. 299.

21. Dow, p. 133.

54. "OUR ELEANOR"

1. Parks, p. 270.

2. Lash, *Eleanor and Franklin*, pp. 651–52; Helm, p. 212.

3. Helm, pp. 207–8, 234.

4. Helm, pp. 236–38.

5. Lash, *Eleanor and Franklin*, p. 680; *Prologue*, Summer 1987, p. 97; Lash, *Love Eleanor*, p. 458.

6. Means, p. 202; Rexford Tugwell, *Roosevelt's Revolution* (New York: Macmillan, 1977), pp. 203–4.

7. Author interview with J. B. West, Apr. 5, 1980.

8. Lash, *Eleanor and Franklin*, pp. 655–57.

9. Lash, *Eleanor and Franklin*, pp. 661–68.

10. D. L. Kimball, *I Remember Mamie* (Fayette, Ia.: Trends and Events, 1981), p. 129; Elliott Roosevelt to author, Apr. 4, 1988; author interview with

Milton Eisenhower, Apr. 1, 1984; Means, p. 258; Mamie Doud Eisenhower (hereafter MDE) file folders 3 and 4, box 173, Pre-Presidential Papers, (hereafter PPP), DDEL; Dwight D. Eisenhower, *Letters to Mamie*, edited with commentary by John S. D. Eisenhower (New York: Doubleday, 1978), pp. 102, 104.

11. John S. D. Eisenhower, *Letters to Mamie*, pp. 104–5, 155.

12. *New York Times*, Jan. 1, 1978; *Letters to Mamie*, pp. 11–12.

13. DDE to MDE, Aug. 24, 1942; DDE to MDE, Dec. 3, 1944; DDE to MDE, Sept. 1, 1945, DDE to MDE, Aug. 23, 1942, all copies in PPP, DDEL—see sections for these periods also in *Letters to Mamie*.

14. DDE to MDE, Apr. 24, 1943, and MDE to DDE, Apr. 24, 1943, file 7, DDE to MDE, July 1, 1943, and July 14, 1943, file 6, box 173, PPP, DDEL.

15. DDE to MDE, Sept. 8, 1943, file 6, box 173, PPP, DDEL.

16. Means, p. 211; Dow, p. 138.

17. Lash, *Eleanor and Franklin*, pp. 683, 685, 687, 688, 690–91, 695.

18. Author conversation with William Howard Taft III, Mar. 1988; Ross, *The Tafts: An American Family*, p. 392.

19. Ross, *Grace Coolidge*, pp. 314–17, Nancy Reagan to author, Apr. 27, 1988; Leighton, pp. 18–21, 26, 27; NR, *Nancy*, pp. 21, 59–66; Leamer, pp. 45, 61; Barbara Bush to author, May 30, 1989; *Time*, Jan. 23, 1989; *Life*, Oct. 1988.

20. *Washington Post*, Apr. 28, 1988.

21. Ross, *Edith Wilson*, pp. 300–301; Marie Forrest to EBW, Jan. 25, 1944, "N" file, box 27, EBW Papers, LC; Arthur Schlesinger, Jr., quote on ER and the ERA, from *Washington Post*, Oct. 15, 1984, p. c4.

22. Julie Nixon Eisenhower, *Pat Nixon*, pp. 73, 75, 79, 82.

23. Steven Birmingham, *Jacqueline Bouvier Kennedy Onassis* (New York: Grossett & Dunlap, 1978), pp. 51–52, 46; *People*, n.d. (article on Janet Auchincloss reminiscences of Hammersmith Farm), author's files.

24. RC, *First Lady from Plains*, pp. 19–23.

25. BF, *Times*, pp. 33–43; BF, *Awakening*, p. 32.

26. Barbara Bush to author, May 30, 1989; *Time*, Jan. 23, 1989; *Life*, Oct., 1988.

27. Alden Hatch, *Red Carpet for Mamie* (New York: Henry Holt, 1954), p. 183; author interview with Milton Eisenhower, Apr. 1, 1984; *Washington Post*, Aug. 2, 1942.

28. Author interview with Mary Jane McCaffree Monroe, May 31, 1988; author interview with Barbara Eisenhower (Foltz), Oct. 22, 1983; Merle Miller, *Ike the Soldier: As They Knew Him* (New York: G. P. Putnam's Sons, 1987), p. 604, calls Ruth Butcher a "formidable drinking companion," a statement corroborated by two primary sources who wish to remain confidential.

Captain C. Craig Cannon to Newton Tarble, Apr. 8, 1946, Tarble to Cannon, June 5, 1946, Cannon to Tarble, July 16, 1946, box 173, file 5, MDE, Jan. to Oct. 1946, PPP, DDEL.

Captain C. Craig Cannon, who looked after the Eisenhowers' requests during this period, later wrote to a liquor distributor that "Mrs. Eisenhower has been informed that her preferred blend of bourbon, Barklay's [sic], is no longer stocked or available in Washington. . . . Would it be possible for such a shipment to be consigned and billed to Washington Distributors for delivery by them to Mrs. Eisenhower." If that was impossible, Cannon asked for any "other means by which we can comply with Mrs. Eisenhower's wishes?" Newton Tarble responded, "Although this Barclay brand has been withdrawn from the market," he would request a Washington distributor to "hold back and earmark a supply of this brand especially for Mrs. Eisenhower. Will you please advise us from time to time when her supply gets low and we will see to it that it is replenished with our compliments."

Although the letters were written after the war, when Eisenhower was back in Washington with Mamie, they state that the Barclay bourbon was her "preferred blend" and was "no longer" in stock, clearly indicating that she had been ordering the liquor since the war. However, the date and the amount ordered make it clear that the purchase of a supply was a result of the entertaining needs of the returned hero General Eisenhower, and not just a group of women playing mah-jongg. If there was one realm in which none questioned Mamie's authority over Ike, it was as homemaker and hostess, roles in which she would be charged with not only ordering foods and liquor, but also keeping all the finances. It is not unreasonable, however, to surmise that since this correspondence was handled through several channels, gossips could make what they wished of "Mrs." Eisenhower ordering the bourbon, and not General Eisenhower.

29. Henry Jameson quoted in David, pp. 160–61.
30. Milton Eisenhower interview, Apr. 1, 1984.
31. David, p. 124.
32. Means, p. 212; Lash, *Eleanor and Franklin,* p. 693.
33. J. B. West, pp. 25–26.
34. Eleanor Roosevelt Seagraves to author, Apr. 28, 1988, with photocopy of letter from William R. Emerson, director of FDR Library, enclosing list of "FDR Contacts with Mrs. Rutherford, 1944–1945."
35. David, p. 123; Museum of Broadcasting recording, June 6, 1944.
36. Furman, *By-Line,* p. 308; MacLeish, p. 80.

55. UNPRECEDENTED

1. Author interview with J. B. West, Apr. 5, 1980; Robert F. Batchelder Autograph Catalogue, late 1970's, n.d., author's files; Edith Helm to EBW, May 3, 1944, ER to EBW, Dec. 21, 1944, box 30, EBW Papers, LC.
2. Author interview with Jack Cadman, Dec. 28, 1982; author interview with Barbara Eisenhower (Foltz), Oct. 22, 1983, and phone conversation, Sept. 1988.
3. Confidential source, former resident of Wardman Park, Mar. 9, 1988.
4. Julie Nixon Eisenhower, *Special People* (New York: Simon and Schuster, 1977), pp. 198, 202; Steve Neal, *The Eisenhowers* (Lawrence, Kan.: University Press of Kansas, 1984), pp. 177–78.
5. Brandon, pp. 206, 222; Hatch, *Mamie,* p. 152.
6. *American Heritage Book of Presidents,* Vol. 11 (New York: American Heritage Publishing Company, 1967), p. 923; Jhan Robbins, *Harry and Bess* (New York: G. P. Putnam's Sons, 1980), p. 66.
7. Arden Davis, p. 74: *New York Times,* Oct. 19, 1982; *Washington Post,* Oct. 19, 1982; Margaret Truman, *Bess Truman,* p. 126.

8. Furman, *By-Line*, p. 308.

9. Furman, *By-Line*, pp. 309–10.

10. Furman, *By-Line*, pp. 310–12; invitation to Inaugural and explanatory note of Randolph Bolling, container 30, EBW Papers, LC.

11. EBW to ER, and invitation, Apr. 2, 1945, container 30, EBW Papers, LC.

12. Eleanor Roosevelt Seagraves to author, Apr. 28, 1988, enclosing letter from William B. Emerson, director of FDR Library, including "FDR contacts with Mrs. Rutherford 1944–1945."

13. J. B. West, p. 59.

14. Hatch, *Mamie*, pp. 184–85.

15. Hatch, p. 198.

16. Miller, *Ike*, p. 604; Neal, p. 464.

17. Furman, *By-Line*, p. 313.

18. Elliott Roosevelt, *Hyde Park*, pp. 307, 308.

19. Lash, p. 721; story related from Grace Tully to Sarah McClendon, told to author, White House Press Briefing Room, Apr. 28, 1988.

20. Ross, *Grace Coolidge*, p. 319; Morris, p. 511; Richard Norton Smith, p. 338.

21. Margaret Truman, *Bess Truman*, p. 250; author telephone conversation with Eleanor Roosevelt Seagraves, Apr. 28, 1988.

22. Elliott Roosevelt, *Hyde Park*, p. 308.

23. Helm, p. 250.

24. Helm, p. 248; Frances Perkins Oral History, Columbia University Oral History Project, quoted in Robbins, pp. 80–81.

25. EBW to ER, Apr. 13, 1945, and Apr. 21, 1945, container 30, EBW Papers, LC.

26. Bassett, p. 352.

56. "I HAVE NOTHING TO SAY TO THE PUBLIC"

1. Furman, *By-Line*, pp. 316–17.

2. Robbins, p. 78.

3. "Biographical Sketch of Mrs. Harry S Truman," Jan. 7, 1980, Harry S Truman Library, p. 6; Dow, p. 165; Robbins, p. 82; Lait and Mortimer, p. 135.

4. Furman, *By-Line*, p. 325; Helm, pp. 256–58; draft of "The Boss," p. 2, box G3, Katie Louchheim Papers, LC.

5. Reathel Odum to Bess Truman, Oct. 11, 1946, with answer, box 4, Reathel Odum Papers, Harry S Truman Library, as cited by Maurine Beasley in her draft chapter on Bess Truman, 1988, courtesy National Archives; Margaret Truman, *Bess Truman*, pp. 276–77.

6. Bess Truman to Mary Paxton Keeley, May 12, 1945, box 1, Keeley Papers, Harry S Truman Library, as cited by Maurine Beasley in her draft chapter on Bess Truman, 1988, courtesy National Archives; see index reference to Bess Truman in *The Presidential Papers of Harry S Truman*.

7. Author interview with Liz Carpenter, Oct., 4, 1987; Katie Lochheim Oral History, Harry S Truman Library.

8. Dow, pp. 157, 160, 164, 176, 204.

9. Reathel Odum to author, Nov. 18, 1983.

10. Margaret Truman, *Bess Truman*, p. 277.

11. Lait and Mortimer, p. 41; Merle Miller, *Plain Speaking: An Oral Biography of Harry S Truman* (New York: Berkley Medallion Books, 1974), p. 237.

12. Dow, p. 184; Peter Hay, *All the Presidents' Women* (New York: Viking Press, 1988), pp. 171, 296.

13. ER to DDE, June 20, 1945, "Eleanor Roosevelt" file, box 100, PPP, DDEL.

14. Captain Harry C. Butcher, USNR, *My Three Years with Eisenhower* (New York: Simon and Schuster, 1946), pp. 870–71, 874–75; Merle Miller, *Plain Speaking*, pp. 367–69; regarding Eisenhower's letter to Marshall asking permission for Mamie to join him when he returned to Europe, author interview with Barbara Eisenhower (Foltz), Oct. 22, 1983; several historians and journalists of World War II steadfastly refute Truman's claim that Eisenhower wrote Marshall asking permission to divorce Mamie and marry Kay, most prominent among them Dr. Forrest C. Pogue, who conducted extensive research for the reputed letter or even documentation of its existence or Truman's claimed destruction of it. He found no evidence of its truth. Robert Sherrod, then of *Time*, later wrote of Truman's equally caustic recollections of his meeting with General MacArthur: "At age seventy-eight, the late President had come to confuse the wish with the deed—something I noticed in a series of interviews with him in 1964. Historians are painfully aware of the fallibility of old men's memories." See Lester and Irene David, *Ike and Mamie*, "Kay—The Myth of the Letters," pp. 127–41. See also Robert Ferrell, ed., *The Eisenhower Diaries* (New York: W. W. Norton, 1981), xv. There was not even a glint of suggestion that Eisenhower ever had any devotion for a woman other than Mamie or that she in any way had alcoholic bouts.

15. *Parade* magazine, July 21, 1985.

16. Mamie Eisenhower 1945 passport, MDE Papers, folder 1, instruments, DDEL.

17. Arden Davis, p. 75; confidential source to author, July 1, 1983.

18. Frances Perkins Oral History, Columbia University Oral History Project; Bess Truman to Mary Paxton Keeley, May 12, 1945, box 1, Keeley Papers, Harry S Truman Library, as cited by Maurine Beasley in her draft chapter on Bess Truman, 1988, courtesy National Archives; Robbins, p. 118.

19. "Biographical Sketch of Mrs. Harry S Truman," Jan. 7, 1980, Harry S Truman Library; Katie Louchheim, draft of "The Boss," p. 3, box B3, Katie Louchheim Papers, LC; Margaret Truman, *Bess Truman*, p. 266; Bess Truman television interview, *Person to Person*, CBS.

20. Katie Louchheim, draft of "Mrs. T," p. 5, box B3, Katie Louchheim Papers, LC; Reathel Odum to author, Nov. 18, 1983.

21. Author interview with Jane Lingo, Nov. 22, 1982; Bess Truman to Mary Paxton Keeley, Apr. 4, 1947, box 1, Keeley Papers, Harry S Truman Library, as cited by Maurine Beasley in her draft chapter on Bess Truman, 1988, courtesy National Archives.

22. *Philadelphia Inquirer*, Oct. 19, 1982; Margaret Truman, *Bess Truman*, pp. 106–7; *Washington Post*, May 11, 1986; Geoffrey Ward, *New York Times Book Review*, "From Harry to Bess," Aug. 7, 1983; "Valentine for Bess," *McCall's*,

Feb. 1975; Clifton Daniel, *Lords, Ladies and Gentlemen: A Memoir* (New York: Arbor House, 1984), p. 80.

23. Robbins, pp. 28, 30, 90; Bess Truman to Katie Louchheim, Apr. 1959 [no other date], and Katie Louchheim, draft of "The Boss," p. 4, box B3, Katie Louchheim Papers, LC; author interview with Jane Lingo, Nov. 22, 1982.

24. Means, p. 241; regarding President Truman's confiding of the deliberations at Potsdam to First Lady Truman, see *Dear Bess: The Letters from Harry to Bess Truman, 1910–1959* (New York: W. W. Norton, 1983), pp. 513–42; Laura Vernon, *Harry Truman Slept Here* (Independence, Mo.: Posy Publications, 1987), p. 46; Robbins, p. 110; Margaret Truman, *Bess Truman*, p. 270; author telephone interview with Clark Clifford, Oct. 27, 1982.

25. RC, pp. 21, 24, 29, 36–37.

26. Ross, *Edith Wilson*, pp. 304, 326; author conversation with Frances Saunders, Mar. 22, 1988; David Levy, Lt. (jg), USNR, chief, Radio Section, to EBW, Oct. 3, 1945, and John Randolph Bolling to David Levy, Oct. 7, 1945, EBW Papers, LC.

27. Ross, *Grace Coolidge*, pp. 320, 325; Division of Prints and Photographs, LC.

28. Joseph P. Lash, *Eleanor: The Years Alone* (New York: W. W. Norton, 1972), p. 225; Joseph P. Lash, *A World of Love: Eleanor Roosevelt and Her Friends, 1943–1962* (New York: McGraw-Hill, 1984), p. 188.

29. *Buffalo Evening News Magazine*, Nov. 27, 1977; Frances Cleveland Preston, Memorial Service eulogy; author interview with Jack Cadman, Dec. 28, 1982; Frances Cleveland Preston letter of Sept. 22, 1947, courtesy Jack Cadman.

30. Margaret Truman, *Bess Truman*, pp. 263, 272; Vernon, p. 37.

31. Arden Davis, p. 74; "Biographical Sketch of Mrs. Harry S Truman," Jan. 7, 1980, Harry S Truman Library.

32. Bess Truman to Mary Paxton Keeley, n.d., 1945, box 1, Keeley Papers, Harry S Truman Library, as cited by Maurine Beasley in her draft chapter on Bess Truman, 1988, courtesy National Archives; "Biographical Sketch of Mrs. Harry S Truman," Jan. 7, 1980, Harry S Truman Library; Bess Truman's public statement on the controversy is cited in Robbins, pp. 113–14; Margaret Truman, *Bess Truman*, pp. 278–79.

33. Elizabeth Burnette to Mrs. Harry S Truman, Oct. 12, 1945, box 24, White House Social Correspondence File, Harry S Truman Library, as cited by Maurine Beasley in her draft chapter on Bess Truman, 1988, courtesy National Archives; Bluma Jacobsen cited in Miller, *Plain Speaking*, p. 106; in reference to Harry Truman's use of racial epithets, within the context of his background and times, see Geoffrey Ward, *New York Times Book Review*, "From Harry to Bess," Aug. 7, 1983; Margaret Truman, *Bess Truman*, p. 301; *The Crisis*, Vol. LII, Nov. 1945, pp. 313, 362.

34. Margaret Truman, *Bess Truman*, p. 280; Harry Truman to Bess Truman, Nov. 18, 1945, quoted in *Dear Bess*, p. 540.

35. J. B. West, pp. 74–78.

36. Robbins, p. 41; *Washington Post*, Oct. 19, 1982; combined newsreel footages of President and Mrs. Truman at time of Bess Truman's death, Oct. 1982, audiotape, author's collection.

37. Author interview with Jane Lingo, Nov. 22, 1983; author telephone interview with Clark Clifford, Oct. 27, 1982.

38. Vernon, p. 37; author telephone interview with Clark Clifford, Oct. 27, 1982; author interview with Liz Carpenter, Oct. 4, 1987.
39. Margaret Truman, *Bess Truman*, pp. 303, 341; *Washington Post Book World*, Sept. 18, 1983.
40. Robbins, pp. 58, 67; Bess Truman to Katie Louchheim, n.d., box B3, Katie Louchheim Papers, LC.
41. *Washington Post*, Oct. 19, 1982; Carrie A. Scott to author, May 29, 1988.

57. THE BOSS

1. Robbins, pp. 96, 140; Merle Miller, *Plain Speaking*, p. 110
2. "Biographical Sketch of Mrs. Harry S Truman," Jan. 7, 1980, Harry S Truman Library; Bess Truman to Katie Louchheim, May 1958, and n.d., box 3, Katie Louchheim Papers, LC.
3. Helm, p. 255; Robbins, p. 87.
4. Robbins, p. 87; Bess Truman to Katie Louchheim, n.d., box B3, Katie Louchheim Papers, LC; Furman, *By-Line*, p. 330.
5. Author interview with Jane Lingo, Nov. 22, 1982; Helm, p. 257; Margaret Truman, *Bess Truman*, p. 282.
6. Helm, pp. 259–60; author interview with Jane Lingo, Nov. 22, 1983; Robbins, p. 85.
7. Helm, p. 253; Julie Eisenhower, *Special People*, p. 213; Margaret Truman, p. 296; J. B. West, p. 89.
8. Memo from "Stack" to MDE, through Captain Hull, Aug. 21, 1946, and variety of notes and other memos, file 5, box 173, PPP, DDEL.
9. MDE to Lady Butterfield, Dec. 16, 1947, and MDE to American:Soviet Friendship, Nov. 7, 1946, file 4, box 173, PPP, DDEL.
10. MDE to Florence E. Witter, Aug. 7, 1950, file 1, letters to MDE, Aug. 30, 1948, June 29, 1948, file 2, box 173, PPP, DDEL; Kimball, *I Remember Mamie*, p. 152.
11. *Brownsville Herald*, Apr. 8, 1948; *Buffalo Evening News*, Oct. 29, 1947.
12. Helm, p. 262; Neal, p. 240.
13. Series of Eleanor Roosevelt letters to General Dwight D. Eisenhower, 1948–1950, "Eleanor Roosevelt" file, box 100, PPP, DDEL; author interview with Milton Eisenhower, Apr. 1, 1984.
14. *Washington Post*, Oct. 15, 1984.
15. Eleanor Roosevelt and Perle Mesta as quoted in Elliott Roosevelt to author, Apr. 4, 1988.
16. Margaret Truman, *Bess Truman*, p. 318.
17. Audio recording of Bess Truman's voice during 1948 campaign on whistle-stop tour, national news broadcast following the death of Mrs. Truman, Oct. 1982, author's collection.
18. Robbins, p. 125.
19. Robbins, pp. 125–26; Furman, *By-Line*, p. 337; Margaret Truman, *Bess Truman*, p. 328; audio recording of broadcast interview of Robert Ferrell and Gerry van der Hueval, network morning news, "Remembering Bess Truman," Oct. 1982, author's collection; Margaret Truman, *Bess Truman*, p. 245; regarding Tallulah Bankhead campaigning for Truman, the Countess von Wehberg to author, Jan. 3, 1989.

20. Ross, *Grace Coolidge*, pp. 323, 326.

21. Margaret Truman, *Bess Truman*, p. 309; Robbins, pp. 132–33.

22. The Pledge of the American Housewife, June 7, 1946, cited in Robbins, p. 97.

23. Helm, p. 263.

24. Robbins, p. 130; Furman, *White House Profile*, p. 336.

25. Author interview with Betty Ford, Nov. 7, 1983, and phone interview, Apr. 18, 1988.

26. Caro, p. 759; author interview with Lady Bird Johnson, Oct. 3, 1987.

27. Pat Nixon to author, through Julie Eisenhower, June 2, 1988.

28. Julie Eisenhower, *Pat Nixon*, pp. 87–101, 109, 111; author interview with Lady Bird Johnson, Oct. 3, 1987.

29. *Philadelphia Inquirer*, Oct. 19, 1982.

30. Author interview with Jane Lingo, Nov. 22, 1983; Helm, p. 275; J. B. West, p. 117.

31. Robbins, pp. 135, 140.

32. Robbins, pp. 114–15.

33. As quoted in Margaret Truman, *Bess Truman*, p. 351.

34. J. B. West, p. 112.

35. Robbins, p. 105; Margaret Truman, p. 419.

36. Robbins, pp. 16, 139, 143; author telephone interview with Clark Clifford, Oct. 27, 1982; *New York Times*, Aug. 16, 1949, as cited by Maurine Beasley in her draft chapter on Bess Truman, 1988, courtesy National Archives.

37. NR, pp. 80–84, 100; Laurence Leamer, *Make-Believe: The Story of Nancy and Ronald Reagan* (New York: Harper & Row, 1983), pp. 63–64, 67, 157; *People* magazine, May 23, 1988.

38. Lash, *Eleanor: The Years Alone*, pp. 184–85.

39. Hatch, *Mamie*, pp. 181–85; David, pp. 172–76.

40. Jacqueline Onassis to author, through Nancy Tuckerman, Dec. 3, 1987; Hall and Pinchot, pp. 83–84; John H. Davis, *The Kennedys* (New York: McGraw-Hill, 1984), pp. 239, 243–44, 251; Birmingham, p. 61.

41. Hatch, *Mamie*, p. 186; Elliott Roosevelt to author, Apr. 4, 1988; David, p. 258; Virgil Pinklye, *Eisenhower Declassified* (New York: Old Tappan, 1979), p. 373.

42. Kimball, p. 166.

43. Dr. and Mrs. Loyal Davis invitation to DDE and MDE, Mar. 1952, "America—Personal Friends (1)," file, box 2, SHAPE correspondence, DDEL; DDE to the Ronald Reagans, Mar. 17, 1952, "Cables-Outgoing," file, box 130, SHAPE correspondence, PPP, DDEL; Nancy Reagan would come to know Mamie Eisenhower through Edie Davis. Mrs. Reagan's adoptive father, Loyal Davis, was a surgeon in World War II, working with General Eisenhower: Nancy Reagan to author, through Wendy Weber, June 1988; NR, pp. 90–91, 123; Barbara Walters joint interview with Nancy and Ronald Reagan, *20/20*, ABC, Oct. 1989.

44. J. B. West, pp. 121–23; Nancy Reagan, *My Turn* (Simon and Schuster, 1989), pp. 100–101.

45. ER to EBW, Apr. 18, 1945, ER to EBW, Oct. 14, 1952, and invitation to Mar. 14, 1946, dinner honoring ER, box 34, EBW Papers, LC; author interview with Lady Bird Johnson, Oct. 3, 1987.

46. Julie Eisenhower, *Pat Nixon*, p. 116; Dwight D. Eisenhower, *Mandate for Change* (New York: Doubleday, 1963), p. 44; Hatch, *Mamie*, p. 243.

58. LOOK AHEAD, NEIGHBOR

1. Campaign songs recorded on EL-T 73-C, and EL-T 80-A, Magnetic Audio-Tapes, A & C Series, DDEL; Mamie Eisenhower campaign tape dispenser, collection of political memorabilia, Division of Political History, Museum of American History, Smithsonian Institution; photocopy of DDE wearing "I Like Mamie" pin, author's collection; David, p. 178; *Life*, Oct. 15, 1952.

2. MDE file, box 40, Bess Furman Papers, LC; David, p. 178; author interview with Milton Eisenhower, Apr. 1, 1984.

3. Author interview with Mary Jane McCaffree Monroe, May 31, 1988; DDE, *Mandate*, p. 63; Merriam Smith, *Meet Mr. Eisenhower* (New York: Harper & Row, 1955), p. 42.

4. Author interview with Milton Eisenhower, Apr. 1, 1984; as quoted in Nick Thimmesch, "Mamie Eisenhower at 80," *McCall's*, Oct. 1976; author interview with Barbara Eisenhower (Foltz), Oct. 22, 1983.

5. George Dixon, "Washington Scene," column, n.d., 1956, MDE file, box 40, Bess Furman Papers, LC.

6. Hatch, *Mamie*, pp. 248–49; MDE to Mary Willock, Aug. 7, 1952, WI (1) file, box 46, MDE Personal Papers, DDEL; author interview with Milton Eisenhower, Apr. 1, 1984.

7. David, p. 183; Neal, p. 281; author interview with Milton Eisenhower, Apr. 1, 1984; Brendon, *Ike*, p. 213.

8. Julie Eisenhower, *Pat Nixon*, pp. 119–27; DDE, *Mandate*, p. 73.

9. Harry Truman to Bess Truman, as cited in Margaret Truman, *Bess Truman*, p. 388; Katie Louchheim, draft of "Mrs. T," p. 2, Katie Louchheim Papers, LC.

10. Margaret Truman, *Bess Truman*, pp. 344, 379; Helm, p. 291.

11. *Washington Evening Star*, Dec. 2, 1952; *Washington Post*, Dec. 2, 1952; Hatch, *Mamie*, p. 257; Caroli, p. 210; cartoon of MDE, #56-684.38, DDEL.

12. James Edward Shaaf, *Mamie Doud Eisenhower and Her Chicken Farmer Cousin* (n.d., n.p., photostat pages in author's collection, original in LC), "1953" chapter.

13. DDE, *Mandate*, p. 100; *Washington Times-Herald*, Jan. 20–22, 1953.

14. Bess Furman to Jacqueline Bouvier, Nov. 18, 1952, quoted in Mary Van Rensselaer Thayer, *Jacqueline Kennedy: The White House Years* (Boston: Little, Brown, 1971), p. 292; Jacqueline Bouvier to Bess Furman, Nov. 20, 1952, Jacqueline Kennedy file, Bess Furman Papers, LC.

15. Jacqueline Onassis, "Jacqueline Kennedy Onassis Talks About Working," *Ms.* magazine, March 1979, p. 50.

16. Ellis D. Slater, *The Ike I Knew*, material collected by Ernestine Durr, edited and typed by Elsie Maki, privately printed, 1980, p. 33, Library of the National Museum of American History, Smithsonian Institution; Hall and Pinchot, pp. 110–112; Davis, *The Kennedys*, pp. 187–88.

17. J. B. West, pp. 129–30; author interview with J. B. West, Apr. 5, 1980.

59. IN THE PINK

1. Shaaf, p. 58; Slater, p. 32; *Washington Post,* Sept. 30, 1984; notes on tour of Eisenhower home, Gettysburg, National Park Service, Nov. 24, 1989; Parks, pp. 312–16.

2. *Washington Post,* Sept. 30, 1984; J. B. West, p. 131.

3. *Prologue,* Summer 1987; J. B. West, pp. 132–33, 140, 155, 157.

4. *Prologue,* Summer 1987; Mamie Eisenhower file, box 41, Bess Furman Papers, LC; Merriman Smith, p. 240; *Life,* Oct. 15, 1952.

5. Slater, p. 33; *Prologue,* Summer 1987; Maxine Cheshire, *Maxine Cheshire, Reporter* (Boston: Houghton Mifflin, 1978), p. 26; author interview with J. B. West, Apr. 5, 1980.

6. Elizabeth Arden to MDE, "Elizabeth Arden only" file, box 2, MDE Personal Papers, White House Series, DDEL; MDE to *Life* editor, Nov. 10, 1953, "Press (1952–1952)," folder 2, box 35, MDE Personal Papers, White House Social Files, DDEL; *Prologue,* Summer 1987; Jolie Gabor and Cindy Adams, *Jolie* (New York: Mason, Charter Books, 1975), p. 291; Marie Smith, *Entertaining in the White House* (New York: McFadden Books, 1970), pp. 216–221.

7. Slater, p. 75; J. B. West, p. 146; *Prologue,* Summer 1987.

8. David, p. 195; Kirk, p. 272; Brendon, p. 277; author interview with Barbara Eisenhower (Foltz), Oct. 22, 1983; author interview with Milton Eisenhower, Apr. 1, 1984; author telephone interview with David Eisenhower, Oct. 18, 1987.

9. MDE press-conference transcript, Mar. 11, 1953, "Press (1952–1953)" file, box 35, Personal Files of MDE, White House Social Files (hereafter WHSF), DDEL.

10. MDE press-conference transcript, Mar. 11, 1953, "Press (1952–1953)" file, box 35, Personal Files of MDE; Inez Robb, "Mamie Is Just What Country Ordered," International News Service, n.d. (early 1953); Merriman Smith, p. 245; DDE to Jack Foster, Rocky Mountain *News,* Aug. 12, 1957, "August 1957" file, box 545, DDE Central Files, PPF/2, DDEL; author interview with Liz Carpenter, Oct. 4, 1987.

11. James Hagerty to John S. D. Eisenhower, Mar. 29, 1954, "Press, 1954 (1)" file, box 35, MDE Personal Papers, WHSF, DDEL; *Prologue,* Summer 1987; *Life,* Oct. 20, 1958.

12. James Hagerty memo to Mary Jane McCaffree, Jan. 16, 1954, "January 1954" file, box 541, PPF/2, DDE Central Files, DDEL; author interview with Mary Jane McCaffree, May 31, 1988.

13. Memo from Charles F. Willis, Jr., to Sherman Adams, Mar. 12, 1954, "March 1954" file, box 541, PPF/2, DDE Central Files, DDEL.

14. Regarding relationship between MDE and Ann Whitman, see all index references to MDE in Robert Donovan, *Confidential Secretary* (New York: E. P. Dutton, 1988); author interview with Mary Jane McCaffree, May 31, 1988; J. B. West, p. 141.

15. *Prologue,* Summer 1987; Sherman Adams memo, Mar. 11, 1953, Sherman Adams to Delia Evenson, Mar. 26, 1953, "March 1953" file, Sherman Adams to Mrs. Arthur Horneyer, Apr. 11, 1953, "April 1953" file, Mary Burns memo to Mary Jane McCaffree, Feb. 24, 1953, "February 1953 (2)" file, PPF/2, DDE Central Files, DDEL; author interview with Mary Jane McCaffree, May 31, 1988.

16. Typed memo to MDE for approval of *Life* magazine story text, n.d., box 34, MDE Personal Papers, White House Series, DDEL; Barbara Walters interview with Mamie Eisenhower, 1970, Audio-Visual Department, DDEL; Merriman Smith, p. 240; Julie Eisenhower, *Special People*, p. 208; Richard P. Yardley cartoon of MDE, n.d.; author interview with Barbara Eisenhower (Foltz), Oct. 22, 1983; *Prologue*, Summer 1987; *Washington Post*, Sept. 30, 1984.

17. J. B. West, p. 159; Neal, p. 463; author interview with Milton Eisenhower, Apr. 1, 1984.

18. Author interview with Betty Ford, Nov. 7, 1983, and telephone interview, Apr. 18, 1988.

19. Barbara Bush to author, May 15, 1989; *Time*, Jan. 23, 1989; *Life*, Oct. 1988.

20. Slater, p. 33; J. B. West, pp. 140, 163–64; Merriman Smith, pp. 77–78; MDE Press Conference transcript, Mar. 11, 1953, "Press (1952–1953)" file, box 35, Personal Files of MDE, WHSF, DDEL; Bart Andrews, *Lucy and Ricky and Fred and Ethel: The Story of I Love Lucy* (New York: Fawcett Books, 1977), p. 125; the *I Love Lucy* episode mentioning MDE: Audio-Visual Department, EL-MP16-300, DDEL.

21. Julie Eisenhower, *Special People*, p. 211; West, pp. 130, 136, 142–43.

22. Abilene *Reflector-Chronicle*, Eisenhower Memorial Edition, 1979, p. 22.

23. *Buffalo Evening News*, Nov. 13, 1979; Means, pp. 246, 248; Neal, p. 462.

24. Author interview with Mary Jane McCaffree Monroe, May 31, 1988; author interview with Barbara Eisenhower (Foltz), Oct. 22, 1983; author telephone interview with David Eisenhower, Oct. 18, 1987; Mamie Eisenhower file, box 41, Bess Furman Papers, LC.

25. MDE press-conference transcript, Mar. 11, 1953, "Press (1952–1953)" file, box 35, Personal Files of MDE, WHSF, DDEL; *Life*, Oct. 15, 1952; Means, pp. 248–249.

26. Julie Eisenhower, *Special People*, p. 203; author interview with Robert Keith Gray, Spring 1982 (n.d.); Means, p. 253; Neal, p. 401.

27. Slater, p. 149.

28. Smith, p. 22; Max Rabb memo to Mary Jane McCaffree, Jan. 29, 1958, "January 1958" file, box 546, PPF/2, DDE Central Files, DDEL; Brendon, pp. 285–86.

29. Homer Gruenther memo to Max Rabb, Mar. 14, 1953, "March 1953" file, box 540, PPF/2, DDE Central Files, DDEL; Merriman Smith, p. 22; Slater, p. 37.

30. J. B. West, p. 160.

31. Barbara Walters interview with MDE, 1970, Audio-Visual Department, DDEL; David, pp. 16–19.

32. Slater, pp. 57–58.

33. MDE press-conference transcript, Mar. 11, 1953, "Press (1952–1953)" file, box 35, Personal Files of MDE, WHSF, DDEL; letter of June 26, 1953, "June 1953" file, Box 541, PPF/2, DDE Central Files.

34. Hall and Pinchot, pp. 95–96.

35. Mamie Eisenhower file, box 40, Bess Furman Papers, LC; *Washington Daily News*, May 20, 1953; "Mamie Saves Mitt from Wringer," "Press (1952–1953)" file, box 35, WHSF, DDEL.

36. *New York Times*, Apr. 19, 1953, pp. 55–57; Merriman Smith, p. 194; Henry Roemer McPhee, assistant special counsel to the president, to M. F. deTurkheim, ed., Apr. 17, 1957, "May 1957" file, box 545, and all material in "February 1956," "May 1956," and "September 1956" files, box 544, PPF/2, DDE Central Files, DDEL.

37. MDE to Mrs. Donald K. Redding, Sept. 9, 1952, box 36, MDE Personal Papers, White House Series, DDEL.

38. MDE to the following: National Federation of Republican Women, n.d.; New York Cancer Office, May 21, 1953; Civil Defense, n.d.; Red Cross, Mar. 21, 1953; U.S. Savings Bonds, July 29, 1953; U.N. Week, July 30, 1953; Federation of American Women's Clubs, May 7, 1953; USO Mothers, May 8, 1953, all in "Statements (Public Service)" file, box 41, MDE Personal Papers, White House Series; Ad Council's "Women in Service" statement, "April 1953" file, box 540, PPF/2, DDE Central Files, DDEL.

39. *Prologue*, Summer 1987; MDE, "If I Were a Bride Today," appeared in *Today's Woman* magazine, "September 1954" file, box 542, PPF/2, DDE Central Files, DDEL.

40. MDE press-conference transcript, Mar. 11, 1953, "Press (1952–1953)" file, box 35, Personal Files of MDE, WHSF, DDEL; Peter Collier and David Horowitz, *The Kennedys: An American Drama* (New York: Warner Books, 1984), pp. 239, 241–42; Ralph G. Martin, *A Hero for Our Time: An Intimate Story of the Kennedy Years* (New York: Fawcett Crest, 1983), p. 83.

41. Julie Eisenhower, *Pat Nixon*, pp. 133–34, 138–43, 149.

42. Author interview with Barbara Eisenhower (Foltz), Oct. 22, 1983; author interview with Mary Jane McCaffree Monroe, May 31, 1988; Merriman Smith, p. 242; Earle D. Chesney to Mary Jane McCaffree, Mar. 8, 1957, "March 1957" file, box 545, PPF/2, DDE Central Files, DDEL.

43. *Los Angeles Times*, Dec. 9, 1952; MDE statement to National Federation of Republican Women, n.d. (early 1953), "Statements (Public Service)" file, box 41, MDE Personal Papers, White House Series, DDEL; Ann Whitman memo to Mary Jane McCaffree, May 3, 1956, "Mamie Eisenhower" file, box 12, Name Series, Ann Whitman Papers, DDEL; *McCall's*, Oct. 1976; Means, pp. 248, 258; author telephone interview with David Eisenhower, Oct. 18, 1987.

44. Grace Coolidge to MDE, Jan. 10, 1953, Nov. 10, 1953, Jan. 6, 1955, and MDE to Grace Coolidge, Dec. 17, 1952, Mar. 31, 1953, Oct. 28, 1953, "Coo" file, box 9, MDE Personal Papers, White House Series, DDEL.

45. MDE scrapbook, Jan. 19, 1954, pastings; Pat Nixon to author, through Julie Eisenhower, June 1988; John H. Taylor, office of Richard M. Nixon, to author, Sept. 24, 1987; MDE first befriended EBW during the Second World War. As First Lady, Mrs. Eisenhower began inviting Mrs. Wilson to co-receive with her at the annual Veterans' Garden Party. MDE and EBW letters, Feb. 4, 1954, Mar. 10, 1954, Mar. 17, 1954, Mar. 23, 1954, May 25, 1955, and June 14, 1955, Jan. 2, 1957, "WI (2)" file, box 46, MDE Personal Papers, White House Series, Barbara Walters interview with MDE, 1970, Audio-Visual Department, DDEL; Ross, *Edith Wilson*, pp. 327, 332.

46. "Eleanor Roosevelt" file, box 41, Bess Furman Papers, LC; Elliott Roosevelt to author, Apr. 4, 1988; Lash, *A World of Love*, pp. 384–85; Lash, *Eleanor: The Years Alone*, pp. 237–38; Lait and Mortimer, p. 43.

47. Author telephone interview with David Eisenhower, Oct. 18, 1987; *Prologue*, Summer 1987.
48. Author interview with J. B. West, Apr. 5, 1980; J. F. terHorst and Col. Ralph Albertazzie, *The Flying White House: The Story of Air Force One* (New York: Coward, McCann, Geoghegan, 1979), pp. 176–78; author interview with Mary Jane McCaffree Monroe, May 31, 1988.
49. Betty Beale to MDE, July 18, 1955, with questions, and three pages of shorthand responses, "Press (1955–1956)" file, box 35, MDE Personal Papers, WHSF, DDEL.
50. Merriman Smith, pp. 289–90.
51. Howard M. Snyder, draft ms., on President Eisenhower's heart attack, Apr. 19, 1965, "September 1955 (1)" file, pp. 6, 9, 12, box 11, Howard M. Snyder Papers, DDEL.

60. SWEETHEART OF THE GOP

1. David, pp. 235–36.
2. DDE, *Mandate for Change*, p. 542.
3. Mary Jane McCaffree to Andrew J. Goodpaster, Sept. 28, 1955, "Mamie Eisenhower" file, box 12, Name Series, Ann Whitman Papers, and Neil Wickersham to MDE, Nov. 10, 1955, "WI (1)" file, box 46, MDE Personal Papers, White House Series, DDEL.
4. Nineteen Sixty-one Inaugural Program, Lady Bird Johnson biography, prepared by Liz Carpenter; "To Lady Bird Johnson with Esteem and Affection from the Ladies of the Senate on the Occasion of the Luncheon in her Honor, Senate Caucus Room, April 26, 1966," pp. 41, 50, box C34, Katie Louchheim Papers, LC; author interview with Lady Bird Johnson, Oct. 3, 1987.
5. Jacqueline Bouvier Kennedy (hereafter JBK) to Lyndon Baines Johnson, Nov. 9, 1954, "Kennedy, Mrs. John F." file, WH Famous Names Collection, Lyndon Baines Johnson Library (hereafter LBJL).
6. Howard M. Snyder, draft ms., on the Eisenhowers relocating to Fort Myer, Apr. 19, 1965, "DDE 1945–46 (1)" file, pp. 2–4, 15–16, box 11, Howard M. Snyder Papers, DDEL. If her doctor continued to prescribe tranquilizers to the First Lady without her knowledge or permission, it would make the situation not in the least bit atypical of the times. Many women were routinely prescribed tranquilizers without their full realization during the era, the "sales of which boomed . . ." in the fifties—Brendon, pp. 276–77.
7. Neal, p. 464.
8. Author interview with Barbara Eisenhower (Foltz), Oct. 22, 1983; Barbara Walters interview with MDE, Nov. 1979, Audio-Visual Department, DDEL; Robert H. Ferrell, ed., *The Eisenhower Diaries*, xv.
9. MDE to Ellis and Priscilla Slater, Jan. 10, 1956, "Slater" file, box 39, MDE Personal Papers, White House Series, DDEL; author interview with Mary Jane McCaffree Monroe, May 31, 1988; West, pp. 160–61.
10. Slater, pp. 44, 107, 123; *New York Times*, Dec. 23, 1955; author telephone interview with David Eisenhower, Oct. 18, 1987; Mamie Eisenhower interview with Barbara Walters, 1970, Audio-Visual Department, DDEL; DDE, *Mandate for Change*, p. 571.

11. Nick Thimmesch, "Mamie Eisenhower at 80," *McCall's*, Oct. 1976.
12. *Washington Evening Star*, June 22, 1956; MDE to Ellis and Priscilla Slater, June 15, 1956, "Slater" file, box 39, MDE Personal Papers, White House Series, DDEL.
13. Julie Eisenhower, *Pat Nixon*, pp. 153, 157, 161–62; David, p. 19.
14. Author interview with Milton Eisenhower, Apr. 1, 1984; Murray Snyder memo to Mary Jane McCaffree, Nov. 28, 1956, "November 1956" file, box 544, PPF/2, DDE Central Files, DDEL; recording of "Sweetheart of the GOP," EL-MP16-193 Audio-Visual Department, DDEL; *Life*, Aug. 27, 1956; author telephone interview with Betty Ford, Apr. 18, 1988; Charles A. H. Thomson and Frances M. Shattuck, *The 1956 President Campaign* (Washington, D.C.: the Brookings Institution, 1960), p. 298; Mamie Eisenhower file, Box 40 and 41, Bess Furman Papers, LC.
15. JBK to MDE, May 10, 1956, "F-K" file, Box 288, WH Social Files, DDEL; Jacqueline Onassis to author, through Nancy Tuckerman, Dec. 3, 1987.
16. Jacqueline Onassis to author, through Nancy Tuckerman, Dec. 3, 1987; Arthur M. Schlesinger, Jr., *A Thousand Days: John F. Kennedy in the White House* (New York, Fawcett Premier, 1965), pp. 24–25; *Jackie Kennedy: Her Fashions, Her Home, Her Words* (New York: Wykagyl Publications, 1961), no author, no page numbers; Collier and Horowitz, p. 386.
17. Schlesinger, pp. 73, 102; Ralph G. Martin, *A Hero for Our Time* (New York: Fawcett Crest Books, 1983), pp. 93, 179, 209, 86, 92.
18. Author interview with Dave Powers, July 30, 1987; Hall and Pinchot, p. 131.
19. Martin, pp. 75, 92, 94; Deane and David Heller, *Jacqueline Kennedy* (Connecticut: Monarch Books, 1961), p. 118.
20. Hall and Pinchot, p. 140.
21. Schlesinger, pp. 36–37, 101.
22. Ross, *Grace Coolidge*, p. 312, 333–39; MDE to Grace Coolidge, May 9, 1955, Dec. 21, 1955, Grace Coolidge to MDE, Dec. 16, 1955, "Coo" file, box 9, MDE Personal Papers, White House Series, DDEL; author interview with Lady Bird Johnson, Oct. 3, 1987.
23. Two handwritten pages by JBK, on Senate stationery, "1956, K51-K59" file, box 40, Pre-Presidential Doodles, JFK Personal Papers, John F. Kennedy Library (hereafter JFKL).
24. Lee Israel, *Miss Tallulah Bankhead* (New York: Berkley Publishing Co., 1972), pp. 294–95; Lash, *Eleanor: The Years Alone*, pp. 243, 279, 303, 311–12; Lash, *A World of Love*, p. 498; Robert H. Ferrell, *Truman: A Centenary Remembrance* (New York: W. W. Norton, 1984), p. 246; Martin, p. 100.
25. Martin, pp. 93, 101, 105, 111; Cheshire, p. 30; Hall and Pinchot, pp. 145, 147; Kathleen Bouvier, *To Jack with Love: Black Jack Bouvier, a Remembrance* (New York: Zebra Books, 1979), p. 278; Schlesinger, p. 84.
26. Ross, *Edith Wilson*, pp. 331, 339, 341; EBW to MDE, Jan. 2, 1957, and Jan. 24, 1957, "Wi (2)" file, box 46, White House Series, MDE Personal Papers, White House Series, DDEL; MDE to EBW, May 2, 1957, and Feb. 2, 1960, "Mamie Eisenhower" file, EBW Papers, LC.
27. Author interview with Mary Jane McCaffree Monroe, May 31, 1988; Homer Gruenther memo to Wilton Persons, Apr. 22, 1958, "May 1958" file, box 546, PPF/2, DDE Central Files, DDEL; Slater, p. 149; *Christmas at the White House*, White House Historical Association, p. 28.

28. Brendon, p. 277; "Mamie Eisenhower" files, boxes 40 (Apr. 6, 1953) and 41, Bess Furman Papers, LC; material in "Press Conferences" file, box 35, MDE Personal Papers, WHSF, DDEL; Mar. 22, 1956, EL-MP16-96, Audio-Visual Department, DDEL.

29. Mary Jane McCaffree to Irvin Feld, Feb. 18, 1953, Mary Burns memo to Mary Jane McCaffree, Feb. 24, 1953, "February 1953 (2)" file, box 540; press release from Murray Snyder, Aug. 1, 1954, "August 1954" file, box 542, draft of Mary Jane McCaffree to Mrs. Patterson, n.d., "March 1956" file, Box 544, PPF/2, DDE Central Files; Box 35, "Press (1953)" file, MDE Personal Papers, WHSF, DDEL; Traphes Bryant *Dog Days at the White House* (New York: Macmillan, 1975), p. 17.

30. Author interview with Barbara Eisenhower (Foltz), Oct. 22, 1983; author interview with Milton Eisenhower, Apr. 1, 1984.

31. RC, pp. 43, 45, 47, 48.

32. Dwight D. Eisenhower, *Waging Peace: 1955–1961* (New York: Doubleday, 1965), p. 228; J. B. West, pp. 177, 183–84; cartoon of MDE, #56-684.39, DDEL; Thimmesch, "Mamie Eisenhower at 80," *McCall's*, Oct. 1976, p. 214; Howard M. Snyder diary entries of July 7, 1958, and July 20, 1958, "July 1, 1958–December 31, 1958" file, box 8, Howard M. Snyder Medical Diary, DDEL; Slater, pp. 210–11; Julie Eisenhower, *Special People*, p. 207.

33. Slater, p. 212; Julie Eisenhower, *Pat Nixon*, pp. 167, 170, 174–78, 184; author interview with Lady Bird Johnson, Oct. 3, 1987; Barbara Walters interview with MDE, Nov. 1979, Audio-Visual Department, DDEL; author interview with Milton Eisenhower, Apr. 1, 1984; office of Richard Nixon to author, Sept. 24, 1987.

34. Author interview with Barbara Eisenhower (Foltz), Oct. 22, 1984; John S. D. Eisenhower, *Strictly Personal* (New York: Doubleday, 1974), p. 262; Julie Eisenhower, *Pat Nixon*, p. 185.

35. Alfred Allan Lewis and Constance Woodward, *Miss Elizabeth Arden: An Unretouched Portrait* (New York: Coward, McCann, Geoghegan, 1972), pp. 282, 284–86; Elizabeth Arden to MDE, July 8, 1958, and Mar. 25, 1959, "Elizabeth Arden" file, box 2, Personal Papers of MDE, White House Series, DDEL; David, p. 211.

36. Pearson article attached to letter of Mar. 26, 1959, "September 1959" file, box 547, PPF/2, DDE Central Files, DDEL.

37. John J. Miller column, June 7, 1959, *National Enquirer*, attached to letter of July 14, 1959, "July 1959" file, box 547, PPF/2, DDE Central Files, DDEL.

38. Slater, pp. 46, 173; Mary Jane McCaffree to Edward Wimmer, National Federation of Independent Business, July 3, 1957, "July 1957" file, box 545, L. A. Minnich, Jr., White House assistant staff secretary, memo to Wendell B. Barnes, Small Business Administration, May 1, 1958, "May 1958" file, secretary of labor Memo, Oct. 13, 1958, "October 1958" file, box 546, PPF/2, DDE Central Files, DDEL.

39. Draft of letter by DDE for MDE to Mr. Haynes, Mar. 2, 1957, "Mamie Eisenhower" file, box 12, Name Series, Ann Whitman Papers, DDEL; "Mamie Eisenhower" file, box 41, Bess Furman Papers, LC.

40. MDE to Jacelyn Moran, Jan. 6, 1953, file, opening page of "A Valentine for You" booklet, press release "First Lady Receives Heart Sunday," Feb. 7, 1955, carbon of MDE to "Dear Friends," Feb. 14, 1955, "Suggested Photo Caption" (n.d., ca. 1956), "Heart, District of Columbia (1)" file, MDE to

Marian McGarraghy, Feb. 7, 1957, "Heart, District of Columbia (2)" file; Edgar Allen to MDE, Feb. 21, 1957, MDE to Dr. Wilkins, June 10, 1957, MDE to Lena Horne, Feb. 24, 1958, "Heart (National) (Only) (1)" file; letterhead of patrons for *Richard III*, Feb. 20, 1956; news release, Feb. 2, 1960, "Heart, (National) (Only) (3)," box 547, White House Social Office Records, MDE Personal Papers, Ernest E. Mulch to MDE, Mar. 17, 1958, "March 1958" file, box 546, PPF/2, DDE Central Files, DDEL.

41. "Mamie Eisenhower" file, box 41, Bess Furman Papers, LC; David, p. 19; author conversation with Nancy Reagan, Marine One helicopter, July 18, 1985; NR, *Nancy*, pp. 91–92; Michael Reagan, *On the Outside Looking In* (New York: Zebra Books, 1988), pp. 75–79, 83, 84.

61. RACE FOR THE LADYSHIP

1. Author interview with Dave Powers, July 30, 1987; Martin, pp. 122, 142–43; Heller, p. 135; Joseph Cerrell Oral History Transcript (hereafter OHT), JFKL; William Manchester, *Remembering Kennedy: One Brief Shining Moment* (Boston: Little, Brown, 1983), p. 93.

2. Author interview with Dave Powers, July 30, 1987; Alfred Chapman OHT, JFKL, p. 9; Martin, pp. 145, 139.

3. Jacqueline Onassis to author, through Lisa Drew, Aug. 1988; quoted in *Jackie Kennedy . . . Fashions . . . Home . . . Words* (no page numbers), Arthur Chapin OHT, p. 26, JFKL; Martin, p. 135.

4. Lash, *A World of Love*, p. 523; Martin, pp. 206, 523; Lash, *Eleanor: The Years Alone*, p. 295; Manchester, p. 113.

5. Schlesinger, pp. 51, 53; Merle Miller, *Lyndon: An Oral History* (New York: G. P. Putnam's Sons, 1980), p. 244.

6. Lash, *A World of Love*, pp. 524–26.

7. Barbara Bush to author, June 1989.

8. BF, *The Times of My Life*, p. 117; Julie Eisenhower, *Pat Nixon*, pp. 180, 186, 187, 189, 190.

9. Nineteen Sixty-one Inaugural Program, Lady Bird Johnson biography prepared by Liz Carpenter; *Austin Mirror*, May 5, 1960.

10. Martin, pp. 172, 214, 210–11; newspaper clipping from the 1960 campaign about Mrs. Kennedy, "Jacqueline Kennedy" file, Bess Furman Papers, LC.

11. Martin, pp. 137–38, 195, 210; Hall and Pinchot, p. 154; *Washington Post*, May 29, 1987.

12. Martin, pp. 138, 141; *Life*, Aug. 24, 1959; author interview with Arthur Schlesinger, Jr., Mar. 30, 1984; Collier and Horowitz, p. 296.

13. "B-2536" file, Democratic National Committee (DNC) News Release, Oct. 11, 1960, and Jacqueline Kennedy, "Campaign Wife" column, Oct. 19, 1960, DNC Papers, JFKL.

14. Correspondence between Jacqueline Kennedy and Lady Bird Johnson, Oct. 1, 1960–Oct. 20, 1960, and Oct. 24, 1960, "Mrs. John F. Kennedy, 1960," file, White House Famous Names File Collection, Lyndon Baines Johnson Library (hereafter LBJL).

15. "Press Releases" file, box 19, "B2639" and "B2857" files, box 21, DNC Papers, JFKL; Jacqueline Kennedy, "Campaign Wife" column, Oct. 16, 1960.

16. Hall and Pinchot, pp. 157–58; Martin, p. 214.

17. Press clippings and letter from "A Virginia Democrat" to EBW, box 65, EBW Papers, LC; Hatch, *Edith Wilson*, p. 272.

18. Julie Eisenhower, *Pat Nixon*, pp. 195–201; author interview with Barbara Eisenhower (Foltz), Oct. 22, 1983.

19. Hall and Pinchot, pp. 153, 161; Martin, p. 223.

20. Cheshire, p. 40; West, p. 187; Bill Draper memo to MDE, Oct. 25, 1960, "Flying Log" file, box 13, MDE Personal Papers, White House Series, DDEL; author interview with Barbara Eisenhower (Foltz), Oct. 22, 1983.

21. J. B. West, p. 187; *Washington Evening Star*, Nov. 26, 1960.

22. Shaaf, p. 23; author interview with Barbara Eisenhower (Foltz), Oct. 22, 1983; Thayer, pp. 7–8, 14–15; "Reaction to Telecast" memo, June 21, 1962, "PP5/Jacqueline Kennedy" files, box 705, White House Central Subject Files, JFKL; West, pp. 192–194; Jacqueline Onassis to author, through Lisa Drew, Aug. 1988.

23. J. B. West, p. 194; author interview with J. B. West, Apr. 5, 1980.

62. LADIES' DAY

1. References for "Ladies' Day" include: Hatch, *Edith Wilson: First Lady Extraordinary*, p. 275; *Jacqueline Kennedy: Beauty in the White House* (New York: Magnum Publications, 1961), p. 54; E. J. Hughes, *The Ordeal of Power* (New York: 1963), p. 7; Carol Felsenthal, *Alice Roosevelt Longworth* (New York: G. P. Putnam's Sons, 1988), p. 243; Ishbel Ross, *Edith Wilson*, p. 327; Heller, p. 122; Hall and Pinchot, p. 165; Leamer, *Make-Believe*, p. 4; Robbins, p. 181; Thayer, pp. 20–25, 69–70, 72, 75, 85, 94; ER to Lorena Hickok, Jan. 23, 1961, FDRL, as cited in Lash, *A World of Love*, p. 533; David, *The Lonely Lady of San Clemente*, pp. 120–121; Reg Gadney, *Kennedy*, p. 85; Lash, *Eleanor: The Years Alone*, p. 300; Julie Eisenhower, *Pat Nixon*, pp. 201, 204; *John Fitzgerald Kennedy: As We Remember Him* (New York: Macmillan, 1965), p. 110; DDE, *Waging Peace*, p. 618; *Washington Post, New York Times, Washington Evening Star*, Jan. 14–22, 1961; author telephone interviews, Edna Gurewitsch, July 26, 1988, Molly Thayer, Nov. 1981, Betty Ford, Apr. 18, 1988, Alice Longworth, Sept. 7, 1977; author interviews, J. B. West, Apr. 5, 1980, Mary Jane McCaffree Monroe, May 31, 1988, Barbara Eisenhower (Foltz), Oct. 22, 1983; Elliott Roosevelt to author, Apr. 4, 1988; Nancy Reagan to author through Wendy Weber, First Lady's Press Office, June 30, 1988; Pat Nixon to author through Julie Eisenhower, June 1988; Edith Wilson to Jacqueline Kennedy, draft, Nov. 9, 1960, box 22, EBW Papers, LC; Bess Truman to Katie Louchheim, May 18, 1957, Dec. 1958, n.d. (1961), box B3, Kennedy Inaugural data, box C32, Katie Louchheim Oral History Interview, June 14, 1968, JFKL, copy in Katie Louchheim Papers, Box G9, Katie Louchheim Papers, LC.

INDEX

Acheson, Dean, 530, 540, 576
Adams, Abigail Smith, 44, 77, 85,
    104–105
  character and personality of,
    60–62, 64, 65, 67–68,
    69–70, 79, 105
  political interests and power of,
    32–33, 49–50, 51, 59–61,
    63–65, 68, 69–72, 92, 187,
    379
  public role of, 61–63, 71–72
  relationship with John Adams,
    49–50, 59–65, 67–68
Adams, Eliza, 68
Adams, Florence, 400–401, 473
Adams, George, 108, 110
Adams, Henry, 210, 251, 312
Adams, John, 33, 46, 49–50, 56,
    59–65, 66–69, 103, 347
Adams, John Quincy, 50, 60, 69,
    77, 79, 105–110, 126, 143,
    261
Adams, Louisa Catherine Johnson,
    69, 79, 103, 104–105, 133,
    156, 183
  character and personality of,
    108–111, 143
  relationship with John Quincy
    Adams, 107, 108–110, 143
  social and political skills of,
    106–107, 109–111
Adams, Sherman, 547, 556, 583
Adams, Thomas, 60, 68, 69
Adventures of a Nobody (Adams),
    109
Alexander, Minnie R., 258

Alexander I, czar of Russia, 110
American Battlefields of France, The
    (Eisenhower), 417
American Revolution, 31, 32,
    41–42, 54–55, 60, 76, 113
Ames, Mary Clemmer, 181, 226,
    237
Anderson, Jennie Herron, 326
Anderson, Marian, 479–480, 581
Anderson, Mary, 457
Anthony, Susan B., 219, 246, 279
Arden, Elizabeth, 583–584
Arthur, Chester Alan, 238, 239,
    242–244, 246–248, 249
Arthur, Ellen Lewis Herndon,
    246–248
Ashum, George, 193
Astor, John Jacob, 85, 88, 122
Auchincloss, Hugh D., 486

Babcock, Orville, 214, 215
Bache, Benjamin, 63
Badeau, Adam, 191, 196, 214, 218
Baker, Ray Stannard, 367
Bankhead, Tallulah, 536, 578
Barbary Wars, 77
Barker, Harry, 392
Barker, Jacob, 84
Barlow, Joel, 87
Baruch, Belle, 475
Baruch, Bernard, 359, 429, 468,
    474–475, 479, 504–505
Bateman, Frieda, 277
Beale, Betty, 569–570, 583
Beecher, Henry Ward, 301
Beer, William, 288–289

Behind the Scenes (Keckley), 208
Belknap, William, 216
Bell, Alexander Graham, 228
Bennett, James Gordon, 180
Bernstorff, Johann von, 352, 355, 370
Bethune, Mary McLeod, 480–481
Bidault, George, 576
Billings, Lem, 565
Birney, Frank, 488, 491–492
Blaine, Harriet, 227, 239–240, 242, 268
Blaine, James G., 236–240
Bliss, Tasker, 364
Bloom, Vera, 404
Boardman, Mabel, 318
Bodley, Rachel, 230
Bok, Edward, 359
Bolling, John, 228
Bolling, Sally, 338
Bones, Helen, 345, 350–351, 352, 357
"Bonus Army," 447–448, 452, 454
Booth, John Wilkes, 199, 207
Bouvier, John Vernou, 475, 486, 579
Boxer Rebellion, 435
Bradford, Gamaliel, 399
Bradley, Omar, 566
Bradwell, Myra, 221
Bremer, Fredrika, 218
Briggs, Emily, 230
Britton, Nan, 358, 377, 398
Brown, Aaron V., 137
Brown, Helen, 517
Bryan, William Jennings, 327, 335, 352
Buchan, John, 118
Buchanan, James, 123, 136–137, 140, 141, 143–144, 155, 159, 161–162, 165–167, 248
Bull Run, Battle of, 186
Bunker Hill, Battle of, 61
Burke, Billie, 338–339
Burr, Aaron, 54, 71, 86, 106

Burr, Theodosia, 86
Burritt, Elihu, 158–159
Bush, Barbara Pierce, 461, 500, 503, 558, 590
Bush, George Herbert Walker, 500, 503, 558
Bush, Neil, 558
Bush, Robin, 558
Butcher, Harry, 521
Butcher, Mollie Ford, 521
Butcher, Ruth, 521
Butler, Philippi, 442–443
Butt, Archibald, 307, 314, 322, 327–329, 330–331
Byrnes, James, 507, 530

Cadman, Jack, 488
Calhoun, John, 86, 131
Calhoun, Lucia, 236
Capen, Nahum, 163
Carnegie, Andrew, 291, 328
Carpenter, Frank "Carp," 279
Carpenter, Fred, 318
Carpenter, Liz, 464, 518, 530, 554
Carroll, Margaret, 36–37
Carter, Eleanor Rosalynn Smith, 470, 502, 524, 558, 582
Carter, Jimmy, 524, 582
Carter, Lillian, 502
Catherine II, empress of Russia, 31
Catt, Carrie, 471
Cermak, Anton, 465
Cerrell, Joseph, 588
Chambers, Whittaker, 538
Chaney, Mayris, 493
Chapman, Alfred, 589
Chapman, Arthur, 589
Charlotte, queen of England, 31–33, 36, 61, 69
Chase, Salmon, 171–172, 177–178, 179–180
Cheshire, Maxine, 597
Chiang Kai-shek, Madame, 445, 494
Christy, Howard Chandler, 410, 414

Churchill, Winston, 494, 495, 523, 580

Civil War, U.S., 171–172, 178–179, 182–197, 203–204, 247–248, 305

Clark, Ted, 416

Clay, Henry, 86, 107, 114, 128, 140, 142, 146

Clemenceau, George, 368

Cleveland, Esther, 277, 278, 312

Cleveland, Frances Folsom, *see* Preston, Frances Folsom Cleveland

Cleveland, Francis, 300

Cleveland, Grover, 169, 230, 248–250, 253–256, 261–267, 273–282, 312–313

Cleveland, Marion, 277

Cleveland, Richard, 300

Cleveland, Rose Elizabeth, 248–249, 250, 253, 258, 263

Cleveland, Ruth, 273, 277, 278, 300

Clifford, Clark, 524, 529, 540

Clinton, Dewitt, 88

Clinton, Henry, 38

Cobb, Howell, 166, 167

Cobb, Mary Ann, 162, 165, 166, 167

Cochran, Hannah, 136

Colby, Bainbridge, 379

Coleman, Ann, 136

Coleman, Edna, 415

Comer, Donald, 463

Congress, U.S., 66–68, 72, 76, 80, 88, 94, 97, 106–107, 115–116, 143, 200, 207, 212, 220, 235, 244, 277, 347, 369

Conkling, Roscoe, 209, 215, 217, 227, 239

Conner, Virginia, 417

Cook, Nancy, 390

Cooke, George, 83

Coolidge, Calvin, 286, 311, 358–359, 368, 381, 388–389, 394, 396, 399–404, 407–409, 413–416, 419, 421–428, 432, 473–474

Coolidge, Calvin, Jr., 311, 402, 404, 453

Coolidge, Grace Anna Goodhue, 248, 285–286, 332, 358–359, 381–382, 388–389, 396–428, 431–432

character and personality of, 285–286, 311, 368, 383, 389, 393–394, 397–400, 404–408, 410–416, 421–428

physical appearance of, 286, 383, 389

popularity and fame of, 394, 406–410, 413–414, 424, 426, 440

post-presidency life of, 431–432, 440–441, 452, 453, 473–474, 490–491, 499–500, 567, 576–577

relationship with Coolidge, 311, 381, 389, 394, 399–401, 407–409, 415–416, 422–428, 432, 473

special projects of, 418–422

Coolidge, John, 396

Coolidge, John (grandson), 311, 402, 414, 473

Cortelyou, George, 275

Coughlin, Charles, 484

Cox, Jacob, 215

Cox, James, 381

Cramer, Charles, 395

Crauford-Stuart, Charles, 355, 377–378

Crook, Colonel, 173, 205, 208, 210, 227, 262, 270, 283, 288, 297

Curtis, William, 78–79

Custis, Daniel, 40
Custis, Jacky, 52, 57
Custis, Nellie, 57–58, 88
Cutts, Anna Payne, 53, 80, 81–82,
    86, 87, 88, 90, 95
Cutts, Richard, 80, 81, 86

Dallas, George, 140
Dandridge, John, 40
Daniel, Clifton, 523
Daniel, Margaret Truman, 510,
    517, 522–523, 540
Daugherty, Harry, 381, 383, 395
Daughters of the American
    Revolution (DAR),
    270–271, 437, 479, 528,
    563
Davis, Edie Robbins, 412, 465, 488,
    587
Davis, James J., 404
Davis, Jefferson, 147
Davis, Loyal, 465, 587
Davis, Varima, 158, 188, 197, 205
Dawes, Caroline, 405
Dayton, Dorothy, 423
Dayton, John N., 131
Declaration of Independence, 76,
    144, 234
Democracy (Adams), 210, 251
Dent, Fred (son), 217, 219
Dent, Frederick, 113–114
Dent, George, 217
Dent, John, 216, 217
Dent, Louis, 220
Depression, Great, 438–439, 441,
    444–445, 447–449, 455,
    469, 471, 474
DePriest, Oscar, 446, 451
Dering, Henry T., 131
Dewey, George, 288, 291
Dewey, Thomas E., 536, 567
DeWolfe, Elsie, 541
de Wolfe, Henry, 382
de Wolfe, Marshall, 382
Dewson, Mollie, 468–469, 472
Dickens, Charles, 155
Dickerman, Marion, 390, 430

Di Donato, Pietro, 484–485
Dirksen, Everett, 567
Donelson, Emily, 114
Doud, Elvira, 326
Doud, John, 326
Douglas, Stephen, 128, 158, 170
Douglass, Frederick, 188, 200
Dow, Dorothy, 487, 519–520
Duncan, Gladys, 455, 480–482
Duncan, Todd, 480

Earhart, Amelia, 461
Early, Steve, 482
Eaton, John, 114
Eaton, Peggy, 114
Eden, Anthony, 495, 569
Edison, Thomas, 228, 295
Edward, Prince of Wales, 166
Edwards, Elizabeth Todd, 128–129,
    181, 221, 246
Edwards, Ninian, 128, 178
Eisenhower, Anne, 534
Eisenhower, Barbara Thompson,
    534, 557, 558, 559–560,
    581
Eisenhower, David, 534, 560, 562
Eisenhower, Doud, 363–364, 390,
    417
Eisenhower, Dwight David, 363,
    390, 417–418, 448,
    456–457, 495–497,
    506–507, 510, 520–521,
    534, 543, 546–548,
    558–562, 570–574,
    581–582, 596
Eisenhower, John, 418, 456, 535,
    558
Eisenhower, Marie Geneva
    "Mamie" Doud, 456–547
    character and personality of, 326,
    417–418, 503–504, 510,
    533–535, 543–568,
    570–574, 579–587,
    597–599
    relationship with Eisenhower,
    363–364, 390, 417–418,
    448, 495–497, 506–507,

520–521, 546–548, 559–563, 570–574
Eisenhower, Milton, 504, 534, 547, 548
Eisenhower, Susan, 534
Elizabeth I, queen of England, 32, 180
Ellett, Elizabeth Lummis, 95
Ellis, Katherine, 162, 183
Emancipation Proclamation, 188
Eppes, John, 86
Evarts, William, 229, 231

Fairfax, Sally, 41
Fall, Albert, 375, 378, 383, 388, 395
Federalists, 62, 64, 65, 70–71, 78–79, 80, 92
Fessler, Ruth, 442–443
Fillmore, Abigail Powers, 151–156
Fillmore, Mary, 151, 155
Fillmore, Millard, 146, 151–156, 169, 176
Fillmore, Powers, 169
first ladies:
    criticism of, 47, 50, 63–64, 85–86, 96, 110, 164–165, 167, 269–270, 375, 446–447
    fashion influence of, 85, 163–164, 174–175, 253, 263, 264–265, 409–410, 564, 600–601
    official recognition and social position of, 79, 84–85, 119, 221, 233, 241, 295, 303
    patronage sought from, 86–87, 88–89, 128, 129–130, 140–141, 146–147, 163, 167, 169, 176, 177–179, 193, 205, 227, 240, 299, 315, 320, 323, 391–392
    portraits of, 91, 127, 144, 146, 151, 152, 164, 213, 230, 233, 302, 410, 414, 442
    post-presidency benefits of, 67–68, 116, 121, 124, 200, 207, 212–213, 231, 235, 244, 336–337, 429, 473
    presidential responsibilities assumed by, 89, 106, 360, 371–381
    press coverage of, 83, 92–93, 110, 129–130, 138–139, 164, 169, 170, 210, 225–226, 233, 235, 239, 253–259, 269–270, 284, 320–321, 366, 379–380, 387, 406, 443–444, 446–447, 456–457
    special projects of, 94, 152, 163, 187–188, 233–234, 240–241, 267–268, 320–323, 384, 418–420
    staffs of, 227, 258, 268, 275, 295, 298–299, 319, 336, 356, 380, 392, 399, 442–443, 458
    titles of, 36, 46, 62, 81, 103, 108, 127–128, 147, 164–165, 175, 298–299, 332
    women influenced by, 95–96, 260, 275, 414–415
First Lady (Kaufman), 465
First Lady of the Land (Nirdlinger), 332
Fish, Hamilton, 214–215
Fisk, Jim, 211–212
Fitzgerald, John J., 425
Folsom, Emma, 230, 248, 249, 250, 266
Folsom, Oscar, 169, 230
Forbes, Charlie, 383, 388, 391, 392, 395
Ford, Elizabeth Anne "Betty" Bloomer Warren, 410, 470, 486–487, 503, 537–538, 558, 565
Ford, Gerald R., 537, 557, 565
Forster, Rudolph, 307
Francis Ferdinand, archduke of Austria, 349
Franklin, Benjamin, 77

Franklyn, Lucy Jenkins, 414
Fraunces, Samuel, 44
Fremont, Elizabeth, 141
Fremont, Jessie, 128, 161
Fremont, John, 161, 176
French, B. B., 171, 172, 193
From Lady Washington to Mrs.
      Cleveland (Gordon), 261
Fugitive Slave Bill, 153–154
Fuller, Margaret, 99, 145
Fulton, Robert, 83
Furman, Bess, 439, 443–444, 451,
      455–457, 465, 479, 535,
      545–546, 550

Galbraith, John Kenneth, 463, 464
Gallatin, Albert, 48, 63, 86
Galt, Alexander, 273
Galt, Norman, 273, 280–281, 302,
      325, 348
Gardiner, Alexander, 121, 123,
      124, 130–133
Gardiner, David, 118, 125
Gardiner, David (son), 121, 189,
      192, 199
Gardiner, Ezra, 131
Gardiner, John D., 131
Gardiner, Juliana, 118, 124, 129,
      130, 182, 189, 192
Gardiner, Lion, 118
Gardiner, Margaret, 118, 120–121,
      124, 127, 128, 129,
      132–133, 139
Gardiner, Samuel, 131
Garfield, James A., 234, 235–244,
      261
Garfield, Lucretia "Crete" Rudolph,
      223, 234, 235–244
   character and personality of,
      236–237, 238, 243–244
   post-presidency life of, 255, 261,
      278, 291, 300, 303, 330,
      335, 362
   relationship with Garfield,
      235–237, 239, 241–244
Garnet, H. H., 200

George III, king of England, 31–32,
      60
George VI, king of England, 483
George Eliot's Poetry and Other
      Studies (Cleveland),
      248–249
Gettysburg, Battle of, 189
Gilder, Richard Watson, 278
Girl Scouts of America, 406, 407,
      420, 436, 440, 443, 451,
      474
Glass, Carter, 376–377
Goodhue, Andrew, 248
Goodhue, Lemira, 248
Gordon, Altrude, 343, 349, 357
Goss, Doris, 442–443
Gould, Jay, 211
Graham, Martha, 470, 486–487
Grant, Fred, 217, 220, 279
Grant, Julia Boggs Dent, 113–114,
      154, 209–225, 333
   character and personality of,
      184–185, 191, 195,
      196–199, 200, 210–212,
      218–225, 232, 234, 351
   political and social ambitions of,
      183–184, 194–195, 206,
      209–211, 214–218,
      221–225, 231–232,
      234–235, 244–246, 274,
      278–280, 321, 379
   post-presidency life of, 224–225,
      229, 231–232, 234–235,
      244–246, 249–250, 255,
      261, 271, 273, 274,
      278–280, 291, 302–303
   relationship with Grant,
      142–143, 183–185,
      194–195, 206, 207,
      209–210, 214–218,
      222–223, 225, 232,
      234–235
Grant, Ulysses S., 142, 183–185,
      190–191, 194–195,
      197–200, 206–210,
      214–219, 222–225,

231–232, 234–235, 246,
   249–250, 261
Grant, Ulysses S., Jr., 278
Gray, Bob, 561
Grayson, Cary, 302, 343, 347, 349,
   350–351, 352, 355, 357,
   360, 367, 369, 370–371,
   373–375, 377
Greeley, Horace, 219
Greene, Nathaniel, 43
Guiteau, Charles, 241, 242
Gurewitsch, David, 590

Hagerty, James, 554–555, 562
Hagner, Isabella, 295, 298, 304,
   305, 319, 324–325, 336,
   345
Haley, James, 411, 418, 422–423,
   425–426
Hall, Mildred, 442–443
Halsey, William F., 498–499
Hamilton, Alexander, 50, 71, 241
Hanna, Mark, 279, 283
Harding, Florence Kling De Wolfe,
   329, 333–334, 362, 364,
   381–384, 387–388,
   391–397, 406
   character and personality of, 358,
      364, 381, 384
   political activism of, 391–393
   post-presidency life of, 401–402,
      404
   relationship with Harding, 377,
      381, 393–396, 398
Harding, Warren G., 329,
   333–334, 358, 364, 377,
   381–384, 387–388,
   393–396, 398, 437
Harper's Weekly, 164, 185, 257, 258
Harriman, Averell, 567
Harriman, Daisy, 378
Harris, Ellen, 567
Harrison, Anna Tuthill Symmes,
   57, 88, 120–121, 183, 207
Harrison, Benjamin, 183, 267–269,
   271, 273, 336

Harrison, Caroline Lavinia Scott,
   263, 267–271, 273, 290,
   336, 435
Harrison, Mary Scott Lord
   Dimmick, 268, 336–337
Harrison, Russell, 336
Harrison, William Henry, 88,
   119–121, 273
Hawthorne, Nathaniel, 158
Hay, Eliza Monroe, 102, 103, 104
Hay, George, 106
Hay, John, 172
Hayes, Lucy Wake Webb, 222–231,
   233–234, 238, 302, 307,
   435
   character and personality of,
      223–224, 226–228, 231
Hayes, Rutherford B., 222–224,
   227–230, 233–234, 238,
   249
Hearst, William Randolph,
   440–441
Helm, Edith Benham, 356, 366,
   380, 458, 471, 476, 483,
   517–518, 532, 536, 539,
   556
Helm, Emilie Todd, 189–190
Hemings, Betty, 75
Hemings, Madison, 96
Hemings, Sally, 75–76, 77, 96
Henry, Patrick, 70
Herndon, William, 207–208
Herron, Maria, 326
Heston, Isaac, 52–53
Heth, William, 35
Hickok, Lorena "Hick," 449, 451,
   452, 455, 456, 460, 472
Hirohito, emperor of Japan, 485
Hitler, Adolf, 479, 483–484, 485,
   490, 491, 494
Hobart, Jennie, 287
Hobby, Oveta Culp, 566
Hoes, Rose, 332
Holloway, Laura, 261
Hooker, Joseph, 186, 305
Hoover, Herbert, 361–362, 364,

Hoover, Herbert (*cont.*)
376, 383, 388, 429, 432,
435, 438, 443–451, 453,
490
Hoover, Ike, 276, 281, 297,
318–319, 326, 337, 338,
370–371, 375, 404, 414,
446
Hoover, J. Edgar, 484, 568
Hoover, Lou Henry, 361–362, 384,
388, 395, 401, 407, 429,
450–451, 453
character and personality of, 431,
435–439, 442–449,
453–454
post-presidency life of, 452–454,
490, 511
public and political work of,
435–439, 441–446
relationship with Hoover, 435,
438, 445, 446, 450–451,
452
Hopkins, Charlotte, 345
Hopkins, Harry, 452, 463, 468,
472, 482
Houckgeest, Andreas Everardus van
Braam, 46
House, Edward M., 350, 352–355,
357, 360, 361, 364, 365,
367, 369, 376, 378
Howe, Louis, 334, 336, 358,
381–382, 389–390, 430,
454, 472
Hoyt, Mary Cleveland, 248
Huntington, Daniel, 230

Ickes, Harold, 461–462, 468
Irving, Washington, 87, 155
Isabella I, queen of Spain, 32, 232

Jackson, Andrew, 93, 105–108,
111–115, 137
Jackson, Edward, 367
Jackson, Rachel Donelson Robards,
105, 111–115
character and personality of, 93,
107–108, 111–112

criticism of, 93, 107–108,
111–112, 114–115
physical appearance of, 105, 107,
112
relationship with Jackson, 93,
107–108, 111, 112, 115
Jackson, Sarah, 114
Jaffray, Elizabeth, 314, 319, 322
James, Henry, 217–218
Jameson, Henry, 504, 559
Jarvis, Russell, 110
Jefferson, Maria, 77
Jefferson, Martha Wayles, 75–77
Jefferson, Patsy, 77
Jefferson, Thomas, 49, 50, 51, 59,
61, 71, 72, 75–79, 80, 82,
96, 97, 111, 115
Jennings, Paul, 126
Jewell, Marshall, 215
Johnson, Andrew, 161, 194, 199,
200, 203–209
Johnson, Andrew, Jr., 203
Johnson, Claudia Alta "Lady Bird"
Taylor, 501, 537–539, 572,
594–595, 596
character and personality of, 331,
457–458, 467, 590–591
Johnson, Eliza McCardle, 203–206,
208–209
Johnson, Joshua, 69
Johnson, Lynda Bird, 537
Johnson, Lyndon Baines, 458, 467,
501, 537–538, 571–572, 589
Johnson, Reverdy, 147
Johnson, Robert, 203, 204
Johnston, Frances Benjamin, 304
Jonas, Charles Raper, 580
Jones, Jesse, 429, 488
Jones, Leonard, 138
Judd, Norman, 169

Kaufman, George S., 465
Keckley, Elizabeth, 173–174, 177,
187, 193, 194, 197–200,
208
Keeley, Mary Paxton, 518, 521,
522, 528

Keller, Helen, 421–422
Kennedy, Jacqueline Lee Bouvier,
        486, 550–551, 563,
        575–579, 587–603
    character and personality of,
        475–476, 542
    relationship with Kennedy, 565,
        572, 575, 576, 587–589,
        591–592
Kennedy, John F., 550–551, 565,
        572, 575–579, 587–589,
        591–592, 598, 600–603
Kennedy, John F., Jr., 598, 600
Kennedy, Joseph P., 475
Kennedy, Robert F., 590–591
Kennedy, Thomas, 111
Key, Francis Scott, 90
Keyes, Frances Parkinson, 394, 453
Khrushchev, Nikita, 583
Khrushchev, Nina, 583
King, Coretta Scott, 583
King, Martin Luther, Jr., 583
King, William Rufus Devane,
        136–137, 155, 162, 183
Kohlsaat, H. H., 376–377
Korean War, 539, 561, 564
Kossuth, Louis, 152
Ku Klux Klan, 413
Kuyper, Elizabeth, 414

Ladies of the White House
        (Holloway), 261
Lafayette, Madame de, 68
Lafayette, Marquis de, 105, 107
Lait, Jack, 483
Lamon, Ward, 142
Lane, Franklin K., 356, 373
Lane, Harriet, 143, 159–168, 169,
        183, 187, 203, 207, 244,
        267, 276, 278
    relationship with Buchanan,
        161–167
Lansing, Robert, 352, 364, 367,
        374, 375, 377–379
Lape, Esther, 390, 430
Lash, Joseph, 472, 484, 568
Lasker, Mary, 472

Lathrop, Julia, 321
Latrobe, Henry, 96
League of Nations, 364–365, 368,
        369, 371, 373, 375–378,
        380, 383, 393
League of Women Voters, 429, 430,
        437
Lear, Polly, 44
Lear, Tobias, 58
Lee, Eliza, 94, 97
LeHand, Marguerite "Missy," 382,
        452, 472, 505
LeRoy, Mervyn, 541
Levasseur, Auguste, 105
Lewis, Robert, 35–37, 44
Life, 496, 542, 553, 555
Life and Letters of Dolley Madison,
        The (Clark), 332
Lincoln, Abraham, 129, 142, 145,
        154, 166, 168–169,
        176–182, 185–186, 188,
        191–194, 196–199, 247,
        418
Lincoln, Edward, 190
Lincoln, Mary Ann Todd, 114,
        168–182, 185–200, 241,
        332, 337
    character and personality of,
        169–172, 185–188, 190,
        195–198, 351
    criticism of, 169–170, 172, 174,
        176, 180–181, 185,
        192–194, 200, 226
    political interests of, 119–120,
        128, 142, 145, 154,
        168–172, 173, 185–188,
        191, 246, 379
    post-presidency life of, 207–208,
        212–213, 220–221, 231,
        232, 234, 235, 244, 246,
        250
    relationship with Lincoln,
        128–129, 142, 145, 154,
        166, 168–169, 176–182,
        185–186, 191, 193–194
Lincoln, Robert Todd, 170, 181,
        189, 190, 221

Lincoln, Thomas "Tad," 171, 173, 181, 185, 198, 220

Lincoln, William "Willie" Wallace, 171, 173, 181–182, 190, 194

Lind, Jenny, 152

Lindbergh, Anne Morrow, 422

Lindbergh, Charles A., 422

Lindsay, Chandlor, 590

Lingo, Jane, 522, 529, 539

Lockwood, Belva, 255

Lodge, Henry Cabot, 327, 368–369, 376–377, 401, 590

Longworth, Alice Roosevelt, 249, 280, 291, 296, 307–309, 349, 355, 357–358, 362, 377, 378, 389, 405, 454, 598

character and personality of, 295, 304–305, 307–308, 314, 315, 316, 325, 329, 334, 477

public interest in, 303–305, 308, 311–312

Longworth, Nicholas, 312, 315, 327, 333–334, 403

Louchheim, Katie, 518–519, 530, 531–532, 549

Louis IX, king of France, 32

Louis XVI, king of France, 31, 49

Louis Philippe, king of France, 117, 118, 127, 159

Lovejoy, Owen, 187

Low, Juliette, 436

Lowenstein, Allard, 578

Luce, Clare Boothe, 508, 534

Ludlow, Louis, 468

Lusitania, 352

McAdoo, Nell, 351, 401

McAdoo, William, 344–345, 346, 349, 354, 360

MacArthur, Arthur, 290

MacArthur, Douglas, 448, 456, 539

McCaffree, Mary Jane, 555, 569–570, 581, 583

McCann, Kevin, 547, 562, 567

McCarthy, Frank, 396

McCarthy, Joseph R., 540, 560, 566, 579

McClellan, George, 180, 182, 186

McCormick, Ruth Hanna, 357

McElroy, Mary Arthur, 244, 246, 271

McFeely, William S., 211

McHenry, James, 37

McKean, Mary, 85

McKee, Mary Harrison, 336

McKim, Charles, 296, 300, 302

McKinley, Ida Saxton, 227, 282–292, 307, 405

relationship with McKinley, 282–283, 284–289, 292

McKinley, William, 282–292

McLean, Evalyn, 355, 357–358, 377, 387, 396–397

McLean, John, 131

McLean, Ned, 355

McPherson, Edward, 167

Madison, Dorothea "Dolley" Payne Todd, 49, 66, 72, 79–80, 164, 175, 233, 247, 258, 302

character and personality of, 53–54, 56, 66, 72, 75, 79–81, 82–85, 90–93, 95–96, 103–104, 125–126, 133, 134, 139–140

fame and popularity of, 72, 83–84, 92–93, 95–96, 97, 103, 145, 147, 156, 332, 394, 455

physical appearance of, 72, 80, 84–85, 87, 96, 115, 127, 145

post-presidency life of, 103–104, 115, 122, 124–126, 127, 133, 134, 139–140, 143, 145, 147, 213, 274

public role of, 77–78, 81–90, 94–97, 134, 143, 145, 147, 260, 372

relationship with Madison, 55–56, 67, 77–78, 80–83,

85–86, 87, 89–90, 94, 95,
103–104, 372
social and political skills of, 56,
72, 75, 77–78, 81–98, 107,
122, 127, 187, 261, 379
Madison, James, 55–56, 67, 72,
77–78, 80–83, 85–86,
88–90, 94, 95, 97,
102–104, 115
Maine, 288
Malone, Dudley Field, 335–336,
359
Marbury, Elisabeth, 405
Marie, queen of Romania, 367
Marie Antoinette, queen of France,
31, 32, 42, 49, 75, 98
Marshall, Thomas, 374
Martineau, Harriet, 95, 103–104
Meredith, Edward, 376
Mesta, Perle, 504, 521, 535, 543,
568
Mexican War, 141–144
Miller, Earl, 452
Miller, John J., 585
Millet, Francis David, 307,
330–331
Milligan, Maurice, 530
Milliken, Seth, 267–268
Mitchell, Samuel, 84
Monroe, Elizabeth Kortright, 55,
56, 80, 90, 107, 332, 435
character and personality of,
68–69, 97–98, 101–103
illnesses of, 98, 102–103
physical appearance of, 102, 103
political involvement of,
105–106
relationship with Monroe,
104–106
Monroe, James, 55, 68, 80, 97,
102–106
Monroe Doctrine, 106, 347
Montgomery, Benjamin, 289
Moore, Gordon, 585
More, Eleanor Herron, 326
Morgan, Kay Summersby, 496–497,
543

Morris, Augusta Heath, 172, 176
Morris, Marcia, 38, 45, 51
Morrow, Dwight, 422
Morrow, E. Fred, 581
Mortimer, Lee, 483
Murphy, Charles, 529
Mussolini, Benito, 485
"My Day," 458, 463, 466, 492, 541
My Memoir (Wilson), 479, 484

Napoleon I, emperor of the French,
68
Neal, Steve, 561
New Deal, 454, 459, 463–464, 466,
470, 473, 476, 487
Newman, Larry, 591
New York Herald, 175–176, 181,
215, 222, 250, 334, 430
New York Times, 156, 164, 169,
254, 303, 318, 391, 405,
406, 427, 447, 545, 600
Nichols, Roy, 136
Nicolay, Helen, 281
Nicolay, John, 172
Niebuhr, Reinhold, 592–593
Nirdlinger, Charles, 332
Nixon, Richard Milhous, 487, 502,
538, 539, 545, 548, 560,
568, 574, 584, 587, 596
Nixon, Thelma Catherine "Pat"
Ryan, 331–332, 568, 584,
585, 596–597
character and personality of,
469–470, 538–539, 548,
565–566, 574, 590–591
relationship with Nixon, 487,
502, 596
Nixon, Tricia, 538
Noah, Mordecai, 97

O'Day, Caroline, 472
Odum, Reathel, 518, 519, 522
Onassis, Aristotle, 580
Orne, Sally, 212
Otis, Harrison, 103
Otis, Sally Foster, 79
Ozaki, Yukio, 323

Paine, Tom, 68
Panic of 1893, 276–278
Parish, Susan, 309, 311
Parker, John F., 198
Parks, Lillian, 472
Patterson, Cissy, 418, 472
Patterson, Martha Johnson, 161,
      203, 205
Patti, Adelina, 259, 281
Payne, John, 49
Payne, Mary, 49, 53, 82
Pearson, Drew, 532, 540, 584
Peck, Mary Hulbert, 301, 335, 354,
      359, 370
Pendleton, C. H., 266
Pennsylvania Gazette, 38, 44, 46, 47,
      55
Perkins, Frances, 468, 478,
      512–513, 521
Pershing, John, 416–417
Personal Memoirs of U. S. Grant
      (Grant), 249–250, 279
Philippines, 288–290, 295,
      456–457
Phillips, Carrie, 358, 377, 382
Pierce, Benjamin, 157–158
Pierce, Franklin, 140, 155–159,
      183
Pierce, Jane Means Appleton,
      156–159, 183
Pierce, Marvin, 461
Pierce, Pauline, 461
Pinchot, Gifford, 330
Pinckney, Charles, 63–64, 81, 107
Pleasants, Debbie, 87
Pocahontas, 356
Polk, James Knox, 132, 134–136,
      137–142, 156–157
Polk, Sarah Childress, 132–145,
      154, 162, 203, 233, 242,
      244, 255, 261, 302
   character and personality of, 133,
      134, 135, 137–140,
      143–144, 183, 226–227,
      229
   physical appearance of, 134, 138

   political involvement of,
      134–135, 137, 140–142
   relationship with Polk, 134–135,
      137, 138, 139–142
Ponceau, Pierre Etienne du, 41
Poore, Ben Perley, 175
Pound, Thaddeus, 237
Powell, Adam Clayton, 527–528
Powers, Dave, 576, 588
Powers, David, 154
Presiding Ladies of the White House
      (Sangster), 293
Preston, Frances Folsom Cleveland,
      230, 248, 249, 250,
      253–267, 271, 273–282,
      299, 414
   character and personality of,
      257–258, 260–261, 267,
      276–278, 281–282, 337
   physical appearance of, 257–258,
      275
   post-presidency life of, 271, 300,
      312–313, 332, 335–338,
      362, 393, 429, 451–452,
      473, 526–527
   public interest in, 253–261,
      263–267, 273–274, 275,
      337
   relationship with Cleveland, 230,
      248, 250, 253–256,
      258–259, 261–263,
      265–267, 273–274,
      276–278
Preston, Thomas Jex, Jr., 337
Profiles in Courage (Kennedy), 572
Prohibition, 387–388, 389, 413,
      430, 445, 453
Purdy, Lovel, 128

Rabb, Maxwell, 562
Randolph, Jennings, 466–467
Randolph, John, 80, 86, 106
Randolph, Polly, 399, 443
Rathbone, Henry R., 198
Rayburn, Samuel, 536, 537, 590
Read, Elizabeth, 390

Reagan, Anne Frances "Nancy"
    Robbins Davis, 411–412,
    418, 465, 490–491,
    500–501, 541, 543–544,
    549, 558, 587
Reagan, Maureen, 587
Reagan, Michael, 587
Reagan, Ronald W., 541, 543–544,
    549, 587
Real, Mary, 196
Reed, Thomas B., 268
Reid, Edith Gittings, 479
Reid, Whitelaw, 310, 325
Reston, James, 545
Reuther, Walter, 472
Richmond, Battle of, 182
Riis, Jacob, 312
Robbins, Kenneth, 412
Robinson, Charles, 159
Robinson, Corinne Roosevelt, 297,
    309, 368
Rockefeller, John D., 328, 329
Rodney, Thomas, 48
Rogers, Maude, 359
Rogers, Will, 407, 423·
Roosevelt, Alice Lee, 249
Roosevelt, Anna, 471, 476, 505,
    512
Roosevelt, Anna Eleanor Roosevelt,
    280, 286, 297, 310–312,
    328, 331, 338, 362, 368,
    378, 445, 452–473,
    476–499, 504–506
  character and personality of,
    315–316, 334–335,
    348–349, 358, 359, 361,
    390–391, 460, 471–473,
    476–486, 494–495, 506
  political activism of, 336, 358,
    381–382, 389–391,
    403–404, 429–431,
    449–450, 454–456,
    459–469, 476–485,
    487–489
  post-presidency life of, 519–520,
    541, 568–569, 578, 588–590

relationship with Franklin
    Roosevelt, 308–309,
    310–311, 358, 364, 366,
    381–382, 389–391, 430,
    450, 452, 454–455,
    462–465, 511
Roosevelt, Bye, 297, 298, 309
Roosevelt, Edith Kermit Carow,
    199, 223–224, 268, 273,
    279–280, 281, 286, 291,
    295–300, 303–308, 325,
    329–330, 362, 452
  character and personality of,
    295–296, 298–300,
    304–306, 307, 312, 316,
    335, 389
  political involvement of, 310
  post-presidency life of, 336, 402,
    451–452, 527
  private vs. public role of,
    295–296, 298–300,
    304–305, 307–308, 312
  relationship with Theodore
    Roosevelt, 223, 249, 292,
    295–298, 304, 307,
    309–310, 312, 333–334
Roosevelt, Elliott, 199, 280, 311
Roosevelt, Elliott (grandson), 334,
    464, 471, 496, 511, 535,
    568
Roosevelt, Ethel, 312
Roosevelt, Franklin D., 308–313,
    315, 328, 334–336, 338,
    348, 358, 361, 364, 366,
    368, 378, 381–382, 402,
    429–431, 449–450, 452,
    458, 462–463, 469,
    474–476, 484, 487–489,
    492–495, 504–507, 511
Roosevelt, Franklin D., Jr., 334,
    358, 471, 488
Roosevelt, James, 334, 471, 490
Roosevelt, Quentin, 295
Roosevelt, Sara Delano, 309, 315,
    348, 364, 389, 390–391,
    431, 471–472, 474, 476, 490

Roosevelt, Theodore, 199, 223, 249, 268, 279–280, 291, 292, 295–298, 300, 302–303, 306–307, 309–313, 316, 323, 327–330, 333–335, 338, 362, 454
Roosevelt, Theodore, Jr., 295
Root, Elihu, 279, 306, 313
Rosenman, Sam, 463
Ross, Nellie Tayloe, 414
Royall, Anne, 95
Russo-Japanese War, 310, 323
Rutherford, Lucy Mercer, 348, 358, 403, 505, 509–510, 511, 512
Rutledge, Ann, 207–208

Sanders, Everett, 416
Sanger, Margaret, 320
Sangster, Margaret E., 293
Sargent, John Singer, 367
Sartoris, Nellie Grant, 217–218, 247
Sawyer, Charles "Doc," 383, 388, 392–395
Schell, Augustus, 163
Schlesinger, Arthur M., Jr., 575, 576, 592
Schneiderman, Rose, 390
Scidmore, Eliza, 323
Scott, Thomas, 186–187
Scott, Winfield, 171
Seagraves, Ellie, 464
Seaton, Josephine, 135
Seaton, Sarah Gales, 83, 93
Seaton, William, 83
Secret Service, 278, 312, 319, 355, 369, 392, 411, 422–423, 425–428, 442
Seward, William, 171–172, 177–178, 179
Singleton, Marian, 116
Singleton, Richard, 116
Sioussat, "French John," 90–91
Slade, William, 200

Slater, Priscilla, 562
slavery, 40, 58, 70–72, 75, 79, 96, 111, 113, 114, 121, 134, 144, 145–146
abolition of, 70, 123, 134–135, 144, 159, 162, 172, 183, 187–188, 228
Slayden, Ellen, 286–287, 329, 332, 343
Slemp, C. Bascom, 416
Smith, Alfred E., 403, 416, 429, 469
Smith, B. Kirby, 204
Smith, Ira, 307, 359
Smith, James, 219–220
Smith, Jesse, 387–388, 395
Smith, Margaret Bayard, 83
Smith, Merriman, 510, 546, 561
Smith, Samuel, 83
Smithsonian Institution, 246, 332–333, 473
Snyder, Howard, 570, 572–573
Sousa, John Philip, 255
Spanish-American War, 288, 291
Sprague, Kate Chase, 227
Spring-Rice, Cecil, 258, 268, 310
Stalin, Joseph, 523
Stanford, Leland, 267–268
Stanton, Edward, 178–179, 186, 196, 206, 217
Stark, Lloyd, 530
Starling, Edmund S., 355, 425–426, 428
Stearns, Frank, 368, 428
Stevenson, Adlai, 544–545, 576–579, 589, 592, 601
Stevenson, Andrew, 116
Stewart, A. T., 174, 193, 215, 216
Stoddart, William O., 171, 172, 185
Stone, Thomas E., 298
Stover, Mary Johnson, 203, 204
Stuart, David, 48
Stuart, Gilbert, 91
Sumner, Charles, 180, 187, 188, 197, 198, 200
Swisshelm, Jane Grey, 188, 196

Taft, Charles, 290, 317, 323
Taft, Helen, 290, 317, 326
Taft, Helen "Nellie" Herron, 227,
    259–260, 292, 306–334,
    338, 358
  character and ambition of, 227,
    259–260, 273, 289–291,
    306–307, 311, 313–324,
    330, 338, 389, 413
  political activism of, 289–291,
    313–315, 317–324,
    328–333, 379
  post-presidency life of, 362,
    383–384, 393, 401–402,
    439–440, 452, 488, 490,
    499
  relationship with Taft, 259–260,
    307, 311, 313–320,
    323–324, 326–330
Taft, Horace, 325
Taft, Martha, 536–537
Taft, Robert, 290, 317, 490, 537
Taft, William Howard, 259–260,
    289–290, 306–307,
    311–334, 358, 362, 383,
    389, 402, 421, 439
Takamine, Jakicki, 323
Taylor, Betty, 146
Taylor, Margaret Mackall Smith,
    145–147, 151, 156, 183,
    207
  public perception of, 145–147
  relationship with Taylor,
    145–147, 151
Taylor, T. J., 331
Taylor, Zachary, 141, 145–147,
    151
Teapot Dome scandal, 395, 398,
    401, 403, 416, 437
Terrell, Mary Church, 581
Thackeray, William Makepeace,
    155
Thomas, F. W., 129, 132
Thompson, Charles Willis, 379
Thompson, Kate, 162, 165, 166,
    167

Thompson, Malvina "Tommy,"
    452, 454, 458, 459, 466,
    476, 478, 489, 568
Thornton, William, 79
Thurmond, Strom, 536
Tilden, Samuel J., 223, 224
Tingey, Thomas, 81
Tippecanoe, Battle of, 119
Titanic, 330–331
Todd, Alec, 190
Todd, John, 52–54
Todd, Lyman, 178
Todd, Payne, 53, 81, 93, 115–116,
    126, 143
Todd, Robert, 114, 128
Todd, William, 53
Toklas, Alice B., 493
Trohan, Walter, 456
Truman, Elizabeth Virginia "Bess"
    Wallace, 507–510
  character and personality of,
    517–521, 527–532,
    535–537, 539, 544
  relationship with Truman,
    522–524, 527–532, 535,
    539, 540
Truman, Harry S, 507–508,
    519–520, 522–524,
    527–532, 535–536,
    539–540, 544, 548–549,
    589, 591
Tuckerman, Nancy, 475
Tugwell, Rexford, 463, 494
Tully, Grace, 490, 511
Tumulty, Joseph, 327, 335,
    353–354, 357, 359–360,
    369, 370, 374–375, 376,
    391, 401, 596
Twain, Mark, 250, 301
Tyler, John, 121–127, 130–134,
    168, 182, 272
Tyler, John, Jr., 123
Tyler, Julia Gardiner, 117–118,
    120–121, 302, 333, 379
  physical appearance and
    personality of, 118,

Tyler, Julia Gardiner (*cont.*)
128–130, 133, 168, 213,
261
post-presidency life of, 138–139,
145–146, 154, 157,
182–183, 188–189,
191–192, 199, 205–206,
213–214, 223, 231, 233,
235, 242–244, 249, 250,
255, 261, 271–273, 274,
429
social style and impact of,
120–121, 123–124,
126–130, 131–134,
138–139, 154, 160, 161,
163, 168, 213–214, 249,
261, 273
relationship with Tyler, 123–127,
130–134, 138, 168, 182
Tyler, Letitia Christian, 121–122,
123, 156
Tyler, Priscilla Cooper, 121–123
Tyson, Job, 163

Uchida, Yasuya, 323
United Nations, 519, 524–526,
534–535, 541, 569

Van Buren, Abraham, 116–117
Van Buren, Angelica Singleton,
116–117, 118–119, 183
Van Buren, Hannah Hoes, 116
Van Buren, John, 116–117
Van Buren, Martin, 116, 118–119
Van Horne, Gabriel, 35, 36, 37
Van Ness, Maria, 94, 103
Victoria, queen of England,
116–117, 129, 159, 160,
164, 166, 167, 199, 232,
255
Vindication of the Rights of Women
(Wollstonecraft), 67
Volstead Act, 445

Wald, Lillian, 472
Wallace, Henry, 487, 488

Wallace, Madge Gates, 522–523,
548–549
Wallace, William, 178
Waller, William, 125
Walton, Bill, 576
Wanamaker, John, 269
Ward, Ferdinand, 235, 246
War of 1812, 88–92, 139, 145
Warren, Mercy, 32, 55
Washington, Booker T., 301, 305
Washington, George, 31–33,
40–45, 49–52, 57, 65, 69,
71, 72, 79, 111, 115, 139,
166, 271
Washington, George Steptoe, 49,
53
Washington, Lucy Payne, 49, 53,
80, 81
Washington, Martha Dandridge
Custis, 31–52, 56–60,
65–67, 102, 119, 143, 166,
187, 233, 258, 271, 310,
332
character and personality of,
40–45, 50–51, 54–55,
57–59, 66–67, 71, 72,
78–79
physical appearance of, 39–40,
44, 46, 48
post-presidency life of, 65–67,
71–72, 78–79
public role of, 37–38, 42–48, 50,
54–55, 59–60, 62, 65–67,
76, 156
relationship with Washington,
33, 40–41, 43–44, 49,
50–52, 57
Washington Post, 244, 254,
255–256, 315, 355, 557
Watterson, Henry, 265–266
Wayles, John, 75–76
Welles, Gideon, 178, 215
West, J. B., 464–465, 466, 471,
482, 529, 540, 551–552,
559, 597, 599
Whiskey Rebellion, 50

Whiskey Ring, 214, 216
White, Henry, 315, 364–365, 367, 376–377
White, Martha Todd, 190
White, Walter, 481, 528
White, William Allen, 399, 405, 432
White House, 78, 80, 83, 92–93, 253–255
   descriptions of, 69, 101–102, 108
   restoration and decoration of, 101, 171, 212, 214, 223, 240–241, 295–296, 300, 301–302, 418–419, 442
Wickersham, George, 323–324
Wikander, Lawrence E., 420
Wikoff, Henry, 175–176
Williams, Aubrey, 463
Willis, Charles F., Jr., 555
Willkie, Wendell, 488–489
Wilson, Edith Bolling Galt, 228, 280–281, 310, 327, 335, 347–357, 359–363, 364–381, 384
   character and personality of, 272, 273, 281, 302, 325–326, 357, 370, 389, 391, 401–402, 429
   physical appearance of, 272, 307, 351–352, 365–366
   political activism of, 353–355, 356–357, 364–365, 371–381, 469
   post-presidency life of, 391, 393, 401–402, 404, 429, 431, 439–440, 449, 452, 474–475, 488, 501–502, 524–525, 544–545, 568, 579–580, 595–596
   relationship with Wilson, 338–339, 343, 347, 351–357, 359–360, 365, 371–381, 391
Wilson, Ellen Louise Axson, 334–339, 343–351, 355, 525

   character and personality of, 300–301, 327, 343–346
   political activism of, 335–336, 343–347, 350
   relationship with Wilson, 300–301, 334–335, 344, 347, 349–350, 380
Wilson, Jessie, 346, 380
Wilson, Margaret, 352
Wilson, Nell, 380
Wilson, Woodrow, 300–301, 327, 334–335, 338–339, 343–360, 362, 364–381, 391, 395, 401–402
Winthrop, Hannah, 32
Wiseman, William, 370
Wister, Owen, 310
Wolf, Simon, 229, 327
Wollstonecraft, Mary, 67–68
Woman in the Nineteenth Century (Fuller), 99, 145
Women's Christian Temperance Union (WCTU), 229–230, 259, 264–265
women's rights, 67–68, 95, 109–111, 144–145, 195–196, 218–219, 230, 234, 240, 246, 270, 321, 334–335, 348, 359, 381, 392–393, 414–415, 438
Wood, Leonard, 288
Wood, William, 176
Woodhull, Victoria, 219
Woods, Rose Mary, 539
World War I, 349, 352, 359–364, 435
World War II, 492–499, 502–504
Wright, Orville, 325
Wright, Wilbur, 325
Wyman, Jane, 543, 587

Young, Brigham, 218